Lecture Notes in Artificial Intelligence 7297

Subseries of Lecture Notes in Computer Science

LNAI Series Editors

Randy Goebel
University of Alberta, Edmonton, Canada
Yuzuru Tanaka
Hokkaido University, Sapporo, Japan
Wolfgang Wahlster
DFKI and Saarland University, Saarbrücken, Germany

LNAI Founding Series Editor

Joerg Siekmann
DFKI and Saarland University, Saarbrücken, Germany

W0193314

Ilias Maglogiannis   Vassilis Plagianakos
Ioannis Vlahavas (Eds.)

Artificial Intelligence: Theories and Applications

7th Hellenic Conference on AI, SETN 2012
Lamia, Greece, May 28-31, 2012
Proceedings

 Springer

Series Editors

Randy Goebel, University of Alberta, Edmonton, Canada
Jörg Siekmann, University of Saarland, Saarbrücken, Germany
Wolfgang Wahlster, DFKI and University of Saarland, Saarbrücken, Germany

Volume Editors

Ilias Maglogiannis
Vassilis Plagianakos
University of Central Greece
Department of Computer Science and Biomedical Informatics
2-4 Papassiopoulou Street, Lamia 35100, Greece
E-mail: {imaglo,vpp}@ucg.gr

Ioannis Vlahavas
Aristotle University of Thessaloniki
Department of Informatics
Thessaloniki 54124, Greece
E-mail: vlahavas@csd.auth.gr

ISSN 0302-9743   e-ISSN 1611-3349
ISBN 978-3-642-30447-7   e-ISBN 978-3-642-30448-4
DOI 10.1007/978-3-642-30448-4
Springer Heidelberg Dordrecht London New York

Library of Congress Control Number: 2012937659

CR Subject Classification (1998): I.2, F.1, I.4, J.3, I.5, H.3-4, H.2.8

LNCS Sublibrary: SL 7 – Artificial Intelligence

Typesetting: Camera-ready by author, data conversion by Scientific Publishing Services, Chennai, India

Printed on acid-free paper

Springer is part of Springer Science+Business Media (www.springer.com)

Preface

It is our pleasure to welcome you to the proceedings of the 7th Hellenic Conference on Artificial Intelligence (SETN 2012) held during May 28–31, 2012, in Lamia, Greece. SETN 2012 was organized by the Hellenic AI Society (EETN), in collaboration with the Department of Computer Science and Biomedical Informatics of the University of Central Greece. Previous conferences were held at the University of Piraeus (1996), at the Aristotle University of Thessaloniki (2002), at the University of the Aegean (Samos, 2004, and Syros, 2008), jointly at the Foundation for Research and Technology Hellas (FORTH) and the University of Crete (2006), and at NCSR "Demokritos" (2010).

SETN conferences have already been established as the most prominent forums for Greek and international AI scientists to present original and high-quality research on emergent topics of artificial intelligence. The SETN 2012 conference aimed to:

- Bring together researchers who work actively in the field of artificial intelligence, to support the exchange of opinions and the formation of new research groups and collaborations
- Disseminate original and highly qualitative results of the Greek AI community and Greek research labs, fostering international collaborations
- Inform undergraduate and postgraduate students about the current state of affairs of AI research as conducted by scientists in Greece and worldwide
- Promote research results to companies and facilitate the development of innovative products

The task of the Technical Program Committee was very challenging putting together a program containing 48 high-quality contributions out of 81 submissions. The collection of papers included in the proceedings offer stimulating insights into emerging AI fields and describe advanced methodologies, systems, tools and techniques. The SETN conference series allows and encourages international participation and the language of the conference is English. Thus, this year the conference proceedings include papers from Germany, Belgium, USA and Taiwan.

Five Special Sessions dedicated to specific AI fields were also affiliated within the SETN 2012 conference:

- Advancing Translational Biological Research Through the Incorporation of Artificial Intelligence Methodologies (Aristotelis Chatziioannou, National Hellenic Research Foundation, Anastasios Bezerianos, University of Patras, and Konstantina Nikita, National Technical University of Athens)
- Artificial Intelligence in Bioinformatics (Pantelis Bagos, University of Central Greece)
- Intelligent Annotation of Digital Content (Dimitris K. Iakovidis, Technological Educational Institute of Lamia)

- Affective and Natural Interfaces (George Caridakis, National Technical University of Athens, Kostas Karpouzis, National Technical University of Athens, and Panagiotis Bamidis, Aristotle University of Thessaloniki)
- Unified Multimedia Knowledge Representation and Processing (Evaggelos Spyrou, Technological Educational Institute of Lamia, Manolis Wallace, University of Peloponnese, Phivos Mylonas, Ionian University, and Ioannis Anagnostopoulos, University of Central Greece)

The wide range of topics and high level of contributions guaranteed a very successful conference. We express our special thanks to all who contributed to the organization and scientific content of this conference. First to the authors of the papers, then to the special session organizers and finally to the reviewers and members of the Program and Organizing Committees. Last but not least, we also thank Alfred Hofmann, Frank Holzwarth, Anna Kramer, Christine Reiss, and the rest of the Springer team for their continuous help and support.

May 2012

Ilias Maglogiannis
Vassilis Plagianakos
Ioannis Vlahavas

Organization

SETN 2012 was organized by the Hellenic AI Society (EETN), in collaboration with the Department of Computer Science and Biomedical Informatics of the University of Central Greece.

Committees

Program Chairs

Ilias Maglogiannis	University of Central Greece
Vassilis Plagianakos	University of Central Greece
Ioannis Vlahavas	Aristotle University of Thessaloniki (EETN President)

Steering Committee

Constantine D. Spyropoulos	NCSR "Demokritos" (SETN 2010 Co-chair)
George Vouros	University of Piraeus, EETN President (SETN 2004 Co-chair)
Grigoris Antoniou	FORTH and University of Crete (SETN 2006 Chair)
Ioannis Vlahavas	Aristotle University (SETN 2002 Chair)
John Darzentas	University of the Aegean (SETN 2008 Chair)
Nikos Fakotakis	University of Patras (ECAI 2008 Chair)
Themistoklis Panayiotopoulos	University of Piraeus (SETN 2004 Co-chair)
Vangelis Karkaletsis	NCSR "Demokritos" (SETN 2010 Co-chair)

Program Committee

Aristotelis Chatziioannou	NHRF
Grigoris Antoniou	University of Crete
Grigorios Beligiannis	University of Ioannina
Stavros Karkanis	Technological Educational Institute of Lamia
Theodoros Soldatos	AIT
Demosthenes Vouyioukas	University of the Aegean
Nikos Papamarkos	Democritus University of Thrace
Michail Lagoudakis	Technical University of Crete
George Caridakis	NTUA
Basilis Gatos	NCSR "Demokritos"
Kyriakos Sgarbas	University of Patras
Achilles Kameas	Hellenic Open University
Katerina Kabassi	TEI Ionian

Maria Virvou	University of Piraeus
Alexander Artikis	NCSR "Demokritos"
George Potamias	FORTH
Vassilis Plagianakos	University of Central Greece
Charalampos Doukas	University of the Aegean
Nikos Hatziargyriou	National Technical University of Athens
Grigorios Tsoumakas	Aristotle University of Thessaloniki
Dimitrios Kosmopoulos	UTA, USA
Michael N. Vrahatis	University of Patras
Efstathios Stamatatos	University of the Aegean
Dimitrios Vergados	University of Piraeus
Sergios Petridis	NCSR "Demokritos"
Manolis Wallace	NTUA
Dimitrios Vogiatzis	NCSR "Demokritos"
George Tsihrintzis	University of Piraeus
Themis Panayiotopoulos	University of Piraeus
Georgios A. Pavlopoulos	Katholieke Universiteit Leuven
Nick Bassiliades	Aristotle University of Thessaloniki
Christos Papatheodorou	Ionian University
Ioannis Tsamardinos	University of Crete and FORTH
Kostas Karpouzis	National Technical University of Athens
Dimitris Iakovidis	Technological Educational Institute of Lamia
Lazaros Iliadis	Democritus University of Thrace
Dimitris Plexousakis	FORTH and University of Crete
Konstantinos Parsopoulos	University of Ioannina
Ilias Sakellariou	University of Macedonia
Petros Kefalas	City College, University of Sheffield
Aristidis Likas	University of Ioannina
Todor Ganchev	University of Patras
Manolis Koubarakis	National and Kapodistrian University of Athens
Konstantinos Dimopoulos	University of Sheffield
Jim Prentzas	Democritus University of Thrace
Vassilis Moustakis	Technical University of Crete
Yiannis Kompatsiaris	CERTH
Michalis Savelonas	University of Houston
Ioannis Refanidis	University of Macedonia
Dimirtis Tasoulis	Winton Capital, UK
Christos-Nikolaos Anagnostopoulos	University of the Aegean
Michalis Vazirgiannis	Athens University of Economics and Business
Giorgos Stoilos	Oxford University, UK
Daniel Schober	IMBI UKLFR
Pantelis Bagos	University of Central Greece
Kostas Karatzas	Aristotle University of Thessaloniki

Panos Trahanias	FORTH and University of Crete
Elpiniki Papageorgiou	Technological Educational Institute of Lamia
Efthyvoulos Kyriacou	University of Cyprus
Dimitris Apostolou	University of Piraeus
Vasileios Mezaris	Informatics and Telematics Institute
Andreas Andreou	Technical University of Cyprus
Spyros Vosinakis	University of the Aegean
Theodore Dalamagas	IMIS Institute/"Athena" Research Center
Georgios Paliouras	NCSR "Demokritos"
Ilias Maglogiannis	University of Central Greece
Georgios Dounias	University of the Aegean
Nicos Pavlidis	Lancaster University, UK
Stasinos Konstantopoulos	NCSR "Demokritos"
Ioannis Anagnostopoulos	University of Central Greece
Ion Androutsopoulos	Athens University of Economics and Business
Manolis Gergatsoulis	Ionian University
Nikos Fakotakis	University of Patras
George Magoulas	Birkbeck College, University of London, UK
Ioannis Hatzilygeroudis	University of Patras
Michael Epitropakis	University of Patras
Christos Douligeris	University of Piraeus
Katia Lida Kermanidis	Ionian University
Stathes Hadjiefthymiades	University of Athens
Ioanna Stamatopoulou	City College, University of Sheffield
Vangelis Karkaletsis	NCSR "Demokritos"
Pavlos Peppas	University of Patras
Dimitris Kalles	Hellenic Open University
Kostas Stergiou	University of Western Macedonia
Konstantinos Koutroumbas	National Observatory of Athens
Constantine Kotropoulos	Aristotle University of Thessaloniki
Evangelos Sakkopoulos	University of Patras
Argyris Arnellos	University of the Basque Country
Constantinos Pattichis	University of Cyprus
Dimitrios Karras	TEI Chalkis
Dimitris Vrakas	Aristotle University of Thessaloniki
Efstratios Georgopoulos	TEI Kalamata
Eleni Galiotou	TEI Athens
George Papanagnou	Lamia General Hospital
Konstantina S. Nikita	NTUA
Manolis Maragoudakis	University of the Aegean
Nikos Vasilas	TEI Athens
Ioannis Pratikakis	Democritus University of Thrace
Panagiotis Stamatopoulos	National and Kapodistrian University of Athens
Panayiotis Tsanakas	NTUA

Sophia Tsekeridou	AIT
Stavros Perantonis	NCSR "Demokritos"
Stefanos Kollias	National Technical University of Athens
Stelios Piperidis	ILSP-Athena RC
Yannis Dimopoulos	University of Cyprus

Local Organizing Committee

Theodosios Goudas	University of Central Greece
Vassilis Pigadas	University of Central Greece
Sotirios Tasoulis	University of Central Greece
Charalampos Doukas	University of the Aegean

Table of Contents

SETN 2012 Main Conference

Special Session: Advancing Translational Biological Research through the Incorporation of Artificial Intelligence Methodologies

Special Session: Artificial Intelligence in Bioinformatics

Special Session: Intelligent Annotation of Digital Content

Special Session: Intelligent, Affective, and Natural Interfaces

Special Session: Unified Multimedia Knowledge Representation and Processing

Application of the Ant Colony Optimization Algorithm to Competitive Viral Marketing

Wan-Shiou Yang and Shi-Xin Weng

Department of Information Management, National Changhua University of Education,
No. 1, Jin-De Rd., Changhua 50007, Taiwan
{wsyang,sxweng}@cc.ncue.edu.tw

Abstract. Consumers often form complex social networks based on a multitude of different relations and interactions. By virtue of these interactions, they influence each other's decisions in adopting products or behaviors. Therefore, it is essential for companies to identify influential consumers to target, in the hopes that influencing them will lead to a large cascade of further recommendations. Several studies, based on approximation algorithms and assume that the objective function is monotonic and submodular, have been addressed this issue of viral marketing. However, there is a complex and broad family of diffusion models in competitive environment, and the properties of monotonic and submodular may not be upheld. Therefore, in this research, we borrowed from swarm intelligence-specifically the ant colony optimization algorithm-to address the competitive influence-maximization problem. The proposed approaches were evaluated using a coauthorship data set from the arXiv e-print (http://www.arxiv.org), and the obtained experimental results demonstrated that our approaches outperform two well-known benchmark heuristics.

Keywords: Ant Colony Optimization Algorithm, Viral Marketing, Social Network, E-Commerce.

1 Introduction

Consumers often form complex social networks based on a multitude of different relations and interactions. By virtue of these interactions, they influence each other's decisions in adopting products or behaviors. Therefore, it is essential for companies to identify influential consumers to target, in the hopes that influencing them will lead to a large cascade of further recommendations. This influence-maximization problem can be defined as the following: Given a social network, pick the k most influential individuals that will function as the initial adopters of a new product, so as to maximize the final number of infected individuals, subject to a specified model of influence diffusion.

Several studies have been addressed this influence-maximization problem. Kempe et al. [8] showed that the problem is NP-hard and many underlying diffusion models have monotonicity and submodularity properties. Hence, they applied a well-known greedy

I. Maglogiannis, V. Plagianakos, and I. Vlahavas (Eds.): SETN 2012, LNAI 7297, pp. 1–8, 2012.

approximation to solve the problem. Many of the existing approaches for solving the influence-maximization problem are based on approximation algorithms and assume that the objective function is monotonic and submodular [1] [3] [5] [10] [11].

This influence-maximization problem has been extended to introduce a new product into a market where competing products exist [4]: Given the competitor's choice of initial adopters of technology B, maximize the spread of technology A by choosing a set of initial adopters such that the expected spread of technology A will be maximal. As identified by Borodin et al. [2], however, there is a complex and broad family of competitive diffusion models, and the properties of monotonic and submodular may not be upheld-in which case the greedy approach cannot be used.

Therefore, in this research, we borrowed from the swarm intelligence-specifically the ant colony optimization (ACO) algorithm-to address the competitive influence-maximization problem. Our proposed approaches do not use the properties of monotonicity and submodularity and hence are general approaches. The proposed approaches were evaluated using a coauthorship data set from the arXiv e-print (http://www.arxiv.org), and the obtained experimental results demonstrated that our approaches outperform two well-known benchmark heuristics.

This paper is organized as follows. Section 2 reviews related studies, and Section 3 describes the proposed approaches applying the ACO algorithm to the competitive influence-maximization problem. The results of evaluating the proposed approaches are reported in Section 4, and Section 5 concludes with a summary of this study and a discussion of future research directions.

2   Literature Review

Motivated by applications to marketing, Domingos and Richardson [6] defined the original influence-maximization problem as finding a k-node set that maximizes the expected number of convinced nodes at the end of the diffusion process. In [13], authors further extended their models to the continuous case. In [8], the authors introduced various diffusion models. They showed that determining an optimal seeding set is NP-hard, and that a natural greedy strategy yields provable approximation guarantees if the diffusion model has the properties of monotonicity and submodularity. This line of research was extended by introducing other competitors so as to produce the most far-ranging influence [1] [3] [4] [5] [9] [10] [11].

As noted by Borodin et al. [2], however, certain diffusion models-particular those for investigating competitive influence in social networks-may not be monotonic or submodular, and hence the original greedy approach cannot be used. In this research, we exploited the search capacity of the ACO algorithm to find an (approximated) solution for the competitive influence-maximization problem. ACO, initially proposed by Dorigo [7], is a new meta-heuristic developed for composing approximated solutions. ACO is inspired by the collective foraging behavior in real ant colonies and represents problems as graphs, with solutions being constructed within a stochastic iterative process by adding solution components to partial solutions. Each individual ant constructs a part of the solution using an artificial pheromone and heuristic information dependent on the problem. ACO has been receiving extensive attention due to its successful applications to many NP-hard combinatorial optimization problems today [7].

3   Proposed Approaches

In this research, we transform consumer's connectedness data into a social network and represent the network as a directed graph, where each node represents a consumer and each edge represents the connectedness between two nodes. In this research, we assume that a company has a fixed budget for targeting k consumers who will trigger a cascade of influence. We consider the competitive influence-maximization problem from the follower's perspective. Therefore, given a social network $SN=(V, E)$ and a set C of initial adopters of a competing product, our goal is to choose a set of nodes S, $S \subseteq V-C$ and $|S|=k$, that maximizes the spread of our new product.

The inspiration for ACO is the foraging behavior of real ants [7]. When searching for food, ants initially explore the area surrounding their nest in a random manner. As soon as an ant finds a food source, it evaluates the quantity and the quality of the food and carries some of it back to the nest. During the return trip, the ant deposits a chemical pheromone trail on the ground. The quantity of pheromone deposited depends on the quantity and quality of the food, and this will guide other ants to the food source. Indirect communication between the ants via pheromone trails enables them to find the shortest paths between their nest and food sources. This characteristic of real ant colonies is exploited in artificial ant colonies, and the ACO algorithm utilizes a graph representation to find (approximated) solutions for the target problem.

In order to utilize graph representation to find (approximated) solutions, in this research, we construct a complete digraph to represent the original social network. Then, we transform the defined competitive influence-maximization problem into a problem of finding a circle of prescribed length so as to maximize the expected spread from the set of nodes in the circle.

The central component of an ACO algorithm is a parameterized probabilistic model, which is called the pheromone model. This model is used to probabilistically generate solutions to the problem under consideration by assembling them using a finite set of solution components. At run-time, ACO algorithms update the pheromone values using previously generated solutions. The update aims to concentrate the search within regions of the search space containing high-quality solutions. We therefore design a basic ACO algorithm as shown in Figure 1, which works as follows. The algorithm first initializes all of the pheromone values according to the InitializePheromoneValue() function. An iterative process then starts, with the GenerateSolution() functionbeing used by all ants to probabilistically construct solutions to the problem based on a given pheromone model in each iteration. The EvaluateSolution() function is used to evaluate the quality of the constructed solutions and some of the solutions are used by the UpdatePheromoneValue() function to update the pheromone before the next iteration starts.

```
ACO_InfluenceMaximization()
{
    InitializePheromoneValue();
    While (termination conditions not met)
    {
        GenerateSolution();
        EvaluateSolution();
        UpdatePheromoneValue();
    }
    Return best solution;
}
```

Fig. 1. The basic ACO algorithm for the competitive influence-maximization problem

The InitializePheromoneValue() function is used to initialize the pheromone values of all nodes of the constructed complete digraph. Initially, each node has a very small pheromone value of $\varepsilon \neq 0$. A possible solution is then created for each node by assembling the solution components as follows. Starting node i is added first, and each of its first-level neighbors are independently selected with probability p; then its second-level neighbors are selected, and so on, until k nodes are assembled in the solution. The influence of the solution-which corresponds to the expected number of the adopters at the end of the diffusion process-is then evaluated. The influences of the top-m solutions are then used as the pheromone and lay down on all component nodes of the solution. Different solutions may lay down pheromone values on the same nodes, in which case all pheromone values of the same node are summarized.

Figure 2(a) shows an example of a social network of size 7, and Figure 2(b) shows the corresponding complete digraph. Suppose each solution has 3 nodes and that each node has an initial pheromone value of 1. The InitializePheromoneValue() function creates 7 solutions since there are 7 nodes in the complete digraph. Suppose each solution is created and the influence of each solution is evaluated as listed in Table 1. Then nodes 3, 4, and 5 will have a pheromone value of 7, and the other nodes all have a pheromone value of 1 if only the best solution (i.e., solution 4) lay down its pheromone.

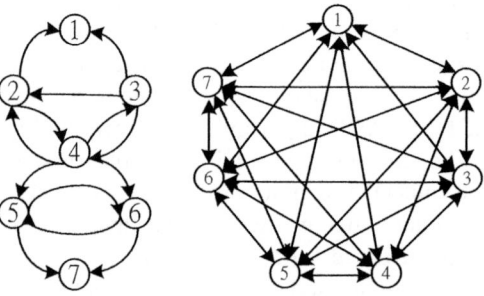

(a)   A social network   (b) The corresponding complete digraph

Fig. 2. A social network and its corresponding complete digraph

Table 1. An example of pheromone values

Solution #	Nodes	Influence
1	1,2,6	4
2	2,1,4	5
3	3,1,2	4
4	4,3,5	6
5	5,6,7	3
6	6,5,7	3
7	7,6,2	4

Then, in the iterative process, all ants probabilistically construct solutions to the problem. In the GenerateSolution() function, each artificial ant generates a complete target set by choosing the nodes according to a probabilistic state-transition rule: an ant positioned on node r chooses the node s to move to by applying the rule given by (1). In (1), q is a random number uniformly distributed in $[0,1]$, q_0 is a parameter ($0 \le q_0 \le 1$), and S is a random variable selected according to the probability distribution given in (2). In both (1) and (2), τ is the pheromone value and η is the heuristic value respectively.

$$s = \begin{cases} \arg \max_{u \in V-r} \left\{ [\tau(u)]^\alpha * [\eta(u)]^\beta \right\} & \text{if } q \le q_0 \\ S, \text{otherwise} \end{cases} \tag{1}$$

$$p(u) = \frac{[\tau(u)]^\alpha * [\eta(u)]^\beta}{\sum [\tau(u)]^\alpha * [\eta(u)]^\beta} \tag{2}$$

Also, in this research, we propose using two methods for determining the heuristic values of nodes:

(a) Degree centrality approach: Degree centrality is defined as the number of links incident upon a node [12]. Since outdegree is often interpreted as a form of gregariousness in a social network, we define the number of links that the node directs to others as its degree heuristic value. For the example shown in Figure 2(a), the degree heuristic of node 4 is 4.

(b) Distance centrality approach: Distance centrality is another commonly used influence measure [12]. The distance centrality of a node is defined as the average distance from this node to all of the other nodes in the graph. Again considering node 4 in Figure 2(a), its distance centrality is 1.33 since its distances from nodes 1, 2, 3, 5, 6, 7 are 2, 1, 1, 1, 1, and 2, respectively. We define the distance heuristic value of a node as the number of all nodes minus its distance centrality.

Suppose the pheromone and the heuristic values of all nodes in Figure 2 are updated as listed in Table 2. Then suppose that an artificial ant is going to choose a 3-node solution, and that three random numbers are generated: 0.6, 0.9, and 0.5. Let $\alpha = 1$, $\beta = 1$, and $q_0 = 0.8$. For the first node, the ant will select node 4 since this has the largest value according to (1); for the second node, since $0.9 > q_0$, the ant will select one node according to the probability distribution given in (2); suppose that node 6 is selected in this step. Finally, the ant will select node 3 since this node has the largest value among the leaving nodes. A set of nodes {4,6,3} is then be generated as the solution.

Table 2. An example of the pheromone values and the heuristic values of nodes

Node	1	2	3	4	5	6	7
Pheromone value	1	1	7	7	7	1	1
Heuristic value	0	2	3	4	2	2	0

The EvaluateSolution() function is then used to evaluate the performance of each solution. To evaluate the performance of a solution, we need to compute the expect spread of the solution. Again, we obtain estimates by simulating the diffusion models in a random process. Specifically, given a particular diffusion model, we simulate the process 1000 times, and compute the average number of influenced nodes for each solution.

Once all ants have found their target sets, the pheromone is updated on all nodes. In our system, the global updating rule is implemented according to (3). Similar to the InitializePheromoneValue() function, the influences of the top-m solutions are used as the pheromone and lay down on all component nodes of the solution and all pheromone values of the same node are summarized. The parameter ρ is the evaporation rate and is implemented to avoid the algorithm converging too rapidly toward a suboptimal region.

$$\tau(u) = (1-\rho) * \tau(u) + \sum_{k=1}^{M} \tau(u)^k \tag{3}$$

Considering the example in Table 2. Let ρ be 0.9. Suppose there is an artificial ant who finds a 3-node solution {3,4,6}, whose expected influence is 5, and the current pheromone values of nodes 3, 4, and 6 are 7, 7, and 1 respectively. After updating the pheromone, these values will be set as 11.3 (= 7 * 0.9 + 5), 11.3 (= 7 * 0.9 + 5), and 5.9 (= 1 * 0.9 + 5) respectively.

The iterative process of the ACO_InfluenceMaximization() function ends when some termination condition is met, such as exceeding the execution time limit or a certain ratio of the nodes being influenced. The result, which is the best target set, is then returned.

4   Evaluation

In this section, we evaluated the efficacy of the proposed approaches by conducting experiments on a real world coauthorship data set. The coauthorship network was compiled from the complete list of papers on the arXiv e-print (www.arxiv.org) dated between January 1, 2006 and December 31, 2010. We constructed a coauthorship network as a directed graph in which each node represents an author and each directed edge represents a coauthor relationship from the author to another if they have coauthored at least one paper. Each edge (s_i , s_j) in the constructed coauthorship network is associated with a weight defined as $\frac{|A_i \cap A_j|}{A_i}$, where A_i and A_j denote the sets of papers authored by s_i and s_j respectively. The coauthorship network contained 8,436 nodes representing all of the authors of the included papers and 168,712 edges representing the co-author relationships between these authors.

We compared the performances of the proposed approaches in the competitive environment. We used the weight-proportional competitive linear threshold model [2] as the diffusion model. In this model, each node v initially chooses a threshold $\theta_v \in [0,1]$, and each directed edge (u,v) is assigned a weight $w_{u,v} \in [0,1]$. Given the sets I_A and I_B of initial adopters, the diffusion process unfolds as follows. In each step t, every inactive node v checks the set of edges incoming from its active neighbors. If their collective weight exceeds the threshold values, the node becomes active. In that case, the node will adopt technology A with probability equal to the ratio between the collective weight of edges outgoing from A-active neighbors and the total collective weight of edges out going from all active neighbors. It has been proven that the competitive model does not have the properties of monotonicity and submodularity [2]. We conducted several preliminary experiments to determine the ACO's parameters α, β, ρ for the proposed approaches. The best combination of parameters α-β-ρ is 1-2-0.8, and therefore this setting was used in the subsequent experiment.

We compared the performances of the proposed approaches in the competitive case. In this experiment, two benchmarks-the maximum degree approach and the minimum distance approach-were used as baselines for our comparisons. In the maximum degree approach, we simply pick k nodes in the coauthorship network having the k highest degree centrality values. In the minimum distance centrality approach, we pick k nodes in the coauthorship network having the k lowest distance centrality values. For our approach the two different heuristics described in Section 3 were used. These values were averaged over 1000 runs. Figure 3 shows the averaged spread of the approximated solution generated by our approaches and two benchmarks when solution size k was 10, 20, 30, 40, 50, 60, 70, 80, and 90.

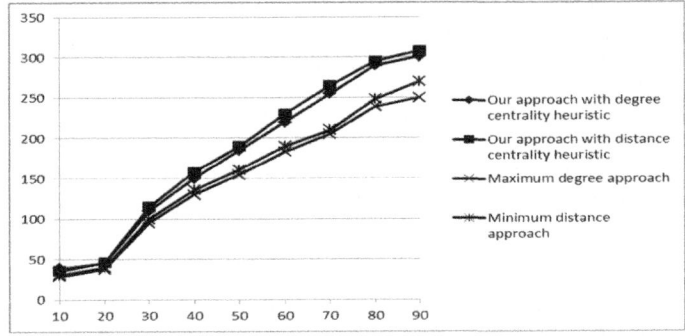

Fig. 3. Comparison of the performances of the proposed approaches and benchmarks in competitive case

It can be seen that our approach using distance heuristic value has the best performance, followed by our approach using degree heuristic value, the minimum distance centrality approach, and the maximum degree approach in order. The performances of both of our two proposed approaches were better than those of the two benchmarks. The experimental results demonstrate the effectiveness of the search capacity of the ACO algorithm. Also, in the two proposed approaches, the approach using distance heuristic value has the highest diffusion values. It indicates that the distance centrality heuristic superior than the degree centrality heuristic.

5   Conclusions

This research used the search capacity of the ACO algorithm to solve the competitive influence-maximization problem. Experiments revealed that the proposed approach using distance heuristic value resulted in best performance. Our work could be extended in several directions, such as testing the proposed approaches in different social networks and using different diffusion models.

References

1. Bharathi, S., Kempe, D., Salek, M.: Competitive Influence Maximization in Social Networks. In: Deng, X., Graham, F.C. (eds.) WINE 2007. LNCS, vol. 4858, pp. 306–311. Springer, Heidelberg (2007)
2. Borodin, A., Filmus, Y., Oren, J.: Threshold Models for Competitive Influence in Social Networks. In: Saberi, A. (ed.) WINE 2010. LNCS, vol. 6484, pp. 539–550. Springer, Heidelberg (2010)
3. Cao, T., Wu, X., Wang, S., Hu, X.: Maximizing Influence Spread in Modular Social Networks by Optimal Resource Allocation. Expert Systems with Applications 38(10), 13128–13135 (2011)
4. Carnes, T., Nagarajan, C., Wild, S.M., Zuylen, A.: Maximizing Influence in a Competitive Social Network: A Follower's Perspective. In: International Conference on Electronic Commerce (2007)
5. Chen, W., Wang, Y., Yang, S.: Efficient Influence Maximization in Social Networks. In: International Conference on Knowledge Discovery and Data Mining (2009)
6. Domingos, P., Richardson, M.: Mining the Network Value of Customers. In: International Conference on Knowledge Discovery and Data Mining (2001)
7. Dorigo, M., Blum, C.: Ant Colony Optimization Theory: A Survey. Theoretical Computer Science 344 (2005)
8. Kempe, D., Kleinberg, J., Tardos, E.: Maximizing the Spread of Influence through a Social Network. In: International Conference on Knowledge Discovery and Data Mining (2003)
9. Kempe, D., Kleinberg, J., Tardos, É.: Influential Nodes in a Diffusion Model for Social Networks. In: Caires, L., Italiano, G.F., Monteiro, L., Palamidessi, C., Yung, M. (eds.) ICALP 2005. LNCS, vol. 3580, pp. 1127–1138. Springer, Heidelberg (2005)
10. Kostka, J., Oswald, Y.A., Wattenhofer, R.: Word of Mouth: Rumor Dissemination in Social Networks. In: Shvartsman, A.A., Felber, P. (eds.) SIROCCO 2008. LNCS, vol. 5058, pp. 185–196. Springer, Heidelberg (2008)
11. Mossel, E., Roch, S.: Submodularity of Influence in Social Networks: From Local to Global. SIAM Journal on Computing 39(6), 2176–2188 (2010)
12. Opsahl, T., Agneessens, F., Skvoretz, J.: Node Centrality in Weighted Networks: Generalizing Degree and Shortest Paths. Social Networks 32(245), 245–251 (2010)
13. Richardson, M., Domingos, P.: Mining Knowledge-sharing Sites for Viral Marketing. In: International Conference on Knowledge Discovery and Data Mining (2002)

Constraint Propagation
as the Core of Local Search

Nikolaos Pothitos, George Kastrinis, and Panagiotis Stamatopoulos

Department of Informatics and Telecommunications, University of Athens,
Panepistimiopolis, 157 84 Athens, Greece
{pothitos,g.kastrinis,takis}@di.uoa.gr

Abstract. Constraint programming is a powerful paradigm for solving constraint satisfaction problems, using various techniques. Amongst them, local search is a prominent methodology, particularly for large instances. However, it lacks uniformity, as it includes many variations accompanied by complex data structures, that cannot be easily brought under the same "umbrella." In this work we embrace their wide diversity by adopting propagation algorithms. Our *constraint based local search* (CBLS) system provides declarative alternative tools to express search methods, by exploiting conflict-sets of constraints and variables. Their maintenance is straightforward as it does not employ queues, unlike the state of the art CBLS systems. Thus, the propagation complexity is kept linear in the number of changes required after each assignment. Experimental results illustrate the capabilities, not only of the already implemented methods, such as hill climbing, simulated annealing, etc., but also the robustness of the underlying propagation engine.

Keywords: constraint based local search, constraint programming, constraint satisfaction problem, solver, indirect methods, metaheuristics.

1 Introduction

Constraint programming (CP) is nowadays a well-established Computer Science field, that facilitates the expression of contemporary or difficult problems and, on the other hand, solves them through generic search methods. What makes this approach unique is not only the independence between the problem description and solution processes, but also the plethora of the solving mechanisms that one may leverage on; *constraint based local search* (CBLS) is one of them.

While in constructive search we build a solution to a *constraint satisfaction problem* (CSP) from scratch and take care to satisfy every constraint after each assignment, CBLS solvers assemble a *candidate* solution, and then try to fix it, by eliminating conflicting sets of variables and constraints.

Recent work on the area includes KANGAROO, a CBLS system that appeared only in 2011 [11]. It is presented as a more efficient alternative to the COMET platform [23]. Both CBLS systems internally employ queues in the constraint propagation and externally provide high level control structures and interfaces, that permit their use by inexperienced users, although it is not easy for the

I. Maglogiannis, V. Plagianakos, and I. Vlahavas (Eds.): SETN 2012, LNAI 7297, pp. 9–16, 2012.

local search method programmer to surpass the already implemented variants and access immediately the conflict sets.[1] IOPT toolkit offers many local search variants, but does not favour internal methods reprogramming [24].

Previous frameworks, like EASYLOCAL++ [4] and HOTFRAME [6] are flexible for the design of new local search methods, but the CSP description is effortful for the average user, as new C++ classes have to be built. They effectively implement local search but it is not bridged with other famous paradigms, such as constructive search. Last but not least, there are also CBLS solvers that are specialized only for specific problems like SAT [12].

A CBLS system should support the design and implementation of most local search variants by facilitating the problem description and by allowing the user/programmer to access every conflict set. Our contribution focuses on these two aspects. First of all, we provide an expressive mechanism to state CSPs by using NAXOS SOLVER, a constraint programming platform [13], that supports constructive search as well. And second, we build generic conflict sets that are updated after each assignment. Our constructs are theoretically defined, algorithmically supported and experimentally tested for solving CSPs.

2   CSPs and Multidisciplinary Contributions

Constraint satisfaction problems appear in many areas not only in Computer Science, but in daily routine too. Common problems such as timetabling for educational institutes are now easily formulated as CSPs [20] and efficiently solved via Constraint Programming [15], while many new CSPs come from Bioinformatics [1]. A known interdisciplinary CSP is the satisfiability problem [21].

Definition 1. *A* CSP *consists of the following triptych* [22]:

- *Constrained* Variables *that compose the set* $\mathscr{X} = \{X_1, X_2, \ldots, X_n\}$.
- Domains *of the variables that make up the set* $\mathscr{D} = \{D_{X_1}, D_{X_2}, \ldots, D_{X_n}\}$. *In this work it is presumed that each domain is a finite set of integers.*
- Constraints *between the variables, composing the set* $\mathscr{C}$. *Each* C_i *in* $\mathscr{C}$ *is a relation between the variables of a set* $S_i \subseteq \mathscr{X}$. *Formally, we define* $C_i = (S_i, T_i)$, *where* $T_i \subseteq D_{i_1} \times D_{i_2} \times \cdots \times D_{i_q}$ *is the set with all the allowed combinations for the variables in* $S_i = \{X_{i_1}, X_{i_2}, \ldots, X_{i_q}\}$.

When every domain becomes singleton, in other words when each constrained variable "equals" a specific value, we have an *assignment*. If an assignment satisfies the constraints of the problem, it is also a *solution*.

2.1   Solving Phase and Thrashing

After a CSP description, we select a procedure to seek a solution. There are *direct search methods* that *construct* a solution step by step, by assigning a value to a variable each time, that is why they are also called *systematic* [14].

---

[1] We did not analyze COMET further, because it has not sufficient implementation details (see also [11]), whilst the KANGAROO executable is currently unavailable.

But when it comes to solve large-scale instances, constructive search suffers by the so-called *combinatorial explosion* that ends up in *thrashing,* because of the many steps and constraints checks required to build a solution.

2.2   Local Search and Variants

An alternative is to start with an assignment and to iteratively try to *repair* it, in order to satisfy the constraints a posteriori [8].

Definition 2. *In the general case, an* assignment *or* location *L is a non-empty subset of $D_{X_1} \times D_{X_2} \times \cdots \times D_{X_n}$. If the assignment contains more than one tuples, i.e. if $|L| > 1$, then it is called a* partial assignment.[2]

Example 1. Let $\mathscr{D} = \{D_{X_1}, D_{X_2}, D_{X_3}\}$ and $D_{X_1} = D_{X_2} = D_{X_3} = \{0, 1, 2\}$. The location $L_1 = \{1\} \times \{1, 2\} \times \{0\}$ is a partial assignment, while $L_2 = \{1\} \times \{1\} \times \{0\}$ is a complete assignment—with all the domains made singleton.

In *local search* we begin with an initial assignment L_{init} and, if it is not a solution, we modify it, so as to move on to an improved assignment L'.

Definition 3. *A* neighborhood *for a (complete or partial) assignment L is a set $\mathsf{N}(L)$ with all the possible successors of L in the search space. The* step function step(L) *is used to return the specific successor of L, with step$(L) \in \mathsf{N}(L)$.*

Each local search variant is described by its neighborhood and step function.

Hill Climbing. A well-known variant is *hill climbing* (HC), also known as *iterative improvement* [3]. Normally, its neighborhood $\mathsf{N}(L)$ contains the locations L' which differ in one variable assignment with regard to L (*1-exchange*).

The step functions of HC variants usually employ an eval-uation function that quantifies each location quality. So, the step(L) function selects a location L' with eval$(L') <$ eval(L). To define this metric we utilize the conflict set notion.

Definition 4. *We have three* conflict set *kinds:*

- CS$(\mathscr{C})$ *consists of the constraints in $\mathscr{C}$, violated by the current assignment.*
- CS$(\mathscr{C}, X)$ *contains the constraints in CS$(\mathscr{C})$ that refer to the variable X.*
- CS$(\mathscr{X})$ *is composed of all the variables $X \in \mathscr{X}$, with CS$(\mathscr{C}, X) \neq \emptyset$.*

An ordinary measure for eval(L) is $|\mathsf{CS}(\mathscr{C})|$. E.g. in the *iterative best improvement,* we select the location L' in $\mathsf{N}(L)$ with the minimum $|\mathsf{CS}(\mathscr{C})|$.

Simulated Annealing. The above practice is prone to be trapped into *local minima* of the evaluation function. In this case we need a *meta-heuristic* to escape the current local minimum by making a random step. *Simulated annealing* (SA) was introduced in 1983 as one of the first meta-heuristics [10].

SA permits random steps—to skip local minima—while a parameter called *temperature* is high; as time passes by and temperature drops, the method becomes less tolerant in random steps, especially if their evaluation is poor.

---

[2] In Definition 2 we extended the more traditional definition: *"partial assignment* is an assignment where not all variables are given values."

3 An Augmented CSP Schema

To cope with the needs of a generic CBLS system, that integrates the above methods and supports the design of new ones, an enhanced CSP outline is suggested by extending the variable notion. At first, the variables in $\mathscr{X}$, specified in the CSP description, are marked as *non-intermediate*; then $\mathscr{X}$ is augmented by adding into it the implied *intermediate* variables. These variables do not alter the CSP semantics; they are completely auxiliary, as they satisfy the following.

Property 1. If a constrained variable $Y \in \mathscr{X}$ is *intermediate* (in other words, if it is *invariant* or *dependent*) *with regard to* the variables $\{X_{i_1}, X_{i_2}, \ldots, X_{i_m}\}$, it holds that $|D_{X_{i_1}}| = 1 \wedge |D_{X_{i_2}}| = 1 \wedge \cdots \wedge |D_{X_{i_m}}| = 1 \implies |D_Y| = 1$.

Example 2. Let $\mathscr{X} = \{X, Y\}$ and $\mathscr{C} = \{Y = X + 1\}$, where Y is intermediate. Due to Property 1, the variable Y is intermediate *with regard to* X, because if we instantiate X (i.e. if we set $D_X = \{3\}$), the domain D_Y must be also made singleton ($D_Y = \{4\}$) in order to satisfy the constraint.

In some cases Property 1 may hold for non-intermediate variables too. Thus, it is *not* Property 1 that makes a variable intermediate; CP solvers automatically generate intermediate variables, to produce amalgamated constraints.

3.1 Intermediate Variables in the N-Queens Problem

Take for example the N-Queens problem; the goal here is to place N queens on a $N \times N$ chessboard, so that no two queens "attack" each other.

Problem 1. In the normal chessboard we have $\mathscr{X} = \{X_1, X_2, \ldots, X_8\}$. Each X_i corresponds to the queen on the ith *line*. The values in D_{X_i} are the possible *columns* to place the queen on. The constraint "*no X_i attacks X_j*" is decomposed into the constraints triplet $X_i \neq X_j \wedge X_i + i \neq X_j + j \wedge X_i - i \neq X_j - j$ [19].

The above three sub-constraints, imply that no two queens share the same column, minor diagonal, and principal diagonal respectively. These can be stated in most CP solvers [5,9] as three *individual* constraints, while the compound statement "*X_i does not attack X_j*" is only used in theoretical bibliography, where ad hoc and not generic constraints often occur. Besides, the inequality constraint ($\neq$) is reusable in many CSPs [7], while the complex constraint "*X_i does not attack X_j*" is not generic. Figure 1 depicts the automatically generated *intermediate* variables X_i', X_i'', X_j', and X_j'' that are eventually added into $\mathscr{X}$.

3.2 Issues in Local Search

Intermediate variables facilitate the CSPs specification and adapt smoothly to direct search methods. However, they do not "fit" well in local search, as it does not usually incorporate constraint propagation [18], that is mainly integrated in systematic search [17]. Actually, in local search, when we assign a value to a

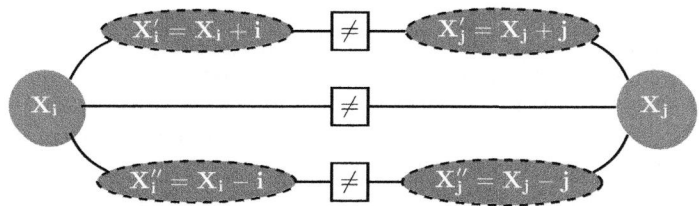

Fig. 1. Non-intermediate and intermediate (*dotted*) variables in the constraint network

variable, the assignment is not propagated to its dependent intermediate variables; their assignment is dependent exclusively to the heuristics and the declared neighborhood and step functions (cf. Definition 3).

Another issue is that the conflict sets are made inefficient to maintain, due to the significant number of redundant (intermediate) variables in them. This makes it also difficult for the heuristics to select the next move to go on, out from a cumbersome set—with the intermediate variables included in it.

3.3   Conflicting Assignments and Violated Constraints

In the new schema, we make the conflict sets transparent to invariants.

Proposition 1. *If a constraint which involves the variables $X_{i_1}, \ldots, X_{i_m}$ is violated, then it holds* $\mathsf{depend}(X_{i_1}) \cup \cdots \cup \mathsf{depend}(X_{i_m}) \subseteq \mathsf{CS}(\mathscr{X})$, *where* $\mathsf{depend}(X)$ *is the set of* non-intermediate *variables that the intermediate X depends on. If X is not intermediate, then we suppose* $\mathsf{depend}(X) = \{X\}$.

With the above proposition we can identify a composite constraint, even if we do not know about its inherent sub-constraints and intermediate variables. For instance, in this work we label each constraint with the *non-intermediate* variables it depends on. Consequently, the conflict sets $\mathsf{CS}(\mathscr{C})$ and $\mathsf{CS}(\mathscr{C}, X)$ contain tuples of variables that are involved into the corresponding violated constraints.

4   Unqueued Constraint Propagation

In light of this theoretical background we designed lightweight algorithms for the assignment propagation and conflict sets maintenance. The assignment of a value to a variable is the focal point of our framework.

Figure 2 illustrates what happens when we ASSIGN a *value* to X. If X is already bound to *another* value, then there is a conflict; we build the *conflictTuples* and add them to $\mathsf{CS}(\mathscr{C})$. Note that $\mathsf{CS}(\mathscr{C}, X)$ and $\mathsf{CS}(\mathscr{X})$ are also updated.

Each intermediate variable has its own *supportTuples* containing the sets of the variables that support its current assignment. When there is a conflict, $X.supportTuples$ collides with *supportVars*, i.e. the variables that fired the assignment. Hence, the conflict set here is $X.supportTuples \times \{supportVars\}$. We used the Cartesian product, because we may have multiple *supportTuples* for an

procedure X.ASSIGN($value, supportVars$)
if X is assigned another value **then**
   $conflictTuples \leftarrow \{\{\}\}$
   X.GETSUPPORT($conflictTuples$)
   for each $Y \in supportVars$ **do**
      Y.GETSUPPORT($conflictTuples$)
   end for
   Add $conflictTuples$ to $\mathsf{CS}(\mathscr{C})$
else
   Commit the assignment of $value$ to X
   Add $supportVars$ to $X.supportTuples$
   for each $c \in \mathscr{C}$, with X involved **do**
      c.FIXEDCONS( )
   end for
end if
end procedure

procedure X.GETSUPPORT($csTuples$)
for each $tuple \in X.supportTuples$ **do**
   $suppTuple \leftarrow \{\{\}\}$
   for each $Y \in tuple$ **do**
      $suppY \leftarrow \{\{\}\}$
      Y.GETSUPPORT($suppY$)
      $suppTuple \leftarrow suppTuple \times suppY$
   end for
   $csTuples \leftarrow csTuples \times suppTuple$
end for
if X is non-intermediate **then**
   $csTuples \leftarrow csTuples \times \{\{X\}\}$
end if
end procedure

Fig. 2. Algorithms to propagate assignments and to update conflict sets

assignment. But before inserting the product into $\mathsf{CS}(\mathscr{C})$, we must "dig" into it to find the non-intermediate variables it depends on, in view of Proposition 1; this is performed via GETSUPPORT, a recursive function in Fig. 2.

If ASSIGN is called by the user/programmer, $supportVars$ is empty and the assignment is permitted in any case. ASSIGN may be also called inside FIXEDCONS, a constraint-specific procedure which imposes *fixed consistency*.

Definition 5. *A constraint $C_i = (S_i, T_i)^3$ is* fixed consistent, *iff for each unassigned variable $X_{i_m} \in S_i$, there exist at least two values $v_1, v_2 \in D_{X_{i_m}}$ that satisfy it, i.e., formally, $\left| T_i \cap \left(D_{i_1} \times \cdots \times \{v\} \times \cdots \times D_{i_q} \right) \right| \geq 1, \ v \in \{v_1, v_2\}$.*

FIXEDCONS imposes fixed consistency w.r.t. C_i, by making singleton every variable in S_i that has only one value supported by the rest of the variables in S_i. Apparently, each constraint type has its own FIXEDCONS implementation.

5   Empirical Results

On top of the above algorithmic ground, we implemented several local search variants, including hill climbing and simulated annealing, outlined in Sect. 2.2. We integrated them into NAXOS SOLVER, a library for an object-oriented programming environment, written in C++ [13].

We used the above methods to find a solution to the N-Queens (Problem 1), on a Dell computer with an Intel Pentium D 2.8 GHz dual-core processor and 1 GB of memory, running Ubuntu 8.04.[4] Figure 3 depicts the performance of the

---

[3] See also Definition 1.
[4] The experiments code is available at http://di.uoa.gr/~pothitos/setn2012 with other instances, such as *graph coloring,* also solved.

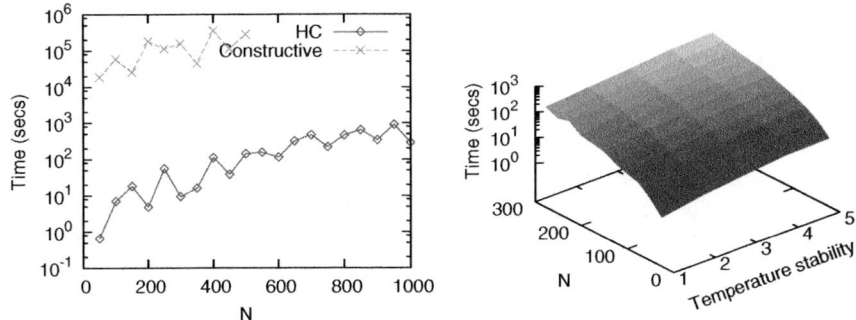

Fig. 3. Solving N-Queens using Constructive Search, Hill Climbing (*left*), and Simulated Annealing (*right*)

two methods, while the problem scales. In the *left* subfigure, constructive search time is also shown; besides, NAXOS SOLVER is capable of using it to solve exactly the same instances, as we did not need to modify the problem descriptions. Nevertheless, local search is orders of magnitude faster than constructive search. ECL^{i}PS^e 5.10 (Interval Constraints) constructive search gave even slower results.

Simulated Annealing performance depends on how fast the "temperature" drops. A low temperature means less random moves. In Fig. 3 the *temperature stability* factor defines for how many steps the temperature will remain the same. In these instances a rapid temperature decrease gives better results.

6 Conclusions and Future Directions

Our goal is to provide a freely available flexible platform—implemented as a C++ library—for both the specification of a problem and the design of local search methods. Beyond facilitating the compound constraints expression, intermediate variables were the key feature for propagating assignments.

A future direction is to enrich the available methods, by adopting e.g. genetic algorithms. It will be also interesting and easy, to describe a methodology for exploiting NAXOS hybrid framework to mix direct and indirect methods [2].

Acknowledgements. Nikolaos Pothitos is financially supported by a Bodossaki Foundation Ph.D. scholarship.

The work infrastructure was supported by the Special Account Research Grants of the National and Kapodistrian University of Athens, in the context of the project "C++ Libraries for Constraint Programming" (project no. 70/4/4639).

References

1. Barahona, P., Krippahl, L., Perriquet, O.: Bioinformatics: A challenge to constraint programming. In: Van Hentenryck, P., Milano, M. (eds.) Hybrid Optimization. Springer Opt. and Its Applications, vol. 45, pp. 463–487. Springer, New York (2011)

2. Chatzikokolakis, K., Boukeas, G., Stamatopoulos, P.: Construction and Repair: A Hybrid Approach to Search in CSPs. In: Vouros, G.A., Panayiotopoulos, T. (eds.) SETN 2004. LNCS (LNAI), vol. 3025, pp. 342–351. Springer, Heidelberg (2004)
3. Cohen, W., Greiner, R., Schuurmans, D.: Probabilistic hill-climbing. In: Hanson, S.J., Petsche, T., Kearns, M., Rivest, R.L. (eds.) Comp. Learn. Theory and Natural Learn. Syst., vol. II, pp. 171–181. The MIT Press, Cambridge (1994)
4. Di Gaspero, L., Schaerf, A.: EasyLocal++: An object-oriented framework for the flexible design of local-search algorithms. S/W Pract. Exp. 33(8), 733–765 (2003)
5. ECL^{i}PS^e constraint programming system (2011), http://eclipseclp.org
6. Fink, A., Voß, S.: HotFrame: A heuristic optimization framework. In: Voß, S., Woodruff, D. (eds.) Opt. S/W Cl. Lib., vol. 18, pp. 81–154. Kluwer, Boston (2002)
7. Gent, I.P., Walsh, T.: CSPLib: A Benchmark Library for Constraints. In: Jaffar, J. (ed.) CP 1999. LNCS, vol. 1713, pp. 480–481. Springer, Heidelberg (1999), http://CSPLib.org
8. Hoos, H.H., Tsang, E.: Local search methods. In: Rossi, et al. (eds.) [16], ch. 5, pp. 135–167
9. Ilog Solver (2010), http://ilog.com/products/cp
10. Kirkpatrick, S., Gelatt Jr., C.D., Vecchi, M.P.: Optimization by simulated annealing. Science 220(4598), 671–680 (1983)
11. Hakim Newton, M.A., Pham, D.N., Sattar, A., Maher, M.: Kangaroo: An Efficient Constraint-Based Local Search System Using Lazy Propagation. In: Lee, J. (ed.) CP 2011. LNCS, vol. 6876, pp. 645–659. Springer, Heidelberg (2011)
12. Pham, D.N., Thornton, J., Sattar, A.: Building structure into local search for SAT. In: Veloso, M.M. (ed.) IJCAI 2007, pp. 2359–2364. AAAI Press, Menlo Park (2007)
13. Pothitos, N.: Naxos Solver (2011), http://di.uoa.gr/~pothitos/naxos
14. Prosser, P., Unsworth, C.: Limited discrepancy search revisited. Journal of Experimental Algorithmics 16(1), 1.6:1–1.6:18 (2011)
15. Qu, R., Burke, E.K., McCollum, B., Merlot, L.T.G., Lee, S.Y.: A survey of search methodologies and automated system development for examination timetabling. Journal of Scheduling 12(1), 55–89 (2009)
16. Rossi, F., van Beek, P., Walsh, T. (eds.): Handbook of Constraint Programming. Foundations of Artificial Intelligence. Elsevier Science, Amsterdam (2006)
17. Sabin, D., Freuder, E.C.: Contradicting Conventional Wisdom in Constraint Satisfaction. In: Borning, A. (ed.) PPCP 1994. LNCS, vol. 874, pp. 10–20. Springer, Heidelberg (1994)
18. Schulte, C., Stuckey, P.J.: Efficient constraint propagation engines. ACM Transactions on Programming Languages and Systems 31(1), 2:1–2:43 (2008)
19. Smith, B.M.: Modelling. In: Rossi, et al. (eds.) [16], ch. 11, pp. 377–406
20. Stamatopoulos, P., Viglas, E., Karaboyas, S.: Nearly optimum timetable construction through CLP and intelligent search. Int'l J. on AI Tools 7(4), 415–442 (1998)
21. Tamura, N., Taga, A., Kitagawa, S., Banbara, M.: Compiling finite linear CSP into SAT. Constraints 14(2), 254–272 (2009)
22. Tsang, E.: A glimpse of constraint satisfaction. AI Review 13(3), 215–227 (1999)
23. Van Hentenryck, P., Michel, L.: Constraint-Based Local Search. Logic Programming. The MIT Press, Cambridge (2009)
24. Voudouris, C., Dorne, R., Lesaint, D., Liret, A.: iOpt: A Software Toolkit for Heuristic Search Methods. In: Walsh, T. (ed.) CP 2001. LNCS, vol. 2239, pp. 716–729. Springer, Heidelberg (2001)

Semantic Query Answering in Digital Libraries

Ilianna Kollia, Kostas Rapantzikos, Giorgos Stamou, and Andreas Stafylopatis

School of Electrical and Computer Engineering, National Technical University of Athens, Zographou Campus 15780, Athens, Greece

Abstract. A large activity for digitization, access and preservation of cultural heritage is taking place in Europe and the United States, which involves all types of cultural institutions, i.e., galleries, libraries, museums, archives and all types of cultural content. Semantic interoperability is a key issue in these developments. Content metadata constitute the main features of cultural items that are analysed and used to interpret users' queries, so that the most appropriate content is presented to the users. This paper presents a new semantic search methodology, including a query answering mechanism which meets the semantics of users' queries and enriches the answers by exploiting appropriate visual features, through an interweaved knowledge and machine learning based approach. An experimental study is presented, using content from the Europeana digital library, illustrating the improved performance of the proposed semantic search approach.

1 Introduction

Digital evolution of the Cultural Heritage Field has grown rapidly in the last few years. Following the early developments at European level and the Lund principles[1], massive digitisation and annotation activities have been taking place all over Europe and the United States. The creation and evolution of Europeana[2], as a unique point of access to European Cultural Heritage, has been one of the major achievements in this procedure. More than 19 million objects, expressing the European cultural richness, are currently accessible through Europeana, aiming at including all European masterpieces.

Due to the diversity of content types and of metadata schemas used to annotate the content, semantic interoperability has been identified as a key issue during the last few years. The main approach to interoperability of cultural content metadata has been the usage of well-known standards in the specific museum, archive and library sectors (Dublin Core, Cidoc-CRM, LIDO, EAD, METS) and their mapping to a common data model used - at the Europeana level: European Semantic Element (ESE, 2008), European Data Model (EDM, 2010) - to provide unified access to the centrally accessed, distributed all over Europe, cultural content. Semantic search targets on answering user queries, or enriching content providers' metadata by exploiting both explicit and implicit related knowledge. Reasoning on available knowledge bases, based on appropriate representations and languages, such as description logics, Resource Description Framework (RDF), Web Ontology Language (OWL) has been identified as the means to

---

[1] http://www.cordis.europa.eu/pub/ist/docs/digicult/lund
[2] http://www.europeana.eu

I. Maglogiannis, V. Plagianakos, and I. Vlahavas (Eds.): SETN 2012, LNAI 7297, pp. 17–24, 2012.
© Springer-Verlag Berlin Heidelberg 2012

move ahead in this direction [4]. The creation of linked data stores from digital cultural heritage resources enables the linking of multiple data, assisting efficiency by permitting combined or linked searches. Semantic search and linking of data can enrich the actual content and make it useful in wider environments and contexts.

In this paper, we exploit semantic metadata representations using knowledge-based reasoning. Moreover, we show that improved query answering results can be obtained if we interweave semantic technologies with machine learning paradigms applied to appropriate features extracted from the images of the Digital Library items. Advanced semantic search based on query answering is presented in Section 2. Section 3 presents a scheme in which the knowledge used in the semantic search is interweaved with machine learning, the latter operating on features extracted from the cultural images included in the items of the Digital Library. The extraction of image features is described in Section 4. An evaluation study illustrating the performance of the proposed approach is presented in Section 5. Conclusions are given in Section 6.

2 Semantic Search in Digital Libraries

Semantic query answering refers to construction of answers to queries posed by users, based not only on string matching over data that are stored in databases, but also on the implicit meaning that can be found by reasoning based on detailed domain terminological knowledge [2]. The key is to semantically connect metadata with ontological domain knowledge through appropriate mappings. The representation formalism used for the terminological descriptions is OWL 2 (the W3C Standard for Ontology representations on the web) [4]. The theoretical framework underpinning the OWL 2 ontology representation language is *Description Logics* (DL) [1]. The DL language underpinning OWL 2 is $\mathcal{SROIQ}$. The building blocks of DL knowledge bases are atomic concepts, atomic roles and individuals that are elements of the denumerable, disjoint sets $\mathbf{C}, \mathbf{R}, \mathbf{I}$, respectively. A DL knowledge base (KB) is denoted by $\mathcal{K} = \langle \mathcal{T}, \mathcal{A} \rangle$, where $\mathcal{T}$ is the terminology (usually called TBox) representing the entities of the domain and $\mathcal{A}$ is the assertional knowledge (usually called ABox) describing the objects of the world in terms of the above entities. Formally, $\mathcal{T}$ is a set of terminological axioms of the form $C_1 \sqsubseteq C_2$ or $R_1 \sqsubseteq R_2$, where C_1, C_2 are $\mathcal{SROIQ}$-concept descriptions and R_1, R_2 are $\mathcal{SROIQ}$-role descriptions. $\mathcal{SROIQ}$-concept expressivity employs conjunction $(C_1 \sqcap C_2)$, disjunction $(C_1 \sqcup C_2)$, universal and existential quantification $(\forall R.C, \exists R.C)$, qualified number restrictions $(\geq R.C, \leq R.C)$ and nominals $(\{a\})$, while $\mathcal{SROIQ}$-role expressivity allows for the definition of role inverse (R^-) and role compositions $(R_1 \circ R_2)$ in the left part of the role inclusion axioms. The TBox $\mathcal{T}$ describes the restrictions of the modeled domain. The ABox $\mathcal{A}$ is a finite set of *assertions* of the form $A(a)$ or $R(a, b)$, where $a, b \in \mathbf{I}$, $A \in \mathbf{C}$ and $R \in \mathbf{R}$. An interpretation $\mathcal{I}$ maps concepts to subsets of the object domain, roles to pairs of elements from the object domain and individuals to elements of the object domain. For an interpretation to be a model several conditions have to be satisfied [1]. If an axiom ax is satisfied in every model of a knowledge base $\mathcal{K}$ we say that $\mathcal{K}$ entails ax, written $\mathcal{K} \models ax$.

We next consider concept based queries. A concept based query q is of the form $q : Q(x) \leftarrow \bigwedge_{i=1}^{n} C_i(x)$, where x is a variable and $C_i(x)$ are predicates-concept atoms.

Algorithm 1. Query Evaluation Procedure using the high level knowledge

---

Input: $\mathcal{K} \langle \mathcal{T}, \mathcal{A} \rangle$: the $\mathcal{SROIQ}$ knowledge base
       q: a concept based query
Output: Ans: the set of answers to the query q
   $Ans := \emptyset$
   $C_1, \ldots, C_n := queryAtomsOf(q)$
   for j=1, ..., n **do**
     for all *individual* $a \in \mathcal{A}$ **do**
       if $\mathcal{K} \models C_j(a)$ **then**
         $Ans := Ans \cup a$
       else
         if $a \in Ans$ **then**
           $Ans := Ans \setminus a$
         end if
       end if
     end for
   end for
   return Ans

An individual a is an answer/instance of a concept based query q posed over the DL knowledge base $\mathcal{K}$ iff $\mathcal{K} \models C_i(a)$ for i=1,...,n. The procedure we follow to find the answers to concept based queries is shown in Algorithm 1. The algorithm takes as input a knowledge base $\mathcal{K}$ and a query q and returns the individuals of the knowledge base that satisfy the query. This is done by iterating over the concept atoms C_j of q and over the individuals a appearing in the knowledge base $\mathcal{K}$ and by checking whether $\mathcal{K}$ entails that a is an instance of C_i. If the instantiated concept atom is entailed we add the individual to the set of answers Ans else, if it is not, we have to check whether a is already contained in Ans. In this case we remove it from the set or else we leave the set as it is. More information about the use of semantic techniques in the cultural heritage domain can be found in [6].

3 Interweaving Semantics with Machine Learning

In Section 2 we used ontologies in order to classify cultural objects to various categories and then used queries for semantic search of cultural heritage content. The creation of global axioms that hold over all items of a digital library, such as Europeana, is however, very difficult. One approach to deal with this is to use only axioms containing constraints that are known to hold over all data and leave out of the knowledge base any constraint that holds over most (but not all) of the data. In any case, the inherent, or resulting, incompleteness of the knowledge bases poses limitations to their usage in answering queries over cultural heritage content. In the current section we show that this problem can be partially overcome by interweaving the knowledge base with feature based image representations of the Digital Library items appropriately exploited by machine learning techniques; the target being to improve semantic search of cultural heritage content. The specific features of cultural heritage images that we use are presented in the next sections.

Algorithm 2. Query Evaluation Procedure using the low level visual features

---

Input: *trainedSVM*: a vector of trained SVM
  data: the queried data
  features: the features of the *data*
  q: a concept based query
Output: Ans: the set of answers to query *q*
  $Ans := \emptyset$
  $C_1, \ldots, C_n := queryAtomsOf(q)$
  for j=1, ..., n **do**
    for all $a \in data$ **do**
      $output(a) := SVMpredict(features(a), trainedSVM_j)$
      if $output(a) = 1$ **then**
        $Ans := Ans \cup a$
      else
        if $output(a) = 0$ **then**
          if $a \in Ans$ **then**
            $Ans := Ans \setminus a$
          end if
        end if
      end if
    end for
  end for
  return *Ans*

The scope of using machine learning techniques in our method is their ability to learn from examples, in particular from the extracted features, to classify the cultural items in various concepts that can appear in queries. As a consequence, these techniques can determine the items that satisfy the corresponding query concept atoms, irrespectively of whether these items have been identified by the knowledge based component of our approach. This results in bridging the gap between restrictions imposed by ontologies and actual restrictions (visual features) that each cultural heritage item possesses. Support Vector Machines (SVMs) constitute a well known method which is based on kernel functions to efficiently induce classifiers that work by mapping the image features, and the corresponding items, onto an embedding space, where they can be discriminated by means of a linear classifier. As such, they can be used for effectively exploiting the extracted features and classify the cultural items in the different concept categories that are included in the formal knowledge. The kernel used to encode the visual knowledge through similarity between different images with respect to low level features, i.e., the feature vectors/values, is a normalized linear kernel defined as follows:

$$k_l(x, y) := \frac{x^T y + c}{\|x\|\|y\|} \tag{1}$$

where x, y are vectors of features, $\|\cdot\|$ is the Euclidean norm and c is considered zero.

Furthermore, it is possible to extend the SVM kernel so as to include individuals within ontologies [7,5]. The extension comes from a family of kernel functions defined as $k_p^F : Ind(A) \times Ind(A) \to [0, 1]$, for a knowledge base $\mathcal{K} = \langle \mathcal{T}, \mathcal{A} \rangle$. $Ind(A)$ indicates the set of individuals appearing in A, and $F = \{F_1, F_2, \ldots, F_m\}$ is a set of concept descriptions. These functions are defined as the L_p mean of the, say m, simple concept kernel functions κ_i, $i = 1, \ldots, m$, where, for every two individuals a,b, and $p > 0$,

$$\kappa_i(a, b) = \begin{cases} 1 & \begin{aligned} &(F_i(a) \in A \land F_i(b) \in A) \lor \\ &(\neg F_i(a) \in A \land \neg F_i(b) \in A); \end{aligned} \\ 0 & \begin{aligned} &(F_i(a) \in A \land \neg F_i(b) \in A) \lor \\ &(\neg F_i(a) \in A \land F_i(b) \in A); \end{aligned} \\ \frac{1}{2} & \text{otherwise.} \end{cases} \tag{2}$$

$$\forall a, b \in Ind(A) \quad k_p^F(a, b) := \left[\sum_{i=1}^{m} \left| \frac{\kappa_i(a, b)^p}{m} \right| \right]^{1/p} \tag{3}$$

The above kernel encodes the formal knowledge for the problem under analysis through the similarity of pairs of individuals with respect to high level features, i.e. concepts of the knowledge base. The rationale of these kernels is that similarity between items is determined by their similarity with respect to each concept F_i, i.e., if two items are instances of the concept or of its negation. A value of p = 1 is generally used for implementing (3). The extension we can use is a combined SVM kernel, computed as the mean value of the above described two kernels, i.e., $k_c(a, b) = k_p^F(a, b) + k_l(a, b)$ where k_p^F is the above knowledge driven kernel and k_l is the normalized linear kernel.

Let us now describe the way that queries are evaluated using SVMs that have already been trained to classify cultural items to concepts. Algorithm 2 shows the procedure. The algorithm takes as input the data we want to query together with their visual features and uses trained SVMs to check which items simultaneously belong to all concepts appearing in the query. $SVMpredict$ predicts the label of an item w.r.t. a concept C_j using the SVM trained to classify items to this concept. The interweaving of the two approaches, the knowledge based and the kernel based, is done by first performing Algorithms 1 and 2 for extracting the query answers from the two methods (Ans_{KB} and Ans_{SVM}) and by then disjuncting these two answer sets ($Ans = Ans_{KB} \cup Ans_{SVM}$). The enriched, in this way, results are then presented to the user.

4 Image Features Exploited by the Machine Learning Approach

The MPEG-7 standard [10] that focuses on the description of multimedia content provides among others, a set of low-level descriptors useful for tasks such as image classification, high-level concept detection and image/video retrieval. It is these features that we use as global image descriptors, i.e., *Dominant Color Descriptor* (DCD), *Color Structure Descriptor* (CSD), *Color Layout Descriptor* (CLD), *Scalable Color Descriptor* (SCD) and *Homogeneous Texture Descriptor* (HTD) and *Edge Histogram Descriptor* (EHD).

Global features do not capture local deformations and therefore are not robust to change of viewpoint or to affine transformations. For this reason we also focus on local features that are located on *interest points* of the image, like corners, blobs, salient edges, and describe their surrounding neighborhood by compact histograms (e.g. histogram of local gradients). Such points are nearly invariant to various image transformations, illumination and appearance. In particular, we use SURF (Speeded-Up Robust Features) [9] features to capture the visual properties of the images. These features have been proven to achieve high repeatability and distinctiveness. The SURF descriptor captures the intensity content distribution around the points of interest in the image.

Then, based on the extracted features, we create a visual vocabulary and we exploit it to represent the images. To understand the notion of a visual vocabulary, one should consider it as an equivalent to a typical language vocabulary, with an image corresponding to a text document. In the same way that text may be decomposed to a set of words, an image can also be decomposed to a set of *visual* words. Then, in order to compare two images, their corresponding visual words may be compared instead. To do so, we create clusters in the space of descriptors and assign each feature to the closest centroid (i.e. visual word). We do this through a fast variant of the k-means algorithm that uses approximate nearest neighbor search, in which nearest cluster centers at each iteration are assigned using randomized kd-trees. We use the FLANN [11] both in vocabulary creation and to assign visual words to image features. A histogram of constant-length can be constructed for each image, containing the appearance frequencies per visual word. This is called the *Bag-of-words* vector of the image, and it is a N_{vw}-dimensional vector, where N_{vw} is the size of the visual vocabulary. Specifically, the bag-of-words vector $bow(I)$ of an image I is a vector with elements $[tf_I(0), tf_I(1), \ldots, tf_I(N_{vw})]$ where $tf_I(i)$ denotes the number of times that the visual word i was selected as a nearest neighbor of one of the interest points extracted from image I.

5   Evaluation Study

The experimental study presented in this section aims at illustrating the performance of the advanced search which exploits both semantic and visual aspects of cultural content that is accessible through the Europeana portal. We focus on the Hellenic content, which consists of 40.000 items, since for this content we also possess thematic knowledge. The thematic ontology that was manually created contains 55 categories of cultural objects (such as pottery, jewelry, stamps, wall paintings, engravings, coins) and more than 300 types. The TBox of the used knowledge base consists of the EDM together with the thematic ontology. The ABox consists of the EDM instances each one of which is described by its type, its creation date, its material, the museum it can be found at. Apart from the metadata, the visual features of the cultural objects were extracted according to the methodology presented in Section 4. Figure 1 (middle) presents images of items belonging to the 'brooch' category, that are made either of gold or copper. The binary masks of the foreground objects are also computed and used to extract color descriptors from the corresponding regions, while discarding the background. Items made of copper share similar color distributions, with these distributions being different from the item made of gold, as shown in Figure 1 (right). Based on this, the SVM classifier can separate the different categories of brooches.

In the following we apply the techniques described in Sections 2 and 3 for semantic query answering and its interweaving with the extracted visual information on the

Table 1. Accuracy (%) of Query Answering

Query	Accuracy(Algorithm 1)	Accuracy(Algorithm 2)	Accuracy(Combination)
1. $Q(x) \leftarrow OpenVase(x)$	85.5	78.4	96.9

above mentioned Europeana items. In particular we use the HermiT reasoner [3,2] and the LIBSVM library[3]. To achieve semantic search, we use the thematic knowledge for Hellenic monuments, particularly for vases (for which metadata and images are provided) that has been created in the framework of the Polemon and 'Digitalisation of the Collections of Movable Monuments of the Hellenic Ministry of Culture' Projects of the Directorate of the National Archive of Monuments[4] and which has been included in the Polydefkis terminology Thesaurus of Archaeological Collections and Monuments [8]. The knowledge used contains axioms about vases in ancient Greece, i.e., class hierarchy axioms referring to the different types of vases, such as amphora, alabaster, crater, as well as axioms regarding the appearance, usage, creation period and the material vases were made of. Using the resulting ontologies and data sets, we applied the proposed methodology to generate queries and provide semantic answers to them.

Let us assume that the user addresses a query asking for 'open vases'. Table 1 reports the accuracy of the query answering task when Algorithm 1 of Section 2 is used, based on the above mentioned terminological knowledge and instance data. It also presents the accuracy of query answering when we use Algorithm 2 of Section 3. In this case we first train SVMs (one for each concept of the query) using the extracted visual features of the items which are returned as query answers by the knowledge base. In particular, the SVMs are trained using the normalized linear kernel described in Section 3, based on the visual features and the annotated labels of the images. After that, we test the remaining data, which - erroneously - have or have not been returned as query answers based on the knowledge, using the trained SVMs according to Algorithm 2. The above means that column 3 shows the percentage of the data that the SVM 'correctly' predicts as query answers among those that were not predicted as such by the knowledge. Table 1 also shows the accuracy of query answering when we combine the results of the knowledge based

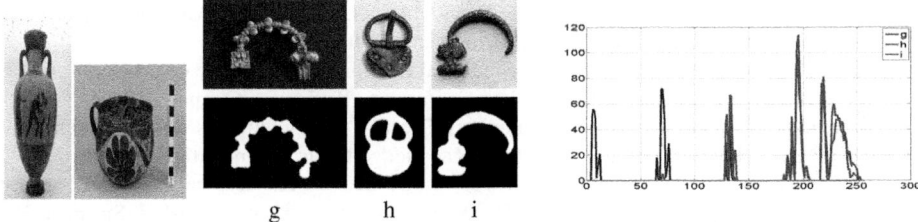

g   h   i

Fig. 1. A close and an open vase (left), Sample images and corresponding segmentation masks. g: made of gold, h-i: made of copper (middle), Histogram comparison for CST MPEG descriptor extracted from the regions defined by the shown binary masks (right).

---

[3] http://www.csie.ntu.edu.tw/~cjlin/libsvm/

[4] http://nam.culture.gr

and visual kernel based approaches. We see that the accuracy in this case, computed as the number of generated query answers that are true over all test data, has been significantly increased. This illustrates the improved performance of the proposed advanced semantic search approach.

6 Conclusions

The current paper presents a new semantic search methodology, including a query answering mechanism that can meet the semantics of users' queries and enrich these answers by exploiting appropriate visual features, both local and MPEG-7, through an extended knowledge and machine learning based approach. We have applied this approach in the framework of a large content base (about 4 million objects) that our team – through our MINT mapping tool – has injected into Europeana. Applying this approach in a variety of subareas, such as archaeology, photography, modern arts, fashion, where specific thematic knowledge can be derived and used, as well as combining it with the evolving field of linked open data for cultural heritage are future extensions of the presented work.

Acknowledgment. The authors wish to thank the Hellenic Ministry of Culture and Tourism for providing the cultural content of the www.collections.culture.gr.

References

1. Baader, F., Calvanese, D., McGuinness, D., Nardi, D., Patel-Schneider, P.F.: The Description Logic Handbook: Theory, Implementation, Applications. Cambridge University Press (2007)
2. Kollia, I., Glimm, B., Horrocks, I.: SPARQL Query Answering over OWL Ontologies. In: Antoniou, G., Grobelnik, M., Simperl, E., Parsia, B., Plexousakis, D., De Leenheer, P., Pan, J. (eds.) ESWC 2011, Part I. LNCS, vol. 6643, pp. 382–396. Springer, Heidelberg (2011)
3. Shearer, R., Motik, B., Horrocks, I.: HermiT: A Highly-Efficient OWL Reasoner. In: Proc. of the 5th Int. Workshop on OWL: Experiences and Directions (2008)
4. Motik, B., Patel-Schneider, P., Parsia, B.: OWL 2 Web Ontology Language: Structural Specification and Functional-Style Syntax. W3C Recommendation (2009)
5. Kollia, I., Simou, N., Stafylopatis, A., Kollias, S.: Semantic Image Analysis using a Symbolic Neural Architecture. Journal of Image Analysis and Stereology (2010)
6. Kollia, I., Tzouvaras, V., Drosopoulos, N., Stamou, G.: A Systemic Approach for Effective Semantic Access to Cultural Content. Semantic Web Journal (2012)
7. Fanizzi, N., d'Amato, C., Esposit, F.: Statistical Learning for Inductive Query Answering on OWL Ontologies. In: Intl. Semantic Web Conference, Karlsruhe, Germany (2008)
8. Kalomirakis, D.: Polydefkis: A Terminology Thesauri for Monuments. In: Tsipopoulou, M. (ed.) Proc. of Digital Heritage in the New Knowledge Environment, Athens (2008)
9. Bay, H., Tuytelaars, T., Van Gool, L.: SURF: Speeded Up Robust Features. In: Leonardis, A., Bischof, H., Pinz, A. (eds.) ECCV 2006. LNCS, vol. 3951, pp. 404–417. Springer, Heidelberg (2006)
10. Chang, S., Sikora, T., Puri, A.: Overview of the MPEG-7 Standard. IEEE Trans. on Circuits and Systems for Video Technology 11, 688–695 (2001)
11. Muja, M., Lowe, D.G.: Fast approximate nearest neighbors with automatic algorithm configuration. In: Intl. Conf. on Computer Vision Theory and Application, pp. 331–340. INSTICC Press (2009)

A SOM-Based Validation Approach to a Neural Circuit Theory of Autism

Spyridon Revithis[1] and Georgios Tagalakis[2]

[1] School of Computer Science and Engineering, University of New South Wales,
UNSW-Sydney, NSW 2052, Australia
revithiss@cse.unsw.edu.au
[2] School of Computer Science and Informatics, University College Dublin,
Dublin 4, Ireland

Abstract. The neural network class of self organizing maps (SOMs) is a promising cognitive modeling tool in the study of the autistic spectrum pervasive developmental disorder. This work offers a novel validation of Gustafsson's neural circuit theory, according to which autism relates to formation characteristics of cortical brain maps. A previously constructed spatial SOM behavioral model is used here as a cognitive model, and by incorporating formation deficiencies related to the topological neighborhood (TN) function. The resulting cognitive SOM maps, being sensitive to the width of TN during SOM formation, point to a model that exhibits marked behavioral characteristics of autism. The simulation results support the causal hypothesis that associates autistic behavior with certain functional and structural characteristics of the human nervous system and, specifically, Gustafsson's theoretical proposition of the role of inhibitory lateral feedback synaptic connection strengths in autism.

Keywords. Neural Networks, Self-Organizing Maps, Cognitive Modeling, Autism.

1 Introduction

Computational modeling offers a powerful way of studying human behavior. It has been applied to numerous areas of Psychology and provides a framework superior to those proposed by the social sciences in terms of methodological diversity, empirical accuracy, and procedural clarity [1]. An increasing number of studies are dedicated to the modeling of developmental cognitive phenomena using neural networks [2-3].

This study investigates neurocomputational aspects of autism. Section 2 presents some key characteristics of the autistic spectrum disorder and a current neural circuit theory. In Section 3, the details of an autistic SOM model, and the computational simulations performed in order to investigate and evaluate its efficacy, are introduced. Section 4 informs of the model and simulation technical details with supporting statistical evaluation of the results. The concluding Section 5 discusses some planned and other possible directions of future work.

I. Maglogiannis, V. Plagianakos, and I. Vlahavas (Eds.): SETN 2012, LNAI 7297, pp. 25–32, 2012.

2   The Neuropsychology of a Neural Circuit Theory of Autism

Since Kanner's [4] and Asperger's [5] publications, autism, a pervasive developmental disorder, is studied by an ever-expanding interdisciplinary research community. Its etiology remains unknown, but it is considered to be neurobiological in nature [6]. Unfortunately, the current diagnostic tools (DSM-IV and ICD-10) dictate a socio-psychological behavioral approach that does not inform of the causes of autism.

Autism is associated with atypical perception and its internal representation. Sensory input often fails to integrate into existing memory (schemas) due to abstraction impairment [7]. There is difficulty to detect the important features among the non-essential details [8]. Elaborating on internal representations is also problematic, where it appears that central executive control is required [9].

Gustafsson's neural circuit theory of autism [10] is based on these empirically based concepts of autistic perception and proposes a neural-level explanation for the lack of drive for central coherence, a key element in autistic behavior [11]. Specifically, important attributes in autism are derived from neurological deficiencies in the formation of brain cortical maps; this leads to problematic feature extraction since "autistic raw data memory" operates in place of "feature memory" due to "inadequate cortical feature maps". Raw data memory is intrinsically linked at the behavioral level to the diagnostic criteria for autism [10]. Autistic maps lack feature distinction and preservation, and fail to provide an internal representation of salient perceptual data. This leads to raw data memory that lacks sophisticated representations [12].

According to Gustafsson [10], the artificial neural network class of self-organizing maps (SOMs) [13-14] provides a biologically plausible way to model characteristics of autistic brain cortical maps. A SOM can represent input features just like a brain map retains salient perceptual stimuli, and can exhibit comparable properties to an autistic brain map if its formation mechanism is impaired. The modeling premise of the impairment is suggested not by the biological map, but by its model. Specifically, Gustafsson argued that a biologically plausible cause of impairment in a SOM is the excessive lateral feedback inhibitory synaptic strengths that can degrade a map's generalization and feature representation capacity, resulting in high sensory discrimination and feature specificity, even to the point of instability.

3   The Autistic SOM Model

3.1   IPSOM: A Spatial Model

IPSOM (Interlocking Puzzle SOM) is a prototype SOM spatial behavioral model of how humans complete interlocking (jigsaw) puzzles [15]. The mathematical and algorithmic form of the neural network employed is according to Haykin [16]. When trained, using a representative sample of puzzle completion sessions, it forms a behavioral SOM of the statistically dominant patterns (strategies) of puzzle completion. IPSOM has been evaluated for the case of 4x5 (20-piece) puzzles against a simulated group of virtual people. Each virtual person was assumed to use one of four predetermined puzzle completion strategies (Fig. 1). The design principles behind the selected strategies were the generation of a small number of straightforward, real-life based patterns, the utilization of topological clustering, and the prioritization of the basic strategy of determining the board periphery during the puzzle completion. IPSOM was conclusively found to be efficient in modeling the behavioral domain [15].

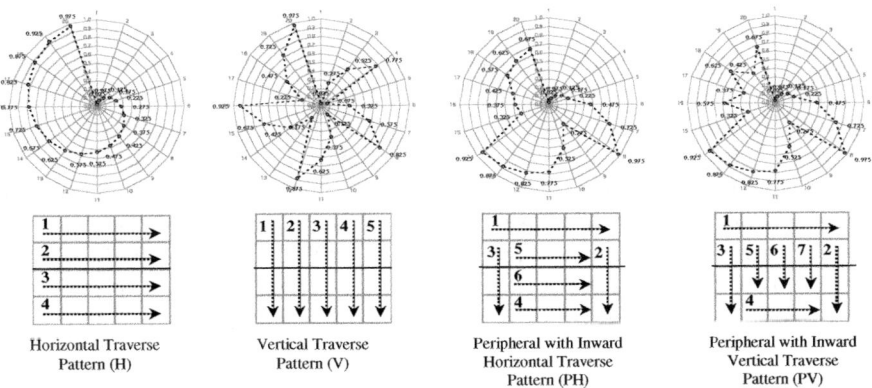

| Horizontal Traverse Pattern (H) | Vertical Traverse Pattern (V) | Peripheral with Inward Horizontal Traverse Pattern (PH) | Peripheral with Inward Vertical Traverse Pattern (PV) |

Fig. 1. An illustration of the four puzzle completion strategies used to evaluate IPSOM. A radar-graph depicts the order of puzzle completion for each pattern (H, V, PH, PV). The radial axis shows the encoded numerical position values on the puzzle board (i.e., which puzzle piece), and the angular axis shows the discrete completion sequence numbers (i.e., which piece is first, second, etc.) By connecting the points on the graph, a distinct visual pattern is formed. Attached to each graph, a puzzle board contains the puzzle completion order conventionally.

In this paper, IPSOM is employed as a modeling test-bed for cortical map spatial perception. The working hypothesis is that IPSOM not only is a behavioral model but also a cognitive model of how humans perceive puzzle completion strategies when presented with puzzle completion examples. It is assumed that an average person would form an internal representation of the dominant strategies; a cortical map would retain the domain specific knowledge, modeled by a trained SOM. The IPSOM map is expected to effectively depict the training patterns in a topologically ordered fashion, where neighboring patterns are also visually similar (Fig. 2).

	1	2	3	4	5	6
1	**PV**	PV	PV-	V-	V	**V**
2	PV	PV-	PV-	V-	V-	V
3	PV-	PV-	~	~	V-	V-
4	PH-	PH-	~	~	H-	H-
5	PH	PH-	PH-	H-	H-	H-
6	**PH**	PH	PH-	H-	H	**H**

X Primary core neuron: Optimal pattern representation
X Core neuron: Good pattern representation
X-   Weak neuron: Poor pattern representation
~   Undecided neuron: Transitionally excessive pattern

Fig. 2. An abstract illustration of a possible IPSOM 6x6 cognitive behavioral map, after being trained using the predesigned four-pattern set. Each SOM neuron is best-matched to one of the data set patterns (H, V, PH, PV) with a corresponding pattern-representation strength.

3.2   The Autistic IPSOM

Gustafsson's theory of autism [10] postulates that autistic cortical maps are inadequate or even undeveloped, and suggests the excessive lateral feedback inhibitory synaptic strengths as the best candidate causal factor. In a SOM, this can be expressed as a premature narrowing of the topological neighborhood (TN) during training; TN can be regarded as the "source of power" [17] in the autistic cognitive model. We maintain that the initial width of the TN function affects the map's representational capacity in a way directly applied to Gustafsson's ideas. By using a modified version of IPSOM, we perform an evaluation with a complex weight-encoding model. A non-autistic brain is expected to successfully represent all the dominant puzzle completion strategies. This can be modeled using IPSOM in its original parameter configuration.

A series of simulations have been performed with the initial width of the TN function set to a typical value of 3 (i.e., equal to the network's radius, as suggested by Haykin [16]). As a representative example, we visualized the last row of a resulting cognitive behavioral map that closely matches the topological configuration of Fig. 2, and calculated the Euclidean distance of Pattern H to all neurons in the map. Here, a smooth transition between patterns is apparent (Fig. 3a and 4a) and illustrates the map's ability to generalize without losing its capacity to accurately represent all statistically important features (i.e., puzzle completion strategies) from the input space (i.e., perceptual stimuli). Thus, feature memory is enabled, in which a subsequent perceptual stimuli session of a slightly different puzzle completion strategy can be associated with one of the existing patterns already stored in the map without significant matching errors. Transitional neurons are not only present but they also meaningfully indicate the map's perceptual stability. The resulting map is non-autistic.

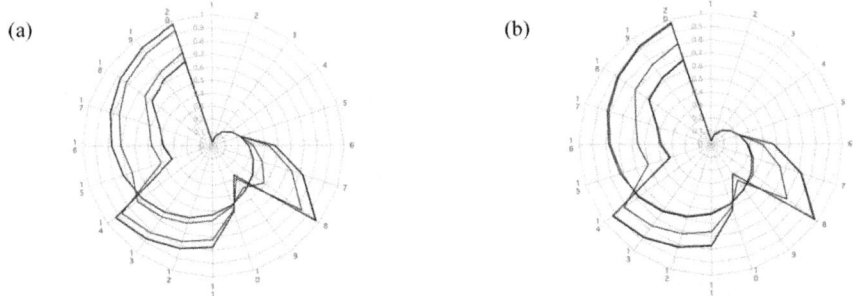

(a)   (b)

Fig. 3. Combined illustration of IPSOM map's last-row (six) neurons after two separate simulations (initial η_0=.1) for different initial TN widths (all other parameters identical). In (a), an initial width of 3 facilitates the representation of transition between patterns. In (b), a smaller width of 1.1 results in neurons tightly grouped into two patterns with impaired transition.

In a second series of simulations, the initial width of the TN function was narrowed to 1.1. Again, as a representative example, we visualized the last row of the resulting cognitive behavioral map that is directly comparable to the previous map discussed (i.e., using the same pseudorandom seed to randomly generate the network's initial synaptic weights), and calculated the Euclidean distance of Pattern H to all neurons in the map. Here, it is evident that there is high pattern discrimination with poor transition between patterns (Fig. 3b and 4b). The map's topological ordering is largely reduced to jumps from pattern to pattern and to hit-or-miss representations indicating an inability to generalize from the input space. The feature memory becomes impaired; a subsequent perceptual stimuli session of a slightly different puzzle completion strategy cannot be associated with one of the existing patterns in the map without significant matching errors, if at all. Evidently, the resulting map exhibits autistic traits.

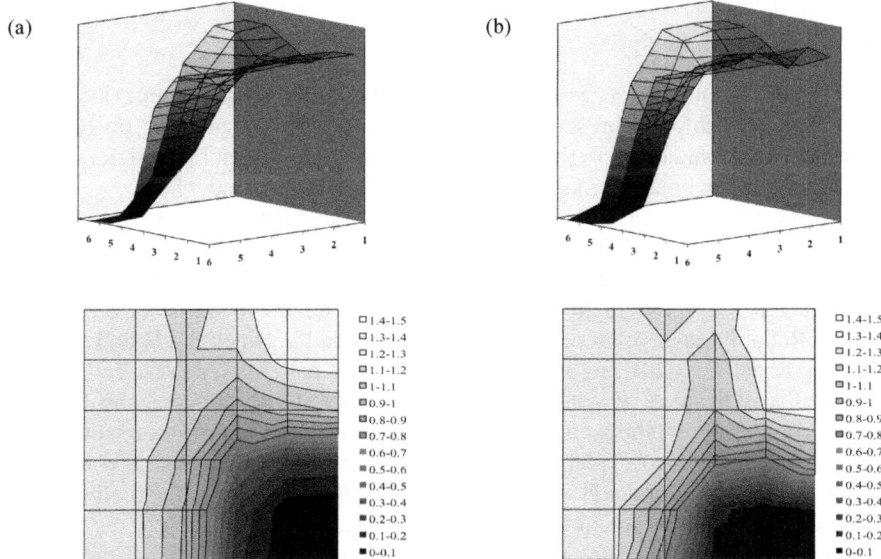

Fig. 4. The Euclidean distance of Pattern H to each neuron in the map is depicted on 3D and 2D graphs after two simulations (initial learning rate η_0=.1) for different initial TN widths (all other parameters identical). The darker and closer to the horizontal 3D base-plane (the IPSOM map) areas signify smaller distance and, thus, higher representational accuracy of Pattern H. In (a), an initial width of 3 facilitates a smoother transition from Pattern H to other patterns on the map, whereas in (b) a width of 1.1 results in steeper increase of the Euclidean distance indicating transitional impairment.

4   Implementation Details and Statistical Analysis

4.1   Technical Aspects of the Model

The IPSOM model is constructed in ANSI C. Its SOM is implemented in a three-dimensional lattice containing the synaptic weight vectors of the neural network. The first two dimensions represent the coordinates needed to refer to a specific neuron in the lattice, while the third dimension is used for holding the synaptic weight vector of that neuron. The training set used exhibited no bias towards any of the H, V, PH, and PV patterns. Each training was concluded in 950 epochs, with an initial learning rate of

.1, and consisted of lattice initialization, neuron competition, neuron cooperation, and synaptic adaptation. The TN of the winning neuron is specified by a translation invariant Gaussian function with exponential decay and it is based on the lateral distance between the winning neuron and the excited neuron. IPSOM uses stochastic approximation, which is implemented by a time-varying learning rate with exponential decay. Again, since the 'standard' SOM network was followed, Haykin [16] provides details on the mathematical formulas used. Each resulting map consists of 36 topologically ordered neurons, each of which holds a synaptic weight vector containing a pattern with varying degree of similarity to the four training patterns as discussed.

4.2   Statistical Analysis

Each pattern is encoded as a vector of 20 numbers representing a puzzle completion strategy; each number represents a specific puzzle piece. Depending on each piece's numerical value and order in the vector, it is possible to determine which puzzle piece was placed on the board during the puzzle completion task, and when.

In order to assess the strength of the association between the puzzle completion patterns of the training set, bivariate non-parametric correlation analysis was performed for each of them against the others. The analysis revealed that there is a highly significant positive association between the PH and PV patterns (ρ=.974, P<.001, N=20). Reliably positive associations were also found between the H and PH patterns (ρ=.523, P=.018, N=20), and between the H and PV patterns (ρ=.507, P=.023, N=20). The results indicate a very strong strategy-wise similarity between the PH and PV puzzle completion methods, and a strong strategy-wise similarity between the H and PH patterns. They also explain the partial visual compatibility observed between the H and PH patterns and the H and PV patterns. These results are in agreement with the patterns topology of a typical IPSOM (see also Fig. 2).

Since the IPSOM neurons have identical structure with the training patterns, bivariate linkage analysis was performed again as an exploratory examination method of the non-autistic and autistic SOM variants of IPSOM. For each SOM, the correlation coefficients of all the horizontally neighboring (immediate and more distant) neurons were computed. Table 1 presents results based on the last row of neurons of each IPSOM variant; the contents of these neurons are visualized in Fig. 3.

The results show that the pattern transition between the neurons in the non-autistic model (N1...N6) is smoother than in the autistic model (A1...A6) (see also Fig. 3). Specifically, the pattern transition from PH to H is completed in two neurons (N3, N4) in the non-autistic map, whereas it only takes a 'weak' PH neuron (A3) in the autistic map. The characteristically very high pattern discrimination in autistic brain cortical maps is evident in this case. In the last row of the autistic map, the neurons practically represent two tightly grouped patterns; the representational variation within each group (PH and H) is almost non-existent. Notably, in the selected case for this analysis, the correlation between any two neurons is by default statistically significant since the represented pattern is either a PH or an H, and a reliably positive association between the latter two has already been mentioned above. However, the degree of this positive association varies, as described, in exactly the way that would indicate an autistic phenotype.

Table 1. Correlation analysis of the non-autistic (N) and autistic (A) variants of IPSOM. The neurons N/A1…N/A6 correspond to non-autistic/autistic IPSOM neurons with map coordinates (6,1), …, (6,6), respectively, which are all the neurons of the last row on each map.

Spearman's ρ		N1	N2	N3	N4	N5	N6		A1	A2	A3	A4	A5	A6
Cor. Coef.	N1	1.0	$1.0^\#$	$.979^\#$	$.595^\#$	$.523^*$	$.523^*$	A1	1.0	$1.0^\#$	$.896^\#$	$.523^*$	$.523^*$	$.523^*$
Sig.		.	.	.000	.006	.018	.018		.	.	.000	.018	.018	.018
Cor. Coef.	N2	$1.0^\#$	1.0	$.979^\#$	$.595^\#$	$.523^*$	$.523^*$	A2	$1.0^\#$	1.0	$.896^\#$	$.523^*$	$.523^*$	$.523^*$
Sig.		.	.	.000	.006	.018	.018		.	.	.000	.018	.018	.018
Cor. Coef.	N3	$.979^\#$	$.979^\#$	1.0	$.714^\#$	$.642^\#$	$.642^\#$	A3	$.896^\#$	$.896^\#$	1.0	$.797^\#$	$.797^\#$	$.797^\#$
Sig.		.000	.000	.	.000	.002	.002		.000	.000	.	.000	.000	.000
Cor. Coef.	N4	$.595^\#$	$.595^\#$	$.714^\#$	1.0	$.991^\#$	$.991^\#$	A4	$.523^*$	$.523^*$	$.797^\#$	1.0	$1.0^\#$	$1.0^\#$
Sig.		.006	.006	.000	.	.000	.000		.018	.018	.000	.	.000	.000
Cor. Coef.	N5	$.523^*$	$.523^*$	$.642^\#$	$.991^\#$	1.0	$1.0^\#$	A5	$.523^*$	$.523^*$	$.797^\#$	$1.0^\#$	1.0	$1.0^\#$
Sig.		.018	.018	.002	.000	.	.		.018	.018	.000	.	.	.
Cor. Coef.	N6	$.523^*$	$.523^*$	$.642^\#$	$.991^\#$	$1.0^\#$	1.0	A6	$.523^*$	$.523^*$	$.797^\#$	$1.0^\#$	$1.0^\#$	1.0
Sig.		.018	.018	.002	.000	.	.		.018	.018	.000	.	.	.

N(pairwise)=20; Sig. (2-tailed): Correlation is significant at the 0.05 level (*) and at the 0.01 level (#).

5   Conclusion and Future Work

It is reported in the literature that SOM neural networks resist formal analysis [18]. Nevertheless, we have been able to show that they can be very efficient in modeling even hard problems, like facets of autism, and can offer valuable scientific insights past the behavioral level. This study is part of an ongoing effort to provide a computational account of how autistic behavior is associated with specific functional and structural characteristics of the human nervous system, and, in particular, to investigate Gustafsson's claims about the role of inhibitory lateral feedback synaptic connection strengths in autism [10]. Analysis of the output of IPSOM, a novel and weight-encoding complex model, has provided evidence to support the latter.

Additional research is under way to investigate alternative formulations of the TN function with higher biological plausibility for a number of brain disorders including autism and delusions in schizophrenia [19]. In the course of this research, empirical examinations on impaired brain cortical maps of humans situated in controlled environments, as well as neurocomputational investigations of existing neuroscientific clinical data, will hopefully aid in revealing further critical modeling parameters.

References

1. Sun, R., Coward, L.A., Zenzen, M.J.: On Levels of Cognitive Modeling. Philosophical Psychology 18, 613–637 (2005)
2. Thomas, M.S.C., Karmiloff-Smith, A.: Connectionist Models of Cognitive Development, Atypical Development and Individual Differences. In: Sternberg, R.J., Lautrey, J., Lubart, T. (eds.) Models of Intelligence: International Perspectives, vol. 44, pp. 133–150. American Psychological Association, Washington, DC (2003)

3. Munakata, Y., McClelland, J.L.: Connectionist Models of Development. Developmental Science 6, 413–429 (2003)
4. Kanner, L.: Autistic Disturbances of Affective Contact. Nervous Child 2, 217–250 (1943)
5. Asperger, H.: Die Autistischen Psychopathen im Kindesalter. Archiv für Psychiatrie und Nervenkrankheiten 117, 76–136 (1944)
6. Gillberg, C., Coleman, M.: The Biology of the Autistic Syndromes. Cambridge University Press, Cambridge (2000)
7. Hermelin, B.: Images and Language. In: Rutter, M., Schopler, E. (eds.) Autism: A Reappraisal of Concept and Treatment. Plenum, New York (1978)
8. Happe, F.: The Autobiographical Writings of Three Asperger Syndrome Adults: Problems of Interpretation and Implications for Theory. In: Frith, U. (ed.) Autism and Asperger Syndrome. Cambridge University Press, Cambridge (1991)
9. Shulman, C., Yirmiya, N., Greenbaum, C.W.: From Categorization to Classification: A Comparison Among Individuals with Autism, Mental Retardation, and Normal Development. Journal of Abnormal Psychology 104, 601–609 (1995)
10. Gustafsson, L.: Inadequate Cortical Feature Maps: A Neural Circuit Theory of Autism. Biological Psychiatry 42, 1138–1147 (1997)
11. Frith, U.: Autism: Explaining the Enigma. Blackwell Publishers, Oxford (1989)
12. Hermelin, B., O'Connor, N.: Psychological Experiments with Autistic Children. Pergammon Press, Oxford (1970)
13. Willshaw, D.J., vor der Malsburg, C.: How Patterned Neural Connections Can Be Set Up by Self-Organization. In: Proceedings of the Royal Society of London, Series B, vol. 194, pp. 431–445. Royal Society, London (1976)
14. Kohonen, T.: Self-Organized Formation of Topologically Correct Feature Maps. Biological Cybernetics 43, 59–69 (1982)
15. Revithis, S., Wilson, W.H., Marcus, N.: IPSOM: A Self-organizing Map Spatial Model of How Humans Complete Interlocking Puzzles. In: Sattar, A., Kang, B.H. (eds.) AI 2006. LNCS (LNAI), vol. 4304, pp. 285–294. Springer, Heidelberg (2006)
16. Haykin, S.: Neural Networks: A Comprehensive Foundation. Prentice-Hall, NJ (1999)
17. Sun, R., Ling, C.: Computational Cognitive Modeling, the Source of Power and Other Related Issues. AI Magazine 19, 113–120 (1997)
18. Cottrell, M., Fort, J.C., Pagès, G.: Theoretical Aspects of the SOM Algorithm. Neurocomputing 21, 119–138 (1998)
19. Revithis, S.: Significance of Topological Neighborhood in SOM Cognitive Modeling of Brain Disorders: Current Neurocomputational Simulations. Book of Abstracts of the 16th International Conference of the Association of Psychology & Psychiatry for Adults & Children - APPAC Journal, vol. 18(2), p. 26. APPAC, Athens (2011)

Word Sense Disambiguation as an Integer Linear Programming Problem

Vicky Panagiotopoulou[1], Iraklis Varlamis[2],
Ion Androutsopoulos[1], and George Tsatsaronis[3]

[1] Department of Informatics, Athens University of Economics and Business, Greece
[2] Department of Informatics and Telematics, Harokopio University, Athens, Greece
[3] Biotechnology Center (BIOTEC), Technische Universität Dresden, Germany

Abstract. We present an integer linear programming model of word sense disambiguation. Given a sentence, an inventory of possible senses per word, and a sense relatedness measure, the model assigns to the sentence's word occurrences the senses that maximize the total pairwise sense relatedness. Experimental results show that our model, with two unsupervised sense relatedness measures, compares well against two other prominent unsupervised word sense disambiguation methods.

1 Introduction

Word sense disambiguation (WSD) aims to identify the correct sense of each word occurrence in a given sentence or other text span [11]. When the possible senses per word are known, supervised learning methods currently achieve the best results [3,7], but they require manually sense-tagged corpora as training data. Constructing such corpora is costly; and the performance of supervised WSD methods may degrade on texts of different topics or genres than those of the training data [1]. Here we focus on *unsupervised* methods, meaning methods that do not require sense-tagged corpora [2,5,10]. We assume, however, that the possible word senses are known, unlike other unsupervised methods that also discover the inventory of possible senses [17].

Many state of the art unsupervised WSD methods construct a large semantic graph for each input sentence. There are nodes for all the possible senses of the sentence's words, but also for all the possible senses of words that a thesaurus, typically WordNet, shows as related to the sentence's words. The graph's edges correspond to lexical relations (e.g., hyponymy, synonymy) retrieved from the thesaurus and they may be weighted (e.g., depending on the types of the lexical relations). Algorithms like PageRank or activation propagation are then used to select the most active node (sense) of each word [2,18,19].

By contrast, we model WSD as an integer linear programming (ILP) problem, where the goal is to select exactly one possible sense of each word in the input sentence, so as to maximize the total pairwise relatedness between the selected senses. Our model can also be seen as operating on a graph of word senses, but the graph includes nodes only for the possible senses of the words in the input sentence, not other related words; hence, it is much smaller compared

I. Maglogiannis, V. Plagianakos, and I. Vlahavas (Eds.): SETN 2012, LNAI 7297, pp. 33–40, 2012.

to the graphs of previous methods. Furthermore, the (weighted) edges of our graphs do not necessarily correspond to single lexical relations of a thesaurus; they represent the scores of a sense relatedness measure. Any pairwise sense relatedness (or similarity) measure can be used, including measures that consider all the possible paths (not single lexical relations) in WordNet connecting the two senses [20], or statistical distributional similarity measures. It is unclear how measures of this kind could be used with previous graph-based WSD approaches, where the graph's edges correspond to single lexical relations of a thesaurus.

To our knowledge, our model is the first ILP formulation of WSD. Although ILP is NP-hard, efficient solvers are available, and in practice our method is faster than implementations of other unsupervised WSD methods, because of its much smaller graphs. A major advantage of our ILP model is that it can be used with any sense relatedness measure. As a starting point, we test it with (i) *SR* [20], a measure that considers all the possible WordNet paths between two senses, and (ii) a Lesk-like [5] measure that computes the similarity between the WordNet glosses of two senses using pointwise mutual information (PMI) [6,22] and word co-occurrence statistics from a large corpus without sense tags. With these two measures, our overall method is unsupervised. It is also possible to use statistical sense relatedness measures estimated from sense-tagged corpora, turning our method into a supervised one, but we reserve this for future work.

Section 2 below introduces our ILP model; Section 3 defines the two sense relatedness measures we adopted; Section 4 presents experimental results against two other prominent unsupervised WSD methods; and Section 5 concludes.

2   Our ILP Model of Word Sense Disambiguation

Let $w_1, \ldots, w_n$ be the word occurrences of an input sentence; s_{ij} denotes the j-th possible sense of w_i, and $rel(s_{ij}, s_{i'j'})$ the relatedness between senses s_{ij} and $s_{i'j'}$. The goal is to select exactly one of the possible senses s_{ij} of each w_i, so that the total pairwise relatedness of the selected senses will be maximum. For each sense s_{ij}, a binary variable a_{ij} indicates if the sense is active, i.e., if it has been selected ($a_{ij} = 1$) or not ($a_{ij} = 0$). A first approach would be to maximize the objective function (1) below, where we require $i < i'$ assuming that the relatedness measure is symmetric, subject to the constraints (2). The last constraint ensures that exactly one sense s_{ij} is active for each w_i.

$$\text{maximize} \quad \sum_{i,j,i',j',i<i'} rel(s_{ij}, s_{i'j'}) \cdot a_{ij} \cdot a_{i'j'} \tag{1}$$

$$\text{subject to} \quad a_{ij} \in \{0, 1\}, \ \forall i, j \quad \text{and} \quad \sum_j a_{ij} = 1, \ \forall i. \tag{2}$$

The objective (1) is *quadratic*, because it is the weighted sum of products of variable pairs ($a_{ij} \cdot a_{i'j'}$). To obtain an ILP problem, we introduce a binary variable $\delta_{ij,i'j'}$ for each pair of senses $s_{ij}, s_{i'j'}$ with $i \neq i'$. Figure 1 illustrates the new formulation of the problem. Each one of the large circles, hereafter called *clouds*, contains the possible senses (small circles) of a particular word occurrence w_i. There must be exactly one active sense in each cloud. Each $\delta_{ij,i'j'}$ variable shows if the edge that connects two senses s_{ij} and $s_{i'j'}$ from different clouds is active ($\delta_{ij,i'j'} = 1$) or not ($\delta_{ij,i'j'} = 0$). We want an edge to be active if and only if both of the senses it connects are active ($a_{ij} = a_{i'j'} = 1$).

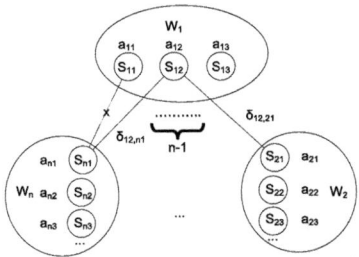

Fig. 1. Illustration of our ILP model of word sense disambiguation

The problem can now be formulated as follows, where $i, i' \in \{1, \ldots, n\}$, $i \neq i'$, and $(i, j), (i', j')$ range over the indices of the possible s_{ij} and $s_{i'j'}$, respectively.

$$\text{maximize} \quad \sum_{i,j,i',j',i<i'} rel(s_{ij}, s_{i'j'}) \cdot \delta_{ij,i'j'} \tag{3}$$

$$\text{such that} \quad a_{ij} \in \{0,1\}, \ \forall i, j \quad \text{and} \quad \sum_j a_{ij} = 1, \ \forall i \tag{4}$$

$$\delta_{ij,i'j'} \in \{0,1\} \quad \text{and} \quad \delta_{ij,i'j'} = \delta_{i'j',ij}, \ \forall i, j, i', j' \tag{5}$$

$$\text{and} \quad \sum_{j'} \delta_{ij,i'j'} = a_{ij}, \ \forall i, j, i'. \tag{6}$$

The second constraint of (5) reflects the fact that the edges (and their activations) are not directed. Constraint (6) can be understood by considering separately the possible values of a_{ij}:

- If $a_{ij} = 0$ (s_{ij} is inactive), $\sum_{j'} \delta_{ij,i'j'} = 0$, $\forall i'$, i.e., all the edges that connect s_{ij} to the senses $s_{i'j'}$ of each other word (cloud) $w_{i'}$ are inactive, enforcing the requirement that any edge connecting an inactive sense must be inactive.
- If $a_{ij} = 1$ (s_{ij} is active), then $\sum_{j'} \delta_{ij,i'j'} = 1$, $\forall i'$, i.e., there is exactly one active edge connecting s_{ij} to the senses $s_{i'j'}$ of each other word (cloud) $w_{i'}$. The active edge from s_{ij} connects to the (single) active sense in the cloud of $w_{i'}$, because if it connected to a non-active sense in that cloud, the edge would have to be inactive, as in the previous case. Hence, the active edge connects two active senses (from different clouds), as required.

An advantage of ILP solvers is that they guarantee finding an optimal solution, if one exists. As already noted, ILP is NP-hard, but efficient solvers are available, and they are very fast when the number of variables and constraints is reasonably small, as in our case.[1] We also implemented a pruning variant of our ILP method, which removes from the graph of Fig. 1 any sense s_{ij} whose WordNet gloss contains none of the other word occurrences being disambiguated; the pruning is not applied to the senses of word occurrences that would be left without any sense after the pruning. This pruning significantly reduces the number of candidate senses and, consequently, the execution time of our method.

3   Relatedness Measures

Lexical relatedness measures can be classified in three categories: (i) measures based on dictionaries, thesauri, ontologies, or Wikipedia hyperlinks, collectively called knowledge-based measures [4,14]; (ii) corpus-based measures, which use word or sense co-occurrence statistics, like PMI and χ^2 [6,22]; and (iii) hybrid measures [16,9]. Some measures are actually intended to assess the relatedness between words (or phrases), not word senses, but they can often be modified to work with senses. Other measures are intended to measure similarity, not relatedness, though the distinction is not always clear. The first measure that we adopt, SR, uses WordNet and belongs in the first category. The second measure is a hybrid one, since it uses both word co-occurrence statistics (to compute PMI scores) and WordNet's glosses.

SR [20] requires a hierarchical thesaurus O with lexical relations, in our case WordNet, and a weighting scheme for lexical relations. Given a pair of senses s_1, s_2 and a path (sequence) $P = \langle p_1, \ldots, p_l \rangle$ of senses connecting $s_1 = p_1$ to $s_2 = p_l$ via lexical relations, P's "semantic compactness" (SCM) is defined as below; $w_{i \to i+1}$ are the weights of the lexical relations (sense to sense transitions) of P.[2] The "semantic path elaboration" (SPE) of P is also defined below; d_i is the depth of p_i in O's hierarchy, and d_{max} is the maximum depth of O.

$$SCM(P) = \prod_{i=1}^{l-1} w_{i \to i+1} \qquad SPE(P) = \prod_{i=1}^{l} \frac{2d_i d_{i+1}}{d_i + d_{i+1}} \cdot \frac{1}{d_{max}}$$

The semantic relatedness SR between s_1 and s_2 is defined below, where P ranges over all the paths connecting s_1 to s_2. If no such path exists, then $SR(s_1, s_2) = 0$.

$$SR(s_1, s_2) = \max_{P = \langle s_1, \ldots, s_2 \rangle} \{ SCM(P) \cdot SPE(P) \}$$

Instead of $SR(s_1, s_2)$, we use $e^{SR(s_1, s_2)}$, which leads to slightly better results.

For two words w_1, w_2, their PMI score is $PMI(w_1, w_2) = \log \frac{P(w_1, w_2)}{P(w_1) \cdot P(w_2)}$, where $P(w_1, w_2)$ is the probability of w_1, w_2 co-occurring (e.g., in the same sentence). If w_1, w_2 are independent, their PMI score is zero. If w_1, w_2 always co-occur, the score is maximum, equal to $-\log P(w_1) = -\log P(w_2)$. With sense-tagged

---

[1] We use LP_SOLVE; see http://lpsolve.sourceforge.net/.

[2] P is a path on WordNet's entire graph, not the graph of Fig. 1 that we construct for each sentence. A Web service implementation of SR with precomputed SR scores for all WordNet senses is available; consult http://omiotis.hua.gr/.

corpora, the PMI score of two senses s_1, s_2 can be estimated similarly. In this paper, however, where we do not use sense-tagged corpora, we use the WordNet glosses $g(s_1)$ and $g(s_2)$ of s_1 and s_2, and the PMI scores of all word pairs w_1, w_2 from $g(s_1)$ and $g(s_2)$, respectively, excluding stop-words:

$$PMI(s_1, s_2) = \frac{\sum_{w_1 \in g(s_1),\, w_2 \in g(s_2)} PMI(w_1, w_2)}{|g(s_1)| \cdot |g(s_2)|}$$

Here $|g(s)|$ is the length of $g(s)$ in words. The intuition is that if s_1 and s_2 are related, the words that are used in their glosses will also co-occur frequently. We use an untagged corpus of approx. 953 million tokens to estimate $PMI(w_1, w_2)$.

4 Experimental Evaluation

We call ILP-SR-FULL and ILP-SR-PRUN the versions of our ILP method with and without sense pruning when the *SR* measure is used, and ILP-PMI-FULL and ILP-PMI-PRUN the versions with the PMI-based measure. We experimented with the widely used Senseval 2 and 3 datasets, whose word occurrences are tagged with the correct WordNet senses. Both datasets have training and test parts.

We compare our ILP approach against two other prominent unsupervised WSD methods, both of which construct a large semantic graph for each input sentence. The graph has nodes not only for all the possible senses of the sentence's words, but also for all the possible senses of the words that WordNet shows as related to the sentence's words. The edges of the graph correspond to single lexical relations of WordNet. (Recall that, by contrast, our ILP approach constructs a much smaller graph for each sentence, which only contains nodes for the possible senses of the sentence's words; and the edges of our graph do not necessarily correspond to single WordNet lexical relations.) The first method we compare against, Spreading Activation Network (SAN), consequently applies a spreading activation to the semantic graph, and eventually retains the most active sense (node) of each word of the input sentence. We use the SAN method of Tsatsaronis et al. [21], which is an improved version and, hence, representative of several other SAN methods for WSD going back to Quillian [15]. The second method we compare against, hereafter called PR, applies PageRank on the semantic graph and retains the most highly ranked sense (node) of each word in the input sentence. PageRank was first used in WSD by Mihalcea et al. [8], but with different improvements it has also been used by others [2,19]. We use the PR method that was recently evaluated by Tsatsaronis et al. [19]. The SAN and PR methods were chosen because they are well-known and implementations of both were available to us, unlike other unsupervised WSD methods [18,12,2].

When they cannot disambiguate (at all, or with high confidence) a word occurrence, many unsupervised WSD methods resort to the *first-sense heuristic*, which selects the first sense of each word, as listed in WordNet. Te first sense is the most common one, based on frequencies from sense-tagged corpora; hence, the heuristic is actually a *supervised* baseline. Unfortunately, the heuristic on

Table 1. Coverage (C), precision (P), recall (R), and F_1-measure (F) of WSD methods on the Senseval 2 and 3 datasets, *polysemous words only*, excluding adverbs, *without using the first-sense heuristic*. The results are percentages.

Senseval 2	Noun				Verb				Adjective				All			
Method	C	P	R	F	C	P	R	F	C	P	R	F	C	P	R	F
san	72.2	27.8	20.0	23.3	71.1	19.6	13.9	16.3	72.4	39.6	28.7	33.3	71.9	27.9	20.0	23.3
pr	72.2	45.5	32.8	38.1	71.1	30.0	21.3	24.9	72.4	38.8	28.1	32.6	71.9	39.4	28.4	33.0
ilp-sr-full	99.6	38.6	38.4	38.5	99.6	25.0	24.9	24.9	92.8	37.4	34.7	36.0	98.1	34.2	33.5	**33.8**
ilp-sr-prun	99.6	38.6	38.4	38.5	99.6	24.6	24.5	24.5	92.8	37.7	35.0	36.3	98.1	34.1	34.4	**33.8**
ilp-pmi-full	99.6	27.9	27.7	27.8	98.9	23.4	23.2	23.3	100.0	37.9	37.9	37.9	99.5	28.6	28.4	28.5
ilp-pmi-prun	99.6	28.6	28.5	28.6	98.9	24.7	24.5	24.6	100.0	43.5	43.5	43.5	99.5	30.5	30.4	30.5

Senseval 3	Noun				Verb				Adjective				All			
Method	C	P	R	F	C	P	R	F	C	P	R	F	C	P	R	F
san	97.9	30.6	29.9	30.2	94.2	28.8	27.1	27.9	94.9	37.8	35.9	36.8	95.8	31.0	29.7	30.4
pr	97.9	38.3	37.5	37.9	94.2	39.6	37.3	38.4	94.9	40.5	38.4	39.4	95.8	39.2	37.6	**38.4**
ilp-sr-full	99.9	32.3	32.2	32.3	98.0	25.8	25.3	25.6	97.0	38.3	37.1	37.7	98.6	30.6	30.2	30.4
ilp-sr-prun	99.9	32.0	31.9	32.0	98.0	25.8	25.3	25.6	97.0	38.7	37.5	38.1	98.6	30.5	30.1	30.3
ilp-pmi-full	96.7	30.2	29.2	29.7	94.1	18.1	17.1	17.6	96.9	39.4	38.2	38.8	95.7	26.9	25.8	26.3
ilp-pmi-prun	96.7	27.3	26.4	26.8	94.1	19.3	18.2	18.7	96.9	39.0	37.8	38.4	95.7	26.1	24.9	25.5

its own outperforms all existing unsupervised WSD methods.[3] Hence, the experimental results of most unsupervised WSD methods, including ours, can be drastically improved by frequently invoking the first-sense heuristic, even for randomly selected word occurrences. We, therefore, believe that unsupervised WSD methods should not be allowed to use the heuristic in evaluations.

Table 1 lists the results of our experiments. We follow common practice and exclude adverbs. We consider only polysemous words, i.e., we ignore words with only one possible meaning (trivial cases), which is why the results may appear to be lower than results published elsewhere; the first-sense heuristic is also not used. Since all six methods may fail to assign a sense to some word occurrences, we show results in terms of coverage (percentage of word occurrences assigned senses), precision (correctly assigned senses over total assigned senses), recall (correctly assigned senses over word occurrences to be assigned senses), and F_1 measure.[4] A reasonable upper bound is human interannotator agreement [11]. For fine-grained sense inventories, like WordNet's, interannotator agreement is between 67% and 80% [13]. A random baseline, assigning senses randomly with uniform probability, achieves approx. 20% and 14% accuracy on Senseval 2 and 3, respectively, counting both monosemous and polysemous words.

On the Senseval 2 dataset, the coverage of our ILP method (with both measures, with and without sense pruning) was significantly higher than that of SAN

---

[3] When both monosemous and polysemous words are considered, the first-sense heuristic achieves 63.7% and 61.3% accuracy on the Senseval 2 and 3 datasets, respectively, with 100% coverage. At 100% coverage, precision and recall are equal to accuracy.

[4] We do not assign a sense to a word occurrence when the relatedness of all of its senses to all the senses of all the other word occurrences is zero.

and PR. In terms of F_1-measure, ILP-SR-FULL performed overall better than SAN and PR, outperforming SAN by a wide margin. Our method performed worse with the PMI-based measure (ILP-PMI-FULL) than with SR on the Senseval 2 dataset, though it still outperformed SAN, but not PR. The pruned versions (ILP-SR-PRUN, ILP-PMI-PRUN) performed as well as or better than the corresponding unpruned ones (ILP-SR-FULL, ILP-PMI-FULL), indicating that sense pruning successfully managed to remove mostly irrelevant senses. Sense pruning also leads to considerable improvements in execution time. The average execuation time per sentence (collectively on both datasets) was 82.81, 23.45, 81.46, 17.40 seconds for ILP-SR-FULL, ILP-SR-PRUN, ILP-PMI-FULL, ILP-PMI-PRUN, respectively. The corresponding times for SAN and PR were 101.38 and 91.92, i.e., our ILP methods are in practice faster than the implementations of SAN and PR we had available, even though the computational complexity of SAN and PR is polynomial.[5]

On the Senseval 3 dataset, the coverage of all ILP methods remains very high, with a small decline when the PMI-based measure is used. The F_1 scores of the ILP methods are now lower, compared to their respective scores in Senseval 2; this is due to the larger average polysemy of Senseval 3 (8.41 vs. 6.48 for polysemous words). Surprisingly, however, SAN and PR now perform better than in Senseval 2; and PR outperforms our ILP methods , with the overall difference between SAN and ILP-SR-FULL now being negligible. We can only speculate at this point that the improved performance of SAN and PR may be due to the higher polysemy of Senseval 3, which allows them to construct larger graphs, which in turn allows them to assign more reliable rank or activation scores to the nodes (senses). The coverage of SAN and PR is also now much higher, which may indicate that as their graphs become larger, it becomes easier for SAN and PR to construct connected graphs; both methods require a connected graph, in order to rank the nodes or spread the activation, respectively. Also, the pruned ILP methods now perform worse than the corresponding unpruned ones, indicating that sense pruning is less successful in discarding irrelevant senses as polysemy increases.

We aim to investigate the differences between the Senseval 2 and 3 results further in future work. For the moment, we conclude that our ILP approach seems to work better with lower polysemy. We believe, though, that our experiments against SAN and PR already show the potential of our ILP model.

5   Conclusions

We presented an ILP model of WSD, which can be used with off-the-shelf solvers and any sense relatedness measure. We experimented with SR and a hybrid PMI-based measure on the Senseval 2 and 3 datasets, against two well-known methods based on PageRank (PR) and Spreading Activation Networks (SAN). Overall, our ILP model performed better with SR. With that measure, it performed better than both PR and SAN on the Senseval 2 dataset, outperforming SAN by a wide margin. By contrast, PR performed much better than our ILP methods on the

---

[5] The complexity of SAN is $O(n^2 \cdot k^{2l+3})$, and PR's is $O(n^2 \cdot k^{\frac{3}{2}l+3})$, where k is the maximum branching factor of the hierarchical thesaurus, l its height, and n the number of word occurrences to be disambiguated [19].

Senseval 3 dataset, and the difference between SAN and our best ILP method was negligible. In practice, our ILP methods run faster than the PR and SAN implementations we had available. We hope that our ILP model will prove useful to others who may wish to experiment with different relatedness measures.

References

1. Agirre, E., Lopez de Lacalle, O.: Supervised domain adaption for word sense disambiguation. In: EACL (2009)
2. Agirre, E., Soroa, A.: Personalizing PageRank for word sense disambiguation. In: EACL (2009)
3. Florian, R., Cucerzan, S., Schafer, C., Yarowsky, D.: Combining classifiers for word sense disambiguation. Natural Language Engineering 8(4), 327–341 (2002)
4. Gabrilovich, E., Markovitch, S.: Computing semantic relatedness using Wikipedia-based explicit semantic analysis. In: IJCAI (2007)
5. Lesk, M.: Automated sense disambiguation using machine-readable dictionaries: How to tell a pine cone from an ice cream cone. In: SIGDOC (1986)
6. Manning, C., Schutze, H.: Foundations of Statistical NLP. MIT Press (2000)
7. Mihalcea, R., Csomai, A.: SenseLearner: Word sense disambiguation for all words in unrestricted text. In: ACL (2005)
8. Mihalcea, R., Tarau, P., Figa, E.: PageRank on semantic networks with application to word sense disambiguation. In: COLING (2004)
9. Montoyo, A., Suarez, A., Rigau, G., Palomar, M.: Combining knowledge-and corpus-based word-sense-disambiguation methods. JAIR 23, 299–330 (2005)
10. Navigli, R.: Online word sense disambiguation with structural semantic interconnections. In: EACL (2006)
11. Navigli, R.: Word sense disambiguation: A survey. ACM Computing Surveys 41(2), 10:1–10:69 (2009)
12. Navigli, R., Lapata, M.: Graph connectivity measures for unsupervised word sense disambiguation. In: IJCAI, pp. 1683–1688 (2007)
13. Palmer, M., Dang, H., Fellbaum, C.: Making fine-grained and coarse-grained sense distinctions, both manually and automatically. NLE 13(2), 137–163 (2007)
14. Ponzetto, S., Strube, M.: Knowledge derived from Wikipedia for computing semantic relatedness. J. of Artificial Intelligence Research 30, 181–212 (2007)
15. Quillian, R.: The teachable language comprehender: a simulation program and theory of language. Communications of ACM 12(8), 459–476 (1969)
16. Resnik, P.: Using inform. content to evaluate semantic similarity. In: IJCAI (1995)
17. Schütze, H.: Automatic word sense discrimination. Computational Linguistics 24(1), 97–123 (1998)
18. Sinha, R., Mihalcea, R.: Unsupervised graph-based word sense disambiguation using measures of word semantic similarity. In: IEEE ICSC (2007)
19. Tsatsaronis, G., Varlamis, I., Nørvåg, K.: An Experimental Study on Unsupervised Graph-based Word Sense Disambiguation. In: Gelbukh, A. (ed.) CICLing 2010. LNCS, vol. 6008, pp. 184–198. Springer, Heidelberg (2010)
20. Tsatsaronis, G., Varlamis, I., Vazirgiannis, M.: Text relatedness based on a word thesaurus. JAIR 37, 1–39 (2010)
21. Tsatsaronis, G., Vazirgiannis, M., Androutsopoulos, I.: Word sense disambiguation with spreading activation networks generated from thesauri. In: IJCAI (2007)
22. Turney, P.D.: Mining the Web for Synonyms: PMI-IR versus LSA on TOEFL. In: Flach, P.A., De Raedt, L. (eds.) ECML 2001. LNCS (LNAI), vol. 2167, pp. 491–502. Springer, Heidelberg (2001)

Parallelism, Localization and Chain Gradient Tuning Combinations for Fast Scalable Probabilistic Neural Networks in Data Mining Applications

Yiannis Kokkinos and Konstantinos Margaritis[*]

Parallel and Distributed Processing Laboratory, Department of Applied Informatics,
University of Macedonia, 156 Egnatia str., P.O. Box 1591, 54006, Thessaloniki, Greece

Abstract. This work investigates the scalability of Probabilistic Neural Networks via parallelization and localization, and a chain gradient tuning. Since PNN model is inherently parallel three common parallel approaches are studied here, namely data parallel, neuron parallel and pipelining. Localization methods via clustering algorithms are utilized to reduce the hidden layer size of PNNs. A problem of localization may be present in the case of multi-class data. In this paper we propose two simple fast approximate solutions. The first is using sigma smoothing parameters obtained from the parallel PNN initial training directly to clustering. In this case a substantial reduction of neurons is achieved without significant loss of recognition accuracy. The second is an effort for an additional tuning. Via confidence outputs we employ a chain training approach to tune for the best possible PNN architecture.

Keywords: Parallel processing, Probabilistic Neural networks, data mining.

1 Introduction

Data mining tries to unlock and exploit the hidden patterns in databases [1]. Probabilistic Neural Networks (PNN) [2] are known intelligence tools for classification that derive knowledge directly from data and represent it in the form of simple well understood Bayesian models, which are most suitable for data mining applications that also need confidence levels. Bayesian classifier methods represent a powerful class of techniques to data mining, as they can in a strict mathematical sense to work under uncertainty. However the PNN hidden neuron size is usually of the order of the whole dataset size and the PNN operation is slow and demanding in memory and CPU resources. Thus for large scale systems and datasets the PNN usage is hindered. This encourages more research into the scalability of these techniques. Hence during the last five years, various works have been presented for mapping Probabilistic Neural Network in parallel processing systems, such as parallel PNN in Beowulf Clusters [3], in Grid mining with Map/Reduce [4], and in Graphic Processing Units [5]. All these works mainly focus on splitting the data-neuron matrix to speed up the slow execution

---

[*] Corresponding author.

I. Maglogiannis, V. Plagianakos, and I. Vlahavas (Eds.): SETN 2012, LNAI 7297, pp. 41–48, 2012.
© Springer-Verlag Berlin Heidelberg 2012

times due to PNNs quadratic computational complexity, and in this way demonstrate that PNNs can be efficiently parallelized.

Yet the quadratic complexity of the original problem remains since Parallelism is only one path towards speedups. While run time can be reduced by parallelism, the computational complexity can be reduced by localization techniques which need fewer locally important neurons, to sum up for the probability distribution functions estimation. Use fewer units in PNN pattern layer but try to place them at optimal places. Like previous works clustering algorithms are also considered here to reduce the hidden layer size of PNNs.

A problem of such localization may be present in the case of multi-class data. In principle there exist no unsupervised algorithm that can sample by clustering the data points inside each class and select the best possible representative center points from every class such as a global accuracy criterion is simultaneously been satisfied. This problem is an extension of the well known k-centers problem and is NP hard [19]. In this paper we propose two simple fast approximate solutions for the above mentioned problem. The first is using sigma smoothing parameters obtained from the parallel PNN initial training directly to clustering. In this way a substantial reduction of neurons is achieved with negligible losses of classification performance. The second is an effort for an additional tuning. Via confidence outputs we employ a chain training approach to tune and test for the best possible PNN architecture. Details and experimental results from all methods are presented next.

2   PNN Architecture and Parallelization Mappings

The Probabilistic Neural Network [2-5] has four layers, namely input, pattern, summation and output. There are M classes in the output layer and each has N_m pattern neurons in the pattern layer, and a single $G_m()$, summation neuron in the summation layer. The d input layer neurons are the data features. The pattern layer is where train patterns are loaded and divided in M groups, one for each class. For an unknown sample X, the pattern neuron i of group m compute a Gaussian kernel of the form:

$$F_{m,i}(X) = \frac{1}{(2\pi\sigma^2)^{d/2}} \exp\left(-\left\|X - X_{m,i}\right\|^2 /(2\sigma^2)\right)$$

(1)

where $X_{m,i}$ is the center of the Parzen kernel and sigma σ is the smoothing parameter (the width), that defines the range of each receptive field. The summation layer computes the conditional density functions by sum up the previous densities in $G_m(X)=(1/N_m)\Sigma F_{m,i}(X)$, and finally the output layer classifies the unknown X in class C_m that have maximum $G_m(X) \cdot h(C_m)$, where $h(C_m)$ is the class prior. The conditional probability for class C_m, can give also the confidence levels of this class and it is $Conf(C_m|X)= G_m(X) \cdot h(C_m)/(\Sigma G_m(X) \cdot h(C_m))$. A PNN with a single sigma parameter called homoscedastic, while the multi-sigma PNN called heteroscedastic. The normalization factor in the denominator of confidence (the prior of X) is the sum of all numerators for all categories C_m.

The main disadvantage of PNN network is that it has one hidden neuron for each training sample and thus requires more computational resources during execution than other models. On a serial machine, O(n) cost is required to classify a single input.

Exploitation of parallel mappings in Neural Networks can be achieved in many different levels from coarse grained to fine grained. The first, the session parallelism level (also called inter model parallelism in parallel data mining) places a different training model session to each processor. The next, the data parallelism, simultaneously learns in different training examples within the same train model session. The layer parallelism use concurrent computation for different layers. The neuron parallelism, use the same model and split the neurons to different processors. These last three levels also belong to intra model parallelism. A taxonomy review is in [6] and general guidelines on breaking any NN structure are in [7]. If the algorithm permits it, one can minimize point-to-point communication by pipelining the neuron calculations. Beyond selecting a representative training sample, PNN training phase is essentially a model selection procedure for the definition of sigma parameters and pattern neurons.

In PNN data Parallelism in Master/Worker architecture the Master node sends to all Workers the same copy of Neural Network, after that Master partition the data set and send a different partition to a different processor. Then for each epoch (a pass through all local data) each Worker independently process its local test set, exchanges its weight updates with other nodes, applies the weight updates to its copy of Neural Network, and computes local error rate and determines if local training is complete. The Search for best sigma parameters can be done by several repetitions of an epoch. This approach ensures that all parameter values required during the training phase, are locally available, decreasing the communication between the nodes and the synchronization of the parallel algorithm. The synchronization appears in the end of an epoch.

In PNN neuron parallelism the neurons are distributed in the processors. An algorithm of neuron parallelism in Master/Worker architecture is the following: 1) Master split data set into train and test (uses stratified sampling) and partition and distribute train set instances across workers to set up the local distributed pattern neurons. 2) Each Worker uses its local train set for the local pattern neurons. 3) Master broadcast the same train parameters to all workers. 4) For each test set instance Master sequentially Broadcast an instance X (or a batch B) of test set data to all workers, all workers compute local distances, kernels and send back partial sums for each class, Master reduce all partial sums for each class from all workers, and find the class of X.

In the PNN pipelined neuron parallelism, the communication time between processors is minimised to point-to-point, allowing each one node to receive-send messages with only his 2 neighbours (previous - next). Each machine keeps a partition of neurons, as in the PNN Neuron Parallel. In batches B, the evaluation points are loaded in the first node. For each batch, is calculated a list of partial sums of the class conditional probabilities for each class. The list and batch together are propagated to the next node in the pipeline that makes the same operation on them. A label of class is finally set in the ending node. This requires only point-to-point communication.

Model selection methods like leave-one-out cross-validation are often used in PNN training and evaluation for selecting the best sigma parameters. This is the one approach we use in the parallel implementations.

3   PNN Localization Problem and k-Centers Sampling

While PNN run time can be reduced by parallelism, the computational complexity can be reduced by localization techniques which need fewer locally important kernels, or neurons, to sum up for the probability density functions estimation. Localization tries to obey the parsimonious principle. The smaller and simpler is the better. All localization techniques require some additional regional information, specifically a list of k local points which are close to any given point x. Various clustering or sampling approaches are proposed to reduce neurons [8] for PNNs like LVQ in [9], k-means clustering [10], hierarchical clustering [11], the DDA algorithm in [12], Gaussian ARTMAP in [13], global k-means with Expectation–Maximization in [14] and k-medoids in [15]. After finding "representative" vectors for each class every sigma parameter depends on the clusters. The modified density equation for the PNN is:

$$F(x \mid c_m) = \frac{1}{\sum_{k=1}^{Nm} N_k^m} \sum_{k=1}^{Nm} \frac{N_k^m}{\prod_{i=1}^{d} \sigma_{ik}^m} \exp\left[-\sum_{i=1}^{d} \frac{(x_i - X_{ik}^m)^2}{2\sigma_{ik}^2} \right] \tag{2}$$

where N_k^m is the number of initial samples that covered from the kth cluster in class m, while σ_{ik}^m and X_{ik}^m are the smoothing parameter and the mean (or the medoid) in ith dimension for the cluster kth in class m, respectively. However the cluster based sigma parameters estimation tends to deteriorate the classification performance and optimization of sigma parameters, as well as of the network weights, is necessary.

In this work we compare many existing samplers like Affinity Propagation (AP) [16], k-Medoids (KM) [1], Subtractive Clustering (SC) [17] and Farthest Point clustering (FPC) [18] to sample important points inside classes.

A problem of such localization may be evident in the case of multi-class data. An efficient algorithm must select the best samples from a class and doing this with respect to the best samples from the other classes. Yet this problem is a multi-class extension of the well known k-centers problem or k median objective and is NP hard [19]. In this paper we propose two simple fast approximate solutions to work around the problem. The first we will demonstrate is using the sigma smoothing parameters obtained from the parallel PNN initial training directly to Subtractive Clustering. In this way a substantial reduction is achieved without significant loss of recognition accuracy. The second is an effort for chain training for an additional tuning.

Affinity Propagation and k-Medoids are accurate but very slow and not incremental in the sense that the next cluster point is not dependent than the previous. They are included for comparison only. We parallelise Subtractive clustering and Farthest Point clustering (FPC) as they are the only incremental, and fast and more suitable for large scaling. Extensive details will be presented elsewhere. Note that FPC needs to predefine the number of centers while Subtractive Clustering not. Nevertheless, to select sufficiently the best centers SC requires a training phase to find a suitable sigma parameter. Fortunately in this work we obtain such a sigma parameter already from the previously supervised parallel PNN training and propose here to use it.

4   Tuning by Chain Gradient Training Paradigm

Using sigmas from PNN training in the SC clustering procedure as proposed in the previous chapter may be efficient enough. Though in the localized version of PNN there is no generic method for selecting the best number of representative points from every class population in all cases. If needed, chain gradient training approach can provide additional tuning to test for the best possible tuned PNN architecture. First by using incremental clustering algorithms like subtractive clustering one can potentially sample most possible representative points from every class in an ordered fashion. Then the method gradually reduces the neuron size, equally from every class, and monitors an average 'gradient' of confidence levels from a whole inter-connected chain of network solutions. In localized PNN case this tuning is not meant for classification performance improvement, but rather for an additional reduction of neuron size without affecting its current performance.

Recall now that PNN is a data model and a data descriptor and also produce confidence levels. Let us suppose that a chain of two PNN instances namely A and B different only in the number of hidden neurons and a evaluation set ES is present.

Initially PNN(A) classifies its own A points to produce A-A confidence measure. PNN(B) classifies its own B points to produce B-B measure. Then PNN(A) classifies B points to produce A-B measure and PNN(B) classifies A points to produce B-A measure. In the third step PNN(A) classifies evaluation set ES to produce A-ES measure and PNN(B) classifies ES to produce B-ES measure. Finally, ES set classifies A and B patterns. The first two are internal measures, the next two are local and the last four are external. A schematic representation is given in fig. 1.

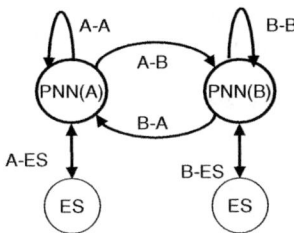

Fig. 1. A chain of two Probabilistic Neural Networks A and B different in the number of patterns, inter-connected with each other via confidence-based measures, indicated by arrows

One can have a sequence of several PNNs different in the number k of hidden neurons only. This chain training tuning scheme must be robust against oscillating local minima. The representative sampled points from every class, in an ordered fashion, are loaded to the hidden layer. If the hidden neuron size is gradually increased then we expect the chain global measure to soon reach a plateau. Confidence levels produced by the output neurons must progressively be increased for correctly classified patterns and be decreased for the falsely classified patterns. An efficient measure that can be used, is the (1+ sum of confidences for falsely classified patterns) / (1+ sum of confidences for correctly classified patterns) ratio. The next paragraphs present some experimental results.

5   Experimental Results

The experimental results for PNN data parallel, PNN neuron parallel and PNN neuron pipelined simulations are determined for 1..2..4.. 6..8 .. 10.. 12.. 14.. 16..24 machines. The speedup is S / P, where S the sequential run time in a single processor and P the time that simulates the network in parallel. All PNN Neural Network implementations are written in C using MPI library. PNN-CV train by cross-validation and PNN-SC with Subtractive Clustering are included.

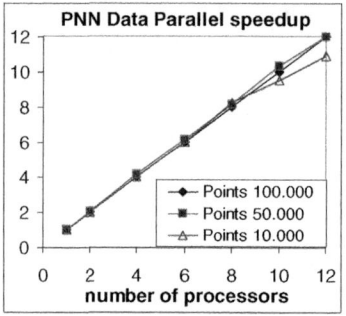
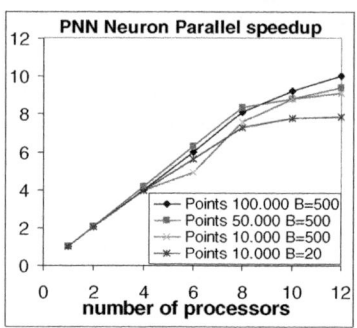

Fig. 2. (A) PNN Data Parallel, speed ups for data sizes of 10.000, 50.000 and 100.000 points, (B) PNN Neuron Parallel speedups respectively for two batch sizes B

In fig.2A for PNN data parallel with 10.000 points a linear speedup is observed up to 8 processors and when the size of problem is increased to 50.000 and 100.000 points we observe linear speedup up to 12 processors. In Fig. 2B for neuron parallelism results it appears a sub-linear speedup (9/12) up to 12 processors. This divergence is improved evidently when the size of problem is increased to 50.000 and 100.000 points and when the number of points in the batch increasing from 20 to 500.

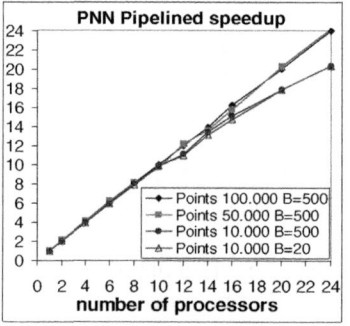
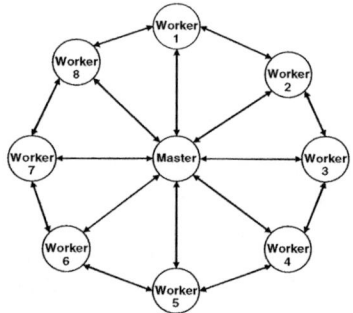

Fig. 3. (A) PNN neuron Pipelined speedups for two sets of 10.000, 50.000 and 100.000 points respectively for two batch sizes B, where one observes an impressive linear acceleration up to 24 processors. (B) The parallel programming model Master/Worker + Pipeline.

It is clearly show in fig. 3A for Pipelined calculations of 50.000 and 100.000 points an impressive linear speedup (24/24) that it is achieved up to all 24 processors we have tried. Results of PNN neuron pipelined are the best of all the previous methods.

For each network we compute error on the validation set. The network with the highest sum of confidences is then picked as one with the best generalization ability.

As standard we use several benchmark datasets downloaded from UCI ML Repository [20]. In table 1 average classification results are presented after 20 runs (10 with 50% train set and 10 with 80% train set) of each algorithm. The 1-NN is the one Nearest Neighbour rule, parallel PNN-CV is standard PNN with cross-validation, parallel PNN-FPC is localized PNN with Farthest point clustering, in where S means a single-sigma parameter used in equation 2, M means multi-sigma as a max distance from center and V means using variances and equation 2. PNN-AP is localized PNN with Affinity Propagation, PNN-KM is PNN with k-medoids. The best results are obtained with PNN-SC localized via the parallel Subtractive Clustering algorithm in which we use the same single sigma parameter founded by PNN-CV.

Table 1. Classification rates on the cross-validated test set for several benchmark datasets

Database	size	Classes	1-NN	PNN-CV	PNN-FPC			PNN-AP	PNN-KM	PNN-SC
					S	M	V	S	S	S
Iris	150	3	96	97 (σ=0.10)	93	95	92	96	96	**97**
Wine	178	3	94	95 (σ=0.22)	89	93	93	93	93	**95**
Wisconsin	683	2	97.5	98.5 (σ=0.25)	98	98	98	98	98	**98.5**
Yeast	1484	10	51	56 (σ=0.18)	45	25	25	47	49	**55**
Diabetes	768	2	70	76 (σ=0.25)	74	63	63	74	74	**75**

Sampling by AP or KM is very slow with a cost $O(n^2 \log n)$ for both and difficult to parallelise, but are included for comparison only. We parallelise efficiently PNN-SC and PNN-FPC. Only PNN-SC recovers the original performance, by using sigma parameter from previous PNN-CV in it. At most 10% points were extracted from each dataset. We observe that AP on average has similar results. Thus this localized approach produce at least 10 times faster PNN, in addition to 24 times speed up obtained from the 24 processors pipelined.

6   Conclusions

The first goal of this work is to speed up PNN. Using 24 processors the PNN training with cross validation and subtractive clustering approaches can impressively be speed up by 24 times. The next goal is to answer the question of preserving the sigma parameter founded by PNN cross-validation how many and which points can be omitted from the pattern layer without significant loss in the PNN performance. Using the sigmas found from the standard PNN directly on the Subtractive Clustering inside classes one can select most representative points and produce a localized PNN with small pattern neuron size and excellent performance that is 10 times even faster than the original version. If needed, additional tuning can be done by the chain gradient to test for the best possible PNN architecture. This approach could also be used in the training phase of other reduced nearest neighbour types of classifiers.

References

1. Dunham, M.H.: Data mining introductory and advanced topics. Prentice Hall (2004)
2. Specht, D.: Probabilistic neural networks. Neural Networks 3, 109–118 (1990)
3. Secretan, J., Georgiopoulos, M., Maidhof, I., Shibly, P., Hecker, J.: Methods for Parallelizing the Probabilistic Neural Network on a Beowulf Cluster Computer. In: International Joint Conference on Neural Networks, IJCNN 2006, Vancouver, pp. 2378–2385 (2006)
4. Cardona, K., Secretan, J., Georgiopoulos, M., Anagnostopoulos, G.: A Grid Based System for Data Mining Using MapReduce. Technical Report, TR-2007-02 (2007)
5. Bastke, S., Deml, M., Schmidt, S.: Combining statistical network data, probabilistic neural networks and the computational power of GPUs for anomaly detection in computer networks. In: 19th International Conference on Automated Planning and Scheduling, Workshop on Intelligent Security (SecArt 2009), Thessaloniki, Greece (2009)
6. Šerbedžija, N.: Simulating Artificial Neural Networks on Parallel Architectures. IEEE Computer, Special Issue on Neural Computing 29(3), 56–63 (1996)
7. Pethick, M., Liddle, M., Werstein, P., Huang, Z.: Parallelization of a backpropagation neural network on a cluster computer. In: 15th IASTED International Conference on Parallel and Distributed Computing and Systems, CA, USA, November 3-5, pp. 574–582 (2003)
8. Specht, D.F.: Enhancements to the probabilistic neural networks. In: Proc. IEEE Int. Joint Conf. Neural Networks, Baltimore, MD, pp. 761–768 (1992)
9. Burrascano, P.: Learning vector quantization for the probabilistic neural network. IEEE Transactions on Neural Networks 2, 458–461 (1991)
10. Traven, H.G.C.: A neural network approach to statistical pattern classification by "semiparametric" estimation of probability density functions. IEEE Transactions on Neural Networks 2, 366–377 (1991)
11. Babich, G.A., Camps, O.I.: Weighted Parzen windows for pattern classification. IEEE Trans. Pattern Anal. Mach. Intell. 18(5), 567–570 (1996)
12. Berthold, M., Diamond, J.: Constructive training of probabilistic neural networks. Neurocomputing 19, 167–183 (1998)
13. Zhong, M., et al.: Gap-Based Estimation: Choosing the Smoothing Parameters for Probabilistic and General Regression Neural Networks. Neural Computation 19, 2840–2864 (2007)
14. Chang, R.K.Y., Loo, C.K., Rao, M.V.C.: A Global k-means Approach for Autonomous Cluster Initialization of Probabilistic Neural Network. Informatica 32, 219–225 (2008)
15. Georgiou, V.L., Alevizos, P.D., Vrahatis, M.N.: Novel approaches to probabilistic neural networks through bagging and evolutionary estimating of prior probabilities. Neural Processing Letters 27, 153–162 (2008)
16. Frey, B.J., Dueck, D.: Clustering by passing messages between data points. Science 315(5814), 972–976 (2007)
17. Sarimveis, H., Alexandridis, A., Bafas, G.: A fast training algorithm for RBF networks based on subtractive clustering. Neurocomputing, 501–505 (2003)
18. Gonzalez, T.F.: Clustering to minimize the maximum intercluster distance. Theoretical Computer Science 38(2-3), 293–306 (1985)
19. Bern, M., Eppstein, D.: Approximation Algorithms for Geometric Problems. In: Approximation algorithms for NP-hard problems, pp. 296–345. PWS Publishing (1997)
20. Frank, A., Asuncion, A.: UCI Machine Learning Repository. University of California, Irvine (2010), http://archive.ics.uci.edu/ml

SWRL2COOL: Object-Oriented Transformation of SWRL in the CLIPS Production Rule Engine

Emmanouil Rigas[1], Georgios Meditskos[2], and Nick Bassiliades[2]

[1] School of Electronics and Computer Science, University of Southampton, UK
er2g11@soton.ac.uk
[2] Department of Informatics, Aristotle University of Thessaloniki, Greece
{gmeditsk,nbassili}@csd.auth.gr

Abstract. The Semantic Web Rule Language (SWRL) is a W3C member submission rule language for ontologies. It is based on a combination of the OWL DL and OWL Lite sublanguages of the OWL Web Ontology Language with the Unary/Binary Datalog RuleML sublanguages of the Rule Markup Language. In this paper we propose a transformation of SWRL rules into the object-oriented rule language of CLIPS (COOL). The purpose of this transformation is to enhance an already existing CLIPS-based OWL ontology reasoner, namely O-DEVICE, with the ability to import and execute SWRL rules during the process of building custom ontology-based production rule programs.

Keywords: SWRL, Production Rules, CLIPS, OWL.

1   Introduction

SWRL [1] is a rule language based on a combination of OWL with the Unary/ Binary Datalog sublanguages of RuleML. SWRL enables Horn-like rules to be combined with an OWL knowledge base. Negation is not explicitly supported but only indirectly through OWL DL (e.g. complements). Its main purpose is to provide a formal meaning of OWL ontologies and extend OWL DL with rules.

In existing ontology reasoning implementations, although it is possible to manipulate ontologies using the SWRL rule notation, for example in KAON2 [2] and Pellet [3], it is not possible (or it is not efficient at least) to define a complete rule program over the ontology since they are not native rule engines. To this end, the use of a rule system that is able to reason over ontologies gives the opportunity to utilize directly the ontology information by building knowledge-based systems. Ontologies can be inserted into the system, and after the materialization of the semantics through the reasoning procedure, that is, the application of inference rules in order to deduce new information (entailment), user-defined rules can operate over the materialized knowledge. Based on this idea, we have developed O-DEVICE [4] on top of the CLIPS production rule engine. Its reasoning process is characterized by the transformation of ontological information into the object-oriented model of the COOL language of CLIPS and the application of inference production rules over the generated object-oriented

I. Maglogiannis, V. Plagianakos, and I. Vlahavas (Eds.): SETN 2012, LNAI 7297, pp. 49–56, 2012.

schema. In that way, custom object-oriented rule programs can be developed on top of the transformed ontological knowledge using the efficient RETE engine of CLIPS. An example of such an application is Software Antipatterns [5].

In this paper, we propose an object-oriented transformation of SWRL rules into the COOL language of CLIPS in order to be able to operate on top of the transformed object-oriented ontological model that is created by O-DEVICE. Our goal is to enable O-DEVICE to import and execute SWRL rules and therefore, easing the development of knowledge-based systems on top of ontologies in CLIPS using a well-defined and widely adopted ontology rule language.

The rest of the paper is structured as follows: Section 2 overviews the syntax of the COOL production rules in CLIPS. Section 3 describes the XSLT transformations that are applied by SWRL2COOL and present a complete example. Finally, in sections 4 and 5 we present related work and we conclude, respectively.

2   The CLIPS Production Rule Engine

CLIPS[1] is a RETE-based production rule engine written in C that was developed in 1985 by NASA's Johnson Space Center and it has undergone continual refinement and improvement ever since. One of the most interesting capabilities of CLIPS is that it integrates the production rule paradigm with the OO model, which can be defined using the COOL (CLIPS Object-Oriented Language) language. In that way, classes, attributes and objects can be matched on the production rule conditions, as well as to be altered on rules actions.

2.1   COOL Production Rules in CLIPS

A production rule in CLIPS is defined using the `defrule` construct that consists of conditions and actions separated with the symbol =>. The conditions can match both facts and objects, whereas the actions define the actions that should be taken upon the satisfaction of all the conditions.

Objects of user-defined classes in COOL can be pattern-matched on the left-hand side of rules using object patterns of the form

```
<object-pattern> ::= (object <attribute-constraint>*)
<attribute-constraint> ::= (is-a <constraint>) |
(name <constraint>) | (<slot-name> <constraint>*)
```

The `is-a` constraint is used for specifying class constraints and it also encompasses subclasses of the matching classes. The `name` constraint is used for specifying a specific object on which to pattern-match. Constraints are also used in slots/multislots in order to restrict certain type of values. Both in fact and object patterns, it is possible to use variables in order to be matched with certain values. A single-value variable is denoted as `?x`, whereas a multivalue variable is denoted as `$?x`. An example rule that prints all the objects of the class `Person` is presented below.

---

[1] `http://clipsrules.sourceforge.net/`

```
(defrule test-rule2
    (object (is-a Person) (name ?x))
=> (printout t ?x crlf))
```

3 Transformation Procedure

SWRL2COOL is based on the XML syntax of SWRL and its main functionality is to transform SWRL rules into the COOL rule language of CLIPS. Currently, the transformed rules are used in the O-DEVICE reasoner [4] in order to allow the definition of custom production rule programs on top of ontologies.

The transformation procedure takes place in two phases (Fig. 1). In the first phase the rules which are written in SWRL are being processed by an XSLT file named `swrl2cool.xsl`. The procedure produces a file which represents the rules in an intermediate format, where SWRL constructs are transformed into CLIPS format, but properties are not yet encapsulated into object patterns. In the second phase this file is given as input to the main SWRL2COOL application (a java program), which produces the final file with the COOL rules. In parallel, the ontology classes and instances are transformed with O-DEVICE into COOL classes and objects. Finally, the two transformed pieces of knowledge (rules and ontology) are joined together to produce the object-oriented rule-based application.

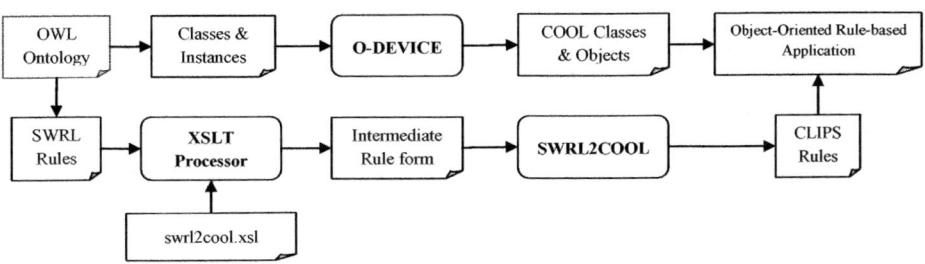

Fig. 1. The transformation procedure

3.1 XSLT Transformations

The SWRL rules have two parts: the body and the head. In most of the cases, the constructs of SWRL correspond to different constructs in COOL depending on whether they are in the head or the body of the rule. In order to handle these two cases, the XSLT transformation procedure is based on the use of modes in the `xsl:template` and `xsl:apply-templates` expressions. The modes allow an element to be processed many times, each time producing a different output. An `xsl:apply-templates` element with a mode argument, is applied to a template rule with a matching mode. The above are being used in this stylesheet as follows:

```
<xsl:template match="ruleml:imp">
<xsl:apply-templates select="ruleml:_body" mode="body" />
=>
<xsl:apply-templates select="ruleml:_head" mode="head" />
  end-of-rule
</xsl:template>
```

The "=>" symbol gets before the head of the rule in order to line-up with the CLIPS syntax and the phrase "end-of-rule" gets at the end of each rule in order to be a point of reference considering the line where one rule ends and another begins. This is used during the second phase of the transformation.

swrl:classAtom. The classAtom consists of a description, which is usually the name of a class and the name of a variable. When a classAtom is in the body of a rule then the description is matched in COOL as object is-a "name of class" and the variable as name "name of variable". Essentially, we refer to an instance of a class that has already been set earlier. On the other hand, when a classAtom is in the head of a rule then the variable is matched in COOL as make-instance <name of variable> and the description as of <name of class>. The head of the rules contains actions that have to be performed in relation to the elements that exist in the body of the rule. For this reason when there is a classAtom in the head of a rule, then we create a new instance of a class that was set before.

```
<xsl:template match="swrlx:classAtom" mode="body" >
   object (is-a <xsl:value-of select="owlx:Class/@owlx:name" /> )
   (name <xsl:apply-templates />)
</xsl:template>
<xsl:template match="swrlx:classAtom" mode="head" >
   (make-instance <xsl:apply-templates /> of <xsl:value-of
   select="owlx:Class/@owlx:name" />)
</xsl:template>
```

swrl:individualPropertyAtom. The individualPropertyAtom consists of the name of a property and the names of two variables. When it is in the body of the rule, the property must be matched to an object that has been defined earlier inside the rule. Thus, the first variable is the name of the object and the second variable is the value of the property. For example:

```
<swrlx:individualPropertyAtom swrlx:property="property_name">
      <ruleml:var>var1</ruleml:var>
      <ruleml:var>var2</ruleml:var>
</swrlx:individualPropertyAtom>
```

The output of the processing begins with the qualifier "property", followed by the "object name" of the object that the second property refers to. The qualifiers are used in the second phase of the transformation process, where COOL rules take their final format.

```
<xsl:template match="swrlx:individualPropertyAtom" mode="body">
  property
    (object (name<xsl:apply-templates select="ruleml:var[1]"/>)
    (<xsl:value-of select="@swrlx:property"/>
    <xsl:apply-templates  select="ruleml:var[2]"/> )
</xsl:template>
```

When an individualPropertyAtom is in the head of the rule, then the property must be matched to an object that has been defined earlier and change its value.

```
<xsl:template match="swrlx:individualPropertyAtom" mode="head">
  (slot-insert$ <xsl:apply-templates  select="ruleml:var[1]"/>
  <xsl:value-of select="@swrlx:property" />
  1 <xsl:apply-templates  select="ruleml:var[2]"/>)
</xsl:template>
```

The above stylesheet makes use of the (slot-insert$ <ins> <p> <i> <v>) function of CLIPS that inserts the value v in the slot p of the object ins at position i.

swrlx:datavaluedPropertyAtom. The datavaluedPropertyAtom consists of the name of the property, a name of a variable and a name of a constant. The datavaluedPropertyAtoms are being processed like the individualPropertyAtoms with one difference. The property takes as a constant value and not a variable.

```
<xsl:template match="swrlx:datavaluedPropertyAtom" mode="body">
  property
    (object (name<xsl:apply-templates select="ruleml:var[1]"/>)
      (<xsl:value-of select="@swrlx:property" />
      <xsl:value-of select="owlx:DataValue" /> )
</xsl:template>
<xsl:template match="swrlx:datavaluedPropertyAtom" mode="head">
  (slot-insert$ <xsl:apply-templates  select="ruleml:var[1]"/>
  <xsl:value-of select="@swrlx:property" />
  1 <xsl:value-of select="owlx:DataValue" />)
</xsl:template>
```

swrlx:builtInAtom. SWRL supports a large amount of built in functions, for comparisons, mathematical expressions, Booleans, strings, date, time and lists. Currently, SWRL2COOL handles only built in functions for comparisons and mathematical expressions and it is assumed that the body of the rule contains functions for comparisons and the head functions for mathematical expressions. The functions for comparisons are treated with the test construct of CLIPS and the functions for mathematical expressions are treated with the bind CLIPS function, to compute a new value that must be added or updated.

```
<xsl:template match="swrlx:builtinAtom" mode="body">
test ( <xsl:value-of select="@swrlx:builtin" />
  <xsl:apply-templates  select="ruleml:var[1] "/>
  <xsl:apply-templates select="ruleml:var[2]|owlx:DataValue"/>)
</xsl:template>
<xsl:template match="swrlx:builtinAtom" mode="head">
  bind <xsl:apply-templates select="ruleml:var[1]"/>
( <xsl:value-of select="@swrlx:builtin" />
  <xsl:apply-templates  select="ruleml:var[2]"/>
<xsl:apply-templates select="ruleml:var[3]|owlx:DataValue[1]"/>)
</xsl:template>
```

3.2   Transformation Example

We now present a transformation example of a complete SWRL rule (below in presentation syntax) and the results of all transformation phases.

```
Car(?c), tank-capacity(?c,?tc), fuel-consumption(?c,?fc)
 -> swrlb:divide(?a,?tc,?fc), autonomy(?c,?a)
```

SWRL Rule - XML syntax:

```
<ruleml:imp>
<ruleml:_body>
  <swrlx:classAtom>
    <owlx:Class owlx:name="car"/>    <ruleml:var>c</ruleml:var>
  </swrlx:classAtom>
  <swrlx:individualPropertyAtom swrlx:property="tank-capacity">
    <ruleml:var>c</ruleml:var>       <ruleml:var>tc</ruleml:var>
  </swrlx:individualPropertyAtom>
  <swrlx:individualPropertyAtom swrlx:property="fuel-consumption">
    <ruleml:var>c</ruleml:var>       <ruleml:var>fc</ruleml:var>
  </swrlx:individualPropertyAtom>
</ruleml:_body>
<ruleml:_head>
  <swrlx:builtinAtom swrlx:builtin="divide">
    <ruleml:var>a</ruleml:var>
     <ruleml:var>tc</ruleml:var> <ruleml:var>fc</ruleml:var>
    </swrlx:builtinAtom>
    <swrlx:individualPropertyAtom swrlx:property="autonomy">
      <ruleml:var>c</ruleml:var> <ruleml:var>a</ruleml:var>
    </swrlx:individualPropertyAtom>
</ruleml:_head>
</ruleml:imp>
```

Intermediate rule format:

```
object (is-a car) (name ?c)
property (object (name ?c) (tank-capacity ?tc)
property (object (name ?c) (fuel-consumption ?fc)
=>
bind ?a (divide ?tc ?fc)
(slot-insert$ ?c autonomy 1 ?a)
end-of-rule
```

Final CLIPS rule:

```
(defrule r2
  (object (is-a car ) (name ?c)
    (tank-capacity $? ?tc $?) (fuel-consumption $? ?fc $?))
=>
  (bind ?a (/ ?tc ?fc))
  (slot-insert$ ?c autonomy 1 ?a))
```

4   Related Work

A lot of approaches have been proposed towards the development of frameworks able to execute SWRL rules on top of OWL ontologies in native rule engines. Many of them use the Jess[2] rule engine and follow a fact-based approach, where both rules and OWL ontologies are mapped on fact-based Jess constructs, in contrast to our approach that follows an object-oriented implementation using the COOL language of CLIPS. To the best of our knowledge, this is the first effort that enables the CLIPS rule engine to import and execute SWRL rules in an object-oriented manner. In the following, we briefly present existing SWRL transformation approaches.

SWRLJessTab [6] is a plugin in Protege that allows the execution of SWRL rules using the Jess rule engine. The interaction between OWL and the Jess rule engine is user-driven. The user controls when OWL knowledge and SWRL rules are transferred to Jess, when inference is performed using those knowledge and rules, and when the resulting Jess facts are transferred back to Protege as OWL knowledge. SWRLJessTab actually maps SWRL rules on fact-based Jess rules that match facts, in contrast to our approach that SWRL rules are transformed into object-oriented rules and match objects in CLIPS.

In [7] the authors reuse the SWRLJessTab along with SweetRules[3] and other standard tools [8] in order to transform an extended version of SWRL suitable in teaching scenarios into Jess fact-based rules. This is also a fact-based approach where the knowledge and the rules are represented in terms of Jess facts.

A similar approach to SWRLJessTab is the OWL2Jess [9] tool that enables the transformation of OWL ontologies to Jess and thus enables OWL models to

---

[2] http://herzberg.ca.sandia.gov/jess
[3] http://sweetrules.projects.semwebcentral.org/

be extended by means of rules. Facts are derived from an initial OWL file by one XSLT stylesheet, while the RDF(S) and OWL Semantics are pre-defined as Jess rules.

5   Conclusions

In this paper, we presented an object-oriented transformation of SWRL rules into the COOL language of CLIPS. The approach is based on XSLT transformations over the XML syntax of SWRL. In that way, we enable the CLIPS production rule engine to import and execute SWRL rules over object-oriented COOL models.

Currently, we use our tool in the O-DEVICE reasoner that processes and maps OWL ontologies on the COOL model of CLIPS. In that way, SWRL rules can be combined with classes and instances from an OWL ontology that has been transformed into classes and instances in the COOL model using the O-DEVICE. In the future, we plan to add support for more built-in SWRL constructs and to implement SWRL2COOL as a Protege plugin.

References

1. Horrocks, I., Patel-Schneider, P.F., Boley, H., Tabet, S., Grosof, B., Dean, M.: SWRL: A semantic web rule language combining OWL and RuleML. W3C member submission, World Wide Web Consortium
2. Motik, B.: KAON2 - scalable reasoning over ontologies with large data sets. ERCIM News 2008(72) (2008)
3. Sirina, E., Parsia, B., Grau, B., Kalyanpur, A., Katz, Y.: Pellet: A practical OWL-DL reasoner. Journal of Web Semantics 5(2), 51–53 (2007)
4. Meditskos, G., Bassiliades, N.: A rule-based object-oriented OWL reasoner. IEEE Transactions on Knowledge and Data Engineering 20(3), 397–410 (2008)
5. Settas, D., Meditskos, G., Stamelos, I., Bassiliades, N.: SPARSE: A symptom-based antipattern retrieval knowledge-based system using semantic web technologies. Expert Syst. Appl. 38(6), 7633–7646 (2011)
6. Golbreich, C., Imai, A.: Combining SWRL rules and OWL ontologies with Protege OWL plugin, Jess, and Racer. In: 7th International Protege Conference (2004)
7. Wang, E., Kim, Y.S.: Using SWRL for ITS through keyword extensions and rewrite meta-rules. In: 5th Int'l Workshop on Ontologies and Semantic Web for E-Learning, SWEL@AIED 2007 (2007)
8. Wang, E., Kim, Y.S.: A teaching strategies engine using translation from SWRL to Jess. In: Intelligent Tutoring Systems 2006, pp. 51–60 (2006)
9. Mei, J., Bontas, E.P., Lin, Z.: OWL2Jess: A Transformational Implementation of the OWL Semantics. In: Chen, G., Pan, Y., Guo, M., Lu, J. (eds.) ISPA-WS 2005. LNCS, vol. 3759, pp. 599–608. Springer, Heidelberg (2005)

Forecasting Fraudulent Financial Statements with Committee of Cost-Sensitive Decision Tree Classifiers

Elias Zouboulidis[1] and Sotiris Kotsiantis[2]

[1] Hellenic Open University, Greece
eliaszouboulidis@yahoo.com
[2] Department of Mathematics, University of Patras, Greece
sotos@math.upatras.gr

Abstract. This paper uses machine learning techniques in detecting firms that issue fraudulent financial statements (FFS) and deals with the identification of factors associated to FFS. To this end, a number of experiments have been conducted using representative learning algorithms, which were trained using a data set of 164 fraud and non-fraud Greek firms. A random committee of cost-sensitive decision tree classifiers is the best choice according to our experiments.

1   Introduction

Even though it is not a new phenomenon, the number of corporate earnings restatements due to aggressive accounting practices, accounting irregularities, or accounting fraud has raised significantly during the past few years, and it has drawn much awareness from investors, analysts, and regulators. After many high profile accounting frauds and corporate scandals (Enron, WorldCom, Adelphia etc) fraudulent events have been followed by increased governmental intervention and regulation. In 2002, the U.S. congress passed the Sarbanes-Oxley Act to improve the accuracy and reliability of corporate financial reporting and disclosures. Europe also had financial scandals over this same period (with the Parmalat scandal being the most notorious) even if most of which were characteristically different from the US style [8]. In this context, Bollen et. al [5] in order to identify the true causes of Europe's biggest business failures over the past 25 years discovered that high leveraging and management fraud were the only two characteristics common in more than half the cases investigated. However, the authors conclude that even though accounting issues found to play a role in a number of business failures in their study, it is less important compared with large US business failures.

Accounting frauds can be characterized as either fraudulent financial reporting or misappropriation of assets, or both. Fraudulent financial reporting is universally known as cooking the books. Researchers have used a variety of techniques and models to detect accounting fraud in circumstances in which, a priori, is likely to exist. In this study, we perform an in-depth examination of publicly available data from the

I. Maglogiannis, V. Plagianakos, and I. Vlahavas (Eds.): SETN 2012, LNAI 7297, pp. 57–64, 2012.
© Springer-Verlag Berlin Heidelberg 2012

financial statements of various firms so as to detect FFS by using supervised machine learning methods. The goal of this research is to identify the financial factors to be used by auditors in assessing the likelihood of FFS. The detection of fraudulent financial statements, along with the qualification of financial statements, have also been in the limelight in Greece because of the increase in the number of companies listed on the Athens Stock Exchange (and raising capital through public offerings) and the attempts to decrease taxation on profits. There is an increasing demand for greater transparency, reliability and more information to be incorporated within financial statements.

The following section attempts a brief literature review. Section 3 describes the data set of our study and the feature selection process. Section 4 presents the experimental results for the number of representative compared algorithms and a combining technique that produce better accuracy. Finally, section 5 discusses the conclusions and some future research directions.

2   Literature Review

As Watts and Zimmerman [22] argue the financial statement audit is a monitoring mechanism that helps reduce information asymmetry and protect the interests of the principals, particularly, stockholders and potential stockholders, by providing sound assurance that management's financial statements are free from material misstatements. However, in real life, detecting management fraud is a hard task when using normal audit procedures since there is a lack of knowledge concerning the characteristics of management fraud. Furthermore, given its infrequency, most auditors lack the experience required to detect it. Last but not least, managers purposely try to deceive auditors. Albrecht et al. [1] review the fraud detection aspects of auditing standards and the empirical research conducted on fraud detection. Ansah et al. [2] investigate the relative influence of the size of audit firms, auditor's position tenure and auditor's year of experience in auditing on the likelihood of detecting fraud in the stock and warehouse cycle. They conclude that such factors are statistically significant predictors of the likelihood of detecting fraud, and enlarge the likelihood of fraud detection.

Lin et al [15] developed a Neural Network fraud classification model. Deng [9] used support vector machines (SVMs) to detecting FFS. Hoogs et al. [13] used a genetic algorithm approach to detecting FFS. Bell and Carcello [4] developed and tested a logistic regression to estimate the likelihood of fraudulent financial reporting. Dianmin Yue et al [10] also used Logistic Regression for Detecting Fraudulent Financial Statement of Listed Companies in China.

Ravisankar et al [18] uses data mining techniques such as Multilayer Feed Forward Neural Network, Support Vector Machines, Genetic Programming, Logistic Regression, and Probabilistic Neural Network to identify companies that resort to financial statement fraud. Each of these techniques is tested on a dataset involving 202 Chinese companies and compared with and without feature selection. Probabilistic Neural Network outperformed all the techniques without feature selection.

For Greek data, Spathis et al [20] constructed a model to detect falsified financial statements. He employed the statistical method of logistic regression. Kirkos et al [14] investigate the usefulness of Decision Trees, Neural Networks and Bayesian Belief Networks in the identification of fraudulent financial statements. For both studies [27] and [18] a balanced sample of a total of 76 manufacturing firms was used; 38 firms with FFS were matched with 38 with non-FFS (the sample did not include financial companies).

3   Data Description

Our dataset contains data from 164 Greek listed on the Athens Stock Exchange (ASE) manufacturing firms (no financial companies are included). Auditors checked all the firms in the sample. For 41 of these firms, there was published indication or proof of involvement in issuing FFS. The classification of a financial statement as false was based on the following parameters: inclusion in the auditors' report of serious doubts as to the precision of the accounts, observations by the tax authorities regarding serious taxation intransigencies which drastically altered the company's annual balance sheet and income statement, the application of Greek legislation regarding negative net worth, the inclusion of the company in the Athens Stock Ex-change categories of under observation and negotiation suspended for reasons associated with the falsification of the company's financial data and, the existence of court proceedings pending with respect to FFS or serious taxation contraventions.

The 41 FFS firms were matched with 123 non-FFS firms. All the variables used in the dataset were mined from formal financial statements, such as balance sheets and income statements. This implies that the worth of this study is not restricted by the fact that only Greek company data was used.

The selection of variables to be used as candidates for participation in the input vector was based upon prior research work connected to the topic of FFS. Such work carried out by [7], [15], [20]. Additional variables were also added so as to catch as many as possible predictors not up to that time identified. Table 1 presents a brief description of the financial variables used in the present study.

In an attempt to show how much each attribute influences the induction, we rank the influence of each one according to different statistical measures e.g. Information Gain, Gain Ratio and Relief Score [23]. The attributes that mostly influence the induction are: RLTC/RCR02, AR/TA01, TL/TA02, AR/TA02, WC/TA02, DC/CA02, NFA/TA02, NDAP02 (see ReliefF Score in Table 1). With regard to the remaining variables, it seems that they do not influence the induction.

In general, the identification of the aforementioned variables as crucial factors agrees with the results of previous studies in this field.

Table 1. Research Variables description and Average ReliefF score of each variable

Variables	Variable Description	ReliefF score
RLTC/RCR02	Return on Long -term capital / Return on Capital and Reserves 2002	0.02603371
AR/TA 01	Accounts Receivable/Total Assets 2001	0.02587121
TL/TA02	Total liabilities/Total assets 2002	0.02577709
AR/TA02	Accounts Receivable/Total Assets 2002	0.02257509
WC/TA 02	Working capital/total assets 2002	0.02118785
DC/CA02	Deposits and cash/current assets 2002	0.01364156
NFA/TA	Net Fixed Assets/Total Assets	0.0133596
NDAP02	Number of days accounts payable 2002	0.01085013
LTD/TCR02	Long term debt/total capital and reserves 2002	0.00798901
S/TA02	Sales/total assets 2002	0.00395956
RCF/TA02	Results carried forward/total assets 2002	0.00384807
NDAR02	Number of days accounts receivable 2002	0.00327257
CAR/TA	Change Accounts Receivable/Total Assets	0.00320415
WCL02	Working capital leveraged 2002	0.00254562
ITURN02	Inventory turnover 2002	0.00215535
TA/CR02	Total Assets/Capital and Reserves 2002	0.00208717
EBIT/TA02	Earnings before interest and tax/total assets 2002	0.00206301
CFO02	Cash flows from operations 2002	0.00169573
CFO01	Cash flows from operations 2001	0.0009421
CR02	Current assets to current liabilities 2002	0.00082761
GOCF	Growth of Operational Cash Flow	0.00073566
CAR/NS	Change Accounts Receivable/Net Sales	0.00071853
EBT02/EBIT02	Earnings before tax 2002/Earnings before interest and tax 2002	0.00049986
Z-SCORE02	Altman z-score 2002	0.00047192
CR/TL02	Capital and Reserves/total liabilities 2002	0.00041943

4   Experimental Results and Proposed Technique

Supervised machine learning is the exploration for algorithms that reason from externally supplied examples to produce general hypotheses, which will make predictions about future examples. For the purpose of this study, a representative algorithm for each learning technique was used. The most commonly used C4.5 algorithm [17] was the representative of the decision trees in our study. Back Propagation (BP) algorithm [23] - was the representative of the ANNs. The 1-NN algorithm was also used as a representative of lazy learners [23]. The Naïve Bayes algorithm [23] was the representative of the Bayesian networks in our study. Finally, the Sequential Minimal Optimization (or SMO) algorithm was the representative of the SVMs [23].

All accuracy estimates were obtained by averaging the results from stratified 10-fold cross-validation in our dataset. It must be mentioned that we used the free available source code for our experiments by the book [23]. The results are presented in Table 2 as far as the total accuracy and the accuracy per class are concerned.

Table 2. Accuracy of simple models in our dataset

	NB	C4.5	1NN	BP	LR	SMO
Total Accuracy	78.7	90.2	80.5	79.3	75.0	75.0
Fraud	56.1	73.2	61.0	58.5	34.1	7.3
Non-Fraud	82.2	95.9	87.0	86.2	88.6	97.4

From Table 2, we can conclude that decision tree outperforms the other models. In an attempt to further improve the accuracy, we try to combine a number of decision tree classifiers.

The most popular ensemble algorithms are bagging [6], boosting [12], decorate [16], rotation forest [19] and random subspace methods [21]. In bagging [6], the training set is randomly sampled k times with replacement, producing k training sets with sizes equal to the original training set. Boosting, induces the ensemble of learners by adaptively changing the distribution of the training set based on the accuracy of the previously created classifiers. There are several boosting variants; AdaBoost [12] is the most well-known. The final classification is obtained from a weighted vote of the base classifiers. On the other hand, in random subspace method [21] the classifier consists of multiple learners constructed by pseudo-randomly selecting subsets of the feature vector, that is, classifiers constructed in randomly chosen subspaces. The main idea of Rotation Forest [19] is to simultaneously encourage diversity by using Principal Components Analysis (PCA) to do feature extraction for each base classifier and accuracy is sought by keeping all principal components and also using the whole data set to train each base learner. Decorate [16] uses a strong learner to construct a diverse committee. This is accomplished by adding different randomly constructed examples to the training set when building new committee members. These artificially constructed examples are given category labels that disagree with the current classification of the committee, thereby directly increasing diversity.

Decision tree classifiers, frequently, employ post-pruning techniques that evaluate the performance of decision trees as they are pruned using a validation set [17]. Any node can be removed and assigned the most frequent class of the training examples that are sorted to the node in question. Thus, if a class is rare, decision tree algorithms often prune the tree down to a single node that classifies all instances as members of the frequent class leading to poor accuracy on the examples of minority class.

A simple method that can be used to imbalanced datasets is to reweigh training examples according to the total cost assigned to each class [3]. The idea is to change the class distributions in the training set towards the most costly class. In our case the instances of the positive (Non Fraud) class are about 3 times more than the instances of the negative class (Fraud). If the number of negative instances are artificially increased by a factor of three, then the learning system, aiming to reduce the number of classification errors, will come up with a classifier that is skewed towards the avoidance of error in the small class, since any such errors are penalized three times more. We implemented an algorithm for building an ensemble of randomizable reweighing base decision tree classifiers. Each of base decision tree classifiers is built using a reweighed different random number seed (but based one the same data). The final prediction is a straight average of the predictions generated by the individual base classifiers. Our approach is schematically represented in Fig. 1. In our case R equals to 15 (5*3). In an ensemble of classifiers about such as a number of sub-classifiers is effective [6], [12], [21]. We could use more sub-classifiers but the accuracy would not be improved enough to worth the additional training time.

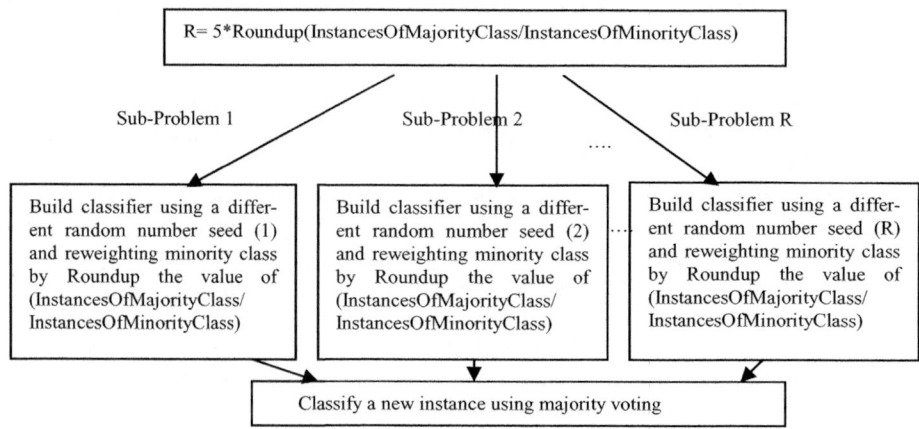

Fig. 1. The presented method

The results of the presented ensemble and that of other well known combining techniques using 25 sub-classifiers are presented in Table 3. It must be mentioned that in the experiment we also include MetaCost [11]. MetaCost is another combining method for making a classifier cost-sensitive. The procedure begins to learn an internal cost-sensitive model by applying a cost-sensitive procedure, which employs a base learning algorithm. Then, MetaCost procedure approximates class probabilities using bagging and then re-labels the training instances with their minimum expected cost classes, and finally relearns a model using the modified training set.

Table 3. Accuracy of ensembles in our dataset

ALGORITHMS	Accuracy	Fraud	Non-Fraud
Adaboost C4.5	92.1	75.6	97.6
Bagging C4.5	92.1	80.5	95.9
Decorate C4.5	86.6	61.0	95.1
Rotation Forest C4.5	85.4	51.2	96.7
Random subspace C4.5	85.4	46.3	98.4
Metacost C4.5	92.1	85.4	94.3
Random Committee of Cost-Sensitive C4.5	94.5	90.2	95.9

The presented algorithm correctly classifies 94.5% of the total sample, 90.2% of the fraud cases and 95.9% of the non-fraud cases. As a conclusion, our approach performs better than other examined ensemble methods.

5   Conclusion

Auditing practices at the present time have to cope with an increasing number of management fraud cases. Supervised machine learning techniques can assist auditors in accomplishing the task of management fraud detection. A relatively small list of financial ratios largely determines the classification results. This knowledge, coupled with machine learning algorithms, can provide models capable of achieving considerable classification accuracies.

Tracking progress is a time-consuming job that can be handled automatically by a learning tool. A screenshot of the implemented tool is presented in Fig 2. While the experts will still have an essential role in monitoring and evaluating progress, the tool can use the data required for reasonable and efficient monitoring.

It must be mentioned that our input vector solely consists of financial ratios. Enriching the input vector with qualitative information, such as previous auditors' qualifications or the composition of the administrative board, could boost the accuracy rate.

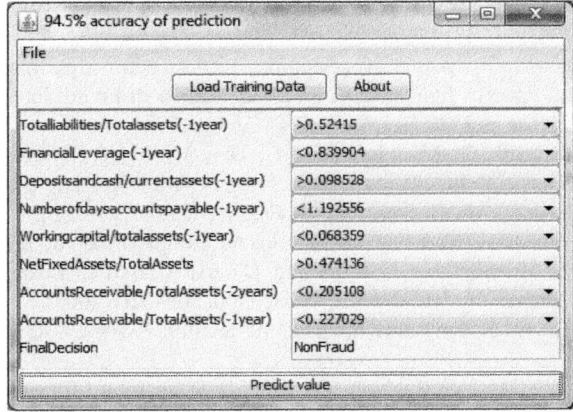

Fig. 2. A screenshot of the implemented decision support tool

References

1. Albrecht, C.C., Albrecht, W.S., Dunn, J.G.: Can auditors detect fraud: a review of the research evidence. Journal of Forensic Accounting 2(1), 1–12 (2001)
2. Ansah, S.O., Moyes, G.D., Oyelere, P.B., Hay, D.: An empirical analysis of the likelihood of detecting fraud in New Zealand. Managerial Auditing Journal 17(4), 192–204 (2002)
3. Barandela, R., Sánchez, J.S., García, V., Rangel, E.: Strategies for learning in class imbalance problems. Pattern Recognition 36(3), 849–851 (2003)
4. Bell, T., Carcello, J.: A decision aid for assessing the likelihood of fraudulent financial reporting. Auditing: A Journal of Practice & Theory 9(1), 169–178 (2000)

5. Bollen, L., Mertens, G., Meuwissen, R., VanRaak, J., Scelleman, C.: Classification and Analysis of Major European Business Failures. Maastricht Accounting, Auditing and Information Management Research Center (MARC) of University Maastricht and RSM (2005)
6. Breiman, L.: Bagging Predictors. Machine Learning 24(3), 123–140 (1996)
7. Calderon, T.G., Cheh, J.J.: A roadmap for future neural networks research in auditing and risk assessment. International Journal of Accounting Information Systems 3(4), 203–236 (2002)
8. Coffee, J.: A theory of corporate scandals: Why the USA and Europe differ. Oxford Review of Economic Policy 21(2), 198–211 (2005)
9. Deng, Q.: Application of Support Vector Machine in the Detection of Fraudulent Financial Statements. In: 4th International Conference on Computer Science & Education, pp. 1056–1059 (2009)
10. Yue, D., Wu, X., Shen, N., Chu, C.-H.: Logistic Regression for Detecting Fraudulent Financial Statement of Listed Companies in China. In: International Conference on Artificial Intelligence and Computational Intelligence, pp. 104–108 (2009)
11. Domingos, P.: MetaCost: A General Method for Making Classifiers Cost-Sensitive. In: Proceedings of the Fifth International Conference on Knowledge Discovery and Data Mining, pp. 155–164. ACM Press (1999)
12. Freund, Y., Schapire, R.E.: Experiments with a New Boosting Algorithm. In: Proceedings of ICML 1996, pp. 148–156 (1996)
13. Hoogs, B., Kiehl, T., Lacomb, C., Senturk, D.: A Genetic Algorithm Approach to Detecting Temporal Patterns Indicative of Financial Statement Fraud. Intelligent Systems in Accounting, Finance and Management 15, 41–56 (2007)
14. Kirkos, S., Spathis, C., Manolopoulos, Y.: Data Mining Techniques for the Detection of Fraudulent Financial Statements. Expert Systems with Applications 32, 995–1003 (2007)
15. Lin, J.W., Hwang, M., Becker, J.K.: A Fuzzy Neural Network for Assessing the Risk of Fraudulent Financial Reporting. Managerial Auditing Journal 18, 657–665 (2003)
16. Melville, P., Mooney, R.: Constructing Diverse Classifier Ensembles using Artificial Training Examples. In: IJCAI 2003, Mexico, pp. 505–510 (2003)
17. Quinlan, J.R.: C4.5: Programs for machine learning. Morgan Kaufmann, San Francisco (1993)
18. Ravisankar, P., Ravi, V., Raghava, G., Bose, I.: Detection of financial statement fraud and feature selection using data mining techniques. Decision Sup. Systems 50, 491–500 (2011)
19. Rodríguez, J.J., Kuncheva, L.I., Alonso, C.J.: Rotation forest: A new classifier ensemble method. IEEE Trans. Pattern Anal. Machine Intell. 28(10), 1619–1630 (2006)
20. Spathis, C., Doumpos, M., Zopounidis, C.: Detecting falsified financial statements: a comparative study using multicriteria analysis and multivariate statistical techniques. The European Accounting Review 11(3), 509–535 (2002)
21. Ho, T.K.: The Random Subspace Method for Constructing Decision Forests. IEEE Transactions on Pattern Analysis and Machine Intelligence 20(8), 832–844 (1998)
22. Watts, R.L., Zimmerman, J.L.: Positive Accounting Theory. Prentice-Hall (1986)
23. Witten, I., Frank, E., Hall, M.: Data Mining: Practical Machine Learning Tools and Techniques, 3rd edn. Morgan Kaufmann (2011) ISBN 978-0-12-374856-0 and Techniques (Third Edition), Morgan Kaufmann, (2011), ISBN 978-0-12-374856-0

Forecasting Corporate Bankruptcy with an Ensemble of Classifiers

Despina Deligianni[1] and Sotiris Kotsiantis[2]

[1] Hellenic Open University, Greece
devi287@hotmail.com
[2] Department of Mathematics, University of Patras, Greece
sotos@math.upatras.gr

Abstract. Prediction of corporate bankruptcy is a phenomenon of growing interest to investors, creditors, borrowing firms, and governments alike. Timely identification of firms' impending failure is really wanted. The aim of this research is to use supervised machine learning techniques in such an environment. A number of experiments have been conducted using representative machine learning algorithms, which were trained using a data set of 150 failed and solvent Greek firms. It was found that an ensemble of classifiers could enable users to predict bankruptcies with satisfying precision long before the final bankruptcy.

1   Introduction

The problem of Bankruptcy prediction is a classical one in the financial literature (see e.g. [3] for a review). The main impact of Bankruptcy prediction is in bank lending. Banks need to forecast the possibility of default of a potential counterparty before they expand a loan. This can lead to sounder lending decisions, and consequently result in important savings.

There are two main approaches to loan default/bankruptcy prediction. The first approach, the structural approach, is based on modeling the underlying dynamics of interest rates and firm attributes and deriving the default probability based on these dynamics. The second approach is the statistical approach. Instead of modeling the relationship of default with the attributes of a firm, this relationship is discovered from the data. The focus of this article is on the empirical approach, particularly the use of supervised machine learning in bankruptcy prediction. The automated system uses financial ratios as predictors of performance, and assesses posterior probabilities of financial health (on the other hand, financial distress).

Balcaen and Ooghe [4] provide an overview of the standard statistical methodologies applied on business failure. Kumar and Ravi [15] present a survey of bankruptcy prediction via statistical and intelligent techniques. These techniques of corporate bankruptcy prediction have their own strengths and weaknesses and, hence, choosing a particular model may not be easy. Searching for best distress prediction models is still in progress [26]. This study provides a critical analysis of most frequently used

I. Maglogiannis, V. Plagianakos, and I. Vlahavas (Eds.): SETN 2012, LNAI 7297, pp. 65–72, 2012.

corporate bankruptcy learning models. Accordingly, we use a representative algorithm for each one of the most widespread machine learning techniques so as to investigate the efficiency of ML techniques in such an environment. Finally, it was found that an ensemble of classifiers could enable users to predict bankruptcies with satisfying precision long before the final bankruptcy.

The following section provides a short literature review in the domain of corporate bankruptcy learning models. Section 3 describes the data set of our study and the variable selection process. Section 4 presents the experimental results for the compared algorithms. Finally, section 5 discusses the conclusions and some future research directions.

2   Literature Review

Many studies have been conducted for bankruptcy prediction using models such as neural networks [16], [7], instance based learners [1], Bayesian models [21], rule learners [23], decision trees algorithms [8] and Support Vector Machines [22], [29]. Olson et al [18] applies a variety of data mining tools to bankruptcy data, with the purpose of comparing accuracy and number of rules. For that data, decision trees were found to be relatively more accurate compared to neural networks and support vector machines, but there were more rule nodes than desired.

Verikas et al [27] present a comprehensive review of hybrid and ensemble-based soft computing techniques applied to bankruptcy prediction. Tsai and Hsu [24] presented a meta-learning framework, which is composed of two-level classifiers for bankruptcy prediction. The first-level multiple classifiers perform the data reduction task by filtering out unrepresentative training data. Then, the outputs of the first-level classifiers are used to create the second-level single (meta) classifier. Hung and Chen [14] propose a selective ensemble of three classifiers, i.e. the decision tree, the back propagation neural network and the support vector machine, based on the expected probabilities of both bankruptcy and non-bankruptcy.

In the Greek context, logit analysis, probit analysis, and the linear probability model are the most commonly used techniques applied [17]. The performance of alternative non-parametric approaches has been explored in the Greek context to overcome the aforementioned shortcomings of the statistical and econometric techniques such as rough sets [9] and multicriteria discrimination method [12]. Tsakonas et al [25] used neural logic networks for bankruptcy prediction.

3   Data Description

Bankruptcy filings in the years 2003 and 2004 were supplied directly from the National Bank of Greece directories and the business database of the financial information services company called ICAP, in Greece. Financial statement data for the fiscal years prior to bankruptcy were supplied from ICAP financial directories. The financial statements of these firms were gathered for a period of three years. The critical year of failure denoted as year 0, three years before as year −3 and year −1 is the final year prior to bankruptcy filing. As the control sample, each selected bankrupt firm was matched with two non-bankrupt (healthy) firms of exactly the same industry, by care-fully comparing the year of the reported data (year −1) assets size and the number of employees. The selected non-bankrupt corporations were within 20% of the selection criteria. Following the prior literature, we examine the probability of a firm's initial filing for bankruptcy and eliminate any observations for a firm after it has filed for bankruptcy during our sample period. Our final bankruptcy sample consists of 50 initial bankruptcies in the year period 2003-2004 and is similar in size but more complete compared to previous studies. The final pooled set of failed and healthy firms is composed of 150 individual firms with financial data for a three-year period, which attributes 450 firm-year observations. Through extensive literature review on bankruptcy prediction about 50 financial ratios were traced. The final set of the calculated input features is 21 because of missing financial data and financial ratio duplication. Table 1 provides a brief description of the financial variables. in order to show how much each attribute influences the induction, we rank the influence of each one according to different statistical measures e.g. Information Gain, Gain Ration and Relief Score [28]. The attributes that mainly influence the induction are: *WC/TA*, EQ/CE and GRNI (see ReliefF Score in Table 1). It seems that the attributes: CA/CL, NIMAR, ROCE, GRNS, ROE, QA/CL, S/TA and OPIMAR do not influence the induction in any way.

Table 1. Research Variables description and Average ReliefF score of each variable

Independent variable	Variable Description	Average Score
WC/TA	Working capital divided by total assets	0.035
EQ/CE	Shareholder's equity to capital employed	0.011
GRNI	Growth rate of net income	0.012
SIZE	Size of firm is the ln(Total Assets/GDP price index)	0.006
GRTA	Growth rate of total assets $(TA_t - TA_{t-1})/(ABS(TA_t)+ ABS(TA_{t-1})$	0.004
TD/EQ	Total debt to shareholder's equity capital	0.003
S/CE	Sales divided by capital employed	0.003
COLPER	Average collection period for receivables	0.002
S/EQ	Sales divided by Shareholder's equity capital	0.002
CE/NFA	Capital employed to net fixed assets	0.002
PAYPER	Average payment period to creditors	0.001
INVTURN	Average turnover period for inventories	0.001
GIMAR	Gross income divided by sales	0.001
CA/CL	Current assets to current liabilities	0
NIMAR	Net income divided by sales	0
ROCE	Net income pre tax divided by capital employed	0
GRNS	Growth rate of net sales	0
ROE	Net income pre tax divided by Shareholder's equity capital	0
QA/CL	Quick assets to current liabilities	0
S/TA	Sales divided by Total Assets	0
OPIMAR	Operating income divided by net sales	0

4   Experimental Results and Proposed Technique

Supervised machine learning is the investigation for algorithms that reason from externally supplied examples to produce general hypotheses, which will make predictions about future examples. For the purpose of this study, a representative algorithm for each learning technique was used. The most commonly used C4.5 algorithm [20] was the representative of the decision trees in our study. RBF algorithm [28] - was the representative of the ANNs. The RIPPER algorithm [6] was the representative of the rule-learners in our study. The Naïve Bayes algorithm [11] was the representative of the Bayesian networks in our study. The 1-NN algorithm was also used as a representative of lazy learners [28]. Finally, the Sequential Minimal Optimization (or SMO) algorithm was the representative of the SVMs [19].

The algorithms discussed here aim at achieving high classification accuracy that is lower error rate in the prediction of unseen instances. However, these algorithms do not differentiate the types of errors. That is for these algorithms classifying a bankrupt case as a non-bankrupt has the same error as classifying a non-bankrupt as a bankrupt. However, in real life, these costs is not the same for the decision maker. For example, the cost of predicting a case as non-bankrupt that is actually bankrupt is higher than vice versa. For our experiments, we used in the cost matrix 2 times more cost in the case that a non-bankrupt instance is actually bankrupt. We made this choice because in our data the set of non-bankrupt firms is two times the set of bankrupt firms, too. Cost-sensitive meta-learning converts existing cost insensitive base learning algorithms into cost-sensitive ones without modifying them. Therefore, it can be regarded as a middleware component that pre-processes the training set. All accuracy approximations were obtained by averaging the results from stratified 10-fold cross-validation in our data. It must be mentioned that we used the free available source code for our experiments by the book [28]. The results are presented in Table 2.

To facilitate the presentation and discussion of the results, each year prior to financial distress is denoted as year –1, year –2, year –3, Year –1 refers to the first year prior to financial distress (e.g., for the firms that faced financial distress in 2004, year –1 refers to 2003); year –2 refers to the second year prior to financial distress (e.g., for the firms that faced financial distress in 2004, year –2 refers to 2002), etc.

Table 2. Accuracy of the algorithms in each testing step

		Naive Bayes	1-NN	RIPPER	C4.5	SMO	RBF
Year(-3)	Bankrupt	26.5	49.0	63.3	69.4	30.6	40.8
	Non Bankrupt	85.4	71.9	49.0	35.4	81.3	67.7
Year(-2)	Bankrupt	26.5	40.8	59.2	55.1	38.8	38.8
	Non Bankrupt	92.7	82.3	51.0	57.3	78.1	81.3
Year(-1)	Bankrupt	26.5	40.8	65.3	59.2	65.3	46.9
	Non Bankrupt	94.8	82.3	75.0	75.0	70.8	77.1

In a comparative assessment of the models' performance we can conclude that RIPPER predicts more right the true positive bankrupt cases and NB the true positive non-bankrupt cases. For this reason, we implemented an algorithm that is based in RIPPER and NB decisions.

The concept of combining classifiers is proposed as a direction for the improvement of the performance of individual learners [5]. The goal of combining classification algorithms is to generate more certain, precise and accurate system results.

The most direct method for dealing with skewed class distributions with unequal misclassification costs is to use cost sensitive learning [13]. For our implementation, we used in the cost matrix 2 times more cost in the case that a non-bankrupt instance is actually bankrupt. As we have already mentioned, we made this choice because in our dataset the sample of non-bankrupt firms is two times the sample of bankrupt firms. The proposed ensemble algorithm is illustrated in Fig. 1.

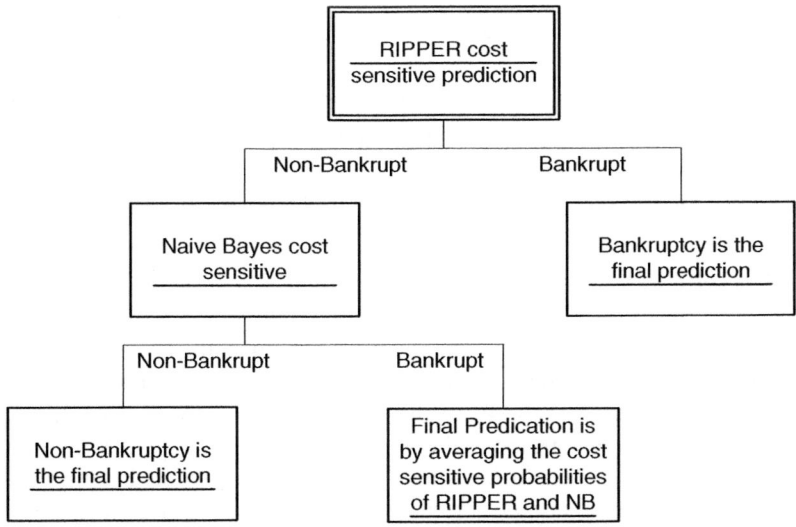

Fig. 1. The presented method

Since RIPPER predicts more right the true positive bankrupt cases, in the presented ensemble we choose RIPPER algorithm to start the classification process. The cost of predicting a case as non-bankrupt that is actually bankrupt is higher than vice versa. NB predicts more right the true positive non-bankrupt cases and for this reason, in the presented ensemble we choose to trust the decision of NB classifier for non-bankrupt cases in the second step. In the remaining cases, the presented model gives the final prediction by averaging the cost sensitive probabilities of the two chosen classifiers.

The results of the presented ensemble are compared with the well known cost-sensitive ensemble MetaCost [10] and the well known voting technique. MetaCost's procedure begins to learn an internal cost-sensitive model by applying a cost-sensitive procedure, which utilizes a base learning algorithm. Then, MetaCost procedure approximates class probabilities using bagging and then re-labels the training instances with their minimum expected cost classes, and as a final point relearns a model using the modified training set.

Table 3. Accuracy of ensembles in our dataset

		Metacost Naive Bayes	Metacost RIPPER	Voting RIPPER & Naive Bayes	Presented Method
Year(-3)	Bankrupt	26.5	46.9	36.7	63.3
	Non Bankrupt	85.4	70.8	79.2	69.0
Year(-2)	Bankrupt	28.6	44.9	30.6	64.2
	Non Bankrupt	89.6	70.8	86.5	71.0
Year(-1)	Bankrupt	28.6	49.9	42.9	71.3
	Non Bankrupt	89.6	85.4	84.4	78.1

According to Table 3, our approach performs better than other examined ensemble methods as far as the average value of the true positive precision in both classes in the examined dataset. Both the training and classification time cost of the presented model is comparable with that of simple voting and less than the cost of Metacost.

5   Conclusion

With the help of supervised machine learning techniques, the experts are in the position to know which of the firms will bankrupt or not with satisfactory accuracy. For this reason, a prototype version of a software support tool has been constructed implementing the presented ensemble of classifiers (see Figure 2). Tracking progress is a time-consuming job that could be handled automatically by such a tool. While the experts will still have the crucial role in monitoring and evaluating progress, the tool could use the data required for reasonable and efficient monitoring. The prediction model developed from the present study proposes the importance of liquidity defined by the ratio working capital to total assets, capital structure defined as equity to capital employed and profitability growth defined as net income growth.

Nevertheless, there were a number of limitations in this study that must be noted. First, the sample size was fairly small. Thus, the generalization of the research results is somewhat limited. The second limitation was that only financial ratio attributes were included in this study. There may be other essential quantitative attributes (i.e. market value, stock data, age) as well as qualitative variables (leadership, type of ownership, reputation, etc.) and there is enough literature in organization theory that reports the value of these attributes. These limitations open up a open opportunity for future research.

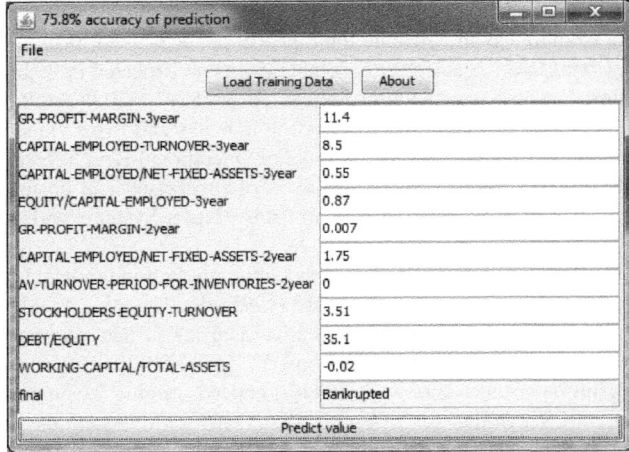

Fig. 2. A screenshot of the implemented decision support tool

References

1. Ahn, H., Kim, K.-J.: Bankruptcy prediction modeling with hybrid case-based reasoning and genetic algorithms approach. Applied Soft Computing Journal 9(2), 599–607 (2009)
2. Alfaro, E., García, N., Gámez, M., Elizondo, D.: Bankruptcy forecasting: an empirical comparison of AdaBoost and neural networks. Decision Support Systems 45(1), 110–122 (2008)
3. Altman, E.L.: Corporate Financial Distress and Bankruptcy. John Wiley and Sons (1993)
4. Balcaen, S., Ooghe, H.: 35 years of studies on business failure: An overview of the classic statistical methodologies and their related problems. The British Accounting Review 38, 63–93 (2006)
5. Berg, D.: Bankruptcy prediction by generalized additive models. Applied Stochastic Models in Business and Industry 23(2), 129–143 (2007)
6. Cohen, W.: Fast Effective Rule Induction. In: Proceeding of International Conference on Machine Learning, pp. 115–123 (1995)
7. Cho, S., Kim, J., Bae, J.K.: An integrative model with subject weight based on neural network learning for bankruptcy prediction. Expert Systems with Applications 36(1), 403–410 (2009)
8. Cho, S., Hong, H., Ha, B.-C.: A hybrid approach based on the combination of variable selection using decision trees and case-based reasoning using the Mahalanobis distance: for bankruptcy prediction. Expert Systems with Applications 37(4), 3482–3488 (2010)
9. Dimitras, A.I., Slowinski, R., Susmaga, R., Zopounidis, C.: Business failure prediction using rough sets. European Journal of Operational Research 114, 263–280 (1999)
10. Domingos, P.: MetaCost: A General Method for Making Classifiers Cost-Sensitive. In: Proceedings of the Fifth International Conference on Knowledge Discovery and Data Mining, pp. 155–164. ACM Press (1999)
11. Domingos, P., Pazzani, M.: On the optimality of the simple Bayesian classifier under zero-one loss. Machine Learning 29, 103–130 (1997)
12. Doumpos, M., Zopounidis, C.: A Multicriteria Discrimination Method for the Prediction of Financial Distress: The Case of Greece. Multinational Finance Journal 3(2), 71–101 (1999)

13. Elkan, C.: The foundations of cost-sensitive learning. In: Proceedings of the 17th International Joint Conference on Artificial Intelligence, pp. 973–978 (2001)
14. Hung, C., Chen, J.-H.: A selective ensemble based on expected probabilities for bankruptcy prediction. Expert Systems with Applications 36, 5297–5303 (2009)
15. Kumar, P.R., Ravi, V.: Bankruptcy prediction in banks and firms via statistical and intelligent techniques: a review. European Journal of Operational Research 180, 1–28 (2007)
16. Lee, K., Booth, D., Alam, P.: A comparison of supervised and unsupervised neural networks in predicting bankruptcy of Korean firms. Expert Systems with Applications 29, 1–16 (2005)
17. Negakis, C.: Robustness of Greek business failure prediction models. International Review of Economics and Business 42(3), 203–215 (1995)
18. Olson, D., Delen, D., Meng, Y.: Comparative analysis of data mining methods for bankruptcy prediction. Decision Support Systems 52, 464–473 (2012)
19. Platt, J.: Using sparseness and analytic QP to speed training of support vector machines. In: Kearns, M.S., Solla, S.A., Cohn, D.A. (eds.) Advances in Neural Information Processing Systems, vol. 11. MIT Press, MA (1999)
20. Quinlan, J.R.: C4.5: Programs for machine learning. Morgan Kaufmann, San Francisco (1993)
21. Sarkar, S., Sriram, R.S.: Bayesian Models for Early Warning of Bank Failures. Management Science 47(11), 1457–1475 (2001)
22. Shin, K., Lee, T., Kim, H.: An application of support vector machines in bankruptcy prediction model. Expert Systems with Applications 28, 127–135 (2005)
23. Thomaidis, N., Gounias, G., Zopounidis, C.: A fuzzy rule based learning method for corporate bankruptcy prediction. In: ACAI 1999, Chania, Greece (1999)
24. Tsai, C.-F., Hsu, Y.-F.: A Meta-learning Framework for Bankruptcy Prediction. Journal of Forecasting (2011), doi:10.1002/for.1264
25. Tsakonas, A., Dounias, G., Doumpos, M., Zopounidis, C.: Bankruptcy prediction with neural logic networks by means of grammar-guided genetic programming. Expert Systems with Applications 30(3), 449–461 (2006)
26. Tseng, F.-M., Hu, Y.-C.: Comparing four bankruptcy prediction models: logit, quadratic interval logit, neural and fuzzy neural networks. Expert Systems with Applications 37(3), 1846–1853 (2010)
27. Verikas, A., Kalsyte, Z., Bacauskiene, M., Gelzinis, A.: Hybrid and ensemble-based soft computing techniques in bankruptcy prediction: a survey. Soft. Comput. 14, 995–1010 (2010)
28. Witten, I., Frank, E., Hall, M.: Data Mining: Practical Machine Learning Tools and Techniques, 3rd edn. Morgan Kaufmann (2011) ISBN 978-0-12-374856-0
29. Zijiang, Y., Wenjie, Y., Guoli, J.: Using partial least squares and support vector machines for bankruptcy prediction. Expert Systems with Applications 38, 8336–8342 (2011)

Greedy Unsupervised Multiple Kernel Learning

Grigorios Tzortzis and Aristidis Likas

Department of Computer Science, University of Ioannina,
GR 45110, Ioannina, Greece
{gtzortzi,arly}@cs.uoi.gr

Abstract. Multiple kernel learning (MKL) has emerged as a powerful tool for considering multiple kernels when the appropriate representation of the data is unknown. Some of these kernels may be complementary, while others irrelevant to the learning task. In this work we present an MKL method for clustering. The intra-cluster variance objective is extended by learning a linear combination of kernels, together with the cluster labels, through an iterative procedure. Closed-form updates for the combination weights are derived, that greatly simplify the optimization. Moreover, to allow for robust kernel mixtures, a parameter that regulates the sparsity of the weights is incorporated into our framework. Experiments conducted on a collection of images reveal the effectiveness of the proposed method.

1 Introduction

Despite the widespread interest in kernel methods in various fields, such as machine learning, computer vision and bioinformatics, their application is severely limited by the sensitivity to the choice of kernel. In recent years, multiple kernel learning (MKL) techniques [5], that determine the weights for combining a set of predefined (base) kernels as part of the learning process, have been developed to alleviate the kernel selection problem. These multiple kernels may describe different notions of similarity in the data, or, even, different modalities.

In this work, we focus on MKL clustering and employ the k-means *intra-cluster variance objective* together with a *linear combination for the base kernels*. Linearly mixing the kernels is the most common approach [2,9,6,7,11,12], although lately effort has been put into considering nonlinear combinations [10,3]. A simple iterative procedure is devised to recover the partitioning, using k-medoids [1], and the kernel mixing coefficients, which are estimated by *closed-form expressions*. Moreover, to avoid multiple restarts for k-medoids, a greedy initialization strategy is developed.

An important aspect of MKL is the sparsity of the kernel combination. Sparse approaches rely on the assumption that some kernels are irrelevant for the underlying problem and retain a few base kernels through an ℓ_1-norm regularizer on the weights [9,12]. They are appealing since they greatly enhance interpretability and their models are distinguished by small capacity. However, *different kernels may capture different aspects of the data* and thus all kernels are important in

I. Maglogiannis, V. Plagianakos, and I. Vlahavas (Eds.): SETN 2012, LNAI 7297, pp. 73–80, 2012.
© Springer-Verlag Berlin Heidelberg 2012

this case, *albeit to a different degree.* Therefore, to provide a more robust ranking of the kernels, based on their quality, the ℓ_2-norm regularizer was applied in [13, 2], while in [6, 11] the general ℓ_p-norm regularizer was introduced, that forces weights to become less sparse as p increases. Also, Lange and Buhmann [7] learned a linear mixture of similarity matrices using an entropy criterion to regulate sparsity. In our approach, a parameter that must be set beforehand controls the weights similarly to the ℓ_p-norm regularizer, allowing the *exploitation of the complementary information of the kernels.* As shown in the experiments, the results of using a single kernel or evenly all kernels can be vastly improved.

The rest of this paper is organized as follows. Next section contains the basics about kernel-based clustering and the greedy initialization scheme. Our MKL framework is detailed in Sect. 3. The empirical results are reported in Sect. 4, before the concluding remarks of Sect. 5.

2   Feature Space Clustering

To uncover the hidden structures of a dataset $\mathcal{X} = \{\mathbf{x}_i\}_{i=1}^N$, $\mathbf{x}_i \in \Re^d$ it is common practice to map the instances to a higher dimensional reproducing kernel Hilbert space $\mathcal{H}$, *a.k.a.* feature space, via a nonlinear transformation $\phi : \mathcal{X} \to \mathcal{H}$ and then perform clustering in space $\mathcal{H}$. Thus it is possible to get nonlinear separators in input space through linear separators in feature space.

Usually a kernel function $\mathcal{K} : \mathcal{X} \times \mathcal{X} \to \Re$ [4] is applied to directly provide the inner products in feature space without explicitly defining transformation ϕ (for certain kernel functions the transformations are intractable). This gives rise to the kernel matrix $K \in \Re^{N \times N}$, $K_{ij} = \mathcal{K}(\mathbf{x}_i, \mathbf{x}_j) = \phi(\mathbf{x}_i)^\top \phi(\mathbf{x}_j)$, which is the most common way of representing similarity in feature space. An important property is that the squared Euclidean distances in feature space can be computed using solely the kernel matrix entries:

$$\|\phi(\mathbf{x}_i) - \phi(\mathbf{x}_j)\|^2 = K_{ii} - 2K_{ij} + K_{jj} \ . \tag{1}$$

2.1 k-Medoids

To partition dataset $\mathcal{X}$ into M disjoint clusters, $\{\mathcal{C}_k\}_{k=1}^M$, using a kernel matrix, k-medoids [1] can be utilized to minimize the intra-cluster variance in feature space (2) over $\mathbf{m}_k$ and δ_{ik}, where $\mathbf{m}_k \in \mathcal{X}$ is the k-th cluster medoid, δ_{ik} is an indicator variable with $\delta_{ik} = 1$ if $\mathbf{x}_i \in \mathcal{C}_k$ and 0 otherwise and l_k is the index of the data point corresponding to the k-th medoid, *i.e.* $\mathbf{m}_k = \mathbf{x}_{l_k}$.

$$\mathcal{E}_\mathcal{H} = \sum_{i=1}^N \sum_{k=1}^M \delta_{ik} \|\phi(\mathbf{x}_i) - \phi(\mathbf{m}_k)\|^2 = \sum_{i=1}^N \sum_{k=1}^M \delta_{ik}(K_{ii} - 2K_{il_k} + K_{l_k l_k}) \tag{2}$$

An analogous to typical k-means iterative procedure is employed to optimize the objective, where the medoids and the cluster assignments are updated in turn. This procedure converges to a local minimum that strongly depends on the initialization of the medoids. To circumvent this problem and avoid multiple restarts, we have adopted a greedy method for selecting initial medoids.

2.2   Greedy Medoid Initialization

The greedy medoid initialization algorithm is an incremental approach for deterministically finding a set of M medoids to initialize the k-medoids algorithm. The clusters are added to the solution one by one, such that the clustering objective (2) is minimized.

In detail, given a kernel K, we start by considering the whole dataset as one cluster, choosing the medoid of the dataset as the first medoid $\mathbf{m}_1$. Suppose that $k-1$ medoids have already been added and $d_i^{(k-1)}$ denotes the squared distance in feature space of instance $\mathbf{x}_i$ to its cluster medoid in the solution with $k-1$ clusters. In order to select the k-th medoid, a search is performed over all dataset points to find the one that provides the greatest reduction of the objective (2). If $\mathbf{x}_j$ is chosen as the k-th medoid then it will allocate all instances that are closer to it in feature space $\mathcal{H}$ than to their cluster medoid in the solution with $k-1$ clusters ($d_i^{(k-1)}$ distance). For each such reallocation the objective will decrease by $d_i^{(k-1)} - \|\phi(\mathbf{x}_j) - \phi(\mathbf{x}_i)\|^2$. Therefore, the overall reduction caused by considering $\mathbf{x}_j$ as the k-th medoid can be quantified as:

$$b_j^{(k)} = \sum_{i=1}^{N} \max \left\{ d_i^{(k-1)} - \|\phi(\mathbf{x}_j) - \phi(\mathbf{x}_i)\|^2, 0 \right\} \ . \tag{3}$$

Obviously, the point $\mathbf{x}_j$ that yields the highest $b_j^{(k)}$ value (denoted by $\mathbf{x}_{j*}$) is appointed as the k-th medoid, i.e. $\mathbf{m}_k = \mathbf{x}_{j*}$, and all points $\mathbf{x}_i$ for which $d_i^{(k-1)} > \|\phi(\mathbf{x}_{j*}) - \phi(\mathbf{x}_i)\|^2$ are assigned to the new cluster. It must be stressed that the $k-1$ medoids remain the same. The above is repeated until $k = M$. After initial medoids have been located, k-medoids can be executed to refine the result.

3   Learning a Linear Kernel Combination for Clustering

The integration of multiple high quality base kernels in the clustering process can enhance the potential of clustering algorithms, whereas the inclusion of uninformative or noisy kernels may lead to performance degradation. Therefore, it is extremely important to develop algorithms that *differentiate and rank the kernels according to the conveyed information*. To this end, we learn a weighted linear combination of base kernels, together with the cluster assignments.

3.1   Problem Formulation

Let $\mathcal{X} = \{\mathbf{x}_i\}_{i=1}^N$, $\mathbf{x}_i \in \Re^d$ be a dataset with N instances and assume that V kernel matrices, $\{K^{(v)}\}_{v=1}^V$, with corresponding feature spaces $\{\mathcal{H}^{(v)}\}_{v=1}^V$, are available. Those kernels can be thought of as *providing different views*[1] of the original instances. Our target is to partition dataset $\mathcal{X}$ into M disjoint clusters,

---

[1] On the following we use the term view to refer to the different representations-perspectives of the original dataset, implied by the different kernels.

$\{C_k\}_{k=1}^M$, by optimizing the intra-cluster variance objective in a feature space $\widetilde{\mathcal{H}}$, whose definition is based on all available views.

A convenient way is to mix the kernels by considering their linear combination (4), where w_v are the kernel weights and p is an exponent that controls the distribution of the weights across the views.

$$\widetilde{K} = \sum_{v=1}^V w_v^p K^{(v)} \,, w_v \geq 0 \,, \sum_{v=1}^V w_v = 1 \,, p \geq 1 \tag{4}$$

The composite matrix $\widetilde{K}$ *is also a kernel matrix*, to which a transformation $\widetilde{\phi}$ corresponds, *i.e.* $\widetilde{K}_{ij} = \widetilde{\phi}(\mathbf{x}_i)^\top \widetilde{\phi}(\mathbf{x}_j)$. The weights reflect the contribution of the individual kernels in $\widetilde{K}$ and an appropriate weight estimation should remove the irrelevant kernels (zero weight), while allowing less informative ones to contribute with a smaller degree (smaller weight). Weights are required to have unit sum to avoid overfitting. The clustering optimization task can now be posed as:

$$\min_{\{C_k\}_{k=1}^M, \{w_v\}_{v=1}^V} \underbrace{\sum_{i=1}^N \sum_{k=1}^M \delta_{ik} \|\widetilde{\phi}(\mathbf{x}_i) - \widetilde{\phi}(\mathbf{m}_k)\|^2}_{\mathcal{E}_{\widetilde{\mathcal{H}}}} \,, \; s.t. \; w_v \geq 0 \,, \sum_{v=1}^V w_v = 1 \,. \tag{5}$$

Note that the exponent p must be set a priori and is not part of the optimization. From (4) and (5) it easy to verify that that the intra-cluster variance in space $\widetilde{\mathcal{H}}$ is the weighted sum of the intra-cluster variances in the individual feature spaces $\mathcal{H}^{(v)}$, *under a common clustering* (6).

$$\mathcal{E}_{\widetilde{\mathcal{H}}} = \sum_{v=1}^V w_v^p \sum_{i=1}^N \sum_{k=1}^M \delta_{ik} (K_{ii}^{(v)} - 2K_{il_k}^{(v)} + K_{l_k l_k}^{(v)}) = \sum_{v=1}^V w_v^p \mathcal{E}_{\mathcal{H}^{(v)}} \,. \tag{6}$$

3.2 The Algorithm

A two step iterative scheme, called **G**reedy **U**nsupervised **MKL** (GUMKL), that alternates between computing the clusters for fixed weights and estimating the weights for fixed clusters, is proposed. Note that weights are uniformly initialized, as outlined in Algorithm 1.

Cluster Update. Given the weights, kernel $\widetilde{K}$ is calculated and the greedy method is applied to pick initial medoids for the current iteration. After that k-medoids is employed to get the cluster assignments and their representatives. Note that we elect to reinitialize the medoids at each iteration to avoid poor minima, since the feature space $\widetilde{\mathcal{H}}$ may change considerably after updating the weights, making the previous iteration medoids inappropriate for initialization.

Weight Estimation. For $p > 1$ the intra-cluster variance $\mathcal{E}_{\widetilde{\mathcal{H}}}$ is convex *w.r.t.* the (constrained) weights, as can be confirmed from (6). Hence, the *optimal values for the weights for the current clusters* can be determined by plugging into (6) the constraints from (5), through a Lagrange multiplier, and setting the

---

Algorithm 1. Greedy Unsupervised MKL

Input: Kernel matrices $\{K^{(v)}\}_{v=1}^V$, Number of clusters M, Exponent p $(p \geq 1)$.
Output: Clustering solution $\{\mathcal{C}_k\}_{k=1}^M$, Weights $\{w_v\}_{v=1}^V$.

1: $t = 0$
2: $w_v^{(0)} = 1/V$, $v = 1, \ldots, V$ //Initial weights.
3: **repeat**
4:     $t = t + 1$
5:     $\widetilde{K}^{(t)} = \sum_{v=1}^V \left(w_v^{(t-1)} \right)^p K^{(v)}$
6:     $(\{l_k^{(t)}\}_{k=1}^M) = $greedy-medoids-initialization$(\widetilde{K}^{(t)})$
7:     $(\{l_k^{(t)}\}_{k=1}^M, \{\mathcal{C}_k^{(t)}\}_{k=1}^M, \mathcal{E}_{\widetilde{\mathcal{H}}}^{(t)}) = k$-medoids$(\widetilde{K}^{(t)}, \{l_k^{(t)}\}_{k=1}^M)$
8:     Update the view weights $w_v^{(t)}$, $v = 1, \ldots, V$, through (7), (8).
9: **until** $|\mathcal{E}_{\widetilde{\mathcal{H}}}^{(t)} - \mathcal{E}_{\widetilde{\mathcal{H}}}^{(t-1)}| < \epsilon$

---

derivatives *w.r.t.* w_v to zero. After some manipulation the following closed-form solution is derived:

$$w_v = 1 / \sum_{v'=1}^V \left(\frac{\mathcal{E}_{\mathcal{H}^{(v)}}}{\mathcal{E}_{\mathcal{H}^{(v')}}} \right)^{\frac{1}{p-1}} , p > 1 . \tag{7}$$

For $p = 1$ the optimization (5) is actually a linear program and the solution lies on the corners of the simplex (8).

$$w_v = \begin{cases} 1 , v = \operatorname{argmin}_{v'} \mathcal{E}_{\mathcal{H}^{(v')}} \\ 0 , \text{otherwise} \end{cases} , p = 1 \tag{8}$$

Note that for $0 < p < 1$, $\mathcal{E}_{\widetilde{\mathcal{H}}}$ becomes concave (6), thus the updates (7) would increase $\mathcal{E}_{\widetilde{\mathcal{H}}}$, which, of course, is not desired.

From (7) it can be observed that views with lower intra-cluster variance $\mathcal{E}_{\mathcal{H}^{(v)}}$ are assigned higher weights, hence *kernels are ranked according to their quality as reflected through* $\mathcal{E}_{\mathcal{H}^{(v)}}$. The exponent p acts as a regularizer on the ranking. The greater (smaller) the p value is, the differences between the views are suppressed (amplified) and the weights become more uniform (sparser) (*i.e.* their distribution is more flat (more peaky)). Moreover, for $p = 1$ a completely sparse outcome emerges, where all views, except one, are discarded (8). In the limit $p \to \infty$, we get that $w_v = 1/V$ from (7), *i.e.* all views are equally considered, irrespectively of their quality. Naturally, the most appropriate p value will depend on the underlying problem and the relative quality of kernels.

Convergence and Refinement. k-medoids monotonically decreases the intra-cluster variance and the subsequent weight updates yield a further reduction. However, the greedily selected medoids at the beginning of each iteration may increase the objective. Therefore, GUMKL cannot be guaranteed to monotonically converge, although this scenario rarely occurred during our experimentation.

It is possible to refine GUMKL results by running a kernel-based algorithm, using the composite kernel produced by GUMKL. In the empirical study we applied kernel k-means [4] and the clustering solution was further improved.

Table 1. Category composition of the tested corel datasets

Dataset	Categories			
D1	*owls*	*hippos*	*trains*	*animal paintings*
D2	*owls*	*hippos*	*trains*	*cargo ships*
D3	*buses*	*leopards*	*trains*	*cargo ships*
D4	*eagles*	*elephants*	*trains*	*passenger ships*
D5	*owls*	*mammals with horns*	*roses*	*cargo ships*

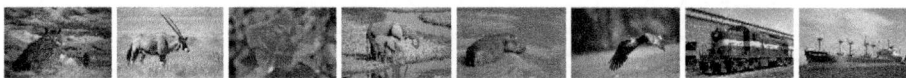

Fig. 1. Examples of images used in the experiments

4   Experimental Results

The effectiveness of GUMKL is evaluated on the task of unsupervised object category recognition on the corel images collection. There are 34 categories in total, each with 100 images that mainly consist of a salient foreground object (Fig. 1). Seven modalities, three color-related and four texture-related modalities, are available[2] in the form of attribute vectors, which naturally produce seven base kernels (each view corresponds to a modality).

To determine whether the proposed technique combines the kernels effectively and investigate the influence of the exponent p on the weight distribution and the returned clusters, GUMKL has been executed for various $p > 1$ values. It is compared to two baselines; i) selecting the best view in terms of intra-cluster variance and splitting the dataset using the corresponding kernel only (GUMKL for $p = 1$) and ii) evenly considering all views by taking a uniform sum of the kernels (GUMKL for $p \to \infty$). For the second baseline, a single iteration of Algorithm 1 is executed without updating the weights.

Regarding the setup of the experiments, five four class datasets were created from the collection, whose classes are described in Table 1. The linear kernel function was applied on the attribute vectors of each modality to compute the seven kernels, which makes the second baseline ($p \to \infty$) equivalent to merging the modalities. The number of clusters was always set equal to the true number of classes. To assess the quality of the returned clusters, the NMI criterion [8] is used. Higher NMI values indicate a better partitioning. Finally, the reported results were always refined by a run of kernel k-means as discussed in Sect. 3.2.

The obtained results are depicted in Figs. 2 and 3. It is evident that GUMKL systematically and considerably outperforms the baselines. Hence, exploiting multiple kernels, by adjusting the mixing coefficients according to the properties of each view, can improve clustering accuracy. A single kernel ($p = 1$) is always inferior to using multiple kernels, even to the simplest case of equal weights ($p \to \infty$), showing that the modalities contain complementary information. Therefore, an aggressive weighting strategy results in loss of useful information. To add to

---

[2] http://www.cs.virginia.edu/~xj3a/research/CBIR/Download.htm

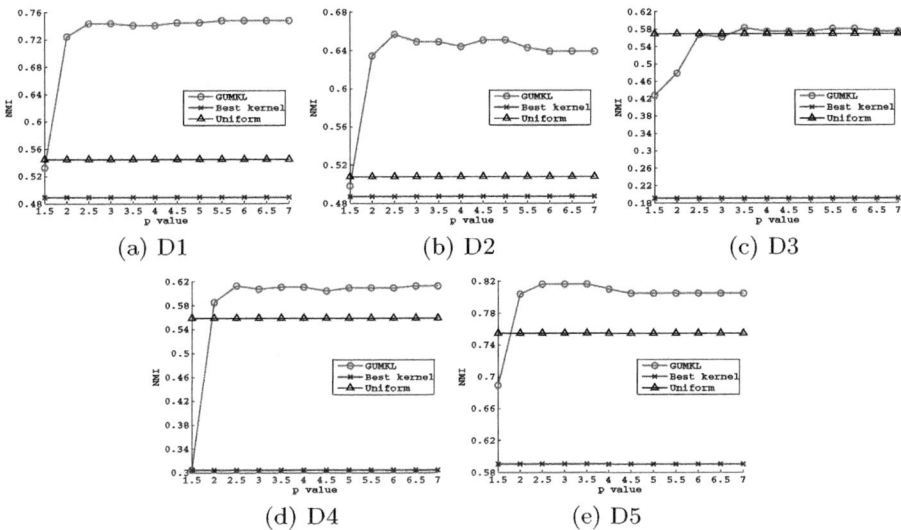

Fig. 2. Clustering performance comparison of GUMKL, for various p values, to the two baselines (best kernel, uniform)

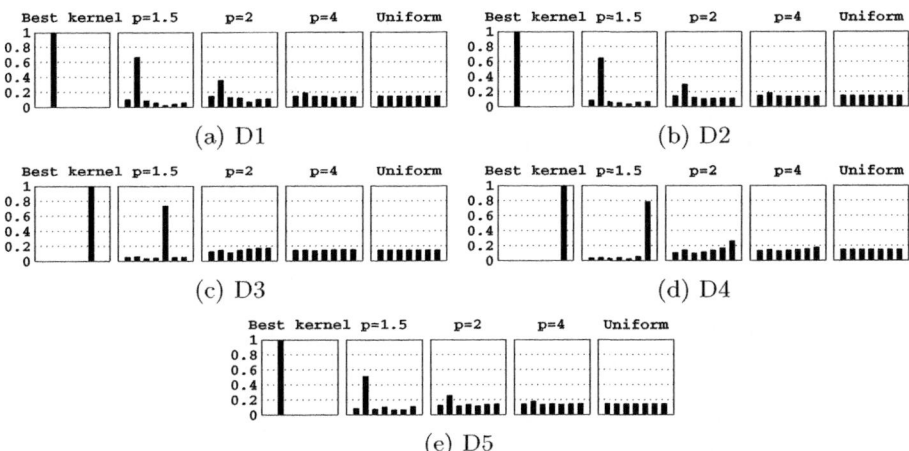

Fig. 3. Weight distribution of GUMKL for indicative p values and of the two baselines (best kernel, uniform). The modalities, left to right, are color histogram, moment and coherence, coarseness and directionality of tamura texture, wavelet and mrsar texture.

that, GUMKL for $p = 1.5$ that produces a very sparse solution (Fig. 3), clearly underperforms. As p increases, coefficients exhibit a more uniform distribution, but the proposed method seems to be quite insensitive to p, if a reasonable value is chosen that avoids extremes ($2 < p < \infty$). The highest NMI is usually attained for $p \in [2.5, 3.5]$, which provides a nice balance between high sparsity and high uniformity. Finally, similar conclusions to the above can be drawn when the kernel k-means refinement is not applied, however the NMI values are lower.

5   Conclusions

We have proposed an unsupervised multiple kernel learning method for linearly combining a set of base kernels under the intra-cluster variance objective. Closed-form expressions are obtained for the combination weights, whose distribution is moderated by a parameter p that allows all kernels to contribute to the solution with distinct degrees. Stable performance is demonstrated in the experiments for a wide range of p, surpassing the compared baselines of single kernel clustering and uniform kernel summation.

In future work, a rigorous comparison to other MKL methods will be carried out. As the appropriate choice of p depends on the dataset, possible ways of automatically adjusting p will be explored. Moreover, implementing nonlinear MKL under the presented framework is in our plans.

References

1. Bishop, C.M.: Pattern Recognition and Machine Learning. Springer-Verlag New York, Inc. (2006)
2. Cortes, C., Mohri, M., Rostamizadeh, A.: L2 regularization for learning kernels. In: Conf. on Uncertainty in Artificial Intelligence, pp. 109–116 (2009)
3. Cortes, C., Mohri, M., Rostamizadeh, A.: Learning non-linear combinations of kernels. In: Advances in Neural Information Processing Systems, pp. 396–404 (2009)
4. Filippone, M., Camastra, F., Masulli, F., Rovetta, S.: A survey of kernel and spectral methods for clustering. Pattern Recognition 41(1), 176–190 (2008)
5. Gönen, M., Alpaydin, E.: Multiple kernel learning algorithms. J. of Machine Learning Research 12, 2211–2268 (2011)
6. Kloft, M., Brefeld, U., Sonnenburg, S., Laskov, P., Müller, K.R., Zien, A.: Efficient and accurate lp-norm multiple kernel learning. In: Advances in Neural Information Processing Systems, pp. 997–1005 (2009)
7. Lange, T., Buhmann, J.M.: Fusion of similarity data in clustering. In: Advances in Neural Information Processing Systems, pp. 723–730 (2005)
8. Tzortzis, G., Likas, A.: The global kernel k-means algorithm for clustering in feature space. IEEE Trans. on Neural Networks 20(7), 1181–1194 (2009)
9. Valizadegan, H., Jin, R.: Generalized maximum margin clustering and unsupervised kernel learning. In: Advances in Neural Information Processing Systems, pp. 1417–1424 (2006)
10. Varma, M., Babu, B.R.: More generality in efficient multiple kernel learning. In: Int. Conf. on Machine Learning, pp. 1065–1072 (2009)
11. Xu, Z., Jin, R., Yang, H., King, I., Lyu, M.R.: Simple and efficient multiple kernel learning by group lasso. In: Int. Conf. on Machine Learning, pp. 1175–1182 (2010)
12. Zeng, H., Cheung, Y.-M.: Kernel Learning for Local Learning Based Clustering. In: Alippi, C., Polycarpou, M., Panayiotou, C., Ellinas, G. (eds.) ICANN 2009, Part I. LNCS, vol. 5768, pp. 10–19. Springer, Heidelberg (2009)
13. Zhao, B., Kwok, J.T., Zhang, C.: Multiple kernel clustering. In: SIAM Int. Conf. on Data Mining, pp. 638–649 (2009)

An AZP-ACO Method for Region-Building

Angelos Mimis[*], Antonis Rovolis, and Marianthi Stamou

Panteion University, Department of Economic and Regional Development, Athens, Greece
{mimis,rovolis}@panteion.gr,
marianthi_stamou@hotmail.com

Abstract. In this paper a regionalization algorithm which groups spatial areal objects into homogeneous zones is presented. The proposed method is based on Automatic Zoning Problem (AZP) procedure which is extended to use the Ant Colony Optimization (ACO) technique. The results produced are compared to the original AZP method. Both methods are applied into the classification of economic data in a post code level on the area of Athens.

Keywords: Region building, constrained clustering, Ant colony optimization, Automatic Zoning Problem.

1 Introduction

The zone design problem involves the aggregation of k regions into n zones while optimizing an objective function and preserving the internal connectivity of the zones [1-2]. This problem is also known as redistricting, regionalization or p-region problem, and in terms of computational complexity, it belongs to the family of nondeterministic polynomial-time hard problems (N-P hard) [3-4].

The zone design is a geographical problem that has been applied to many fields such as climate zoning [5], location optimization [6], in socio-economic [2], [7] and epidemiological analysis [8], in electoral and school districting [4], [9] and many more. The problems mentioned may differ into the data types (numerical or categorical) the different objective functions used (e.g. capturing intra-region homogeneity or compactness) or the constraints imposed (e.g. minimum population within zones). All of these approaches can be classified into the following three categories, 1) linear programming techniques, 2) heuristic-based optimization and 3) contiguity constrained clustering [10-12].

In the first group of methods, Duque et al [12-13] have formulated the regionalization as a mixed integer programming problem and incorporated the contiguity within zones in the solution space searched. This approach is computational expensive and thus its use is limited to small data sets.

In the second group, the heuristic-based optimization techniques are included, which optimize a given function while preserving the contiguity constraints. The first method developed was the Automatic Zoning Problem (AZP) by Openshaw [1] which

---

[*] Corresponding author.

I. Maglogiannis, V. Plagianakos, and I. Vlahavas (Eds.): SETN 2012, LNAI 7297, pp. 81–89, 2012.

starts with an initial solution and by randomly adding neighboring regions to various zones, converges to a better solution. This approach was later improved by applying Tabu search and Simulating Annealing in order to avoid the local optimum in the search space (ZDES software) [2]. In a more recent approach by Bacao et al. [4], a Genetic Algorithms was developed and compared with the ZDES results. These methods have two inherited limitations. Firstly, they are computational intensive and secondly, some variants give significantly different results with each run.

The third approach is based on hierarchical clustering and its more recent form is performed into two steps. Initially a hierarchical constrained clustering is performed to create the tree of aggregated regions, followed by an optimization method in order to determine the cut of level in the hierarchical tree [7], [10-11]. In the hierarchical step various methods have been implemented such as the single, average, complete linkage and Ward method. The drawback of this methodology is the limited solution space that is explored.

In this paper the second approach is adopted, aiming to an improvement to the current methodology in use. The AZP method is extended to use the Ant Colony Optimization (ACO) technique and the results produced are compared to the initial AZP method. The advantages of our method are threefold: to avoid local optimum, to provide improved solutions and a tool that can be used alongside the Geographical Information System (GIS) software.

In the next section the proposed methodology is presented. In section 3 the algorithm is applied on a case study on the city of Athens, where the data and results are presented. Finally in the last section some concluding remarks are drawn.

2   Methodology

In the problem at hand, a study area which is completely divided into regions is given. These regions are aggregated into zones so that each region is assigned to only one zone and that the zones are contiguous internally (regions within a zone) and externally (zones together). In order to measure the quality of a partition an objective function of the attribute values of the regions for the current zone-design is examined, aiming in optimum performance.

In the initial work of Openshaw [1], a mildly steepest descent algorithm was proposed (AZP). This algorithm consists by the following steps:

— Step 1. An initial solution is found, or in terms of the problem an initial classification of n regions into a given number of m zones (m<n).
— Step 2. A list of the zones L={$Z_1,Z_2,...,Z_m$} is made.
— Step 3. A zone Z_k is randomly selected and removed from L.
— Step 4. For Z_k a list of contiguous regions B={$R_1,R_2,...$} is composed.
— Step 5. Until this set of regions B is empty, a region R_j is selected randomly and removed from B.
— Step 6. The zone in which R_j belongs is found and it is examined if it can be removed from it. If by aggregating R_j into zone Z_k the zone remains contiguous then the algorithm continues to step 7, otherwise to step 5.

— Step 7. The value of the objective function is calculated for the new classification.
— Step 8. If an improvement is made, the new zonation is kept, otherwise it is rejected and the algorithm moves to step 5.
— Step 9. Set B is re-composed and the algorithm moves to step 5.

The steps 2-9 are repeated until convergence is achieved.
ACO is inspired by nature, where ants select the shortest path to food by laying and following chemical trails called phenomone. After the initial paper by Dorigo and Cambardella [14], it has been applied to various problems except Travelling Salesman Problem (TSP) such as vehicle routing, graph coloring, sequential ordering [15-16]. The algorithm is performed by a number of iterations. In each iteration, in a typical ACO application, the steps are the following:

— Step 1. A set of m ants are located at randomly selected regions.
— Step 2. Each ant is making a tour through the neighboring regions, visiting each region once.
— Step 3. For each ant, say k, the next region q to be visited is selected, based on the probability

$$P_{qk} = \frac{\tau_{zk}^a * v_{zk}^b}{\sum_q \tau_{zk}^a * v_{zk}^b} \tag{1}$$

where τ is the phenomone strength, v is the visibility and a, b are two constants. If a=0, the closest region in attribute values is chosen. Also in the case where b=0 the visibility between regions is ignored.

— Step 4. When the ants has explored the space, the phenomone trails are updated by:

$$\tau_{qz} = (1 - \rho)\tau_{qz} + \Delta\tau_{qz} \tag{2}$$

where ρ is the evaporation constant, and $\Delta\tau_{qz}$ is the reinforcement achieved by region inclusion in zone.

In our version of AZP, called AZP-ACO, the steps 5-6, are replaced by the ACO algorithm described. The initial values, for pheromone, are evaluated in the first step of the algorithm, by examining the difference between the attribute values of contiguous regions. Typical values for the AZP-ACO method are a=b=1, ρ=0.5 and m is equal to the number of neighboring regions.
As an objective function a homogeneity measure is used, which is defined as the sum of squared differences between attributes allocated on each region and the mean values of each zone. The Sum of Squared Differences (SSD) is given by:

$$SSD = \sum_L \sum_i \sum_j (x_{ij} - \overline{x}_j)^2 \tag{3}$$

where $\overline{x}_j$ is the mean   value of j attribute on a zone in L set and x_{ij} is the value of j attribute on region i, classified on a zone in L [7], [11]. The SSD is a measure of dispersion of attribute values for the regions in a zone. Also homogeneous zones contribute small values into the objective function.

The algorithms of AZP and AZP-ACO were implemented in C++ and were loosely coupled with ArcGIS 9.3. In ArcGIS, which is the main tool in our analysis, the regions are defined and are accompanied by the relative attribute data. In ArcGIS the W contiguity matrix is evaluated and exported with the attribute values into the C++ program. In our approach the W matrix has the values of 1 for regions with common part of an edge and 0 otherwise (rook contiguity). Finally the output of the custom program, which is the regions classification, is passed into the GIS software to display and further examine the result.

3   Data

Our empirical analysis is based on the postcode on the city of Athens. More specifically, the area of our analysis contains of 207 postcodes (Figure 1). The variable considered for classification is the average annual income, published by the Greek Ministry of Finance in 2002 (Available at http://www.gsis.gr/ggps/statistika/statistika.html).

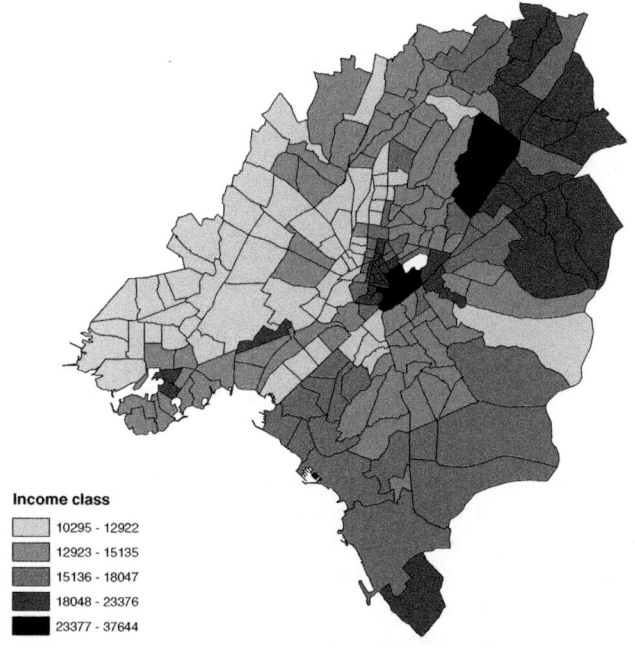

Income class

	10295 - 12922
	12923 - 15135
	15136 - 18047
	18048 - 23376
	23377 - 37644

Fig. 1. Study area

4   Results

The AZP and the AZP-ACO were applied to the regionalization of the post codes in the study area of Athens. The spatial objects, in our case, have only one attribute, the mean income.

The methods have been compared for speed and quality of the solution. Four experiments were made, in which the number of spatial objects are the same (207) as well as the number of attributes. In the first case, the resulting clusters were 5 and in the other experiments were 10, 15 and 20 respectively. The experiments were run 30 times for each method and the average results are presented in Table 1, where the number of function evaluations, the time needed and the value of the objective function are presented.

Table 1. Results of the AZP and AZP-ACO algorithm

	AZP			AZP-ACO		
#regions	#evaluations	time(sec)	value	#evaluations	time(sec)	value
5	437	10.8	14.9	7310	140.6	10.9
10	559	8.4	11.5	6843	112.6	7.5
15	645	7.2	10.0	6660	102.5	5.7
20	721	6.8	8.9	5987	86.4	4.5

As far as the quality criterion is concerned, the internal homogeneity of the resulting zones was measured by Equation (3), where smaller values are better. In all the tests the AZP-ACO produces improved results. As it can be seen from the Table 1, as the number of regions increases, the ratio $SSD_{AZP}/SSD_{AZP-ACO}$ increases as well, starting from 1.37 for 5 regions and ending up to 1.97 for 20 regions. On the other hand, the time needed to perform the clustering is around 13 times more for AZP-ACO than for the AZP. Further, as can be seen in Table 2, AZP-ACO is superior to classic AZP not only in the mean value of the objective function but in the standard deviation as well.

Another important issue that is usually ignored in the literature is to visualize the zoning proposed by the methods and compare the results in terms of geography. For that purpose in mind a typical zoning for the two algorithms is presented in Figures 2-5. In the first case, regions are aggregated into 5 zones. The difference in Figures 2 and 3 is substantial. The AZP-ACO method (Figure 3) has captured the areal changes in income and has divided the region, as expected, into the city center area (zone 1), the surrounding of the city center (zone 3), the north-west (zone 5), the south-east (zone 4) and the north-east zones (zone 2). On the other hand AZP, did not distinguish the north-east zone from south-east zone (zone 3 in Figure 2) and has displayed a limited area surrounding the city center (zone 2). In the second case, 10 zones were used and both methods have captured the characteristics of the data set. As can be seen in Figures 4 and 5 both methods have created zones for the high, medium and low income regions (Figure 1). A striking difference in the two zoning-designs lies in zone 6 in Figure 4, which by looking into the data it can be seen, that AZP has included non-homogeneous regions. A more robust approach has been adopted by

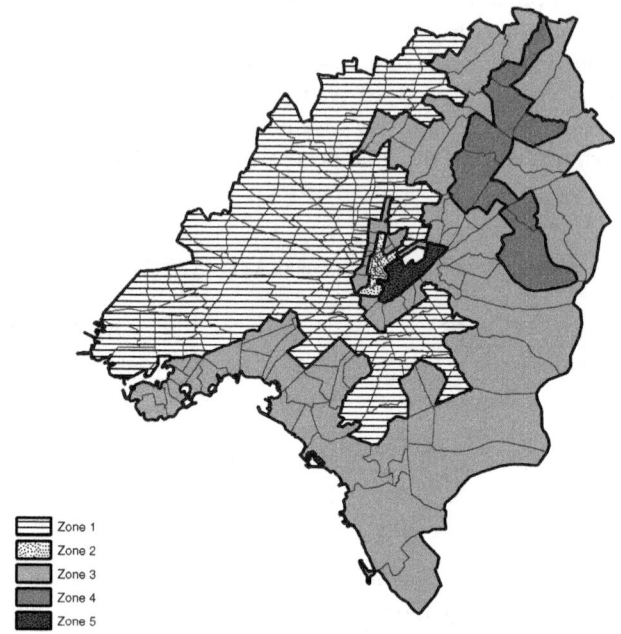

Fig. 2. The region-design proposed by AZP for 5 regions

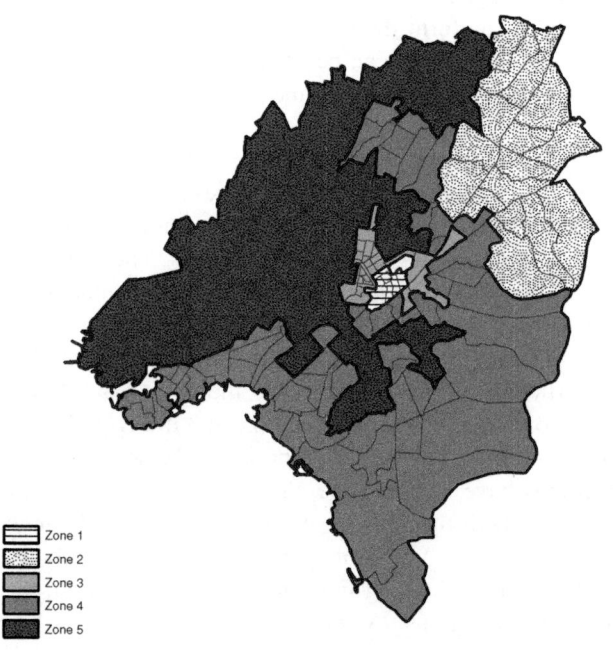

Fig. 3. The region-design proposed by AZP-ACO for 5 regions

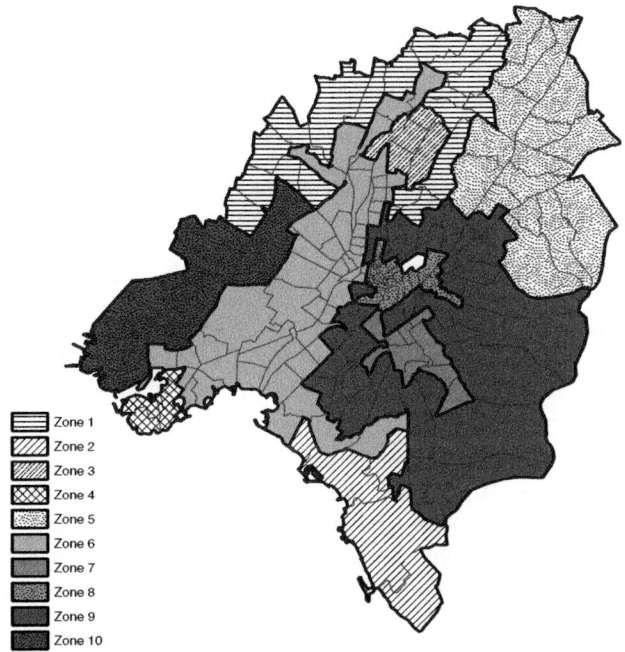

Zone 1
Zone 2
Zone 3
Zone 4
Zone 5
Zone 6
Zone 7
Zone 8
Zone 9
Zone 10

Fig. 4. The region-design proposed by AZP for 10 regions

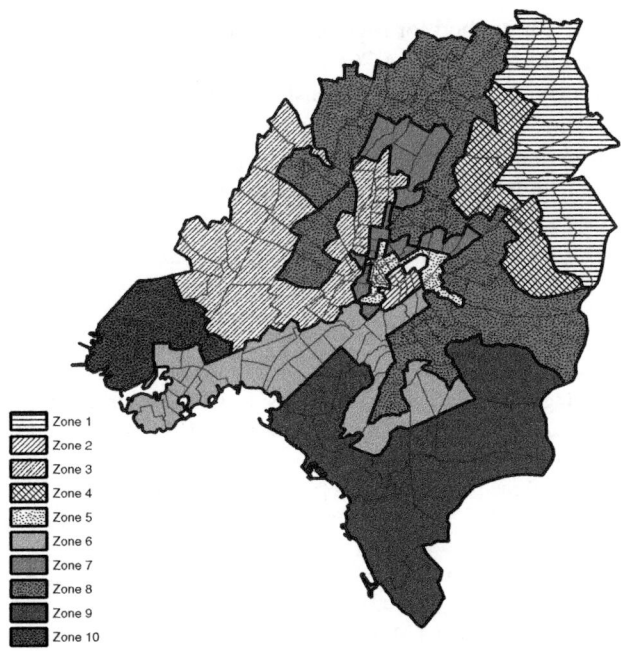

Zone 1
Zone 2
Zone 3
Zone 4
Zone 5
Zone 6
Zone 7
Zone 8
Zone 9
Zone 10

Fig. 5. The region-design proposed by AZP-ACO for 10 regions

AZP-ACO (Figure 5) where the same area has been partition and aggregated into zones 6 and 3 resulting in a more natural partitioning. Further, a drawback of the illustrated clustering, for both cases, is the presence of long zones (e.g. zone 1 in Figure 4 and zone 8 in Figure 5). This is attributed to the data set used (Figure 1) and can be treated by including into the objective function a term for compactness of the zones.

Table 2. Descriptive statistics of the results

| | AZP | | | AZP-ACO | | |
#regions	median	mean	stdev	median	mean	stdev
5	14.5	14.9	3.8	9.8	10.9	3.1
10	11.0	11.5	3.2	7.5	7.5	2.1
15	9.6	10.0	2.7	5.5	5.7	1.3
20	8.5	8.9	2.3	4.3	4.5	1.1

Finally, an issue commonly arising in region clustering is the number of zones that should be used. As Guo [10] pointed out, for explanatory spatial data analysis, the number of zones is a problem parameter and the results are examined for various values. On the other hand, it can be seen that for particular applications, the problem definitions depicts the number of zones as in the case of electoral or school districting [4].

5   Conclusions

In this paper, an efficient method for regionalization is presented, which combines the original AZP methodology with the ACO method of optimization. This approach was compared with the original method of Openshaw and illustrated an improvement of more than 30% in terms of the objective function.

The region-design method proposed can be applied into different domains and permits the use of different definitions for contiguity and objective function in terms of compactness, dissimilarity or heterogeneity.

References

1. Openshaw, S.: A geographical solution to scale and aggregation problems in region-building, partitioning and spatial modeling. Trans. Inst. Br. Geogr. 2, 459–472 (1977)
2. Openshaw, S., Rao, L.: Algorithms for reengineering 1991 census geography. Environ. Plann. A 27, 425–446 (1995)
3. Keane, M.: The size of the region-building problem. Environ. Plann. A 7, 575–577 (1975)
4. Bacao, F., Lobo, V., Painho, M.: Applying genetic algorithms to zone design. Soft. Comput. 9, 341–348 (2005)
5. Fovel, R.G., Fovell, M.-Y.C.: Climate zones of the conterminous United States defined using cluster analysis. J. Clim. 2, 2103–2135 (1993)
6. Goodchild, M.F.: The aggregated problem in location allocation. Geogr. Anal. 11, 240–255 (1979)

7. Assuncao, R.M., Neves, M.C., Gamara, G., Da Costa Freitas, C.: Efficient regionalization techniques for socio-economic geographical units using minimum spanning trees. Int. J. Geogr. Inform. Syst. 20(7), 797–811 (2006)

8. Haining, R., Wise, S., Blake, M.: Constructing regions for small-area analysis material deprivation and colorectal cancer. J. Public Health Med. 16, 457–469 (1994)

9. Martin, D.: Automated zone design in GIS. In: Atkinson, P., Martin, D. (eds.) GIS and Geocomputation, Innovations in GIS, vol. 7, pp. 103–111. Taylor and Francis, London (2000)

10. Guo, D.: Regionilization with dynamically constrained agglomeration clustering and partitioning. Int. J. Geogr. Inform. Sci. 22(7), 801–823 (2008)

11. Guo, D., Wand, H.: Automatic region building for spatial analysis. Transactions in GIS 15, 29–45 (2011)

12. Duque, J.C., Ramos, R., Surinach, J.: Supervised regionalization methods: A survey. Int. Reg. Sci. Rev. 30, 195–220 (2007)

13. Duque, J.C., Church, R.L., Middleton, R.S.: The p-regions problem. Geogr. Anal. 43, 104–126 (2011)

14. Dorigo, M., Gambardella, L.M.: Ant colonies for the travelling salesman problem. BioSystems 43, 73–81 (1997)

15. Bonabeau, E., Dorigo, M., Theraulaz, G.: Inspiration for optimization from social insect behavior. Nature 406, 39–42 (2000)

16. Dorigo, M., Stutzle, T.: Ant colony optimization. The MIT Press, Cambridge (2004)

Exploiting Quadratic Mutual Information for Discriminant Analysis

Vasileios Gavriilidis and Anastasios Tefas

Aristotle University of Thessaloniki, Department of Informatics,
Thessaloniki, Greece
vgavril@csd.auth.gr, tefas@aiia.csd.auth.gr

Abstract. Novel criteria that reformulate the Quadratic Mutual Information according to Fisher's Discriminant Analysis are proposed for supervised dimensionality reduction. The proposed method uses a quadratic divergence measure and requires no prior assumptions about class densities. The criteria are optimized using gradient ascent with initialization using random or LDA based projections. Experiments on various datasets are conducted and highlight the superiority of the proposed approach compared to the standard QMI criterion.

Keywords: Renyi Entropy, Parzen estimator, Feature transform, Feature extraction, Mutual information.

1 Introduction

Dimensionality reduction is a commonly used step in machine learning, especially when dealing with a high dimensional space of features. The original feature space is mapped onto a new, reduced dimensionality space and the examples to be used by machine learning algorithms are represented in that new space. Dimensionality reduction saves memory usage for storing training patterns and reduces the computation required for distance calculation. This way we improve performance and alleviate the effect of the curse of dimensionality [2]. Apart from time, dimensionality reduction is also crucial in terms of separability, thus a good selection or extraction lies to the criterion to be evaluated and enhanced.

Feature extraction, uses a transform to lower dimensions such as a projection matrix, which maximizes or minimizes a given criterion. The data transformation may be linear, as in Principal Component Analysis (PCA) [6] or Independent Component Analysis (ICA) [1], but many nonlinear dimensionality reduction techniques also exist such as kernel PCA [10].

In pattern classification, we are interested in methods that best separate the classes. Such a technique is Linear Discriminant Analysis (LDA), where a transform is produced that enhances the discrimination between data in different classes [5]. LDA assumes that samples are normally distributed, although techniques have been proposed for bypassing that problem [7]. In addition, LDA is limited to the number of features it can produce which is, $N_c - 1$ where N_c is the number of classes, but extensions have been proposed to overcome this [8].

I. Maglogiannis, V. Plagianakos, and I. Vlahavas (Eds.): SETN 2012, LNAI 7297, pp. 90–97, 2012.
© Springer-Verlag Berlin Heidelberg 2012

Information theory provides us measures that can be used to optimize class separability. Mutual information between the class labels and the transformed data to fewer dimensions acts as a more general criterion that overcomes many limitations of the methods discussed above. An even more sophisticated approach is given in [12]. This approximation is inspired by the quadratic Renyi entropy, it is differentiable and it can both avoid the knowledge of density of the classes and be applied to large training datasets. It can provide the ability to perform linear mappings for clustering [13] and even feature extraction [9].

A combination of QMI and LDA is introduced in this paper to provide a novel dimensionality reduction method that enhances class separability. The proposed approach uses the definition of QMI in order to reformulate criteria inspired by LDA. The proposed criteria are given in the form of ratios that enforce the within class similarity and between class dissimilarity. The novel optimization criteria then can be efficiently optimized using gradient ascent and update rules are derived for the projection matrix.

The manuscript is organized as follows. The derivation of QMI starting from Shannon's entropy definition is described in Section 2. The novel criteria that are inspired by LDA and combine measures that appear in QMI criterion are presented in Section 3. Classification results using nearest neighbor classifier in several datasets from the UCI machine learning repository are given in Section 4. Finally, conclusions are drawn in Section 5.

2   Prior Work and Problem Statement

Assume a random variable Y that models, $\mathbf{y}_i \in R^d$, that represent the projected input data, $\mathbf{x}_i \in R^D$, where $D > d$, and a discrete-value random variable C representing class labels taking values from 1 to N_c. The projected data are calculated by the product of each sample $\mathbf{x}_i$ with the projection matrix $\mathbf{W} \in R^{D \times d}$ hence, $\mathbf{y}_i = \mathbf{W}^T \mathbf{x}_i$.

Using Shannon's definition [11], the entropy of the discrete distribution, which is a measure of the randomness or unpredictability of a sequence of symbols, is $H(C) = -\sum_c P(c) log\,(P(c))$, where P denotes a probability while a lower case p denotes probability density. In general, the mutual information expresses the reduction in uncertainty about one variable due to the knowledge of the other variable, hence it can measure dependence between two variables, in our case the difference $H(C) - H(C|Y)$ is the uncertainty about the class C by observing the feature vector $\mathbf{y}$. It is defined as:

$$I(C,Y) = H(C) - H(C|Y)$$
$$= \sum_c \int_\mathbf{y} p(c,\mathbf{y}) \, log\left(\frac{p(c,\mathbf{y})}{P(c)\,p(\mathbf{y})}\right) dy \qquad (1)$$

Torkkola [12] has proposed the quadratic mutual information between the data sample and the corresponding class labels to be calculated as:

$$I_T(C,Y) = V_{IN} + V_{ALL} - 2V_{BTW} \qquad (2)$$

where:

- V_{IN} is expressing the interactions between pairs of samples inside each class, summed over all classes.
- V_{ALL} is expressing the interactions between all pairs of samples, regardless of class, weighted by the sum of squared class priors.
- V_{BTW} is expressing the interactions between samples of a particular class against all samples weighed by the class prior and summed over all classes.

Details can be found on [12]. The objective is to find a transform g such that $\mathbf{y} = g(\mathbf{x}_i)$ maximizes $I_T(C, Y)$.

3   Update Methods Inspired by Discriminant Analysis

The objective of LDA is to perform dimensionality reduction while preserving as much of the class discriminatory information as possible. In general, in order to use LDA for multiple classes, we first define the scatter matrices, $\mathbf{S}_B$ and $\mathbf{S}_W$ which are the between classes scatter matrix and the within class scatter matrix, respectively. Those matrices are computed as:

$$\mathbf{S}_B = \sum_{c-1}^{N_c} P(c)(\boldsymbol{\mu}_c - \boldsymbol{\mu})(\boldsymbol{\mu}_c - \boldsymbol{\mu})^T \tag{3}$$

$$\mathbf{S}_W = \sum_{c=1}^{N_c} \sum_{i \in c} (\mathbf{x}_i - \boldsymbol{\mu}_c)(\mathbf{x}_i - \boldsymbol{\mu}_c)^T \tag{4}$$

where $\boldsymbol{\mu}$ is the overall mean vector of the data, $\boldsymbol{\mu}_c$ is the mean vector of class c and $\mathbf{x}_i$ is the i-th vector that belongs to class c. Scatter matrices are quite similar to V_{IN} and V_{BTW}, however, whereas V_{IN} and V_{BTW} represent similarity, $\mathbf{S}_B$ and $\mathbf{S}_W$ represent dissimilarity. The corresponding criterion that needs maximization in the case of LDA is the following:

$$J(\mathbf{w}) = \frac{\mathbf{w}^T \mathbf{S}_B \mathbf{w}}{\mathbf{w}^T \mathbf{S}_W \mathbf{w}} \tag{5}$$

That is, based on (5), we propose a criterion inspired by QMI that has the form of (5). In order to increase the sample interactions inside each class while decreasing the sample interactions of different classes, we propose the transform of (2) to any of the following two criteria:

$$I_B(C, Y) = \frac{V_{IN}}{V_{BTW}} \tag{6}$$

$$I_A(C, Y) = \frac{V_{IN}}{V_{ALL}} \tag{7}$$

Let N be the number of samples, J_p the number of samples for each class, c_p, and $G(\mathbf{y}, \boldsymbol{\Sigma})$, be a n–dimensional Gaussian function where $\boldsymbol{\Sigma}$ is the covariance matrix. The prior probability of each class is $P(c_p) = \frac{J_p}{N}$, thus, $\sum_{p=1}^{N_c} J_p = N$. The Parzen density estimation, that corresponds to the density of each class, the joint density, as well as the density of all classes is given by:

$$p(\mathbf{y}|c_p) = \frac{1}{J_p} \sum_{j=1}^{J_p} G\left(\mathbf{y} - \mathbf{y}_{pj}, \sigma^2 I\right) \tag{8}$$

$$p(c_p, \mathbf{y}) = \frac{1}{N} \sum_{j=1}^{J_p} G\left(\mathbf{y} - \mathbf{y}_{pj}, \sigma^2 I\right) \tag{9}$$

$$p(\mathbf{y}) = \frac{1}{N} \sum_{i=1}^{N} G\left(\mathbf{y} - \mathbf{y}_i, \sigma^2 I\right) \tag{10}$$

respectively, where I is the identity matrix. Now analysing, and computing components in (6) and (7) while using Parzen density estimation given in (8), (9) and (10) we obtain:

$$V_{IN} = \sum_c \int_{\mathbf{y}} p(c, \mathbf{y})^2 \, dy = \frac{1}{N^2} \sum_{p=1}^{N_c} \sum_{k=1}^{J_p} \sum_{l=1}^{J_p} G\left(\mathbf{y}_{pk} - \mathbf{y}_{pl}, 2\sigma^2 I\right) \tag{11}$$

$$V_{ALL} = \sum_c \int_{\mathbf{y}} P(c)^2 \, p(\mathbf{y})^2 \, dy = \frac{1}{N^2} \left(\sum_{p=1}^{N_c} \left(\frac{J_p}{N}\right)^2\right) \sum_{k=1}^{N} \sum_{l=1}^{N} G\left(\mathbf{y}_k - \mathbf{y}_l, 2\sigma^2 I\right) \tag{12}$$

$$V_{BTW} = \sum_c \int_{\mathbf{y}} p(c, \mathbf{y}) P(c) p(\mathbf{y}) \, dy = \frac{1}{N^2} \sum_{p=1}^{N_c} \frac{J_p}{N} \sum_{j=1}^{J_p} \sum_{k=1}^{N} G\left(\mathbf{y}_{pj} - \mathbf{y}_k, 2\sigma^2 I\right) \tag{13}$$

It is straightforward to show that if all classes have the same number of samples then $V_{ALL} = V_{BTW}$ that is, if all classes have the same probability to occur then (12) becomes equal to (13).

All different measures given in (2), (6) and (7), need a maximization update rule for the given projection matrix $\mathbf{W}$. The projections of the input data, derive directly from the projection matrix $\mathbf{W}$, thus:

$$\mathbf{W} = \arg\max_{\mathbf{W}} \left(I(\{c_i, \mathbf{y}_i\})\right) \tag{14}$$

Unfortunately, the optimization of the criterion in (14) can not be solved analytically, hence, a numerical optimization is needed. Using gradient ascent with learning rate, ρ for updating $\mathbf{W}$, the update rule of the projection matrix can be the following:

$$\mathbf{W}_{t+1} = \mathbf{W}_t + \rho \frac{\partial I}{\partial \mathbf{W}} \tag{15}$$

Using the chain rule, one can obtain the following:

$$\frac{\partial I}{\partial \mathbf{W}} = \sum_{i=1}^{N} \frac{\partial I}{\partial \mathbf{y}_i} \frac{\partial \mathbf{y}_i}{\partial \mathbf{W}} = \sum_{i=1}^{N} \frac{\partial I}{\partial \mathbf{y}_i} \mathbf{x}_i^T \tag{16}$$

hence, we need to find the derivatives of (2), (6) and (7). We also impose the constraint, $\mathbf{W}^T\mathbf{W} = I$, in order to have an orthonormal subspace as solution and prevent convergence to trivial infinite solutions, hence after updating $\mathbf{W}$ Gram–Schmidt orthonormalization is used.

Derivatives represent the direction where each sample would likely move after the transformation is applied. Firstly, we know that the derivative of the potential between two samples is computed as:

$$\frac{\partial}{\partial \mathbf{y}_i} G\left(\mathbf{y}_i - \mathbf{y}_j, 2\sigma^2 I\right) = G\left(\mathbf{y}_i - \mathbf{y}_j, 2\sigma^2 I\right) \frac{(\mathbf{y}_j - \mathbf{y}_i)}{2\sigma^2} \tag{17}$$

We can now perform gradient ascent using the derivatives of (11), (12) and (13), which are given by:

$$\frac{\partial}{\partial \mathbf{y}_{ci}} V_{IN} = \frac{1}{N^2\sigma^2} \sum_{k=1}^{J_c} G\left(\mathbf{y}_{ck} - \mathbf{y}_{ci}, 2\sigma^2 I\right)\left(\mathbf{y}_{ck} - \mathbf{y}_{ci}\right) \tag{18}$$

$$\frac{\partial}{\partial \mathbf{y}_{ci}} V_{ALL} = \frac{1}{N^2\sigma^2} \left(\sum_{p=1}^{N_c} \left(\frac{J_p}{N}\right)^2\right) \sum_{k=1}^{N} G\left(\mathbf{y}_k - \mathbf{y}_i, 2\sigma^2 I\right)\left(\mathbf{y}_k - \mathbf{y}_i\right) \tag{19}$$

$$\frac{\partial}{\partial \mathbf{y}_{ci}} V_{BTW} = \frac{1}{N^2\sigma^2} \sum_{p=1}^{N_c} \frac{J_p + J_c}{2N} \sum_{j=1}^{J_p} G\left(\mathbf{y}_{pj} - \mathbf{y}_{ci}, 2\sigma^2 I\right)\left(\mathbf{y}_{pj} - \mathbf{y}_{ci}\right) \tag{20}$$

We can now calculate the gradient of (2), (6) and (7) as follows:

$$\frac{\partial I_T}{\partial \mathbf{y}_i} = \frac{\partial V_{IN}}{\partial \mathbf{y}_i} + \frac{\partial V_{ALL}}{\partial \mathbf{y}_i} - 2\frac{\partial V_{BTW}}{\partial \mathbf{y}_i} \tag{21}$$

$$\frac{\partial I_B}{\partial \mathbf{y}_i} = \frac{V_{BTW}}{V_{BTW}^2} \frac{\partial V_{IN}}{\partial \mathbf{y}_i} - \frac{V_{IN}}{V_{BTW}^2} \frac{\partial V_{BTW}}{\partial \mathbf{y}_i} \tag{22}$$

$$\frac{\partial I_A}{\partial \mathbf{y}_i} = \frac{V_{ALL}}{V_{ALL}^2} \frac{\partial V_{IN}}{\partial \mathbf{y}_i} - \frac{V_{IN}}{V_{ALL}^2} \frac{\partial V_{ALL}}{\partial \mathbf{y}_i} \tag{23}$$

These gradients can be calculated using (18), (19) and (20). Using (21), (22) and (23) in (16) and the result in (15) we derive the update rules for updating the projection matrix $\mathbf{W}$ until convergence.

Except for the calculation of gradients, we also need to somehow initialize $\mathbf{W}$. There are many options, among them initializations based on linear feature extraction, that one can find in the literature, like PCA, ICA and LDA can be used. In the proposed approach we use random values and LDA as proposed in [12].

4   Experimental Results

We compared the performance of dimensionality reduction using the standard QMI definition against the criteria proposed in (6) and (7) which are called for simplicity MI_B and MI_A, respectively. To do so, several databases from the UCI machine learning repository [4] have been used in the experiments. The datasets that were used are presented in Table 1.

All these datasets were scaled to the interval $[0, 1]$. To evaluate the test error on the various experiments we used 5×2 fold cross validation. Moreover, the classifier that was used was a k–nearest neighbor and we provide results for $\mathbf{W}$ initializations using both random projections and LDA projections. We should also mention that the same random initializations have been used for all criteria.

In addition, the number of dimensions that we tested are from 1 to $N_c - 1$ due to LDA limitations, although we do not show all the results in CMU face images because of the large number of classes it possess. As explained earlier, measures MI_B in (6) and MI_A in (7) have no difference when all classes have the same number of samples, so test results of these measures are substituted with the test results of the measure MI_{BA} which can be either one. Tables 2 - 4 show classifications test error results, where in the first column the measure to be maximized and the initialization of $\mathbf{W}$ is given.

Table 1. UCI Machine Learning Repository Data Sets Characteristics

Database	Samples	Dimension	Classes
CMU faces	640	960	20
Balance	625	4	3
Ionosphere	351	34	2
Ecoli	336	7	8
Wine	178	13	3
Iris	150	4	3

CMU Face Images. This data consists of 640 greyscale face images of people taken with varying pose, expression, eyes (wearing sunglasses or not). There are 32 images for each person capturing every variation combination. Each sample image was resized to 30×32. Observing Table 2, we can notice that the proposed MI_{BA} criterion is much better when $\mathbf{W}$ is initialized by LDA. In addition we performed Dieterich f statistical test [3], and gained a value over 8, on LDA initialization, hence the error rates difference between the criteria is statistically significant.

Ecoli. This dataset contains protein localization sites. As can be seen in Table 3, proposed criteria are better than the standard QMI criterion in both initialization methods. In addition, in figure 1 a projection in two dimensions revealing

Table 2. Error rates on CMU faces Images

Dimension	1	2	3	4	8	12	15	16	17	18	19
QMI, Random	52.50	28.94	22.69	15.06	17.50	19.62	13.56	15.62	13.81	15.44	**10.94**
MI_{BA}, Random	74.19	59.75	48.06	42.00	19.19	19.94	13.56	15.62	13.81	15.44	**10.94**
QMI, LDA	49.50	24.00	12.00	7.19	5.94	4.50	4.87	6.12	3.44	4.94	4.56
MI_{BA}, LDA	27.25	4.38	3.44	3.25	2.81	2.25	2.69	**1.94**	2.94	3.81	5.25

information about class separability and compactness is given. MI_A has produced a projection that attempts to separate all the classes. Standard QMI is very compact but fails to provide any separability between classes, while MI_A is superior for classification but is not as compact as the standard QMI.

Table 3. Error rates on Ecoli

Dimension	1	2	3	4	5	6	7
QMI, Random	36.63	32.29	25.90	20.60	19.76	17.23	15.66
MI_B, Random	35.90	23.37	17.71	17.47	16.75	15.78	15.66
MI_A, Random	32.77	22.89	18.31	16.99	16.99	**15.42**	15.66
QMI, LDA	36.27	28.31	29.40	22.53	20.72	17.59	13.13
MI_B, LDA	36.51	20.72	18.31	16.87	17.35	15.90	**13.01**
MI_A, LDA	36.39	21.33	18.07	16.87	17.95	16.14	13.13

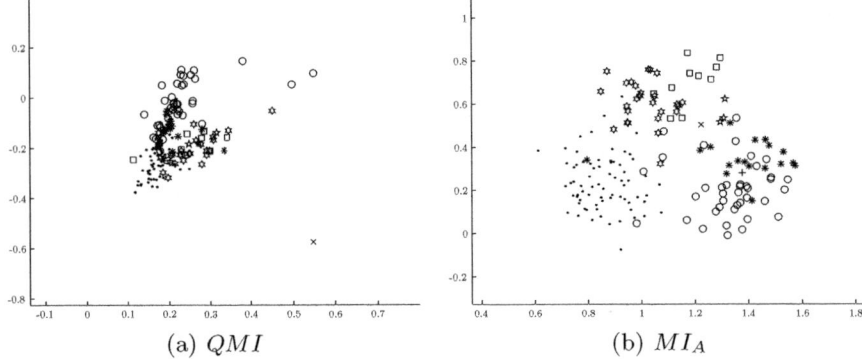

(a) QMI (b) MI_A

Fig. 1. Projected samples of the Ecoli dataset using the same random initialization. The QMI criterion is given in (a) and MI_A criterion in (b).

Datasets with Small Number of Classes. Balance, Ionosphere, Wine and Iris are some datasets that possess a small number of classes and all results are shown in Table 4. Overall, MI_B or MI_A is superior against standard QMI.

Table 4. Error rates on databases with small number of classes

Database	Balance		Ionosphere	Wine		Iris	
Dimension	1	2	1	1	2	1	2
QMI, Random	23.78	**20.19**	42.40	33.18	**30.68**	4.53	4.80
MI_B, Random	65.77	36.73	44.11	32.95	30.91	4.27	**3.73**
MI_A, Random	66.09	37.24	**42.29**	32.95	31.36	4.27	**3.73**
QMI, LDA	8.97	10.26	39.20	32.73	30.45	8.53	3.47
MI_B, LDA	9.29	10.26	33.83	34.77	**29.55**	3.47	**2.67**
MI_A, LDA	**8.91**	10.26	**32.57**	34.77	29.77	3.47	**2.67**

5   Conclusions

A novel method for dimensionality reduction and feature extraction inspired by mutual information between features and class labels and using Linear Discriminant Analysis criteria is proposed. As it has been illustrated, we can substitute the standard QMI with the MI_{BA} criterion which attains in most cases better classification and separability characteristics. Future work will be directed on overcoming the limitation of LDA initialization.

References

1. Comon, P.: Independent component analysis, a new concept? Signal Processing 36(3), 287–314 (1994); Higher Order Statistics
2. Corporation, B.: Dynamic programming. Princeton University Press, City (1957)
3. Dietterich, T.G.: Approximate statistical tests for comparing supervised classification learning algorithms. Neural Computation 10(7), 1895–1923 (1998)
4. Frank, A., Asuncion, A.: UCI machine learning repository (2010), http://archive.ics.uci.edu/ml
5. Fukunaga, K.: Introduction to Statistical Pattern Recognition, 2nd edn. Academic Press (1990)
6. Kittler, J., Devijver, P.A.: Statistical properties of error estimators in performance assessment of recognition systems. IEEE Transactions on Pattern Analysis and Machine Intelligence, PAMI 4(2), 215–220 (1982)
7. Kumar, N., Andreou, A.G.: Heteroscedastic discriminant analysis and reduced rank HMMs for improved speech recognition. Speech Communication 26(4), 283–297 (1998)
8. Okada, T., Tomita, S.: An optimal orthonormal system for discriminant analysis. Pattern Recognition, 139–144 (1985)
9. Ozertem, U., Erdogmus, D., Jenssen, R.: Spectral feature projections that maximize shannon mutual information with class labels. Pattern Recogn. 39, 1241–1252 (2006)
10. Schölkopf, B., Smola, A., Müller, K.R.: Kernel principal component analysis (1999)
11. Shannon, C.: A mathematical theory of communication. Bell Systems Techn. Journal 27, 623–656 (1948)
12. Torkkola, K.: Feature extraction by non-parametric mutual information maximization. Journal of Machine Learning Research 3, 1415–1438 (2003)
13. Vera, P.A., Estévez, P.A., Principe, J.C.: Linear Projection Method Based on Information Theoretic Learning. In: Diamantaras, K., Duch, W., Iliadis, L.S. (eds.) ICANN 2010, Part III. LNCS, vol. 6354, pp. 178–187. Springer, Heidelberg (2010)

Emerge-Sort: Swarm Intelligence Sorting

Dimitris Kalles[1,2], Vassiliki Mperoukli[1], and Andreas Papandreadis[2]

[1] Hellenic Open University, Patras, Greece
kalles@eap.gr, vickybergr@yahoo.gr, bp@hol.gr
[2] Open University of Cyprus, Nicosia, Cyprus

Abstract. We examine sorting on the assumption we do **not** know in advance which way to sort. We use simple local comparison and swap operators and demonstrate that their repeated application ends up in sorted sequences. These are the basic elements of Emerge-Sort, an approach to self-organizing sorting, which we experimentally validate and observe a run-time behavior of $O(n^2)$.

1   Introduction

Sorting has been one of the first areas of computer science to showcase efficient algorithms to stand the test of time. Our key motivation to examine sorting is to investigate what is the minimum structure of local operators whose repetitive application ends up in sorted sequences. We relax the assumption that we know which way to sort, yet arrive at a sorted sequence by simple local interactions, which are also able to address on-the-fly modifications of the sequence-to-be-sorted. Accordingly, our contribution lies with the development of several such operators and the validation of their **emergent** sorting efficiency independently of any global sorting direction bias.

A simple example may help to visualize such a context. Consider a database which is distributed across several sites, with each site maintaining a sorting that best suits its local needs (either largest-first or smallest-first). If there is a need to redistribute objects across the sites, according to their order, so as to avoid asking all sites where an object might be located, one can either opt for some sort of centralized control over who-comes-first or, simply, let each object re-arrange itself in the local neighborhood. Additionally, when new objects are inserted dynamically into any of the available sites, one can either explicitly direct each one of them to the correct database partition or, simply, wait until the object finds its way to a partition. Similar problems have been long studied in the distributed computing literature [1][2][3], have attracted the attention of the multiagent systems community [4][5] and the consensus reaching community [6].

Locality is central to the swarm intelligence and game theory areas too. Swarm intelligence has gathered significant momentum since many traditional problems (graph partitioning and clustering, among others) have been recast in terms of swarm behavior. Swarm intelligence is at the junction of randomized behavior and local operations and has been demonstrated to solve difficult problems such as task scheduling [7]. Now, emergent sorting is a behavior that has been documented in insect societies and modeled via swarm intelligence principles [5][8], albeit in an unconventional

I. Maglogiannis, V. Plagianakos, and I. Vlahavas (Eds.): SETN 2012, LNAI 7297, pp. 98–105, 2012.

way; therein, sorting takes place in 2-D and consists of forming concentric circles where items of similar size are at roughly the same distance from the centre. 2-D sorting has received relatively scant attention since it is usually seen as a (difficult) case of clustering, another classic problem that has been also recently addressed with swarm intelligence [9]. It is interesting to note that swarm intelligence, beyond emergent sorting [4], has been also related to autonomic computing research, mainly through the observation of autonomic computing principles in biology inspired systems and the transfer of relevant concepts to problems in distributed computing [10].

Game theory, on another front, directs huge research effort at studying various computational games from the point of view of reaching a Nash equilibrium; therein, one usually favors algorithms that make little use of global knowledge and where agents act competitively yet manage to converge to a state that satisfies them all [11]. In such settings, one asks what expense such anarchy incurs when seen from an optimization point of view; in other words, if one could centrally design what each agent will do, it is interesting to know how much effort one would save. The beauty of localized behavior in that setting usually comes from the appreciation of its robustness and graceful behavior in adversarial contexts as well. The similarity to our problems is quite straightforward: we are, what is the cost of not knowing which way we need to sort and how can we induce our sequences to self-sort.

Seen from a more conventional computer science perspective, swarm intelligence draws on several aspects of distributed computing [1][12][13], where, however, the underlying algorithm usually assumes a sequence of distinct passes over the data to achieve sorting. It is interesting to see that $O(n^2)$ seems to be the minimum one has to pay for such sorting but we note that our local operators achieve such performance without any knowledge of further steps. From that perspective, we view cellular automata to be also related to our approach [14][15, also taking into account the genetic discovery of interesting behaviors for such automata [16][17] and their influence on distributed co-ordination in consensus reaching problems [18][19].

The rest of this paper is structured in three sections. The next one is the core of the paper: we sketch out the basic principles that have lead to Emerge-Sort by showing how various modifications in simple local operators influence their capacity to finally deliver sorted sequences. Following that, we show a brief experimental validation of these fundamental concepts and, finally, we conclude the paper by drawing key connecting lines from our research to swarm intelligence and by setting forth the key future research viewpoint.

2   Developing Emerge-Sort

There are six possible ways to permute a triple (a,b,c) of distinct numbers (Fig. 1); additionally, un-sorted triples require a single swap between two elements to turn into sorted ones.

It turns out that this simple operator cannot scale to arbitrarily selected triples of any unordered sequence (it is not difficult to devise a counter-example demonstrating eternal oscillation between two sequences), so the next best attempt is to minimally extend this operator.

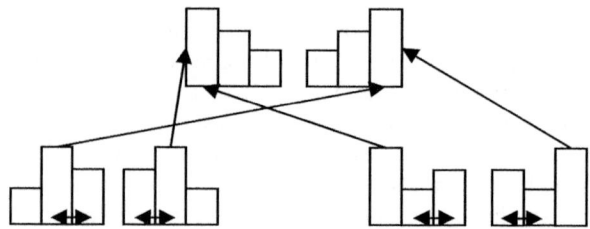

Fig. 1. Possible permutations and swaps to sort any three numbers

Interestingly, the extension is quite simple: sort the triple in the direction indicated by a majority vote among all triple members' direction preferences. Such direction preference (bias) can be initialized at random for each member. In effect, the new local sorting operator (which, we stress, is confined to the triple's limits):

-    First, establishes a preference for a sorting direction,
-    Then, enforces that direction by locally sorting the triple,
-    Finally, modifies the sorting direction bias of the minority vote items.

So, we have substituted the "to make as few moves as possible" approach with a still very simple one, namely "to make as few direction bias changes as possible" (which, of course, means that the arrows shown in Fig. 1, about how permutations are turned into sorted triples, are no longer valid). The new approach creates overlapping triples that compete for setting the sorting direction of the sequence. But, this suffices for the sequence to be eventually sorted.

2.1   A Proof of Concept

As a convention, let us use A to denote an ascending sorting bias (for left-to-right), and D to denote a descending sorting bias (again, for left-to-right). Let us also assume that we have a sequence of length n to sort. A triple is uniquely identified by the location of its middle element, i, with $1 \leq i \leq n$ and we employ a simple wrapping that arranges the sequence in a circle (ring).

Now, assume that at initialization, all numbers in the sequence have equal probability of having a sorting bias direction of A or D. Note that the sorting bias in a triple only conveys information as to what sorting direction it *plans* to employ.

We now show an example of a neck-to-neck competition for establishing the bias; it will then be easier to develop a general probabilistic argument.

Let us assume that a sequence has the following bias distribution: *DDDDAAAA*. Some locations (underlined) belong to triples with competing biases: *DDD**D**_A_AA**A**_*; let us examine one such contest point at the centre of triple 5. For this point, triples 4, 5 and 6 compete to set its bias. Even if all triples act purely parallel, the one to fire last gets the final opportunity to modify that location's bias. If we examine all contest points for the particular configuration set out above and enumerate all possibilities of alternative triple firing orders, it turns out that, there is a 1/3 probability that there will again be four As and four Ds and there is a 2/3 probability that either As or Ds will overwhelm the other.

However, establishing a majority of one sorting direction bias will, quite probably, create more triples of the same bias, increasing the probability that all triples will end up with the same bias. Eventually, this sorts the sequence.

2.2   A Global Sorting Direction Bias Delivers a Sorted Sequence

When all triples have the same sorting direction bias, any triple that is being picked to sort itself will contribute to the overall sorting.

A simple measure of unsorted-ness of any sequence is the number of alternating runs, as defined by the times one has to change the upwards or downwards direction when traversing the sequence, end-to-end. For example, the sequence $(3, 5, 6, 2)$ has 2 alternating runs; a triple can have at most 2 alternating runs.

Assume that one has achieved a global sorting direction bias of A (of course, no triple is aware that its bias is also a global one). Then, any time a triple is locally sorted, it either decreases the number of alternating runs of its extended neighborhood (and of the whole sequence, as a result) or it leaves that number unchanged. Each alternative has a probability of ½.

Now, consider a sequence of length n, where, in one parallel round, all triples sort themselves. Of course, we have no guarantee that the actual number distributions in these triples will mean that a particular local sorting will decrease the overall number of alternating runs with a probability of ½. However, we can approximate as $1/2^n$ the probability that no individual triple sorting will affect the overall sequence's number of alternating runs. Since this number converges very fast down to 0, an incremental improvement (decrease) of 1 in the unsorted-ness measure is almost certain to happen.

Note that, whenever large chunks of the sequence are already sorted, there exist fewer points which serve as ends of the alternating runs and the previous argument does not hold. But, to compensate for that, we note that the actual numbers of alternating runs is now much smaller itself, compared to when the sequence is shuffled. The number of alternating runs can be viewed as a potential function, which, at every point, strictly does not increase.

With a settled sorting direction bias, the maximum distance one number needs to travel is n-1, so $O(n)$ parallel steps suffice to sort the sequence. If we allow each triple to fire independently of each other and randomly, then it may take $O(n^2)$ individual triple local sorting operations to deliver the final sorted sequence.

2.3   Converging to a Global Sorting Direction Bias

Considering any triple in isolation, just one operation suffices to switch it to a common bias; any minority item cannot avoid having its flag overturned.

The next more complex case is to consider a quadruple with evenly distributed flags. When examined in triples, it will also have a global direction bias settled fast; the first step will change one flag and, then, a single flag cannot survive.

Things become more complicated with longer sequences. When examining an *ADDAA* quintuple, oscillations can occur *ad nauseam* between alternating configurations (for example, if we first examine a triple centered around a *D* item, then the majority of flags features a *D*, which can change again if we examine a triple centered around one of the remaining *A*s).

The probability of oscillations strictly decreases the longer we examine local triples and eventually one ends up in a sequence with a common flag; this happens because we have a Markov chain with two equilibrium distributions, all *A*s or all *D*s, whose stationary distribution (denoted as M^i for a square $n \times n$ matrix, with n being the length of sequence) converges to a single column of 1's. This is a probabilistic guarantee that all sub-sequences with the same flag will be eventually washed out.

$$M^i_{n \times n} = \begin{bmatrix} 1 & 0 & & \cdots & & 0 \\ 1 & 0 & & \cdots & & 0 \\ 1 & 0 & 0 & \cdots & 0 & 0 \\ {\scriptstyle i \to \infty} & {\scriptstyle i \to \infty} & {\scriptstyle i \to \infty} & & {\scriptstyle i \to \infty} & {\scriptstyle i \to \infty} \\ \vdots & 0 & \ddots & \cdots & \cdots & 0 \\ & {\scriptstyle i \to \infty} & & & & {\scriptstyle i \to \infty} \\ \vdots & \vdots & \vdots & & \vdots & \vdots \\ 1 & 0 & 0 & \cdots & \cdots & 0 \\ {\scriptstyle i \to \infty} & {\scriptstyle i \to \infty} & {\scriptstyle i \to \infty} & & & {\scriptstyle i \to \infty} \end{bmatrix}$$

Brief experimentation with several variants of the matrix above revealed that they converged within 1% of the stationary form in $O(n^3 \log n)$. But, as we shall see in the experimental section below, this is an unwarranted pessimistic estimate when compared to the average sorting time for a variety of sequences.

3   Experimental Validation

To validate the principle of Emerge-Sort we describe a series of experiments we have carried out across a range of input sizes and with several initial distributions of *A* and *D* biases.

We review in Table 1 the results for $n = 128$. Each line corresponds to 100 experiments. The **% A** column indicates the percentage of elements that have been initialized with an *A* sorting direction bias. It is reasonable, of course, that when a large majority of elements has the same sorting direction bias, there is a high probability that the sequence will eventually be sorted according to that bias. The **% sorted Ascending** column confirms just that.

Note that, as earlier argued, it is also reasonable that the faster all sequence elements converge to a common sorting direction bias, the faster it will be able to eventually sort itself. This is confirmed by the **# Rounds** column, which reports the individual number of triples examined. It is also confirmed by the **# Moves** columns, which shows how many numbers are moved per round on average. Since triples are fired at random, rounds are measured in terms of individual triple inspections.

Table 1. Results for $n = 128$ (100 experiments)

% A	% sorted Ascending	# Rounds	# Moves
99	100	4614	51
95	100	5163	52
90	99	6099	53
80	97	7778	58
70	96	9346	64
60	68	10697	74
55	63	10985	76
50	54	10949	76

We present in Fig. 2 a clear $O(n^2)$ pattern for larger values of n.

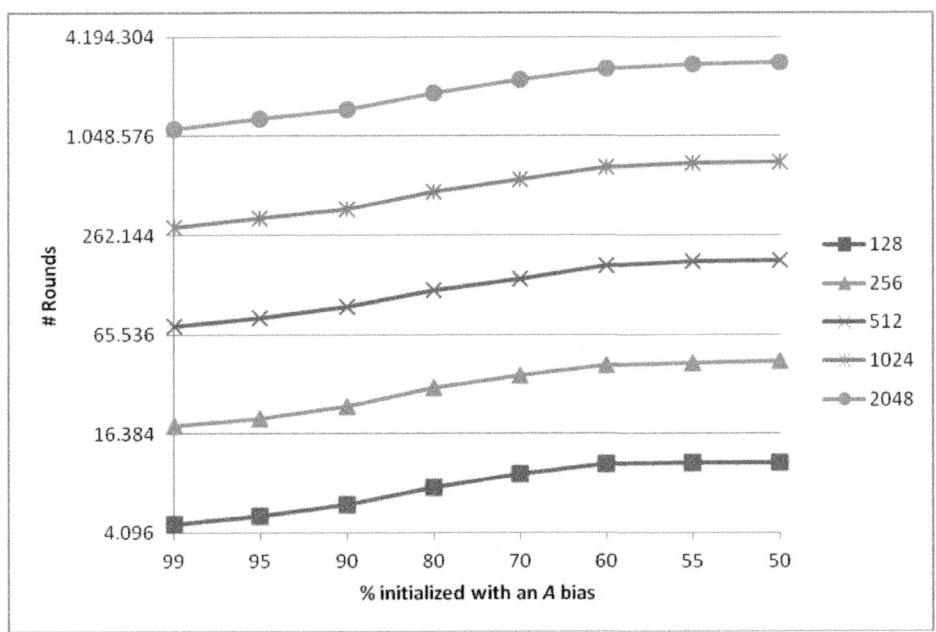

Fig. 2. Results for $n = 128, 256, 512, 1024, 2048$

4   Conclusions and Future Directions

We have described the concepts and a brief experimental validation of Emerge-sort, a sorting algorithm that does not depend on being told which way a sequence should be sorted and yet manages to sort that sequence, usually alongside a dominant preference among the sequence numbers, based on randomly applied simple local operators.

Emerge-sort closely follows the concepts of ant based algorithms, where sequences of numbers are societies of individuals who act locally and are unaware of the consequences of their actions on the sequence as a whole. Therein no shared knowledge, control or logic exists; individuals are only triggered into action via messaging by objects within their reach. Direction bias flags act as pheromones that are laid on the ground (this is the *stigmergy* concept), inviting others to follow a certain direction (this is the *chemotaxis* concept). Although the society has no hierarchies, large numbers can be viewed as foraging agents who influence others by helping settle direction issues (much like how taller children act when a group of children self-arranges itself in a circle according to height in a schoolyard). Furthermore, when a triple finds itself ordered it remains idle, being oblivious to a grander common global goal. But this delivers the $n/\log n$ penalty which this society pays for not having an *a priori* leader to settle the direction issue.

Research in Emerge-sort started as an experimental effort into investigating the dynamics of local operators regarding their ability to generate order. But, in computing, the trade-off between local operators and co-ordination has been studied in several directions, ranging from distributed systems to approximation algorithms and to algorithmic game theory, also drawing on cellular automata from computational physics. So, we expect that by studying Emerge-Sort alongside established and solidly founded paradigms we will be able to research termination and complexity issues of its algorithmic nature using arguments that may have been applied in these domains; this will also allow us to gain more insight into the crossing lines between such paradigms.

Acknowledgements. Loizos Michael and Ioannis Stamatiu have offered valuable comments on mathematical properties of card shuffling and ring networks. Emerge-Sort is fully implemented in Java and is available on demand for academic purposes. An earlier version was implemented in Maple. It is temporarily hosted at http://student-support2.ouc.ac.cy:8080/emergesort/index.html, where a few variants are also demonstrated.

References

1. Flocchini, P., Kranakis, E., Krizanc, D., Luccio, F.L., Santoro, N.: Sorting and election in anonymous asynchronous rings. Journal of Parallel and Distributed Computing 64, 254–265 (2004)
2. Prasath, R.: Algorithms for Distributed Sorting and Prefix Computation in Static Ad Hoc Mobile Networks. In: 2010 International Conference on Electronics and Information Engineering, vol. 2, pp. 144–148 (2010)
3. Israeli, A., Jalfon, M.: Uniform Self-Stabilizing Ring Orientation. Information and Computation 104(2-3), 175–196 (1993)
4. Casadei, M., Gardelli, L., Viroli, M.: Collective Sorting Tuple Spaces. In: 11th International Workshop on Cooperative Information Agents, Delft, The Netherlands, pp. 255–269 (2006)
5. Casadei, M., Menezes, R., Viroli, M., Tolksdorf, R.: Using Ant's Brood Sorting to Increase Fault Tolerance in Linda's Tuple Distribution Mechanism. In: Klusch, M., Hindriks, K.V., Papazoglou, M.P., Sterling, L. (eds.) CIA 2007. LNCS (LNAI), vol. 4676, pp. 255–269. Springer, Heidelberg (2007)

6. Bénézit, F., Thiran, P., Vetterli, M.: The Distributed Multiple Voting Problem. IEEE Journal of Selected Topics in Signal Processing 5(4), 791–804 (2011)
7. Bonabeau, E., Theraulaz, G., Deneubourg, J.-L.: Fixed Response Thresholds and the Regulation of Division of Labour in Insect Societies. Bulletin of Mathematical Biology 60, 753–807 (1998)
8. Bonabeau, E., Dorigo, M., Theraulaz, G.: Swarm Intelligence: From Natural to Artificial Systems. Oxford University Press, New York (1999)
9. Handl, J., Meyer, B.: Ant-based and swarm-based clustering. Swarm Intelligence 1(2), 95–113 (2008)
10. Babaoglu, O., Canright, G., Deutsch, A., Di Caro, G., Ducatelle, F., Gambardella, L., Ganguly, N., Jelasity, M., Montemanni, R., Montresor, A., Urnes, T.: Design patterns from biology to distributed computing. ACM Transactions on Autonomous and Adaptive Systems 1(1), 26–66 (2006)
11. Koutsoupias, E., Papadimitriou, C.: Worst case equilibria. In: Annual Symposium on Theoretical Aspects of Computer, pp. 404–413. Springer (1999)
12. Dijkstra, E.W.: Self-stabilizing systems in spite of distributed control. Communications of the ACM 17(11), 643–644 (1974)
13. Loui, M.C.: The complexity of sorting on distributed systems. Information and Control 60, 70–85 (1984)
14. Gonzaga de Sa, P., Maes, C.: The Gacs-Kurdyumov-Levin automaton revisited. Journal of Statistical Physics 67(3-4), 507–522 (1992)
15. Gordillo, J.L., Luna, J.V.: Parallel sort on a linear array of cellular automata. In: International Conference on Systems, Man and Cybernetics, vol. 2, pp. 1903–1907 (1994)
16. Mitchell, M., Hraber, P.T., Crutchfield, J.P.: Revisiting the edge of chaos: Evolving cellular automata to perform computations. Complex Systems 7, 89–130 (1993)
17. Andre, D., Bennett III, F.H., Koza, J.R.: Discovery by genetic programming of a cellular automata rule that is better than any known rule for the majority classification problem. In: First Annual Conference on Genetic Programming, Stanford, CA, pp. 3–11 (1996)
18. Boyd, S., Ghosh, A., Prabhakar, B., Shah, D.: Gossip algorithms: Design, analysis and applications. In: 24th Annual Joint Conference of the IEEE and Communication Societies, pp. 1653–1664 (2005)
19. Kempe, D., Dobra, A., Gehrke, J.: Gossip-based computation of aggregate information. In: IEEE Conference on Foundations of Computer Science, pp. 482–491 (2003)

iThink: A Library for Classical Planning in Video-Games

Vassileios-Marios Anastassiou, Panagiotis Diamantopoulos,
Stavros Vassos, and Manolis Koubarakis

Department of Informatics and Telecommunications
National and Kapodistrian University of Athens
Athens 15784, Greece
{astyanax,panos_10d,stavrosv,koubarak}@di.uoa.gr

Abstract. Academic artificial intelligence (AI) techniques have recently started to play a more central role in the development of commercial video games. In particular, classical planning methods for specifying a goal-oriented behavior have proven to be useful to game developers in an increasingly number of cases. Motivated by the fact that there is no clear standard for developing a goal-oriented behavior in video games, we present iThink, a framework that allows the use of academic techniques for classical planning in order to achieve goal-oriented behavior in a real game developing environment. In our work we focus on STRIPS, a well-studied framework for classical planning, and Unity3D, a popular game engine that is becoming an emerging standard for, so-called, "indie" game development. Except for being a useful tool for game developers, we believe that iThink can be used in education, providing a modern and fun environment for learning and experimenting with classical planning.

1 Introduction

Traditionally, the artificial intelligence (AI) methods used in video games have not relied on techniques that have been developed in the academic field of AI. Essentially, game developers create an illusion of intelligence using a few programming tricks without the need to rely on deliberation or other sophisticated techniques from academic AI [6,13]. As a fast and robust implementation is very critical for the video game industry, this approach proved to be effective and convenient. In particular, this meant that for most video games the behavior of non-player characters (NPCs) involved a number of pre-programmed responses that vary depending on conditions about the game-world and the player.

This was not a problem for many years as the video game industry was able to evolve remarkably well based on the advances in other areas such as computer graphics whose impact on the game-play was celebrated by the players. The design of more challenging NPCs was typically counter-weighed by giving them more power than the human players (e.g., extra strength or speed, omniscience). Nonetheless, it seems that in the last few years the game industry has reached a point where more sophisticated techniques for NPC behavior are necessary. This

I. Maglogiannis, V. Plagianakos, and I. Vlahavas (Eds.): SETN 2012, LNAI 7297, pp. 106–113, 2012.
© Springer-Verlag Berlin Heidelberg 2012

has been acknowledged both by gamers who thirst for smarter opponents that give the perception of truly autonomous human-like entities with their own agendas and realistic acting and sensing capabilities [4,7], as well as game developers who seek a scalable, maintainable, and reusable decision-making framework for implementing NPCs as the complexity of the game-world increases [9].

A notable academic AI technique that proved to be useful for this purpose is *classical planning*, which is often referred to in video game industry as *goal-oriented action planning (GOAP)*. The main idea of this technique is to provide an NPC with a set of *actions*, a description of the *effects* of these actions in the game-world, and a *goal* the NPC should try to achieve by using the available actions. This approach has received much attention in the video game industry mainly due to the noted case of the commercial game "F.E.A.R." [8] that used a simplified version of STRIPS planning [3] for NPC behavior.

The implementation of STRIPS planning in the game of "F.E.A.R" relies on important restrictions and optimizations in order to achieve real-time performance. Similarly, in subsequent games that planning has been used, the implementation is game-specific and cannot easily be reused in other games. On the other hand, existing academic frameworks for classical planning that aim for generality, such as planners that conform to the Planning Domain Definition Language (PDDL) [5], cannot be directly used in a game engine: apart from performance issues that cannot be easily overcome (e.g., academic planners typically assume no restrictions in memory resources), a major problem is connecting the *"real"* objects in a game-world with their corresponding *"symbolic"* ones in the underlying logic-based representation used for planning.

In this paper we address the practical problem of providing an planning framework that can be used in a wide game development environment. We report on our work on developing iThink, a STRIPS planning framework that aims for generality, ease of use, and is integrated in a real game engine. iThink is targeted to Unity3D, a popular game engine that is becoming an emerging standard for, so-called, "indie" game development but is also used in "AAA" titles, that is, commercial games of the highest quality. Except for being a useful tool for game developers, we believe that iThink can be used in education, providing a modern and fun environment for learning and experimenting with classical planning.

The rest of the paper is organized as follows. In Section 2 we go over the basic details of STRIPS planning. In Section 3 we present the iThink framework that implements STRIPS planning in the game engine Unity3D. In Sections 4 and 5 we discuss related and future work, and in Section 6 we draw some conclusions.

2   STRIPS Planning

In the area of classical planning one is faced with the following task: given i) a complete specification of the *initial state* of the world, ii) a set of *action schemas* that describe how the world may change, and iii) a *goal condition*, one has to find a sequence of actions such that when applied one after the other in the initial state, they transform the state into one that satisfies the goal condition.

In this work we focus on the STRIPS formalism for representing planning tasks [3]. In STRIPS, the representation of the initial state, the action schemas, and the goal condition is based on literals from predicate logic. For example, in a video game scenario the positive literal $Gun(o)$ may be used to represent that o is a gun, and $Holding(knife_{23})$ to represent the fact that the NPC is holding a particular knife. Similarly, the negative literal $\neg Holding(o)$ may be used to represent that the NPC is not holding the gun o.

The *initial state* is specified as a set of positive literals. This set provides a complete specification of the state based on a *closed-world assumption*. That is, for all ground literals not included in the set, it is assumed that the negative version of the literal is true. The *actions* then of the domain affect the current state by means of adding and deleting literals. For example, $pick\text{-}up(o, room_1)$ may be used to represent the action of the NPC picking up the gun o that is located in $room_1$, which affects the current state by adding the literal $Holding(o)$.

The *action schemas* are the general rules that specify the available ground actions in the domain. For $pick\text{-}up(o, room_1)$, the corresponding action schema may look like $pick\text{-}up(x_1, x_2)$, followed by two sets of literals that specify the preconditions and the effects of any particular action that is a ground instance of this schema. The set of preconditions specifies what literals need to be present in a state in order for the action to be executable in that state. The set of effects specifies how the state should be transformed when the action is executed: positive literals are added in the state description, and negative literals are removed.

Finally, a *goal condition* is also a set of positive literals, and the intuition is that the goal is satisfied in a state if all the literals listed in the goal condition are included in the set that describes the state. A solution then to a planning problem is a *sequence of actions* such that if they are executed sequentially starting from the initial state, checking for corresponding preconditions and applying the effects of each action one after the other, they lead to a state description that satisfies the goal condition.

In the next section we will present iThink, a framework for STRIPS planning that is embedded in the Unity3D game developing environment.

3   The iThink Framework in Unity3D

Unity3D[1] is an integrated authoring tool that provides out-of-the-box functionality for building video-games and simulations. Unity3D implements a full-featured high-quality game engine, and provides tools for developing and managing content. The developers can code the functionality of the game-world using Javascript, C#, and Boo (a python-inspired .Net language), in a programming environment that is based on the FOSS Mono platform.

A free license supporting a basic feature set is available, providing easy access to any developer. Along with its potential portability across different systems, Unity3D is a promising ground for easy development and deployment of educational, research or commercial projects. The features of Unity3D along with

---

[1] http://unity3d.com/

the increasing popularity and the extensive documentation freely available online led us to choose Unity3D as the ideal game developing environment for implementing iThink.

3.1 iThink Overview

The development of iThink was done with two goals in mind. The first one concerns game developing and aims for ease of use and modularity for the programmers, while the second concerns academic research and aims for providing the ground for studying planning techniques in a real software development setting. In order to achieve these (sometimes contradictory) goals, we had to make a few compromises so as to serve both worlds.

iThink provides the necessary methods for specifying a STRIPS planning problem about elements of the game-world in Unity3D. As STRIPS is based on predicate logic, we had to come up with a convenient way of initializing logical literals that refer directly to objects in the software programming sense. For this purpose we utilized the tag functionality of Unity3D according to which any object of the game-world (including items, way-points, NPCs, and the human player) may be associated with a number of tags. Using the integrated developing environment of Unity3D, a developer can specify easily the types of available objects, which iThink can then use for planning purposes. For instance, for a particular object o that is tagged with the label "gun", the literal $Gun(o)$ will be added to the iThink knowledge base to be used for planning purposes.

The initial state of the planning problem is specified using literals that are built automatically using the specified tags, as well as others that are specified by the developer via appropriate methods. Similarly, the goal condition is specified by the developer as a set of literals. The tag functionality is also used in the specification of action schema strings in order to restrict the generated actions to those that make sense in the current state of the game-world. For example, the $pick\text{-}up(x_1, x_2)$ action schema may only be used to instantiate actions where x_1 is an item and x_2 a location of the game-world.

As far as finding a solution to a planning problem is concerned, iThink provides methods for employing a forward-search method that works in the state-space in a breadth-first or depth-first manner for the uninformed case and a best-first manner when a heuristic is provided[12]. Note that iThink is general enough to allow the implementation of other available methods for classical planning as well. iThink classes are organized in a way that can be easily extended and adapted to meet the particular needs of the developer. Each iThink class implements an atomic building block for representing STRIPS planning problems in Unity3D and effectively searching for solutions. The most important classes of iThink are presented in the next section. The full implementation is available online at the project's webpage: `http://code.google.com/p/ithink-unity3d/`

3.2 Implementation Details of iThink

The core functionality of iThink is implemented in nine C# classes as follows.

```
 1  public class SimpleFPSAgent : MonoBehaviour
 2  {
 3      iThinkBrain brain;
 4      public string[] schemaList = {
 5          "ActionMove-3-Tag~loc-Tag~loc-Tag~dir",
 6          "ActionTurn-2-Tag~dir-Tag~dir",
 7          "ActionShoot-4-Tag~loc-Tag~loc-Tag~dir-Tag~gun",
 8          "ActionStab-2-Tag~loc-Tag~knife",
 9          "PickUp-2-Tag~knife-Tag~loc",
10          "ActionPickUp-2-Tag~gun-Tag~loc"
11      };
12      public void Awake() //executed when NPC is constructed
13      {
14          brain = new iThinkBrain();
15
16          List<String> tags = new List<String>();
17          tags.Add("dir"); tags.Add("loc"); tags.Add("player");
18          tags.Add("npc"); tags.Add("gun"); tags.Add("knife");
19          brain.sensorySystem.OmniUpdate(this.gameObject, tags);
20
21          brain.ActionManager = new iThinkActionManager();
22          brain.ActionManager.initActionList(
23              this.gameObject,
24              schemaList,
25              brain.getKnownObjects(),
26              brain.getKnownFacts()
27          );
28      }
29      public void Update() //executed at every frame of the game
30      {
31          //... code that specifies the initial state and goal
32
33          brain.planner.forwardSearch(   //invokes planner
34              brain.startState,
35              brain.goalState,
36              brain.ActionManager,
37              1); //specifies the search method
38          brain.planner.getPlan().debugPrintPlan();
39
40          //... code that uses the plan for NPC behavior
41      }
42  }
```

Fig. 1. Example of iThink usage in a simplified game-world

- **iThinkFact** is used to specify STRIPS literals. An iThinkFact instance specifies the predicate name of the literal, a collection of game objects as the arguments of the literal, and the polarity of the literal (positive or negative).
- **iThinkState** is used to specify STRIPS states. An iThinkState instance is simply a set of literals, i.e., iThinkFacts instances.

- **iThinkAction** is used to specify ground actions. An iThinkAction instance specifies the name of the action, a set of preconditions as a set of positive literals, and a set of effects as a set of positive and negative literals.
- **iThinkActionSchema** is used to specify STRIPS action schemas. An instance of iThinkActionSchema specifies the name of the action schema, the number of arguments, and the type of objects that can be used as arguments when generating a ground action using the schema. This information is given to the constructor of the class using a properly formatted string.
- **iThinkActionManager** generates and stores a collection of all the available ground actions that can be generated using the information about the available action schemas and the iThink knowledge base of available objects.
- **iThinkSensorySystem** facilitates an automatic generation of literals that describe the current state of the game-world using Unity3D tags on objects.
- **iThinkPlan** is used to specify STRIPS plans, that is, solutions to a STRIPS planning problem. An instance of iThinkPlan specifies a sequence of actions, i.e. iThinkAction instances, and is also used to represent partial plans.
- **iThinkPlanner** provides search utilities and is responsible for the execution of the planning process. Currently, a forward-search method is implemented that works in a breadth-first or depth-first manner for uninformed search and in a best-first manner when a heuristic is provided.
- **iThinkBrain** is the main class that manages a planning problem using the other iThink classes. iThinkBrain can be the basis of specifying any planning problem that concerns objects of the game-world.

We proceed to show the usage of iThink with an example involving an NPC.

3.3   iThink Usage Example

An intended use of iThink is to associate an instance of iThinkBrain with an NPC. In this case, whenever the NPC needs to find a high-level plan for achieving a goal in the game-world, the implementation of the NPC can use the iThink functionality to update the initial state of the planning problem according to the current state of the game-world, specify a goal, and use the available planning methods to find a sequence of actions that achieves this goal.

In Figure 1 we show an example, omitting some details due to space limitations. The main tasks that the developer needs to do are the following.

1. Define an NPC class that contains an iThinkBrain object (lines 1–3).
2. Specify, as properly formatted strings, the action schemas that iThinkBrain will evaluate. The strings show the available actions and the types of objects of the game-world that can be used to initialize them (lines 4–11).
3. In the initialization of the NPC, use a sensor method of iThinkSensorySystem to identify the available objects of the game-world (lines 16–19), and initialize the iThinkActionManager that generates the available actions (lines 21–27).
4. In the method that updates the behavior of the NPC, inform iThinkBrain about the initial state and the desired goal condition to pursue (insert code at line 31), invoke the iThinkBrain planner (lines 33–38), and then use the result to specify the NPC behavior (insert code at line 40).

4   Related Work

There are many implementations of planning techniques in the literature. The novelty of iThink is that it departs from the strictly symbolic approach typically adopted in academic AI and aims for a planning capability that operates directly on the software programming objects. In order to embed the symbolic STRIPS approach in Unity3D in a way that is easy to inter-operate with the existing methods and tools of the developing environment, we had to deal with problems that are usually not considered in academic AI research. This is often no easy task and our approach succeeded in remaining faithful to the original STRIPS formalism, while providing a programming framework that expresses the logical background of STRIPS using familiar constructs such as tags and variables.

Similarly, there are a few approaches that attempt the incorporation of GOAP in video games. Orkin used a simplified STRIPS approach in the notable case of the game "F.E.A.R.' [8]. Bjarnolf investigated threat analysis using a GOAP system that worked in an "Observe, Orient, Decide, Act" manner [1]. Long compared a GOAP implementation with a finite-state machine implementations, suggesting that planning techniques are superior when considering both practicality and performance [2]. Peikidis investigated the application of GOAP techniques in a strategy game [10] and Pittman studied command hierarchies in a GOAP setting as a solution to code maintenance issues [11].

All these approaches follow closely the architectural decisions of F.E.A.R in order to achieve real-time efficiency. Nonetheless, these approaches are based on strong simplifications of the STRIPS paradigm that drastically reduce the expressiveness of the approach. Moreover, each approach focuses on specific game constructs and details, essentially making it appropriate only for the particular application case. In contrast, iThink aims for generality and modularity. By being faithful to the STRIPS logical background, iThink provides a powerful framework for representing different planning environments in Unity3D.

5   Future Work and Extensions

Our ultimate goal is to evolve iThink into an efficient AI module that can be used in the development of commercial video games. For our future work we intend to implement and experiment with heuristic planning methods that are specifically tailored for particular video game genres, such as for example the first-person shooter (FPS) genre. We also want to investigate how iThink may be extended to account for planning that involves multiple agents using a blackboard architecture and the possibility of taking advantage of multi-threading for achieving better performance and response times.

There are also some parts of iThink that we want to improve, such as for example the way the action schemas are specified in the current version. Our intention is to fully integrate iThink in the Unity3D editor so that the developer can specify such information using a visual interface that will further simplify the modeling of the underlying planning domain. Along these lines, we also plan on building debugging tools for testing and visualizing the planning process.

6   Conclusions

Classical planning has proven to be useful for achieving a dynamic, emergent behavior for NPCs in video games. Our approach is a novel way of employing academic techniques for classical planning in a real video game developing environment. iThink aims for generality and modularity, providing the means for specifying a wide range of planning problems according to the particular needs of game developing. Except for being a useful tool for game developers, we believe that iThink can be used in education, providing a modern and fun environment for learning and experimenting with classical planning.

References

1. Bjarnolf, P.: Threat analysis using goal-oriented action planning. B.Sc. Thesis, University of Skovde, School of Humanities and Informatics (2008)
2. Edmund, L.: Enhanced NPC Behaviour using Goal Oriented Action Planning. Master's thesis, University of Abertay Dundee, School of Computing and Advanced Technologies, Division of Software Engineering (2007)
3. Fikes, R.E., Nilsson, N.J.: STRIPS: A new approach to the application of theorem proving to problem solving. Artificial Intelligence 2, 189–208 (1971)
4. Funge, J.D.: Artificial Intelligence For Computer Games: An Introduction. A.K. Peters, Ltd., MA (2004)
5. Mcdermott, D., Ghallab, M., Howe, A., Knoblock, C., Ram, A., Veloso, M., Weld, D., Wilkins, D.: PDDL - the planning domain definition language. Tech. rep., CVC TR-98-003/DCS TR-1165, Yale Center for Comp. Vision and Control (1998)
6. Millington, I., Funge, J.: Artificial Intelligence for Games, 2nd edn. Morgan Kaufmann Publishers Inc., San Francisco (2009)
7. Nareyek, A.: Artificial intelligence in computer games - State of the art and future directions. ACM Queue 10(1), 58–65 (2004)
8. Orkin, J.: Three states and a plan: The AI of F.E.A.R. In: Proceedings of the Game Developer's Conference, GDC (2006)
9. Orkin, J.: Agent architecture considerations for Real-Time planning in games. In: Artificial Intelligence & Interactive Digital Entertainment, AIIDE (2005)
10. Peikidis, P.: Demonstrating the use of planning in a video game. B.Sc. Thesis, University of Sheffield, CITY Liberal Studies, Dept. of Computer Science (2010)
11. Pittman, D.L.: Enhanced NPC Behaviour using Goal Oriented Action Planning. Master's thesis, University of Nebraska-Lincoln (2007)
12. Russell, S.J., Norvig, P.: Artificial Intelligence: A Modern Approach, 2nd edn. Prentice Hall (2002)
13. Schaeffer, J., Bulitko, V., Buro, M.: Bots get smart. IEEE Spectrum 45(12), 44–49 (2008)

Detecting Human Features in Summaries – Symbol Sequence Statistical Regularity

George Giannakopoulos[1], Vangelis Karkaletsis[1], and George A. Vouros[2]

[1] Software and Knowledge Engineering Laboratory,
National Center of Scientific Research "Demokritos", Greece
{ggianna,vangelis}@iit.demokritos.gr
[2] Department of Digital Systems, University of Pireaus, Greece
georgev@unipi.gr

Abstract. The presented work studies textual summaries, aiming to detect the qualities of human multi-document summaries, in contrast to automatically extracted ones. The measured features are based on a generic statistical regularity measure, named Symbol Sequence Statistical Regularity (*SSR*). The measure is calculated over both character and word n-grams of various ranks, given a set of human and automatically extracted multi-document summaries from two different corpora. The results of the experiments indicate that the proposed measure provides enough distinctive power to discriminate between the human and non-human summaries. The results hint on the qualities a human summary holds, increasing intuition related to how a good summary should be generated.

1 Introduction

In the domain of natural language processing numerous attempts have been made to identify what is the set of qualities that renders a text understandable and fluent. This problem has been apparent in machine translation (MT), natural language generation (NLG) and automatic summarization. In addition, linguists and tutors have been grading various degrees of fluency of given texts, usually judging L2 authors (authors judged on their second, non-native, language). Within this study we focus on a notion of regularity, apparently a concept related to grammaticality and fluency more than other textual features.

Grammaticality is the quality of conforming to a given grammar. Fluency, on the other hand, is referred to mostly as a measure of text production or reading rate – *i.e.* fluent writers write more quickly than less fluent ones [3] and fluent readers read faster than non-fluent ones. However, the notion of fluency has also been used to describe well-formed, easily understood text [17].

In existing bibliography, there are methods that use grammaticality as a measure of acceptability [1]. Similarly, grammaticality has been considered to be a measure of performance for machine translation systems [9] and summarization systems [6]. The quantification of grammaticallity is a non-trivial task, which has led various researchers towards methodologies concerning the calculation of a grammaticality measure. Most approaches stand upon either parsers [17] or constraint satisfaction models [13].

I. Maglogiannis, V. Plagianakos, and I. Vlahavas (Eds.): SETN 2012, LNAI 7297, pp. 114–123, 2012.
© Springer-Verlag Berlin Heidelberg 2012

In summary texts, the grammar considered for grammaticality is that of the used language (*e.g.* English). In our approach, we do not use a given grammar: we use a measure we term Symbol Sequence Statistical Regularity (*SSSR*). This measure indicates, in a graded fashion, whether sequences of symbols (*e.g.* words, characters) have been found to be neighbours in a manner similar to the sequences in a set of given, training texts. With the use of *SSSR*, we try to determine statistically the differences of human and automatic summary texts, to gain intuition required to create better summarization systems.

The rest of the paper is structured as follows. In section 2 we provide background information and a brief review of related works. Then, we present the Symbol Sequence Statistical Regularity definition, along with the proposed methodology for its usage, in section 3. Experiments follow, in section 4, providing the validation of our anaysis. We close the paper with the conclusions and the lessons learned from the study, in section 5.

2   Related Work

In the research quest for fluency and grammaticality evaluation, the works of various linguists and philosophers concerning grammars and acceptability have provided both the foundations and a constant source of research. The work of N. Chomsky for many years has delved upon the notion of grammaticality [4,5]. Both in statistical as well as non-statistical aspects of grammaticality, it has been considered that there can be either a binary decision upon whether a text segment is grammatical, or a graded decision.

Research considering how grammaticality can be graded in a non-binary way has treated grammar as a set of constraints that are either realized or not within a text. There have been distinctions between soft and hard constraints, related to how important a constraint is to the acceptability of a clause [13,22]. Much of the existing work has been based on Optimality Theory (see [21]), which declares that output language is based on a procedure that uses a "candidate analysis" generation function, called *GEN* and a *harmonic* evaluation function, called *H-eval*, which evaluates candidates according to a harmony criterion. The GEN function is part of a Universal Grammar that generates candidate alternatives of analysis for the input, while and the H-eval function is created based on well-formedness rules of a given language. The methodology using GEN and H-eval describes a loop between the two components, until no analysis generated by GEN can give better harmonical results.

In [1], we find an approach based on Property Grammars, which is also a constraint based syntactic formalism. Using Property Grammars tha authors, in the process of analysis, detect the number of properties related to a constituent. Then, these properties are evaluated, and a quantization is performed by measuring the number of violations, non-violations and the number of all the properties evaluated. Highly grammatical text chunks will have a low number of violations for a given set of evaluated properties. The method also applies constraint weighting, which has been used in other works as well [22]. The output is a *grammaticality index* that is shown to correlate to human acceptability evaluations.

From the domain of machine translation, we find the X-Score evaluation process [9], which computes a "target language", consisting of morphology and relationships extracted from a model corpus called "fluency corpus". Then a tagger is used to apply morhological and relation tags to terms of the evaluated text. The assumption used by the authors of X-Score is that the fluency score of a text should be linearly dependent on the frequencies of tags. A prediction function is estimated based on the fluency corpus and then the function is applied to the frequencies of tags of any evaluated text, returning the estimated fluency index of the evaluated text. In the work described in [17] the prediction of acceptability is viewed as a machine learning problem, where the output of a set of parsers is used as input to a learner, trying to discern human from machine generated sentences. Then, the distance of evaluated texts from the support vectors output by the SVM learner determine a metric that correlates to human judgements of fluency.

Here, we should note that a number of other methods of evaluation have been used in the domain of summarization and machine translation, like the ROUGE/BE family of evaluators [14,10] or their "Machine Translation"-related predecessor BLEU [19]. These use word n-grams or sets of terms (*e.g.* head-relation pairs) extracted from the evaluated text and compare them to similarly extracted n-grams or sets of terms from a model corpus. Then, recall and precision related measures can be used to evaluate the given text. These methods however, together with they Pyramid method [20] and the AutoSummENG family of methods [8,7], are mostly meant to evaluate content and not grammaticality.

Studies that analyse human summarization in order to understand the process have been conducted in the past, revealing the abstractive nature of human summarization. In [11], the section on Corpus Analysis indicates that a number of sentences in human summary texts had no equivalent in the source documents. Furthermore, most of the sentences that indeed had an equivalent in the original texts were transformed and combined in various ways to form the summary. Various aspects of the summarization process have been examined in [18] as well, in terms of the processes that define the content and the methodology of rewriting sentences. A series of studies, also apparent in [6], show that automatic systems lack in various domains of text quality, even though they do well in content selection.

The state of the art contains various kinds of evaluators concerning grammaticality and fluency, which are both indicators of acceptability and regularity of text. Our method is related to various of these evaluators, because it: uses a model corpus; derives patterns from the model corpus; uses machine learning methods to discriminate between human and machine-generated texts. The differentiating factors of the presented method, on the other hand, are the following. First, we do not extract a grammar from a text; we determine *regularity*, given an input corpus. This regularity may correlate to various qualities that render a text normal and not only grammar. Second, we do not apply preprocessing of any kind to the input text. Only word splitting is used, *if* we want to use word n-grams. Third, our method requires no underlying language knowledge. This way it functions independently of language. The model of *regularity* is extracted from a given corpus. Fourth, we use sub-word structure information, by the use of character n-grams. Last, the method supports variable granularity, allowing to detect different types of regularity, from word spelling to syntax.

At this point, we want to focus on the fact that the presented study used the analysis methodology as a *means* to derive important lessons. Therefore, we have not studied in full the application spectrum of the analysis method itself.

3 Symbol Sequence Statistical Regularity

In order to analyse the differences between human summary texts and automatically generated ones, we have created a representation of text that includes sequence information. We wanted our representation to be parametric in terms of desired granularity and also allow comparison between its instances. We also wanted to add the ability to cope with fuzziness and ambiguity of expression.

The produced representation, which we call Statistical Symbol Sequence Representation (*SSS-Rep*), is *a set of triples*, including a *pair* and *a corresponding distribution for each pair*. The first part F of each pair is a sequence of symbols; each symbol can in fact be either a single letter, a word or a whole sentence. The second part S is a single symbol[1]. The distribution D for a given pair describes the number of co-occurences of F and S in the text as a function of distance between them, up to a maximum distance d_{max}. This distance is measured as the (integer) number of symbols from F to S in the text, so if we talk about words the distance is measured in words, if we talk about characters, in characters. From now on we denote such a representation as a set of triplets in the form: $F \to S(D)$, where $D \equiv$ (distance1 $\Rightarrow$ numberOfOccurences1|distance2 $\Rightarrow$ numberOfOccurences2...) in a sparse distribution representation. $D(x)$ identifies the number of occurences for a given distance x. We cosider $\mathbb{D}$ to be the powerset of sparse distribution representations. So, if distance1 is 1 and distance2 is 4 and their numberOfOccurences are 2, 5 correspondingly, then we have found 2 times S to be in a distance of 1 from F in the text and 5 times in a distance of 4.

The *SSS-Rep* has a set of parameters, indicative of its granularity and fuzziness: the r-gram rank r of F, the maximum distance d_{max} of co-occurence as well as the type of symbol (*e.g.* character, word, sentence). Thus, we will use the form *SSS-Rep*(r, d_{max}, symbolType) to fully describe an *SSS-Rep* and we will call every triplet that can be derived from a given *SSS-Rep* an *instance of* SSS-Rep.

Example 1. The sentence:
"A_big_big_test."
is represented as *SSS-Rep*(1,1,character) by:
$t \to e(1 \Rightarrow 1.0); \_ \to b(1 \Rightarrow 2.0); A \to \_(1 \Rightarrow 1.0); \_ \to t(1 \Rightarrow 1.0); b \to i(1 \Rightarrow 2.0); t \to .(1 \Rightarrow 1.0); e \to s(1 \Rightarrow 1.0); g \to \_(1 \Rightarrow 2.0); s \to t(1 \Rightarrow 1.0); i \to g(1 \Rightarrow 2.0)$
while in *SSS-Rep*(2,2,word) by:
$big, big \to test(1 \Rightarrow 1.0); a, big \to test(2 \Rightarrow 1.0); a, big \to big(1 \Rightarrow 1.0)$
    We say that the first set of triplets is an *instance of SSS-Rep*(1,1,character), while the second an *instance of SSS-Rep*(2,2,word).

We note that, essentialy, *SSS-Rep*(1,1,word) can directly map to a bigram language model [15]. Thus, some *SSS-Rep* configurations are n-gram language models. However, in general *SSS-Rep* configurations are not n-gram models. The study of the exact

---

[1] Using a single symbol in the second part allows efficient calculation of the *SSS-Rep*.

relation between *SSS-Rep* and n-gram models is, however, outside the scope of this work.

Having defined *SSS-Rep*, we define a measure of similarity between two instances of an *SSS-Rep*, given the fact that they share the *same parameters*. First we prepare our functional tools:

If T_1, T_2 are two instances of *SSS-Rep*$(r, d_{max}, symbolType)$, we define the membership operator:

$$SSS\text{-}Rep(r, d_{max}, \text{symbolType}) \vdash T_1 \iff$$
$$T_1 \dashv SSS\text{-}Rep(r, d_{max}, \text{symbolType}) \iff$$
$$T_1\text{is an instance of } SSS\text{-}Rep(r, d_{max}, \text{symbolType}) \iff$$
$$T_1 = \{(x, y, z) : \text{isA}(y, \text{symbolType}),$$
$$\text{isNGramOf}(x, \text{symbolType}), \text{rank}(x) = r,$$
$$\{z\} \in \mathbb{D}\}$$

where rank(x) gives the n-gram rank of x, and isA$(x, \text{symbolType})$ returns true if x is a symbol of type symbolType and isNGramOf$(y, \text{symbolType})$ returns true if y is a sequence of symbols $y = \{y_1, y_2, ..., y_n\}, n \in \mathbb{N}^* : \forall 1 \leq i \leq n, i \in \mathbb{N}, \text{isA}(y_i, symbolType)$.

We also define a membership function connecting triplets to an *SSS-Rep* instance T: $A \equiv (F \to S(D)) \in T \iff$ there exists an identical triplet A in the set of triples representing T.

We define a similarity measure *sim* between distributions D_1, D_2, even though existing similarity measures like KL-divergence or chi-square can be used as well. We used a simple sum of absolute differences, because it cost less processing time to calculate. In fact the similarity between two distributions is the sum of the absolute differences *for all the non-zero elements for either distribution*. If X are the values of $\{x : D_1(x) > 0 \text{ or } D_2(x) > 0\}$, then: $sim(D_1, D_2) = \sum_{i \in X}(abs(D_1(i) - D_2(i)))$, where abs is the absolute value function.

On the same basis, the similarity of two triplets A, A', simT(A, A') equals to the similarity of their distributions D, D', sim(D, D') if the two first elements of the triples are identical, else we define simT$(A, A') = 0$. For T_1, T_2,
$T_1 \dashv SSS\text{-}Rep(r, d_{max}, \text{symbolType})$,
$T_2 \dashv SSS\text{-}Rep(r, d_{max}, \text{symbolType})$ we define the regularity function of T_1 given T_2 and its corresponding operator "$\sim$":

Definition 1. $T_1 \sim T_2 \equiv$
$regularity(T1|T2) = \frac{\sum_{A \in T_1, A' \in T_2} sim(A, A')}{|T_1|}$, *where* $|T_1|$ *is the number of triplets in* T_1. *We use the* $|T_1|$ *in the denominator because* T_1 *is the triplet judged and* T_2 *the a-priori evidence: we need the regularity function to be anti-symmetrical.*

In order to define the *SSS-Rep* of a corpus $C = T_1, T_2, ..., T_n, n \in \mathbb{N}^*$, we can simply concatenate the corpus texts in a single super-text. Given this definition, we can also define the comparison between a corpus and a text, by comparing the corresponding super-document and the document *SSS-Reps*. This is what we call *SSSR*.

4   Experiments

The data on which our experiments were conducted were the summary and evaluation corpus of DUC 2006. The corpus consists of summaries for 50 different topics, as well as the corresponding 25 input documents per topic from which the summaries were generated. Each topic had a number of automatically extracted summaries, one for each participating system, and 4 human created summaries. The human summaries were differentiated by means of an identifier, as were the baseline system summaries, which originated from a baseline system created by NIST, which simply took the first 250 words of the most recent document for each topic. All summaries were truncated to 250 words before being evaluated. To verify some of our experiments using a second corpus, we have used the corpus of DUC 2007 as well. The corpus, similarly to the one of DUC 2006, consists of summaries for 45 different topics. All topics had 4 human summaries each, as well as 28 machine generated summaries. In the corpora the human summaries appeared both as models and peers (i.e., twice each). In this study we have kept both duplicates of human summaries as "human" instances, so the count of human summaries will appear to be double the expected.

In order to use baseline-quality texts, we created a single automatic summary for each topic in the DUC2006 corpus. The summary was created by randomly adding words from the 25 input documents in a way that the statistics of the words (frequency) would tend to be the same as the input documents. The length of the summaries is about 250 words (length chosen from a Poisson distribution averaging to 250).

To determine whether the presented methodology extracts features that discern between human and automatic summaries, we have conducted the following process over two different corpora. For a given topic, the set of input documents were analysed to determine the $\{SSS\text{-}Rep(i, j, character), 1 \leq i \leq 8, j = i\}$ set of representations for each topic. We also performed word analysis to get the set of representations $\{SSS\text{-}Rep(k, l, word),$ where $1 \leq k \leq 3, l = k\}$. Both character and word $SSS\text{-}Rep$ created the representation $C_{SSS\text{-}Rep}$ of the analyzed topic. For each summary document, either human or automatically-generated, we extracted the same set of representations as those of the corresponding topic. We compared each summary text representation $T_{SSS\text{-}Rep}$ to the corresponding topic representation $C_{SSS\text{-}Rep}$, creating a feature vector, the values of which were the results of $T_{SSS\text{-}Rep} \sim C_{SSS\text{-}Rep}$ for the $SSS\text{-}Rep$ configurations. This gave a 11-dimensional vector, which we matched to a label $L \in \{human, peer\}$. The "peer" label was assigned to automatic summarizer documents plus our baseline documents. We used a simple Naive Bayes and a kernel-estimating Naive Bayes classifier [12] to determine whether the vectors were enough to classify human and non-human (peer) texts effectively. In both cases 10-fold stratified cross-validation was performed to determine the effectiveness of the method (see the WEKA toolkit [23]). Then, we used an SVM classifier as well, to validate the results. We calculated each feature's Information Gain and performed Principal Component Analysis to determine important features.

4.1   Classification between Human and Machine-Generated Summaries

The naive Bayes classification using the full feature vector managed to provide an F-measure that exeeds 90%, for both classes. It is impressive that we need not apply more complex classifiers (like SVM or neural networks); this identifies the features used as appropriate. In Table 1 we see the breakdown of correctly classified and misclassified instances. We see that the count of automatic summary texts is much higher than the one of human summaries. This would be expected to lower the effectiveness of the simple naive Bayes; but that has not happened. Once more, the features are shown to be appropriate. We apply a more complex classifier to see if it is easy to maximize the attained F-measure. Using Multinomial Bayes [16], as well as an Radial Basis Function kernel SVM classifier (C-SVM) with a high cost parameter (LibSVM implementation [2]) we got the results shown in Table 1.

Table 1. Confusion Matrix — DUC 2006: (left to right) Naive Bayes (NB), Multinomial NB, C-SVM

Classified As			Classified As			Classified As		
Peer	Human	Actual Class	Peer	Human	Actual Class	Peer	Human	Actual Class
1740	60	Peer	1780	20	Peer	1797	3	Peer
13	387	Human	4	396	Human	1	399	Human

At this point we wanted to check whether the SVM model we produced was only overfitting the DUC 2006 corpus data. Thus, we evaluated the model on the DUC 2007 corpus data. Impressively, the results were quite similar, as can be seen in Table 2, amounting to an F-measure of over 97% for both classes. Then, we evaluated the model of DUC 2007 on the DUC 2006 data. The results of this experiment, which are described in Table 2, show that we had an increased number of false negatives for the Human class. This is probably the effect of not including baseline texts in the experiments conducted on the corpus of DUC 2007, which reduced available information on negatives. In any case, the application of the extraction and learning process by itself yields comparable results for both corpora.

Table 2. Confusion Matrix — C-SVM model: DUC2006 on DUC2007 (left); DUC2007 on DUC2006 (right)

Classified As			Classified As		
Peer	Human	Actual Class	Peer	Human	Actual Class
1439	1	Peer	1797	3	Peer
18	342	Human	335	65	Human

The experimental results, therefore, illustrated that the use of *SSS-Rep* as the means to represent the corpus and the texts, along with the use of *SSSR* for the extraction of regularity, provide good enough features to tell human and automatically generated summaries apart.

4.2　Feature Importance

At this point, we wanted to see, given the success of the classification process, what the key features in the classification are. We used two methods to decide upon the answer. First, we ranked the features according to their Information Gain (see [15, p. 583] for linguistic uses of the measure), concerning the human-peer classification. Second, we performed Principal Component Analysis [24] to extract complex features that hold the most useful pieces of information.

The information gain calculation gave the ranking of Table 3. In the table, attributes are named according to the *SSS-Rep* used, where the first part ("char" or "word") indicates what kind of symbol was used and the second part what was $r = d_{max}$ paramteter value was. For example, Char2 indicates character symbols with $r = d_{max} = 2$. The Table presents both ranking for DUC 2006 and 2007 corpus on the left and right part correspondingly.

Table 3. Feature Importance Based on Information Gain (left), PCA analysis (right)

Rank	IG 2006	SSS-Rep	IG 2007	SSS-Rep
1	0.6528	Char8	0.6769	Char7
2	0.6527	Char7	0.67525	Char8
3	0.6463	Char6	0.67394	Char6
4	0.6161	Char5	0.61962	Char5
5	0.3703	Char4	0.35862	Char4
6	0.0545	Char3	0.06614	Char3
7	0.0256	Word3	0.01098	Char1
8	0.0196	Char1	0.0078	Char2
9	0.0133	Word1	0	Word2
10	0	Word2	0	Word3
11	0	Char2	0	Word1

Corpus	Eigenvalue	Feature Formula
DUC 2006	5.62218	0.414Char4+0.409Char5 +0.389Char6
DUC 2007	5.70926	-0.411Char4-0.397Char5 -0.372Char6

The application of PCA on both the corpora of DUC 2006 and DUC 2007 brought a pleasant surprise: the most important Principal Components (according to their eigenvalue) extracted from both corpora were very similar. Both the absolute values of weights of the original features in the complex features, as well as the eigenvalues of the major principal components themselves were similar (see Table 3), giving high importance to non-word units (character n-grams). This indicates emergent important features, only partially dependent on the corpus.

It seems that the low-ranked character n-grams simply reproduce the spelling constraints of a language and offer no useful information. The most important features appeared to be high-ranked character n-grams, because those overlap more than one word. These features are the ones detecting word collocations and other similar phenomena. Using *only Char7 and Char8 features* with Multinomial Naive Bayes we reached a performance of 99% accuracy (only 16 misclassified peer texts and 8 misclassified human, on a whole of 2176 texts). In Figure 1, the light colored (yellow) areas indicate human instances and the dark colored (blue) peer instances. We see that higher rank character n-grams discriminate between classes: humans have *lower SSSR* in high ranks than automatic summaries, but *higher SSSR* than random texts.

What is easily noted from the above is that importance is focused in sub-word (character) features. However, it is not the spelling that makes the difference, but the joining

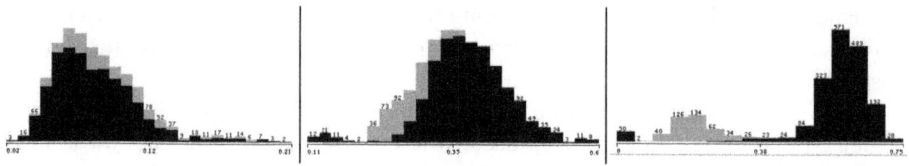

Fig. 1. Distribution of (left to right) character uni-grams, 4-grams, 8-grams *SSR* for DUC 2006

of words. We interpret the results as an indication that regularity is not a measure of quality: it is mostly a measure of whether a text is result of an abstraction or reformulation process. That is why people have lower *SSR* performance than automatic summarization systems, but higher than random texts.

5 Conclusions and Future Work

From the study presented we have inferred a number of facts, concerning mostly the summarization process. First, many existing automatic summarization systems, which are based mostly on extractive techniques, appear to share statistical features. There is such a feature that can tell human summaries apart from automatically generated ones. This is called Symbol Sequence Statistical Regularity, *SSR*. Second, human summaries tend to have *lower SSR* values than automatically generated summaries. This may be directly connected to the abstractive nature of multi-document summarization. On the other hand, human summaries tend to have *higher SSR* values than summaries generated as random text. It would be better, however, if more research was conducted as to what values of *SSR* would text generated by language models like HMM have. Would *SSR* remain useful then? Last, the principal components, based on *SSR*, that discriminate human from automatically-generated summaries for a given language seem to be rather specific. This indicates that humans do follow statistically tracable patterns of text generation if we get to the character level.

In an effort to evaluate automatic texts, with respect to human perception of fluency and grammaticality, the presented *SSR* measure adds one more scientific tool, which holds such abilities like language-neutrality and objectivity. It would be very important to determine other, perhaps similar measures that will be able to detect other aspects of human texts. This includes existing n-gram-based methods which can be leveraged to increase our intuition of the complex process of summarization. Such intuition will in turn, hopefully, give birth to better automatic summarization systems. In our research, we have begun to utilize *SSR* in the process of sentence reformulation for summarization and expect results soon.

The corpora of DUC 2006, 2007 were kindly provided by NIST and have been used according to the ACQUAINT directions. The whole range of experiments for this paper, as well as the editing process and statistical analysis were conducted on Open Source software. The JINSECT toolbox used in the paper can be found at
`http://sf.net/projects/jinsect`.

References

[1] Blache, P., Hemforth, B., Rauzy, S.: Acceptability prediction by means of grammaticality quantification. In: Proceedings of the 21st International Conference on Computational Linguistics and the 44th Annual Meeting of the ACL, pp. 57–64 (2006)

[2] Chang, C., Lin, C.: LIBSVM: a library for support vector machines, vol. 80, pp. 604–611 (2001), Software http://www.csie.ntu.edu.tw/cjlin/libsvm

[3] Chenowith, N., Hayes, J.: Fluency in Writing: Generating Text in L1 and L2. Written Communication 18(1), 80 (2001)

[4] Chomsky, N.: Grammaticality in the Logical Structure of Linguistic Theory (1955)

[5] Chomsky, N.: Rules And Representations. Columbia University Press (2005)

[6] Dang, H.T.: Overview of DUC 2006. In: Proceedings of HLT-NAACL 2006 (2006)

[7] Giannakopoulos, G., Karkaletsis, V.: Summarization system evaluation variations based on n-gram graphs. In: TAC 2010 (2010)

[8] Giannakopoulos, G., Karkaletsis, V., Vouros, G., Stamatopoulos, P.: Summarization system evaluation revisited: N-gram graphs. ACM Trans. Speech Lang. Process. 5(3), 1–39 (2008)

[9] Hamon, O., Rajman, M.: X-Score: Automatic Evaluation of Machine Translation Grammaticality. In: Proceedings of the 5th International Conference on Language Resources and Evaluation, LREC (2006)

[10] Hovy, E., Lin, C., Zhou, L., Fukumoto, J.: Basic Elements (2005)

[11] Jing, H.: Using hidden Markov modeling to decompose human-written summaries. Computational Linguistics 28(4), 527–543 (2002)

[12] John, G., Langley, P.: Estimating continuous distributions in bayesian classifiers. In: Proceedings of the Eleventh Conference on Uncertainty in Artificial Intelligence, San Mateo, vol. 1, pp. 338–345 (1995)

[13] Keller, F.: Gradience in Grammar. Ph.D. thesis, University of Edinburgh (2000)

[14] Lin, C.: Rouge: A Package for Automatic Evaluation of Summaries. Proceedings of the Workshop on Text Summarization Branches Out (WAS 2004), 25–26 (2004)

[15] Manning, C., Schütze, H.: Foundations of Statistical Natural Language Processing. The MIT Press (1999)

[16] McCallum, A., Nigam, K.: A comparison of event models for naive bayes text classification. In: AAAI 1998 Workshop on Learning for Text Categorization, vol. 752, pp. 41–48 (1998)

[17] Mutton, A., Dras, M., Wan, S., Dale, R.: GLEU: Automatic Evaluation of Sentence-Level Fluency. In: Proceedings of the 45th Annual Meeting of the Association of Computational Linguistics, pp. 344–351 (2007)

[18] Nenkova, A.: Understanding the process of multi-document summarization: content selection, rewriting and evaluation. PhD in Philosophy, Columbia University (2006)

[19] Papineni, K., Roukos, S., Ward, T., Zhu, W.: BLEU: a method for automatic evaluation of machine translation. In: Proceedings of the 40th Annual Meeting on Association for Computational Linguistics, pp. 311–318 (2001)

[20] Passonneau, R., McKeown, K., Sigelman, S., Goodkind, A.: Applying the Pyramid Method in the 2006 Document Understanding Conference (2006)

[21] Prince, C., Smolensky, P.: Optimality Theory: Constraint Interaction in Generative Grammar. Optimality Theory in Phonology: A Reader (2004)

[22] Sorace, A., Keller, F.: Gradience in linguistic data. Lingua 115(11), 1497–1524 (2005)

[23] Witten, I., Frank, E., Trigg, L., Hall, M., Holmes, G., Cunningham, S.: Weka: Practical Machine Learning Tools and Techniques with Java Implementations. In: ICONIP/ANZIIS/ANNES, pp. 192–196 (1999)

[24] Wold, S.: Principal component analysis. Chemometrics and Intelligent Laboratory Systems 2(1), 37–52 (1987)

Learning from Mixture of Experimental Data: A Constraint–Based Approach

Vincenzo Lagani[1], Ioannis Tsamardinos[1,2], and Sofia Triantafillou[1,2,*]

[1] BioInformatics Laboratory - FORTH-ICS
Vassilika Vouton 100, Heraklion - Greece
[2] Computer Science Department, University of Crete
Knossou Ave., Heraklion - Greece

Abstract. We propose a novel approach for learning graphical models when data coming from different experimental conditions are available. We argue that classical constraint–based algorithms can be easily applied to mixture of experimental data given an appropriate conditional independence test. We show that, when perfect statistical inference are assumed, a sound conditional independence test for mixtures of experimental data can consist in evaluating the null hypothesis of conditional independence separately for each experimental condition. We successively indicate how this test can be modified in order to take in account statistical errors. Finally, we provide "Proof-of-Concept" results for demonstrating the validity of our claims.

Keywords: Graphical Models, Mixture of Experimental data, Conditional independence test, Constraint Based learning.

1 Introduction

Graphical models are mathematical tools that have become widely known in the last decades. Structural Equation Models (SEM), Hidden Markov Models (HMM), Bayesian Networks (just to name the most common examples) are currently employed for addressing a wide range of real world applications, e.g. text recognition, information retrieval, gene regulatory network reconstruction. Despite years of research, when it comes to learning graphical models from data, there are still several open–to–debate issues; a particularly challenging problem is dealing with experimental interventions that alter the distribution of the data.

Experimental interventions are commonly employed in any area of scientific research. Patient randomization during clinical trials, as well as gene knock–outs in gene expression studies are prominent examples of experimental manipulations, that are usually essential for confirming scientific hypotheses. The same system must often been analyzed under different experimental conditions, to better investigate its operation. Unfortunately, standard graphical–model learning

---

* This research was partially supported by the EU funded project REACTION, Grant Agreement no. 248590.

I. Maglogiannis, V. Plagianakos, and I. Vlahavas (Eds.): SETN 2012, LNAI 7297, pp. 124–131, 2012.

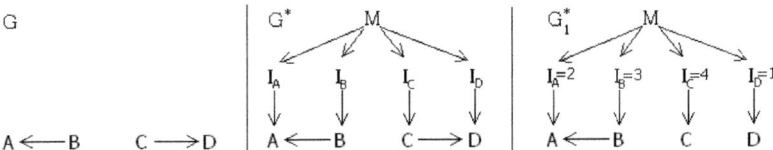

Fig. 1. A simple DAG (left), the augmented graph $\mathcal{G}^*$ (center) and the DAG corresponding to the experiment $E_1 = \{I_A = 2, I_B = 3, I_C = 4, I_D = 1\}$ (right). $I_D = 1$ is a hard intervention, causing the deletion of the edges pointing to D.

algorithms can not be directly employed on mixtures of experimental data; the naïve solution of pooling all data together can lead to spurious (in)dependencies [1], that negatively affect the learning performances. This means that a huge amount of scientific data can not be analyzed with current graphical–model learning methods.

We argue that *any constraint–based algorithm, in principle, can be extended for data coming from different experimental conditions*. Constraint–based methods are a class of algorithms for learning graphical models that have recently proved to be particularly effective[2,3]. This type of algorithms are built on the basis of conditional independence tests; depending on the embedded test, the same algorithm can deal with different types of data [4]. In this work, we employ tests specifically devised for mixtures of experimental data within algorithms originally conceived for data from a single experimental condition. This approach significantly differs from previous works, which are mainly based on a) computationally expensive Search–and–Score paradigms [5], or b) constraint–based algorithms that are specific for a particular experimentation protocol and can not address the general case [6].

To the best of our knowledge, no conditional independence test for experimental data has been proposed yet. We suggest a conceptually simple test: the null hypothesis "variables X and Y are independent given the conditioning set Z" is separately tested for each experiment, and the null hypothesis is rejected if X and Y are found associated at least once. In the next sections we demonstrate that this simple procedure is sound when perfect statistical inferences are assumed. Moreover, we propose an alternative, practical procedure for taking into account both type II and type I statistical errors. Our experimental results indicate that adopting our conditional independence tests leads to better results than naïvely pooling data from different experimental conditions.

2   Notation and Problem Statement

Simply put, a sound conditional independence test for mixtures of experimental data should be able to detect the conditional (in)dependencies characterizing the passive obeservational case on the basis of datasets sampled under various experimental conditions. Section 3 introduces a simple procedure, namely the

Basic approach, that fulfils this objective. A short introduction to the basic theories used to develop this method is presented in this section.

We assume that the data-generating procedure can be described by a Bayesian Network. Let $\mathcal{G} = \{\mathbf{N}, \mathbf{A}\}$ be a Directed Acyclic Graph (DAG), where $\mathbf{A}$ is a set of oriented edges and $\mathbf{N} = \{N_1, \ldots, N_n\}$ a set of nodes, each one representing a variable. Under the Markov Condition and the Faithfulness Assumption, $\mathcal{G}$ encodes the set of (in)dependencies of the joint probability distribution (JPD) of the set of variables $\mathbf{N}$ according to a graphical criterion, called d-separation [7]. We consider two types of interventions: hard (surgical) interventions, in which the manipulated variables' values are set solely by the experimental procedure, and therefore all incoming edges to the manipulated variable are removed from the graph; and soft interventions, in which the skeleton of the graph remains intact, and the parameters of the distribution of the manipulated variables are altered by the experimental procedure [8].

When we pool together data sampled under different conditions, we obtain a new JPD which encodes certain (in)dependencies. We define $\mathcal{G}^* = \{\mathbf{N}, \mathbf{A}^*, \mathbf{I}\mathcal{M}\}$ as the DAG representing these independencies. Node $\mathcal{M}$ corresponds to the "manipulating" variable $\mathcal{M} \in \{1, 2, \ldots m\}$ representing the scientist performing the m different experiments. Nodes $\mathbf{I}$ correspond to the interventional variables $\mathbf{I} = \{I_1, \ldots, I_n\}$ representing the manipulations that the scientist performs on each variable. Variable I_i can take q_i integer values $D(I_i) = \{I_i^1, I_i^2, \ldots, I_i^{q_i}\}$, each corresponding to a different manipulation of the distribution of N_i. $\mathbf{A}^* = \{\mathbf{A} \cup \{\mathcal{M} \to I_i\}_{i=1}^n \cup \{I_i \to N_i\}_{i=1}^n\}$(see Fig. 1).

Let $\{\mathbf{E}_k\}_{k=1}^m$ be a set of m different experiments. An experiment $\mathbf{E}_k$ corresponds to the k-th value of $\mathcal{M}$, and is fully identified by the fixed values that the interventional variables take during its execution. Moreover, each $\mathbf{E_k}$ is related to a DAG $\mathcal{G}_k^*$, obtained from $\mathcal{G}^*$ after removing the edges pointing to variables targeted by hard interventions. D_k is the dataset sampled/produced during the experiment $\mathbf{E}_k$, while P_k is the JPD of the variables in D_k. Similarly, the distribution over the pooled dataset $D_T = \bigcup_{k=1}^m D_k$ is indicated as P_T.

We use $(\neg)ind_k(N_i, N_j|\mathbf{C})$ to denote that "N_i and N_j are (not) independent in P_k given $\mathbf{C}$", where $N_i, N_j \in \mathbf{N}$ and $\mathbf{C} \subseteq \mathbf{N} \setminus \{N_i, N_j\}$. By convention, a conditional independence that holds in the observational case is indicated as $ind(N_i, N_j|\mathbf{C})$. Finally, a generic statistical procedure that evaluates the null hypothesis "N_i and N_j are independent given $\mathbf{C}$ in the data distribution P_k" is indicated as $TestInd(N_i, N_j|\mathbf{C}; P_k)$.

3   Assuming Perfect Statistical Inferences: Basic Approach

Let $TestInd_{Oracle}(N_i, N_j|\mathbf{C}; P_k)$ be an *oracle*, i.e. a conditional independence test that makes no statistical errors. We now define the conditional independence test for a mixture of experimental data $TestInd_{Basic}(N_i, N_j|\mathbf{C}; P_1 \ldots P_m)$:

Basic approach. *Let* $D_1, \ldots, D_m$ *be* m *datasets sampled under different experimental conditions, and* $P_1, \ldots, P_m$ *the respective joint probability distributions.* $TestInd_{Basic}(N_i, N_j|\mathbf{C}; P_1 \ldots P_m)$ *rejects the null (independence)* hypothesis iff $TestInd_{Oracle}(N_i, N_j|\mathbf{C}; P_k)$ rejects the null hypothesis for at least one $P_k, k = 1, \ldots, m$.

It is easy to demonstrate that $TestInd_{Basic}$ detects the *preserved* conditional dependencies entailed in $\mathcal{G}$:

Proposition 1. *Given the set of experiments* $\mathbf{E}_1, \ldots, \mathbf{E}_m$, *the conditional dependency* $\neg ind(N_i, N_j|\mathbf{C})$ *is preserved if at least one* $\neg ind_k(N_i, N_j|\mathbf{C}), k = 1, \ldots, m$ *holds.*

If the dependency is preserved, then $TestInd_{Oracle}$ rejects the null hypothesis at least once, and thus $TestInd_{Basic}$ also rejects its null hypothesis. Conversely, if $ind(N_i, N_j|\mathbf{C})$ holds, then $TestInd_{Basic}$ will accept the null hypothesis of independence, because (a) we assume that the oracle does not perform Type I statistical errors and (b) our settings ensure that *no spurious association can be created within an experiment by experimental manipulations*, as described in the following theorem.

Theorem 1. *No dependency* $\neg ind_k(N_i, N_j|\mathbf{C})$ *can hold if* $\neg ind(N_i, N_j|\mathbf{C})$ *does not hold in the observational case.*

Proof. W assume faithfulness and Markov condition for both $\mathcal{G}$ and $\mathcal{G}_k^*$, thus a spurious association in D_k can be created iff $\mathcal{G}_k^*$ encodes an artificial d-connecting path not present in $\mathcal{G}$. Such an artificial d-connecting path should either (a) be encoded in the part of the $\mathcal{G}_k^*$ structure that is in common with $\mathcal{G}$ or (b) pass through the interventional nodes and $\mathcal{M}$. Both cases are not possible, because (a) soft interventions do not change $\mathcal{G}$ structure, and deletion of arcs due to surgical interventions can only destroy d-connecting paths; (b) the values of the interventional variables are held constant during each experiment, and this implies that $ind_k(N_i, N_j|\mathbf{C}) \equiv ind_k(N_i, N_j|\mathbf{C}, I_1 = I_1^k, \ldots, I_n = I_n^k)$, where $\{I_1 = I_1^k, \ldots, I_n = I_n^k\}$ are the values assumed by the interventional variables in the k-th experiment. Conditioning on all interventional variables blocks all d-connecting paths that pass through the interventional nodes, thus excluding any spurious association. □

4   Considering Statistical Errors: Merging Approach

The *Basic* approach depends on a number of assumptions that affect its practical applicability. In a more realistic setting, type II statistical errors are possible, i.e. the statistical power may be low. A possible solution for increasing the statistical power may consist in merging different datasets; however, when data from different experimental conditions are pooled together, Theorem 1 does not hold anymore, and *spurious associations not encoded in $\mathcal{G}$ may be created*.

We now define a sufficient condition that ensures the absence of spurious associations in mixtures of data from different experiments. Let $D_\mathbf{u}, \mathbf{u} \subseteq \{1, \ldots, m\}$ be the pooled dataset from a subset of the experiments $\mathbf{E}_1, \ldots, \mathbf{E}_m$. $P_\mathbf{u}$ is the joint probability distribution of $D_\mathbf{u}$. We furthermore define the set of experimental modifications $\mathbf{S}_\mathbf{u}$ as the set of the interventional variables whose values change, even once, across the experiments pooled in $D_\mathbf{u}$.

Theorem 2. *The probability distribution $P_{\mathbf{u}}$ entails no spurious association iff $|\mathbf{S_u}| \leq 1$.*

Proof. When $|\mathbf{S_u}| \geq 2$, at least two interventional variables, namely I_r and I_s, are not conditioned upon anymore, and thus at least one d-connecting path, namely $N_r \leftarrow I_r \leftarrow \mathcal{M} \rightarrow I_s \rightarrow N_s$, is present.

When $|\mathbf{S_u}| = 1$, all interventional variables are constant, except one, namely I_r. However, no d-connecting path between two nodes $N_i, N_j \in \mathcal{G}$ can pass through I_r, because such a path would be blocked by the other interventional variables that are all conditioned upon.

When $|\mathbf{S_u}| = 0$ the data were produced under the same experimental conditions, i.e., results of Theorem 1 still hold.   □

The results of Theorem 2 allow us to define the following conditional independence test for mixture of experimental data, namely the *S–Merging* approach:

S–Merging approach. *Given m experiments $\mathbf{E}_1, \ldots, \mathbf{E}_m$ and their respective JPDs $P_1, \ldots, P_m$, the test $TestInd_{S-Merging}(N_i, N_j|\mathbf{C}; P_1, \ldots, P_m)$ rejects the null hypothesis of independence iff $TestInd_{Oracle}(N_i, N_j|\mathbf{C}; P_{\mathbf{u}})$ rejects the null hypothesis of independence for any $P_{\mathbf{u}}$ with $|\mathbf{S_u}| \leq 1$, $\mathbf{u} \subseteq \{1, \ldots, m\}$.*

The *S–Merging* approach tests the existence of a dependency in any single dataset *and* in any pooled dataset $D_{\mathbf{u}}$ where $|\mathbf{S_u}| \leq 1$ (i.e., the tests performed by the *Basic* approach are always a subset of the tests performed by the *S–Merging* approach). Merging different distributions does not ensure an increment of statistical power; under this respect, the *S–Merging* approach is clearly heuristic: it *tries* to maximize the available statistical power by evaluating any subset of datasets that can be pooled together without creating spurious associations.

Finally, both the *Basic* and *S–Merging* approaches internally perform multiple statistical inferences, increasing the probability of type I statistical errors. We employ a Family Wise Error Rate (FWER) correction procedure, namely the Holm-Bonferroni method [9]. More sophisticated procedures could be adopted for correcting for multiple tests.

5   Experiments

We considered the following experimental scenario for evaluating our approaches: the observational case E_1, two experiments E_2 and E_3 with 5 randomly chosen manipulated variables each, and two experiments E_4 and E_5 such that $|\mathbf{S}_{\{2,4\}}| = 1$ and $|\mathbf{S}_{\{3,5\}}| = 1$ (i.e. the experiments within each couple differ between each other only for a single intervention). We only considered hard (surgical) interventions. We employed three prototypical Bayesian Networks, namely ALARM, INSURANCE and HAILFINDER, for generating synthetic discrete data. For each network we simulated 6 mixtures of experimental data, by varying the single–experiment sample size among $\{50, 100, 300, 500, 700, 1000\}$.

On each mixture of experimental data we applied the well known, constraint–based PC algorithm [7,10], with in turn the $TestInd_{Basic}$ and $TestInd_{S-Merging}$

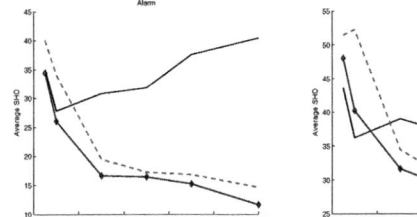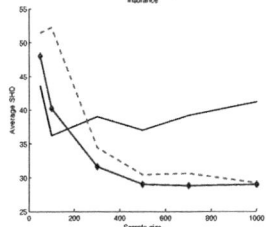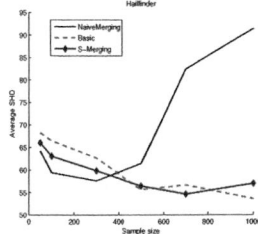

Fig. 2. Results of the experiments on synthetic data. Each graph refers to a different network (from left to right: ALARM, INSURANCE and HAILFINDER). The x axis reports the sample size for each experiment, while the y axis the SHD values averaged over 5 repetitions. Each line represents a different approach, respectively: *NaïveMerging* (black solid line), *Basic* (red dashed line) and *S–Mergin* (blue line with diamonds).

tests. The G^2 conditional independence test was employed internally, and the *fan–in* parameter of the PC algorithm was set to 3. Furthermore, we applied the PC algorithm equipped with the G^2 test on all data pooled together; we call this simple procedure the *NaïveMerging* approach. We employed the *NaïveMerging* approach in order to demonstrate that indiscriminately pooling data from different experimental conditions leads to systematic errors. The whole procedure was repeated 5 times, with significance threshold always set to 0.05.

The Structural Hamming Distance (SHD) was employed for comparing the Partially Directed Acyclic Graph (PDAG) provided by the PC method with the Complete Partially Directed Acyclic Graphs (CPDAG) corresponding to the structures of the three networks [11]. The SHD metric has an intuitive interpretation: it indicates the number of arcs that must be added, deleted, reversed or oriented in order to transform a partial directed graph into another one.

The results of our analysis are summarized in Fig. 2. $TestInd_{S-Merging}$ usually allows a better reconstruction of the true CPDAG than $TestInd_{Basic}$; this result indicates that the additional tests performed by the $S - Merging$ approach are effective in order to retrieve the true dependencies, i.e., merging data coming from different experimental conditions can lead to an increment of statistical power (given that the condition $|\mathbf{S_u}| \leq 1$ stated in Theorem 2 is respected). Moreover, both the $S - Merging$ and *Basic* approach show better performance when the sample size increments. Conversely, the performance of the *NaïveMerging* approach decreases with the increment of the sample size. This trend was expected: the spurious associations created by pooling all data together become stronger as more samples are available. Thus, the PC algorithm retrieves an increasing number of false associations, and these errors are "propagated" through the network.

6 Discussion

This work constitutes a first step towards the creation of a new class of graphical–model learning algorithms for mixtures of experimental data. Our intuition is conceptually simple: constraint–based methods, in principle, can be applied on experimental data, by simply coupling a suitable conditional independence test.

Following our intuition we provided the first conditional independence tests for mixtures of experimental data, $TestInd_{Basic}$ and $TestInd_{S-Merging}$. Our tests deal with datasets sampled under different experimental conditions, and attempt to retrieve the conditional (in)dependencies entailed in the observational data distribution. While $TestInd_{Basic}$ relies on the assumption of perfect statistical inferences, $TestInd_{S-Merging}$ is devised in order to avoid type II statistical errors by maximally exploiting all the available statistical power.

Furthermore, we provided a sufficient condition (Theorem 2) for avoiding the creation of spurious associations when data from different experiments are pooled together. Even though the rule $|\mathbf{S_u}| \leq 1$ can seem quite strict, this condition has interesting potential applications. For example, it demonstrates that a medical study where patients are randomized between two groups can be safely merged with a successive, follow up observational study carried on the same patients, for increasing the statistical power of the analysis.

Finally, the experimental results obtained with the PC algorithm seem to confirm the validity of our methods. Both the *Basic* and *S–Merging* approaches outperform the simplistic solution of pooling all data together; as the sample size increases, the spurious associations become stronger, and the difference among the approaches becomes more evident. Moreover, the *S–Merging* approach demonstrated to be usually more powerful than the *Basic* one, as expected.

The class of constraint–based algorithms is particularly large, and different algorithms show different interesting features, e.g. the possibility of learning rich causal models like Maximal Ancestral Graphs (MAGs, [12]), or the possibility of learning only part of the structure [11]. Our further researches will keep exploring the possibility of extending constraint–based methods for mixtures of experimental data.

7   Related Work

A possible approach for learning graphical models from different experiments consists in learning a first skeleton of the graph from observational data and then to exploit external interventions for orienting edges [13]. These methods consider each dataset in isolation, and thus underutilize the available information, and cannot be employed in absence observational data. Search-and-Score methods in conjunction with modified score functions [5,8] have also been employed for learning from mixtures of experimental data. The main drawback of these algorithms is that Search-and-Score procedures are usually highly computationally demanding. Other algorithms assume that interactions among variables can be represented with a specific type of function (e.g., noisy OR functions among binary variables [14]), but they are applicable only when their respective, strict assumptions hold. Constraint–based algorithms were also proposed for learning from multiple experiments. An algorithm for learning causal models in systems where only one variable is manipulated at a time (per dataset) is proposed in [6]. This algorithm is not general as it can only address cases that follow a specific experimental process. A method for inferring causal relations from (in)dependence models derived from different experiments was proposed in [15]. However, this approach can not be applied in presence of hard interventions.

Finally, to the best of our knowledge only one work identifies a sufficient condition for pooling together data from different experiments [1]. However, checking this condition requires the knowledge of the underlying causal structure, that is almost always unknown.

References

1. Eberhardt, F.: Sufficient condition for pooling data from different distributions. In: ERROR (2006)
2. Aliferis, C.F., Statnikov, A., Tsamardinos, I., Mani, S., Koutsoukos, X.D.: Local causal and markov blanket induction for causal discovery and feature selection for classification part i: Algorithms and empirical evaluation. J. Mach. Learn. Res. 11, 171–234 (2010)
3. Aliferis, C.F., Statnikov, A., Tsamardinos, I., Mani, S., Koutsoukos, X.D.: Local Causal and Markov Blanket Induction for Causal Discovery and Feature Selection for Classification Part II: Analysis and Extensions. J. Mach. Learn. Res. 11, 235–284 (2010)
4. Lagani, V., Tsamardinos, I.: Structure-based variable selection for survival data. Bioinformatics 26(15), 1887–1894 (2010)
5. Cooper, G.F., Yoo, C.: Causal Discovery from a Mixture of Experimental and Observational Data. In: UAI (1999)
6. Tian, J., Pearl, J.: Causal discovery from changes. In: UAI (2001)
7. Pearl, J.: Causality: Models, Reasoning, and Inference. Cambridge University Press (March 2000)
8. Eaton, D., Murphy, K.: Exact bayesian structure learning from uncertain interventions. In: AISTAT (2007)
9. Holm, S.: A Simple Sequentially Rejective Multiple Test Procedure. Scandinavian Journal of Statistics 6(2), 65–70 (1979)
10. Murphy, K.P.: The Bayes Net Toolbox for MATLAB
11. Tsamardinos, I., Brown, L., Constantin, A.: The max-min hill-climbing Bayesian network structure learning algorithm. Machine Learning 65(1), 31–78 (2006)
12. Richardson, T., Spirtes, P.: Ancestral Graph Markov Models. The Annals of Statistics 30(4), 962–1030 (2002)
13. He, Y.-B., Geng, Z.: Active Learning of Causal Networks with Intervention Experiments and Optimal Designs. Journal of Machine Learning Research 9, 2523–2547 (2008)
14. Hyttinen, A., Hoyer, P.O., Eberhardt, F.: Noisy-OR Models with Latent Confounding. In: UAI (2011)
15. Claassen, T., Heskes, T.: Learning causal network structure from multiple (in)dependence models. In: PGM (2010)

Information Sharing and Searching via Collaborative Reinforcement Learning

George A. Vouros

Department of Digital Systems, University of Piraeus, Piraeus Greece
georgev@unipi.gr

Abstract. This paper proposes a method for computing a routing policy-value function for effective information sharing and searching in arbitrary networks of agents through collaborative reinforcement learning. This is done by means of local computations performed by agents and payoff propagation. The aim is to 'tune' a network of agents for efficient and effective information searching and sharing, without altering the topology or imposing an overlay structure.

1   Introduction

'Tuning' networks of agents to perform information searching and sharing requires agents to gather the *necessary* knowledge so as to decide their routing policies and propagate requests to the *right* agents, minimizing the searching effort, thus increasing the efficiency (i.e. speed/cost ratio) and the efficacy (i.e. retrieved results) of the task.

Considering to be a decentralized control problem, information searching and sharing in large-scale systems of cooperative agents is a hard problem in the general case: The computation of an optimal policy, when each agent possesses an approximate partial view of the state of the environment and when agents' observations and activities are interdependent (i.e. one agent's actions affect the observations and the state of an other) [2], is hard. This fact, has resulted to efforts that either require agents to have a global view of the system [14], to heuristics [3], to the pre-computation of agents' information needs and information provision capabilities for proactive communication [15], to localized reasoning processes built on incoming information [11,12,13], to mathematical frameworks for coordination, whose optimal policies can be approximated for small (sub-) networks of associated agents [10], and to reinforcement learning algorithms for hierarchical peer-to-peer information retrieval systems [16]. On the other hand, there is a lot of research on semantic peer to peer search networks and social networks many of which deal with tuning a network of peers for effective information searching and sharing. They do it mostly by imposing logical and semantic overlay structures.

To address the limitations (related to scalability and the assumptions made) of the above-mentioned approaches, the information sharing and searching algorithms reported in [8,9] use routing indices and agents' profiles. There are three important issues regarding these methods: (a) Given that random information sharing and searching is a hard competitor for any such task [7], the effectiveness of these methods concerning the number of information items retrieved is not that high, even if they manage to gradually increase the efficiency of the searching task. (b) Agents do not consider the cost or delay of their task even if the overall benefit increases. For instance, requests may be propagated via specific agents whose load (thus throughput time) increases; and finally, (c) the convergence of the method cannot be guaranteed.

To address the limitations of previous works, this paper proposes using the agent-based update of the edge-based decomposition Sparse Cooperative Q-learning method proposed in [5], so as agents to estimate the value of their routing policies in a distributed and scalable way, by exploiting the dependencies of their routing actions. The proposed method, to a greater extent than other proposals concerning the use of reinforcement learning techniques for information retrieval [16] exploits the structure of the problem by means of coordination graphs [4] and thus, can result to very effective tuning, even to non-hierarchical (arbitrarily organized) systems. Also, the proposed approach generalizes approaches that exploit routing indices [8,9] in two directions: (a) It estimates routing policy-value functions via payoff propagation, and (b) it has the potential to incorporate any problem/context specific parameter concerning routing actions value.

2   Problem Specification

The setting: Let $N=\{A_1, A_2, ..., A_n\}$ be the set of agents in the system. The network of agents is modelled as an acquaintances graph $G=(N,E)$, where N is the set of agents and E is a set of bidirectional edges denoted as non-ordered pairs (A_i,A_j). The neighbourhood of an agent A_i (denoted by $N(A_i)$) includes all the acquaintances of A_j such that $(A_i,A_j) \in E$. Each edge is associated with a communication cost, $Cost(A_i,A_j)$ and each agent has a specific service rate $SR(A_i)$ that specifies its maximum throughput rate (i.e. the number of queries that it processes in the unit of time). The (mean) delay of each agent A_i to process a query, is determined as follows: $Delay(A_i)= Number\_of\_Waiting\_Queries/SR(A_i)$. We assume that the cost and the delay are associated to comparable values. It must be noticed that in contrast to costs, delays change over time.

The agents in the network share the same set of information categories C. Each agent assigns a value (*i-Value*) to each information category. This specifies the reward one gets by obtaining an information item from that category. Also, any agent has an *expertise,* which is represented by a specific information category, and it possesses a unique *information item* (e.g. a document) of that category. Additionally, we consider a set of k queries $\{q_1,..., q_k\}$. Each query asks for an information item under a specific category c in $C,$ and is represented by a triple $<id,c,TTL>$, where id is the identity of the query, and TTL (Time To Live) is a positive integer that specifies the *maximum* number of hops that *any* query can reach.

Definitions: Considering a specific query $q=<id,c,TTL>$, a *search session* for this query is associated with a specific path in the network and starts when the query is generated by a specific agent and finishes either when the query has been answered (*served*) or when it has traversed a path in the network whose length is equal to the specified Time To Live (*TTL*) without being served (*unfulfilled*).

At a specific point of time, the *state of a search session* for a specific query comprises the variables *path* (which initially is empty, and each agent adds its id in the path before propagating the query), *ttl* (which is initially equal to *TTL* and it is reduced by one for each hop), and the variable *agent* (specifying the agent currently processing the query). Thus, given a session at state $<path,ttl,A_i>$, and in case A_i routes the query to A_j, then the new state for this session is $<A_j \oplus path, (ttl-1), A_j>$, where $(A_j \oplus path)$ is the extension of *path* with A_j. The *joint state* comprises the variables of all search sessions.

The finite set of routing actions available to each agent A_i with respect to the query q correspond to its G-neighbors $N(A_i)$: More precisely, given the state of the search session $<path,ttl,A_i>$ for $q=<id,c,TTL>$, A_i may send that query to any of its G-neighbors that has the "best" potential among neighbours to route a query for c so as to be served with a minimum cost and delay (compared to the other G-neighbors) in $ttl' \le (ttl-1)$ hops (i.e. in less hops than those required).

Coordination Graphs: In the following we consider that agents are organized in *coordination graphs* [4]. Generally, these are structured according to the dependencies between agents' actions, revealing the structure of the coordination problem: Coordination graphs allow decomposing a global value function for any joint action of agents, into a sum of local functions: Each local function depends on the combination of actions of the involved agents. In contrast to the acquaintance graph $G=(N,E)$, we denote coordination graphs as $CG=(N_{CG},E_{CG})$. Also, when it is not clear, we distinguish between G-neighbors (i.e. neighbors in the acquaintance graph) and CG-neighbors (i.e. neighbors in the coordination graph).

Given the acquaintance graph G, the coordination graph $CG=(N_{CG},E_{CG})$ is as follows: Each node in N_{CG} corresponds to an agent A_i in the acquaintance graph with two additional attributes: The type of the requested information and the *ttl* of the request (we denote such an agent by $A_{i,c,ttl}$, where $c \in C$ and $ttl=1...TTL$). Therefore, for each agent in G there are $|C| \times TTL$ nodes in CG. Two nodes $A_{i,c,ttl}$ $A_{j,c',ttl'}$ with $i \ne j$ are connected with a directed edge $(A_{i,c,ttl} A_{j,c',ttl'})$ iff A_j is in $N(A_i)$, $c=c'$ and $ttl'<ttl$. In this case $A_{j,c',ttl'}$ (resp. $A_{i,c,ttl}$) is a CG-neighbor (resp. *inverse* CG-neighbor) of $A_{i,c,ttl}$ (resp. of $A_{j,c',ttl'}$). Indeed, the routing action of A_i given the state $<path,ttl,A_i>$ of a search session for $q=<id,c,TTL>$, denoted by $act_{i,c,ttl}$, depends on the routing action $act_{j,c,ttl'}$, $ttl' \le (ttl-1)$, of any G-neighbor A_j, given that, the return received by A_i, in case it propagates the query to A_j, depends on the routing decision of A_j.

It must be noticed that CG is not constructed in an explicit way by the proposed method. CG provides a structure to the information searching and sharing task and differs substantially from G: (a) While routing actions concern propagating queries in the "actual network", i.e. in G, the necessary information for valuating routing actions is gathered and propagated in CG; (b) CG has $|C| \times TTL$ more nodes than G; (c) if A_j is in $N(A_i)$, then not any pair of nodes $A_{i,c,ttl}$ $A_{j,c',ttl'}$ is connected (e.g. there is not any edge from $A_{i,c,3}$ to $A_{j,c,5}$); (d) CG is a directed and acyclic graph: Indeed, there can not be any path $(A_{i,c,ttl},...,A_{i,c,ttl})$ since a pair of nodes $A_{i,c,ttl}$ $A_{j,c,ttl'}$ is connected iff $ttl'<ttl$.

The problem: Each agent A_i has a finite set of routing actions $Act_i{}^1$. This set comprises all the routing options an agent has for any information category and state of a search

---

[1] To distinguish symbols, we have used lowercase letters for atomic states/actions/policies/rewards, uppercase letters for joint states/actions/policies/rewards and uppercase-bold letters for sets of states/actions/policies.

session. The joint action is the combination of agents' individual actions, and thus a member of $Act=Act_1 \times \ldots \times Act_n$. Given a set of discrete state variables S_i (whose values depend on the state of specific query sessions), the joined state of the system at a specific time point t is defined to be a member of $S=S_1 \times \ldots \times S_m$. A state transition function $T:S \times Act \times S \rightarrow [0,1]$ gives the transition probability $p(S^{t+1}|S^t, Act)$ that the system will reach state S^{t+1} when the joint action Act is performed at the time point t, when the system is at state S. A reward function $r_i:S \times Act \rightarrow \mathbb{R}$ provides each agent A_i with an individual reward, depending on the joint action Act performed in state S.

Given that the model assumes the Markov property and that the reward and transition probabilities are independent of the time t, the successor of a state S (or s) given an action Act (resp. act), is denoted by S' (resp. s').

A policy $\Pi:S \rightarrow Act$ specifies a joint action Act for each joint state S.

The objective of tuning the information sharing and searching task is to find an optimal policy Π^* that maximizes the expected discounted future return $V^*(s) = max_\Pi$ $E[\Sigma_t \gamma^t R(S^t, \Pi(S^t))|\Pi, S^0 = S]$ for each state S. The expectation operator $E[.]$ averages over stochastic transitions, R is the global reward and $\gamma \in [0,1)$ is the discount factor.

3 The Proposed Approach

Briefly, the overall process is as follows: Each agent gets payoff updates from its *CG*-neighbors, it propagates updated local payoffs to its *inverse CG*-neighbors, uses computed payoffs to estimate routing action values, and processes/ routes own queries. The estimation of the routing action values happens through collaborative reinforcement learning, while the estimation of payoffs – which are exploited by the learning method- via the max-plus algorithm.

The objective of collaborative reinforcement learning is to support agents to select a joint policy that provides them the highest possible reward. Agents have no prior knowledge about the effect of their actions, but this information has to be learned based on the received rewards. We use the collaborative multiagent Markov decision process (collaborative multiagent MDP) model [4], also used in [5]. In this model each agent selects an individual action, given a particular state. Based on the resulting joint action the system transitions to a new state and the agents receive an individual reward. The global reward is the sum of all individual rewards. No agent can observe the global reward. In a collaborative MDP, the goal of the agents is to optimize the global reward. The individually received rewards allow for solution techniques that take advantage of the problem structure revealed by coordination graphs.

Recall that the objective is to find an optimal policy Π^* that maximizes the expected discounted future return. Q-functions (action-value functions) represent the expected future discount reward for a state S when selecting an action Act and behaving optimally from then on. To approximate the global Q-function we use the agent-based update of the edge-based decomposition Sparse Cooperative Q-learning method proposed in [5].

Therefore, given a coordination graph of agents, each edge $(A_{i,c,ttl}, A_{j,c,ttl'})$ in E_{CG} corresponds to a local Q-function Q_{ij}. The global Q-function is the sum of all local functions

$$Q(S,Act) = \sum_{(A_{i,c,ttl}, A_{j,c,ttl}')} Q_{ij}(S_{ij}, act_{i,c,ttl}, act_{j,c,ttl}') \tag{1}$$

where $S_{ij} \subseteq S_i \cup S_j$ is the subset of state variables that are relevant to the dependency between agents A_i and A_j with respect to c. The local Q-function Q_i of agent A_i is defined as the summation of half the value of all Q-functions Q_{ij}, where $A_{j,c,ttl}' \in N_{CG}(A_{i,c,ttl})$:

$$Q_i(S_i, act_{i,c,ttl}) = \sum_{(A_{i,c,ttl}, A_{j,c,ttl}')} Q_{ij}(S_{ij}, act_{i,c,ttl}, act_{j,c,ttl}') \tag{2}$$

The agent update (edge decomposition) method computes the temporal difference error per agent and divides this value over the edges. The Q-function of an edge incorporates the information from *all* edges of *each of* the involved agents:

$$Q_{ij}(S_{ij}, act_{i,c,ttl}, act_{j,c,ttl}') = Q_{ij}(S_{ij}, act_{i,c,ttl}, act_{j,c,ttl}') +$$
$$a \sum_{A_{k,c,t} \in \{A_{i,c,ttl}, A_{j,c,ttl'}\}} \frac{r_k(S,Act) + \gamma Q_k(s'_k, act^*_{k,c,t}) - Q_k(s_k, act_{k,c,t})}{|N_{CG}(A_{k,c,t})|} \tag{3}$$

The discount factor γ is set to 0.3 and the learning rate α to 0.2. act^*_k is the maximizing action of agent A_k in the state s'_k. The reward $r_k(S,Act)$ for each of the agents A_k in an edge is set to be equal to the i-*Value* ($iValue(A_k,c)$) of the searched information category c for the agent A_k. The value of the maximizing action of agent A_k for a search session at state $s'_k = (path, ttl, A_k)$ is estimated as follows: $Q_k(s'_k, act^*_{k,c,ttl}) = max(g_k(act_{k,c,ttl}))$, where g_k depends on the payoffs propagated via the max-plus algorithm (explained in the next paragraphs). $Q_k(s_k, act_k)$ is computed as specified by equation (2).

Thus, each local Q-function Q_{ij} is updated with a proportional part of the received reward of the two agents it is related to and with the contribution of this edge to the maximizing joint action $act_{k,c,ttl}*$ in the state s_k. As already said, this is approximated by the max-plus algorithm. Using this combination of methods, as it is shown in [8], the edge-based decomposition scales linearly in the number of *CG*-neighbors. The update of the action-value for an agent is based on the current Q-value and the local contribution of this agent to the global return.

In order to compute the optimal joint action that maximizes the sum of agents' local payoffs (i.e. the global payoff), we use message passing algorithms [6], and particularly the max-plus algorithm. According to this algorithm, given a query $<id,c,TTL>$ a session of which is at state $<path,ttl, A_i>$, each agent sends a message μ_{ij} to each of its *CG*-neighbors. Allowing only payoff functions defined over at most two agents in *CG* the computation of payoffs is as follows:

$$\mu_{ij}(act_{j,c,ttl}) = \max_{act_{i,c,ttl}} \left\{ F_{ij}(act_{i,c,ttl'}, act_{j,c,ttl}) + \sum_{A_k \in N_{CG}(A_i) - \{A_j\}} \sum_{t=1}^{ttl'} \mu_{ki}(act_{i,c,t}) \right\} + c_{ij} \tag{4}$$

The sums concern the local payoffs of all *CG*-neighbors of $A_{i,c,ttl'}$, except those related to A_j. Given that $F_{ij}(act_i, act_j) = f_i(act_i) + f_i^j(act_i, act_j)$, f_i specifies the payoff contribution of $A_{i,c,ttl'}$. Formally, $f_i(act_{i,c,ttl}) = iValue(A_i,c) - Delay(A_i)$.

Also, f_i^j is the payoff contribution of the pair of neighbors $A_{i,c,ttl}$ and $A_{j,c,ttl'}$, given their actions $act_{i,c,ttl}$, $act_{j,c,ttl'}$. Formally,

$$f_i^j(act_{i,c,ttl}, act_{j,c,ttl'}) = \begin{cases} -Cost(A_i,A_j) & if \quad act_{i,c,ttl} \ routes \ \ to \ A_j \\ \\ -COST & otherwise \end{cases}$$

where *COST* is a very large number[2]. It must be pointed out that these functions specifying payoff contributions are rather simple and independent of the *ttl* parameter. Future work concerns elaborating them further by taking into account further attributes of the problem and of the setting.

Given a query *<id,c,TTL>* a session of which is at state *<path,ttl, A_i>*, the agent A_i may at any time step compute

$$g_i(act_{i,c,ttl}) = f_i(act_{i,c,ttl}) + \sum_{A_k \in N(A_i)} \mu_{ki}(act_{i,c,ttl}) \qquad (5)$$

which equals the contribution to the global payoff function achieved via A_i's subtrees. Thus, each agent can form a decision by approximating its optimal choice regarding *c* and *ttl:*

$$act_{i,c,ttl}^* = \underset{act_{i,c,ttl}}{\arg\max} \, g_i(act_{i,c,ttl}) \qquad (6)$$

Although the max-plus algorithm converges to fixed message values, Q-learning does not converges to the optimal Q* values for multiple, independent learners, since the decisions of one agent affect in a dynamic way the actions of the others [5].

Overall, the task is as follows: Given an agent A_i in *G*, and a query *<id,c,TTL>* whose session is at state *<path,ttl, A_i>*, A_i routes the query to a percentage of its *G*-neighbors (let that be *AP – AcquaintancesPercentage*). Routing decisions are formed by exploiting routing action values estimated by means of equation (3), or, initially, purely randomly: Initially, agents have no estimation about the information provision abilities and costs associated to any of their neighbors. Also, even in the case that an agent has an estimation of routing actions' values, it explores further possibilities by propagating the queries to randomly chosen *G*-neighbors, as well. When the query reaches an agent A_k that possesses an item in category *c*, then this agent sends the answer directly to the originator of the query. Given that the search session for the corresponding query is at state *<path',ttl', A_k>*, A_k calculates and propagates its payoff to the *inverse CG*-neighbors of $A_{k,c,ttl'}$. Then, payoff propagation due to this update proceeds concurrently to the routing of other queries and, of course, to the estimation of agents' routing action values. Payoffs are getting propagated until they converge to fixed values: This is always the case, given that the constructed *CG*s are acyclic.

4   Experimental Results

To validate the proposed approach we have built a prototype that simulates information sharing in networks of agents. To test our approach we have run several experiments with random and small-word networks. Due to space reasons, we present results for random networks only. Networks comprise 50 agents (|*N*|=50). Results are

---

[2] The rationale behind this, is that, when A_i considers selecting a routing action to A_j, then the payoffs of the other neighbors become irrelevant.

representative for cases with larger networks of agents. The average number of acquaintances per agent in our experiments is 13. Each experiment ran 5 times for 40 rounds at each round. At each round a constant number of 330 queries are being generated. Each query is randomly assigned to an originator agent and is set to request one information item of a randomly chosen category. The *TTL* for every query is set to be equal to 7. In such a setting, the demand for information items is high, given agents' information provision abilities and the *TTL* of queries. To end a round, all query sessions must have been ended, and all payoff messages must have been converged to fixed values. Information used in the experiments is synthetic and is being classified in 15 distinct categories: Agents' expertise and information values for each of the categories is determined randomly. The percentage of acquaintances (*AP*) to which a query can be propagated is set to 1,10 or 20, so as to show the efficacy of the method, even if agents perform restricted exploration. To demonstrate the advantages of our method we provide results for different configurations: (a) Agents propagate queries according to the best routing action estimated using only the max-plus algorithm (equation (6)). This configuration is indicated by "MS"; (b) Agents propagate their payoff estimations *only* to the inverse-*CG* neighbors that show high interested to each corresponding category of information *c* (indicated by "P"). The estimation of agents' interests is done as proposed in [8,9]. (c) We also provide results from a baseline method where agents select their routing actions randomly (indicated by "R"). The experimental settings are denoted by X-Y-AP-W, where X denotes the type of network, Y the number of agents, *AP* the percentage of acquaintances to which queries are propagated, and W is either "MS", "R", or unspecified for the "standard" cooperative Q-learning setting. For instance, Rand-50-10-MS denotes a setting with a random network of 50 agents where each query is being propagated to at most 10% of an agent's acquaintances (*AP=10*), and agents decide on their routing actions using equation (6). Results computed in each experiment show the total number of query-propagation messages (*q-messages*), the total number of messages for the propagating payoffs (*p-messages*), the *benefit* of the system, i.e. the percentage of served queries, and the *message gain,* i.e. the ratio of benefit to the total number of messages. Experimental results are depicted in Figure 1.

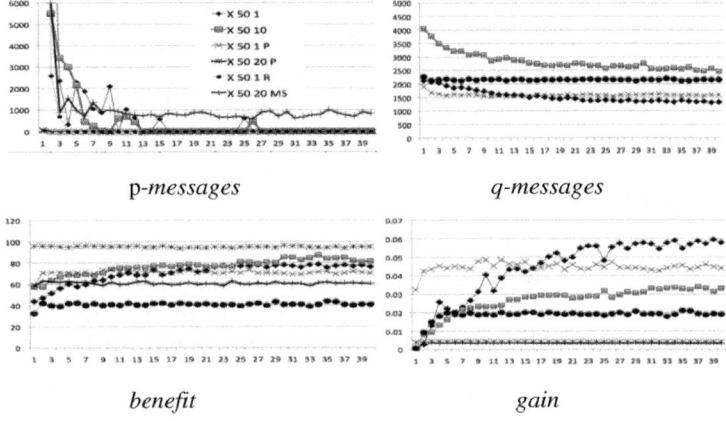

Fig. 1. Results for X=Rand. The horizontal axis shows the round number.

Results lead us to the following conclusions: (a) In any configuration of the method, the number of *p-messages* in the network is drastically reduced to 0. Actually, random routing achieves the greater reduction of *p-messages* in the first 5 rounds. As *AP* increases, in all settings, the number of *p-messages* decreases more quickly. In the "MS" configuration, the number of p-messages reaches a plateau far above zero. On the contrary, in the "P" settings, where agents exploit profiles of acquaintances, the number of *p-messages* is very small and they reach zero very fast. (b) The number of *q-messages* is also gradually reduced: Greater *AP* results to a greater number of messages. Also, the "R" and "P" configurations do not manage to decrease the number of *q-messages* (these are constantly very large - not shown in the diagram). This makes us concern about "when and how profiles should be used?". (c) Things are different for the benefit achieved: Random routing proves to be competitive, while routing taking into account agents' profiles is very effective even from the first rounds: It achieves nearly 100% benefit when messages are propagated to 20% of agents' acquaintances. However, when agents use the cooperative Q-learning method proposed they increase the benefit considerably: Increasing *AP* results to slightly larger benefit. (d) Concerning gain, in all settings, it increases as *AP* reduces: Configurations exploiting 1% of acquaintances are more effective given that they achieve high benefit, with a small number of messages.

5   Concluding Remarks

Aiming to tuning the information searching task in arbitrary networks of agents, we compute an approximation of the global routing policy-value function through collaborative reinforcement learning. Specifically we use the agent-based update of the edge-based decomposition Sparse Cooperative Q-learning method proposed in [5]. The proposed method exploits dependencies between agents' actions and thus, can result to very effective tuning, even to non-hierarchical (arbitrarily organized) systems. This is demonstrated by the results in a number of experimental settings discussed: The method is very effective even if we restrict exploration or payoff propagation. Future work aims to study optimality in various settings, studying deeply the exploitation of profiles.

References

1. Cooper, B.F., Garcia-Molina, H.: Ad hoc, self-supervising peer-to-peer search networks. ACM Transactions on Information Systems (TOIS)archive 23(2), 169–200 (2005)
2. Goldman, C., Zilberstein, S.: Decentralized Control of Cooperative Systems: Categorization and Complexity Analysis. JAIR 22, 143–174 (2004)
3. Goldman, C., Zilberstein, S.: Optimizing Information Exchange in Cooperative Multi-agent Systems. In: Proc. of AAMAS 2003 (July 2003)
4. Guestrin, C., Koller, D., Parr, R.: Multiagent planning with factored MDPs. In: NIPS, vol. 14 (2002)
5. Kok, J.R., Vlassis, N.: Collaborative Reinforcement Learning by Payoff Propagation. JMLR 7, 1789–1828 (2006)

6. Kschischang, F.R., Frey, B.J., Loeliger, H.-A.: Factor graphs and the sum-product algorithm. IEEE Transactions on Information Theory 47(2) (2001)
7. Velagapudi, P., Prokopyev, O., Scerri, P., Sycara, P.: Analyzing the Performance of Randomized Information Sharing. In: Proc. of AAMAS 2009, pp. 821–828 (2009)
8. Vouros, G.: Information Searching and Sharing in Large-Scale Dynamic Networks. In: Proc. of AAMAS 2007, pp. 235–242 (2007)
9. Vouros, G.: Searching and Sharing Information in Networks of Heterogeneous Agents. In: Proc. of AAMAS 2008, Poster (2008)
10. Xu, Y., Scerri, P., Yu, B., Lewis, M., Sycara, K.: A POMDP Approach to Token-Based Team Coordination. In: Proc. of AAMAS 2005, Utrecht, July 25-29. ACM Press (2005)
11. Xu, Y., Lewis, M., Sycara, K., Scerri, P.: Information Sharing in Large Scale Teams. In: Proc. of Workshop on Challenges in Coordination of Large Scale MultiAgent Systems (2004)
12. Xu, Y., Liao, E., Scerri, P., Yu, B., Lewis, M., Sycara, K.: Towards Flexible Coordination of Large Scale Multi-Agent Systems. In: Challenges of Large Scale Coordination (2005)
13. Xu, Y., Scerri, P., Yu, B., Okamoto, S., Lewis, M., Sycara, K.: An Integrated Token Based Algorithm for Scalable Coordination. In: Proc. of AAMAS 2005, pp. 407–414 (2005)
14. Xuan, P., Lesser, V., Zilberstein, S.: Communication Decisions in Multi-agent Cooperation: Model and Experiments. In: Proc. of AGENTS 2001, pp. 616–623 (2001)
15. Zhang, Y., Volz, R., Ioeger, T.R., Yen, J.: A Decision Theoretic Approach for Designing Proactive Communication in Multi-Agent Teamwork. In: SAC 2004, pp. 64–71 (2004)
16. Zhang, H., Lesser, V.: A Reinforcement Learning based Distributed Search Algorithm For Hierarchical Peer-to-Peer Information Retrieval Systems. In: Proc. of AAMAS 2007, pp. 231–238 (2007)

Distributed Instance Retrieval in $E_{HQ^+}^{DDL} \, \mathcal{SHIQ}$ Representation Framework

George M. Santipantakis[1] and George A. Vouros[2]

[1] ICSD, University of the Aegean, Greece
[2] Digital Systems, University of Piraeus, Greece

Abstract. While there has been a great deal of work concerning distributed reasoning with ontologies, in most cases either only TBox reasoning is concerned, or ABox reasoning is supported for languages of limited expressivity. To a greater extent than other representation frameworks, the proposed $E_{HQ^+}^{DDL} \, \mathcal{SHIQ}$ framework allows peers to establish concept-to-concept semantic correspondences to acquaintances' ontologies via bridge rules, and relate individuals by equivalence correspondences or link assertions for the $\mathcal{SHIQ}$ fragment of Description Logics. The paper presents $E_{HQ^+}^{DDL} \, \mathcal{SHIQ}$ and proposes an algorithm for the retrieval of individuals in a distributed setting.

1 Introduction

In this paper we study settings where heterogeneous, connected peers (i.e. peers with distinct and independently developed ontologies) aim to combine their conceptual and assertional knowledge towards the distributed retrieval of instances. To do so, we need to establish semantic correspondences between concepts and interlink instances from the different ontologies. Several applications can benefit from the combination of the distinct ontologies located in peers. This may also be the case for peers that may decide to modularize their knowledge, so as to enhance their reasoning performance.

Intrigued to provide a solution for such settings, we propose the $E_{HQ^+}^{DDL} \, \mathcal{SHIQ}$ representation framework. This framework, to a greater extent than other frameworks/languages for distributed reasoning with distinct ontologies, allows subjective semantic correspondences to be applied between concepts, allows equivalence correspondences between pairs of individuals and it provides a special type of roles, namely links, which relate individuals in distinct ontologies. Links can be transitive or applied to cardinality and qualitative restrictions, be applied to existential and universal restrictions, as well as hierarchically related to other relations. $E_{HQ^+}^{DDL} \, \mathcal{SHIQ}$ has been inspired by Distributed Description Logics, originally introduced by [1] and $\mathcal{E}$-connections [4]. The framework therefore naturally inherits the semantic constructors available in these frameworks for the conceptual and assertional part of the ontology and places further restrictions so as to preserve decidability, and distinguish clearly between representation cases.

I. Maglogiannis, V. Plagianakos, and I. Vlahavas (Eds.): SETN 2012, LNAI 7297, pp. 141–148, 2012.

This paper presents the $E_{HQ^+}^{DDL}$ $\mathcal{SHIQ}$ framework and discusses idiosyncrasies of that framework for distributed information retrieval. Finally, it presents an algorithm for retrieving instances in distributed settings of interconnected heterogeneous peers.

2   A Motivating Scenario

To clearly consider the issues that the proposed framework aims to address, we assume the ontology for the centralized semantic information system (SIS) presented in [11]: SIS aims to support the location of markets that trade computational resources in a democratized grid or cloud environment. The concepts in the ontology describe the different types of markets that agents may participate in, the different types of agents that participate in these markets, as well as the types of resources. Aiming to a distributed implementation of SIS, participating peers may possess this ontology, or parts of this ontology according to subjective priorities, expertise or interests. This may result to any arbitrary decomposition of the formalized information. Alternative conceptualizations of the domain elements are also possible between different peers.

In this setting we require peers to combine their knowledge about markets and tradable resources (i.e. resources advertised and requested in markets) and retrieve instances with specific characteristics. Thus, the problem is that, given a query Q formalized as a concept in any of the peers, retrieve all instances of Q that are implied by the distributed knowledge base (i.e. implied by all of its models). The problem that this work addresses, concerns combining heterogenous knowledge bases so as peers to retrieve instances effectively.

3   Related Work

There are several prominent works presented for efficient reasoning over large (trillions of triples) knowledge bases. The majority of the methods apply the same idea: construct an abstraction from the specifications of these triples, and use it for reasoning. The abstraction can be either a product of Map-Reduce tasks e.g. [8], or be a summary ABox [2]. Such methods can be complementary to the proposed framework, so as to make reasoning efficient, locally to each peer.

Among the frameworks that can apply distributed reasoning at the assertional level, we distinguish [12] which separates the assertional part of the ontology into modules. The method however cannot support qualified cardinality restrictions and the expressivity has upper bound to $\mathcal{SHI}$. DDL is another framework that clearly supports instance retrieval for $\mathcal{SHIQ}$ [10]. Reasoning is performed by tableaux algorithms in each peer, and subsumptions, as well as instances' specifications are propagated via semantic correspondences. This means that the framework is applicable to ontologies with overlapping domains, where there are no further relations between pairs of instances beyond (unrestricted) correspondences. As shown in Section 6, extending the framework with relations between instances in different ontologies, and restricting correspondences to equalities between instances, as it is done in E_{HQ+}^{DDL}, the retrieval task is getting more complicated. Furthermore, as far as we know, there is not any work describing distributed instance retrieval for $\mathcal{E}$-connections: This totally resides on local means, which is also justified by the assumption that ontologies cover distinct domains.

In addition to the above, we emphasize on the "locality" of knowledge: Peers must not be forced to share their axioms and assertions with others, and distributed reasoning must result from combinations of local reasoning chunks performed in distinct ontology units.

4   Introduction to E_{HQ+}^{DDL} $\mathcal{SHIQ}$

Preliminaries : In this section we present preliminaries on $\mathcal{SHIQ}$, Distributed Discription Logics and $\mathcal{E}$-connections.

Let $\mathcal{N_C}$ be a set of concept names, $\mathcal{N_R}$ be a set of role names and $\mathcal{N_O}$ the set of individual names. Let $Inv(R)$ denote the inverse role of R and $(\mathcal{N_R} \cup \{Inv(R)|R \in \mathcal{N_R}\})$ be the set of $\mathcal{SHIQ}$-roles. The set of $\mathcal{SHIQ}$-concepts is the smallest set constructed by the constructors in Table 1. In order to preserve decidability, number restrictions are restricted to *simple* roles only, i.e. roles that are neither transitive nor they have any transitive sub-roles. An interpretation $\mathcal{I} = \langle \Delta^{\mathcal{I}}, \cdot^{\mathcal{I}} \rangle$ consists of a non empty domain $\Delta^{\mathcal{I}}$ and the interpretation function $\cdot^{\mathcal{I}}$ which maps every concept to a subset of $\Delta^{\mathcal{I}}$ and every role to a subset of $\Delta^{\mathcal{I}} \times \Delta^{\mathcal{I}}$.

Table 1. $\mathcal{SHIQ}$ fragment of Description Logics

Atomic Concept	$C^{\mathcal{I}} \subseteq \Delta^{\mathcal{I}}$	
Universal Concept	$\top^{\mathcal{I}} = \Delta^{\mathcal{I}}$	
Bottom Concept	$\bot^{\mathcal{I}} = \emptyset$	
Atomic Role	$R^{\mathcal{I}} \subseteq \Delta^{\mathcal{I}} \times \Delta^{\mathcal{I}}$	
Conjunction	$(C \sqcap D)^{\mathcal{I}} = C^{\mathcal{I}} \cap D^{\mathcal{I}}$	$\mathcal{S}$
Disjunction	$(C \sqcup D)^{\mathcal{I}} = C^{\mathcal{I}} \cup D^{\mathcal{I}}$	
Negation	$(\neg C)^{\mathcal{I}} = \Delta^{\mathcal{I}} \setminus C^{\mathcal{I}}$	
Existential Restriction	$(\exists R.C)^{\mathcal{I}} = \{x \in \Delta^{\mathcal{I}}|\exists y \in \Delta^{\mathcal{I}}, (x,y) \in R^{\mathcal{I}}, y \in C^{\mathcal{I}}\}$	
Value Restriction	$(\forall R.C)^{\mathcal{I}} = \{x \in \Delta^{\mathcal{I}}|\forall y \in \Delta^{\mathcal{I}}, (x,y) \in R^{\mathcal{I}} \rightarrow y \in C^{\mathcal{I}}\}$	
Transitive Role	$\mathcal{I} \vDash Trans(R) \leftrightarrow R^{\mathcal{I}} = (R^{\mathcal{I}})^{+}$	
Role Hierarchy	$\mathcal{I} \vDash (P \sqsubseteq R)^{\mathcal{I}} \leftrightarrow P^{\mathcal{I}} \subseteq R^{\mathcal{I}}$	$\mathcal{H}$
Inverse Role	$(Inv(R))^{\mathcal{I}} = \{(x,y)|(y,x) \in R^{\mathcal{I}}\}$	$\mathcal{I}$
Qualified	$(\geq nS.C)^{\mathcal{I}} = \{x \in \Delta^{\mathcal{I}}, ||y, (x,y) \in S^{\mathcal{I}} \wedge y \in C^{\mathcal{I}}|| \geq n\}$	$\mathcal{Q}$
Number Restrictions	$(\leq nS.C)^{\mathcal{I}} = \{x \in \Delta^{\mathcal{I}}, ||y, (x,y) \in S^{\mathcal{I}} \wedge y \in C^{\mathcal{I}}|| \leq n\}$	

Let C and D possibly complex concepts, $C \sqsubseteq D$ is called a general concept inclusion (GCI) axiom. A finite set of GCIs is called a TBox (denoted by $\mathcal{T}$). An interpretation $\mathcal{I}$ satisfies a GCI $C \sqsubseteq D$ if $C^{\mathcal{I}} \subseteq D^{\mathcal{I}}$. $\mathcal{I}$ satisfies a TBox if it satisfies each GCI in it. In this case $\mathcal{I}$ is a model of this TBox. A concept C is satisfiable w.r.t. a role hierarchy $\mathcal{R}$ and a TBox if there is a *model* $\mathcal{I}$ of TBox and $\mathcal{R}$ with $C^{\mathcal{I}} \neq \emptyset$. A concept C subsumes a concept D w.r.t TBox $\mathcal{T}$ and $\mathcal{R}$ if $C^{\mathcal{I}} \subseteq D^{\mathcal{I}}$ holds in every model of $\mathcal{T}$ and $\mathcal{R}$.

For a concept expression C, a role name R, and the individual names a, b, assertions are either *instance assertions* of the form $a : C$ or *role assertions* $(a, b) : R$. Also, $a \doteq b$, $a \neq b$ are *individual equality, inequality assertions*, respectively. The finite set of assertions w.r.t. a TBox $\mathcal{T}$ and a role hierarchy $\mathcal{R}$ is called ABox.

Distributed Description Logics (DDL) is a framework which allows distributed reasoning over $\mathcal{SHIQ}$ [1], [10]. The intuition of the framework is that concepts and individuals in an ontology can be mapped to corresponding elements of remote ontologies. Given a finite index set I, the correspondences between concepts are expressed as *onto*-bridge rules $i : C \overset{\sqsupseteq}{\to} j : G$, or *into*-bridge rules $i : C \overset{\sqsubseteq}{\to} j : G$, where i, j in I denote distinct ontologies, $i : C$, $j : G$ concepts in these ontologies and the direction of the arrow denotes the subjectiveness of the correspondence (i.e. correspondences are under the subjective view of j). For the assertional part, subjective individual correspondences can be either *partial* or *complete*. Given an instance name a_i in a local ABox $\mathcal{A}_i$ and $b_j^1, b_j^2, ..., b_j^n$ instances names in the ABox $\mathcal{A}_j$, a partial individual correspondence (PIC) is an expression of the form $a_i \mapsto b_j^k, k = 1, ..., n$, while a complete individual correspondence (CIC) is an expression of the form $a_i \overset{=}{\mapsto} \{b_j^1, ..., b_j^n\}$. The distributed knowledge base is constructed by the local knowledge bases, and the set of bridge rules and correspondences between mapped elements.

On the other hand, $\mathcal{E}$-connections is a framework which combines representations in different logics ([5]). Concerning DL, as originally proposed in [4], $\mathcal{E}$-connections are intended for modelling scenarios where the respective domains of the ontology units are mutually disjoint, however this assumption has been relaxed in [3]. $\mathcal{E}$-connections $\mathcal{C}_{\mathcal{HQ+}}^{\mathcal{E}}(\mathcal{SHIQ}, \mathcal{SHOQ}, \mathcal{SHIO})$ may combine ontology units in any of the $\mathcal{SHIQ}, \mathcal{SHOQ}, \mathcal{SHIO}$ fragments of DL using link-properties. Link-properties can be hierarchically related, be transitive and, in case they are simple, be restricted by qualitative restrictions.

For a finite index set I, a set of link-properties connecting concepts in the i and j units, $i \neq j \in I$, is defined to be the set $\mathcal{E}_{ij} = \epsilon_{ij}$. In case $i = j$ is the set $\mathcal{E}_{ij} = \epsilon_{ij} \cup \{Inv(E) | E \in \epsilon_{ji}\}$, where ϵ_{ij} are the sets of link-property or role names that are not pairwise disjoint, but are disjoint with respect to the sets of concept names. An ij-property axiom is an assertion of the form $E_{ij}^n \sqsubseteq E_{ij}^m$, where the superscript distinguishes link-properties in $\mathcal{E}_{ij}$. An ij-property box R_{ij} includes a finite set of ij-property inclusion axioms (R_{ii} is the local RBox $\mathcal{R}_i$). The sets of i-concepts (i.e. concepts specified in the i-th unit) are inductively defined as the smallest sets constructed using the constructors provided by the local DL fragment, as well with the link-property specifications' constructors [4].

The $\mathcal{E}$−connections definition of a combined TBox is a family of TBoxes $\mathbf{T} = \{\mathcal{T}_i\}_{i \in I}$, where $\mathcal{T}_i$ is a finite set of i-concept inclusion axioms. A combined knowledge base $\Sigma = \langle \mathbf{T}, \mathcal{R} \rangle$ is composed by the combined TBox $\mathbf{T}$, and the combined RBox $\mathcal{R}$. In addition to instance assertions, assertions between individuals can be of the form $a \cdot E_{ij} \cdot b$, where E_{ij} is a property in $\mathcal{E}_{ij}$.

Both DDL and $\mathcal{E}$-connections apply distributed tableau algorithms for deciding concepts' satisfiability. The algorithms can be found in [9] and [6].

$E_{HQ+}^{DDL} \mathcal{SHIQ}$ combines the features of DDL and $\mathcal{E}-$connections as follows:

Definition 1. ($E_{HQ+}^{DDL} \mathcal{SHIQ}$ Syntax) Let I be a non empty set of indexes, for $i, j \in I$, N_{C_i} are sets of concept names and the set of ij-properties' names is denoted by ϵ_{ij}, not necessarily pairwise disjoint, but disjoint with respect to the sets N_{C_i}. For $i, j \in I$, the set of ij-properties connecting concepts in the i and j units, is defined as $\mathcal{E}_{ij} = \epsilon_{ij}$, and in case $i = j$ is the set $\mathcal{E}_{ij} = \epsilon_{ij} \cup \{Inv(E)|E \in \epsilon_{ji}\}$. An ij-property axiom is an assertion of the form $E_{ij}^n \sqsubseteq E_{ij}^m$, where E_{ij}^* are distinct properties in $\mathcal{E}_{ij}$. Transitive axioms are of the form $Trans(E; (i, j))$, where E is a property name defined for the pair of ontology units $i, j \in I$. Such an axiom is a shorthand for the axiom $Trans(E; (i, i), (i, j))$ as defined in [6], meaning that E is a transitive role in i and a transitive link-property connecting i and j.

An ij-property box R_{ij} includes a finite set of ij-property inclusion axioms, plus all transitivity axioms concerning ij-properties. The combined property box RBox $\mathcal{R}$ contains each of the ij-property boxes. The set of i-concepts, $i \in I$, are inductively defined as in $\mathcal{E}-$connections and cardinality restrictions may hold only for simple properties.

Finally, semantic correspondences are denoted as bridge rules of concept onto concept, or concept into concept rules, as already defined.

Definition 2. ($E_{HQ+}^{DDL} \mathcal{SHIQ}$ Distributed Knowledge Base) A combined TBox is a family of TBoxes $\boldsymbol{T}= \{\mathcal{T}\}_{i \in I}$, where each $\mathcal{T}_i$ is a finite set of i-concept inclusion axioms. A distributed knowledge base $\Sigma = \langle \boldsymbol{T}, \mathcal{R}, \mathcal{A}, \mathcal{B} \rangle$ is composed by the combined TBox $\boldsymbol{T}$, the combined RBox $\mathcal{R}$, and a collection of bridge rules $\mathcal{B} = \{\mathfrak{B}_{ij}\}_{i \neq j \in I}$ between ontology units. A distributed ABox $\mathcal{A} = \langle \{A\}_{i \in I}, \mathcal{C}, \mathfrak{L} \rangle$ consists of the family of ABoxes $\{A\}_{i \in I}$, a collection of individual correspondences $\mathcal{C} = \{\mathfrak{C}_{ij}\}_{i \neq j \in I}$ of the form $i : a \overset{=}{\mapsto} j : b$, and property assertions $\mathfrak{L} = \{\mathfrak{L}_{ij}\}_{i, j \in I}$ of the form $a \cdot E_{ij} \cdot b$, where E_{ij} is a property in $\mathcal{E}_{ij}$.

Each TBox $\mathcal{T}_i$, $i \in I$ is locally interpreted by a local, possibly hole interpretation $\mathcal{I}_i$ that consists of a domain $\Delta^{\mathcal{I}_i}$, a valuation function $\cdot^{\mathcal{I}_i}$ which maps every concept to a subset of $\Delta^{\mathcal{I}_i}$. The ij-property boxes R_{ij} with $i, j \in I$, are interpreted by valuation functions $\cdot^{\mathcal{I}_{ij}}$ that map every ij-property to a subset of $\Delta^{\mathcal{I}_i} \times \Delta^{\mathcal{I}_j}$. Let $\mathcal{I}_{ij} = \langle \Delta^{\mathcal{I}_i}, \Delta^{\mathcal{I}_j}, \cdot^{\mathcal{I}_{ij}} \rangle$, $i, j \in I$. A hole interpretation maps any concept (including the top and bottom ones) to the domain or to the empty set.

Definition 3. ($E_{HQ+}^{DDL} \mathcal{SHIQ}$ Domain relation) A domain relation $r_{ij}, i \neq j$ from $\Delta^{\mathcal{I}_i}$ to $\Delta^{\mathcal{I}_j}$ is a subset of $\Delta^{\mathcal{I}_i} \times \Delta^{\mathcal{I}_j}$, s.t. for each d in $\Delta^{\mathcal{I}_i}$, $r_{ij}(d) = \{d'|d' \in \Delta^{\mathcal{I}_j}$, with $i : d \overset{=}{\mapsto} j : d'\}$ and it holds that in case $r_{ij}(d_1) = d'$ and $r_{ij}(d_2) = d'$, then $d_1 = d_2$. Also, given a subset D of $\Delta^{\mathcal{I}_i}$, $r_{ij}(D)$ denotes $\cup_{d \in D} r_{ij}(d)$.

Definition 4. ($E_{HQ+}^{DDL} \mathcal{SHIQ}$ Distributed Interpretation) Given the index I and $i, j \in I$, a distributed interpretation $\mathfrak{I}$ of a distributed knowledge base Σ is the tuple formed by the set of local interpretations $\mathcal{I}_i = \langle \Delta^{\mathcal{I}_i}, \cdot^{\mathcal{I}_i} \rangle$ for each $\mathcal{T}_i$, the family $\{\mathcal{I}_{ij}\}$, and a set of domain relations r_{ij}. Formally, $\mathfrak{I} = \langle \{\mathcal{I}_i\}_{i \in I}, \{\mathcal{I}_{ij}\}_{i, j \in I}, \{r_{ij}\}_{i \neq j \in I} \rangle$.

A local interpretation $\mathcal{I}_i$ satisfies an i-concept C w.r.t. a distributed knowledge base Σ, i.e. $\mathcal{I}_i \vDash C$ iff $C^{\mathcal{I}_i} \neq \emptyset$. $\mathcal{I}_i$ satisfies an axiom $C \sqsubseteq D$ between i-concepts (i.e. $\mathcal{I}_i \vDash C \sqsubseteq D$) if $C^{\mathcal{I}_i} \subseteq D^{\mathcal{I}_i}$. Also, $\mathcal{I}_{ij}$ satisfies an ij-property axiom $R \sqsubseteq S$ ($\mathcal{I}_{ij} \vDash R \sqsubseteq S$) if $R^{\mathcal{I}_{ij}} \subseteq S^{\mathcal{I}_{ij}}$. A transitivity axiom $Trans(E; (i, j))$ is satisfied by $\mathcal{I}_i$ iff $E^{\mathcal{I}_{ii}} \cup E^{\mathcal{I}_{ij}}$ is transitive.

The distributed interpretation $\mathfrak{I}$ *satisfies* ($\vDash_d$) the elements of a distributed knowledge base, if the following conditions hold:

1. $\mathfrak{I} \vDash_d i : C \sqsubseteq D$, if $\mathcal{I}_i \vDash C \sqsubseteq D$
2. $\mathfrak{I} \vDash_d \mathcal{T}_i$ if $\mathfrak{I} \vDash i : C \sqsubseteq D$ for all $C \sqsubseteq D$ in $\mathcal{T}_i$
3. $\mathfrak{I} \vDash_d i : C \overset{\sqsubseteq}{\to} j : D$, if $r_{ij}(C^{\mathcal{I}_i}) \subseteq D^{\mathcal{I}_j}$
4. $\mathfrak{I} \vDash_d i : C \overset{\sqsupseteq}{\to} j : D$, if $r_{ij}(C^{\mathcal{I}_i}) \supseteq D^{\mathcal{I}_j}$
5. $\mathfrak{I} \vDash_d \mathfrak{B}_{ij}$, if $\mathfrak{I}$ satisfies all bridge rules in $\mathfrak{B}_{ij}$
6. $\mathfrak{I} \vDash_d R \sqsubseteq S$, if $\mathcal{I}_{ij} \vDash R \sqsubseteq S$, where $R \sqsubseteq S$ in R_{ij}
7. $\mathfrak{I} \vDash_d Trans(E; (i, j))$ if $\mathcal{I}_i \vDash Trans(E; (i, j))$, where $Trans(E; (i, j))$ in R_{ij}
8. $\mathfrak{I} \vDash_d R_{ij}$ if $\mathfrak{I} \vDash_d R \sqsubseteq S$ and $\mathfrak{I} \vDash_d Trans(E; (i, j))$ for all inclusion and transitivity axioms in R_{ij}
9. $\mathfrak{I} \vDash_d \Sigma$ if for every $i, j \in I, \mathfrak{I} \vDash_d \mathcal{T}_i$, $\mathfrak{I} \vDash_d \mathcal{R}_{ij}$ and $\mathfrak{I} \vDash_d \mathfrak{B}_{ij}$.

Definition 5. ($E_{HQ+}^{DDL}\mathcal{SHIQ}$ *Distributed entailment and satisfiability*) $\Sigma \vDash_d X \sqsubseteq Y$ *if for every* $\mathfrak{I}$, $\mathfrak{I} \vDash_d \Sigma$ *implies* $\mathfrak{I} \vDash_d X \sqsubseteq Y$, *where* X *and* Y *are either i-concepts, or ij-properties,* $i, j \in I$. Σ *is satisfiable if there exists a* $\mathfrak{I}$ *such that* $\mathfrak{I} \vDash_d \Sigma$. *A concept* $i : C$ *is satisfiable with respect to* Σ *if there is a* $\mathfrak{I}$ *such that* $\mathfrak{I} \vDash_d \Sigma$ *and* $C^{I_i} \neq \emptyset$.

The worst case complexity is 2NexpTime w.r.t. the size of the combined TBox and RBox. Further details on $E_{HQ+}^{DDL}\mathcal{SHIQ}$ can be found in [7].

5   Distributed Instance Retrieval in $E_{HQ+}^{DDL}\ \mathcal{SHIQ}$

The task of instance retrieval in any fragment of Description Logics, is defined as the computation of the set of individuals that instantiate a given concept. For the proposed framework $E_{HQ+}^{DDL}\ \mathcal{SHIQ}$, into-bridge rules and individual correspondences provide the means through which information is "translated" and transferred between peers. Intuitively, an into-bridge rule $i : A \overset{\sqsubseteq}{\to} j : B$ means that if concept $i : A$ has an individual a, then there should exist an individual $j : b$ such that $(a^{I_i}, b^{I_j}) \in r_{ij}$. Formally, given a distributed knowledge base $\Sigma = \langle \mathbf{T}, \mathcal{R}, \mathcal{A}, \mathcal{B} \rangle$, and $i : A \overset{\sqsubseteq}{\to} j : B \in \mathfrak{B}_{ij}$, $\langle i : a \overset{\mapsto}{\to} j : b \rangle \in \mathfrak{C}_{ij}$ then $\Sigma \vDash i : A(a) \Longrightarrow \Sigma \vDash j : B(b)$ (locally to i, j).

According to the semantics of a complete individual correspondence (CIC) such as $\langle i : a \overset{=}{\mapsto} j : b \rangle$, the pair of individuals $\langle a^{I_i}, b^{I_j} \rangle$ belongs to the domain relation r_{ij} and a^{I_i}, b^{I_j} are the same real-world object. Since equality is a transitive relation, given Definition 3 the following holds: if $\langle i : x \overset{=}{\mapsto} j : u \rangle$, $\langle i : y \overset{=}{\mapsto} j : v \rangle$, $x^{I_i} = y^{I_i}$ then $u^{I_j} = r_{ij}(x^{I_i}) = r_{ij}(y^{I_i}) = v^{I_j}$ under the subjective point of view of j. Similarly to the instance retrieval algorithm proposed in [10], we need a transformation function f_{ij}, which transforms individuals from i to individuals of j, such that their interpretations respect the semantics of domain relation r_{ij}. Formally, given a bridge rule $\{i : A \overset{\sqsubseteq}{\rightarrow} j : B\}$, the distributed knowledge base $\Sigma = \langle \mathbf{T}, \mathcal{R}, \mathcal{A}, \mathcal{B} \rangle$, and f_{ij}, then: $\Sigma \vDash i : A(a) \implies \Sigma \vDash j : B(f_{ij}(b))$. Specifically, $f_{ij}(x)$, in case an individual correspondence $\langle i : x \overset{\mapsto}{\rightarrow} j : y \rangle$ exists, the individual x is mapped to y, else injects a new individual $f_{ij}(x)$ and asserts the respective correspondence.

The representation framework E_{HQ+}^{DDL} $\mathcal{SHIQ}$ combines CIC and bridge rules, with link-properties and link assertions. These constructors interact to derive new knowledge. The instance retrieval algorithm presented in [10] can be applied only on those logics where the original ABox can be partitioned into a set of separate ABoxes, where the properties of any individual are specified locally. Obviously, the presence of link assertions do not allow ABoxes to be independently processed.

Similarly to DDL, given a set of bridge rules $\{i : A \overset{\sqsupseteq}{\rightarrow} j : G, i : B_k \overset{\sqsubseteq}{\rightarrow} j : H_k\}$ for $1 \leq k \leq n$, E_{HQ+}^{DDL} $\mathcal{SHIQ}$ can propagate subsumption relations from i-th to j-th module: $\Sigma \vDash_d i : A \sqsubseteq \bigsqcup_{k=1}^{n} B_k \Rightarrow \Sigma \vDash_d j : G \sqsubseteq \bigsqcup_{k=1}^{n} H_k$. But, additionally to DDL, reasoning on the conceptual part of the distributed ontology results to a distributed concept taxonomy that takes into account link-property specifications as well (a specific example is shown below). The method $DTax(C, \mathcal{T}_i)$ computes the set of concepts that are either equal or subsumed by concept C in i. The proposed retrieval algorithm for a concept $j : Q$ is as follows:

$InstRetrieve_j(Q)$

    compute the set $DTax(Q, \mathcal{T}_j)$

    retrieve the set of local individuals S_Q of Q w.r.t. the distributed taxonomy

    for every concept C in $DTax(Q, \mathcal{T}_j)$

        for each bridge rule of the form $i : D \overset{\sqsubseteq}{\rightarrow} j : C$

        compute the set of individuals $S_D = InstRetrieve_i(D)$

        for each individual x in S_D compute $S_Q \leftarrow S_Q \cup \{f_{ij}(x)\}$

    return S_Q

As an example we consider a distributed knowledge base constructed by the following information:

$\mathcal{T}_j : \{CapableToReason \sqsubseteq \forall hasProcessor.QuadCoreCPU\}$,

$\mathcal{A}_j : \{CapableToReason(myPC), hasProcessor(myPC, i7.sn001)\}$,

$\mathcal{T}_i : \{QuadCoreCPU \sqsubseteq CPU\}$,

$\mathfrak{B}_{ij} : \{i : CPU \overset{\sqsubseteq}{\rightarrow} j : Processor\}$,

$\mathfrak{C}_{ij} : \{i : i7.sn001 \overset{=}{\mapsto} j : i7.myPC\}$.

We want to retrieve all the individuals of the concept *Processor*. The process starts by computing the distributed taxonomy. $DTax_j(Processor, \mathcal{T}_j)$ returns the set $\{Processor\}$. Local reasoning will return the empty set of individuals, and the process will propagate the query to peer i through the bridge rule, invoking $InstRetrieval_i(CPU)$. Peer i will reply with the set of individuals $\{i7.sn001\}$: This is the case, since additionally to DDL, the application of $DTax_j(Processor, \mathcal{T}_j)$ for the specification in $\mathcal{T}_j$ and the assertion $hasProcessor(myPC, i7.sn001)$ imply that $QuadCoreCPU(i7.sn001)$, which further implies $CPU(i7.sn001)$ in i. The instance $i7.sn001$ is translated by the f_{ij} function to the $i7.myPC$, and returned by the algorithm.

6   Discussion

The proposed algorithm for the representation framework E^{DDL}_{HQ+} $\mathcal{SHIQ}$ allows reasoning with collective knowledge bases with non-empty ABoxes for the retrieval of individuals. The method inherits from DDL the capability to propagate concept subsumptions across heterogeneous data repositories and in the same time allows object assertions between distinct ontology units. This leads to the conclusion that E^{DDL}_{HQ+} $\mathcal{SHIQ}$ supports more expressive queries than DDL, while extending $\mathcal{E}$-connections to reasoning with ontologies covering overlapping domains.

Further work on this framework requires investigating the combination of ontology units, with more expressive fragments of DL. The framework is implemented using Pellet 2.2.2 and experimental results will be available upon stabilization of the software. Also, the overall system's performance will be measured for a variety of peer architectures and organizations.

Acknowledgement. This research project is being supported by the project "IRAKLITOS II" of the O.P.E.L.L. 2007 - 2013 of the NSRF (2007 - 2013), co-funded by the European Union and National Resources of Greece.

References

1. Borgida, A., Luciano Serafini, L.: Distributed Description Logics: Assimilating Information from Peer Sources. Data Semantics, 153–184 (2003)
2. Dolby, J., Fokoue, A., Kalyanpur, A., Schonberg, E., Srinivas, K.: Scalable highly expressive reasoner (SHER). Web Semantics 7, 357–361 (2009)
3. Grau, C., Kutz, O.: Modular Ontology Languages Revisited. In: Proc. of SWeCKa 2007 (2007)
4. Grau, B.C., Parsia, B., Sirin, E.: Working with Multiple Ontologies on the Semantic Web. In: McIlraith, S.A., Plexousakis, D., van Harmelen, F. (eds.) ISWC 2004. LNCS, vol. 3298, pp. 620–634. Springer, Heidelberg (2004)
5. Kutz, O., Lutz, C., Wolter, F., Zakharyaschev, M.: E-connections of abstract description systems. Artif. Intell. 156(1), 1–73 (2004)
6. Parsia, B., Grau, C.: Generalized Link Properties for Expressive epsilon-Connections of Description Logics. In: Proc. of AAAI 2005 (2005)
7. Santipantakis, G., Vouros, G.: $E^{DDL}_{HQ+}\mathcal{SHIQ}$ Representation framework. Technical Report (2011),
   http://ai-lab-webserver.aegean.gr/gsant/TechnicalReports.html
8. Schlicht, A., Stuckenschmidt, H.: MapResolve. In: Rudolph, S., Gutierrez, C. (eds.) RR 2011. LNCS, vol. 6902, pp. 294–299. Springer, Heidelberg (2011)
9. Serafini, L., Borgida, A., Tamilin, A.: Aspects of distributed and modular ontology reasoning. In: Proc. of IJCAI 2005 (2005)
10. Serafini, L., Tamilin, A.: Distributed Instance Retrieval in Heterogeneous Ontologies. In: Proc. of the 2nd Italian Semantic Web Workshop (2005)
11. Vouros, G., et al.: A Semantic Information System for Services and Traded Resources in Grid e-Markets. FGCS 26(7), 916–933 (2010)
12. Wandelt, S., Müller, R.: Sound and Complete SHI Instance Retrieval for 1 Billion ABox Assertions. In: 10th Int. Semantic Web Conf. on Scalable Semantic Web Knowledge Base Systems Workshop (2011)

Evolutionary Optimization of a Neural Network Controller for Car Racing Simulation

Damianos Galanopoulos, Christos Athanasiadis, and Anastasios Tefas

Department of Informatics, Aristotle University of Thessaloniki
Box 451, 54124, Greece
`tefas@aiia.csd.auth.gr`

Abstract. In this paper a novel method for car racing controller learning is proposed. Car racing simulation is an active research field where new advances in aerodynamics, consumption and engine power are modelled and tested. The proposed approach is based on Neural Networks that learn the driving behaviour of other rule-based bots. Additionally, the resulted neural-networks controllers are evolved in order to adapt and increase their performance to a given racing track using genetic algorithms. The proposed bots are implemented and tested on several tracks of the open racing car simulator (TORCS) providing smoother driving behaviour than the corresponding rule-based bots and increased performance using the evolutionary adaptation.

Keywords: TORCS, Neural networks, Genetic algorithms, Evolutionary Optimization.

1 Introduction

Nowadays, video games are becoming more and more important, as a hot consumer product, as well as a great opportunity for research in artificial intelligence. The main goal is to offer fun to the player. In previous years this goal has been achieved partly through the visual realism and interesting game scenarios. But every video game player knew that the current AI in the games was way far from the actual human behaviour. When we are playing a game versus one or more NPC (non-character player) we can easily realize that we are not playing versus another human because either the other player is too simple to beat, figuring out a specific efficient strategy, or the AI is so complicated that the human loses every time. Artificial intelligence in computer games is infused into non-playable characters with a view to giving the human player the illusion of a clever human opponent. Initially we have to create a NPC that imitates the behaviour of a human player [3]. However, we have to bear in mind that the NPC must also have the ability to adapt depending on the current state and environment and the current opponents in the game. Computational intelligence methods can be implemented to deal with the adaptation task. Such methods can be retrieved from evolutionary algorithms and Neural Networks [2].

I. Maglogiannis, V. Plagianakos, and I. Vlahavas (Eds.): SETN 2012, LNAI 7297, pp. 149–156, 2012.

Previous approaches to car racing were already developed for the forerunner of TORCS, the robot auto racing simulator (RARS) [7]. For example, Stanley et al. [8] developed a car racing strategy that depended on range-finders and developed a sensory-motor mapping with the incremental neural evolution of augmenting topologies (NEAT) approach.

The Cognitive BOdySpaces for Torcs-based Adaptive Racing (COBOSTAR), which was developed by B. Martin V. Butz and Thies D.Lonneker [9], is divided in two parts: on-track optimization and off-track optimization. Actually, they implemented heuristic functions for mapping input data into decision. These functions were different when the controller was on-track or off-track.

Another approach has been proposed in [4]. The idea behind this bot was to have a driving architecture based on a set of simple controllers. Each controller is applied as a separate module in charge of a basic driving action. Two important modules are the learning module, which finds where the bot have to increase or reduce its speed, and the opponents management module, which adapts the agent behaviour when the opponents are close.

Luigi Cardamore's approach [10] consists of an evolved neural network, implementing a basic driver behaviour, compounded with code for basic tasks such as the start, the crash-recovery, the gear change, and the overtaking. They use neuroevolution of augmented topologies(NEAT)[8] for predicting target speed and target position for a given input configuration. The implemented fitness functions is the error between the actual values and the predicted ones.

The combination of a fuzzy logic module with a classifier module and a finite state machine is proposed [11] with a view to tackling the great variety of TORCS commands from Diego Perez and Yago Saez.

The basic idea in our controller is to use Neural Networks for the decisions of the driver bot. That is, the bot is trained using back-propagation in a single hidden layer NN. The training data are collected by using other bots that are using rule-based AI to control the car. That is, the proposed bot is trained by other bots. We expect to enhance the performance of the rule-based bots since the NN will smoothly imitate their behaviour. Moreover, in order to improve its performance, the proposed bot has the ability to evolve its NN using evolutionary algorithms. That is, the proposed bot, firstly, learns from other bots how to drive and adapts the weights of its NN using genetic algorithms in order to improve its lap time for given racing tracks. The novelty of our method is the use of the time performance as the fitness function, which changes the NN weights depending on the current lap time.

2   TORCS Environment

The open race car simulator (TORCS) provides an open source car racing environment with a very realistic simulator that has a sophisticated physic engine which takes into consideration real car racing issues such as fuel consumption, collisions or traction. Besides that, TORCS offers a very realistic game-play and graphics. It is a well designed simulator which can be compared with the finest race game titles. Additionally, TORCS provides a very flexible and simple client-server architecture. Server stands for the game's functions, and client stands for the car agent handling. The above characteristics justify why it has been used for research purposes in the scientific community, especially for solving the simulated racing car challenge task. In 2011, three different challenges were held; the EVO-2011 in Torino, ACM GECOO-2011 in Dublin and the IEEE CIG-2011 in Seoul.

The first approaches appeared, were hand-crafted rule-based and only slightly optimized on several aspects. Our approach in this challenging task is based on Neural networks combined with evolutionary algorithms. We tried to tackle the challenge of imitating other players or car agent behaviour.

We have used two different controllers, as trainers of the proposed bot. The first controller is a simple rule-based controller (named "Simple Driver"), which is offered with the client server architecture, and the second one is called "Simplicity". The proposed controller is based on a feed forward ANN (Artificial Neural Networks) that was trained with data generated by other controllers using back-propagation. The final step in our method was to adopt modified genetic algorithms in order to achieve better results.

TORCS consists of a server component that supports the general TORCS setup [1] and returns information sensors about the controller and the track. The client component uses these information to apply its strategy. The controllers (clients) run as external programs and communicate with the server with UDP connections. At each game tic the controller receives sensor data that corresponds to the car's current state and its surrounding environment (the tracks and the components). The controller has to calculate four output parameters (the wheel steering, the gas pedal, the fuel level and the break pedal). Its strategy depends on the current input (information from sensors). In the proposed method we use learning methods in order to build output commands.

The sensors novelty is in that they do not contain the whole track information, but they carry only simulated local information instead. In particular, the available sensors are an angle sensor, which specifies the current angle between the car direction and the track axis, the current speed in longitudinal and transverse axes of the car, 19 range sensors, which sample the free track space in front of the car and they are only valid while on track, 36 opponent sensors, which notice opponents around the car, the current engine speed in rounds per minute, the current gear, the track position with respect to the track edges, and the current rotation speed of the four wheels. Moreover, there is further racing information available including the current lap time, the damage of the car, the distance from the start line along the track line, the total distance raced, the amount of remaining fuel, the last lap time and the standing in the race. For the car control, there is a gas pedal and a brake pedal, gear shifting, and steering values available.

Thus, the agent strategy cannot receive information about tracks morphology (such as which curve comes next) and it depends only on the local information (the sensors they were described before).

3   Proposed Approach

Our agent was trained by applying two rule based controllers in order to collect data fast and for the different sensors cited in the previous section. Data collection was made for several game tracks. More specifically, we use two different tracks, named F-Speedway and CG-Speedway No1 for data capturing. For each track we used approximately 10.000 input states for each controller. Each input state is composed of 9 input data that represent the controller's environment and two output values that correspond to controller acceleration and wheel steering. These two outputs are in fact the desired outputs of the designed Neural Networks. For each output "label", we created a separate Neural Network. That is, one neural network decides about the acceleration and the other decides about the steering. Values are normalized in $[-1, 1]$.

3.1   Off-line Neural Network Learning by Imitation

The first part of our work was to imitate controller's behaviour by implementing Artificial Neural Networks. Initially we obtained the data from the controller we wanted to imitate (trainer) and a neural network was trained with the back-propagation algorithm. We used neural networks with a specific structure [5]. Hecht-Nielsen [6] proved that one hidden layer is sufficient to approximate a bound continuous function with a specific mean square error. Thus, we chose to generate our neural network with one hidden layer with 50 neurons. The number of neurons was selected using cross-validation in the training set in order to avoid over-training. Using the previously described structure we reduced the time and code complexity. As an activation function for the NN we have used the logistic function $f(t) = \frac{1}{1+e^{-t}}$ and the learning rate h was set to 0.5 and the momentum m to 0.1. The Neural Network weights determine the controller decisions, which will define the behaviour of our bot in real-time gaming.

Using the back-propagation algorithm we were able to train neural networks to return the desired output data. Thus, we can use the outputs of the trained neural networks in order to control the acceleration and steering of the car. In fact we are using the following expression:

$$s = \frac{2}{1 + e^{(speed_{currnet} - speed_{target})}} - 1$$

where $speed_{current}$ is the speed in the previous game tic and the $speed_{target}$ is the output of the Neural Network every game tic. This expression takes values in $[-1, 1]$. When this expression returns 1, it means that our controller has to fully accelerate and when it returns -1 controller has to fully break. Similarly, we utilize the same expression for the wheel steering. The objective was to succeed convergence in bots behaviour (between the controller that was used as trainer and our agent). The next step is to modify the NN weights in order to improve controller's behaviour in unknown tracks and simultaneously to increase agent steering smoothness and reduce lap time. To do so, we use adaptation of the NN weights using genetic algorithms.

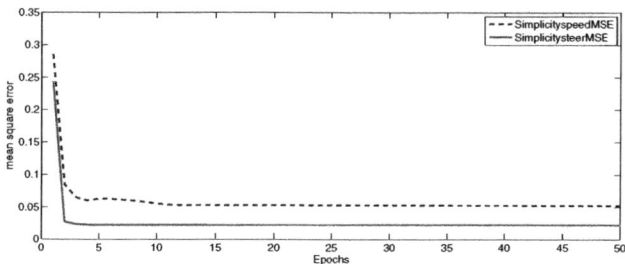

Fig. 1. NN convergence

3.2   On-line Learning Using Genetic Algorithms

Genetic algorithms(GA) are heuristic methods that try to mimic the natural process of evolution. Genetic algorithms became popular through the work of John Holland in the early 1970's. Actually, GA try to generate solutions to optimization and search problems. These solutions are evaluated by a fitness function. To do so, the genetic operations of mutation and cross-over attempt to find an optimal solution. The operation of mutation and cross-over of GA are described in [12].

In our work we employed GA in order to improve the performance of the neural networks trained in the first stage. Thus, the GA try to optimize the fitness function by searching for better weights for the trained NNs. We use as a fitness function the $currentLapTime$, which can be returned from the game with the goal to evaluate the performance of current weights. That is, the trained NNs are evolved trying to achieve the fastest lap.

When the evolution begins we store three different NN weight sets for acceleration control and three for steering control and the lap time that the controller achieved with those weights. These initial weights that will be used for producing the offsprings are produced by training the NN with different learning parameters (e.g., learning rate, initialization, etc). Then, we modify these weights by using mutation and cross-over. Mutation is simulated by adding uniform random noise (transported to $[-1,1]$) to certain probabilistically selected weights. The weights are normalized in $[-1,1]$. We add multiplicative noise on the selected weights as follows:

$$weights_{new} = weights + weights * \frac{noise}{k}$$

, where k is a normalization constant which affects the impact of noise. That is, the selected weights are slightly increased or decreased according to the noise value.

The crossover operation is implemented by combining probabilistically selected solutions (NN weight sets) according to their fitness. The selected NNs exchange randomly selected weights in order to create their offsprings. The agent uses the new weights in three consecutive laps and the time achieved is used as fitness function. The selection procedure keeps only the three best offsprings weights and replace the previous weights accordingly. Our anticipation here is to optimize the current lap time every three-laps. This is expected since GA at least keeps the initial weights in case of non improvement. The procedure is repeated every three laps. We have noticed that the lap time is not continuously decreasing. When we test the same weights multiple times the returned lap time is not exactly the same. Thus, we expect some small fluctuations in the convergence. We let our agent to repeat the above procedure many times. For every track, we have tested the controller for 40 laps.

4   Experiments

In our experiments we used several tracks that TORCS offers. For the sake of convenience we are going to present results for the following tracks Oval B-Speedway, F-Speedway, CG-Speedway No1. Two benchmark observation comparisons to test and reveal differences between trainer and trainee are the current lap time, that indicates the speed performance, and the distance from the track axis, which indicates the wheel steering performance. Our expectations in those two observations are, firstly, our bot to achieve better lap times and, secondly, to accomplish a more smooth driving trajectory. In Figures Fig. 2(a), Fig. 2(b), Fig. 3(a), Fig. 3(b) we can see the performance of the trainer and the trainee in lap time and smooth driving behavior in two TORCS tracks, namely, CG-Speedway-1 and F-speedway.

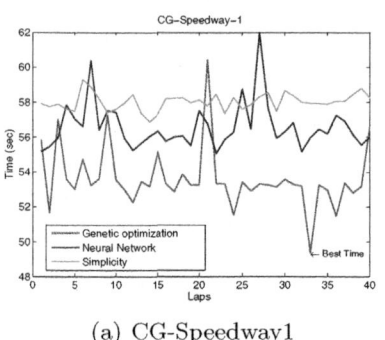
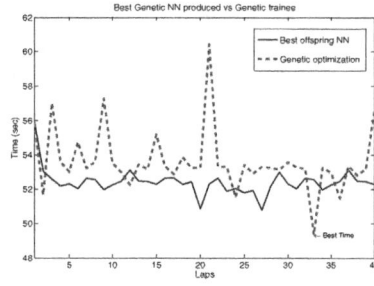

(a) CG-Speedway1

(b) Best offspring NN vs Genetic optimization

Fig. 2.

In Figure 2(a) the lap-time for 40 laps on the CG-Speedway-1 track is shown. The three curves correspond to the performance of the Simplicity driver (trainer), the trained Neural Network that learns from the behavior of the Simplicity driver and the best adapted NN for each generation during the genetic optimization for 40 laps. In Figure 2(a) it is clear that the the trained NN achieves better lap times than the rule-based Simplicity driver. The performance is improved on average by two seconds. Moreover, it is obvious that genetic optimization further improves the performance of the NN trainee and, on average, the performance is improved by 5 seconds compared to the Simplicity driver. The best performance in a single lap is observed in the 34th lap during the genetic optimization. That is, the trained NN has learned the driving behavior from its rule-based trainer and enhanced his performance due to smoother driving trajectories as we will see in the following. Moreover, by genetically evolving its weights during the actual driving procedure the proposed NN based driver further improved the lap-time and during the genetic optimization the global minimum lap time has been reached in the 34th lap.

The NN that achieved the best performance during the genetic optimization is selected as the best offspring and evaluated again for 40 laps. In Fig. 2(b) we compare the performance of the best NN's for each generation during the evolutionary optimization with the overall best NN that was produced on the 34th lap and was the outcome of the evolutionary optimization. It is clear that the genetically optimized NN achieves better results. However, for the tested 40 laps it cannot reach the best time achieved during the optimization. This is easily explained since the performance of the trained drivers is not always the same and we search for a bot that is on average better than the trainer.

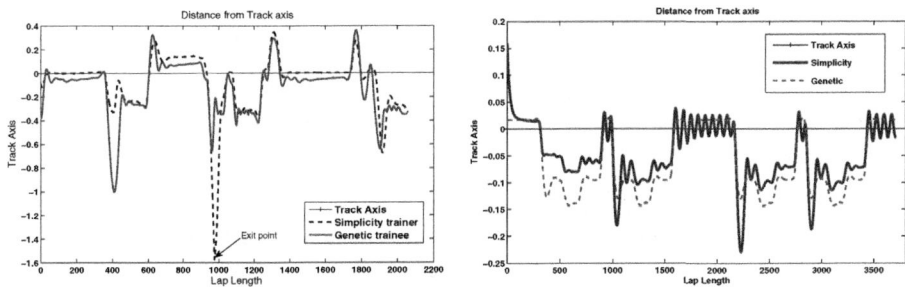

(a) CG-Speedway1 Distance to Track Axis   (b) F-Speedway Distance to Track Axis

Fig. 3.

In Figures Fig. 3(a), Fig. 3(b) we test the smoothness of genetic trainee and simplicity driver trainer in two different tracks. What we can notice, especially in Fig. 3(b), is that the trainee overcame the rule-based decision behaviour and simulated a smoother driving trajectory. Moreover, an interesting noticeable observation is highlighted in Fig. 3(a). At the 980 meter of track there is a sharp turn where the rule-based trainer came out of the track in every lap. The neurogenetic bot manage to stay in the track bounds and save time achieving a smoother driving trajectory at that point.

5   Conclusion

In this work we proposed a computational intelligence method using the combination of neural networks with genetic algorithms so as to develop an agent which can be trained while playing The Open Race Car Simulator (TORCS), attempting, this way, to achieve higher performance compared with the performance of its trainer bot. Our results show that we managed to create a controller that enhances the behaviour of its trainer in regards to acceleration, achieving better lap -times from its trainer and steering by implementing a smoother driving trajectory. Moreover, by utilizing evolutionary adaptation we managed to improve even more the performance of our bot and to gradually achieve the best performance.

References

1. Torcs the open race car simulator, http://torcs.sourceforge.net/
2. Petrakis, S., Tefas, A.: Neural Networks Training for Weapon Selection in First-Person Shooter Games. In: Diamantaras, K., Duch, W., Iliadis, L.S. (eds.) ICANN 2010, Part III. LNCS, vol. 6354, pp. 417–422. Springer, Heidelberg (2010)
3. Laird, J.E., Van Lent, M.: Human-level AI's Killer Application: Interactive Computer Games. In: Proceedings of the Seventeenth National Conference on Artificial Intelligence and Twelfth Conference on Innovative Applications of Artificial Intelligence, pp. 1171–1178 (2000)
4. Onieva, E., Pelta, D.A., Alonso, J., Milanés, V., Pérez, J.: A modular parametric architecture for the TORCS racing engine. In: Proceedings of the 5th International Conference on Computational Intelligence and Games (CIG 2009), pp. 256–262. IEEE Press, Piscataway (2009)
5. Haykin, S.S.: Neural networks and learning machines, 3rd edn. Multi Layer Perceptron, pp. 152–258 (2008)
6. Hecht-Nielsen, R.: Theory of back-propagation neural network. In: Proc. of the Int. Conf. of Neural Networks I, pp. 593–611 (1989)
7. Robot auto racing simulator (2006), http://torcs.sourceforge.net
8. Stanley, K., Kohl, N., Sherony, R., Miikkulainen, R.: Neuroevolution of an automobile crash warning system. In: Genetic and Evolutionary Computation Conference, CECCO 2006, pp. 1977–1984 (2006)
9. Martin, B., Butz, V., Lonneker, T.D.: Optimized Sensory-motor Couplings plus Strategy Extensions for the TORCS car Racing Challenge. In: IEEE Symposium on Computational Intelligence and Games, CIG 2009, pp. 317–324 (2009)
10. Cardamone, L., Loiacono, D., Lanzi, P.L.: Applying cooperative coevolution to compete in the 2009 TORCS Endurance World Championship. In: Evolutionary Computation (CEC), pp. 1–8. IEEE (2010)
11. Perez, D., Saez, Y., Recio, G., Isasi, P.: Evolving a rule system controller for automatic driving in a car racing competition. In: Symposium on Computational Intelligence and Games (CIG), pp. 336–342. IEEE (2009)
12. Holland, J.H.: Adaptation in Natural and Artificial Systems, 2nd edn. MIT Press, Cambridge (1992)

Bagged Nonlinear Hebbian Learning Algorithm for Fuzzy Cognitive Maps Working on Classification Tasks

Elpiniki I. Papageorgiou[1], Panagiotis Oikonomou[2], and Arthi Kannappan[3]

[1] Technological Educational Institute of Lamia, Informatics & Computer Technology Department, 3rd km Old National Road Lamia-Arthens, 35100 Lamia, Greece
epapageorgiou@teilam.gr
http://users.teilam.gr/~epapageorgiou
[2] University of Thessaly, Computer and Communication Engineering Dept,
38221 Volos, Greece
paikonom@uth.gr
[3] RVS College of Computer Applications, Coimbatore-641402, Tamilnadu, India
Sek_art@rediffmail.com

Abstract. Learning of fuzzy cognitive maps (FCMs) is one of the most useful characteristics which have a high impact on modeling and inference capabilities of them. The learning approaches for FCMs are concentrated on learning the connection matrix, based either on expert intervention and/or on the available historical data. Most learning approaches for FCMs are Hebbian-based and evolutionary-based algorithms. A new learning algorithm for FCMs is proposed in this research work, inheriting the main aspects of the bagging approach which is an ensemble based learning approach. The FCM nonlinear Hebbian learning (NHL) algorithm enhanced by the bagging technique is investigated contributing to an approach where the model is trained using NHL algorithm as a base learner classifier. This work is inspired from the neural networks ensembles and it is used to learn the FCM ensembles produced by the NHL exploiting better classification accuracies.

1 Introduction

Fuzzy cognitive mapping is a method for analysing and depicting human perception of a given system. The method produces a conceptual model which is not limited by exact values and measurements, and thus it is well suited to represent relatively unstructured knowledge and causalities expressed in imprecise forms. FCM is a dynamic tool because cause-effect relations and feedback mechanisms are involved [1]. The advantageous modeling features of FCMs, such as simplicity, adaptability and capability of approximating abstractive structures encourage us to use them for complex problems in diverse scientific areas [2][3].

In most cases, FCMs are constructed manually, and, thus, they cannot be applied when dealing with large number of variables. In such cases, their development could be significantly affected by the limited knowledge and skills of the knowledge engineer. Thus, it is essential to use learning algorithms to accomplish this task. The

I. Maglogiannis, V. Plagianakos, and I. Vlahavas (Eds.): SETN 2012, LNAI 7297, pp. 157–164, 2012.

adaptive Hebbian-based learning algorithms, the evolutionary-based such as genetic algorithms and the hybrid approaches composed of Hebbian type and genetic algorithm are the most efficient and widely used methods for training FCMs [4-11].

The aim of this study is to present a new ensemble based learning approach using the bagging technique to enhance the learning capabilities of the FCM-NHL approach [5]. In this research work, we investigated the bagging approach for NHL algorithm to learn FCMs. The NHL algorithm was used as a base learning algorithm in bagging ensemble paradigm. The explored learning approach on bagged FCM-NHL is applied to autism classification to show its functionality. The results were compared with the previous ones produced by NHL algorithm, and showed that the learning approach can further be improved using ensemble FCM approach. Ensemble FCM uses FCM trained with NHL algorithm and incorporates the ideas of ensemble method of bagging. Here, the goal of bagged FCM-NHL construction is to achieve better generalization ability over a single classifier in the case of FCMs. The proposed method uses an autistic data set to train FCMs for constructing ensemble FCMs.

2   Ensemble Learning and Fuzzy Cognitive Map

2.1   Ensemble Learning

Ensemble learning is one of the most promising areas of soft computing, which is used successfully in many real world applications such as text categorization, optical character recognition, face recognition and computer aided medical diagnosis [12][13]. The idea of designing ensembles was originated as an alternative way for improving performance of individual classifiers by exploiting knowledge derived from different sources. Ensemble methods overcome the statistical problem, the computational problem and the representation problem of learning algorithms which output is only a single hypothesis, and thus they overcome the limitation of traditional learning algorithms.

In ensemble learning, an agent takes a number of learning algorithms and combines their output to make a prediction. The algorithms being combined are called base-level algorithms [12]. Base-level algorithms are usually generated from training data by a base learning algorithm which can be decision tree, neural network or other kinds of learning algorithms. Most ensemble methods use a single base learning algorithm to produce homogeneous base-level algorithms, but there are also some methods which use multiple learning algorithms to produce heterogeneous learners.

There are many effective ensemble methods, but the most representative ones are Boosting [14] and Bagging [15]. In bagging, if there are m training examples, the base-level algorithms are trained on sets of m randomly drawn, with replacement, sets of the training examples. In each of these sets, some examples are not chosen, and some are duplicated. On average, each set contains about 63% of the original examples. In boosting, there is a sequence of classifiers in which each classifier uses a weighted set of examples. Those examples that the previous classifiers misclassified are weighted more. Weighting examples can either be incorporated into the base-level algorithms or can affect which examples are chosen as training examples for the future classifiers.

2.2   Main Aspects of Fuzzy Cognitive Maps

An FCM is depicted as a fuzzy causal graph [1], in which nodes represent concepts, whereas directed edges between the concepts denote causal relationships present between them. A given system is defined as a collection of concepts (events, actions, values, goals, etc.) that influence each other through cause-effect relationships, which are quantified and usually normalized to the [-1, 1] interval. Positive values describe promoting effect, whereas negative ones describe inhibiting effect. Other values correspond to different intermediate levels of the causal effect. Figure 1 shows a generic representation of the FCM model.

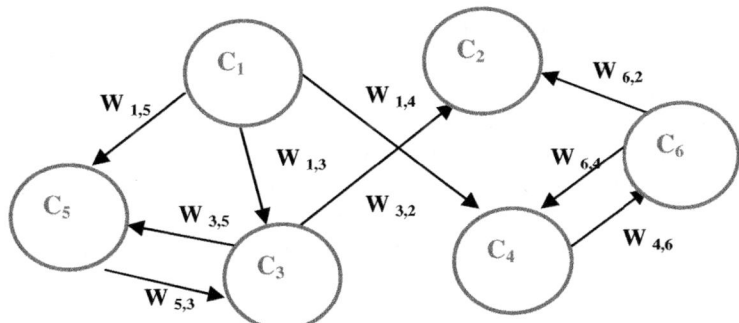

Fig. 1. A Fuzzy Cognitive Map model example

In general, we define FCM as an order pair $< C, W >$, where C is the set of labels and W is the connection matrix. Every label $A_i \in C$ its mapped to its activation value $A_i \in [0,1]$, where 0 means no activation, and 1 means full activation. The labels from C can be interpreted as linguistic terms [1],[2] that point to fuzzy sets. In such case, the activation value A_i is interpreted as the value of fuzzy membership function that measures the degree in which an observed value belongs to the fuzzy set pointed by the related term. The other, simplified interpretation of C can be such that the labels C_i denote the real valued variables, the domains of these variables are assumed as normalized into the [0, 1] interval.

According to the FCM development process, the number and kind of concepts are determined by a group of experts that comprise the FCM model. Then, each interconnection is described by a domain expert either with an if-then rule that infers a fuzzy linguistic variable from a determined set or with a direct fuzzy linguistic weight, which associates the relationship between the two concepts and determines the grade of causality between the two concepts.

In the sequel, all the linguistic variables suggested by experts, are aggregated using the SUM method and an overall linguistic weight is produced. This weight is then transformed into a numerical weight e_{ij}, belonging to the interval [-1, 1], by using the defuzzification method of the center of gravity and finally a numerical weight for e_{ij} is calculated. Using this method, all the weights of the FCM model are inferred.

Once the FCM is constructed, it can receive data from its input concepts, perform reasoning and infer decisions as values of its output concepts. During reasoning the FCM iteratively calculates its state until convergence. The state is represented by a *state vector* A^k, which consists of real node values $A_i(k) \in [0,1]$, $i=1,2,...N$ at an iteration k. The value of each node is calculated by the following equation [16]:

$$A_i(k+1) = f((2A_i(k) - 1) + \sum_{\substack{j \neq i \\ j=1}}^{N} (2A_j(k) - 1) \cdot E_{ji})$$ (1)

which is a rescaled simulation process that removes the spurious influence of inactive concepts (with $C_i = 0$) on other concepts, and avoids the conflicts emerge in cases where the initial values of concepts are 0 or 0.5.

2.3   Learning Algorithms for Fuzzy Cognitive Maps

The learning approaches for FCMs are concentrated on learning the connection matrix **E**, based either on expert intervention and/or on the available historical data. According to the available type of knowledge, the learning techniques can be categorized into three groups: Hebbian-based, population-based and hybrid combining the main aspects of Hebbian-based and evolution-based type learning algorithms. These types of learning algorithms are the most efficient and widely used for training FCMs [4-11]. In the first case, Hebbian-based learning algorithms, such as Active Hebbian Learning (AHL) and NHL were proposed for learning the weight matrix of FCMs based on experts' intervention. On the second case, the experts are substituted by historical data and the underlying learning algorithm used them to estimate the entries of the connection matrix **E**. In the third case of hybrid learning approaches, the learning goal is to modify/update weight matrices based on initial knowledge from experts and historical data at a two stage process.

A recent review study on learning algorithms for FCMs and their advanced applications is presented in [4]. This study summarizes the main features of the Hebbian type learning, population-based type and hybrid learning for FCMs, depicting at the same time their recent applications in diverse research areas by pinpointing the degree of success of each one.

3   Bagged NHL Learning Approach for Fuzzy Cognitive Map

FCM ensemble is a learning paradigm where a collection of finite number of FCMs is trained for the same task and used for specific application domains. Learning many FCMs and combining their predictions provide an FCM ensemble. The objective of FCM ensemble construction with training different FCMs using NHL, as the base classifier, is to achieve better classification ability over a single FCM classifier. The NHL algorithm has already used to train FCMs for classification tasks showing its functionality [5][169]. The main steps of the NHL algorithm are presented in [16].

The performance of NHL for FCM training can be improved by applying ensemble learning of bagging for solving classification tasks. In this proposed algorithm, since cross validation approach is applied to the data sets, the available data set is partitioned into k subsets with equal size, and then we use part of the k subsets for training while the remaining subset used for performance evaluation. In the examined case study, the subsets are $k = 10$, thus the data is divided into ten sets, where one set is stored as test data and the remaining used as training data. The value of each concept and the value of weight are updated. Next the test data is trained using the ensemble method and simple majority method is used to calculate the final accuracy. The proposed bagging learning of FCMs along with NHL algorithm, namely bagged NHL-FCM, is described at follows.

Algorithm: Bagging

```
Input:
  1. D is INPUT DATA of 23 concepts given by experts
  2. W is initial weight matrix
  3. Training data SB (total number of records-40)
  4. Weak-learning algorithm for FCMs, NHL
  5. Integer T=5,10, specifying the number of iteration
  6. Integer k=10 specifying the number of subsets (each
     subset has 4 records)
  7. Percent F (70% or 90%) to create resample training
     set St
Do k=1, ..10
  Do t=1, ..T
  8. Take a resample replica St by 70-90% of SB
  9. Call NHL for FCMs with St and receive the classifi-
     er FCM-t which produce after testing an output
     hk(i) for each k test set consisting of i=4 records
  10. Add hk(i) to the ensemble E
  End
End
```

Test: Simple majority voting method –Given a test set k, with $\mathbf{x}_i$, where i=4 records

```
For i=1, ..4
  For t=1, ..T
    1. Evaluate the ensemble E_i={ht(i)}={h1(i),h2(i),
       ..hT(i)}  for x_i record
```

$$2. \text{ Let } v_{t,j} = \begin{cases} 1, ht - picks - class - \omega_j \\ 0, otherwise \end{cases}$$

```
       be the vote given to class ω_j by classifier ht.
    3. Obtain total vote received by each class
```

$$V_j = \sum_{t=1}^{T} v_{t,j} \text{ for j=1,..C in the case of C classes}$$

```
    4. Choose the class that receives the highest total
       vote as the final classification.
  End
End
```

Diversity in bagging is obtained by using bootstrapped replicas of the training data: different training data subsets are randomly drawn—with replacement—from the entire training data [15]. Each training data subset is used to train a different classifier of the same type. Individual classifiers are then combined by taking mean summed output of their decisions (see Figure 2). For any given instance, the class chosen by most classifiers is the ensemble decision.

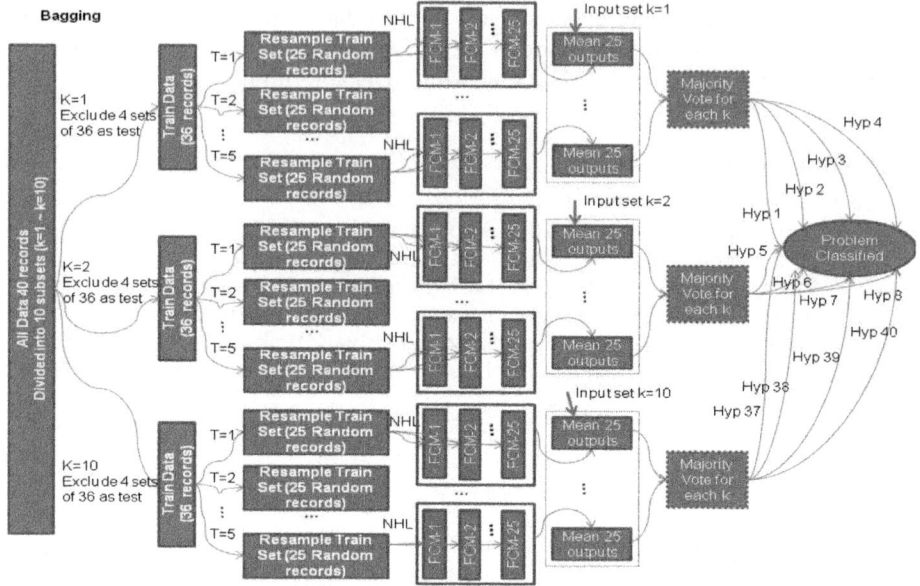

Fig. 2. Bagging approach implemented in FCM-NHL algorithm

Bagging is particularly appealing when available data is of limited size. To ensure that there are sufficient training samples in each subset, relatively large portions of the samples (70% to 90%) are drawn into each subset. This causes individual training subsets to overlap significantly, with many of the same instances appearing in most subsets, and some instances appearing multiple times in a given subset.

4   Experimental Analysis and Results

Autism is a developmental disorder in which attention shifting is known to be restricted. A number of methods have been elicited to study this problem. In a recent work, Arthi K. et al. (2011) analyzed the performance of FCMs on autistic disorder modeling and prediction using NHL algorithm [16]. In that study, the FCM model constructed by physicians to assess three levels of autism (no autism, probable autism and autism) was trained using NHL algorithm for forty real children cases. The produced FCM model consists of 24 concepts. The concept C_{24} has been considered from the experts as DC and could be categorized as Definite Autism (DA), Probable Autism (PA) and No Autism (NA). The overall classification accuracy of that approach was approximately 79% and outperformed other benchmarking machine learning classification techniques [16].

Forty datasets were collected for classification of three different categories, like twenty six as DA, ten as PA and four as NA children. These forty datasets were gathered in [16]. Each one of the three learning approaches was implemented at the 40 records to predict the classification category of each one.

The classification performance results were gathered in Table 1, depicting the confusion matrices of each one learning approach. The classification accuracies of the two examined training approaches for autism disorder assessment was 82.5% and 87.5% (bagging) respectively. The bagged FCM-NHL gave much better results.

Table 1. Confusion matrices & classification accuracies of FCM-NHL and Bagged FCM-NHL

Learning Algorithms	**FCM-NHL**			**Bagged FCM-NHL** (for T=5 and 70% resample)			**Bagged FCM-NHL** (for T=10 and 90% resample)
Confusion matrices	**DA**	**PA**	**NA**	**DA**	**PA**	**NA**	-
DA	24/26	2/26	-	24/26	2/26	-	-
PA	1/10	8/10	1/10	-	7/10	3/10	-
NA	-	3/4	1/4	-	-	4/4	-
True Positive (All)		33/40			35/40		35/40
Accuracy (%)		**82.5%**			**87.5%**		**87.5%**

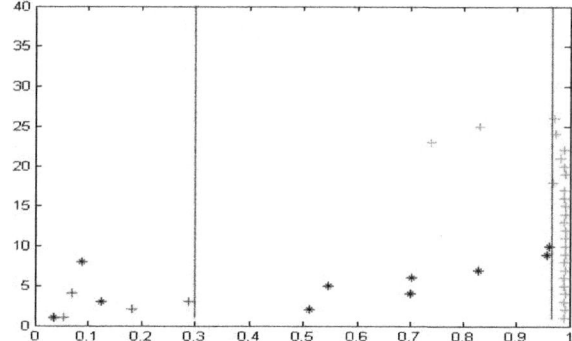

Fig. 3. Classification lines of bagged NHL-FCM algorithm

We also performed a number of experiments for different percentage of resample datasets in the case of bagging, for 70% (25 datasets) and for 90% (33 datasets) and for two different settings of T, for T=5 and T=10. The results were the same for all experimental settings producing correct classes in 35 of 40 cases.

When bagging approaches were implemented, then the 24 records from 26 datasets of "Definite Autism" gave a result of DA and 2 records gave a result of PA. The 7 records from the 10 records of "Probable Autism" gave a result of PA, 0 records were classified as DA and 3 as NA, whereas in the case of "No Autism", the 4 from the 4 records gave the result of NA. Figure 3 presents the classified cases for each one of the three categories. The lines were constructed using the method described in [16]. Applying bagging approach the classification accuracy of FCM-NHL algorithm was improved for the same dataset.

Concluding, the proposed learning methodology was experimentally evaluated in comparison to previous learning algorithm of NHL for autism classification in children exhibiting fast and stable learning. Further research towards a systematic approach to develop FCMs from data could be still carried out. Summarizing, more research work is needed to be done to the extension of the learning capabilities for enhancing and adapting FCM ensembles, as well as the establishment of new FCM learning algorithms.

References

1. Kosko, B.: Fuzzy cognitive maps. Int. J. Man-Machine Studies 24(1), 65–75 (1986)
2. Glykas, G.: Fuzzy Cognitive Maps: Theory, Methodologies, Tools and Applications, 1st edn. Springer, Heidelberg (2010)
3. Papageorgiou, E.I.: A Review Study of FCMs Applications during the last decade. In: Porc. FUZZ-IEEE 2011, Taipei, Taiwan, June 27-30, pp. 828–835 (2011)
4. Papageorgiou, E.I.: Learning Algorithms for Fuzzy Cognitive Maps: A Review Study. IEEE Transactions on SMC Part C (2011) (in press)
5. Papageorgiou, E., Stylios, C., Groumpos, P.: Fuzzy Cognitive Map Learning Based on Nonlinear Hebbian Rule. In: Gedeon, T(T.) D., Fung, L.C.C. (eds.) AI 2003. LNCS (LNAI), vol. 2903, pp. 256–268. Springer, Heidelberg (2003)
6. Froelich, W., Wakulicz-Deja, A.: Mining temporal medical data using adaptive fuzzy cognitive maps. In: Proc. 2nd Conf. on Human System Interactions, HSI 2009, art. no. 5090946, pp. 16–23 (2009)
7. Stach, W., Kurgan, L.A., Pedrycz, W.: M. Reformat, Genetic learning of fuzzy cognitive maps. Fuzzy Sets and Systems 153(3), 371–401 (2005)
8. Papakostas, G.A., Boutalis, Y.S., Koulouriotis, D.E., Mertzios, B.G.: FCMs for pattern recognition applications. Int. J. Pattern Recogn. & Artif. Intel. 22(8), 1461–1486 (2008)
9. Kim, M.-C., Kim, C.O., Hong, S.R., Kwon, I.-H.: Forward-backward analysis of RFID-enabled supply chain using fuzzy cognitive map and genetic algorithm. Expert Systems with Applications 35(3), 1166–1176 (2008)
10. Słoń, G., Yastrebov, A.: Optimization and Adaptation of Dynamic Models of Fuzzy Relational Cognitive Maps. In: Kuznetsov, S.O., Ślęzak, D., Hepting, D.H., Mirkin, B.G. (eds.) RSFDGrC 2011. LNCS, vol. 6743, pp. 95–102. Springer, Heidelberg (2011)
11. Papageorgiou, E.I., Spyridonos, P., Glotsos, D., Stylios, C.D., Ravazoula, P., Nikiforidis, G., Groumpos, P.P.: Brain Tumour Characterization using the Soft. Computing Technique of Fuzzy Cognitive Maps. Applied Soft Computing 8, 820–828 (2008)
12. Policar, R.: Ensemble based systems in decision making, IEEE Circuits and Systems Magazine, third quarter, 21–46 (2006)
13. Zhou, Z.-H.: Ensemble learning. Encyclopedia of Biometrics, 270–273 (2009)
14. Dietterich, T.G.: Machine learning research: Four current directions. AI Magazine 18(4), 97–136 (1997)
15. Breiman, L.: Bagging predictors. Machine Learning 24(2), 123–140 (1996)
16. Kannappan, A., Tamilarasi, A., Papageorgiou, E.I.: Analyzing the performance of fuzzy cognitive maps with non-linear hebbian learning algorithm in predicting autistic disorder. Expert Systems with Applications 38(3), 1282–1292 (2011)

Credit Rating Using a Hybrid Voting Ensemble

Elias Kamos[1], Foteini Matthaiou[1], and Sotiris Kotsiantis[2]

[1] Hellenic Open University, Greece
kamos.h@nbg.gr, fmatthaiou@yahoo.gr
[2] Department of Mathematics, University of Patras, Greece
sotos@math.upatras.gr

Abstract. Credit risk analysis is an essential topic in the financial risk management. Credit risk analysis has been the main focus of financial and banking industry. A number of experiments have been conducted using representative supervised learning algorithms, which were trained using two public available credit datasets. The decision of which specific method to choose is a complex problem. Another option instead of choosing only one method is to create a hybrid ensemble of classifiers.

1   Introduction

One of the important decisions financial institutions have to make as part of their operations is to make a decision whether or not to give a loan to an applicant. With the appearance of large data storing services, huge amounts of data have been stored regarding the repayment performance of past applicants. It is the aim of credit scoring to examine this data and build models that differentiate consistent from bad payers using features such as amount on savings account, purpose of loan, marital status, etc.

Many machine learning techniques have been used to build credit-scoring models [2], [7]. The decision of which specific method to choose is a difficult problem for credit risk analysis [1]. A high-quality alternative to choosing only a method is to create an ensemble of classifiers [18], [11]. In this study, we have implemented a hybrid decision support system that combines representative algorithms using a voting methodology and achieves better accuracy than any simple method.

The following section attempts a brief literature review for credit risk analysis. Section 3 provides a brief description of the used datasets. Section 4 presents the presented method and the experimental results for the representative compared combining techniques. Finally, section 6 discusses the conclusions and some future research directions.

2   Literature Review

Because of credit risk analysis importance, there is a growing research interest about credit risk analysis. A recent survey on credit scoring and credit modeling is [16]. Many different approaches including individual models, such as kernel classifiers [7], classification tree [19], artificial neural networks (ANN) [9], [10], [6] support vector

I. Maglogiannis, V. Plagianakos, and I. Vlahavas (Eds.): SETN 2012, LNAI 7297, pp. 165–173, 2012.
© Springer-Verlag Berlin Heidelberg 2012

machine (SVM) [20], [8] and some hybrid models, such as neuro-fuzzy system [22] and immune classifiers [3] were widely applied to credit risk analysis tasks. In the above individual models, it is difficult to say that the accuracy of one model is consistently better than that of another model in all circumstances.

In most situations, the performance of these individual models is problem-dependent. In the hybrid models [21], [19], some researchers have revealed that these hybrid classifiers which hybridize two or more classification methods can provide higher classification accuracy than that of individual models. Motivated by this finding, we integrate multiple classifiers into an aggregated output to achieve the further performance improvement.

3   Data Description

We used two publicly credit datasets: Credit-a dataset and Credit-g dataset.

Table 1. Credit-a Dataset – List of Attributes

Attribute	Type
Sex	Nominal
Age	Continuous
Mean time at addresses	Continuous
Home status	Nominal
Current occupation	Nominal
Current job status	Nominal
Mean time with employers	Continuous
Other investments	Nominal
Bank account	Nominal
Time with bank	Continuous
Liability reference	Nominal
Account reference	Nominal
Monthly housing expense	Continuous
Savings account balance	Continuous
Class (Reject / Accept)	Nominal

In Credit-a dataset, each case out of 690 represents an application for credit card facilities described by eight discrete and six continuous attributes, with two decision classes (Accept / Reject). The database attributes are shown in Table 1. The German Credit dataset (Credit-g) contains observations on 20 variables for 1000 past applicants for credit. Each applicant was rated as "good credit" (700 cases) or "bad credit" (300 cases). The database attributes are shown in Table 2.

Table 2. Credit-g Dataset – List of Attributes

Attribute	Type
Checking account status	Nominal
Duration of credit in months	Continuous
Credit history	Nominal
Purpose of credit	Nominal
Credit amount	Continuous
Average balance in savings account	Nominal
Present employment	Nominal
Installment rate as % of disposable income	Continuous
Personal status	Nominal
Other parties	Nominal
Present resident since - years	Continuous
Property magnitude	Nominal
Age in years	Continuous
Other payment plans	Nominal
Housing	Nominal
Number of existing credits at this bank	Continuous
Nature of job	Nominal
Number of people for whom liable to provide maintenance	Continuous
Applicant has phone in his or her name	Nominal
Foreign worker	Nominal
Class (Reject / Accept)	Nominal

4 Experimental Results and Proposed Technique

For the purpose of this study, a representative algorithm for each supervised learning technique was used. The most commonly used C4.5 algorithm [13] was the representative of the decision trees in our study. The K2 algorithm [24] was the representative of the Bayesian networks in our study. BP algorithm [24] - was the representative of the ANNs. Ripper [4] was the representative of the rule-learners. The 3-NN algorithm that combines robustness to noise and less time for classification than using a larger k for kNN was also used [24]. Finally, the Sequential Minimal Optimization (or SMO) algorithm was the representative of the SVMs as one of the fastest methods to train SVMs [12].

All accuracy estimates were calculated by averaging the results from stratified 10-fold cross-validation in the datasets. It must be mentioned that we make use of the free available source code for our experiments by the book [24]. The results for the credit-a as well as the credit-g datasets are presented in Table 3. Three evaluation criteria were used to measure the classification results:

- Total accuracy = (number of correct classification) / (the number of evaluation sample)
- Type I accuracy = (number of both observed bad and classified as bad) / (number of observed bad)
- Type II accuracy = (number of both observed good and classified as good) / (number of observed good)

Table 3. Accuracy of simple models in credit datasets

Dataset		K2	C4.5	3NN	BP	RIPPER	SMO	LogReg
credit-a	Total	86.23%	86.08%	84.63%	86.52%	85.79%	84.92%	85.21%
	Type-I	79.8%	83.7%	82.1%	86%	86%	92.2%	86.3 %
	Type-II	91.4%	88%	86.7%	86.9 %	85.6 %	79.1%	84.3 %
credit-g	Total	75.5%	70.5%	73.3%	72.5%	71.7%	75.1%	75.2%
	Type-I	85.9%	84%	86.1%	77.4%	87.3%	87.1%	86.4%
	Type-II	51.3%	39%	43.3%	61%	35.3%	47%	49%

Lately in the area of machine learning and data mining the concept of combining classifiers is suggested as a new direction for the improvement of the accuracy of individual classifiers. Witten & Frank [24] provides an accessible and informal reasoning, from statistical, computational and representational viewpoints, of why ensembles can improve classification results. The most typical method is to use a mixture of learning algorithms on all of the training data and combine their predictions according to a voting scheme. This technique attempts to achieve diversity [23] in the classification errors of the classifiers by using different learning algorithms, which vary in their method of search and representation. The intuition is that the classifiers generated using different learning biases are expected to make errors in different manner [26].

Using a voting methodology as an aggregation rule with the classifiers in the proposed algorithm, we wait for producing good results based on the idea that the majority of classifiers are more probable to be right in their decision when they agree in their estimation. According to the proposed algorithm, during the classification of a test example the ensemble model calculate the votes of each class and if the votes of the base-classifiers of the most possible class is at least two times the votes of the next possible class then the decision is that of the most possible class. But, if the global voting ensemble is not so sure e.g. the votes of the most possible class is less than two times the votes of the next possible class; the model finds the k nearest neighbors using the selected distance metric and train the local voting ensemble using these k instances. Finally, in this case the model uses simple voting of the global voting classifiers with local voting classifiers for the classification of the testing instance.

The proposed ensemble is described by pseudo-code in Fig 1.

```
Training:
Build Global Classifiers using the training set
Classification:
  1. Obtain the test instance
  2. Calculate the decisions of the base-classifiers.
  3. If the votes of the most possible class is at least two
     times the votes of the next possible class then the de-
     cision is the most possible class else
        a. Find the k(=50) nearest neighbors using the se-
           lected distance metric (Manhattan in our imple-
           mentation)
        b. Using as training instances the k instances
           train the local classifiers
        c. Aggregate the decisions of global classifiers
           with local classifiers by simple voting for the
           classification of the testing instance.
```

Fig. 1. Integrating Global and Local Voting

The proposed algorithm requires choosing the value of k. There are quite a few methods to do this. Firstly, simple solution is to fix k a priori before the beginning of the learning process. However, the best k for a specific dataset is clearly not the best for another dataset. A second, more time-consuming solution is to determine this best k automatically through the minimization of a cost criterion. The idea is to apply a model selection process upon which the different hypothesis that may be built. One technique to do that is to evaluate the error on a test set and thus keep as k the value for which the error is the least. In the current implementation we decided to use a fixed value for k (=50) in order to a) keep the training time low and b) since about this size of instances is appropriate for a simple algorithm, to construct a relatively precise model.

Subsequently, we compare in Table 4 the proposed methodology (GlLocVot) for the credit-a as well as the credit-g datasets with:

- The methodology of selecting the best classifier according to 3-cross valida-tion (BestCV) [24].
- Grading methodology using the instance based classifier IBk with ten nearest neighbors as the meta level classifier [14]. In grading, the meta-level classifier predicts whether the base-level classifier is to be trusted. The base-level attributes are used also as meta-level attributes, while the meta-level class val-ues are correct and incorrect. Only the base-level classifiers that are predicted to be correct are taken and their predictions combined by summing up the probability distributions predicted.
- Simple Voting methodology using the same base classifiers [25].
- Stacking that replaces this with a trainable classifier [17]. This is possible, since for the training set, we have both the predictions of the base learners and the true class. The matrix containing the predictions of the base learners as

predictors and the true class for each training case will be called the meta-data set. The classifier trained on this matrix is called the meta-classifier or the classifier at the meta-level. Stacking methodology that constructs the meta-data set by adding the entire predicted class probability distribution instead of only the most likely class using MLR as meta-level classifier was used in our experiments [17].

In Table 4, we represent with "v" that the proposed method looses from the specific algorithm. That is, the specific algorithm performed statistically better than the proposed method according to t-test with p<0.05 [24]. Furthermore, in Table 4, "*" indicates that proposed method performed statistically better than the specific algorithm according to t-test with p<0.05. In all the other cases, there is no significant statistical difference between the results.

Table 4. Accuracy of ensembles in credit datasets

Dataset		GlLocVot	Voting	BestCV	Grading	Stacking
	Total	88.6%	87.39%	84.63% (*)	85.21% (*)	87.39%
Credit-a	Type-I	83.9%	88.3% (v)	82.4%	85%	86.3%
	Type-II	92.4%	86.7% (*)	86.4% (*)	85.4% (*)	88.3% (*)
	Total	78.7%	76% (*)	75.6% (*)	75.9% (*)	76.1% (*)
Credit-g	Type-I	88.2%	88%	87%	88.1%	89.6%
	Type-II	56.7%	48% (*)	49% (*)	47.3% (*)	44.7% (*)

As a conclusion, our approach performs better than selecting the best classifier from the ensemble by cross validation and other tested combining methods in the credits dataset. Because of the encouraging results obtained from these experiments, we can expect that the proposed technique can be effectively applied to the classification task in real world cases, and perform more accurately than traditional data mining approaches.

5   Conclusion

Deciding whether an applicant is a 'good' or a 'bad' risk is known as credit scoring. In general, credit scoring includes any technique for classifying risks into a set of predefined categories [5]. Traditional credit scoring methods award points for certain features that the creditor considers important such as the amount of the applicant's income, whether he or she owns a home, and how many years he has worked in his last job [15].

The aim of this study was to investigate the usefulness and compare the performance of supervised machine learning techniques in credit scoring. In terms of classification accuracy, the proposed new voting methodology achieves better accuracy than any examined simple and ensemble method. The weakness of the proposed method is the decreased comprehensibility. With involvement of multiple classifiers in decision-making, it is more difficult for non-expert users to perceive the underlying reasoning procedure leading to a decision.

Tracking progress is a time-consuming job that can be handled automatically by the implemented tool (see Figure 2). The tool expects the training set as an Attribute-Relation File Format (ARFF). There is not any restriction in attributes' order. However, the class attribute must be in the last column. After the training of the model (this takes some time to complete, from few seconds to few minutes), the user is able to predict the class of the new single instance. While the experts will still have the vital role in evaluating process, the tool can use the data required for reasonable and efficient monitoring.

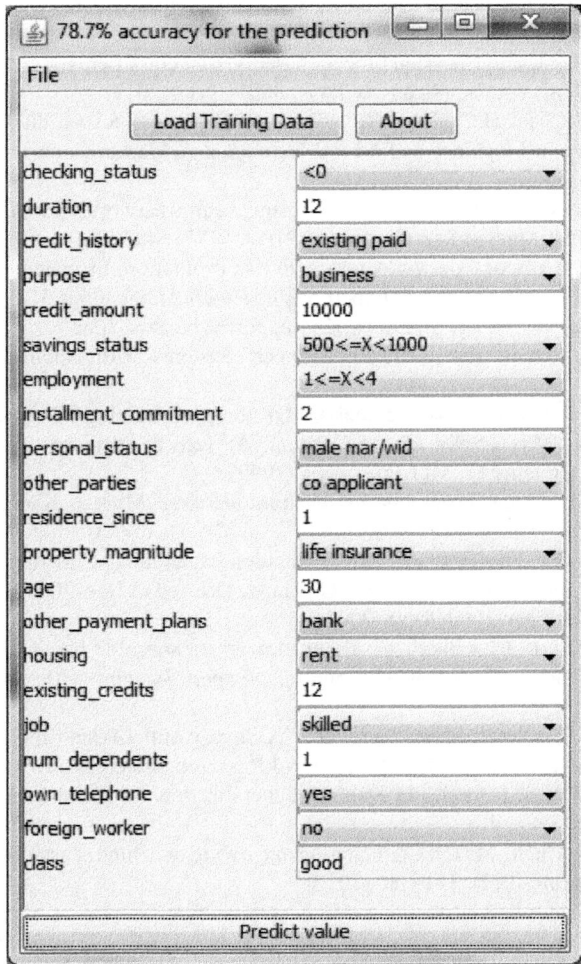

Fig. 2. A screenshot of the implemented decision support tool

References

1. Baesens, B., Van Gestel, T., Viaene, S., Stepanova, M., Suykens, J., Vanthienen, J.: Benchmarking state-of-the-art classification algorithms for credit scoring. Journal of the Operational Research Society 54(6), 627–635 (2003)

2. Yap, B.W., Ong, S.H., Husain, N.H.M.: Using data mining to improve assessment of credit worthiness via credit scoring models. Expert Systems with Applications 38(10), 13274–13283 (2011)
3. Chang, S.-Y., Yeh, T.-Y.: An artificial immune classifier for credit scoring analysis. Applied Soft Computing (November 12, 2011), 10.1016/j.asoc.2011.11.002
4. Cohen, W.: Fast Effective Rule Induction. In: International Conference on ML, pp. 115–123 (1995)
5. Hand, D.J.: Good practice in retail credit scorecard assessment. Journal of the Operational Research Society 56, 1109–1117 (2002)
6. Hájek, P.: Municipal credit rating modelling by neural networks. Decision Support Systems 51(1), 108–118 (2011)
7. Huang, S.-C.: Using Gaussian process based kernel classifiers for credit rating forecasting. Expert Systems with Applications 38(7), 8607–8611 (2011)
8. Huang, Z., Chen, H.C., Hsu, C.J., Chen, W.H., Wu, S.S.: Credit Rating Analysis with Support Vector Machines and Neural Networks: A Market Comparative Study. Decision Support Systems 37, 543–558 (2004)
9. Khashman, A.: Credit risk evaluation using neural networks: Emotional versus conventional models. Applied Soft Computing 11(8), 5477–5484 (2011)
10. Khashman, A.: Neural networks for credit risk evaluation: Investigation of different neural models and learning schemes. Expert Systems with Applications 37(9), 6233–6239 (2010)
11. Yu, L., Yue, W., Wang, S., Lai, K.K.: Support vector machine based multiagent ensemble learning for credit risk evaluation. Expert Systems with Applications 37, 1351–1360 (2010)
12. Platt, J.: Using sparseness and analytic QP to speed training of support vector machines. In: Kearns, M.S., Solla, S.A., Cohn, D.A. (eds.) Advances in Neural Information Processing Systems 11. MIT Press, MA (1999)
13. Quinlan, J.R.: C4.5: Programs for machine learning. Morgan Kaufmann, San Francisco (1993)
14. Seewald, A.K., Fürnkranz, J.: An Evaluation of Grading Classifiers. In: Hoffmann, F., Adams, N., Fisher, D., Guimarães, G., Hand, D.J. (eds.) IDA 2001. LNCS, vol. 2189, pp. 115–124. Springer, Heidelberg (2001)
15. Li, S., Tsang, I., Chaudhari, N.: Relevance vector machine based infinite decision agent ensemble learning for credit risk analysis. Expert Systems with Applications 39, 4947–4953 (2012)
16. Thomas, L.C., Oliver, R.W., Hand, D.J.: A Survey of the Issues in Consumer Credit Modelling Research. Journal of the Operational Research Society 56, 1006–1015 (2005)
17. Ting, K., Witten, I.: Issues in Stacked Generalization. Artificial Intelligence Research 10, 271–289 (1999)
18. Tsai, C.-F., Chen, M.-L.: Credit rating by hybrid machine learning techniques. Applied Soft Computing 10(2), 374–380 (2010)
19. Wang, G., Hao, J., Ma, J., Jiang, H.: A comparative assessment of ensemble learning for credit scoring. Expert Systems with Applications 38(1), 223–230 (2011)
20. Wang, G., Ma, J.: A hybrid ensemble approach for enterprise credit risk assessment based on Support Vector Machine. Expert Systems with Applications 39(5), 5325–5331 (2012)
21. Wang, G., Ma, J.: Study of corporate credit risk prediction based on integrating boosting and random subspace. Expert Systems with Applications 38(11), 13871–13878 (2011)
22. Wang, Y.Q., Wang, S.Y., Lai, K.K.: A New Fuzzy Support Vector Machine to Evaluate Credit Risk. IEEE Transactions on Fuzzy Systems 13, 820–831 (2005)

23. Windeatt, T.: Diversity measures for multiple classifier system analysis and design. Information Fusion 6, 21–36 (2005)
24. Witten, I., Frank, E., Hall, M.: Data Mining: Practical Machine Learning Tools and Techniques, 3rd edn. Morgan Kaufmann (2011) ISBN 978-0-12-374856-0
25. Xiaoyan, M., Watta, P., Hassoun, M.H.: Analysis of a Plurality Voting-based Combination of Classifiers. Neural Process Lett. 29, 89–107 (2009)
26. Zouari, H., Heutte, L., Lecourtier, Y.: Controlling the diversity in classifier ensembles through a measure of agreement. Pattern Recognition 38, 2195–2199 (2005)

Extending Generalized Arc Consistency

Anastasia Paparrizou and Kostas Stergiou

Department of Informatics and Telecommunications Engineering,
University of Western Macedonia, Greece

Abstract. Generalized arc consistency (GAC) is the most widely used local consistency in constraint programming. Several GAC algorithms for specific constraints, as well as generic algorithms that can be used on any constraint, have been proposed in the literature. Stronger local consistencies than GAC have also been studied but algorithms for such consistencies are generally considered too expensive. In this paper we propose an extension to the standard GAC algorithm GAC2001/3.1 that achieves a stronger local consistency than GAC by considering intersections of constraints. Importantly, the worst-case time complexity of the proposed algorithm, called GAC+, is higher than that of GAC2001/3.1 only by a factor e, where e is the number of constraints in the problem. Experimental results demonstrate that in many cases GAC+ can reduce the size of the search tree compared to GAC, resulting in improved cpu times. Also, in cases where there is no gain in search tree size, there is only a negligible overhead in cpu time.

1 Introduction

Constraint Programming (CP) has become one of AI's success stories in recent years and is nowdays an established paradigm for modelling and solving hard combinatorial problems from areas such as planning and scheduling, timetabling, resource allocation, bioinformatics, etc. At the core of CP's success is the wide range of efficient contraint propagation algorithms offered by modern CP solvers for several types of non-binary constraints.

Constraint propagation algorithms typically try to prune values from the domains of variables by enforcing a local consistency property on the constraints of the problem. The most widely used local consistency is generalized arc consistency (GAC), also known as domain consistency. Several specialized GAC algorithms for specific (*global*) constraints have been proposed in the literature. In the absense of specialized algorithms, generic GAC algorithms that can be used on any constraint are applied. Examples of such algorithms are GAC3 [9], GAC4 [10], and GAC2001/3.1 [1].

Stronger local consistencies than GAC have also been studied extensively. Although the application of such methods can result in significant gains in terms of search tree size, they are rarely used in CP solvers. This is because algorithms for strong consistencies are generally considered too expensive, meaning that potential gains in search tree size are very often outweighted by the cpu time overheads.

In this paper we propose an extension to the well-known generic GAC algorithm GAC2001/3.1 that achieves a stronger local consistency than GAC through the intelligent exploitation of simple data structure used by GAC2001/3.1. Importantly, the

I. Maglogiannis, V. Plagianakos, and I. Vlahavas (Eds.): SETN 2012, LNAI 7297, pp. 174–181, 2012.

worst-case time complexity of GAC+, is higher than that of GAC2001/3.1 only by a factor e, where e is the number of constraints in the problem. Experimental results from benchmark problems demonstrate that in many cases GAC+ can reduce the size of the search tree compared to GAC, resulting in improved cpu times. Also, in cases where there is no gain in search tree size, there is only a negligible overhead in cpu time.

2   Background

A *Constraint Satisfaction Problem* (CSP) is defined as a tuple $(\mathcal{X}, \mathcal{D}, \mathcal{C})$ where: $\mathcal{X} = \{x_1, \ldots, x_n\}$ is a set of n variables, $\mathcal{D} = \{D(x_1), \ldots, D(x_n)\}$ is a set of finite domains, one for each variable, with maximum cardinality d, and $\mathcal{C} = \{c_1, \ldots, c_e\}$ is a set of e constraints with maximum arity k. Each constraint c is a pair $(vars(c), rel(c))$, where $vars(c) = \{x_1, \ldots, x_m\}$ is an ordered subset of $\mathcal{X}$, and the relation $rel(c)$ is a subset of the *Cartesian* product $D(x_1) \times \ldots \times D(x_m)$ that specifies the allowed combinations of values for the variables in $var(c)$. Constraints are represented either extensionally by explicitly specifying their relation or intensionally through a predicate or function.

Each tuple $\tau \in rel(c)$ is an ordered list of values $(a_1, \ldots, a_k)$ such that $a_j \in D(x_j), j = 1, \ldots, k$. Given a constraint c, a variable $x_i \in var(c)$, and a tuple $\tau \in rel(c)$, we denote by $\tau[x_i]$ the projection of τ on x_i. A tuple $\tau \in rel(c)$ is *valid* iff none of the values in the tuple has been removed from the domain of the corresponding variable.

Given two constraints c_i and c_j, if $var(c_i) \cap var(c_j) \neq \emptyset$ then we say that the constraints *intersect*. We denote by f_{max} the maximum number of variables that are common to any two constraints that share more than one variable.

A standard way of solving CSPs is by interleaving depth-first search and constraint propagation. The former is typically guided by branching heuristics, while the latter involves repeatedly enforcing some *local consistency* property on the constraints of the problem so that infeasible values are located and pruned.

The most commonly used local consistency is *generalized arc consistency* (GAC) or *domain consistency*, simply referred to as *arc consistency* in the case of binary constraints.

Definition 1. A value $a_i \in D(x_i)$ is GAC iff for every constraint c s.t. $x_i \in vars(c)$ there exists a valid tuple $\tau \in rel(c)$ that includes the assignment of a_i to x_i. In this case τ is called a *support* of a_i. A variable is GAC iff all its values are GAC. A problem is GAC iff there is no empty domain in $\mathcal{D}$ and all the variables in $\mathcal{X}$ are GAC.

When applied, GAC and its weaker variants such as Bounds Consistency (BC), focus on one constraint at a time. In contrast, higher-order local consistencies exploit the fact that very often constraints have two or more variables in common, to achieve stronger pruning than GAC. One of the most promising such consistencies is *max Restricted PairWise Consistency* (maxRPWC) [2].

Definition 2. A value $a_i \in D(x_i)$ is maxRPWC iff $\forall c_j \in C$, where $x_i \in var(c_j)$, a has a support $\tau \in rel(c_j)$ s.t. $\forall c_l \in C$ ($c_l \neq c_j$), s.t. $var(c_j) \cap var(c_l) \neq \emptyset, \exists \tau' \in$

$rel(c_l)$, s.t. $\tau[var(c_j) \cap var(c_l)] = \tau'[var(c_j) \cap var(c_l)]$ and τ' is valid. In this case we say that τ' is a PW-support of τ. A variable is maxRPWC iff all values in its domain are maxRPWC. A problem is maxRPWC iff there is no empty domain in $\mathcal{D}$ and all variables are maxRPWC.

Although the application of maxRPWC, and other strong local consistencies, can result in stronger pruning than GAC, it is not widely used. This is due to the high cost of algorithms for maxRPWC. For example, the standard maxRPWC1 algorithm has $O(e^2 k^2 d^p)$ worst-case time complexity, where p is the maximum number of variables involved in two constraints that share at least two variables [2]. In contrast, GAC2001/3.1 has $O(ek^2 d^k)$ worst-case complexity which is significantly lower considering that $p = 2k - 2$ in the worst case.

Following [4] we call a local consistency A stronger than B iff in any problem in which A holds then B holds, and strictly stronger iff it is stronger and there is at least one problem in which B holds but A does not.

3   GAC+

We now present GAC+, an algorithm that extends GAC2001/3.1 to achieve a local consistency stronger than GAC. Specifically, when GAC+ is applied it deletes all values that are not GAC and in addition it can delete some extra values that are GAC but are not maxRPWC. To achieve this it utilizes the $LastGAC$ data structure of GAC2001/3.1. To recall the use of this data structure, for each constraint c and each value $a_i \in D(x_i)$, where $x_i \in var(c)$, $LastGAC_{c,x_i,a_i}$ gives (i.e. points to) the most recently discovered support of a_i in c.

Algorithm 1. Algorithm GAC+

1: **if** PREPROCESSING **then** L=L $\cup \{x_i\}, \forall x_i \in V$;
2: **else** L={ currently assigned variable };
3: **while** L $\neq \emptyset$ **do**
4:      L=L$-\{x_i\}$;
5:      **for each** $c_k \in C$ s.t. $x_i \in var(c_k)$ **do**
6:          **for each** $x_j \in V$ s.t. $x_j \in var(c_k)$ AND $x_j \neq x_i$ **do**
7:              **if** $revise\_GAC+(c_k, x_j) > 0$ **then**
8:                  **if** DWO(x_j) **then return** FAILURE;
9:                  L=L $\cup \{x_j\}$;
10: **return** SUCCESS;

Algorithm GAC+ utilizes a list L where variables that have their domains pruned are inserted. Once a variable x_i is extracted from L, each constraint c_k that involves x_i is examined (line 5 in Algorithm 1) and all the variables that appear in c_k, except x_i, are revised. This is done by calling Function $reviseGAC+$.

This function takes a constraint c_i and a variable x_j, s.t. $x_j \in var(c_i)$, and for each value $a_j \in D(x_j)$ first checks if a_j has a support in c_i. In case $LastGAC_{c_i,x_j,a_j}$ is valid then this tuple is a support for a_j. If $LastGAC_{c_i,x_j,a_j}$ is not valid anymore, a new support is sought. This is done by iterating through the tuples of c_i in lexicographical order starting from the one immediatelly after $LastGAC_{c_i,x_j,a_j}$ (line 5 in Function 2). In case a tuple τ that is valid and consistent is located, then a support for a_j has been established and $LastGAC_{c_i,x_j,a_j}$ is set to τ. Up to this point GAC+ operates just like a typical GAC algorithm. However, once a support τ is located, GAC+ performs an additional operation which can sometimes determine that τ has no PW-support in some intersecting constraint. Namely, the algorithm iterates over the constraints intersecting with c_i on more than one variable and for each such constraint c_k calls function checkPWtuple[1].

Function 2. reviseGAC+(c_i, x_j)

1: removedValues = 0;
2: **for each** $a_j \in D(x_j)$ **do**
3:     SUPPORT_FOUND=FALSE;
4:     **if** $\neg isValid(LastGAC_{c_i,x_j,a_j})$ **then**
5:         **for each** τ of $c_i > LastGAC_{c_i,x_j,a_j}$, s.t. $\tau[x_j] = a_j$ **do**
6:             **if** $isValid(\tau)$ AND $isConsistent(c_i, \tau)$ **then**
7:                 $LastGAC_{c_i,x_j,a_j} = \tau$;
8:                 PW_CONSISTENCY=TRUE;
9:                 **for each** $c_k \neq c_i$ s.t. $|var(c_k) \cap var(c_i)| > 1$ **do**
10:                     **if** $checkPWtuple(c_i, \tau, c_k)$ **then**
11:                         PW_CONSISTENCY=FALSE; **break**;
12:                 **if** PW_CONSISTENCY **then**
13:                     SUPPORT_FOUND=TRUE; **break**;
14:     **if** $\neg$ SUPPORT_FOUND **then**
15:         remove a_j from $D(x_j)$;
16:         removedValues = removedValues + 1;
17: **return** removedValues;

This function first locates Lex_Max, the lexicographically largest $LastGAC_{c_k,x_k,\tau[x_k]}$ for all variables x_k that belong to the intersection of c_i and c_k (lines 1-4). Then it checks if there can exist a tuple greater or equal to this one that has the same values for the variables of the intersection as τ. Crucially, this check is done in linear time as follows.

Assuming $Lex\_Max = <(x_1, a_1), ..., (x_m, a_m)>$ then this tuple is scanned from left to right. If the currently examined variable x_k belongs to $var(c_k) \cap var(c_i)$ and $a_k > \tau[x_k]$, where a_k is the value of x_k in Lex_Max, then we conclude that there can be no PW-support for τ in c_k (line 10). In the opposite case where $a_k < \tau[x_k]$ (line 10), we infer that a PW-support could be located for τ and thus we stop searching. If x_k does not belong to $var(c_k) \cap var(c_i)$ then if the value it takes in Lex_Max is the last value in its domain, we continue scanning (line 7). Otherwise, the scan is stopped because there may exist a tuple larger or equal to Lex_Max that is a PW-support of τ.

As implied by its description, checkPWtuple can verify the lack of PW-support mainly in cases where the variables in the intersection appear consecutively at the start of

---

[1] Constraints that intersect on exactly one variable are not considered because after making the problem GAC they cannot possibly contribute to any extra pruning [2].

constraint's c_k scope. Hence, this function performs a limited, and cheap, check for PW consistency. That is, it can sometimes determine that a verified support τ is not PW consistent (i.e. it has no PW-support on some constraint). In such a case, the search for a support for a_j is resumed in *reviseGAC+*. The following example illustrates the basic idea behind GAC+.

Function 3. checkPWtuple(c_i, τ, c_k)

1: Lex_Max=NULL;
2: **for each** $x_k \in var(c_k) \cap var(c_i)$ **do**
3:      **if** $\tau' = LastGAC_{c_k,x_k,\tau[x_k]} > Lex\_Max$ **then**
4:          Lex_Max=τ';
5: **for each** $x_k \in var(c_k)$ **do**
6:      **if** $x_k \notin var(c_k) \cap var(c_i)$ **then**
7:          **if** $Lex\_Max[x_k]$ is last value in $D(x_k)$ **then continue**;
8:          **else break**;
9:      **else**
10:         **if** $Lex\_Max[x_k] < \tau[x_k]$ **then break**;
11:         **if** $Lex\_Max[x_k] > \tau[x_k]$ **then return** FALSE;
12: **return** TRUE;

Example 1. Consider two constraints c_1 and c_2 with $var(c_1) = \{x_1, x_2, x_3, x_4\}$ and $var(c_2) = \{x_3, x_4, x_5, x_6\}$. Assume that the support $\tau = \{0, 2, 2, 1\}$ has been located for value 0 of x_1, and that $LastGAC_{c_2,x_3,2}$ is tuple $\tau' = \{2, 2, 0, 1\}$. Since $\tau'[x_4]$ is greater than $\tau[x_4]$, it is clear that there is no valid and consistent tuple in c_2 that includes values 2 and 1 for x_3 and x_4 respectively. That is, no PW-support for τ exists in c_2 and hence value 0 of x_1 is not maxRPWC. If we assume that τ is the last support of $(x_1, 0)$ in c_1 then GAC+ will determine (simply by comparing τ to τ') that 0 should be deleted from $D(x_1)$. In contrast, a GAC algorithm cannot infer this since it does not consider constraint intersections at all.

The following proposition is a direct consequence of the limited check for PW consistency that GAC+ performs. The proof is straightforward if we consider that GAC+ is identical to GAC2001/3.1 plus the calls to Function *checkPWtuple*, which can only result in extra pruning, and is thus ommitted.

Proposition 1. GAC+ achieves a level of local consistency that is strictly stronger than GAC and strictly weaker than maxRPWC.

As mentioned, the ability of GAC+ to delete extra values compared to a GAC algorithm depends on the ordering of the variables in the scope of the constraints. For instance, if the scope of constraint c_2 in Example 1 is $var(c_2) = \{x_3, x_5, x_4, x_6\}$ with $LastGAC_{c_2,x_3,2}$ being $\tau' = \{2, 0, 2, 1\}$ then we cannot deduce that no PW-support for τ exists in c_2 unless 0 is the last value in $D(x_5)$. This is because a tuple that is lexicographically greater than τ', e.g. $\{2, 1, 1, 1\}$ may be a PW-support of τ. However, the ordering of the constraints' scope can be altered if necessary. For example, if a subset of the variables in a constraint appears in many intersections with other constraints then these variables can be moved to the front of the constraint's scope to facilitate pruning by GAC+. This can be done for all constraints in a preprocessing step.

Finally, we discuss the worst-case complexity of GAC+. Since GAC+ uses the same *LastGAC* data structure as GAC2001/3.1, it has the same $O(ekd)$ space complexity.

Proposition 2. The worst-case time complexity of GAC+ is $O(e^2 k^2 d^k)$.

Proof. GAC+ is identical to GAC2001/3.1 with the addition of lines 8-13 to *reviseGAC+*. In *reviseGAC+*, for each variable x_j and each of its d values, d^{k-1} tuples are first checked for GAC consistency with $O(k)$ cost for each check. Then, for each tuple and each constraint c_k interecting c_i *checkPWtuple* is called.

Let us now consider the cost of *checkPWtuple*. Finding the lexicographically largest *LastGAC* among the at most f_{max} variables in $var(c_k) \cap var(c_i)$ costs $O(f_{max})$, assuming that the lexicographic comparison of two tuples is implemented efficiently. The **for** loop of line 5 costs $O(k)$ since in the worst case all values in the tuple must be examined. Hence, the cost of *checkPWtuple* is $O(f_{max} + k)$=$O(k)$.

Hence, *reviseGAC+* costs $O(dd^{k-1}(k+ek)) = O(ekd^k)$. This function can be called at most kd times for each constraint c_i and variable $x_j \in var(c_i)$. However, the cost of *reviseGAC+* for each x_j and each c_i is amortized over all the kd calls because of the use of *LastGAC* (see [1] for details). Since there are at most e constraints and k variables per constraint, the worst-case time complexity of GAC+ is $O(e^2 k^2 d^k)$.   □

4 Experiments

We ran experiments with benchmark non-binary problems taken from C. Lecoutre's repository and used in the CSP Solver Competitions[2]. We tried the following classes: *Golomb rulers, random problems, forced random problems, chessboard coloration, Schurr's lemma, modified Renault, positive table constraints* and *BDD*. The first five classes only include constraints of arity up to 4, while the other three include constraints of large arity (up to 18).

The algorithms were implemented within a CP solver written in Java from scratch. Search used a binary branching scheme, the *dom/wdeg* heuristic for variable ordering [3], and lexicographical value ordering. The searches for GAC on extensional constraints of large arity were performed using the efficient algorithm of [6]. The ordering of variables in the constraint scopes was not altered to facilitate propagation for GAC+, although this is an interesting direction for future work.

In Table 1 we present indicative results from search algorithms that maintain a certain local consistency throughout search. We compare GAC+ to GAC (implemented using algorithm GAC2001/3.1). The results demonstrate that GAC+ improves upon the performance of GAC2001/3.1 in the majority of instances.

Specifically, GAC+ is clearly better than GAC2001/3.1 on *Golomb rulers* instances as well as *random* and *forced random* problems. Often there are large margins between the performances of the two algorithms. For example on *rand-3-20-20-60-632-fcd-15* GAC+ is 3 times faster than GAC2001/3.1. These results are due to the stronger pruning achieved by GAC+ which results in significant reduction in the number of nodes.

---

[2] http://www.cril.univ-artois.fr/CPAI08/

Table 1. Search tree nodes and cpu times in secs from various representative problem instances

Instance	Node visits		CPU time	
	GAC2001/3.1	GAC+	GAC2001/3.1	GAC+
renault-mod-5	1,070	1,038	**326**	332
renault-mod-10	1,532	1,514	48	**47**
renault-mod-24	753	674	217	**206**
renault-mod-25	1,273	545	510	**365**
renault-mod-31	863	796	76	**69**
bdd-21-133-18-78-6	41,199	39,002	3,521	**2,777**
bdd-21-133-18-78-7	36,383	31,713	**4,312**	4,462
ruler-25-8-a4	2,697	2,316	96	**67**
ruler-34-9-a4	8,495	9,430	1,264	**934**
rand-3-20-20-60-632-fcd-4	223,155	113,814	275	**154**
rand-3-20-20-60-632-fcd-8	136,912	110,585	171	**145**
rand-3-20-20-60-632-fcd-15	85,940	25,858	109	**35**
rand-3-20-20-60-632-4	124,450	37,612	165	**51**
rand-3-20-20-60-632-7	114,375	112,592	**150**	155
rand-3-20-20-60-632-9	73,408	48,956	102	**67**
pt-8-20-5-18-800-4	37,466	37,416	1,301	**1,181**
pt-8-20-5-18-800-7	15,845	15,757	505	**464**
cc-8-8-2	13,278	13,762	**7.2**	7.8
cc-9-9-2	12,945	12,828	**12**	13
lemma-20-9	370,992	370,992	**101**	102
lemma-30-9	367,664	367,664	**249**	253

GAC+ does not achieve notable additional pruning on *positive table constraints*. Albeit, it is still faster than GAC2001/3.1. Results are somewhat mixed on the *modified Renault* and *BDD* classes. However, GAC+ is faster than GAC2001/3.1 in the majority of the instances.

GAC+ is not successful, in terms of pruning, on the *chessboard coloration* and *Schurr's lemma* classes. This is due to the structure of the instances in these classes. In *chessboard coloration* constraints have relatively small arity (4) and they are very loose (disjunctions of $\neq$ constraints). This minimizes the extra pruning that can be achieved by GAC+. Note that in some cases GAC+ results in more node visits than GAC2001/3.1, meaning that its few extra value deletions actually mislead the variable ordering heuristic. In *Schurr's lemma* problems there are only a few constraint intersections on more than one variable. As a result, our method cannot exploit the problems' structure for additional pruning. However, despite the lack of additional pruning in these two classes, the overheads of GAC+ do not slow down search notably compared to GAC2001/3.1.

4.1   Discussion

From the experimental results we can conclude that the performance of GAC+ depends largely on the structure of the particular problem class, i.e. on the topology of the constraint graph and the type of constraints. Our method is particularly successful on problems where many intersections between constraints exist, and the constraints are relatively tight. On the other hand, GAC+ does not offer improvements on problems with few intersections or/and when constraints are loose. We believe that these results can be exploited to preselect the appropriate propagation technique by examining the structure of the given problem.

It is important to note that the idea on which GAC+ is based (i.e. the exploitation of the $LastGAC$ data structure) is not only applicable within a generic algorithm. Algorithms for certain specialized constraints can also benefit. Specifically, specialized GAC algorithms for *table constraints* (i.e. extensionally defined constraints) can be enhanced to achieve stronger pruning following the ideas presented here in a straightforward way. The GAC algorithms of [8], [7] and [5] already utilize a structure similar to $LastGAC$. Therefore, it is easy to extend them along the lines of GAC+. We intend to investigate this in the future.

5   Conclusion

We have presented GAC+, an extension to the standard GAC algorithm GAC2001/3.1 that achieves a stronger local consistency level than GAC. This is accomplished through the exploitation of a simple data structure already used by GAC2001/3.1. In contrast to existing methods for strong local consistencies, the worst-case time complexity of GAC+ is very close to that of GAC algorithms. This is reflected on the practical performance of the algorithm as it does not slow down search in a significant way even in cases where no additional pruning compared to GAC is achieved. On the other hand, there exist cases where the additional pruning of GAC+ results in important cpu time gains.

References

1. Bessière, C., Régin, J.C., Yap, R., Zhang, Y.: An Optimal Coarse-grained Arc Consistency Algorithm. Artificial Intelligence 165(2), 165–185 (2005)
2. Bessiere, C., Stergiou, K., Walsh, T.: Domain filtering consistencies for non-binary constraints. Artificial Intelligence 172(6-7), 800–822 (2008)
3. Boussemart, F., Hemery, F., Lecoutre, C., Sais, L.: Boosting systematic search by weighting constraints. In: Proceedings of ECAI 2004, Valencia, Spain (2004)
4. Debruyne, R., Bessière, C.: Domain Filtering Consistencies. JAIR 14, 205–230 (2001)
5. Gent, I.P., Jefferson, C., Miguel, I., Nightingale, P.: Data structures for generalised arc consistency for extensional constraints. In: Proceedings of the Twenty Second Conference on Artificial Intelligence (2007)
6. Lecoutre, C.: Optimization of Simple Tabular Reduction for Table Constraints. In: Stuckey, P.J. (ed.) CP 2008. LNCS, vol. 5202, pp. 128–143. Springer, Heidelberg (2008)
7. Lecoutre, C., Szymanek, R.: Generalized Arc Consistency for Positive Table Constraints. In: Benhamou, F. (ed.) CP 2006. LNCS, vol. 4204, pp. 284–298. Springer, Heidelberg (2006)
8. Lhomme, O., Régin, J.C.: A fast arc consistency algorithm for n-ary constraints. In: Proceedings of AAAI 2005 (2005)
9. Mackworth, A.K.: On reading sketch maps. In: Proceedings IJCAI 1977, pp. 598–606 (1977)
10. Mohr, R., Masini, G.: Good Old Discrete Relaxation. In: Proceedings of ECAI 1988, pp. 651–656 (1988)

An Online Kernel-Based Clustering Approach for Value Function Approximation

Nikolaos Tziortziotis and Konstantinos Blekas

Department of Computer Science, University of Ioannina
P.O. Box 1186, Ioannina 45110 - Greece
{ntziorzi,kblekas}@cs.uoi.gr

Abstract. Value function approximation is a critical task in solving Markov decision processes and accurately modeling reinforcement learning agents. A significant issue is how to construct efficient feature spaces from samples collected by the environment in order to obtain an optimal policy. The particular study addresses this challenge by proposing an on-line kernel-based clustering approach for building appropriate basis functions during the learning process. The method uses a kernel function capable of handling pairs of state-action as sequentially generated by the agent. At each time step, the procedure either adds a new cluster, or adjusts the winning cluster's parameters. By considering the value function as a linear combination of the constructed basis functions, the weights are optimized in a temporal-difference framework in order to minimize the Bellman approximation error. The proposed method is evaluated in numerous known simulated environments.

1 Introduction

The objective of Reinforcement Learning (RL) [1,2] is to control an autonomous agent in usually unknown environments. The agent interacts with the environment which is typically modelled as a Markov Decision Process (MDP), and at each time step receives a scalar reward signal that evaluates the quality of the selected transitions. The decision making procedure is designed so as to choose actions with the optimum expected returns. The quality of a policy is quantified by the so-called value function which associates to every state the expected discounted return which is received starting from the particular state and all decisions are made following this policy. However, in cases with large or continuous state spaces the value function cannot be calculated explicitly. In such domains a common strategy is to employ function approximation, by representing the value function as a linear combination of some predefined set of basis functions.

The Temporal Difference (TD) family of algorithms [3] provide a nice framework for policy evaluation. The parameters of the value function are usually learned from data, as in the case of typical TD and the Least-Squares TD (LSTD) methods [4,5]. Also, kernelized reinforcement learning methods have been paid a lot of attention by employing kernel techniques to standard RL methods [6] and Gaussian Processes for approximating the value function [7,8,9].

I. Maglogiannis, V. Plagianakos, and I. Vlahavas (Eds.): SETN 2012, LNAI 7297, pp. 182–189, 2012.

However, in most cases the basis functions used for estimating the value function remain fixed during the learning process, as for example in [10] where a predefined number of fixed Fourier basis functions are used for value approximation. Alternatively, a steady number of basis functions are tuned in a batch manner, as in the cases presented in [11, 12] that build a graph over the state space after selecting a large number of input data and then generates the k eigenvectors of the graph Laplacian matrix. In another work [13], a set of k RBF basis function are adjusted directly over the Bellman's equation of the value function. Finally, in [14] the probability density function and the reward model, which are assumed to be known, are used for creating basis function from Krylov space vectors (powers of the transition matrix used to systems of linear equations).

In this paper, a novel framework for value function approximation is proposed which addresses the issue of the on-line construction of basis functions. An on-line kernel-based clustering approach is used for separating the input space that contains pairs of state-action by appropriate considered a kernel function that encapsulates both kind of information. The clustering procedure selects iteratively a winning prototype and applies a learning procedure for the adaptation of its parameters based on the stochastic gradient descent. Additionally, it provides a mechanism for automatically adding clusters. The parameters of the clusters can be further used for building a dictionary of basis function which can be employed on the policy evaluation procedure for the adaptation of weights of the value function linear model. These two stages act simultaneously during the learning process aiming at the estimation of an optimal policy. The proposed method has been tested to several known simulated environments where we have made comparisons with a recent value function approximation approach that uses a fixed number of predefined Fourier basis functions.

The remaining of this paper is organized as follows. In Section 2, we briefly present some preliminaries and review the basic TD scheme for value function approximation. Section 3 contains the main contribution of this paper where we describe an efficient on-line kernel-based clustering algorithm for constructing basis functions and how it can be embedded to the basic TD learning scheme. In Section 4, experimental results are provided to illustrate the effectiveness of the proposed method. Finally, in Section 5 we give conclusions and suggestions for future research.

2   Background and Preliminaries

A *Markov Decision Process* (MDP) is a tuple $(\mathcal{S}, \mathcal{A}, P, R, \gamma)$, where $\mathcal{S}$ is the state space; $\mathcal{A}$ is the action space; $P : \mathcal{S} \times \mathcal{A} \times \mathcal{S} \rightarrow [0, 1]$ is a Markovian transition model that specifies the probability $P(s, a, s')$ of transition to a state s' when taken an action a in state s; $R : \mathcal{S} \rightarrow \mathbb{R}$ is the reward function; and $\gamma \in (0, 1)$ is the discount factor for future rewards. A *stationary policy* $\pi : \mathcal{S} \rightarrow \mathcal{A}$ for a MDP is a mapping from states to actions and denotes a mechanism for choosing actions. An *episode* is a sequence of state transitions: $< s_1, a_1, r_1, s_2, \ldots, >$. An agent repeatedly chooses actions until the current episode terminates, and then a new episode starts over again.

The notion of *value function* is of central interest in reinforcement learning tasks. Given a policy π, the value $V^\pi(s)$ of a state s is defined as the expected discounted return obtained when starting from this state and all decisions are made according to policy π until the current episode terminates:

$$V^\pi(s) = E_\pi \left[\sum_{t=0}^{\infty} \gamma^t R(s_t) | s_0 = s \right] . \tag{1}$$

As it is well-known the value function satisfy the following recursive equation:

$$V^\pi(s) = E_\pi \left[R(s_t) + \gamma V^\pi(s_{t+1}) | s_t = s \right] . \tag{2}$$

which expresses a relationship between the values of successive states in the same episode and is known as *Bellman's equation*. In the same way, the state-action value function (Q-function) $Q(s, a)$ denotes the expected cumulative reward as received by taking action a in state s, and thereafter following the policy π:

$$Q^\pi(s, a) = E_\pi \left[\sum_{t=0}^{\infty} \gamma^t R(s_t) | s_0 = s, a_0 = a \right] . \tag{3}$$

In this study we will mainly focus on Q functions dealing with state-action pairs.

The objective of RL problems is to estimate an optimal policy π^* which is equivalent to finding the optimal state-action value function Q^*:

$$\pi^*(s) = \arg \max_a Q^*(s, a). \tag{4}$$

A common choice for representing the value function is through a linear function approximation using a set of k basis functions $\{\phi_j(s, a)\}_{j=1}^k$:

$$Q(s, a; w) = \phi(s, a)^\top w = \sum_{j=1}^{k} \phi_j(s, a) w_j , \tag{5}$$

where $w = (w_1, \ldots, w_k)$ is a vector of weights which are unknown and must be estimated so as to minimize the approximation error. The selection of the basis functions is very important and must be chosen in such a way so as to encode properties of the state and action relevant to the proper determination of the Q values. As we will see later, our method provides an adaptive incremental procedure for discovering appropriate basis functions through on-line clustering.

One of the most popular on-policy TD algorithms is the SARSA [1] which is based on a *bootstrapping* technique. Assuming that an action a_t is taken and the agent moves from belief state s_t to a new state s_{t+1} receiving a reward r_t, a new action a_{t+1} is chosen according to the current policy. Then, the predicted Q value of this new state-action pair and the received reward are used to calculate an improved estimate for the Q value of the previous state-action pair:

$$\delta_t = r_t + \gamma Q(s_{t+1}, a_{t+1}) - Q(s_t, a_t) = r_t + \gamma(\phi(s_{t+1}, a_{t+1}) - \phi(s_t, a_t))^\top w_t , \tag{6}$$

which is the one-step temporal-difference (TD) error. This is used for adjusting the weights of the policy by performing a stochastic gradient descent scheme:

$$\boldsymbol{w}_{t+1} = \boldsymbol{w}_t + \alpha_t \delta_t \nabla_{\boldsymbol{w}} Q(\boldsymbol{s}_t, a_t) , \tag{7}$$

where α_t is the learning rate which set to some small value (e.g. 0.05) and can be decreased over time. Additionally, is useful to combine SARSA with the *eligibility traces*, SARSA(λ), allowing the update rule to propagate the TD error backward over the current trajectory of states. This is achieved by modifying the above equation (Eq. 7) as $\boldsymbol{w}_{t+1} = \boldsymbol{w}_t + \alpha_t \delta_t e_t$, where $e_t = \gamma \lambda e_{t-1} + \nabla_{\boldsymbol{w}} Q(\boldsymbol{s}_t, a_t)$ is a vector of eligibility traces and $\lambda \in [0, 1]$ is the trace-decay parameter.

3   The Proposed Method

The proposed methodology is based on a policy evaluation scheme that incrementally builds a dictionary of basis functions for modelling the value function. This is accomplished by using an on-line clustering scheme that decomposes appropriately an efficient kernel space of the inputs so as to achieve optimal exploration of the value function. To what follows and for simplicity we will assume that the input samples that are generated by the agent are state-action pairs, denoted as $x_i = (\boldsymbol{s}_i, a_i)$. We will also consider that the action space is discrete of size M.

Assuming a given data set of N samples $\{x_1, x_2, \ldots, x_N\}$ the task of clustering aims at partitioning the input set into k disjoint clusters, $c_1, c_2, \ldots, c_k$ containing samples with common properties. The kernel k-means [15,16], which is an extension of the standard k-means algorithm, is based on transforming data to a feature space through appropriate kernel functions and minimizing the clustering error in this space. In particular, the objective function is given by

$$J_k = \sum_i^N \min_{j=1}^k \{-K(x_i, m_j)\} \tag{8}$$

where m_j are some representatives for each cluster. In our study we have considered that every cluster c_j is characterized by the following features:

- $\boldsymbol{\mu}_j$: its centroid in state space $\mathcal{S}$,
- Σ_j: diagonal covariance matrix over the state space,
- $\boldsymbol{p}_j = (p_{j1}, \ldots, p_{jM})$: the density function over the M discrete actions, giving the probabilities of each action ($\sum_{m=1}^M p_{jm} = 1$).

These features constitute the representative vector $m_j = (\boldsymbol{\mu}_j, \Sigma_j, \boldsymbol{p}_j)$ of a cluster.

The kernel function $K(x_i, m_j)$ for an arbitrary sample, $x_i = (\boldsymbol{s}_i, a_i)$, with the c_j cluster is derived as a product of two kernels, one for each space:

$$K(x_i, m_j) = K_s(\boldsymbol{s}_i, \boldsymbol{\mu}_j, \Sigma_j) K_a(a_i, \boldsymbol{p}_j) . \tag{9}$$

For the state space a Gaussian kernel have been used:

$$K_s(s_i, \mu_j, \Sigma_j) = \exp(-\frac{1}{2}(s_i - \mu_j)^\top \Sigma_j^{-1}(s_i - \mu_j)) \,, \tag{10}$$

while for the action space the kernel function is derived from the probability for this action of the cluster action distribution, i.e.

$$K_a(a_i, p_j) = p_{j,a_i} \,. \tag{11}$$

Note that in fact the action kernel is the cosine similarity between the probability vector for actions and an indicator vector of the input action a_i with zeros in all positions except in the position of a_i where has one.

In our case, the samples are non-stationary and are generated sequentially (i.e. time-varying). On-line clustering provides a framework for constructing recursive learning rules taking into account model evolutions over time. The proposed on-line kernel-based clustering method is performed iteratively as follows: For a random taken data point $x_i = (s_i, a_i)$, the method first selects the winning cluster j^* according to the current kernel values, i.e.

$$j^* = \arg \max_{j=1}^{k} K(x_i, m_j) \,. \tag{12}$$

If the maximum kernel value is less than a predefined threshold K_{min}, then a new cluster is created ($k = k + 1$) by initializing it properly. This is done by setting the state s_i as the cluster centroid, $\mu_k = s_i$, while for the action density probability p_k we give a large value for the action probability of action a_i (e.g. $p_{k,a_i} = 0.8$) and normalize the others so as to hold the constraint, $\sum_m p_{km} = 1$.

The next step is the *adaptation phase* where the prototype m_{j^*} of the winning cluster must be adjusted. This is accomplished by using the next update rules:

$$\mu_{j^*}^{(new)} = \mu_{j^*} + \eta K(x_i, m_j)(s_i - \mu_{j^*}) \,, \tag{13}$$

$$\Sigma_{j^*}^{(new)} = \Sigma_{j^*} + \eta K(x_i, m_j) diag((s_i - \mu_{j^*}^{(new)})(s_i - \mu_{j^*}^{(new)})^\top) \,, \tag{14}$$

$$n_{jm}^{(new)} = \begin{cases} n_{jm} + 1, & \text{if } m = a_i \\ n_{jm}, & \text{otherwise} \end{cases} \,, \tag{15}$$

where the term η is the learning rate taking a small value (e.g. 0.05), which can be reduced over time. It must be noted that the density of actions, p_{jm}, is guided by the frequency distribution n_{jm} and thus it is more convenient to keep records of frequencies. Then, the probabilities p_{jm} are calculated by the relative frequencies. From the above rule, it is easily to show that the probability of action a_i will be increased by $(\nu_j - n_{jm})/(\nu_j(\nu_j + 1))$, while the probability of the other $M - 1$ actions will be decreased by $n_{jm}/(\nu_j(\nu_j + 1))$ ($\nu_j = \sum_{m=1}^{M} n_{jm}$ is the total frequency of cluster c_j).

The method starts with a single cluster $k = 1$, where it is initialized as described previously by the first data point collected by the agent $x_1 = (s_1, a_1)$. At every time step the policy evaluation stage uses the k basis functions as (currently) taken by the clustering procedure. Therefore, the on-line clustering approach provides not only the shape, but also the proper number of basis functions for estimating the value function. At a second level, the linear weights are re-estimated following the temporal difference (TD) learning process, as described previously. The above procedure is repeated until convergence, or the number of episodes reaches a prespecified value. The overall scheme of the proposed methodology is given in Algorithm 1.

Algorithm 1. The proposed method for value function approximation

---
1: Start with $k = 1$ and use first point $x_i = (s_1, a_1)$ for initializing it. Set a random value to weight w_1. $t = 0$.
2: **while** convergence or maximum number of episodes not found **do**
3:    Suppose previous input $x_i = (s_i, a_i)$. Observe new state s_{i+1}.
4:    Select action according to the current policy $a_{i+1} = \arg\max_{l=1}^{M} Q(s_{i+1}, l)$.
5:    Find the winning cluster $j^* = \arg\max_{j=1}^{k} K(x_{i+1}, m_j)$.
6:    **if** $K(x_{i+1}, m_{j^*}) < K_{min}$ **then**
7:       Create a new cluster ($k = k + 1$) and initialize its prototype m_k with x_{i+1}.
8:       Create a new weight w_k of linear model initialized randomly. $w_t = w_t \cup w_k$.
9:    **else**
10:       Update the prototype m_{j^*} of the winning cluster using Eqs. 13-15.
11:    **end if**
12:    Obtain the new k basis functions as: $\phi_j(s, a) = K((s, a), m_j) \ \forall \ j = 1, \ldots, k$.
13:    Update the weights w_t of Q function according to Eqs. 6, 7.
14:    $t = t + 1$
15: **end while**

---

4   Experimental Results

A number of experiments have been conducted using three well-known continuous benchmarks in order to assess the performance of the proposed methodology. These environments can be found on the RL-Glue software which are freely available at http://glue.rl-community.org/. Comparison has been made with a recent method presented in [10] that uses fixed Fourier basis functions of order 3, denoted as 'O(3)Fourier' [1]. In all experiments we have set the discount factor γ equal to 1, the parameter λ equal to 0.9, and the threshold for adding a new cluster as $K_{min} = 0.5$.

The first benchmark is the famous *cart pole* where the objective is to keep the pole balanced and the cart within its limits by applying a fixed magnitude force either to the left, or to the right (two actions). There are four continuous variables: the horizontal position and the velocity of the cart, as well as the angle and the angular velocity of the pole, while the reward received is +1.

---

[1] Open source code for this method can be found in the RL-Glue library.

The second environment is the *mountain car*, where the objective is to drive an under-powered car up a steep mountain road from a valley to the right tophill using three actions. The state consists of two continuous variables: the position and the current velocity of the car, while at each time step a negative reward $r = -1$ is received.

In the last domain the agent controls a simulated *acrobot* attached by the hands to a fixed location. The goal is to apply torque to the hips of the robot and swing the feet above a pre-specified threshold. Each state characterized by four continuous variables: the angle and the angular velocity of the two joints. The agent can select between three actions: positive torque, negative torque and zero torque on the second joint. A negative reward ($r = -1$) is received at each time step except for the case where the goal is reached ($r = 0$). An episode is terminated only when the goal is reached.

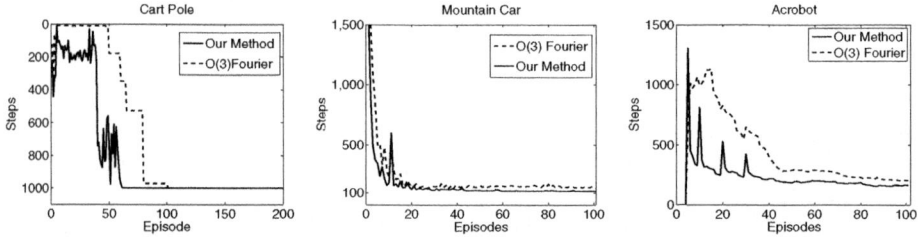

Fig. 1. Comparative results in three simulated environments

The depicted results on these three benchmarks are illustrated in Fig. 1, where each curve gives the number of steps that the agent makes per episode. Note these are the mean curves obtained by 10 runs per problem. As it is obvious our method has the tendency to converge to the optimum solution faster than the 'O(3)Fourier' method that employs (256) fixed Fourier basis function. It is interesting to note that in the case of the 'mountain car' and 'acrobot' environments the proposed method managed to discover better policies.

5   Conclusions and Future Directions

In this study we have presented a novel framework for learning representation of reinforcement learning agents and control in Markov decision processes. An on-line kernel-based clustering approach is used as a mechanism for creating and adjusting clusters over the input state-action pairs generated by the agent. At each step, the current cluster parameters are used for building an efficient kernel space that provides with the appropriate basis functions to the temporal-difference learning framework. Thus, the linear weights used for value function approximation are sequentially adjusted in a more optimal way. The initial results of our method obtained from the comparative study are very promising and promote directions for further research. Since the proposed scheme of constructing basis functions is general, it allows the possibility to study its impact to other temporal difference algorithms for learning the weights of the value function, such as the Least-Squares Temporal Difference (LSTD) or Gaussian Process Temporal Difference (GPTD). Also, alternative schemes of on-line clustering can be examined, as well as to make an extensive comparison with other value function approximation approaches.

References

1. Sutton, R.S., Barto, A.G.: Reinforcement Learning: An Introduction. MIT Press, Cambridge (1998)
2. Kaelbling, L.P., Littman, M.L., Moore, A.W.: Reinforcement learning: A survey. Journal of Artificial Inteligence Research 4, 237–285 (1996)
3. Sutton, R.: Learning to predict by the method of temporal differences. Machine Learning 3(1), 9–44 (1988)
4. Boyan, J.A.: Technical update: Least-squares temporal difference learning. Machine Learning, 233–246 (2002)
5. Lagoudakis, M.G., Parr, R.: Least-squares policy iteration. Journal of Machine Learning Research 4, 1107–1149 (2003)
6. Xu, X., Hu, D., Lu, X.: Kernel-based least squares policy iteration for reinforcement learning. IEEE Transactions on Neural Networks 18(4), 973–992 (2007)
7. Rasmussen, C.E., Kuss, M.: Gaussian processes in reinforcement learning. In: Advances in Neural Information Processing Systems 16, pp. 751–759 (2004)
8. Engel, Y., Mannor, S., Meir, R.: Reinforcement learning with gaussian process. In: International Conference on Machine Learning, pp. 201–208 (2005)
9. Farahmand, A.M., Ghavamzadeh, M., Szepesvári, C., Mannor, S.: Regularized policy iteration. In: NIPS, pp. 441–448 (2008)
10. Konidaris, G.D., Osentoski, S., Thomas, P.S.: Value function approximation in reinforcement learning using the fourier basis. In: AAAI Conf. on Artificial Intelligence, pp. 380–385 (2011)
11. Mahadevan, S.: Samuel meets amarel: Automating value function approximation using global state space analysis. In: AAAI (2005)
12. Mahadevan, S., Maggione, M.: Proto-value Functions: A Laplacian Framework for Learning Repersentation and Control in Markov Decision Porocesses. Journal of Machine Learning Research 8, 2169–2231 (2007)
13. Menache, I., Mannor, S., Shimkin, N.: Basis Function Adaptation in Temporal Difference Reinforcement Learning. Annals of Operations Research 134, 215–238 (2005)
14. Petrik, M.: An analysis of laplacian methods for value function approximation in mdps. In: International Joint Conference on Artificial Intelligence, pp. 2574–2579 (2007)
15. Scholkopf, B., Smola, A.J., Muller, K.-R.: Nonlinear component analysis as a kernel eigenvalue problem. Neural Computation 10(5), 1299–1319 (1998)
16. Tzortzis, G., Likas, A.: The Global Kernel k-Means Clustering Algorithm. IEEE Trans. on Neural Networks 20(7), 1181–1194 (2009)

Acoustic Bird Activity Detection on Real-Field Data

Todor Ganchev[1], Iosif Mporas[1], Olaf Jahn[2], Klaus Riede[2],
Karl-L. Schuchmann[2], and Nikos Fakotakis[1]

[1] Artificial Intelligence Group, Wire Communications Laboratory
Dept. of Electrical and Computer Engineering, University of Patras,
26500 Patras, Greece
[2] Zoologisches Forschungsmuseum Alexander Koenig
53113 Bonn, Germany
tganchev@upatras.gr

Abstract. We report on a research effort aiming at the development of an acoustic bird activity detector (ABAD), which plays an important role for automating traditional biodiversity assessment studies – presently performed by human experts. The proposed on-line ABAD is considered an integral part of an automated system for acoustic identification of bird species, which is currently under development. In particular, taking advantage of real-field audio recordings collected in the Hymettus Mountains east of Athens, we investigate the applicability of various machine learning techniques for the needs of our ABAD, which is intended to run on a mobile device. Performance is reported in terms of recognition accuracy on audio-frame level, due to the restrictions imposed by the requirement of run-time decision making with limited memory and energy resources. We report recognition accuracy of approximately 86% on a frame level, which is quite promising and encourages further research efforts in that direction.

Keywords: acoustic bird activity detection, bioacoustics, biodiversity surveys, real-field data.

1   Introduction

At present biodiversity inventories and monitoring studies are typically performed by expert biologists, who have to visit (periodically) sites and habitats of interest to conduct audiovisual, capture-recapture, or collection surveys. This is a time-consuming and costly task, which, due to multiple reasons, cannot be performed continuously and systematically for extended periods of time. Therefore, even a partial automation of the data collection and analysis procedures are considered to be important for developing future biodiversity assessment approaches.

Birds are an important indicator of the conservation status of habitats and landscapes as well as a proxy for biodiversity patterns. Thus, the detection of the presence and the estimation of population trends and reproductive success of certain bird species groups are of significant importance as they offer a general measurement of the health of an ecosystem [1].

I. Maglogiannis, V. Plagianakos, and I. Vlahavas (Eds.): SETN 2012, LNAI 7297, pp. 190–197, 2012.
© Springer-Verlag Berlin Heidelberg 2012

As birds are heard more often than seen, one promising non-intrusive method for monitoring their presence and activity is the acoustic detection and identification of avian taxa. In the present work, we focus on investigating the feasibility of automatic acoustic detection of bird vocalizations from real-field audio recordings and evaluate the recognition accuracy of the proposed ABAD, when implemented with different classifiers.

In the present paper, all sounds of non-bird origin, e.g. human- or machine-made sounds, sounds due to natural phenomena (e.g., wind and rain), sounds from other animals or unanimated objects co-existing in that environment, are collectively referred to as *background audio* or *noise*. Next, all sounds of bird origin that can be distinguished from the audio background by a human listener are collectively labeled as *bird vocalizations*, regardless of the coexistence of background interference.

2   Acoustic Bird Activity Detection in Real-Field Environment

The acoustic bird activity detector serves as a gateway, which aims to eliminate from the input audio stream these portions of the signal that correspond to sounds of non-bird origin. Thus, the ABAD excludes from storing or passing to the consequent processing stages, such as species identification, the silence intervals and any non-bird sounds, but passes through unaltered these portions of the audio which were recognized as bird vocalizations.

We aimed at an efficient design with respect to computation and memory, and by using frame-by-frame detections of the presence or absence of bird vocalizations in the input audio stream or with at minimal delay (Fig. 1). The acoustic bird activity detection process consists of three main stages *audio acquisition*, *audio parameterization*, and *pattern recognition*. While the audio parameterization step aims at computing descriptors, which capture the generalized acoustic properties of bird vocalizations, the pattern recognition step categorizes the current input audio frame either as *bird vocalization* or as *background noise*. Depending on the machine learning technique employed, this stage either estimates the degree of match between an unknown input signal and the pre-computed general models for the bird vocalizations and the background acoustic environment or, alternatively, makes decision without using any explicit modeling of the class-specific distributions. Lastly, after some post-processing of the binary decisions (or the scores) obtained for the current audio frame, a final decision is made with respect to a predefined threshold: either the current audio frame contains a bird vocalization or not. In the following, we briefly outline the consequent steps of signal acquisition, pre-processing, parameterization, and classification:

Audio acquisition: Audio is captured by a microphone, next amplified and then sampled at 32 kHz, so that the wide frequency range of bird vocalizations from various species is covered. Precision of 16-bits per sample is used to guarantee sufficient resolution of details for the subsequent processing of the signal.

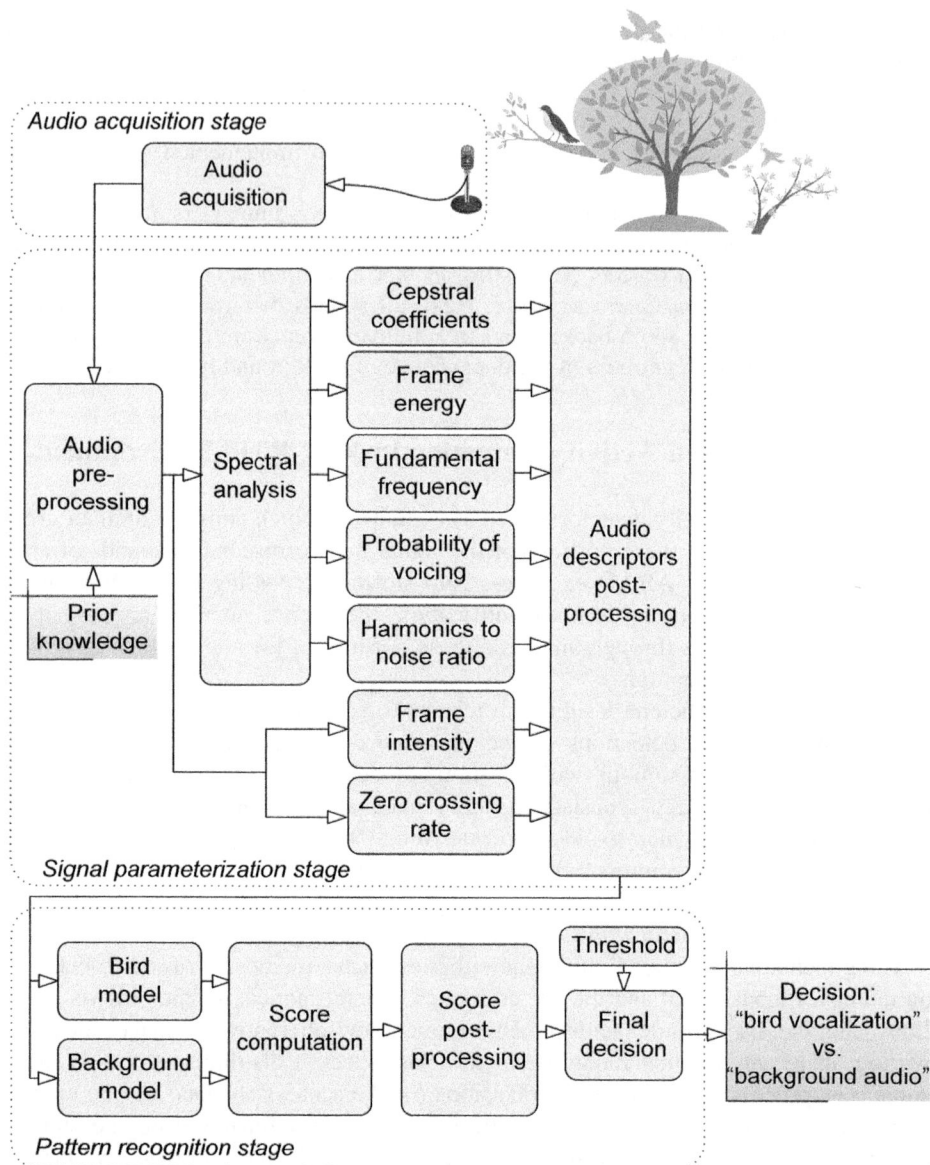

Fig. 1. Block diagram of the acoustic bird activity detection process (see text for details)

Audio Pre-processing: The pre-processing of the input audio stream consists of mean value removal, which is performed on the time domain signal, for eliminating the dc-offset that might have occurred during signal acquisition and amplification. Furthermore, based on prior knowledge we assume that, for most avian species, there is no useful information characterizing the bird vocalizations in the audio signal for the frequency band below 400 Hz. Thus, in order to reduce the influence of any environmental noise and low-frequency interferences, such as wind, vibrations of nearby objects, traffic noise, a high-pass filtering is applied on the amplified audio signal. The high-pass filtering with a low-order filter was found to provide a reasonable trade-off between computational demands and improvement of recognition accuracy, as it requires significantly fewer computational and memory resources when compared to contemporary noise reduction methods, such as those discussed in [2]. Specifically, it was experimentally found that a Butterworth filter of order 6 with cut-off frequency 400 Hz effectively reduces the low-frequency noise and improves the overall recognition accuracy. The audio pre-processing also includes Hamming windowing of the signal, and thus all consequent processing is performed on a frame level. In the following we assume audio frame size of 20 ms and skip step of 10 ms.

Audio Parameterization: Previous work on acoustic bird activity detection from real-world data reported the importance of tonal audio features [3] and their advantage over the traditional Mel-frequency cepstral coefficients (MFCC) in noisy conditions. In the present work, we make use of a more diverse set of audio parameters that facilitates the robust detection of bird vocalizations in non-stationary noise environments. In particular, each audio segment obtained after the audio pre-processing step is zero-padded to 1024 samples and then becomes subject to the audio parameterization procedure. Specifically, we compute two types of complementary audio descriptors: temporal (zero crossing rate, frame intensity) and spectral (MFCC, frame energy, fundamental frequency, probability of voicing, and the harmonics-to-noise ratio). These audio descriptors have been successfully used in audio processing and sound classification tasks, and offer improved robustness in noisy conditions. In the present work, we computed all audio parameters via the openSMILE acoustic parameterization tool [4]. In particular, for each audio frame we computed 12 MFCCs following the default HTK setup [5], the root mean square energy of the frame (E), the voicing probability (Vp), the harmonics-to-noise ratio (HNR) by autocorrelation function, the dominant frequency (Fd) normalized to 500 Hz, the intensity (Int) and the zero crossing rate (ZCR). Stacking together these audio parameters results in a feature vector of 18 audio features. Post-processing for dynamic-range normalization was applied to all audio features for equalizing the range of their numerical values.

A series of feature-ranking and selection tests have shown that the abovementioned *static* audio features are sufficient to carry out the recognition task and that appending to the feature vector their first and second time derivatives contributes less to improving the overall recognition accuracy. Yet, appending the time derivatives to the static features increases significantly the length of the feature vector, and thus, the demand of training data needed for robust model development, but also the computational demands.

Pattern Recognition Stage: The audio features obtained to this end are fed to a binary classifier which is trained to discriminate between the *bird vocalizations* and the *background* acoustic noise. Depending on the machine learning method employed, the decisions obtained (or alternatively the scores computed) for each audio frame are next post-processed. This post-processing aims at eliminating sporadic erroneous labeling of the current audio frame, e.g., due to momentary burst of interference, and thus contributes to the improvement of the overall recognition accuracy. A simple and computationally effective rule for post-processing is smoothing each decision (or score) with respect to its closest temporal neighbors. In particular, when the previous N neighbor audio frames and the following N neighbor frames were recognized as bird vocalization then the current frame is also (re)labeled as bird vocalization. Likewise are processed the frames whose neighbors were recognized as category background audio. The length w of the smoothing window is subject to investigation and in the general case is equal to $w = 2N + 1$, where $N \geq 0$. The case $N = 0$ corresponds to eliminating the post-processing of the recognized labels, while the cases $N = 1, 2, 3$ correspond to window size $w = 3, 5, 7$.

Eventually a final decision about the label of the current audio frame (either *bird vocalization* or *background noise*) is made after applying a predefined threshold on the post-processed scores. This threshold controls the 'sensitivity' of the ABAD and allows for some trading-off of false alarm errors vs. target miss errors, and thus allows for fine-tuning the operational mode and the gating properties of the ABAD. Furthermore, the choice of threshold levels directly affects the amount of the audio data fed to the subsequent audio processing steps.

3   Evaluation Setup and Results

In the following subsections, we describe the evaluation dataset, the experimental setup, and discuss the experimental results.

3.1   Real-World Dataset

The dataset used in the present research is a small excerpt from our collection of audio recordings, obtained in the Hymettus Mountains west of Athens, Greece. The recordings have been manually tagged (labels: bird vocalization vs. background audio) by an engineer with considerable experience in the area of audio processing. The training data representing the category *bird vocalizations* consists of approximately 6 minutes of concatenated bird vocalizations (35636 audio frames) extracted from 50 audio files, each with average duration of approximately 30 seconds. The training data for the category *background audio* was represented by a similar amount of audio, extracted from the same 50 files, and contains environmental sounds typical for our study area.

The test dataset consisted of another subset of 150 files (271024 audio frames), which were processed by each of the machine learning algorithms outlined in the next subsection.

3.2   Experimental Setup

We investigated the applicability of various machine-learning techniques, for the implementation of the binary classifier. Classifiers belonging to different categories of algorithms were selected:

- *k*-nearest neighbors classifier with linear search of the nearest neighbor and without weighting of the distance – also known as instance based classifier (*IBk*) [6],
- Bayes network (*BayesNet*) [7], with Simple Estimator (alpha = 0.5) and the K2 search algorithm (maximum number of parents = 1);
- 3-layer Multilayer perceptron (*MLP*) neural network [8] with architecture 18–10–1 neurons (all sigmoid) trained with 50 000 iterations;
- Pruned C4.5 decision tree (*J48*), with 3 folds for pruning and 7 for growing the tree [9];
- Support vector machine with sequential minimal optimization (*SMO*) algorithm [10] and RBF kernel [11].

We made use of the Weka [12] implementations of these algorithms with the default values of all parameters, which are not specified here.

A common experimental protocol was followed during the evaluation of all classifiers. Specifically, the ABAD implemented with different binary classifiers were treated uniformly and were trained with the dataset outlined in Section 3.1. The recognition accuracy of the ABAD was evaluated on audio-frame level in terms of percentages of correct detections on the test dataset specified in Section 3.1.

3.3   Experimental Results

The ranking of the machine-learning methods was made on the basis of their classification accuracy for the case of no post-processing of the frame decisions ($N = 0$) (Table 1). Specifically, the ABAD implementation based on the Multilayer Perceptron (*MLP*) neural network demonstrated the highest recognition accuracy, followed by the Support Vector Machine with sequential minimal optimization (*SMO*), the *k*-nearest neighbors classifier (*IBk*), the decision tree (*J48*), and finally the Bayes Network (*BayesNet*).

Table 1. Recognition accuracy (reported in percentages) for the acoustic bird activity detection implemented with various machine-learning techniques and different length, *w*, of the smoothing window

Binary Classifier	$w=1$ ($N=0$)	$w=3$ ($N=1$)	$w=5$ ($N=2$)	$w=7$ ($N=3$)
MLP	**85.0**	**86.3**	**86.1**	**86.0**
SMO	79.1	81.4	81.0	80.8
IBk	78.5	82.9	82.1	81.4
J48	74.9	79.1	78.0	77.2
BayesNet	64.9	65.8	65.6	65.5

This ranking is not surprising considering the limited amount of data used for training the binary classifiers, as well as the fact that some of the audio features in the feature vector are correlated to a certain degree. For instance the frame energy (*E*) is correlated with the frame intensity (*Int*), and the voicing probability (*Vp*) is correlated to the harmonics-to-noise ratio (*HNR*). However, it was observed that this redundancy in the feature vector, in fact, contributes to the improvement of the robustness to noise. One explanation for this effect could be that since the audio features in these pairs are computed in dissimilar manner, they are affected in different ways by the interference. Thus, in noisy conditions, depending on the noise type, these audio features complement each other, and thus contribute to the overall improvement of the noise robustness.

We want to emphasize that smoothing the scores (or the decisions) of the binary classifier is beneficial only when the closest temporal neighbors (corresponding to the previous and next audio frame) are used ($N = 1$) but this advantage is reduced when the decisions for the more distant neighbors ($N = 2, 3$) are accounted for.

The highest overall recognition accuracy of 86.3% was obtained for the *MLP* classifier in combination with post-processing with a smoothing window, $w = 3$, i.e., when the scores of the two closest neighbor frames (previous and next) are used. In practice, this smoothing scheme requires delaying the final decisions of the ABAD with one time-step with respect to the decisions made by the binary classifier. In our setup this delay is 10 ms, as the overlapping between two consecutive audio frames is 10 ms.

The relatively low absolute value of the recognition accuracy, 86.3%, can be explained with the non-stationary and fully uncontrolled conditions in our real-field environment (Hymettus Mountains), where interferences resulting from human presence and activities and from natural phenomena, such as wind and rain, are quite common and co-occur in time and space with the bird vocalizations. Nevertheless, when more annotated real-field data become available, we intend to experiment with more advanced statistical modeling techniques which explicitly address the intra-class distribution of the data for each class, which is expected to reduce the false acceptance rates.

In conclusion, it is worth noticing that the ABAD implemented with *MLP*-based binary classifier with architecture 18-10-1 is quite compact. This makes the ABAD computationally inexpensive, and less memory demanding, in contrast to the other implementations, with the instance based *k*-nearest neighbor classifier, or with the *SMO* (with RBF kernel) classifier. All these make the ABAD implementation with the *MLP* classifier followed by smoothing window, $w = 3$, quite suitable for porting as an "*App*" on a contemporary handheld mobile device.

Acknowledgements. The research reported in the present paper was supported by the AmiBio project (LIFE08 NAT/GR/000539), which is implemented with the contribution of the LIFE+ financial instrument of the European Union (project web-site: www.amibio-project.eu).

The authors wish to acknowledge the contribution of Mr. Stavros Ntalampiras, and Mr. Theodoros Kostoulas from the University of Patras and also to the entire team of the Association for the Protection and Development of Hymettus (SPAY), who supported the implementation of the audio data collection campaign in the Hymettus area.

References

1. Dawson, D.K., Efford, M.G.: Bird population density estimated from acoustic signals. Journal of Applied Ecology 46, 1201–1209 (2009)
2. Loizou, P.: Speech Enhancement: Theory and Practice. CRC Press (2007)
3. Jančovič, P., Köküer, M.: Automatic detection and recognition of tonal bird sounds in noisy environments. EURASIP Journal on Advances in Signal Processing 2011, Article ID 982936, 10 (2011), doi:10.1155/2011/982936
4. Eyben, F., Wöllmer, M., Schuller, B.: OpenEAR - introducing the Munich open-source emotion and affect recognition toolkit. In: Proc. of the 4th International HUMAINE Association Conference on Affective Computing and Intelligent Interaction, ACII 2009 (2009)
5. Young, S., Evermann, G., Gales, M., Hain, T., Kershaw, D., Liu, X., Moore, G., Odell, J., Ollason, D., Povey, D., Valtchev, V., Woodland, P.: The HTK book (for HTK Version 3.4), Cambridge University Engineering Department (2006)
6. Aha, D., Kibler, D.: Instance-based learning algorithms. Machine Learning 6, 37–66 (1991)
7. Bouckaert, R.R.: Bayesian networks in Weka. Technical Report 14/2004. Computer Science Department. University of Waikato (2004)
8. Chester, D.L.: Why two hidden layers are better than one. In: Proc. of the International Joint Conference on Neural Networks, vol. 1, pp. 265–268 (1990)
9. Quinlan, R.: C4.5: Programs for machine learning. Morgan Kaufmann Publishers, San Mateo (1993)
10. Keerthi, S.S., Shevade, S.K., Bhattacharyya, C., Murthy, K.R.K.: Improvements to Platt's SMO algorithm for SVM classifier design. Neural Computation 13(3), 637–649 (2001)
11. Scholkopf, B., Smola, A.J.: Learning with Kernels. MIT Press (2002)
12. Witten, H.I., Frank, E.: Data Mining: practical machine learning tools and techniques. Morgan Kaufmann Publishing (2005)

Parameter Tuning of Hybrid Nature-Inspired Intelligent Metaheuristics for Solving Financial Portfolio Optimization Problems

Vassilios Vassiliadis, Georgios Dounias, and Alexandros Tzanetos

Management and Decision Engineering Laboratory,
Department of Financial and Management Engineering, University of the Aegean,
41 Kountouriotou Str. GR-82100, Greece
{v.vassiliadis,fme08099}@fme.aegean.gr, g.dounias@aegean.gr

Abstract. In previous studies, nature-inspired algorithms have been implemented in order to tackle hard NP-optimization problems, in the financial domain. Specifically, the task of finding optimal combination of assets with the aim of efficiently allocating your available capital is of major concern. One of the main reasons, which justifies the difficulties entailed in this problem, is the high level of uncertainty in the financial markets and not only. As mentioned above, artificial intelligent algorithms may provide a solution to this task. However, there is one major drawback concerning these techniques: the large number of open parameters. The aim of this study is twofold. Firstly, results from extended simulations are presented regarding the application of a specific hybrid nature-inspired metaheuristic in a particular formulation of the financial portfolio optimization problem. The main focus is on presenting comparative results regarding the performance of the proposed scheme for various configuration settings. Secondly, it is our intend to enhance the hybrid scheme's performance by incorporating intelligent searching components such as other metaheuristics (simulated annealing).

Keywords: parameter tuning, genetic algorithm, portfolio optimization, hybrid Nature-Inspired Intelligent (NII) algorithm.

1   Introduction

Nowadays, a non-trivial task for investment managers, as well as investors in general, is to find efficient ways to allocate capital. By doing so, the level of risk decreases and in the same time the potential investor's goal is achieved. However, the question remains: which is a proper way to select assets for my portfolio? There are several ways of doing so. Some decision makers may invest on a financial index (such as S&P's 500), or in individual stocks. Nevertheless, there exist more intelligent approaches.

Portfolio optimization problems are concerned with finding the optimal combination of assets, as well as their corresponding weights, i.e optimization in two search spaces: one discrete (for assets) and one continuous (for weights). This kind of problems are considered as NP-hard, i.e. there is no deterministic algorithm known that can find an exact solution within polynomial time. Exhaustive search algorithms,

I. Maglogiannis, V. Plagianakos, and I. Vlahavas (Eds.): SETN 2012, LNAI 7297, pp. 198–205, 2012.

or other traditional approaches from the field of operational research, are inefficient to find the optimal solution or, in the best case, they get stuck in local optima [1]. A potential solution is the introduction of intelligent metaheuristics.

Nature-inspired algorithms in the field of artificial intelligence correspond to techniques that are based on how biological systems and natural networks deal with real-world situations in nature [2]. The main advantage of nature-inspired intelligent algorithms over traditional methodologies which deal with optimization problems is their searching ability. Finally, hybrid schemes combine unique characteristics of two or more intelligent methods so as to enhance searching of the solution space.

The scope of this paper is to present a statistical analysis regarding various combinations of hybrid algorithm's parameter settings. Also, the overall performance of the algorithm is of great importance, as well. In order of achieve this, we incorporate additional searching components in the main strategy of the genetic algorithm. In this study, we provide results regarding the incorporation of a simulated annealing algorithm. As far as the application domain is concerned, the objective function is to maximize a non-linear financial ratio which takes into account both the risk and the expected return of the portfolio. The main contribution of this work lies in detecting useful trends regarding the hybrid algorithm's parameters. This will provide an assistance tool for further investigation in the portfolio optimization domain.

The structure of this paper is as follows. In section 1, an introduction to some main concepts is given. In section 2, findings from the literature review are presented in brief. In section 3, the basic methodological issues are shown. In section 4, the mathematical formulation of the optimization problem is presented. Computational results and a brief discussion are presented in section 5. Finally, in section 6 some basic conclusions and future research potentials are presented.

2   Literature Review

In this section, evidence from the literature is provided regarding the application of nature-inspired algorithms for the portfolio optimization problem. For convenient reasons, the main findings are presented in brief. Studies in this field are limited, and only a selection of them is presented here.

Table 1. Basic studies from the literature

Reference	Applied Methodology	Portfolio Optimization Problem
[1]	Ant Colony Optimization Algorithm & Firefly algorithm (hybrid)	Maximize Sortino ratio with constraint in tracking error volatility
[3]	Evolutionary Algorithm & Quadratic Programming (hybrid)	Minimize tracking error volatility
[4]	- Genetic Algorithms - Evolutionary Algorithms - Memetic Algorithms	Minimize portfolio's risk
[5]	Genetic Algorithm & Levenberg-Marquardt algorithm	Maximize Sortino ratio with constraint in tracking error volatility
[6]	Particle Swarm Optimization	Minimize portfolio's risk Constraint on portfolio's expected return
[7]	Particle Swarm Optimization	Maximize excess return Constraint on tracking error volatility
[8]	Ant Colony Optimization & non linear programming algorithm (hybrid)	Minimize probability of tracking error falling below a threshold

In what follows, interesting points from the literature survey are presented:

- These studies highlight the significance of nature-inspired metaheuristics.
- Another important aspect is the use of combined methodologies (hybrids) in order to deal with the complexities of the financial portfolio management problem.
- In some of these studies, preliminary results regarding the influence of various configuration settings in the performance of hybrid schemes are included.
- To sum up, findings from the literature review highlight the importance of using hybrid NII techniques in order to solve the portfolio optimization problem under the passive and active management framework. Particularly, new, more complex formulations of the problem, offer new challenges to the academia. The combination of unique characteristics from two or even more NII algorithms is encouraged.

3   Methodological Issues

In this section, the implemented hybrid schemes are briefly presented. In this point, it is important to note that the portfolio optimization problem can be divided into two separate optimization tasks. The first task is to find optimal combination of financial assets (stocks) from a specific market (discrete optimization). The second task is to optimally allocate the available capital into the selected assets (continuous optimization). The common characteristic of both hybrid algorithms is that they deal with the optimization problem separately, as described above. The first hybrid method comprises a genetic-based algorithm [9], which deals with the discrete optimization part, and a mathematical optimization technique, namely the Levenberg – Marquardt method[1] [12], which optimally allocates the available capital. The benchmark hybrid scheme applies the same technique in the discrete optimization task, whereas for the continuous optimization a simulated annealing algorithm is implemented [11].

In what follows, pseudocode of both hybrid algorithms is presented.

```
Function Genetic Algorithm - Levenberg_Marquardt
Parameter Initialization
Population Initialization
Calculation of Weights and Fitness Value(Levenberg_Marquardt)
For i=1:generations
   Randomly choose genetic operator
   Apply genetic selection (choose n-best members of population)
   Apply Crossover or Mutation for producing new members
   Calculate weights/evaluate fitness value(Levenberg_Marquardt)
   Adjust population in order to keep best members
End
```

Fig. 1. Hybrid Algorithm 1

---

[1] This is a local search procedure based on a non-linear programming methodology which combines the Gauss – Newton and the steepest descent method.

```
Function Genetic Algorithm - Simulated Annealing
Parameter Initialization
Population Initialization
Calculation of Weights and Fitness Value(Simulated Annealing)
For i=1:generations
   Randomly choose genetic operator
   Apply genetic selection (choose n-best members of population)
   Apply Crossover or Mutation for producing new members
   Calculate weights/evaluate fitness value(Simulated Annealing)
   Adjust population in order to keep best members
End
```

Fig. 2. Hybrid Algorithm 2

4   Application Domain

The portfolio optimization problem deals with finding a combination of assets, as well as the corresponding amount of capital invested in them, with the aim of optimizing a given objective function (investor's goal) under certain constraints. The first person who provided a complete framework for this kind of problem was Harry M. Markowitz, with his seminal paper [10].

In this paper, the objective of the portfolio optimization problem is to maximize a financial ratio, namely the Sortino ratio [5]. Sortino ratio is based on the preliminary work of Sharpe (Sharpe ratio) [5], who developed a reward-to-risk ratio.

The formulation of the financial optimization problem is presented below:

$$Maximize\ Sortino\ Ratio = \frac{E(r_P) - r_f}{\theta_0(r_P)} \tag{1}$$

s.t.

$$\sum_{i=1}^{k} w_i = 1 \tag{2}$$

$$-1 \leq w_i \leq 1 \tag{3}$$

$$k = 10 \tag{4}$$

where,

$E(r_P)$, is the portfolio's expected return, defined as follows: $E(r_P) = \sum_{i=1}^{k} w_i * E(r_i)$

r_f, is the risk-free return, considered as the market's 'safest' asset

$\theta_0(r_P)$, is the volatility of returns which fall below a certain threshold and equals

$$\theta_0(r_P) = \sqrt{\int_{-\infty}^{0} (0 - r_P)^2 * f(r_P) dr_P} \tag{5}$$

w_i, is the percentage of capital invested in the ith asset

k, is the total number of assets contained in a portfolio[2]

r_p, is the daily return of the portfolio, defined as follows: $r_P = \sum_{i=1}^{k} w_i * r_i$

$f(r_P)$, is the probability density function of the portfolio's returns. Assuming that portfolio's returns follow a normal distribution, the probability density function can

be defined as: $f(r_P) = \dfrac{e^{\frac{-(r_P - E(r_P))^2}{2*\sigma^2}}}{\sigma*\sqrt{2*\pi}}$

5   Computational Study

In this section, results regarding the performance of the hybrid algorithms in various configuration settings are presented. The dataset comprised of 93 daily returns, corresponding to the period 04/01/2010 – 28/05/2010, of 49 stocks of the FTSE/ASE40 Index. In this point, it has to be mentioned that all stocks of the Index have been taken into consideration (even those stocks corresponding to firms which have been excluded the Index). The reason for doing this is to eliminate the effect of survivorship bias[3].

In the next table, values for both algorithms' basic parameters are presented.

Table 2. Parameters for hybrid schemes

Parameters for Genetic Algorithm	
Population	100
Generations	20/30/50
Crossover Probability	0,10/0,90
Mutation Probability	0,10/0,90
Percentage of best members for selection (for *n-best* members selection)	10%
Parameters for Simulated Annealing	
Population	100
Generations	100

---

[2] In this study, the number of assets included in the portfolio is 10.

[3] Tendency for failed companies to be excluded from performance indices mainly because they no longer exist. This effect often causes the results of the studies to skew higher because only companies which were successful enough to survive until the end of the time period of the study are included.

These configuration settings represent a range of possible values, which are commonly used in the literature [9]. As far as the experimentation set-up is concerned, due to the stochastic behavior of the nature-inspired intelligent metaheuristics a number of independent simulations (100) were executed for each set of configurations. The aim was to produce a range of solutions in order to draw a distribution of the results. Due to space limitations, a specific statistical measure, namely the quantiles of the distribution, was calculated. As far as the distribution of objective function's values, it is desirable to have two basic properties:

– Fat right tails (large number of quantiles in large confidence levels), which indicate high probability of finding portfolios with large Sortino ratios.
Thin left tails (small number of quantiles in small confidence levels), which indicate low probability of finding portfolios with small Sortino ratios.

Table 3. Statistical results for hybrid schemes (numbers in cells represent Sortino ratios)

	pop=100, crossover probability= 0.90, mutation probability=0.10				
gen=20	**Percentiles of distribution**				
	0.025	*0.25*	*0.50*	*0.75*	*0.975*
GA – LMA	1.9246	2.2555	2.4228	2.5859	2.8664
GA - SA	1.9550	2.4550	2.6890	2.8520	2.9950
gen=50					
	0.025	*0.25*	*0.50*	*0.75*	*0.975*
GA – LMA	2.2492	2.5246	2.6533	2.8228	3.1622
GA - SA	2.4890	2.8880	3.0500	3.1573	3.4597
	pop=100, crossover probability= 0.10, mutation probability=0.90				
gen=20	**Percentiles of distribution**				
	0.025	*0.25*	*0.50*	*0.75*	*0.975*
GA – LMA	1.9856	2.3698	2.4558	2.7589	2.9010
GA - SA	2.1580	2.3607	2.5897	2.9897	3.2540
gen=50					
	0.025	*0.25*	*0.50*	*0.75*	*0.975*
GA – LMA	2.2005	2.3969	2.7859	2.9569	3.0056
GA - SA	2.5860	2.7580	2.9950	3.2530	3.5550
	pop=100, crossover probability= 0.10, mutation probability=0.10				
gen=20	**Percentiles of distribution**				
	0.025	*0.25*	*0.50*	*0.75*	*0.975*
GA – LMA	1.7580	1.8560	1.9580	2.0050	2.1250
GA - SA	1.8050	1.9560	1.9990	2.0150	2.1450
gen=50					
	0.025	*0.25*	*0.50*	*0.75*	*0.975*
GA – LMA	1.9057	1.9840	2.0146	2.1980	2.3057
GA - SA	1.9730	1.9960	2.1897	2.3580	2.4760
	pop=100, crossover probability= 0.90, mutation probability=0.90				
gen=20	**Percentiles of distribution**				
	0.025	*0.25*	*0.50*	*0.75*	*0.975*
GA – LMA	2.1050	2.2480	2.3183	2.4097	2.6897
GA - SA	2.2057	2.3840	2.4747	2.8894	3.0013
gen=50					
	0.025	*0.25*	*0.50*	*0.75*	*0.975*
GA – LMA	2.3546	2.5489	2.6563	2.8597	3.0001
GA - SA	2.4982	2.6290	2.8570	3.0052	3.1551

Regarding the results presented in Table 3, above, the following important remarks can be stated. First of all, for each set of configurations, as the number of generations increases, the distribution of results improves. This is quite sensible, due to the fact that for more generations, the algorithm explores the solution space in a great extend. Another, more important finding, is that the hybrid scheme consisting of the genetic algorithm and the simulated annealing process, yields better distributions of results. This may be attributed to the fact that both the GA and SA components have stochastic, and not deterministic, elements which provide them, in a way, better exploration ability. It seems that the incorporation of an intelligent metaheuristic, such as the SA algorithm, provides a better searching strategy of the weight optimization domain (continuous solution space), thus guiding the GA component towards better solutions in the discrete space. Finally, another interesting conclusion concerns the hybrid schemes' behavior for various values of the crossover and mutation probability. These genetic operators play a vital role in the exploration and exploitation of the solution space. Based on the table's results, the best results are obtained in the case where the crossover probability is set to 0.10, whereas the mutation probability is set to 0.90 (this means that the randomness of the GA component rises). This contrasts to many studies, where the mutation probability is set to low values.

6   Conclusion and Future Research

In this study a hybrid NII scheme, which combined a genetic algorithm and the Levenberg-Marquardt algorithm, was proposed for solving a certain formulation of the constrained portfolio optimization problem. More specifically, the objective was to maximize a financial ratio, namely the Sortino ratio. What is more, for benchmarking reasons, a hybrid scheme consisting of a genetic algorithm and a simulated annealing technique, was applied. The main difference between these two schemes is the component that optimizes the amount of capital invested in each asset of the selected portfolio. Mainly, the first technique is based on a deterministic procedure, whereas the second is a stochastic metaheuristic. The focus of this work was twofold. Firstly, our goal was to provide evidence regarding the performance of the hybrid nature-inspired algorithm for various configuration settings. An important task for the decision-maker is to identify 'good' values for the configuration parameters, in a way that high-quality solution spaces are reached. Secondly, our aim was to compare a deterministic with a stochastic component for this kind of problems. It was our firm belief that the intelligent metaheuristic was going to achieve better results.

Results from this study are not directly comparable to other studies from the literature, due to the fact that the formulation of the optimization problem differs. However, based on our findings, it seems that there is a controversial result: in most studies the mutation probability is set to low values, in order to avoid including more randomness in the algorithm. In our case, setting this probability in large values, provides better results. This may indicate that our algorithm approximates a random search procedure. However, in order to draw safer conclusions more sets of simulations have to be executed. Also, the nature of the solution space itself may provide an explanation to this issue. In this point it has to be mentioned that the simulation results are both preliminary and limited. More simulations have been scheduled, as future research.

Finally, some future research directions might be the following: firstly, other, hybrid or not, NII algorithms should be applied. What is more, further simulations are required in order to come up with safer conclusions about the functionality of the proposed alternative mechanisms in this study. As far as the application domain is concerned, other formulations of the portfolio optimization problem should be investigated, specifically these which reflect up-to-date objectives.

References

1. Giannakouris, G., Vassiliadis, V., Dounias, G.: Experimental Study on a Hybrid Nature-Inspired Algorithm for Financial Portfolio Optimization. In: Konstantopoulos, S., Perantonis, S., Karkaletsis, V., Spyropoulos, C.D., Vouros, G. (eds.) SETN 2010. LNCS, vol. 6040, pp. 101–111. Springer, Heidelberg (2010)
2. Brabazon, A., O'Neill, M.: Bilogically Inspired Algorithms for Financial Modeling. Springer, Heidelberg (2006)
3. Shapcott, J.: Index Tracking: Genetic Algorithms for Investment Portfolio Selection. EPCC-SS92-24, pp. 1–24 (1992)
4. Streichert, F., Ulmer, H., Zell, A.: Evolutionary algorithms and the cardinality constrained portfolio optimization problem. Selected Papers of the International Conference on Operations Research (OR 2003), pp. 253–260 (2003)
5. Vassiliadis, V., Bafa, V., Dounias, G.: On the performance of a hybrid genetic algorithm: application on the portfolio management problem. In: Proceedings of the 8th International Conference on Advances in Applied Financial Economics (AFE 2011), pp. 70–78 (2011)
6. Chen, W., Zhang, R.T., Cai, Y.M., Xu, F.S.: Particle swarm optimization for constrained portfolio selection problems. In: 5th International Conference on Machine Learning and Cybernetics, pp. 2425–2429 (2006)
7. Thomaidis, N.S., Angelidis, T., Vassiliadis, V., Dounias, G.: Active portfolio management with cardinality constraints: an application of particle swarm optimization. New Mathematics and Natural Computation, working paper (2007)
8. Vassiliadis, V., Thomaidis, N., Dounias, G.: Active Portfolio Management under a Downside Risk Framework: Comparison of a Hybrid Nature – Inspired Scheme. In: Corchado, E., Wu, X., Oja, E., Herrero, Á., Baruque, B. (eds.) HAIS 2009. LNCS, vol. 5572, pp. 702–712. Springer, Heidelberg (2009)
9. Miller, B.L., Goldberg, D.E.: Genetic algorithms, tournament selection, and the effects of noise. Complex Systems 9(3), 193–212 (1995)
10. Markowitz, H.: Portfolio Selection. The Journal of Finance 7(1), 77–91 (1952)
11. Corana, A., Marchesi, M., Martini, C., Ridella, S.: Minimizing Multimodal Functions of Continuous Variables with the "Simulated Annealing" Algorithm. ACM Transactions on Mathematical Software 13(3), 262–280 (1987)
12. More, J.J.: The Levenberg-Marquardt algorithm: Implementation and Theory. Lecture Notes in Mathematics, vol. 630, pp. 104–116 (1978)

An Intelligent Tool for Anatomical Object Segmentation Using Deformable Surfaces

Konstantinos K. Delibasis, Argiris Christodoulidis, and Ilias Maglogiannis

Dept. of Computer Science & Biomedical Informatics, University of Central Greece,
Lamia, Greece, Lamia
kdelibasis@yahoo.com,
{axristodoulidhs,imaglo}@ucg.gr

Abstract. Image segmentation is a very active area of research in machine vision. In this work, an innovative methodology is presented that allows the segmentation of objects in three-dimensional images with initial user intervention. The paper describes the adopted approach for implementing the algorithm of deformable / active surfaces (AS), using the explicit scheme for numerical evaluation of the partial derivative equation of the AS evolution. Both the Vector Field Convolution (VFC) and the Gradient Vector Flow (GVF) image dynamic field are investigated for 3D segmentation using the AS. The proposed methodology is implemented as software tool, which allows the initialization of AS using cylinder-like surfaces with user intervention. Initial results are provided for the case of three-dimensional synthetic data and clinical Computed Tomography (CT) images, in terms of segmentation accuracy and speed of convergence.

Keywords: Computer Vision, Deformable surface, Active surfaces, Object segmentation.

1 Introduction

Image segmentation is a central problem in computer vision. Object segmentation from three-dimensional images is a special, more demanding case of this task, which finds numerous applications in automated diagnosis, medical decision support systems and medical treatment planning and assessment. The concept of active contours for image segmentation was first reported for segmenting objects of interest in [1]. Since then, the methodology of active contours and active surfaces has been widely reported in literature [2]. A number of variants have been applied, using several image-based definitions of the external force field. In [3] an internal force component parallel to the contour outward normal vector was introduced to simulate the inflating balloon effect. The image edge strength is utilized in [1], the Gradient Vector flow (GVF) [4], [5] and the Vector Field Convolution (VFC) [6] are more recent advances. Almost all active surface approaches require proper initialization when applied to images with multiple objects. In this work, we propose an explicit scheme for the evolution equation of an Active Surface (AS) model. The AS model is constructed on

I. Maglogiannis, V. Plagianakos, and I. Vlahavas (Eds.): SETN 2012, LNAI 7297, pp. 206–213, 2012.

a rectangular grid rather on a Delaunay triangular mesh, allowing simpler arithmetic operations for calculating partial derivatives. A software tool is developed for providing the AS model with user-based initialization using simple cylinder-like surfaces. The rest of the paper is structured as follows: Section 2 presents the proposed methodology for AS evolution, while Section 3 reports the results obtained by the evaluation of the method. Finally, Section 4 concludes the paper.

2   Methodology

2.1   Active Surface (AS) Explicit Evolution

In this section we present the adopted mathematical modelling approach for the AS evolution. Let us define the deformable contour (snake) consisting of N_p points at time t, as $\mathbf{v}(s,t) = \mathbf{v}_t(s) = \left(x_t(s), y_t(s), z_t(s) \right)^T$, with $s \in \left[1, N_p \right]$. According to [8] the evolution of an active contour $\mathbf{v}(s,t)$, under the influence of external force field $\mathbf{f}_{ext}\left(\mathbf{v}(s,t) \right)$ is given by

$$\frac{\partial \mathbf{v}(s,t)}{\partial t} = a\mathbf{v}''(s,t) - \beta\mathbf{v}'''(s,t) + \mathbf{f}_{ext}\left(\mathbf{v}(s,t) \right) \tag{1}$$

where the $\mathbf{v}''(s,t), \mathbf{v}'''(s,t)$ are the 2nd and 4th derivative order with respect to parameter contour parameter s and a, β are parameters controlling the shape of the snake.

In the case of the active (or deformable) surface $\mathbf{v}(s,u,t)$ at time t, consisting of N_c contours with N_p points each, as $\mathbf{v}(s,u,t) = \left(x_t(s,u), y_t(s,u), z_t(s,u) \right)^T$, with $(s,u) \in \left[1, N_c \right] \times \left[1, N_p \right]$ the AS evolution equation is similar to (1):

$$\frac{\partial \mathbf{v}(s,u,t)}{\partial t} = a\mathbf{v}''(s,u,t) - \beta\mathbf{v}'''(s,u,t) + \mathbf{f}_{ext}\left(\mathbf{v}(s,u,t) \right) \tag{2}$$

Eq. (2) can generate 3 partial differential equations (PDE), one for each Cartesian coordinates of the AS points. The 2nd and forth order derivative in (2) are calculated as following:

$$\mathbf{v}'' = \frac{\partial^2 \mathbf{v}}{\partial s^2} + \frac{\partial^2 \mathbf{v}}{\partial u^2} = \mathbf{v}_{ss} + \mathbf{v}_{uu},$$
$$\mathbf{v}''' = \frac{\partial^4 \mathbf{v}}{\partial s^4} + \frac{\partial^4 \mathbf{v}}{\partial u^4} = \mathbf{v}_{ssss} + \mathbf{v}_{uuuu} \tag{3}$$

The above partial derivatives can be arithmetically approximated using central differences, independently along the s (contours) and u parameters. If we temporarily drop the time parameter symbol t, the partial derivatives of the active surface along the s parameter are approximated as following:

$$
\begin{aligned}
\mathbf{v}_{ss}(s,u) &= [1,-2,1] * \mathbf{v}(s,u) = \mathbf{v}(s+1,u) - 2\mathbf{v}(s,u) + \mathbf{v}(s-1,u) \\
\mathbf{v}_{ssss}(s,u) &= [1,-4,6,-4,1] * \mathbf{v}(s,u) \\
&= \mathbf{v}(s+2,u) - 4\mathbf{v}(s+1,u) + 6\mathbf{v}(s,u) - 4\mathbf{v}(s-1,u) + \mathbf{v}(s-2,u)
\end{aligned}
\tag{4}
$$

where the * stands for the linear convolution operator. We can enforce closed contours along the s or u parameter by using modulo operations for the point parameters [7, p.9] i.e. $\mathbf{v}_{ss}(1,u) = [1,-2,1] * \mathbf{v}(s,u) = \mathbf{v}(s+1,u) - 2\mathbf{v}(s,u) + \mathbf{v}(N_p,u)$.

By discretising the time derivative in (2), we obtain the discrete AS evolution equation, in a manner similar to [5, (A10)]:

$$
\begin{aligned}
\frac{\mathbf{v}^{t+\Delta t}(s,u) - \mathbf{v}^t(s,u)}{\Delta t} &= a\mathbf{v}_{ss}^t + a\mathbf{v}_{uu}^t - \beta\mathbf{v}_{ssss}^t - \beta\mathbf{v}_{uuuu}^t + \mathbf{f}_{ext}\left(\mathbf{v}^t(s,u)\right) \\
\mathbf{v}^{t+\Delta t}(s,u) &= \mathbf{v}^t(s,u) + \Delta t\left(a\mathbf{v}_{ss}^t + a\mathbf{v}_{uu}^t - \beta\mathbf{v}_{ssss}^t - \beta\mathbf{v}_{uuuu}^t + \mathbf{f}_{ext}\left(\mathbf{v}^t(s,u)\right)\right)
\end{aligned}
\tag{5}
$$

The above equation is the forward Euler arithmetic approximation of the active surface PDE, often called explicit PDE scheme [11]. We utilized this approach, since the implicit PDE approximation, as described in [6, Eq.(9)], [7] would require the inversion of an $N \times N$ pentadiagonal matrix, with $N = N_c \times N_p$, for each time iteration. Despite the fact that efficient techniques exist for inverting such tables [9], [10], the size of the matrix imposes prohibitive memory requirements (N may easily be of the order of 10^4 – see Table 1). Eq. (5) converges without numerical instability for $\Delta t < 0.25$ [8]. The parameters a in (2), (5) was set to 0.2 for anatomical objects and 0.25 for synthetic data, whereas and the parameter β was set to 0.1 for anatomical objects and 0.2 for synthetic data, as determined experimentally.

The AS is allowed to iterate until the average positional difference between two consecutive iterations falls below the threshold of 0.1 pixels.

2.2   Definition of External Force Field

In order to calculate the corresponding AS model external forces, we utilize the Vector Field Convolution (VFC) [6], which was reported to be superior to the Gradient Vector Flow image dynamic field, described in [4]. VFC is generated using a kernel **K** containing vectors that point towards the origin of K. The magnitude of the vectors is calculated using [6 (15)] setting the γ parameter to 2.2. The size of the kernel **K** was set to 32 pixels for both trachea/synthetic data in [6 (17)]). The GVF force field is generated using a homogeneous diffusion of the original image gradient vector. Each iteration of the diffusion operation is performed using 2D convolution with the following matrix $\begin{bmatrix} 0 & \mu & 0 \\ \mu & 1-4\mu & \mu \\ 0 & \mu & 0 \end{bmatrix}$ as described in [7, Eq.(26)], with μ=0.2. The number of iterations for implementing the diffusion of the image gradient was set to 100. For the implementation of the VFC and GVF, the Matlab source code, which is available in [6] was used.

2.3   User Intervention

The user may intervene in a number of ways in order to optimise the segmentation results. The most important intervention is the initialization of the Active Surface, since it directly affects the correct convergence and the segmentation accuracy of the AS model. The main objective is the use of simple initializing shapes, easy to be defined by the used, whereas achieving sufficient proximity to the required object. In this work we utilize two kinds of cylinder-like initializing surfaces: a) a homogenous cylinder with a straight vertical axis and b) a non-homogeneous cylinder (variable radius) with C^0 continuous axis. We choose this type of initialization because of its simplicity and ease of user-based input.

3   Results

Results are presented using both 3D synthetic data and anatomical objects from CT images. We used the two-dimensional (2D) synthetic data of [4], [6] to create a 64x64x64 raw volume as shown in Fig.1. This shape has been used extensively for Active Contour / AS testing, since it is characterized by a deep and narrow cut that cannot easily be discovered by the AC/AS methods.

The AS is initialized using variable radius straight axis cylinder (Fig. 1b), consisting of 64 contours with 320 points each. The final AS using the VFC external force field is shown in Fig. 1c, after 260 iterations, with execution time equal to 99 sec using Matlab 7.9.0, running on a laptop with i5 at 2.40 GHz CPU and 4GB of RAM. It is evident that the AS has converged to the correct shape, despite the difficulty presented by the required shape. The intersection of the converged AS with the mid-slice of the synthetic volume data (Fig. d) confirms visually the accuracy of the segmentation. The average distance of the AS points from the shape edge voxels was 0.195 voxels.

In Fig.2 a comparison of the total positional error (in voxels) of the converged AS under the GVF and the VFC external force field is shown for the synthetic volume data. It can be observed that the VFC converges faster and more accurately than the GVF. The intersection of the AS with slice 32 is given for selected iterations (the last iteration for both cases is included).

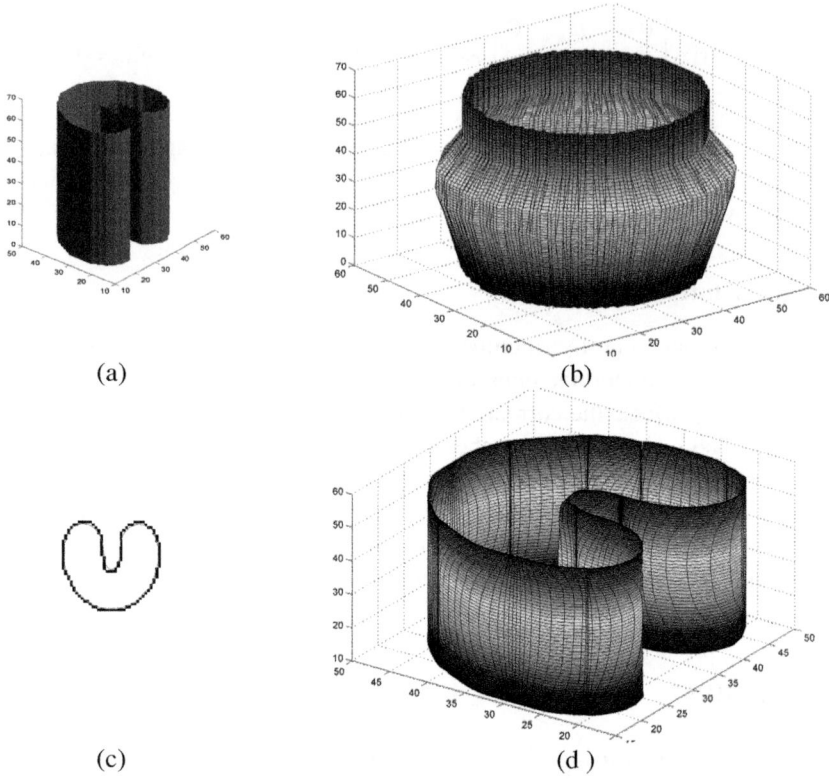

(a)   (b)

(c)   (d)

Fig. 1. Segmentation of 3D synthetic data (a) using AS initialized as a cylinder-like surface (b). The converged AS and its intersection with the mid-slice of the 3D data is shown in (d) and (c).

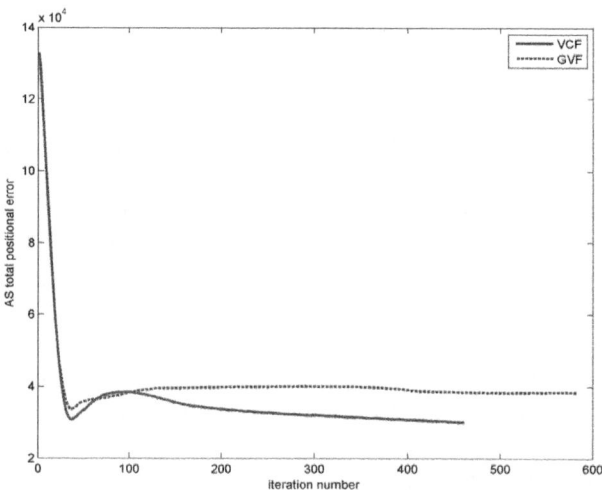

Fig. 2. The evolution of the AS positional error in the case of 3D synthetic data, using VFC and GVF external force field

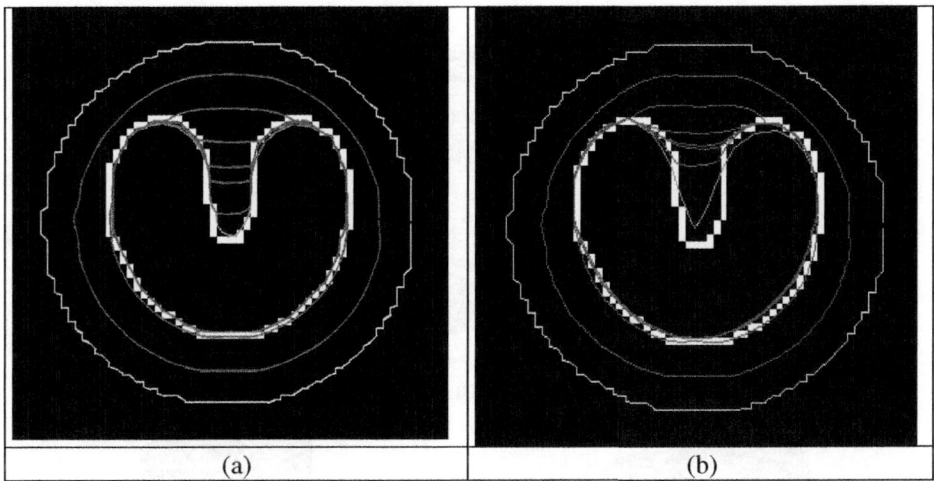

Fig. 3. (a) The evolution of AS under VFC (iterations 1,20,40,60,80,100,200,460) and (b) GVF (iterations 1,20,40,60,80,100,200,581)

In Fig.4 the results of segmenting a part of the trachea are presented using AS with GVF and VFC. The AS is initialized by the used as the cylinder in Fig.3a. User initialization was performed in 5 out of the 40 processed transverse slices, inside the required object. The converged AS using GVF and VFC is shown in (b) and (c) respectively). The intersection of the initial AS model, the AS at the 10th iteration and the converged AS is also given for VFC and GVF in (d) and (e) respectively. It can be observed that the segmentation performed by the VFC appears more accurate than the AS under the GVF external forces.

The numerical results from the performed experiments are presented in Table 1. The average positional error in the case of the anatomical objects was calculated based on object delineation by expert user. It becomes obvious that the proposed tool can find practical use in a research and even in a clinical environment, since it allows object segmentation from 3D data with low degree of user intervention. The VFC appears to converge slightly faster and more accurately both in synthetic data and clinical volumes.

Table 1. Numeric results form the AS-based object segmentation

Object	Method	N_cxN_p	Num. of iterations	Average positional error (voxels)
Synthetic	GVF	64x320	581	0.149
	VFC	64x320	460	0.097
Trachea I	GFV	42x70	155	0.81
	VFC	42x70	148	0.72
Trachea II	GVF	40x80	112	1.02
	VFC	40x80	91	1.12

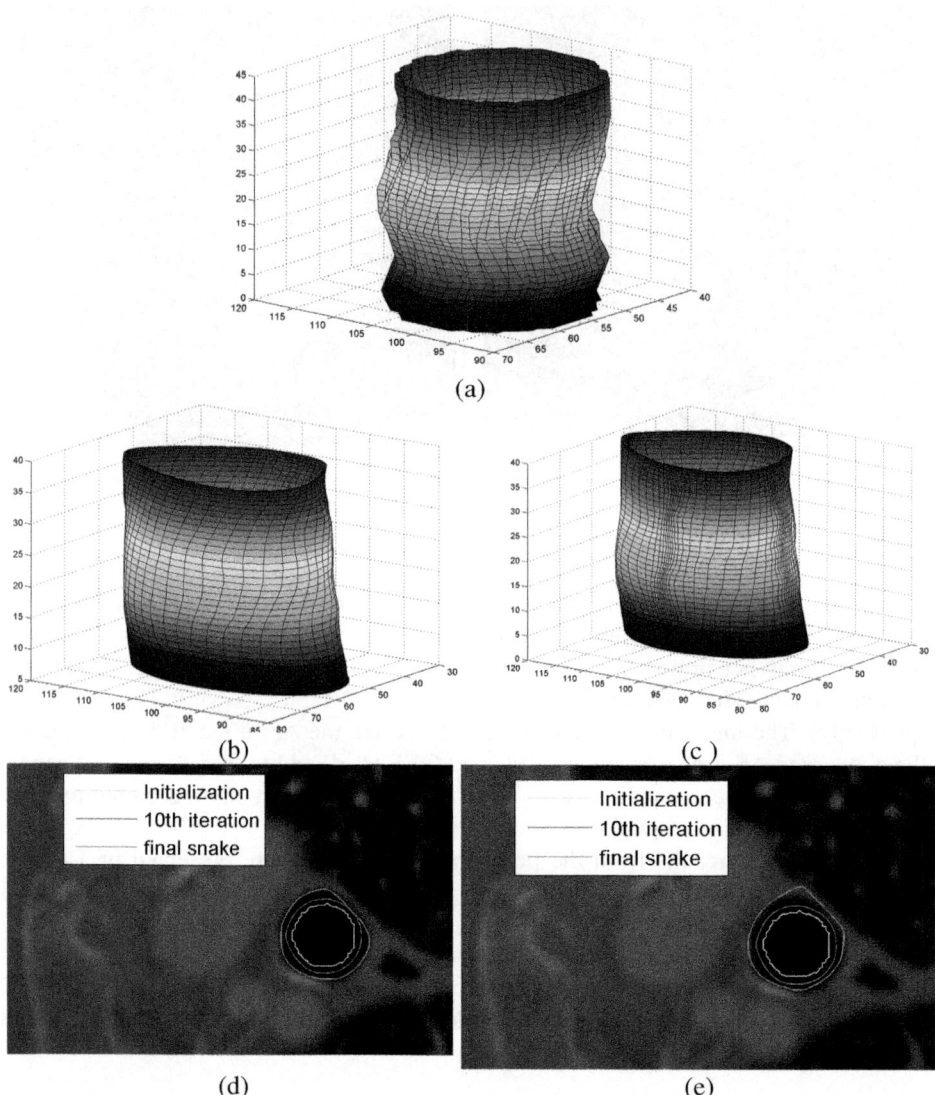

Fig. 4. Segmentation of the trachea with AS initialized in (a), using VFC (b) and GVF (c). The intersection of the initial AS, the AS at the 10th iteration and the converged AS is also given for VFC and GVF in (d) and (e) respectively.

4   Conclusions

In this paper we presented a novel 3D segmentation methodology based on AS modelling, which has been implemented as an intelligent software tool. The developed tool has been tested in both synthetic and clinical data. In both cases the accuracy of the evolved model is quite satisfactory. The corresponding quantitative and qualitative results from the visual assessment show that the proposed method is capable of accurately modeling anatomical structures, requiring only limited user intervention.

References

1. Kass, M., Witkin, A., Terzopoulos, D.: Snakes: Active contour models. International Journal of Computer Vision 1(4), 321–331 (1988)
2. He, L., Peng, Z., Everding, B., Wang, X., Han, C.Y., Weiss, K.L., Wee, W.G.: A comparative study of deformable contour methods, on medical image segmentation. Image and Vision Computing 26, 141–163 (2008)
3. Cohen, L.D.: On active contour models and balloons. Computer Vision, Graphics, and Image Processing. Image Understanding 53(2), 211–218 (1991)
4. Xu, C., Prince, J.L.: Snakes, shapes, and gradient vector. IEEE Transactions on Image Processing 7(3), 359–369 (1998)
5. Xu, C.: Deformable Models with application to human cerebral cortex reconstruction from Magnetic Resonance images, PhD dissertation Johns Hopkins University (1999)
6. Li, B., Acton, S.T.: Active contour external force using vector field convolution for image segmentation. IEEE Transactions on Image Processing 16, 2096–2106 (2007)
7. Acton, S., Ray, N.: Biomedical Image Analysis: Segmentation. Morgan and Claypool Publishers (2009) ISBN: 9781598290219
8. Heat, M.T.: Scientific Computing, An Introductory Survey, 2nd edn. McGraw-Hill (2002) ISBN 007112229X
9. Press, W., Teukolsky, S., Vetterling, W., Flannery, B.: Numerical Recipes in C, 2nd edn. Cambridge Univ. Press, Cambridge (1992)
10. Benson, A., Evans, D.J.: A normalized algorithm for solution of positive definite symmetric quindiagonal systems of linear equations. ACM Trans. Math. Softw. 3, 96–103 (1977)
11. Hall, C.A., Porsching, T.A.: Numerical analysis of partial differential equations. Englewood Cliffs, Prentice Hall (1990)

Tracking Differential Evolution Algorithms: An Adaptive Approach through Multinomial Distribution Tracking with Exponential Forgetting

Michael G. Epitropakis[1,*], Dimirtis K. Tasoulis[2], Nicos G. Pavlidis[3], Vassilis P. Plagianakos[4], and Michael N. Vrahatis[1]

[1] Computational Intelligence Laboratory, Department of Mathematics, University of Patras, GR-26110 Patras, Greece
[2] Winton Capital Management, 1–5 St Mary Abbots Place, London SW8 6LS, U.K.
[3] Department of Management Science, Lancaster University, LA1 4YX, U.K.
[4] Department of Computer Science and Biomedical Informatics, University of Central Greece, GR-35100 Lamia, Greece
{mikeagn,vrahatis}@math.upatras.gr,
d.tasoulis@wintoncapital.com, n.pavlidis@lancaster.ac.uk, vpp@ucg.gr

Abstract. Several Differential Evolution variants with modified search dynamics have been recently proposed, to improve the performance of the method. This work borrows ideas from adaptive filter theory to develop an "online" algorithmic adaptation framework. The proposed framework is based on tracking the parameters of a multinomial distribution to reflect changes in the evolutionary process. As such, we design a multinomial distribution tracker to capture the successful evolution movements of three Differential Evolution algorithms, in an attempt to aggregate their characteristics and their search dynamics. Experimental results on ten benchmark functions and comparisons with five state-of-the-art algorithms indicate that the proposed framework is competitive and very promising.

Keywords: Differential Evolution, Adaptation, Multinomial Distribution, Exponential forgetting.

1 Introduction

The Differential Evolution (DE) algorithm is a population–based stochastic direct search method that utilizes concepts borrowed from the broad class of Evolutionary Algorithms. Several variants of the original DE algorithm have been recently proposed [1,2,3,4,9,10,11,12,14]. Nevertheless, a relatively small number of DE variants have exhibited substantial performance gains in a large number of real-world applications, and hence few variants have attracted the attention of the Evolutionary Computing research community. These variants successfully

---

* Corresponding author.

I. Maglogiannis, V. Plagianakos, and I. Vlahavas (Eds.): SETN 2012, LNAI 7297, pp. 214–222, 2012.
© Springer-Verlag Berlin Heidelberg 2012

exploit different aspects of the DE algorithm, either by utilizing novel mutation strategies that exploit DE's exploratory/exploitative search power, or by incorporating adaptive schemes to capture the structure of the benchmark function at hand. Representative examples of the former type include specialized mutation strategies [9], index neighborhood-based mutations [2], or proximity mutations [4]. Variants of the latter type include schemes such as parameter and strategy adaptation schemes [1,5,10,14].

In this study, we borrow ideas from adaptive filter theory to develop an "online" algorithm adaptation technique and incorporate it in the Differential Evolution algorithm. The proposed framework uses three DE variants, namely JADE [14], jDE [1], and DEGL [2] algorithms. It allows each individual to randomly select amongst them to evolve at each time step. The probability of selecting each variant depends on its history of improving the population at each time step and thus guiding it to promising search regions. Extensive experimental results on 10 benchmark functions demonstrate that the proposed framework is very promising.

The rest of the paper is organized as follows: Section 2 briefly describes the multinomial distribution tracker along with its main characteristics. Its incorporation into the DE algorithm as a new algorithm adaptation framework is briefly described in Section 3. The paper ends with an experimental analysis of the proposed framework, a discussion and some pointers for future work.

2 Multinomial Distribution Tracking through Exponential Forgetting

This section briefly presents the multinomial distribution and its extension to include exponential forgetting. In the multinomial distribution each trial results in one out of a fixed and finite number K of possible outcomes, with probabilities $\theta_1, \theta_2, \ldots, \theta_K$ and N independent trials. The number of times outcome i was observed over the N trials, is represented by a random variable X_i. Thereby, the vector $X = (X_1, X_2, \ldots, X_K)$ follows a multinomial distribution with parameters N, θ, where $\theta = (\theta_1, \theta_2, \ldots, \theta_K)$ and probabilities: $P(X_1 = x_1, \ldots, X_K = x_K | \theta, N) = (N!)/(\prod_{i=1}^{K} x_i!) \prod_{i=1}^{K} \theta_i^{x_i}$. Based on a data sample D we can estimate the parameter $\widehat{\theta} = \theta(D)$ of a multinomial distribution through the Maximum Likelihood Estimation (MLE) procedure. Given a data sample D, the likelihood function can be defined as: $L(\theta; D) = p(D | \theta) = p(x_1, x_2, \ldots, x_K | \theta)$. The MLE estimator of the θ parameter can be easily calculated by applying Lagrange multipliers in the log-likelihood function. Therefore the MLE of the multinomial distribution can be obtained by the following form: $\widehat{\theta}_i^{\mathrm{ML}} = m_k/N$, where $m_k = \sum_{i=1}^{K} x_i$.

We make the assumption that the impact of each observation should be related to the time of observation. This is reasonable since the optimization procedure frequently changes phases through evolution. More recent information about the evolution phase is expected to be more relevant to the optimization procedure while earlier information should be gradually disregarded. In the current study, we develop a tracking framework that is based on the Recursive Least Squares (RLS) adaptive filter [7,8]. To this end, we incorporate weights to the likelihood function and adopt the framework proposed in [8]. Given that a data sample appears as a signal or a data stream in time, $D = \{D_1, D_2, \ldots, D_t, \ldots\}$, where t denotes the current time step. We incorporate an exponential weighting factor in the log-likelihood function and produce a new likelihood which incorporates time, $L^\lambda(\theta|D_1, D_2, \ldots, D_t)$. As in the RLS filter, the new likelihood can be defined as: $L^\lambda(\theta|D_1, D_2, \ldots, D_t) = \sum_{j=1}^{t} \lambda^{t-j} L(\theta|D_1, \ldots, D_j) = L(\theta|D_t) + \lambda L(\theta|D_1, \ldots, D_{t-1})$, where $\lambda \in [0, 1]$ is a weighting factor which is also called the *forgetting factor*. The forgetting factor decreases the impact of past observations on the log-likelihood and thus the estimated parameters are able to adapt to changes. All data examples are assigned equal weights as λ increases to unity, while as λ decreases more recent data samples become more important.

Through the application of Lagrange multipliers we can obtain the MLE $\widehat{\theta}_i^{\mathrm{ML}_\lambda}$ according to the following equation:

$$\widehat{\theta}_i^{\mathrm{ML}_\lambda}(t) = \frac{n_i(t)}{\sum_{k=1}^{K} n_k(t)}. \tag{1}$$

where $n_i(t)$ represents the effective window width which can be recursively calculated through the following equation:

$$n_i(t) = \lambda n_i(t-1) + D_t^i, \tag{2}$$

for $t = 1, 2, \ldots$ and $n_i(0) = 0$, where D_t^i denotes the number of successes of outcome i at time t. If $\lambda = 1$ the aforementioned framework corresponds to the simple case of the $\widehat{\theta}_i^{\mathrm{ML}}$ MLE. Through this framework we can track the parameters of a multinomial distribution with the potential of forgetting the history of past observations in an exponential manner.

3   The Multinomial Distribution-Based Differential Evolution Framework

In this section, we discuss the main concepts behind the proposed framework, namely the Multinomial distribution-based Differential Evolution (MultiDE). The proposed framework is based on the Differential Evolution algorithm (DE) [12]. DE is a population–based stochastic optimization method, which utilizes concepts borrowed from the broad class of Evolutionary Algorithms. For an optimization problem at hand defined in the real D–dimensional space $\mathbb{R}^D$, DE starts by initializing randomly a population of *NP*, potential solutions (*individuals*) in the optimization domain following a uniform probability distribution. The population is subsequently updated at each iteration, called *generation*, by means of three main evolutionary search operations, namely the *mutation*, *recombination*, and *selection* operators. The search operators efficiently shuffle information among the individuals, enabling the search for an optimum to focus on the most promising regions of the solution space. A thorough description of the DE algorithm can be found in [3,4,9,12].

Algorithm 1. The MultiDE algorithmic scheme

1: Initialize individuals of the population
2: Initialize the multinomial distribution tracker, for each algorithm $i : n_i(t_0) = 0$, $\widehat{\theta}_i^{\mathrm{ML}\lambda}(t_0) = \frac{1}{K}$.

3: **for** each time step t **do**
4:     **for** each individual j in the population **do**
5:         **Sample** k_{str} **from the multinomial distribution with parameters** $\widehat{\theta}_i^{\mathrm{ML}\lambda}(t)$.
6:         **Apply the** *mutation* **operator** using algorithm k_{str}, $k_{str} \in \{1)$ JADE, 2) jDE, 3) DEGL$\}$.
7:         **Apply the** *binomial crossover* **operator**
8:         **Apply the** *selection* **operator**
9:     **end for**
10:     **Update the score of the** k_{str} **strategy through Eq. (3)**
11:     **Update the multinomial distribution tracker through Eqs. (1)–(2)**
12: **end for**

The proposed framework introduces two main concepts different from the standard DE. Initially, it probabilistically assigns to each individual one DE variant, chosen from a pool of K candidate algorithms. Subsequently, based on the individuals' movements, it adapts this probability over the evolutionary stages through the aforementioned multinomial distribution tracker. The remaining steps of the DE algorithm remain the same. In the current study we utilize a pool of $K = 3$ state-of-the-art DE variants that have efficiently tackled several real or artificial problem landscapes, namely the JADE [14], the jDE [1], and the DEGL [2] algorithms. Obviously any DE variant could be incorporated into the pool to enhance the exploratory and exploitative power of the proposed framework. Subsequently, one of the available algorithms is assigned to each individual based on a probability. This probability is adapted at each generation through the multinomial distribution tracker, based on the relative fitness improvement of each algorithm [5].

Specifically, let us assume that the ith algorithm $i \in \{1, 2, \ldots, K\}$, will evolve NP_i individuals, with $\sum_{i=1}^{K} NP_i = NP$. For each individual $j, j \in \{1, 2, \ldots, NP_i\}$ we assign a score based on its relative fitness improvement during the last generation according to $w_j = f_{best}|f_{parent}^i - f_{offspring}^i|/f_{offspring}^i$, where f_{best} is the fitness of the best individual, f_{parent}^i is the fitness of the ith individual before the evolution phase, while $f_{offspring}^i$ is its fitness after the evolution phase [5]. The final score, Score(i), of each algorithm can be calculated according to the following formula:

$$\text{Score}(i) = \text{round}\left(100K \frac{\mathrm{W}(i)}{\sum_{i=1}^{K} \mathrm{W}(i)}\right), \tag{3}$$

where $\mathrm{W}(i) = w_{\min} + \sum_{j=1}^{NP_i} w_j$, $w_{\min} = 0.01$ is a small constant that prevents the extinction of an algorithm, in the case where the ith algorithm has not been selected in the previous generation. The rounding procedure as well as the multiplication by $100K$ will fix the score to the required integer value, by the multinomial distribution. The final score assists the algorithm which produces the higher relative fitness improvement in the last generation. Thereby, the multinomial distribution tracker learns from the current evolution stage and promotes the algorithm that is more likely to efficiently evolve the population to promising search regions. Having calculated the final scores, we estimate the probabilities of each algorithm by calculating the aforementioned maximum likelihood estimator $\widehat{\theta}_i^{\mathrm{ML}_\lambda}$, given by Eqs. (1) and (2). The main algorithmic scheme of the proposed framework is briefly demonstrated in Algorithm 1.

4   Experimental Results

In this section we perform an experimental evaluation of the proposed approach. We employ ten high dimensional and scalable benchmark functions with different characteristics. The first six functions have been acquired from the recently CEC'2008 Special Session on Large Scale Global Optimization [13]. The remaining four test functions are hybrid composition functions, proposed recently in [6], and correspond to the $f_{16} - f_{19}$ functions of the suite. A detailed description of the benchmark functions can be found in [6,13]. To demonstrate the efficiency of the proposed framework, we compare it with five state-of-the-art DE variants, namely the DEGL [2], the JADE [14], the jDE [1], the ODE [11], and the SADE [10] variant.

Throughout the experimental results section, all methods have been implemented with the default parameters settings as have been proposed in the literature. The population size has been kept fixed to $NP = 100$ individuals and for each simulation, a budget of max$NFEs = 5000 \cdot D$ function evaluations has been employed [13]. Here we utilize the 50–dimensional versions of the aforementioned function set. To evaluate the performance of the considered algorithms we will use the *solution error measure*, or simply *error* [4]. Each algorithm was executed independently 50 times to obtain an estimation of the median (*Median*), the mean solution error (*Mean*), and its standard deviation (*St.D.*). Moreover to evaluate the statistical significance of the observed performance differences, we apply two-sided Wilcoxon rank sum tests between the proposed DE variants and the other DE variants. Here we have implemented three different forgetting factor values, $\lambda \in \{0.91, 0.99, 1\}$. The first two values force to forget the history of the strategy probabilities with either a fast or a slow rate, respectively, i.e. a sliding window size of $w \approx 11.1$, or $w \approx 100$ generations respectively. The sliding window can be approximated using the λ parameter, through: $w \approx 1/(1 - \lambda)$ [7].

Tables 1 and 2 report the experimental results on the 50–dimensional versions of the considered benchmark set. It can be clearly observed that the synergy of DE variants through the multinomial distribution tracker may result to an enhanced DE scheme, with a lot of potential. In general, for the majority of the considered functions, MultiDE exhibits either a significant performance enhancement, or an equally good performance in comparison to the other five DE variants. Only in three functions the proposed framework exhibits inferior performance in terms of median error values (f_2, f_3 and f_5). Substantial performance gains are mainly exhibited in the most challenging functions of the test suite, i.e. the hybrid composition functions ($f_6 - f_{10}$) and f_4. In these cases the proposed approaches significantly outperform all other DE variants. Comparing the non-forgetting, (MultiDE$_{\lambda=1.00}$), against the forgetting variants (MultiDE$_{\lambda=0.91}$ and

Table 1. Error values of the proposed DE framework, MultiDE, and five state-of-the-art DE variants on the first five 50–dimensional versions of the considered benchmark set (f_1–f_5)

Algorithm	Median	Mean	St.D.	NFE	Success	St. Sig.
		f_1 : Shifted Sphere Function				
DEGL	0.000e+00	0.000e+00	0.000e+00	3.230e+04	100.0	(=/=/=)
JADE	0.000e+00	0.000e+00	0.000e+00	4.363e+04	100.0	(=/=/=)
jDE	0.000e+00	0.000e+00	0.000e+00	1.535e+05	100.0	(=/=/=)
ODE	0.000e+00	0.000e+00	0.000e+00	1.194e+05	100.0	(=/=/=)
SADE	0.000e+00	0.000e+00	0.000e+00	7.779e+04	100.0	(=/=/=)
MultiDE$_{\lambda=0.91}$	0.000e+00	0.000e+00	0.000e+00	5.032e+04	100.0	(=/=/=)
MultiDE$_{\lambda=0.99}$	0.000e+00	0.000e+00	0.000e+00	5.056e+04	100.0	(=/=/=)
MultiDE$_{\lambda=1.00}$	0.000e+00	0.000e+00	0.000e+00	5.002e+04	100.0	(=/=/=)
		f_2 : Shifted Schwefel's Problem 2.21				
DEGL	1.430e+01	1.559e+01	5.660e+00	N/A	0.0	(+/+/+)
JADE	1.115e+00	1.127e+00	2.264e-01	N/A	0.0	(−/−/−)
jDE	2.220e+00	2.543e+00	1.581e+00	N/A	0.0	(−/−/−)
ODE	4.631e+00	6.115e+00	6.306e+00	N/A	0.0	(=/−/−)
SADE	2.925e+01	2.961e+01	3.300e+00	N/A	0.0	(+/+/+)
MultiDE$_{\lambda=0.91}$	5.678e+00	6.471e+00	3.266e+00	N/A	0.0	(=/=/=)
MultiDE$_{\lambda=0.99}$	6.161e+00	6.718e+00	3.269e+00	N/A	0.0	(=/=/=)
MultiDE$_{\lambda=1.00}$	6.396e+00	6.765e+00	2.794e+00	N/A	0.0	(=/=/=)
		f_3 : Shifted Rosenbrock's Function				
DEGL	0.000e+00	1.356e+00	1.908e+00	1.834e+05	66.0	(−/−/−)
JADE	2.286e+00	9.801e+00	1.956e+01	2.284e+05	8.0	(=/=/=)
jDE	3.975e+01	4.698e+01	1.956e+01	N/A	0.0	(+/+/+)
ODE	4.683e+01	9.303e+04	4.997e+05	N/A	0.0	(+/+/+)
SADE	1.918e+01	2.553e+01	2.439e+01	N/A	0.0	(+/+/+)
MultiDE$_{\lambda=0.91}$	3.015e+00	4.210e+00	9.579e+00	2.210e+05	2.0	(=/=/=)
MultiDE$_{\lambda=0.99}$	3.278e+00	4.480e+00	9.818e+00	2.477e+05	2.0	(=/=/=)
MultiDE$_{\lambda=1.00}$	2.873e+00	3.110e+00	3.023e+00	2.498e+05	2.0	(=/=/=)
		f_4 : Shifted Rastrigin's Function				
DEGL	1.492e+02	1.515e+02	2.531e+01	N/A	0.0	(+/+/+)
JADE	0.000e+00	0.000e+00	0.000e+00	2.217e+05	100.0	(=/=/=)
jDE	7.136e+01	7.198e+01	6.070e+00	N/A	0.0	(+/+/+)
ODE	3.651e+02	3.488e+02	4.078e+01	N/A	0.0	(+/+/+)
SADE	0.000e+00	5.680e+00	1.106e+01	2.305e+05	68.0	(+/+/+)
MultiDE$_{\lambda=0.91}$	0.000e+00	0.000e+00	0.000e+00	1.935e+05	100.0	(=/=/=)
MultiDE$_{\lambda=0.99}$	0.000e+00	0.000e+00	0.000e+00	1.962e+05	100.0	(=/=/=)
MultiDE$_{\lambda=1.00}$	0.000e+00	0.000e+00	0.000e+00	2.158e+05	100.0	(=/=/=)
		f_5 : Shifted Griewank's Function				
DEGL	7.000e-03	1.382e-02	2.143e-02	3.251e+04	48.0	(+/+/+)
JADE	0.000e+00	1.020e-03	2.839e-03	4.470e+04	88.0	(=/=/=)
jDE	0.000e+00	0.000e+00	0.000e+00	1.538e+05	100.0	(−/−/−)
ODE	0.000e+00	1.200e-03	3.090e-03	1.212e+05	86.0	(=/=/=)
SADE	0.000e+00	5.760e-03	1.041e-02	7.681e+04	64.0	(+/+/+)
MultiDE$_{\lambda=0.91}$	0.000e+00	6.800e-04	2.369e-03	5.018e+04	92.0	(=/=/=)
MultiDE$_{\lambda=0.99}$	0.000e+00	1.480e-03	3.694e-03	5.118e+04	84.0	(=/=/=)
MultiDE$_{\lambda=1.00}$	0.000e+00	1.320e-03	3.766e-03	5.041e+04	88.0	(=/=/=)

MultiDE$_{\lambda=0.99}$), we can observe that in the majority of cases there is no significant performance difference. Only in f_8 and f_9 the forgetting variants exhibit significantly better behavior. However, in most cases the non-forgetting variants produce lower median and mean error values.

Generally, we have observed that the adaptation of the strategy probabilities behave differently based on the benchmark problem at hand as well as the evolution phase. This indicates that the forgetting factor values should adapt through different evolution phases. This is a very interesting research area that we intend to extensively study in the future.

Table 2. Error values of the proposed DE framework, MultiDE, and five state-of-the-art DE variants on the last five 50–dimensional versions of the considered benchmark set $(f_6 - f_{10})$

Algorithm	Median	Mean	St.D.	NFE	Success	St. Sig.
			f_6 : Shifted Ackley's Function			
DEGL	2.901e+00	3.001e+00	6.213e-01	N/A	0.0	$(+/+/+)$
JADE	**0.000e+00**	**0.000e+00**	0.000e+00	6.353e+04	100.0	$(=/=/=)$
jDE	**0.000e+00**	**0.000e+00**	0.000e+00	2.281e+05	100.0	$(=/=/=)$
ODE	0.000e+00	2.460e-03	1.739e-02	1.753e+05	98.0	$(=/=/=)$
SADE	0.000e+00	3.442e-01	5.674e-01	1.161e+05	72.0	$(+/+/+)$
MultiDE$_{\lambda=0.91}$	**0.000e+00**	**0.000e+00**	0.000e+00	7.363e+04	100.0	$(=/=/=)$
MultiDE$_{\lambda=0.99}$	**0.000e+00**	**0.000e+00**	0.000e+00	7.336e+04	100.0	$(=/=/=)$
MultiDE$_{\lambda=1.00}$	0.000e+00	1.758e-02	1.243e-01	7.362e+04	98.0	$(=/=/=)$
			f_7 : Hybrid Composition Function 1 $(f_{16}$ [6])			
DEGL	8.144e+01	7.839e+01	3.066e+01	N/A	0.0	$(+/+/+)$
JADE	1.167e-05	2.697e-05	5.025e-05	N/A	0.0	$(+/+/+)$
jDE	9.126e-05	9.085e-05	2.451e-05	N/A	0.0	$(+/+/+)$
ODE	5.736e-03	6.463e-03	3.008e-03	N/A	0.0	$(+/+/+)$
SADE	3.124e-02	2.524e-01	1.503e+00	2.188e+05	12.0	$(+/+/+)$
MultiDE$_{\lambda=0.91}$	1.559e-13	1.426e-03	6.143e-03	1.749e+05	94.0	$(=/=/=)$
MultiDE$_{\lambda=0.99}$	**1.165e-13**	2.146e-04	1.517e-03	1.741e+05	98.0	$(=/=/=)$
MultiDE$_{\lambda=1.00}$	1.788e-13	**2.167e-13**	1.990e-13	1.767e+05	100.0	$(=/=/=)$
			f_8 : Hybrid Composition Function 2 $(f_{17}$ [6])			
DEGL	1.157e+02	1.151e+02	3.575e+01	N/A	0.0	$(+/+/+)$
JADE	8.797e+00	9.285e+00	1.551e+00	N/A	0.0	$(+/+/+)$
jDE	6.427e+00	6.320e+00	9.796e-01	N/A	0.0	$(+/+/+)$
ODE	8.416e+00	8.591e+00	8.773e-01	N/A	0.0	$(+/+/+)$
SADE	4.013e-01	1.241e+00	3.015e+00	N/A	0.0	$(+/+/+)$
MultiDE$_{\lambda=0.91}$	1.535e-01	**3.250e-01**	7.725e-01	N/A	0.0	$(=/=/-)$
MultiDE$_{\lambda=0.99}$	**1.213e-01**	3.729e-01	9.330e-01	N/A	0.0	$(=/=/-)$
MultiDE$_{\lambda=1.00}$	1.906e-01	3.587e-01	1.144e+00	N/A	0.0	$(+/+/=)$
			f_9 : Hybrid Composition Function 3 $(f_{18}$ [6])			
DEGL	3.777e+01	3.621e+01	1.070e+01	N/A	0.0	$(+/+/+)$
JADE	2.792e-01	2.787e-01	3.346e-02	N/A	0.0	$(+/+/+)$
jDE	1.098e-01	1.082e-01	3.737e-02	N/A	0.0	$(+/+/+)$
ODE	5.347e+00	7.079e+00	5.950e+00	N/A	0.0	$(+/+/+)$
SADE	9.096e-02	9.885e-02	7.226e-02	N/A	0.0	$(+/+/+)$
MultiDE$_{\lambda=0.91}$	**4.158e-04**	**6.529e-04**	8.106e-04	N/A	0.0	$(=/-/-)$
MultiDE$_{\lambda=0.99}$	1.001e-03	2.019e-03	2.570e-03	N/A	0.0	$(+/=/-)$
MultiDE$_{\lambda=1.00}$	4.474e-02	5.518e-02	2.886e-02	N/A	0.0	$(+/+/=)$
			f_{10} Hybrid Composition Function 4 $(f_{19}$ [6])			
DEGL	1.175e+01	1.114e+01	2.671e+00	N/A	0.0	$(+/+/+)$
JADE	**0.000e+00**	1.823e-01	3.965e-01	5.144e+04	80.0	$(=/=/=)$
jDE	8.186e-15	**9.568e-15**	5.738e-15	1.662e+05	100.0	$(+/+/+)$
ODE	5.526e-17	3.022e-01	6.365e-01	1.535e+05	78.0	$(+/+/+)$
SADE	2.100e+00	2.132e+00	1.442e+00	8.487e+04	12.0	$(+/+/+)$
MultiDE$_{\lambda=0.91}$	**0.000e+00**	2.104e-01	4.452e-01	5.848e+04	76.0	$(=/=/=)$
MultiDE$_{\lambda=0.99}$	**0.000e+00**	2.816e-01	4.340e-01	5.850e+04	66.0	$(=/=/=)$
MultiDE$_{\lambda=1.00}$	**0.000e+00**	3.236e-01	6.636e-01	5.793e+04	72.0	$(=/=/=)$

5   Conclusions

Recent Differential Evolution variations suggest that the advantages of several DE variants can be exploited by integrating them in adaptive schemes. We attempt to exploit the characteristics of different DE variants in an attempt to improve their performance. Borrowing ideas from adaptive filter theory we develop an "online" algorithmic adaptation framework. The proposed framework is based on tracking the parameters of a multinomial distribution to capture the potentially changing probabilities of success of the different algorithms involved.

Experimental results on 10 benchmark functions demonstrate that the proposed framework is very promising. For the majority of the tested cases, it exhibits great performance gains against other five DE variants. The most appropriate degree of forgetting depends on the evolution stage, as well as the problem. It would be interesting to further study its impact and develop an adaptive forgetting factor scheme.

Acknowledgments. M.G. Epitropakis and M.N. Vrahatis would like to thank the European Union (European Social Fund – ESF) and Greek national funds through the Operational Program "Education and Lifelong Learning" of the National Strategic Reference Framework (NSRF) - Research Funding Program: "Heracleitus II: Investing in knowledge society through the European Social Fund" for financially supporting this work.

References

1. Brest, J., Greiner, S., Boskovic, B., Mernik, M., Zumer, V.: Self-Adapting control parameters in differential evolution: A comparative study on numerical benchmark problems. IEEE Transactions on Evolutionary Computation 10(6), 646–657 (2006)
2. Das, S., Abraham, A., Chakraborty, U.K., Konar, A.: Differential evolution using a Neighborhood-Based mutation operator. IEEE Transactions on Evolutionary Computation 13(3), 526–553 (2009)
3. Das, S., Suganthan, P.N.: Differential evolution: A survey of the state-of-the-art. IEEE Transactions on Evolutionary Computation 15(1), 4–31 (2011)
4. Epitropakis, M.G., Tasoulis, D.K., Pavlidis, N.G., Plagianakos, V.P., Vrahatis, M.N.: Enhancing differential evolution utilizing proximity-based mutation operators. IEEE Transactions on Evolutionary Computation 15(1), 99–119 (2011)
5. Gong, W., Fialho, Á., Cai, Z., Li, H.: Adaptive strategy selection in differential evolution for numerical optimization: An empirical study. Information Sciences 181(24), 5364–5386 (2011)
6. Lozano, M., Molina, D., Herrera, F.: Editorial scalability of evolutionary algorithms and other metaheuristics for large-scale continuous optimization problems. Soft Computing - A Fusion of Foundations, Methodologies and Applications 15(11), 2085–2087 (2011)
7. Niedzwiecki, M.: Identification of Time-varying Processes. John Wiley & Sons, New York (2000)
8. Pavlidis, N.G., Tasoulis, D.K., Adams, N.M., Hand, D.J.: λ-perceptron: An adaptive classifier for data streams. Pattern Recognition 44(1), 78–96 (2011)
9. Price, K., Storn, R.M., Lampinen, J.A.: Differential Evolution: A Practical Approach to Global Optimization. Natural Computing Series. Springer-Verlag New York, Inc., Secaucus (2005)
10. Qin, A.K., Huang, V.L., Suganthan, P.N.: Differential evolution algorithm with strategy adaptation for global numerical optimization. IEEE Transactions on Evolutionary Computation 13(2), 398–417 (2009)
11. Rahnamayan, S., Tizhoosh, H.R., Salama, M.M.A.: Opposition-Based differential evolution. IEEE Transactions on Evolutionary Computation 12(1), 64–79 (2008)

12. Storn, R., Price, K.: Differential evolution – a simple and efficient adaptive scheme for global optimization over continuous spaces. Journal of Global Optimization 11, 341–359 (1997)
13. Tang, K., et al.: Benchmark functions for the CEC 2008 special session and competition on large scale global optimization. Tech. rep., Nature Inspired Computation and Applications Laboratory, USTC, China (2007)
14. Zhang, J., Sanderson, A.C.: JADE: adaptive differential evolution with optional external archive. IEEE Transactions on Evolutionary Computation 13(5), 945–958 (2009)

Clustering of High Dimensional Data Streams

Sotiris K. Tasoulis[1], Dimirtis K. Tasoulis[2], and Vassilis P. Plagianakos[1]

[1] Department of Computer Science and Biomedical Informatics,
University of Central Greece,
Papassiopoulou 2–4, Lamia, 35100, Greece
{stas,vpp}@ucg.gr
[2] Winton Capital Management,
1–5 St Mary Abbot's Place, SW8 6LS, United Kingdom
d.tasoulis@wintoncapital.com

Abstract. Clustering of data streams has become a task of great interest in the recent years as such data formats is are becoming increasingly ambiguous. In many cases, these data are also high dimensional and in result more complex for clustering. As such there is a growing need for algorithms that can be applied on streaming data and the at same time can cope with high dimensionality. To this end, here we design a streaming clustering approach by extending a recently proposed high dimensional clustering algorithm.

Keywords: Clustering, Data Streams, Kernel Density Estimation, Incremental Principal Component Analysis.

1 Introduction

Recent technological advances have made the continues collection of data trivial, leading to very large databases that grow at an unlimited rate and usually it is either unnecessary or impractical to store them. These streaming data present new challenges to clustering algorithms.

A streaming clustering process aims to continuously track the clustering structure of the data. Since stream data by nature impose a one pass constraint on the design of the algorithms, this task becomes more difficult. In addition, in many cases, streaming data are also high dimensional and in result more complex to cluster, due to the effect that high dimensionality has on distance or similarity [10,1]. Recently in [11] a density based hierarchical clustering approach (dePDDP) has been proposed that can deal with high dimensional data by projecting them onto a lower dimensional subspace.

Most clustering methods cannot be used for streaming data, since they rely on the assumption that the data are available in a permanent memory structure, from which global information can be obtained at any time. However, in many cases a clustering algorithm can be extended to the concept of data streams. A k-means clustering model for data streams was proposed in [4] and more recently, in [3] the DENSTREAM algorithm was developed by extending the GDBSCAN

I. Maglogiannis, V. Plagianakos, and I. Vlahavas (Eds.): SETN 2012, LNAI 7297, pp. 223–230, 2012.
© Springer-Verlag Berlin Heidelberg 2012

algorithm. In this paper, we extend the recently proposed dePDDP framework and propose a new method for high dimensional data stream clustering.

In the next Section, we present the background material. In Section 3, we summarize the proposed approach and in Section 4 we present the experimental analysis that demonstrate the method's efficiency. Finally, the paper ends with concluding remarks in Section 5.

2 The dePDDP Algorithm

The dePDDP algorithm [11] is an algorithm that can deal with ultra high dimensions and has the ability to automatically retrieve the number of the clusters in the dataset. dePDDP is a divisive hierarchical clustering algorithm, producing a nested sequence of partitions, with a single, all-inclusive cluster at the top. Starting from this all-inclusive cluster the nested sequence of partitions is constructed by iteratively splitting clusters, until a termination criterion is satisfied. The main characteristic of the dePDDP algorithm is that it incorporates information from the density of the projected data onto the first principal component. The dePDDP procedure suggests that by splitting the data based on the global minimizer of the estimated density of the projected data onto the first principal component, is the best we can do to avoid splitting coherent data clusters. The cluster selection criterion and the termination criterion are guided by the same idea.

To formally describe how the principal direction projection based algorithm operates, let us assume that the data at hand is represented by an $n \times a$ matrix D, in which each row represents a data sample $d_i, i = 1, \ldots, n$, and a denotes the dimensionality. If we define the vector b and matrix Σ to represent the mean vector and the covariance of the data respectively:

$$b = \frac{1}{n} \sum_{i=1}^{n} d_i, \quad \Sigma = \frac{1}{n}(D - be)^{\top}(D - be),$$

where e is a column vector of ones. The covariance matrix Σ is symmetric and positive semi-definite, so all its eigenvalues are real and non-negative. The eigenvectors u_j $j = 1, \ldots, k$ corresponding to the k largest eigenvalues are called the principal components or principal directions. The dePDDP algorithm uses the projections p_i:

$$p_i = u_1(d_i - b), \quad i = 1, \ldots, n,$$

onto the first principal component u_1 to initially separate the entire data set into two partitions P_1 and P_2 based on a global minimizer x^*:

Definition 1. *(Global Minimizer) A global minimizer x^* is a point of $\mathbb{R}$ such that $\hat{f}(x^*; h) = \min_x \mathcal{X}$, where $\mathcal{X} = \{x \in R : \exists \delta > 0, \hat{f}(x + \delta; h) > \hat{f}(x; h)$ and $\hat{f}(x - \delta; h) > \hat{f}(x; h)\}$.*

The kernel density estimation $\hat{f}(x; h)$ of the density of the projected data onto the first principal component is given by the equation:

$$\hat{f}(x; h) = n^{-1}h^{-1}\sum_{i=1}^{n} K\left((x - p_i)/h\right).$$ (1)

The kernel choice in this work is the standard multi-variate normal density given by $K(x) = (2\pi)^{-1/2}e^{-0.5|x|}$.

Thus, $\forall d_i \in D, if\, p_i \geqslant x^*$ then the i-th data point belongs to the first partition P_1 $P_1 = P_1 \cup d_i$; otherwise, it belongs to the second partition $P_2 = P_2 \cup d_i$. The algorithm proceeds by splitting the cluster with the lowest global minimizer value and stops the iteration if no minimizer exists for any of the remaining clusters.

3   The Proposed Clustering Algorithm

To extend the dePDDP approach to streaming data we need to online update the hierarchical structure of the algorithm at each data point arrival. Thus, the proposed streaming modification will use the standard dePDDP methodology to assign the data entry to an already defined cluster or to create a new one.

In more detail, at each time instant n for each new data point arrival d_n, the proposed algorithm appropriately updates the hierarchical clustering structure constructed up to that time point. Starting from the root node the data points will be first projected on the u_1 Principal Component (PC) of all the points that have already been assigned to that node. Consequently, they will be assigned to a sub-node as described in Section 2, based on the density estimate $\hat{f}(x; h)$ of all the points assigned to that node.

However, this would imply that all the points assigned to each node need to be kept in memory in order to calculate both the PC u_1 and $\hat{f}(x; h)$, which is unrealistic in the data stream scenario. Nevertheless, online methods have been developed that overcome this constraint for online adaptation of both u_1 and $\hat{f}(x; h)$ respectively. Here, for the principal component u_1 we use the candid covariance-free IPCA (CCIPCA) method [12], which is based on the works of Oja and Karhunen [6] and Sanger [8]. The CCIPCA method is described in Section 3.1. To efficiently calculate the density function over data stream, we employ the method introduced in [14] based on the M-kernels concept. The main characteristic of this methodology is that it only uses a fix-sized main memory, which is irrespective of the total number of data points in the stream and the time complexity is linear to the size of the data stream (see Section 3.2).

The complete algorithmic scheme of the new SPDC (Streaming Principal Direction Clustering) algorithm is presented at Algorithm 1. For each node of the hierarchical structure the algorithm keeps in memory the node identity ID, the PC u_1^{ID}, the Density Function $\hat{f}(x; h)^{ID}$, and the identity of the left and right kid $Rkid^{ID}$ and $Lkid^{ID}$, respectively. For each point arrival d_n, the PC is updated and d_n is projected onto the updated PC. Then the density function is updated and d is assigned to the left or right sub-node based on the minimizer x^* as explained in Section 2. The iteration stops when there is not a minimizer and the algorithms returns the identity ID.

Algorithm 1. The SPDC algorithm summary

1: For each point arrival d_n
2: **Do**
3: $ID = RootNode$
4: Update u_1^{ID} and calculate $p_n^{ID} = u_1^{ID} d_n$
5: Update Density $\hat{f}(x; h)^{ID}$ with p_n^{ID}
6: **if** there is a minimizer $x*$ **then**
7:    If $p_n^{ID} \geqslant x^*$ then $ID = Rkid^{ID}$ else $ID = Lkid^{ID}$
8:    go to 4
9: **end if**

3.1   Incremental PCA

Let $d_1, d_2, \ldots$ be the sample vectors that are acquired sequentially. Each $d_n, n = 1, 2, \ldots$, is a a-dimensional vector. Without loss of generality, we can assume that d_n has a zero mean (the mean may be incrementally estimated and subtracted out). Then the nth step estimate u_1^n of u_1 is given by

$$u_1^n = \frac{n - 1 - l}{n} u_1^{n-1} + \frac{1 + l}{n} d_n d_n^T \frac{u_1^{n-1}}{\|u_1^{n-1}\|},$$

where $(n - 1/n)$ is the weight for the last estimate and $1/n$ is the weight of the new data. The positive parameter l is called the amnesic parameter. With the presence of l, larger weight is given to new samples and the effect of old samples will fade out gradually. In this work, we do not use an amnesic parameter and l is set to 0. Finally, to begin the iteration, we set $u_1^0 = d_1$ as the first direction of data spread. A mathematical proof of the convergence of CCIPCA can be found in [13].

3.2   Density Estimation over Data Streams

To calculate the density of a point at the time frame of the stream n, we need to calculate the sum of n elements as shown in equation (1). To find a minimizer $x*$, we need to calculate the density over n points. As expected when data comes in the form of data stream, the large volume and the endlessness of the data stream make it computationally impossible to keep them in memory.

   To handle data stream efficiently, we can maintain a representative sample of points with appropriately weights in order to accurately approximate $\hat{f}(x; h)$, as described in [14].

   Let m be the number of the sample points that we keep in memory. When a new point arrives at time $m + 1$ in order to update the density function based on this point without increasing the computational complexity of the algorithm, we merge two points based on a merging cost. As a merging cost we use the distance between two consecutive points. Let p_k and p_l be the two points with the smallest merging cost. Then p_k and p_l are substituted by $p_n = (p_k + p_l)/2$. The weight value of the kernel function that corresponds to p_n is the sum of the weight values of the kernel function of p_k and p_l respectively. Then at time point n, the density estimation can be written as

$$\hat{f}_n^*(x; h) = n^{-1}h^{-1} \sum_{i=1}^{m} \rho_i^* K\left((x - p_i)/h\right),$$

where $\sum_{i=1}^{m} \rho_i^* = n$. The bandwidth parameter is very important for the quality of the density estimation. Most well known bandwidth strategies [9] often assign a global bandwidth to all kernels. However, these strategies depend on the complete sample, which is not known in the concept of data streams. To overcome this problem, we use an approximate solution that complies with the processing requirements of data streams similar to the one used in [5]. We use the "normal reference rule" bandwidth strategy, which is the bandwidth that minimizes the Mean Integrated Squared Error (MISE). For a sample with n samples this is given by $h_{opt}^n = \sigma \left(\frac{4}{3n}\right)^{1/5}$, where σ is the standard deviation of the data. The standard deviation here is computed incrementally in constant time.

4 Experimental Analysis

In this Section, we perform an experimental evaluation of the proposed clustering method on streaming data. To achieve this we employ a series of simulated datasets. This gives the opportunity to pre-design and hence know beforehand the structure of the data that the clustering algorithm aims to recover. In particular we construct datasets by randomly drawing points from a finite mixture of k Gaussian distributions that represent the actual clusters in the data. 5000 points are drawn in total for each dataset. The mean of each Gaussian is randomly placed in $[100, 200]^a$ and the covariance matrix is also randomly generated by an appropriate procedure, so as to ensure that it is symmetric and positive definite.

To assess the quality of a data partition, we use the class labels which are not available to the clustering algorithms. We measure the degree of correspondence between the resulting clusters and the classes of each object. In detail, let $\mathcal{L}$ be the set of class labels $l_i \in \mathcal{L}$, for each point $d_i \in \mathcal{D}$, $i = 1, \ldots, n$, with l_i taking values in $\{1, \ldots, L\}$ we define the purity of a k-cluster partitioning as $\Pi = \{\mathcal{C}_1, \ldots, \mathcal{C}_k\}$. The purity of Π is defined by the following formula:

$$p(\Pi) = \frac{\sum_{j=1}^{k} \max\{|\{p_i \in \mathcal{C}_j : l_i = 1, \ldots, L\}|\}}{n},$$

so that $0 \leq p(\Pi) \leq 1$. High values indicate that the majority of vectors in each cluster come from the same class, so in essence the partitioning is "pure" with respect to class labels.

To address the question of whether all members of a given class are included in a single cluster we use the V-measure [7] criterion. The V-measure tries to capture cluster homogeneity and completeness, which summarizes a clustering solution's success in including every point of a single class and no others. Again, high values corresponds to better performance.

Tables 1 and 2 report the clustering performance with respect to the clustering purity, the V-measure and the number of the found clusters for several types of datasets, respectively. For each dataset, 50 experiments have been conducted and the mean values with the standard deviation (in the parenthesis) are presented. The clustering performance is always measured at the last 100 points of the stream. The performance of the proposed method is compared against the well known DENSTREAM algorithm [3]. For DENSTREAM, the ϵ parameter was set to 100. In the case of SPDC (Streaming Principal Direction Clustering), 100 M-kernels were used in all experiments. The bandwidth parameter for the density estimation was set as explained in Section 3.2. As shown the SPDC clustering results yield superior Purity and V-measure in most cases.

Table 1. Mean purity, V-measure and number of the found clusters for the artificial datasets

No. Of Cl.	Dimension 2			Dimension 10		
	Purity	V-measure	Clusters	Purity	V-measure	Clusters
	SPDC			SPDC		
2	1.00 (0.02)	0.68 (0.09)	6.02 (1.59)	0.99 (0.06)	0.81 (0.16)	4.00 (1.43)
5	0.96 (0.07)	0.92 (0.05)	6.90 (1.68)	0.96 (0.07)	0.95 (0.05)	5.64 (1.16)
10	0.72 (0.14)	0.82 (0.09)	8.14 (2.06)	0.82 (0.11)	0.89 (0.06)	10.08 (2.26)
	DENSTREAM			DENSTREAM		
2	0.51 (0.00)	0.00 (0.00)	1.00 (0.00)	0.85 (0.05)	0.70 (0.23)	1.70 (0.23)
5	0.22 (0.00)	0.00 (0.00)	1.00 (0.00)	0.56 (0.07)	0.60 (0.12)	2.70 (1.78)
10	0.12 (0.00)	0.00 (0.00)	1.00 (0.00)	0.23 (0.00)	0.35 (0.02)	2.00 (0.22)

Table 2. Mean purity, V-measure and number of the found clusters for the artificial datasets

No. Of Cl.	Dimension 50			Dimension 100		
	Purity	V-measure	Clusters	Purity	V-measure	Clusters
	SPDC			SPDC		
2	1.00 (0.00)	0.90 (0.10)	2.88 (0.82)	1.00 (0.00)	0.92 (0.08)	2.64 (0.62)
5	0.97 (0.07)	0.97 (0.05)	5.30 (0.78)	0.90 (0.13)	0.93 (0.08)	4.84 (0.86)
10	0.85 (0.11)	0.91 (0.06)	9.18 (1.73)	0.78 (0.13)	0.86 (0.10)	8.26 (1.81)
	DENSTREAM			DENSTREAM		
2	1.00 (0.00)	1.00 (0.00)	2.00 (0.00)	1.00 (0.00)	1.00 (0.00)	2.00 (0.00)
5	1.00 (0.00)	1.00 (0.00)	5.00 (0.00)	0.92 (0.01)	0.95 (0.00)	4.60 (0.26)
10	0.17 (0.00)	0.21 (0.05)	1.50 (0.27)	0.21 (0.00)	0.31 (0.04)	1.90 (0.54)

To examine the sensitivity of the number of M-kernels parameter used by SPDC algorithm we perform a series of experiments for the 50-dimensional 5-cluster case.

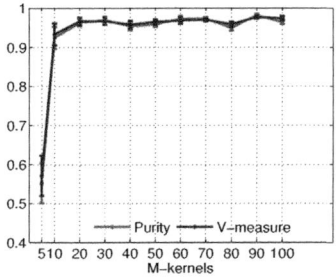

Fig. 1. Mean purity and V-measure with respect to the corresponding number of M-kernels

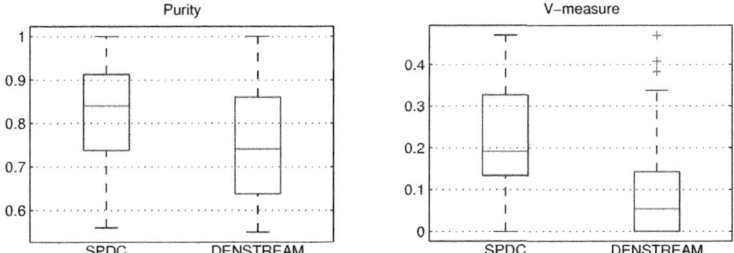

Fig. 2. Boxplots of Purity and V-measure for the Forest CoverType real world dataset

For each parameter value 50 experiments have been made. As shown in Figure 1 a parameter value higher than 10 is enough to achieve high quality results.

Finally, we test the efficiency of SPDC and DENSTREAM at the Forest Cover-Type real world dataset, obtained from the UCI machine learning repository [2]. This dataset is comprised of 581012 observations characterized in 54 attributes, where each observation is labelled in one of seven forest cover classes. Here we only use the 10 numerical attributes. In Figure 2 we can see boxplots of the Purity and the V-measure of the clustering result, obtained in the last 100 points for various time point of the data stream for SPDC and DENSTREAM, respectively. The ϵ parameter for DENSTREAM was set to 30 for better results. As shown the SPDC results are superior in both cases. Purity values are always high, but the V-measure obtain lower values since in most cases the algorithms tend to find more clusters than the actual.

5   Concluding Remarks

Although many data stream clustering algorithms have been proposed in the literature, very few of them can actually deal with high dimensionality. In this work, we present an algorithm that can effectively deal with high dimensional data streams. The proposed method shows promising results in synthetic and real data scenarios. In a future work we intent to extend this approach for clustering on evolving data streams.

Acknowledgments. This research has been co-financed by the European Union (European Social Fund - ESF) and Greek national funds through the Operational Program "Education and Lifelong Learning" of the National Strategic Reference Framework (NSRF) - Research Funding Program: Heracleitus II, Investing in knowledge society through the European Social Fund.

References

1. Beyer, K., Goldstein, J., Ramakrishnan, R., Shaft, U.: When Is Nearest Neighbor Meaningful? In: Beeri, C., Bruneman, P. (eds.) ICDT 1999. LNCS, vol. 1540, pp. 217–235. Springer, Heidelberg (1998)
2. Blake, C., Merz, C.: UCI repository of machine learning databases (1998)
3. Cao, F., Ester, M., Qian, W., Zhou, A.: Density-based clustering over an evolving data stream with noise. In: 2006 SIAM Conference on Data Mining, pp. 328–339 (2006)
4. Domingos, P., Hulten, G., Edu, P.C.W., Edu, C.H.G.W.: A general method for scaling up machine learning algorithms and its application to clustering. In: Proceedings of the Eighteenth International Conference on Machine Learning, pp. 106–113. Morgan Kaufmann (2001)
5. Heinz, C., Seeger, B.: Towards Kernel Density Estimation over Streaming Data. In: International Conference on Management of Data. Computer Society of India, COMAD 2006, Delhi, India (December 2006)
6. Oja, E., Karhunen, J.: On Stochastic Approximation of the Eigenvectors and Eigenvalues of the Expectation of a Random Matrix. Journal of Mathematical Analysis and Applications 106, 69–84 (1985)
7. Rosenberg, A., Hirschberg, J.: V-measure: A conditional entropy-based external cluster evaluation measure. In: 2007 Joint Conference on Empirical Methods in Natural Language Processing and Computational Natural Language Learning (EMNLP-CoNLL), pp. 410–420 (2007)
8. Sanger, T.D.: Optimal unsupervised learning in a single-layer linear feedforward neural network. Neural Networks 2(6), 459–473 (1989)
9. Scott, D.W.: Multivariate Density Estimation: Theory, Practice, and Visualization. Wiley Series in Probability and Statistics. Wiley (September 1992)
10. Steinbach, M., Ertöz, L., Kumar, V.: The challenges of clustering high dimensional data. New Vistas in Statistical Physics: Applications in Econophysics, Bioinformatics, and Pattern Recognition (2003)
11. Tasoulis, S., Tasoulis, D., Plagianakos, V.: Enhancing Principal Direction Divisive Clustering. Pattern Recognition 43, 3391–3411 (2010)
12. Weng, J., Zhang, Y., Hwang, W.: Candid covariance-free incremental principal component analysis (2003)
13. Zhang, Y., Weng, J.: Convergence analysis of complementary candid incremental principal component analysis (2001)
14. Zhou, A., Cai, Z., Wei, L., Qian, W.: M-kernel merging: Towards density estimation over data streams. In: International Conference on Database Systems for Advanced Applications, p. 285 (2003)

Multifactor Dimensionality Reduction for the Analysis of Obesity in a Nutrigenetics Context

Katerina Karayianni[1], Ioannis Valavanis[2],
Keith Grimaldi[3], and Konstantina Nikita[1]

[1] School of Electrical and Computer Engineering, National Technical University of Athens,
9 Iroon Polytechniou Str., 15780, Zografos, Athens, Greece
[2] Institute of Biological Research and Biotechnology, National Hellenic Research Foundation,
Vas. Konstantinou 46, 11635, Athens, Greece
[3] Biomedical Engineering Laboratory, Institute of Communication and Computer Systems,
National Technical University of Athens, Polytechniou Str., 15780, Zografos, Athens, Greece
kkarayian@biosim.ntua.gr, ivalavan@eie.gr,
keith.grimaldi@gmail.com, knikita@ece.ntua.gr

Abstract. The current work aims to study within a nutrigenetics context the multifactorial trait beneath obesity. To this end, the use of parallel Multifactor Dimensionality Reduction (pMDR) is investigated towards the identification of i) factors that have an impact to obesity onset solely or interacting with each other and ii) rules that describe the interactions among them. Data have been obtained from a large scale nutrigenetics study and each subject, characterized as normal or overweight based on Body Mass Index (BMI), is featured a 63-dimensional vector describing his/her genetic variations and nutritional habits. pMDR method was used to reduce the initial set of factors into subsets that can classify a subject into either normal or overweight with a certain accuracy and are further used by corresponding prediction models. Results showed that pMDR selected factors associated to obesity and constructed predictive models showing a good generalization ability. Rules describing interactions of the selected factors were extracted, thus enlightening the classification mechanism of the constructed model.

Keywords: nutrigenetics, obesity, Multifactor Dimensionality Reduction, prediction model.

1 Background

Obesity has been found to have a positive relationship with cardiovascular disease (CVD) mortality in various large scale studies [1-2]. Although obesity onsets mostly as a result of certain environmental exposures, e.g. the high in sugars and fats westernized nutrition, or the lack of physical exercise, it can be also studied as an interactive effect among the genetic profile of a person and its exposure to environmental factors. Such interactive effects, studied by the relatively new field of nutrigenetics [3], can provide insights on the development of obesity and may trigger

I. Maglogiannis, V. Plagianakos, and I. Vlahavas (Eds.): SETN 2012, LNAI 7297, pp. 231–238, 2012.
© Springer-Verlag Berlin Heidelberg 2012

forming new strategies for the control of obesity and CVD, not limited solely to environmental exposures.

The importance of indentifying gene-gene interactions towards the study of diseases has been highlighted in [4], where it is emphasized that epistasis (gene-gene interactions) is ubiquitous in human diseases. Apart from complex gene-gene interactions, which can reveal more biological information than individual gene analysis , various studies have focused on the additional importance of analyzing how gene and environmental factors interact and have an impact towards the development of disease [5]. Various gene-environment interactions that are related to obesity have been identified in [6], where authors conclude the importance of accounting for gene-environment interactions towards the understanding and treatment of obesity. Choosing to study gene-environment interactions in obesity has also be shown to be a justifiable approach in [7], in which the relationship of genetic and environmental factors in a person's BMI was studied, though without reporting over specific genetic variations. The contribution of genes and environmental factors towards BMI has been also studied in [8], where the statistical analysis conducted identified two polymorphisms that in synergy with fats intake contribute to the modulation of waist circumference.

Studies of gene-gene and gene-environment interactions have some inherent difficulties. On one hand, there is a relative difficulty in collecting the appropriate environmental and genetic factors for a significant number of subjects. On the other hand, there is difficulty in analyzing a problem of such complexity due to the high dimensionality of the data [9]. Various advanced computational methods have been proposed and applied to identify interactions among genetic and environmental factors that may trigger perturbations into biological pathways and contribute to the development of diseases [10]. Multifactor Dimensionality Reduction (MDR) is a popular non-parametric, model-free method for detecting gene-gene and gene-environment interactions developed by Ritchie et al. [11]. It has been used for the study of gene-gene interactions in various diseases, e.g. hypertension [12], type 2 diabetes [13] and breast cancer [14].

In the current work, the method chosen to analyze the available data towards the identification of causal interactions beneath obesity is a more recent algorithm developed by Ritchie et al., i.e. parallel Multifactor Dimensionality Reduction (pMDR) [15]. The particular implementation offers various advantages in relation to the prior Dimensionality Reduction method (MDR), as it scales to handle big datasets. In addition, it allows constructing rules that describe the interactions among the selected subset of factors, providing more valuable information that enlightens the interplay of the involving features. This study employs a large scale dataset of more than 2300 subjects and targets i) associations of obesity and interaction rules from a pool of 63 features describing gender, various nutritional elements and genetic variations that have been previously individually associated with obesity and cardiovascular health [16] and ii) corresponding predictive models that can distinguish subjects characterized as normal or overweight based on Body Mass Index (BMI). Regarding previous findings, it comes to take one step further our previous work in [9], in which ANN-based methods were used select the most informative features from the same nutrigenetics data and construct predictive models for obesity status.

2   Dataset

The dataset employed comes from a previous large scale nutrigenetics study [16]. It includes data for 2341 white people, and for each subject a total of 38 nutrition measurements have been collected, e.g. daily intake of cholesterol, supplements of metals, in addition to the recording for 24 genetic variations (Single Nucleodite Polymorphisms-SNPs, or Insertions/Deletions) that have been found to have an influence on daily requirements of various nutritional elements for improving various CVD health aspects [16]. Nutritional elements, genetic variations and additionally gender complete the set of 63 input factors. Each subject is characterized as overweight or normal, according to his/her BMI (calculated as weight $(Kg)/height^2$ (m^2)). 1464 subjects were labeled as overweight (BMI > 25), and the remaining 877 as normal (BMI ≤ 25). Before analyzing the data by pMDR, it was necessary to do a pre-processing of the data to convert them into categorical values. Nutritional factors from intake of supplements were classified into four classes, which are bottom 33.3%, middle 33.3% and top 33.3% of non-zero values and zero, while the rest of the nutritional factors were classified according to the quartiles. Gene variations are categorical variables by themselves, e.g. a SNP corresponds to a three state categorical feature (AA/GG/AG). For each categorical variable, numerics (e.g. 1,2 and 3 for a three class variable) were used when importing data to pMDR. An extensive description of the dataset used can also be found in [9].

3   Methods

The current work investigates the use of the pMDR algorithm as a computational method to derive prediction models from the factors measured for each subject in the dataset and identify interactions among the elements of the models. The method uses a new algorithm in relation to the previous implementation of MDR that is able to analyze and identify interactions among factors from large datasets. The implementation is done with the Message Passing Interface (MPI) that enables parallel processing into multiple processors, which can make possible the handling high-complexity problems. An additional advantage of the method is that it can extract rules of interaction, capturing how the various combinations among the categorical values of the reduced features can predict a two-state result. The pMDR algorithm can be used for extremely large datasets of individuals and with many variable states, making feasible the analysis of small order interactions in very large datasets. The analysis of higher-order interactions in large datasets is also feasible, but is demanding in machine computational power and running time [11].

The pMDR algorithm is a non-parametric and model-free method that uses cross-validation to derive results. Firstly, data are divided into the training and testing set. The desired number of factors to comprise the reduced model is also specified. For all possible groups with this number of elements from the initial set of factors, the algorithm derives the various combinations of states among them. For example, for the two-factor combinations, the model consisting of a nutritional factor with four categorical states and a gene factor with three different types of variations has twelve different states of combinations. Then, each individual from the subjects is grouped to the combination that matches its characteristics. In this way, it can be calculated for each combination the ratio of cases to controls (in our case, obese to non-obese subjects). Then, this ratio is compared to the general ratio of cases to controls for the whole data set. If it is higher or equal to the general ratio, then the particular combination is characterized as high risk, else as low risk. Given the true labeling of subjects, sensitivity and specificity are calculated for each model and are used to compare the performance amongst the various models. The so-called balanced accuracy is the average of sensitivity and specificity of the model and it is calculated for each model for both the training and testing set in each cross-validation step. In addition, for each model there is an estimation of the prediction error in the testing set, based on the proportion of mislabeled subjects by the model. In the final step of the algorithm, the single best model across all combinations and up to the maximum model order selected, i.e. maximum number of factors included, is selected based on the highest cross-validation consistency and prediction accuracy [15]. pMDR allows the configuration of various execution parameters, which can have an impact on both the robustness of the method as well as the computational cost. For example, increasing the number of cross-validations augments the computational cost, yet having a sufficient number of cross-validations is necessary to ensure the validity of results. pMDR was used here in a cluster of two processing nodes of specification Intel(R) Xeon(TM) CPU 3.00GHz dual-core.

4   Results

In this part we present the results obtained by the pMDR method. The particular execution was configured to include models consisting up to seven factors (maximum order: 7) from the total 63 included in the dataset. In addition, it was selected to perform five-fold cross-validation (at each cross-validation step the best model is also kept in order to measure cross validation consistency, see following paragraph).

Table 1. Selected models (of order:1,..,7), based on five-fold cross-validation. For each model, average predicted balanced accuracy, average prediction error (correspond to measurements in testing sets) and CV consistency are presented.

Factors	Average Prediction Balanced Accuracy (%)	Average Prediction Error (%)	CV consistency
Gender (1)	59.34	43.83	5
Saturated Fat-Food Only, Gender (2)	60.57	37.99	5
Vitamin B6-Food Only, Saturated Fat-Food Only, Gender (3)	61.90	38.30	4
Vitamin B6, Vitamin A, Saturated Fat, Caffeine (4)	52.87	46.49	1
Vitamin C-Food Only, Omega 3, Cholesterol, Caffeine, Calcium (5)	55.27	43.72	3
Vitamin B12-Food Only, Vitamin A-Food Only, Refined Carbohydrate, Folic Acid-Supplement Only, Cruciferous, Caffeine (6)	51.00	47.16	1
Vitamin D - Food Only, Vitamin C-, Food Only Refined Carbohydrate, Omega 3, Cholesterol, Caffeine, Calcium - Supplement Only (7)	53.08	44.53	1

Table 2. Interactions among factors included in the best model (For Saturated Fat – Food Only, 0 corresponds to the lowest intake and 3 to the highest intake)

IF Saturated Fat – Food Only = 0 AND Gender = Male   THEN STATUS = Overweight
IF Saturated Fat – Food Only = 0 AND Gender = Female THEN STATUS = Normal
IF Saturated Fat – Food Only = 1 AND Gender = Male   THEN STATUS = Overweight
IF Saturated Fat – Food Only = 1 AND Gender = Female THEN STATUS = Normal
IF Saturated Fat – Food Only = 2 AND Gender = Male   THEN STATUS = Overweight
IF Saturated Fat – Food Only = 2 AND Gender = Female THEN STATUS = Normal
IF Saturated Fat – Food Only = 3 AND Gender = Male   THEN STATUS = Overweight
IF Saturated Fat – Food Only = 3 AND Gender = Female THEN STATUS = Overweight

After completing all cross-validation steps the algorithm evaluates the cross-validation consistency (CV consistency: number of occurrences as best model in the cross-validations) and the average values for balanced accuracy and prediction error for each model. Final results are shown in Table 1. The method identifies the single best model based on the highest CV. In case two or more models have the same CV value the single best model is determined based on the highest average predicted balanced accuracy and least prediction error. The single best model obtained here uses two factors corresponding to saturated fat – food only (factor 20, corresponds to saturated fat contained in food and not in supplements, see [9], [16] as well) and gender (factor 1). pMDR outputs in form of rules the identified interactions among the factors that comprise each model. For the single best model [Saturated Fat - Food Only, Gender] the resulting rules are shown in Table 2. The combinations of factors states that have not resulted into a classifiable status (Normal/ Overweight) have been omitted.

5   Discussion

The average prediction balanced accuracy obtained in testing sets, which is the selected measure for the evaluation of the models, is for the single best model almost 61%. The average prediction error for the same model is about 38%. In addition, the best model is consistently the best in all five cross-validations steps that took place. These values are satisfactory given that dimensionality reduction analysis has been conducted and that models are accompanied by rules that enlighten the classification mechanism of the selected model.

Interpreting the rules generated by the algorithm for the selected model and reported here, we can derive that high values of saturated fat (categorical value 3) can be associated with obesity in both genders, while lower values (categorical value 1) seem to affect males the most.

Comparing the results of the pMDR algorithm with the previous methods of PDM-ANN and GA-ANN used in [9], it is noted that the balanced accuracy of the best model is comparable to the mean accuracy of training with the ANN-based methods, although these do not match directly, since the methods do not use exactly the same fitness measures. The seven-order model consists of factors that are included in the results of methods PDM-ANN (apart from caffeine) and GA-ANN. In addition, method PDM-ANN (when 5 factors are used) has three factors in common with the 5-dimensional model obtained by pMDR. Thus, there is partial accordance of the pMDR results with the other methods, yet it has to be evaluated for higher-order models to confirm the relevance of results. It's noted here that the 7-order model obtained by pMDR comprised environmental factors only, without any genetic factors being included and did not highlight gene-environment interactions. This has to be further examined by obtaining higher order models by pMDR method, which needs further available computational power (e.g. running on a Grid). On the contrary, the methods used in our previous study [9], stochastic based or serially selecting features, could give higher order models, in which genetic variations were included, too.

The computational needs of the algorithm are high. An increase by one of the number of factors per combination increases disproportionately the necessary running time. When the algorithm was set to run for eight factors the running would took more four weeks to complete in the available cluster machine. Thus, the algorithm seems satisfactory to reveal low order interactions in such a large dataset, while demands very powerful computers to run for higher order models.

Future work shall include using pMDR to find higher-order models together with the relevant rules of interactions. This would enable the comparison of the results with the subset of factors derived from the PDM-ANN and GA-ANN methods in our previous work.. This is a very computationally intensive task and could be become possible by executing the pMDR algorithm in parallel processes in a high-performance computer cluster or Grid, appropriate for large-scale bioinformatics applications. Future work may also combine the approach of the current work with the previous ones conducted on the same dataset using the ANN-based methods. The most important factors identified by the latter could be passed into pMDR, in order to construct rules of interaction among them and gain more information.

6   Conclusions

In this study, the pMDR algorithm was used to analyze a large set of data from a nutrigenetics study on almost 2300 people, for all of which 63 genetic/nutritional factors, gender and BMI were recorded. The dimensionality reduction that was feasible with the available computing processing power reduced the 63 factors into seven. From the models derived, the one showing the greatest accuracy and least prediction error consisted of two factors, namely saturated fat intake and gender. The information from the remaining higher order models is also informative, as it gives insights about the interactions among them towards the development of obesity. The higher order models showed some consistency in the factors included with the ones identified by the previously ANN-based methods applied to the same dataset.

Acknowledgement. KK would like to thank the A.G. Leventis Foundation.

References

1. McGee, D.: Diverse Populations Collaboration: Body mass index and mortality: A meta-analysis based on person-level data from twenty-six observational studies. Ann. Epidemio. 15, 87–97 (2004)
2. Wilson, P., D'Agostino, R., Sullivan, L., Parise, H., Kannel, W.: Overweight and obesity as determinants of cardiovascular risk: The Framingham experience. Arch. Intern. Med. 162, 1867–1872 (2002)
3. Ordovas, J., Mooser, V.: Nutrigenomics and nutrigenetics. Curr. Opin. Lipidol. 15, 101–108 (2004)
4. Moore, J.H.: The ubiquitous nature of epistasis in determining susceptibility to common human diseases. Human Heredity 56, 73–82 (2003)
5. Hunter, D.J.: Gene-environment interactions in human diseases. Nature Reviews Genetics 6(4), 287–298 (2005)
6. Andreasen, C.H., Andersen, G.: Gene-environment interactions and obesity–further aspects of genomewide association studies. Nutrition 25(10), 998–1003 (2009)
7. Karnehed, N., Tynelius, P., Heitmann, B.L., Rasmussen, F.: Physical activity, diet and gene-environment interactions in relation to body mass index and waist circumference: the Swedish young male twins study. Public Health Nutr. 9, 851–858 (2006)
8. Robitaille, J., Pérusse, L., Bouchard, C., Vohl, M.C.: Genes, Fat Intake, and Cardiovascular Disease Risk Factors in the Quebec Family Study. Obesity 15, 2336–2347 (2007)

9. Valavanis, I., Mougiakakou, S., Grimaldi, K., Nikita, K.: A multifactorial analysis of obesity as CVD risk factor: Use of neural network based methods in a nutrigenetics context. BMC Bioinformatics 11, 453 (2010)
10. Heidema, A., Boer, J., Nagelkerke, N., Mariman, E., van der, A.D., Feskens, E.: The challenge for genetic epidemiologists: how to analyze large numbers of SNPs in relation to complex diseases. BMC Genet. 7, 23 (2006)
11. Hahn, L., Ritchie, M., Moore, J.: Multifactor dimensionality reduction software for detecting gene-gene and gene-environment interactions. Bioinformatics 19, 376–382 (2003)
12. Williams, S., Ritchie, M., Phillips, J., Dawson, E., Prince, M., Dzhura, E., Willis, A., Semenya, A., Summar, M., White, B., Addy, J., Kpodonu, J., Wong, L., Felder, R., Jose, P., Moore, J.: Multilocus analysis of hypertension: a hierarchical approach. Hum. Hered. 57, 28–38 (2004)
13. Cho, Y., Ritchie, M., Moore, J., Park, J., Lee, K., Shin, H., Lee, H., Park, K.: Multifactor-dimensionality reduction shows a two locus interaction associated with Type 2 diabetes mellitus. Diabetologia. 47, 549–554 (2004)
14. Ritchie, M., Hahn, L., Roodi, N., Bailey, L., Dupont, W., Parl, F., Moore, J.: Multifactor-dimensionality reduction reveals high-order interactions among estrogen-metabolism genes in sporadic breast cancer. Am. J. Hum. Genet. 69, 128–147 (2001)
15. Bush, W., Dudek, S., Ritchie, M.: Parallel Multifactor Dimensionality Reduction: a tool for the large scale analysis of gene-gene interactions. Bioinformatics 22, 2173–2174 (2006)
16. Arkadianos, I., Valdes, A., Marinos, E., Florou, A., Gill, R., Grimaldi, K.: Improved weight management using genetic information to personalize a calorie controlled diet. Nutr. J. 6, 29 (2007)

Coupling Regulatory Networks and Microarays: Revealing Molecular Regulations of Breast Cancer Treatment Responses

Lefteris Koumakis[1], Vassilis Moustakis[1,2], Michalis Zervakis[3], Dimitris Kafetzopoulos[4], and George Potamias[1,*]

[1] Institute of Computer Science, FORTH
{koumakis,potamias}@ics.forth.gr
[2] Department of Production Engineering, Technical Univsrsity of Chania
moustakis@dpem.tuc.gr
[3] Department of Electronic and Computer Engineering, Technical University of Chania
michalis@display.tuc.gr
[4] Institute of Molecular Biology & Biotechnology, FORTH
kafetzo@imbb.forth.gr

Abstract. Moving towards the realization of genomic data in clinical practice, and following an individualized healthcare approach, the function and regulation of genes has to be deciphered and manifested. Two of the most significant forms of molecular data come form microarray gene expression sources, and gene interactions sources – as encoded in Gene Regulatory Networks (GRNs). The usual computational task is the gene selection procedure with the GRNs to be mainly utilized for annotation and enrichment purposes. In this study we present a novel perception of these resources. Initially we locate all functional **path-modules** encoded in GRNs and we try to assess which of them are compatible and match the gene-expression profiles of samples that belong to different phenotypes. The differential power of the selected path-modules is computed and their biological relevance is assessed. The whole approach was applied on a set of microarray studies with the target of revealing putative regulatory mechanisms that govern and putatively guide the treatment responses of BRCA patients. The results were quite satisfactory according to their biological and clinical relevance.

1   Introduction

Advances in highthroughput technologies (e.g., microarrays, SNP mapping and copy-number variations etc.) have put the foundation stones for the vision of contemporary *personalized medicine*. On the other hand, *systems biology* follows a 'holistic' approach in order to explore and study the behavior of biological components, trying to uncover and model cell interaction events and, in a way, reproduce the function of organisms. In such a context, we need computational methods that not only combine information and data from dispersed and heterogeneous data sources but also distil the knowledge and provide a systematic, genome-scale view of biology [1]. The

I. Maglogiannis, V. Plagianakos, and I. Vlahavas (Eds.): SETN 2012, LNAI 7297, pp. 239–246, 2012.
© Springer-Verlag Berlin Heidelberg 2012

advantage of this approach is that it can identify emergent properties of the underlying molecular system as a 'whole' – an endeavor of limited success if targeted genes, reactions or even molecular pathways are studied in isolation. Genes and proteins do not function independently, but participate in complex, interconnected pathways and *gene regulatory networks* (GRN) that govern the function of cells, tissues, organs and organisms seen as functional biological systems and not just as a 'bag of molecules' [2]. At the same time, most of the known and established GNRs are based on laborious wet-lab experiments that make their generation and validation a rather difficult as well as time- and cost-consuming task. A major challenge is to accelerate our understanding of the *molecular mechanisms* of these variations and to produce targeted individualized therapies. Faced with such a challenge we devised and present an integrated methodology that 'amalgamates' knowledge and data from both GRNs and MA gene-expression sources. A preliminary realization of the methodology is implemented in a system called *MinePath*. MinePath aims to uncover potential gene-regulatory 'fingerprints' and mechanisms that underlie and govern the molecular profiles of diseases.

2   Microarrays and GRNs: Techniques and Limitations

MA experiments involve more variables (genes) than samples (patients). This fact, leads to results with poor biological significance. To remedy this there is an open debate whether we should concentrate on gathering more data or on building new algorithms. Simon et al., [3], published a very strict criticism on the common pitfalls of microarray data mining, while in [4] the authors comment about the bias in the gene selection procedure.

   In the light of the these observations, and in order to overcome the posted limitations we have to view MA based gene-expression profiles *just as an instance* of biological information, strongly connected - rather than isolated, from other sources of related biological knowledge, e.g., GRNs. GRNs are network structures that depict the interaction of DNA segments during the transcription of the genes into mRNA. From a computational point of view, GRNs can be conceived as analogue biochemical computers that regulate the level of expression of target genes [5]. The network by itself acts as a mechanism that determines cellular behavior where the nodes are genes and edges are functions that represent the molecular reactions between the nodes. These functions can be perceived as Boolean functions, where nodes have only two possible states ("on" and "off"), and the whole network represented as a simple *directed graph* [6]. It is indicative that most of the relations in known and established GRNs have been derived from laborious and extensive laboratory experiments and careful study of the existing biochemical literature. Thus GRNs are far from complete.

   A number of different methodologies have been proposed to help overcome this, and help to identify useful biological knowledge from GRNs with very few of them to be considered superior to the others - mainly because of the intrinsically noisy property of the data, 'the curse of dimensionality', and the unknown 'true' underlying networks. In this paper we present a novel methodology that couples microarray gene-expression profiles wit GRNs. The methodology aims towards the identification of differentially expressed functional GRN *path-modules*.

3   MinePath: Revealing Phenotype-Specific Regulation

Online public repositories contain a variety of information that includes not only the GRNs per se but links and rich annotations for the respective nodes (genes) and edges (reactions). In the current study we utilize the KEGG pathways repository[1]. KEGG provides a format representation standardized by its own markup description language (KGML[2]). A preliminary implementation of our methodology is implemented in a system called *MinePath*, and it unfolds into four phases. **(i) Pathway decomposition.** MinePath relies on a novel approach for GRN processing that takes into account all possible functional interactions of the network, i.e., the network's functional sub-paths. Different GRNs are downloaded from the KEGG repository. With an XML parser (operated on KEGG's KGML representation scheme of GRNs) the network is **decomposed** into its all-possible sub-paths (see Figure 1.a for an exemplification). After parsing a set of (targeted) GRNs, the decomposed sub-paths are stored in a database that acts as a repository for future reference. As the database repository could contain sub-paths from a variety of different GRNs we may combine different molecular pathways and networks – a major need for molecular biology and a big challenge for systems biology and contemporary bioinformatics research.

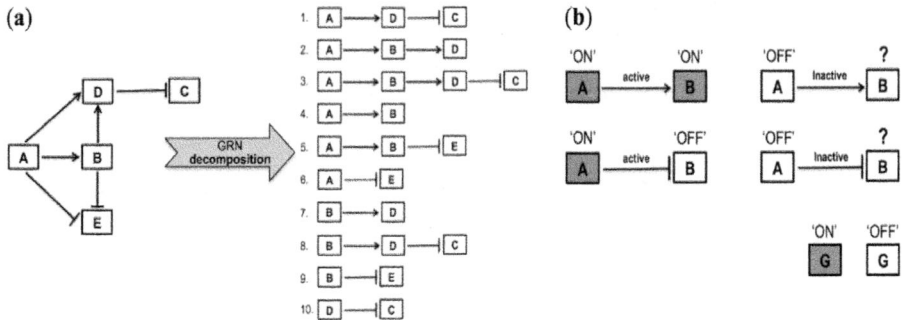

Fig. 1. (a) GRN decomposition: the artificial GRN (left) is decomposed into its all-possible sub-paths (10; right). (b) Functional path-modules: a reaction is considered as 'active' only-and-only-if its starting gene is active (e.g., 'ON' → 'ON' or, 'ON' ⊣ 'OFF' for active activation/expression or, inhibition reactions, respectively; otherwise is considered as inactive, 'OFF' → ? or, 'OFF' ⊣ ?, with the state of the regulated gene on the right of the reaction being undetermined).

(ii) Inference of functional path-modules. Each GRN sub-path is interpreted according to Kauffman's principles and semantics [6]: ① the network is a directed graph with genes (inputs and outputs) being the graph nodes and the edges between them representing the *causal* links between them, i.e., the *regulatory* reactions; ② each node can be in one of the two states, 'ON', the gene is expressed or up-regulated (i.e., the respective substance being present) or, 'OFF', the gene is not-expressed or

[1] KEGG: Kyoto Encyclopedia of Genes and Genomes; http://www.genome.jp/kegg/
[2] KGML (KEGG Markup Language); http://www.genome.jp/kegg/xml/

down-regulated; and ③ time is viewed as proceeding in discrete steps - at each step the new state of a node is a Boolean function of the prior states of the nodes with arrows pointing towards it. In order to cope with and reveal functional regulatory mechanisms we impose over the formed sub-paths the following requirement: for a sub-path to be considered as functional it should be 'active' during the GRN regulation process - in other words we assume that all genes in a sub-path are functional. For example consider the reaction A → B (see Figure 1.b), if A is 'ON' then the activation/expression ('→') regulatory reaction is active, resulting into the activation/expression of gene B ('ON') – the same holds for an inhibition (—⊣) reaction. In the case that gene A is 'OFF' then the reaction is considered as inactive with the state of the regulated gene B to remain undetermined ('?'). Under this assumption, a **path-module** is just a sub-path (atomic or more complex) for which all its reactions are considered as active. So, the state of all genes engaged in a path-module that forms an *ordered regulation pattern*, e.g., the pattern of the complex regulatory mechanism A → D —⊣ C is <'ON', 'ON', 'OFF'>.

(**iii**) **Matching gene-expression profiles and path-modules.** The next step is to locate microarray experiments and respective gene-expression data for which we expect (suspect) the targeted GRNs play an important role - for example, the cell-cycle and apoptosis GRNs play an important role in tumorgenesis and cancer progression. The samples of a binary transformed (discretized) gene-expression matrix are matched against functional path-modules of target GRNs. (retrieved form the described repository). We follow an information-theoretic gene-expression discretization process (detailed in [7]).

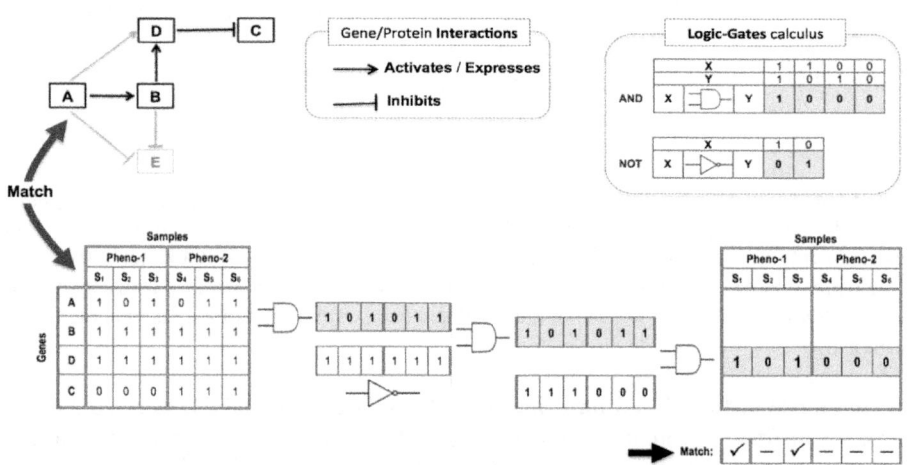

Fig. 2. Matching gene-expression sample profiles with GRN functional path-modules: a logic-gates approach

As an example, assume the gene-expression binary profiles of six artificial samples for genes A, B, D and C - with '1' to denote 'ON' and '0' to denote 'OFF' - three of them are assigned to phenotype-1 (S_1, S_2, and S_3) and the other three to phenotype-2 (S_4, S_5, and S_6) – refer to Figure 2. Furthermore, assume the artificial GRN shown in the lower left part of Figure 2, and its sub-path A → B → D ⊣ C (in bold). We fol-low a **logic-gates** process that aims to match the path-module instance of the sub-path with the respective samples' binary instances. The process results into the formation of an ordered pattern that indicate the samples for which the target sub-path is consis-tent with ('1's) or not ('0's), i.e., the respective path-module A='ON' → B='ON' → D='ON' ⊣ C='OFF' is active.

(iv) The differential-power of path-modules. Note that for the finally inferred pat-tern of Figure 2, <1,0,1,0,0,0>, value '1' occurs in positions one and three which means that the examined path-module is active for samples one and three; in all other samples it is inactive ('0'). As samples one and three belong to phenotype-1, the tar-get path-module matches 2 out of 3 phenotype-1 samples, and zero phenotype-2 sam-ples. In general, assume that there are S_1 and S_2 samples that belong to phenotype-1 and phenotyp2, respectively, and that path-module P_i matches $S_{i;1}$ and $S_{i;2}$ samples form phenotype-1 and phenotype-2, respectively. Formula 1, computes the **differen-tial power** of a path-module with respect to the two phenotypic classes;

$$\frac{S_{i;1}}{S_1} - \frac{S_{i;2}}{S_2} \tag{1}$$

The formula posses a *polarity* characteristic according the class phenotype: positive for class S_1 and negative for class S_2; e.g., for the above example, the differential power of path-module A='ON' → B='ON' → D='ON' ⊣ C='OFF' is (2/3) – 0 = 0.67, and as it positive it is interpreted and considered as a regulation mechanism that governs phenotype-1.

4   The Regulation of Breast Cancer Treatment Response

Most of breast cancer (BRCA) cases are estrogen responsive, a series of growth-promoting pathways are activated, for example, the estrogen receptor (ER) related ErbB signaling GRN. In an effort to reveal the underlying regulatory mechanisms that govern BRCA patients' treatment responses we applied the presented MinePath methodology on a set of four independent gene-expression studies targeting the ER phenotypic status of the respective patients, i.e., ER+ (ER positive) vs. ER- (ER negative). The details of the gene-expression data from the four studies are: GSE2034 (the GEO-Gene Expression Omnibus[3] study code), 286 patients [8]; GSE2990, 183 patients [9]; GSE3494, 247 patients [10]; and GSE7390, 198 patients [11]. We targeted 14 pathways, all of which are engaged within the 'Pathways in Cancer' integrated pathway (KEGG code: hsa05200), e.g., ErbB (hsa04012), MAPK (hsa04010), mTOR (hsa04150) etc. After applying the aforementioned matching process we selected the 100 path-modules with the highest differential power – 50 for ER+ and 50 for the ER- phenotypes, respectively. Inspecting the results we observed that the pathway that engage a significantly larger, with respect to all other targeted pathways, number of the selected sub-paths is the ErbB signaling pathway. Figure 3 shows the ErbB signaling pathway as colored with the help of the KEGG Mapper/Search&Color[4] tool (symbols and coloring scheme are shown at the bottom

---

[3] http://www.ncbi.nlm.nih.gov/geo/
[4] http://www.genome.jp/kegg/mapper.html

of the figure). Note the two different functional path *cascades* for the ER+ (black arrows) and ER- (grey arrows) phenotypes, respectively. Both have extra-cellular origins:

❶ The ER- path originates from TGFα (transforming growth factor, alpha), AR (amphiregulin), BTC (betacellulin), and EPR (epiregulin) epidermal growth factors that activate both **ErbB-1** and **ErbB-2** EGF-receptors; then, the two receptors initiate the path GRB2 → GAB1 → **PI3K** → **PKB/Akt** that guides to the activation of mTOR that activates p70S6K which signals "protein synthesis", and inhibits BAD which signals "cell survival";

❷ The ER+ path originates from the extra-cellular NRG1, NRG2 (neuregulin1,2) growth factors that activate **ErbB-3** and **ErbB-4** viral oncogenes followed by the **PI3K** → **PKB/Akt** activation reaction which is also part of the ER- path. But now, PKB/Akt acts just as an inhibitor of GSK-3 and blocking of "Metabolism". Moreover, PKB/Akt activates mTOR, which now acts as an inhibitor of EIF-4EBP with the result of blocking "protein synthesis". According to the recent biomedical literature the aforementioned results are quite relevant to the estrogen-receptor status - we focused our exploration on the mechanisms underlying the resistance to pure estrogen antagonists (e.g., fulvestrant5).

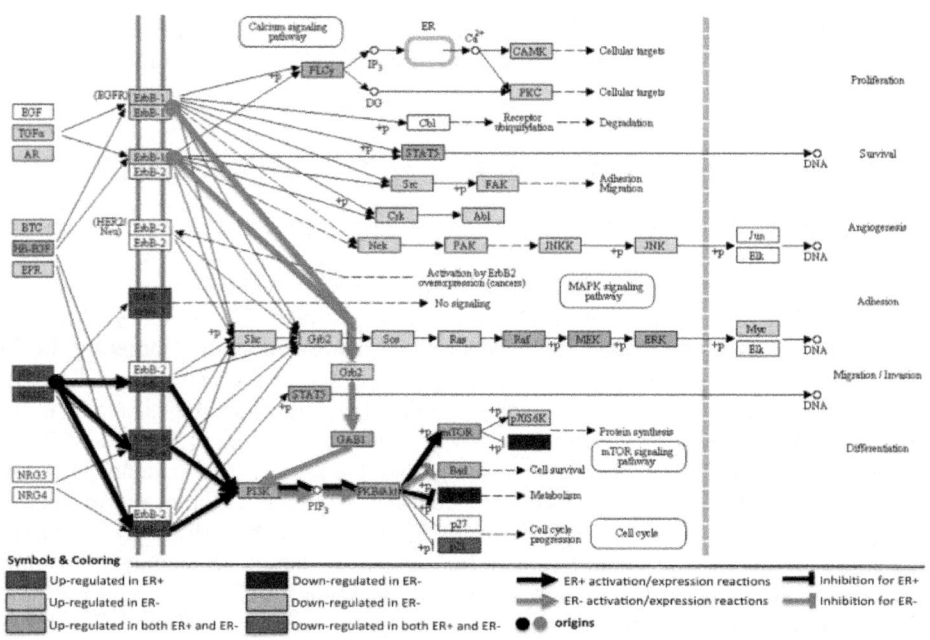

Fig. 3. Regulation of ER+ and ER- phenotypes in the ErbB signaling GRN

---

[5] Fulvestrant (Faslodex, AstraZeneca) is a drug treatment of hormone receptor-positive metastatic BRCA in postmenopausal women with disease progression following anti-estrogen therapy.

Recent studies show the significant role of both ErbB3 and ErbB4 as alternative targets for the treatment of BRCA patients; as Sutherland notes in [12]: "*... recent studies now implicates the other two ErbB family members, ErbB-3 and -4. Exposure of ER+ breast cancer cells to the pure antiestrogen, fulvestrant, increased levels of ErbB-3 or ErbB-4 and sensitivity to the growth-stimulatory effects of heregulin β1, a potent ligand for these receptors. Thus, the initial growth inhibitory effects of fulvestrant appear compromised by cellular plasticity that allows rapid compensatory growth stimulation via ErbB-3/4 ...*"; In addition, Hutcheson et al., [13], investigated whether induction of ErbB3 and/or ErbB4 may provide an alternative resistance mechanism to antihormonal action - their conclusion is that fulvestrant treatment is sensitive to the actions of the ErbB3/4 ligand HRGb1 (NRG1) with enhanced ErbB3/4-driven signaling activity, and significant increases in cell proliferation; the same results are also reported in other relevant studies related to the treatment of BRCA patients [14, 15].

5   Conclusions

We have presented an integrated methodology for the coupling of both GRNs and MA gene expression profiles. In the heart of the methodology are the decomposition of GRNs into functional sub-paths, and the matching of these sub-paths with samples' gene expression profiles, in order to compute their differential power with target phenotypic classes. The whole methodology is preliminary implemented in a system called MinePath. MinePath was applied on a set of four gene-expression studies with the target of identifying putative mechanisms that underlie and govern the treatment response of BRCA patients according to their ER-status profiles. Results were quite indicative and strongly supported by the relevant biomedical literature. Our on-going work and future R&D plans include: (a) further experimentation with various real-world microarray studies and different GRNs; (c) elaboration on more sophisticated path/gene-expression profile matching formulas and operations; (d) incorporation of different gene coding schemes in order to cope with microarray experiments from different platforms and nomenclatures; (e) incorporation of a GRN visualization component, and (e) porting of the whole methodology in a scientific workflow environment enabled by the development of respective Web-Services.

References

1. Ideker, T., Galitski, T., Hood, L.: A new approach to decoding life: systems biology. Annual Review of Genomics and Human Genetics 2, 343–372 (2001)
2. Collins, F.S., Eric, D., Green, E.D., Guttmacher, A.E., Mark, S., Guyer, M.S.: A vision for the future of genomics research. Nature 422, 835–847 (2003)
3. Simon, R., Radmacher, M.D., Dobbin, K., McShane, L.M.: Pitfalls in the Use of DNA Microarray Data for Diagnostic Classification. Journal of the National Cancer Institute 95(1), 14–18 (2003)
4. Ambroise, C., McLachlan, G.J.: Selection bias in gene extraction on the basis of microarray gene-expression data. PNAS 99(10), 6562–6566 (2002)

5. Arkin, A., Ross, J.: Computational functions in biochemical reaction networks. Biophys. J. 67(2), 560–578 (1994)
6. Kauffman, S.A.: The Origins of Order: Self-Organization and Selection in Evolution. Oxford Univ. Press, New York (1993)
7. Potamias, G., Koumakis, L., Moustakis, V.: Gene Selection via Discretized Gene-Expression Profiles and Greedy Feature-Elimination. In: Vouros, G.A., Panayiotopoulos, T. (eds.) SETN 2004. LNCS (LNAI), vol. 3025, pp. 256–266. Springer, Heidelberg (2004)
8. Wang, Y., et al.: Gene-expression profiles to predict distant metastasis of lymph-node-negative primary breast cancer. Lancet. 365(9460), 671–679 (2005)
9. Sotiriou, C., et al.: Gene expression profiling in breast cancer: understanding the molecular basis of histologic grade to improve prognosis. J. Natl. Cancer Inst. 98(4), 262–272 (2006)
10. Miller, L.D., et al.: An expression signature for p53 status in human breast cancer predicts mutation status, transcriptional effects, and patient survival. PNAS 102(38), 13550–13555 (2005)
11. Desmedt, C., et al.: Strong time dependence of the 76-gene prognostic signature for node-negative breast cancer patients in the TRANSBIG multicenter independent validation series. Clin. Cancer Res. 13(11), 3207–3214 (2007)
12. Sutherland, R.L.: Endocrine resistance in breast cancer: new roles for ErbB3 and ErbB4. Breast Cancer Research 13(3), 106 (2011)
13. Hutcheson, I.R., et al.: Heregulin beta1 drives gefitinib-resistant growth and invasion in tamoxifen-resistant MCF-7 breast cancer cells. Breast Cancer Research 9(4), R50 (2007)
14. Zhu, Y., Sullivan, L.L., Nair, S.S., Williams, C.C., Pandey, A.K., Marrero, L., Vadlamudi, R.K., Jones, F.E., et al.: Coregulation of estrogen receptor by ERBB4/HER4 establishes a growth-promoting autocrine signal in breast tumor cells. Cancer Research 66(16), 7991–7998 (2006)
15. Sonne-Hansen, K., et al.: Breast cancer cells can switch between estrogen receptor alpha and ErbB signaling and combined treatment against both signaling pathways postpones development of resistance. Breast Cancer Research and Treatment 121(3), 601–613 (2010)

A Galaxy Workflow for the Functional Annotation of Metagenomic Samples

Eleftherios Pilalis[1], Eythymios Ladoukakis[2],
Fragiskos N. Kolisis[1,2], and Aristotelis Chatziioannou[1]

[1] Metabolic Engineering & Bioinformatics Group Institute of Biological
Research and Biotechnology, National Hellenic Research Foundation, Athens, Greece
{epilalis,kolisis,achatzi}@eie.gr
[2] Laboratory of Biotechnology, School of Chemical Engineering,
National Technical University of Athens, Athens, Greece

Abstract. In this work, an annotation workflow was developed, which performs a series of annotation tasks to sequences originating from metagenomic samples, using standard bioinformatics tools and Perl scripts. The Perl scripts interact with a Mysql database in order to store all annotation results to the respective tables, thus rendering easy the quick access and querying to all data. The whole pipeline was integrated into a Galaxy server, which provides a simple and intuitive interface that allows the user to easily create, run and share workflows for large datasets.

Keywords: Galaxy, Metagenomics, Gene Ontology Terms, Protein Function Prediction.

1   Introduction

Due to the recent advances in high-throughput sequencing, very large amounts of environmental DNA sequence data can be generated in a very short time. As a consequence, Metagenomics represent an emerging field with critical importance, as it describes the collection and analysis of the total DNA that is contained in an environmental niche [1]. Thus, sampling and analyzing environmental DNA is a promising way to identify novel genes, protein functions and enzymes, reflecting evolutionary adaptation to specific environmental conditions and therefore presenting great biotechnological and biomedical interest. However, the analysis of metagenomic data remains challenging, because of the complexity of microbial communities found in a particular environmental niche, the huge as well as heterogeneous genomic data volume   and the inherent noise that characterize these DNA sequence data.

This annotation workflow is part of a large metagenomics 7th Framework project, named Hotzyme, aiming to investigate the global biodiversity in hot terrestrial environments. Metagenomics has a great potential for assessing biodiversity and for enzyme discovery. This technology has been applied mainly to soil and marine water samples which revealed an enormous biological and molecular diversity. But to date,

I. Maglogiannis, V. Plagianakos, and I. Vlahavas (Eds.): SETN 2012, LNAI 7297, pp. 247–253, 2012.

very little work has been done on hot terrestrial environments, mainly due to the difficulty of access to various hot environments and the relatively lower concentration of biomass in such ecological systems [2]. This project aims to address this problem by screening for a new generation of (hyper)thermostable hydrolases from hot terrestial environments. Although thermostable hydrolases have been known for many years, the related research and applications have been limited to cultivated thermophilic microorganisms. Since most microorganisms (>99%) cannot easily be cultivated, many potentially active enzymes have never been characterized. This is particularly true for thermostable enzymes, since the number of isolated and characterized (hyper) thermophiles is very small. Therefore, the diversity of thermophiles and their encoded enzymes remains largely unexplored.

The analysis of metagenomic data begins with the assembly of the small DNA fragments, which are generated from the sequencer, to larger sequences called contigs. Then, the contigs are used as the main input to gene and protein function prediction algorithms. Although various tools have been developed for these purposes, it yet remains challenging from the computational aspect to handle efficiently the versatile different annotation tasks required. Therefore, we developed an automatic annotation workflow for metagenomic samples, integrated into the Galaxy platform. Galaxy [3] is an open-source framework for the integration of computational tools and databases into a cohesive workspace and can be used for data intensive biomedical research. Galaxy provides a user-friendly web interface where users can develop, execute and share workflows of complex analyses that can be repeated on many different datasets, or refactored for different computing purposes. The users have the option of using a public server for their analysis or to install a fully customizable local instance on their own server. The platform itself includes pre-configured tools for NGS analysis but also allows for integration of customized tools by each user with access to the server.

2   The Annotation Workflow

The pipeline (summarized in Figure 1) is initialized, complying with the specifications set by the user regarding the file containing the pair-end reads of the metagenomic experiment (fasta or fastq file). Subsequently, the following tasks are performed:

- Application of the Velvet program [4] for the assembly of the metagenomic reads to larger sequences (contigs)
- Parsing of the fasta file (contig_parser.pl) generated by the assembler, in order to populate the database with the basic information on the contigs (name, sequence and sample description included in the fasta file).

- Application of the Getorf program of the EMBOSS suite [5], in order to obtain putative open reading frames, within the contigs, that encode proteins. The output file of Getorf is parsed by a Perl script (getorf_parser.pl) and the results are stored into the Mysql database (table getorf).
- BlastN [6] search (nucleotidic blast) of the nucleotidic contig sequences against the Refseq [7] genomic database. The default threshold of high-scoring segment pairs (HSP) evalue is set to 0.001. The results of the Blast search are parsed by a Perl script (blastn_parser.pl) and are stored into the Mysql database (table blastn).
- Translation of the contigs to the corresponding aminoacids sequences (for all 6 reading frames) using the Transeq program of the EMBOSS suite, and submission of the peptidic sequences to BlastP [6] search (protein blast) against the Refseq protein database (default threshold HSP evalue set to 0.001). The results of the Blast search are parsed by a Perl script (blastp_parser.pl) and are stored into the Mysql database (table blastp).
- Submission of the peptidic sequences to a Hmmer [8] search against the Pfam [9] database (gathered threshold parameter), in order to obtain the annotation of the protein domains that are comprised in the peptides. The results of the Hmmer search are parsed by a Perl script (hmmer_parser.pl) and are stored into the Mysql database (table hmmer).
- Attribution of Gene Ontology terms [10] to the contigs, based on the protein homologs from the Refseq database (go_refseq.pl).

Consequently, once the pipeline is terminated, the Mysql database is filled with a wide range of annotations related to putative functions of the metagenomics sequences. The nucleotide blast search provides the information about the phylogenetic origin of the sequences that are found in the environmental sample. The protein blast search provides homologous sequences at the protein level, which is the first step of functional annotation. Additionally, the Hmmer search provides the independent protein domains that are found in the sample. It is noteworthy that the Hmmer algorithm uses Markov chain models that render it very sensitive to remote homologies. Thus, it is a very efficient tool for the detection of protein functions even for sequences with very weak conservation compared to known proteins with established function. Finally, the database contains the Gene Ontology Terms that are attributed to the contigs on the basis of the detected homology with the proteins of the Refseq database. Homology is assessed using a maximum user-specified threshold of Blast HSP e-value. The Mysql database provides an easy and immediate access to all aforementioned results. All tables are linked by a unique contig id and hence all annotations of every contig can be easily and intuitively retrieved by SQL queries.

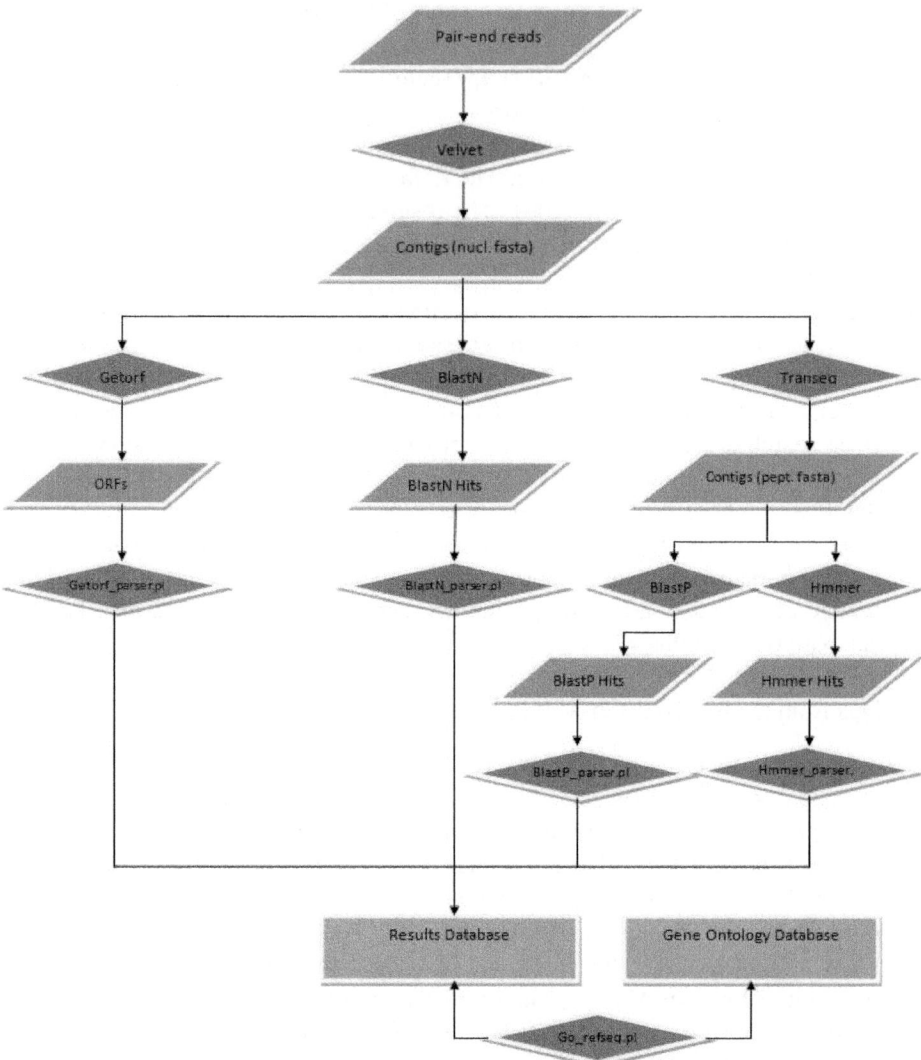

Fig. 1. The metagenomic annotation pipeline

3   Integration of Bioinformatics Tools/Algorithms

3.1   Stand-Alone Programs

- Velvet [4]: de novo metagenomic assembler based on de Bruijn graphs
- Blast + (Basic Local Alignment Search Tool) [6]: Finds regions of local similarity between sequences.

- Hmmer [8]: Implements profile hidden Markov models as probabilistic models to perform sequence comparisons against protein families (alignments) of the Pfam [9] database
- Emboss transeq [5]: Translates nucleotide sequences to peptide sequences
- Emboss getorf [5]: Finds and extracts open reading frames (ORFs) on input nucleotide sequences

3.2 Public Databases

- Refseq (genomic and protein) [7]: A comprehensive, non-redundant and well annotated database of genomes and proteins
- Pfam [9]: An extensive and highly curated database of protein domains, classified in families. It is a valuable resource of information on the functionality of query proteins

3.3 Scripts

contig_parser.pl

Usage: **contig_parser.pl** contig_file.fasta contig_file.log db_name db_user_name db_password

- creates a Mysql database, the name of which is specified by the user (*db_name*)
- creates table *contig* into the database
- parses a fasta file containing the assembled contigs and fills table *contig* with all contigs

getorf_parser.pl

Usage: **getorf_parser.pl** getorf.out getorf_parser.log db_name db_user_name db_password

- creates table *getorf* into the database
- parses a *Getorf* output file and stores the results into the *getorf* table

blastn_parser.pl

Usage: **blastn_parser.pl** blastn.out blastn_parser.log db_name db_user_name db_password

- creates table *blastn* into the Mysql database
- parses a BlastN (nucleotice Blast) output file and stores the Blast results into the *blastn* table

blastp_parser.pl

Usage: **blastp_parser.pl** blastp.out blastp_parser.log db_name db_user_name db_password

- creates table *blastp* into the Mysql database
- parses a BlastP (protein Blast) output file and stores the Blast results into the *blastp* table

hmmer_parser.pl

Usage: **hmmer_parser.pl** hmmer.out hmmer_parser.log db_name
db_user_name db_password
- creates table *hmmer* into the database
- parses a *Hmmer* output file and stores the results into the *hmmer* table

go_refseq.pl

Usage: **go_refseq.pl hsp**_evalue_threshold go_refseq.log
database user_name password

- creates table go_refseq into the database
- uses the BlastP results in order to retrieve the Gene Ontology Terms from the homologous proteins. Homology is assessed using a maximum user-specified threshold of blast HSP e-value (default 0.001), in the Refseq protein database. The Refseq annotations are contained in the Gene Ontology database, which was downloaded as a flat file from the Gene Ontology consortium website [11] and imported into a Mysql database called go.

4   Conclusion

Automated workflows are efficient tools for the performance of data mining tasks by users not expert in computing, but also for the efficient handling and analysis of very large datasets, such as metagenomic sequences. The workflow presented here is a comprehensive tool for annotation of metagenomic datasets, starting from the raw output of DNA sequencers (raw sequence reads) and leading to a complete database of functional annotation of the assembled sequences. The integration of the workflow into the Galaxy platform provides an intuitive and easily accessible tool for every biologist needing to handle very large datasets with little to no expertise in bioinformatics. Further development of the workflow will include ready to apply advanced queries, availability of other genomic/protein databases an integration of functional annotation tools that employ Gene Ontology and pathway enrichment analysis (ex Stranger [12]).

Acknowledgements. The presented work in this paper has been funded by the EU/FP7/KBBE-2010.3.5-04 Microbial diversity and metagenomic mining for biotechnological innovation, "Systematic screening for novel hydrolases from hot environments" project (Hotzyme).

References

1. Desai, N., et al.: From genomics to metagenomics. Curr. Opin. Biotechnol. (2011)
2. Lorenz, P., Eck, J.: Metagenomics and industrial applications. Nat. Rev. Microbiol. 3(6), 510–516 (2005)
3. Giardine, B., et al.: Galaxy: a platform for interactive large-scale genome analysis. Genome Res. 15(10), 1451–1455 (2005)

4. Zerbino, D.R., Birney, E.: Velvet: algorithms for de novo short read assembly using de Bruijn graphs. Genome Res. 18(5), 821–829 (2008)
5. Rice, P., Longden, I., Bleasby, A.: EMBOSS: the European Molecular Biology Open Software Suite. Trends Genet. 16(6), 276–277 (2000)
6. Altschul, S.F., et al.: Basic local alignment search tool. J. Mol. Biol. 215(3), 403–410 (1990)
7. Pruitt, K.D., Tatusova, T., Maglott, D.R.: NCBI reference sequences (RefSeq): a curated non-redundant sequence database of genomes, transcripts and proteins. Nucleic Acids Res. 35(Database issue), D61–D65 (2007)
8. Finn, R.D., Clements, J., Eddy, S.R.: HMMER web server: interactive sequence similarity searching. Nucleic Acids Res. 39(Web Server issue), W29–W37 (2011)
9. Bateman, A., et al.: The Pfam protein families database. Nucleic Acids Res. 32(Database issue), D138–D141 (2004)
10. Ashburner, M., et al.: Gene ontology: tool for the unification of biology. The Gene Ontology Consortium. Nat. Genet. 25(1), 25–29 (2000)
11. http://www.geneontology.org/GO.downloads.database.shtml
12. Chatziioannou, A.A., Moulos, P.: Exploiting Statistical Methodologies and Controlled Vocabularies for Prioritized Functional Analysis of Genomic Experiments: the StRAnGER Web Application. Front Neurosci. 5, 8 (2011)

Bioinformatic Analysis of Expression Data of ApoE Deficient Mice

Olga Papadodima[1], Allan Sirsjo[2], and Aristotelis Chatziioannou[1]

[1] Institute of Biological Research and Biotechnology, National Hellenic Research Foundation,
48 Vas. Constantinou Ave., 11635 Athens, Greece
[2] School of Health and Medical Sciences, Division of Clinical Medicine,
University of Örebro, Sweden

Abstract. Atherosclerosis is a multifactorial disease involving a lot of genes and proteins recruited throughout its manifestation. The present study aims to exploit bioinformatic tools in order to analyze microarray data of atherosclerotic aortic lesions of ApoE knockout mice, a model widely used in atherosclerosis research. In particular, a dynamic analysis was performed among young and aged animals, resulting in a list of 852 significantly altered genes. Pathway analysis indicated alterations in critical cellular processes related to cell communication and signal transduction, immune response, lipid transport and metabolism. Cluster analysis partitioned the significantly differentiated genes in three major clusters of similar expression profile. Promoter analysis applied to functional related groups of the same cluster, revealed shared putative *cis*-elements potentially contributing to a common regulatory mechanism. Finally, by reverse engineering the functional relevance of differentially expressed genes with specific cellular pathways, putative genes acting as hubs were identified, linking functionally disparate cellular processes in the context of traditional molecular description.

Keywords: Microarray analysis, Atherosclerosis, transcriptomic analysis, promoter analysis.

1   Introduction

Atherosclerosis is the leading pathological contributor to cardiovascular morbidity and mortality worldwide, characterized by the progressive accumulation of lipid and fibrous depositions in the vessel wall of medium-sized and large arteries. Although it has traditionally been viewed as simple deposition of lipids within the vessel wall, it is now assumed that atherosclerosis is a multifactorial disease that involves several genes and proteins, activated during its genesis, progress and phenotypic manifestation. During atherogenesis, a complex endothelial activation and dysfunction induced by elevated and modified low-density lipoproteins and many other factors leads to a compensatory inflammatory response (1). Current evidence supports a central role for inflammation, in all phases of the atherosclerotic process. Substantial biological data implicate inflammatory pathways in early atherogenesis, in the progression of lesions, and finally in the thrombotic complications of this disease (2).

I. Maglogiannis, V. Plagianakos, and I. Vlahavas (Eds.): SETN 2012, LNAI 7297, pp. 254–261, 2012.
© Springer-Verlag Berlin Heidelberg 2012

Clinical investigations, population studies, and cell culture experiments have provided important clues to the pathogenesis of atherosclerosis. However, the use of animal models has had a crucial contribution in the research of the atherosclerotic course. Atherosclerosis will not be developed in laboratory mice under normal conditions. However, targeted deletion of the gene for Apolipoprotein E (ApoE knockout mice) leads to severe hypercholesterolemia and spontaneous atherosclerosis (3). For this reason, ApoE deficient mice are widely used to study atherosclerosis (4). ApoE is a ligand for receptors that clear chylomicrons and very low-density lipoprotein remnants. Furthermore, a number of population studies suggest that ApoE genotype predicts the risk of developing atherosclerosis and related diseases (5).

In this study, we present a bioinformatic analysis based on microarray data derived from ApoE knockout mice. Gene expression data of wild type and ApoE knockout 6, 32 and 78-weeks old mice were used. The dataset that we used was presented in a detailed work studying atherosclerosis and inflammatory pathways during aging (6). The workflow of our analysis consists of six basic steps: normalization, statistical selection, pathway analysis, clustering and promoter analysis. It has been successfully applied in a dynamic analysis of mastic oil treatment of cancer cells, providing novel evidence on the molecular basis of its inhibitory action on tumor growth (7). As a further step, in order to expand our knowledge regarding the functional implication of genes in various cellular processes, prioritizing them according to their centrality, we exploited the hierarchical structure of the Gene Ontology (GO) tree, and candidate hub-genes or interacting proteins were identified.

2   Materials and Methods

2.1   Microarray Data

The mouse dataset used is the GSE 10000, available at Gene Expression Omnibus (GEO) database. Microarrays were prepared following MIAME guidelines, as described in (6). Briefly, RNA from aortic tissue of apoE knockout and wild type animals was hybridized on Affymetrix 430 2.0 Arrays. Three different ages were studied: 6, 32 and 78 weeks.

2.2   Microarray Data Analysis and Statistical Analysis

Microarray data analysis was performed in Gene ARMADA (8). Briefly, background correction was performed employing its gcRMA method followed by Quantile Normalization. Data were $\log_2$ transformed to comply with the normality assumption. Differentially expressed genes in at least one among all the experimental conditions were identified using Gene ARMADA, by performing 1-way ANOVA on $\log_2$ transformed fold changes. The resulting gene list was obtained by setting the p-value threshold to 0.01, the False Discovery Rate (FDR) threshold to 0.05 and by removing genes that presented a fold change below |1|, in log2 scale, in all conditions.

2.3   Prioritized Pathway/Functional Analysis

Statistical enrichment analysis was performed using StRAnGER (9), in order to high-light biological processes including statistically significant numbers of the ANOVA derived genes. In order to expand our knowledge regarding the functional implication of genes in various cellular processes, prioritizing them according to their centrality, we used the online tool GORevenge (10) with the following settings: Aspect: BP (Biological Process), Distance: Graph, Algorithm: BubbleGene and Relaxation: 2.

2.4   Cluster and Promoter Analysis

The list derived from ANOVA was subjected to hierarchical clustering (linkage me-thod: Average, distance: Cosine) in Gene ARMADA. Promoter analysis was per-formed as previously described in (5), with the difference that only mouse promoters were considered.

3   Results

3.1   Statistically Significant Differentiated Genes

To obtain the aortic gene expression profile of ApoE deficient mice in 6, 32 and 78 week old mice we analyzed the GSE 10000 dataset, containing expression data of aortic tissue from wild type and ApoE knockout mice. Specifically, in order to identi-fy significant alterations among all three tested ages, 1-way ANOVA was applied to expression fold changes between expression in ApoE knockout and wild type animals (p value<0.01 and FDR<0.05) coupled with further filtering on fold change (>|1| in at least one condition in log2 scale). A list of 1033 significantly differentiated probsets was obtained, depicted per time point using a volcano plot representation (Figure 1). These 1033 probsets correspond to 852 annotated genes. It is characteristic that in 6 weeks old mice the number of significantly altered genes is very limited, in 32 weeks old mice the majority of differentiated genes are upregulated while in 78 weeks old mice we have the greater number of differentiated genes.

3.2   Pathway Analysis

For the scope of gaining further insight concerning the biological functionalities of gene expression alterations in a more systematic way, the list of 852 significantly differentiated genes yielded from ANOVA was subjected to statistical enrichment analysis using StRAnGER, exploiting GO terms and Kegg pathways for the task of the functional annotation of the interrogated genes. GO-based analysis focused on the categories of "Biological Process" with a hypergeometric p-value<0.001 suggested several processes as possibly differentiated which are presented in Table 1. A lot of central molecular mechanisms emerge as altered, as indicated by the GO categories listed in Table 1, like differentiation, proliferation (inferred by cell cycle and cell division GO terms) apoptosis, cell adhesion, signal transduction, and immune response. Kegg–based analysis also indicates alterations in cell adhesion and signal transduction. It is important to note that in conformity to the well established relationship of atherosclerosis and inflammation, the majority (29 out of 32) of the genes under the category "immune response" are upregulated suggesting a stimulation of the immunological mechanisms.

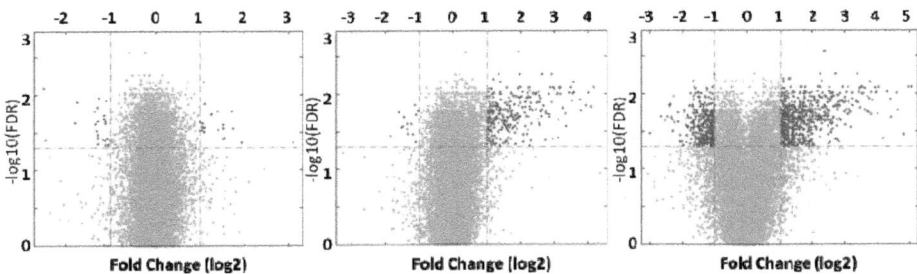

Fig. 1. Volcano plots of the gene list as yielded by ANOVA. Each panel represents filtered and normalized data from each experimental condition (3, 6 and 78 weeks old mice). The horizontal axes depict the fold change ratio between ApoE deficient and wild type mice, for each age in $\log_2$ scale while the vertical axes represent statistical significance by depicting the $-\log_{10}$(FDR).

3.3   Cluster Analysis

In order to identify groups of genes presenting similar expression and possibly comprising regulated "waves" of transcription, the list of 1033 significantly differentiated probesets was subjected to hierarchical clustering (Figure 2). Three major clusters can be distinguished: the first one contains transcripts downregulated in 78 week old mice, while their expression remains close to the control (wild type) level at 6 and 32 weeks. The second cluster groups genes which are upregulated at 32 weeks and their expression at ApoE knockout mice remains at high levels, as compared to wild type, also at 78 weeks. The third cluster groups genes whose expression is late upregulated at 78 week old ApoE knockout, as compared to age-matched wild type mice.

Based on these three major clusters, we performed GO-analysis to the genes of each cluster separately. Genes under cluster 1 are functionally connected to processes involved in cell differentiation, adhesion and signal transduction. Cluster 2 contains the greatest number of genes, which are related mainly to mechanisms involved in immune and inflammatory response as well as lipid metabolism. These processes emerge as significantly altered specifically in the case of cluster 2. Cluster 2 genes are also connected to key cellular processes like signal transduction, apoptosis, cell cycle and differentiation. Cluster 3 genes are mainly related to mechanisms concerning gene transcription.

Table 1. GO-analysis. The list of 852 significantly altered genes was submitted to GO analysis elucidating over-represented GO terms. GOT p-value represents the hypergeometric test p-value score for each GO term. Enrichment represents the ratio of the number of times a GO term occurs in the 852 gene list to the number of times this GO term exists in the list of the Affymetrix 430 2.0 array.

GO Annotation	GOT p-value	Enrichment
ion transport	0.00000000003	33/498
signal transduction	0.00000000004	44/803
cell differentiation	0.00000000005	36/480
immune response	0.00000000005	32/250
metabolic process	0.00000000007	38/542
cell adhesion	0.00000000011	36/387
protein amino acid phosphorylation	0.00000000059	32/497
multicellular organismal development	0.00000000128	41/770
proteolysis	0.00000000690	25/358
apoptosis	0.00000010814	24/383
lipid metabolic process	0.00000328813	15/212
protein transport	0.00003352383	22/465
G-protein coupled receptor signaling	0.00028681297	19/436
oxidation reduction	0.00034119987	21/510
cell cycle	0.00043684087	18/417
cell division	0.00050194998	12/231

3.4   Promoter Analysis

In order to investigate whether there are common regulatory transcriptional mechanisms in functional groups of genes revealed by the cluster-based GO analysis, we performed a representative promoter analysis in genes of cluster 2 belonging to the GO category "immune response" and "inflammatory response". We selected these categories because they are functionally relevant and because they contain an adequate number of genes (the total number of genes in both categories is 36). Table 2 summarizes statistically significant transcription factor (TF) motif families common in promoter sequences of these 36 genes, sorted in descending order in terms of statistical significance.

3.5   Identification of Candidate Hub-Genes

In order to expand our knowledge regarding which genes have critical role, taking into consideration their centrality as described in the GO tree, we used the online tool GORevenge (10). The list of 852 differentiated genes was submitted to GORevenge and the derived list of genes, containing candidate hub-genes, was partitioned to contain only the genes that have been also identified as statistically significantly differentiated. The derived list (Table 3) contains genes that were identified as significant both by ANOVA and by GORevenge analysis. Significant molecules involved in signaling and developmental mechanisms emerge as central players.

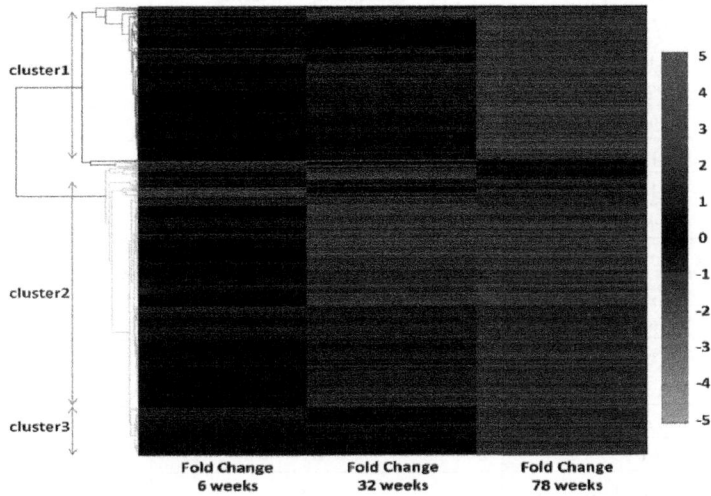

Fig. 2. Hierarchical clustering of the 1033 statistically significant differentiated probesets. Fold changes between the gene expressions in ApoE knockout as compared to age-matched wild type mice are grouped in three major clusters.

Table 2. Common TF motif families in the promoters of 36 genes belonging to cluster 2 and to the categories "immune response" and "inflammatory response". The percentage column depicts the percentage of genes whose promoters have at least one match with the respective motif family.

Family	Description	p-value	%
V$MZF1	Myeloid zinc finger 1 factors	0.00015	91
V$PLAG	Pleomorphic adenoma gene	0.00035	91
V$EREF	Estrogen response elements	0.00038	87
V$CP2F	CP2-erythrocyte Factor, Elf related	0.00046	83
V$SRFF	Serum response element binding factor	0.00060	87
V$CTCF	CTCF and BORIS gene family	0.00062	83
V$KLFS	Krueppel like transcription factors	0.00255	100
V$STAT	Signal transducer and activator of transcription	0.00289	96
V$RXRF	RXR heterodimer binding sites	0.00329	100
V$GREF	Glucocorticoid responsive elements	0.00337	91

Table 3. GOrevenge prioritization. The second column refers to the number of GO terms remaining after Gorevenge pruning, while the third column refers to the original number of bilobical process catecory GO terms of each gene. All presented genes are also differentially expressed. Top 20 genes are shown.

gene symbol	remaining GO terms	original GO terms
Wnt5a	95	112
Fgfr2	75	92
P2rx7	62	73
Igf1	49	56
Tlr2	42	47
Thbs1	41	42
Ptgs2	36	37
Slc11a1	34	40
Psen2	34	37
Ptprc	33	40
Ccnd1	32	37
Foxf1a	32	34
Osr1	30	33
Lyn	28	33
Col1a1	26	29
Adora1	25	25
Adam17	24	29
Cxcl12	24	27
Socs3	24	27

4   Discussion

In this study we presented a detailed bioinformatic analysis of ApoE knockout mice, exploiting different approaches in order to identify critical altered molecular mechanisms and important central players. It was shown that the gene expression profile in atherosclerotic plaques containing arteries of ApoE knockout mice is profoundly different from wild type. Specifically, 852 genes were found as differentially expressed and the majority of them appear after the age of 32 weeks. The indicated altered processes, as revealed by ontology-based enrichment analysis, include adhesion and signal transduction, differentiation, apoptosis and immune response, reflecting the cellular and molecular complexity of atherosclerosis and the cross-talk of endothelial and immune cells in aortic lesions. Cluster analysis revealed three major groups of genes with similar expression profiles which were further analyzed, in order to find functional (GO-based) sub-groups in each cluster. In agreement with the notion that atherosclerosis is an inflammatory disease, immune response and inflammation were the prominent categories indicated as significantly altered in the case of cluster 2, which contains genes upregulated both in 36 and 78 weeks old mice. Promoter analysis of the genes under these categories revealed common binding elements that could contribute to a common transcriptional regulation. In particular, all of the tested genes (100%) contain *cis*-elements of the RXR family. This family groups together motifs related to the receptors of retinoids, which are recognized by various heterodimers of retinoid X receptors (RXRs) and retinoic acid receptors. Interestingly, RXR has been reported to regulate several genes related to metabolic homeostasis and inflammation (11). Noteworthily, among the identified putative TF binding sites there are estrogen response elements (EREs) in the 87 % of the promoters as well as glucocorticoid responsive elements (GREs) in the 91 % of the tested promoters. It is well known that estrogen and glucocorticoid receptors play important roles in both physiological and pathological conditions involving immunity and inflammation (12). Finally, in the list of prioritized genes in table 3 we can distinguish several with important roles in atherosclerosis related mechanisms. It is noteworthy to mention Tlr2, a member of the Toll-like receptors family, which plays a fundamental role in activation of innate immunity (13). Furthermore, the identification of Psen2 (presenillin 2), a gene implicated in Alzheimer's disease, as candidate hub gene is interesting because genes implicated in Alzheimer have been reported to affect cholesterol or lipoprotein function and have also been implicated in atherosclerosis (14). Concluding, this bioinformatic analysis of ApoE knockout mice revealed critical altered cellular mechanisms governing atherosclerosis and indicated important molecular players.

References

1. Stoll, G., et al.: Stroke 37, 1923–1932 (2006)
2. Hansson, G.K.: N. Engl. J. Med. 352, 1685–1695 (2005)
3. Zhang, S.H., et al.: Science 258, 468–471 (1992)
4. Mahley, R.W., et al.: Annu. Rev. Genom. Hum. Genet. 1, 507–537 (2000)
5. Song, Y., et al.: Ann. Intern. Med. 141, 137–147 (2004)
6. Grabner, R., et al.: J. Exp. Med. 206, 233–248 (2009)
7. Moulos, P., Papadodima, O., et al.: BMC Med. Genomics 2, 68 (2009)
8. Chatziioannou, A., et al.: BMC Bioinformaics 10, 354 (2009)
9. Chatziioannou, A., et al.: Front. Neurosci. 5, 8 (2011)
10. Moutselos, K., et al.: IEEE Transactions on Biomedical Engineering 58, 12 (2011)
11. Nohara, A., et al.: J. Atheroscler Thromb 16, 303–318 (2009)
12. Gouni-Berthold, I., et al.: Curr. Drug Targets Cardiov. Haematol. Disord. 5, 513–523 (2005)
13. Borrello, S., et al.: Int. J. Immunopathol Pharmacol. 24(3), 549–556 (2011)
14. Carter, C.J.: Neurochem. Int. 50(1), 12–38 (2007)

Gene Ontology Semi-supervised Possibilistic Clustering of Gene Expression Data

Ioannis A. Maraziotis[1], George Dimitrakopoulos[1,2], and Anastasios Bezerianos[1]

[1] Department of Medical Physics, School of Medicine,
University of Patras, 26500, Patra, Hellas
[2] Department of Electrical and Computer Engineering,
University of Patras, 26500, Patra, Hellas
`imaraziotis@gmail.com, {geodimitrak,bezer}@upatras.gr`

Abstract. Clustering is one of the most important data analysis methods with applications of significant importance in many scientific fields. In computational biology, clustering of gene expression data from microarrays assists biologists to investigate uncharacterized genes by identifying biologically relevant groups of genes. Semi-supervised clustering algorithms have proven to bring substantial improvements in the results of standard clustering methods especially on datasets of increased complexity. In this paper we propose a semi-supervised possibilistic clustering algorithm (SSPCA) utilizing supervision via pair-wise constraints indicating whether a pair of patterns should belong to the same cluster or not. Furthermore we show how external sources of biological information like gene ontology data can provide constraints to guide the clustering process of SSPCA. Our results show that the proposed algorithm outperformed other well established standard and semi-supervised methodologies.

Keywords: possibilistic clustering, semi-supervision, constraints, gene ontology, gene expression.

1 Introduction

Clustering was, and still remains one of the most popular methods for the analysis of gene expression from microarray experiments, used to provide insight into the structure of the data and to aid at the discovery of biologically relevant groups of genes.

Initial computational efforts employed classical clustering techniques [1] for grouping genes according to their expression profile, based on the experimentally validated assumption that genes involved in the same biological process exhibit similar patterns of variation. In most of the cases however, certain peculiarities of the gene expressions at hand, like the large degree of complexity in the measured entities and the amount of inherent noise present in microarray experiments, prevent standard clustering methods to provide adequate results in terms of pattern similarity and biological correlation. Following several studies in the field of functional genomics showing the advantages of integrating different types of biological data [2], a solution in improving clustering results of microarray data would be to incorporate additional sources of

I. Maglogiannis, V. Plagianakos, and I. Vlahavas (Eds.): SETN 2012, LNAI 7297, pp. 262–269, 2012.
© Springer-Verlag Berlin Heidelberg 2012

biological information [3]. An algorithmic family that could utilize prior knowledge on a certain field, is semi-supervised algorithms. Partially supervised clustering methods stand between purely unsupervised and fully supervised methods, benefiting from the advantages of both.

Algorithms performing semi-supervised clustering have recently received a significant amount of interest in the machine learning and data mining communities. It has been shown that even a relatively small amount of supervision significantly improves the accuracy of clustering [3]. Existing methods for semi-supervised clustering can be divided into two general categories known as constraint-based and metric-based approaches. In the metric-based approach an existing clustering algorithm is employed, but the measure of distortion used by this algorithm is first trained to satisfy the labels or constraints in the supervised data. On the other hand in constraint-based methods, the clustering algorithm itself is modified so as to integrate the user-provided labels or constraints, constituting this way a more suitable approach since its operation does not constitute of two steps but it is integrated in a single process.

Given the above considerations, and following the constraint-based approach we propose a novel Semi-Supervised Possibilistic Clustering Algorithm (SSPCA). SSPCA extends the operation of possibilistic clustering [4] in the semi-supervised field, considering sets of constraints either forcing patterns/genes to cluster together or assigning them to different clusters. We apply SSPCA on the intrinsic problem of gene expression clustering. Furthermore we show how external sources of information can guide the selection of constraints. While several types of biological data could serve as a source of external information; Gene Ontology (GO) Consortium currently serves as the dominant approach for machine-legible functional annotation.

Experimental results on real and artificial data prove not only the efficiency of the proposed SSPCA against other clustering algorithms but also the advantages of using external sources of biological information (i.e. GO) in clustering gene expression data.

2   Methods

2.1   Constraints and Semi-supervision

In the proposed methodology additional information (or prior knowledge) on a specific domain, is given on sets of either must-link or cannot-link constraints or both. Let E be the set of must-link constraints to be given in pairs (x_i, x_j) ε E where the instances x_i and x_j should be assigned to the same cluster, while cannot-link constraints in pairs (x_i, x_j) ε Δ where Δ is the set of cannot-link constraints and x_i, x_j should be assigned to different clusters. In the approach we are adapting a specific gene can be associated with more than one pair and kind of constraints. We could for example have three constraints that would impose a gene to be in the same group/class with some other three genes, while at the same time to belong to different classes with another pair of genes. Therefore we will insert a new metric that will calculate the number of constraints that are retained for a specific gene j and the number of violations over the constraints within a certain cluster i:

$$\beta_{ij} = \frac{V_{ij} - R_{ij}}{T_j} \tag{1}$$

where T_j is the total number of given constraints concerning the element or gene j, R_{ij} are the pairs of constraints that are preserved within the cluster, while V_{ij} is the number of constraints that are violated within the same cluster concerning sample j. As we can determine from eq. (1), the range of the score of every member of the cluster is within -1 and 1. Specifically concerning the range of value for β_{ij}, it is:

$$\beta_{ij} = \begin{cases} 1, & \{R_{ij} \to 0 \wedge V_{ij} \to T_j\} \\ 0, & \{R_{ij} = V_{ij} \vee T_j = 0\} \\ -1, & \{R_{ij} \to T_j \wedge V_{ij} \to 0\} \end{cases} \tag{2}$$

When β_{ij} approaches 1, then most of the constraints regarding the specific pattern are violated within the cluster, while when the score approaches -1, most of the constraints are preserved. At this point we should note that the score becomes zero, if there are no constraints regarding a specific pattern at the dataset of supervision and that approaches zero in the case that the percentage of constraints that are violated equals the number of constraints that are retained. We will expand now the metric proposed in (1), in order to account for the validity of a cluster in terms of retained constraints for all of its members:

$$B_i = \frac{1}{2}\left(1 - \frac{1}{N_C} \cdot \sum_{j=1}^{N_C} \frac{R_{ij} - V_{ij}}{T_j}\right) \tag{3}$$

where N_c is the number of the members of a cluster i.   In contrast to the previously proposed metric, the score of a cluster ranges from 0 to 1, where 1 is the case for which there is no violation for any of the members of the group/cluster regarding the constraints known for it, while 0 is the exact opposite case. As we will see later in the analysis of those two metrics will play a central role in SSPCA algorithm.

2.2   Gene Ontology and Constraints Selection

We present a framework (Fig. 1) for selecting constraints from gene ontology terms that will be used as input to SSPCA to guide the clustering process of gene expression data. The Gene Ontology Consortium is one of the most widely used database concerning annotations of gene functions. The number of genes associated with a certain annotation term indicates how specific that term is, therefore based on this criterion we could discriminate between general and more specific terms. Therefore two genes sharing a more specific term are more likely to interact than genes that share a general term. While, there are many GO measures in the literature that provide a quantitative degree of similarity between two specific genes in respect to their GO terms, Resnick's [5] is one of the most widely used.

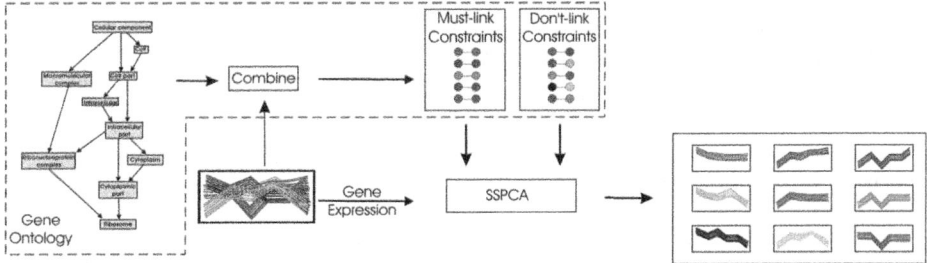

Fig. 1. Schematic representation of the framework we adapt to extract constraints, based on gene ontology terms, used to guide the clustering process of SSPCA on gene expression data

However, the main goal of the proposed method is clustering, hence along with the GO information we must also consider the similarity of the expression profiles for a certain couple of genes. Hence we will insert a measure that will take under consideration both of the aforementioned criteria:

$$G_{ij} = \frac{d_{ij}^2 / s_{ij}}{\sum_{k=1}^{N} d_{ik}^2 / s_{ik}}, \quad \forall j \in [1...N] \tag{4}$$

where i and j correspond to certain genes, d_{ij} is the Euclidean distance between the expression profiles of i and j while s_{ik} is Resnik's similarity measure. As we can depict from (4) the reverse GO similarity between two genes is weighted by their corresponding euclidean expressional distance, since to determine a certain constraint we take under consideration gene expression as well. We finally normalize by the total sum of these scores of i against all other genes. While s_{ij} ranges from 0 to a maximum value, having 0 as worst case the opposite occurs for Euclidean distance. Hence the range of the proposed measure ranges from 0 to a maximum value, having 0 as the best case.

In order to extract the necessary constraints from a given data set, we adapt a methodology where every one of the genes present in the dataset under study, is cross-checked against all others. Each one of these pairs is given a similarity degree based on (4). After the process is concluded for all genes, we sort the similarities degrees of the corresponding pairs. A specific fraction of the pairs that have achieved a minimum score will be used as must-link constraints, while the ones that have the largest values will be used as cannot-link constraints. The exact percentage of the constraints is given as input to the algorithm.

2.3 SSPCA

In this section we will describe the operation of the proposed SSPCA algorithm. SSPCA through its objective function tries to minimize the distance among the patterns and the corresponding centroids of the clusters while at the same time is guided by the pairs of constraints towards the determination of more concise clusters. The mathematical description of the SSPCA objective function expanding the operation of possibilistic clustering in the semi-supervised field is:

$$J_1(U,V;X,\Pi) = \sum_{i=1}^{C}\sum_{j=1}^{N} a_{ij}^m d_{ij}^2 + \sum_{i=1}^{C}\sum_{j=1}^{N}\left(1-a_{ij}\right)^m \left(\gamma_i + D_i d_{ij}^2\right) \tag{5}$$

where:

$$D_i = (1-n)\frac{N_T}{N_C}B_i \quad \text{and} \quad \gamma_i = n\frac{\sum_{k=1}^{N}\alpha_{ik}^m d_{ik}^2}{\sum_{k=1}^{N}\alpha_{ik}^m} \tag{6}$$

N_T represents the number of patterns in a specific cluster and N_C the number of patterns that are part of both the cluster and the constraints data set. The term N_T over N_C ensures that if a small number of constraints is provided in comparison to the total number of patterns in the dataset, these constraints will not dominate the overall clustering process. We will discuss about the effect of the parameters D_i later in the text, while and γ_i is in accordance to the corresponding value described in [4]. The variable a_{ij} is a function of u_{ij} and β_{ij}, assuming a small positive number n, ranging from zero to unity, we set:

$$a_{ij} = n \cdot u_{ij} - (1-n) \cdot \beta_{\phi(ij)} \tag{7}$$

In every iteration the membership value of a_{ij} depends not only on the distance x_j from v_i but also from the number of constraints that are retained or violated concerning a specific pattern j. As we can depict from (6) n is a parameter controlling the degree that constraints will be taken into account in the overall clustering process and can either have a fixed value throughout all the clustering process or can vary during the iterations steps. In cases that we are confident for the accuracy of the constraints and also have a satisfying number of constraints for the majority of the dataset then n can be viewed as a constant whose value can have a small value (i.e. ranging from 0.4 to 0.6) that reflects the quantity and confidence of the semi-supervised information we have. In the case however where either we do not have a satisfying number of constraints for the data set and/or we have either a minimum amount of confidence or even uncertainty concerning the accuracy of the constraints, parameter n could be regarded as a time/iterations dependent variable. In this paper we will study the first case only.

In possibilistic and fuzzy clustering, each pattern is a member of all existing clusters up to a certain degree indicated by the corresponding membership value and hence all pairs of patterns constraints should be checked for violations throughout all clusters. We can however consider that a pattern is part of the cluster for which it has the maximum membership value. Hence, we can check for pattern violations, concerning one cluster per pattern. This is accomplished using a function, which rewards or penalizes membership values only in the case of cluster members, while in the opposite case eliminates the influence of the constraints. Using this technique we reduce the computational complexity, contribute to the faster convergence of the algorithm and at the same time not harming the generality of the solution. Given all the above, we introduce φ as a function returning the set of patterns that have their maximum membership value within a certain cluster (i.e. compared to other clusters) at every iteration. The mathematical interpretation of function φ is:

$$\phi(i) = \begin{cases} 0, & \text{if } \left\{ \arg\left(\max_{k} u_{k\rho}\right) \equiv i \,|\, \forall \rho \in D \right\} \\ 1, & \text{else} \end{cases} \tag{8}$$

$\varphi(i)$ is a function returning the set of patterns that have their maximum membership value is within the i-th cluster at every iteration. Given φ we have that:

$$\beta_{\phi(i,j)} = \begin{cases} \beta_{\phi(i)j}, & j \in C \\ 0, & \text{else} \end{cases} \tag{9}$$

Using partial derivatives and the method of Largange multipliers we solve (5) in respect to membership values u_{ij} and the centroids v_i, hence:

$$u_{ij} = \frac{1/n}{1 + \left(\dfrac{d_{ij}^2}{D_i d_{ij}^2 + \gamma_i}\right)^{\frac{1}{m-1}}} + \frac{1-n}{n} \beta_{\phi(i)j} \tag{10}$$

while for the centroids we have:

$$v_i = \frac{\sum_{j=1}^{N} \left[a_{ij}^m + D_i \left(1 - a_{ij}\right)^m \right] x_j}{\sum_{j=1}^{N} \left[a_{ij}^m + D_i \left(1 - a_{ij}\right)^m \right]} \tag{11}$$

As we can depict from (9) the value of u_{ij} is highly influenced by the value of β_{ij} and D_i. Based on the definition given in (1) and range in (2) we can depict that in order for the value of u_{ij} to be increased the majority of the constraints regarding the j-th pattern in i-th cluster must be retained. Also the value of constraints has a zero effect when the number of violations equals the number of retentions. On the other hand if D_i is high then u_{ij} will be high, if D_i is low then u_{ij} will be low. Indeed as we discussed in the previous section based on (3) the value of D_i (from 0 to unity) increases as the number of patterns for which the majority of constraints is retained increases within the a certain cluster constraints that are retained increases.

3   Results

In this section we will describe the experiments we conducted to test the validity of our approach, based on both artificial and real data sets. In the followings, we com pared the apodosis of SSPCA against two standard clustering techniques PK-means [4] and K-means as well as a semi-supervised method CPK-means [6].

Table 1. Results on the apodosis of the standard clustering techniques PK-means, K-means and the semi-supervised method CPK-means in comparison to the proposed SSPCA

Algorithm	Supervision	ARI	
		DS1	DS2
SSPCA	0	0.39	0.30
	10	0.57	0.50
	30	0.84	0.69
CPK-means	30	0.580	0.517
PK-means	-	0.39	0.30
K-means	-	0.460	0.362

In order to test our method under more controlled conditions we resorted to artificial data (hereafter DS1). This dataset has been artificially created initiating from real data as described in [7]. It consists of 400 patterns across 10 different experimental conditions. The dataset has 10 clusters. The second dataset was based on an experimental study published in [8], consisting of the expression levels of more than 6000 genes measured across 17 time points during two cell cycles of Saccharomyces cerevisiae (SS). From this study we have used a subset of 384 annotated genes (DS2) visually identified as five distinct time points, each one representing a phase of the SS cell cycle. The expression levels of each gene were normalized to zero mean and unity standard deviation.

The constraints for DS1 were extracted by considering the known labels of the patterns and following the methodology described in [3], while for DS2 we acquired constraints as described in previous section. In this study we have used information on the GO domain: molecular function, for the SS micro-organism. Given that the labels in both datasets considered are a priori known we have the adjusted rand index (ARI) metric [9] to measure the efficiency of the considered algorithms. A value of ARI equal to 1 indicate a perfect clustering according to the provided pattern labels while a value of zero the opposite. Clustering was repeated 10 times for the data sets under consideration, by all the algorithms checked and the mean values of the results in terms of adapted metric were used. As we have already mention the key parameter in the operation of SSPCA is n that controls the influence of the provided constraints in the overall clustering process. We have repeatedly executed SSPCA for the following range of n values: 0.4, 0.45, 0.50, 0.55, 0.6. The best results, reported on Table 1, were acquired for a value of n equal to 0.6.

As we can depict from Table 1, the results of SSPCA and PK-means is the same when the percentage of provided constraints equals zero, since PK-means is a special case of SSPCA in the non-supervised field. As we can see on the table the proposed algorithm outperformed both of the considered unsupervised algorithms for a small percentage of supervision (10%). Finally for the same percentage of provided constraints, SSPCA had more than 25% and 30% improved apodosis in DS2 and DS1, respectively than the semi-supervised algorithm CPK-means.

The reported results not only demonstrate the efficiency of SSPCA and the benefits of semi-supervised over standard clustering methods but also indicate the advantages of using external sources of biological information to guide the clustering of gene expression data.

4   Conclusions

In this work we presented a semi-supervised possibilistic clustering algorithm incorporating prior-knowledge in the form pair-wise constraints. Initial results suggested that the proposed algorithm outperformed other crisp and fuzzy methods. Furthermore we showed that under the semi-supervised framework adapting external sources of biological information, such as GO, for constraints selection, can significantly improve the clustering results.

We are working in methodologies that will extend the operation of SSPCA by allowing the algorithm to automatically extract a meaningful number of clusters. Additionally, we are performing a wide range of additional simulations from gene expression data arriving from several organisms and other sources of biological knowledge (i.e. protein-protein interactions) to further validate the findings of this study.

Acknowledgments. This research has been co-financed by the European Union (European Social Fund – ESF) and Greek national funds through the Operational Program "Education and Lifelong Learning" of the National Strategic Reference Framework (NSRF) - Research Funding Program: THALES. Investing in knowledge society through the European Social Fund.

References

1. Wu, L.F., et al.: Large scale prediction of Saccharomyces cerevisiae gene function using overlapping transcriptional clusters. Nat. Genetics 31, 255–265 (2005)
2. Maraziotis, I.A., Dimitrakopoulou, K., Bezerianos, A.: An in silico method for detecting overlapping functional modules from composite biological networks. BMC Systems Biology 2, 93 (2008)
3. Maraziotis, I.A.: A Semi-supervised algorithm applied on gene expression data. Pattern Recognition 45(1), 637–648 (2012)
4. Krishnapuram, R., Keller, J.M.: A possibilistic approach to clustering. IEEE Trans. on Fuzzy Systems 1(2) (1993)
5. Resnik, P.: Using information content to evaluate semantic similarity in taxonomy. In: Proc. of Int. Joint Conf. on Artificial Intelligence, pp. 448–453 (1995)
6. Wagstaff, K., Cardie, C., Rogers, S., Schroedl, S.: Constrained K-Means clustering with background knowledge. In: Proceedings of 18th International Conference on Machine Learning, pp. 577–584 (2001)
7. Yeung, K.Y., Haynor, D.R., Ruzzo, W.L.: Validating clustering for gene expression data. Bioinformatics 17, 309–318 (2001)
8. Cho, R.J., et al.: A genome-wide transcriptional analysis of the mitotic cell cycle. Molecular Cell 2, 65–73 (1998)
9. Yeung, K.Y., Ruzzo, W.L.: An empirical study on principal component analysis for clustering gene expression data. Bioinformatics 17, 763–774 (2001)

Towards Better Prioritization of Epigenetically Modified DNA Regions

Ernesto Iacucci[1], Dusan Popovic[1], Georgios A. Pavlopoulos[1],
Léon-Charles Tranchevent[1], Marijke Bauters[2],
Bart De Moor[1], and Yves Moreau[1]

[1] ESAT-SCD / IBBT-K.U.Leuven Future Health Department, Katholieke Universiteit Leuven,
Kasteelpark Arenberg 10, Box 2446, 3001, Leuven, Belgium
[2] Department of Human Genetics / IBBT-K.U.Leuven Future Health Department, Katholieke
Universiteit Leuven, Kasteelpark Arenberg 10, Box 2446, 3001, Leuven, Belgium
{Ernesto.Iacucci,Dusan.Popovic,Georgios.Pavlopoulos,
Leon-Charles.Tranchevent,Bart.DeMoor,
Yves.Moreau}@esat.kuleuven.be,
marijke.bauters@cme.vib-kuleuven.be.be

Abstract. Epigenetic modifications of the genome can cause profound changes in phenotype of an organism. Experimental methods allow us to detect regions of the DNA that have been epigenetically modified; these regions are said to be *enriched* in a queried state versus a control. Detecting the enriched regions is not a simple matter as making sense of the data involves multiple analytical steps and often results in false calls. In this study, we analyze the utility of using additional features of the data (such as the transcription start site (TSS) and the histone coverage) to detect enrichment. We train a decision tree ensemble using these three features and review how well they identify regions that are truly enriched (as validated by q-PCR). We find that the enrichment score derived directly from ChIP-chip experiment data is less informative than the histone coverage.

Keywords: ChIP-chip, data integration, protein-DNA, machine learning, decision trees.

1 Introduction

The detection of protein-DNA interactions is an important area of research. Protein-DNA interactions account for various cellular events such as DNA repair and transcription factor binding [1-3]. Transcription factors regulate the expression level of gene products that carry out the majority of processes in the cell. Histone-DNA interactions are a specific type of protein-DNA interactions that also influence the expression of genes. Indeed, DNA that is wound around histone-bodies (the complex form of histones) is less accessible to the cellular transcriptional machinery and thus genes located in these regions are less likely to be expressed [4,5]. These

I. Maglogiannis, V. Plagianakos, and I. Vlahavas (Eds.): SETN 2012, LNAI 7297, pp. 270–277, 2012.
© Springer-Verlag Berlin Heidelberg 2012

modifications are considered epigenetic as they alter the expression of genes while not changing their sequences.

A widely used technique to measure protein-DNA interaction is chromatin immunoprecipitation followed by DNA microarray hybridization (ChIP-chip). Using ChIP-chip, one is able to identify areas of the genome that are enriched between two conditions of interest (e.g., disease vs. control) [1,6]. Detecting the enriched regions is not a simple matter as making sense of the data involves multiple analytical steps and often results in false calls [7,8]. In this study, we assess whether using additional features enhance the detection of enriched regions [9,10]. In addition to the enrichment scores, extracted from ChIP-chip data, the transcription start site (TSS) and histone coverage scores are defined and used to train a decision tree based algorithms.

While the primary feature resulting from a ChIP-chip experiment is the enrichment score for a region, the other two features are easily derived. The TSS score is the distance of the region to the nearest predicted TSS. The histone coverage is a unit value which is calculated from a regions size (in base-pairs) in relation to the size of a full turn of the DNA around a histone body (147 base-pairs).

We then review how well these three features perform in predicting the regions that are truly enriched (as validated by q-PCR).

2   Methods

Our dataset consists of 25 DNA regions for which we have ChIP-chip enrichment scores, region sizes and distances to the nearest transcription start site, and validated q-PCR values. Our dataset is derived from ChIP-chip experiments essaying fragile-X patient samples (data unpublished). The q-PCR values define the positive and negative examples and will be considered binary for the purposes of this work.

- The ChIP-chip *enrichment score* is derived from a data analysis procedure described in [11,12]. Briefly, the data is processed as follows:
- The outliers in the data are removed (probes in a 5 probe window are averaged and probes which are over 2 standard deviation from the mean are removed).
- The data is normalized, by adjusting the mean of entire distribution to zero.
- The differences between the two samples are calculated (one sample is the condition/disease sample and the other would be the control).
- The data is smoothed (a 3-point moving average is calculated for each peak).
- The probes, which show significant differences, are identified (those over 2 standard deviations from the mean).
- The regions of consistent difference defined by multiple probes (4 probes of a 5 probe window) are called (flagged as significant).

The *transcription start site (TSS) feature* is calculated as the distance from the nearest TSS. These distances (measured in base-pairs), are then mapped to an integer score which varied from 0 to 5. The *histone coverage* is a feature which is computed from the size (measured in base-pairs) of the enriched region. The size of the region is transformed into a unit value by applying the equation displayed in Figure 1.

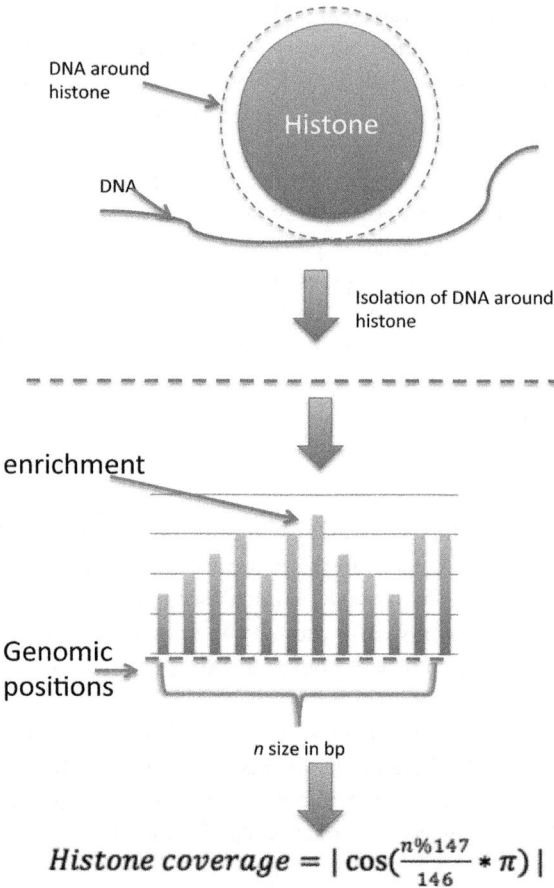

$$Histone\ coverage = \left| \cos\left(\frac{n\%147}{146} * \pi\right) \right|$$

Fig. 1. Histone coverage score calculation

The dataset, consisting of the three features and the validated q-PCR outcomes, is then feed to a decision tree-learning algorithm (classregtree, Matlab v7.10.0). In addition, a bagged decision tree ensemble classifier on the whole dataset is also trained.

This algorithm builds individual trees on the bootstrap replicates of the original dataset and then uses out-of-bag observations to compute unbiased estimates of the classification error. This is often exploited to measure feature importance. For each feature, its values across all the observations are permuted, after which the difference in mean squared error is examined. Eventually, a higher positive difference implies greater importance for that feature. Furthermore, we validated our results using leave-one-out cross validation.

3   Results and Discussion

We run a decision tree learning algorithm on the whole dataset to examine which features are selected as the most informative and in which order. We construct a ROC curve for each feature and examine the AUC as a heuristic to determine which features are the most important. Out of the three features considered, we find that enrichment performs the poorly (AUC TSS: 0.62, AUC Enrichment Score 0.60, AUC Histone score: 0.73). This result suggests that the use of enrichment scores alone is not an optimal strategy to predict truly enriched regions. We observe that the TSS score and histone coverage, are necessary to improve performance in the prediction task. This observation is consistent with the results from the out-of-the-bag feature importance analysis (see Figure 2).

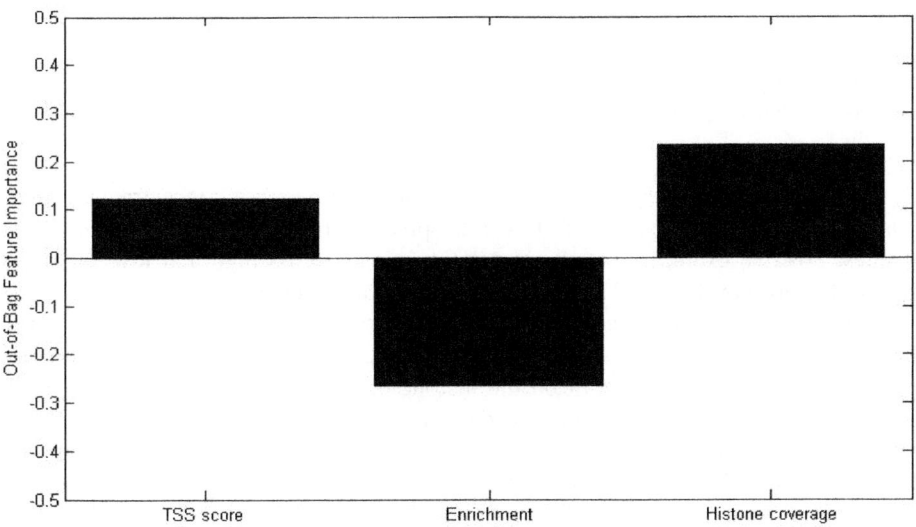

Fig. 2. Out of bag importance of features

Figure 2 demonstrates that the highest positive difference occurs with the histone coverage, which implies greater importance of this feature. Surprisingly, the enrichment feature is associated to a negative difference, indicating that it is the least important of the features. In order to illustrate this finding with the original data, we create a scatter plot that compares the histone coverage with the enrichment value while at the same time indicating the positive and negative regions (see Figure 3).

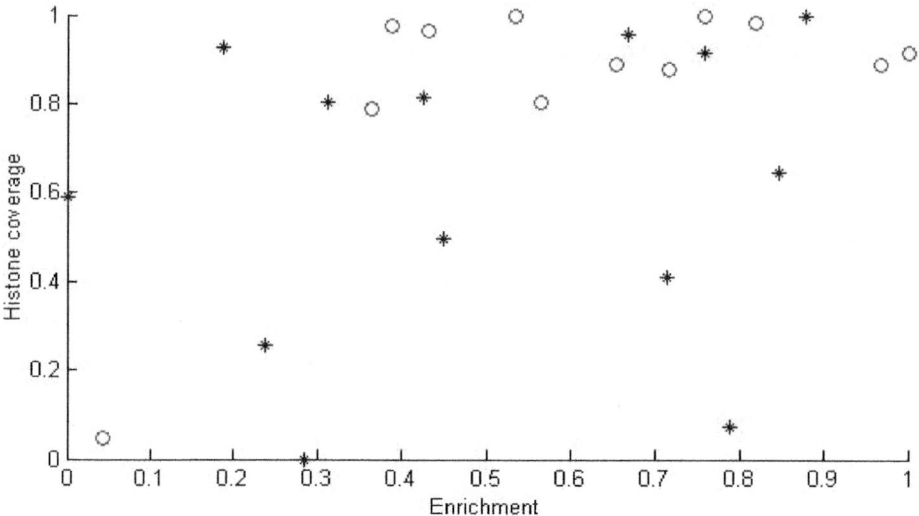

Fig. 3. Scatter plot of histone coverage vs enrichment score. Circles indicate negative examples and crosses indicate positive examples.

Figure 3 demonstrates that negative examples (circles) are concentrated at higher histone coverage values while they are spread across high and low enrichment values. Positive examples (crosses) are also spread across high and low enrichment values but are mostly found at lower histone coverage values.

The utility of the TSS score and the histone coverage is more apparent when one considers that the decision tree constructed using the whole dataset has a topology which determines the first split on the histone coverage and the second split on the TSS score and determines no splits on the enrichment score (see Figure 4).

In order to assess the reliability of this approach, we ran 100 iterations of a leave-one-out cross validation analysis. The results were as follows: using the enrichment feature alone, the random forest algorithm has a mean performance (accuracy) of 0.44 (st. dev. 0.022), when we use all three features the value rises to 0.64 (st. dev. 0.045), when we use the TSS score and the Histone coverage (and no enrichment value), the best value, of 0.76 (st. dev. 0.022), is achieved.

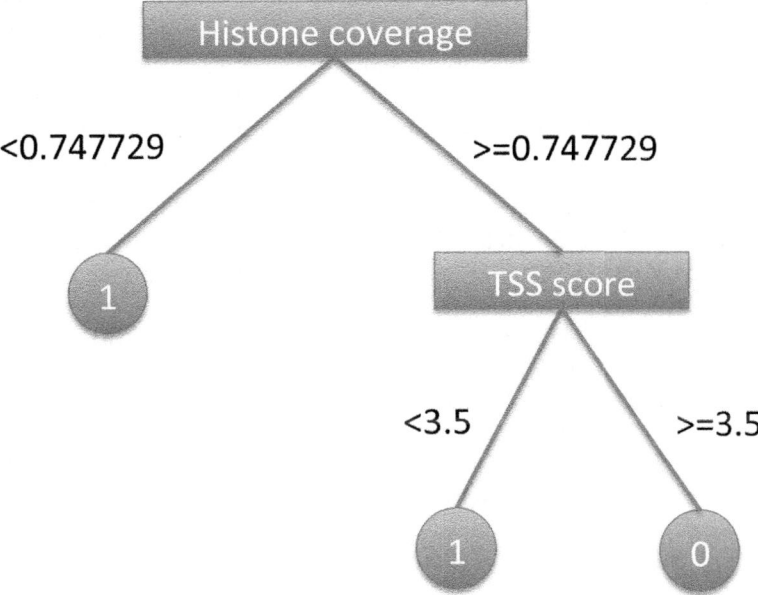

Fig. 4. Decision Tree

As presented in Table 1, the results are consistent with the ones obtained single decision trees using random forests algorithm (Matlab TreeBagger class). The lower accuracy of random forests comparing to single trees in this particular case could be explained by small size of the training data sets thought the iterations. The former performs additional bootstrapping step internally, effectively reducing available training data even more in this way.

Table 1. Metric comparison across 100 experiments

Features	Random forest		Decision trees	
	mean	*std.*	*mean*	*std.*
TSS score, Histone coverage	0.6380	0.0237	0.7600	0.0223
TSS score, Histone coverage, Enrichment	0.5948	0.0315	0.6400	0.0446
Enrichment	0.4508	0.0196	0.4400	0.0223

4   Conclusions

This work present novel insight into the task of predicting true enrichment in regions detected by ChIP-chip experimentation. Our main technical contribution is two-fold.

First, we demonstrate that the use of enrichment scores alone is not an optimal strategy. Second, we show that the use of two additional features, namely TSS and histone coverage, provide unique information, and are necessary to improve the prediction results. Looking forward, we plan to examine the integration of other features and the development of other strategies, which might increase predictive power.

Acknowledgements. *Funding:* The authors would like to acknowledge support from: Research Council KUL:ProMeta, GOA Ambiorics, GOA MaNet, CoE EF/05/007 SymBioSys en KUL PFV/10/016 SymBioSys , START 1, several PhD/postdoc & fellow grants. Flemish Government: FWO: PhD/postdoc grants, projects G.0318.05 (subfunctionalization), G.0553.06 (VitamineD), G.0302.07 (SVM/Kernel), research communities (ICCoS, ANMMM, MLDM); G.0733.09 (3UTR); G.082409 (EGFR) IWT: PhD Grants, Silicos; SBO-BioFrame, SBO-MoKa, TBM-IOTA3 FOD:Cancer plans, IBBT. Bel- gian Federal Science Policy Office: IUAP P6/25 (BioMaGNet, Bioinformatics and Modeling: from Genomes to Networks, 2007- 2011); EU-RTD: ERNSI: European Research Network on System Identification; FP7-HEALTH; CHeartED.

References

1. Bieda, M., Xu, X., Singer, M.A., Green, R., Farnham, P.J.: Unbiased location analysis of E2F1-binding sites suggests a widespread role for E2F1 in the human genome. Genome Res. 16(5), 595–605 (2006)
2. Kreuz, M., Rosolowski, M., Berger, H., Schwaenen, C., Wessendorf, S., Loeffler, M., Hasenclever, D.: Development and implementation of an analysis tool for array-based comparative genomic hybridization. Methods Inf. Med. 46(5), 608–613 (2007)
3. Pelizzola, M., Koga, Y., Urban, A.E., Krauthammer, M., Weissman, S., Halaban, R., Molinaro, A.M.: MEDME: an experimental and analytical methodology for the estimation of DNA methylation levels based on microarray derived MeDIP-enrichment. Genome Res. 18(10), 1652–1659 (2008)
4. Dowell, R.D.: Transcription factor binding variation in the evolution of gene regulation. Trends Genet. 26(11), 468–475 (2010)
5. Gilchrist, D.A., Fargo, D.C., Adelman, K.: Using ChIP-chip and ChIP-seq to study the regulation of gene expression: genome-wide localization studies reveal widespread regulation of transcription elongation. Methods 48(4), 398–408 (2009)
6. MacQuarrie, K.L., Fong, A.P., Morse, R.H., Tapscott, S.J.: Genome-wide transcription factor binding: beyond direct target regulation. Trends Genet. 27(4), 141–148 (2011)
7. Toedling, J., Huber, W.: Analyzing ChIP-chip data using bioconductor. PLoS Comput. Biol. 4(11), e1000227 (2008)
8. Toedling, J., Skylar, O., Krueger, T., Fischer, J.J., Sperling, S., Huber, W.: Ringo–an R/Bioconductor package for analyzing ChIP-chip readouts. BMC Bioinformatics 8, 221 (2007)
9. Chen, K.B., Zhang, Y.: A varying threshold method for ChIP peak-calling using multiple sources of information. Bioinformatics 26(18), i504–i510 (2010)

10. Johnson, D.S., Li, W., Gordon, D.B., Bhattacharjee, A., Curry, B., Ghosh, J., Brizuela, L., Carroll, J.S., Brown, M., Flicek, P., Koch, C.M., Dunham, I., Bieda, M., Xu, X., Farnham, P.J., Kapranov, P., Nix, D.A., Gingeras, T.R., Zhang, X., Holster, H., Jiang, N., Green, R.D., Song, J.S., McCuine, S.A., Anton, E., Nguyen, L., Trinklein, N.D., Ye, Z., Ching, K., Hawkins, D., Ren, B., Scacheri, P.C., Rozowsky, J., Karpikov, A., Euskirchen, G., Weissman, S., Gerstein, M., Snyder, M., Yang, A., Moqtaderi, Z., Hirsch, H., Shulha, H.P., Fu, Y., Weng, Z., Struhl, K., Myers, R.M., Lieb, J.D., Liu, X.S.: Systematic evaluation of variability in ChIP-chip experiments using predefined DNA targets. Genome Res. 18(3), 393–403 (2008)
11. Sharp, A.J., Migliavacca, E., Dupre, Y., Stathaki, E., Sailani, M.R., Baumer, A., Schinzel, A., Mackay, D.J., Robinson, D.O., Cobellis, G., Cobellis, L., Brunner, H.G., Steiner, B., Antonarakis, S.E.: Methylation profiling in individuals with uniparental disomy identifies novel differentially methylated regions on chromosome 15. Genome Res. 20(9), 1271–1278 (2010)
12. Sharp, A.J., Stathaki, E., Migliavacca, E., Brahmachary, M., Montgomery, S.B., Dupre, Y., Antonarakis, S.E.: DNA methylation profiles of human active and inactive X chromosomes. Genome Res. 21(10), 1592–1600 (2011)

Mining Cell Cycle Literature Using Support Vector Machines

Theodoros G. Soldatos[1] and Georgios A. Pavlopoulos[2]

[1] Life Biosystems GmbH, Belfortstr. 2, 69115, Heidelberg, Germany
thsoldat@gmail.com
[2] ESAT-SCD / IBBT-K.U.Leuven Future Health Department, KatholiekeUniversiteit Leuven,
KasteelparkArenberg 10, Box 2446, 3001, Leuven, Belgium
Georgios.Pavlopoulos@esat.kuleuven.be

Abstract. While biomedical literature is rapidly increasing, text classification remains a challenge for researchers, curators and librarians. In the context of this work, we use the Caipirini (http://caipirini.org) service to report on the exploration of a literature corpus related to the G1, S, G2 and M phases of the human cell cycle respectively. We use Support Vector Machines (SVMs) and a well-studied dataset to compare each of the cell cycle phases against all others in order to find abstracts that are related to one specific phase at a time. Finally we measure the performance of the results using the standard accuracy, precision and recall metrics. We find differences between the results of each of the four phases and we compare with previous findings of relevant work. We conclude that the results concur and help interpreting the observed classification performance.

Keywords: supervised machine learning, biomedical literature, cell cycle, support vector machines.

1 Introduction

Classifying literature and identifying a targeted set of articles of interest is frequently a bottleneck in biomedical research. As the number of papers produced per day increases rapidly, several tools that aim to help extracting information from biomedical literature have been developed [1,2]. For example, tools like ETBLAST [3], PubFinder [4], MScanner [5], BibGlimpse [6], Kleio [7], MedlineRanker [8], and Caipirini [9] help search and organise literature according to the interests of users. Mostly, such tools tackle the problem by trying to collect, classify and manipulate articles based on the biomedical terms or keywords that are mentioned in their texts. However, to our knowledge, only Caipirini [9] allows directly to compare and separate literature corpora according to relevance with gene sets. This task, i.e., distinguishing among a set of abstracts which are related more to one category and which are more relevant to another, can be useful in many ways. For example, many biomedical researchers often need to compare sets of genes which are expressed under different conditions or to compare gene lists produced in different ways, e.g., by using different

I. Maglogiannis, V. Plagianakos, and I. Vlahavas (Eds.): SETN 2012, LNAI 7297, pp. 278–284, 2012.

high-throughput experiments, or statistical analyses. Often one such researcher may want to identify literature focused on the specific conditions under consideration, e.g., to separate abstracts in groups that specifically discuss certain developmental stages, or abstracts that discuss the molecular (de)regulation of a plant's circadian rhythm specifically related to a certain season or time-period, or abstracts that discuss a specific disease for certain organisms only, and so on.

For the current study, we chose to work on a similar scenario: we wanted to explore literature corpora related to the human cell cycle and to identify abstracts related to each of the four phases, in specific. For this we relied on a previously studied dataset [10,11], for which a set of genes was assigned to each of the four phases (G1, S, G2 and M) – we used these gene lists as input to Caipirini [9] which allowed us to compare each phase against the other three, and to test the performance for each phase. We found that there were noticeable differences between the classifications of each case.

2   Materials and Methods

Caipirini: For this study, we took advantage of Caipirini [9], a service that allows researchers and curators to classify biomedical literature using support vector machines (SVMs). It mainly accepts as input two user-defined datasets (namely sets A and B). These can be imported directly as lists of PubMed [12] identifiers or as gene lists using Entrez[13] or Ensembl[14] gene identifiers. Sets A and B are used as examples for the training of the supervised learning method. The training relies on vectors extracted directly from the input abstracts or indirectly from the abstracts linked to the input genes. Next, abstracts from a third input set (called set C) are applied on the trained model which in turn assigns them either to set A or B. While Caipirini poses many advantages [9], one of its key features is that its automated pipeline enables users with no computational background to use SVMs, without having to take care of the underlying modelling complexities. This way, an experimental biologist who holds two sets of genes (A and B), can easily compare them directly and search among a relevant set of abstracts (set C) for the specific literature related with each of the sets of available genes. In its background, Caipirini [9] uses the SVM library LIBLINEAR [15], in accordance with the fact that linear SVM models have been found to perform well on text classification tasks. The service of Caipirini is described in detail at [9].

The dataset: We used a human gene set that was previously assigned to the four cell cycle phases by Martini [10]: 113 genes were assigned to the G1-phase, 154 to the S-phase, 82 to the G2-phase and 251 to the M-phase. The exact lists of gene identifiers can be found at the supplementary notes of [11], and at Martini's [10] webpage (under 'Example 1'), while the setup specific for S-Phase can be found in any of Caipirini's [9] examples '2', '3', or '4'.

Table 1. Number of abstracts that remained in Set C after removing from the results of the PubMed queries (a) first the overlap with the training set, and then also (b) the non indexed, by Caipirini's underlying dictionary, abstracts

Cell Cycle Phase	Number of abstracts		Query
	(a)	(b)	
G1	1337	1336	humans[MeSH Terms] AND ("G1 Phase"[MeSH Terms]) NOT ("S Phase"[MeSH Terms] OR "DNA Replication"[MeSH Terms] OR "G2 Phase"[MeSH Terms] OR "Prophase"[MeSH Terms] OR "Prometaphase"[MeSH Terms] OR "Metaphase"[MeSH Terms] OR "Anaphase"[MeSH Terms] OR "Telophase"[MeSH Terms] OR "Cytokinesis"[MeSH Terms]) AND ("2000/01/01"[PDAT] : "2008/06/31"[PDAT])
S	3904	3897	humans[MeSH Terms] AND ("S Phase"[MeSH Terms] OR "DNA Replication"[MeSH Terms]) NOT ("G1 Phase"[MeSH Terms] OR "G2 Phase"[MeSH Terms] OR "Prophase"[MeSH Terms] OR "Prometaphase"[MeSH Terms] OR "Metaphase"[MeSH Terms] OR "Anaphase"[MeSH Terms] OR "Telophase"[MeSH Terms] OR "Cytokinesis"[MeSH Terms]) AND ("2000/01/01"[PDAT] : "2008/06/31"[PDAT])
G2	1134	1134	humans[MeSH Terms] AND ("G2 Phase"[MeSH Terms]) NOT ("G1 Phase"[MeSH Terms] OR "S Phase"[MeSH Terms] OR "DNA Replication"[MeSH Terms] OR "Prophase"[MeSH Terms] OR "Prometaphase"[MeSH Terms] OR "Metaphase"[MeSH Terms] OR "Anaphase"[MeSH Terms] OR "Telophase"[MeSH Terms] OR "Cytokinesis"[MeSH Terms]) AND ("2000/01/01"[PDAT] : "2008/06/31"[PDAT])
M	1263	1260	humans[MeSH Terms] AND ("Prophase"[MeSH Terms] OR "Prometaphase"[MeSH Terms] OR "Metaphase"[MeSH Terms] OR "Anaphase"[MeSH Terms] OR "Telophase"[MeSH Terms] OR "Cytokinesis"[MeSH Terms]) NOT ("G1 Phase"[MeSH Terms] OR "S Phase"[MeSH Terms] OR "DNA Replication"[MeSH Terms] OR "G2 Phase"[MeSH Terms]) AND ("2000/01/01"[PDAT] : "2008/06/31"[PDAT])

The Comparisons: We performed four comparisons: we imported in Caipirini [9] the gene list assigned to each cell cycle phase as Set A and the three remaining gene lists (assigned to the other phases) as Set B. For Set C we used a literature corpus that allowed us to measure the performance for each classification and to evaluate the results, as described next.

The Evaluation: Following the example presented in [9], and in order to evaluate the classification results, we created a test set C by collecting abstracts known via Medical Subject Heading (MeSH) terms [16] to be related to each of the cell cycle phases. From [9] we reused only the S-phase query (that collects the S-phase related abstracts). In addition, we altered the S phase query so that we can assign abstracts specifically to each of the other three phases as well (see Table 1). As expected, the retrieved PubMed results for each query did not overlap - however, we processed these sets further and we removed any abstracts that belonged also to the training set (i.e., abstracts linked to the respective input genes). Last, we excluded abstracts that had not yet been indexed by Caipirini's underlying dictionary; only small differences were observed (see Table 1). Set C was used as a 'control', and was the same in all of the four classification tasks.

3   Results and Discussion

By assigning the genes that are related to each specific cell cycle phase to set A and the rest of the genes to set B we trained Caipirini [9] four times, as follows bellow:

- Set A = G1-Phase gene IDs; Set B = S,G2,M-Phase gene IDs
- Set A = S-Phase gene IDs; Set B = G1,G2,M-Phase gene IDs
- Set A = G2-Phase gene IDs; Set B = G1,S,M-Phase gene IDs
- Set A = M-Phase gene IDs; Set B = G1,S,G2-Phase gene IDs

In all cases, Set C was the same, i.e., the PubMed identifiers retrieved from the queries presented in Table 1. For each of the four cases, we calculated the accuracy, the precision and the recall of Caipirini's classification. The summarized results are presented in Table 2; the accuracy, the precision and the recall calculations were based on the standard formulas, defined next:

- Accuracy = (TP+TN) / (TP+TN+FP+FN)
- Precision = TP / (TP+FP)
- Recall = TP / (TP+FN)

For all measured metrics above, *TP* stands for 'true positives', *TN* stands for 'true negatives', *FP* stands for 'false positives', and *FN* stands for 'false negatives',

Table 2. Comparing each cell cycle-phase against the rest. Accuracy, precision and recall were calculated for each of the four experiments.

	Caipirini	Input Training Sets		Performance Measures		
	Task	Vectors of A	Vectors of B	Accuracy	Precision	Recall
1	G1 vs S,G2,M	5696	28621	0.806	0.404	0.220
2	S vs M,G1,G2	7920	26397	0.660	0.842	0.412
3	G2 vs G1,S,M	4805	29512	0.816	0.192	0.073
4	M vs G1,S,G2	15896	18421	0.634	0.237	0.548

For the S-phase, we used 154 genes associated with the S-phase as set A, 446 genes associated with the other three phases of the human cell cycle (G1, G2, and M) as set B, and as set C we used all abstracts known via MeSH terms to be related to the cell cycle (see Table 1). With this case we verified the performance of Caipirini presented in [9] (see Table 2), and we continued with the remaining three phases similarly:

- (a) We compared the G1 phase with the three other phases and in comparison to the S phase results we found lower precision and recall, but higher accuracy (see Table 2),
- (b) When comparing the G2 phase against the others, we observed that precision and recall were lower than all other three cases, although accuracy remained remarkably the highest (see Table 2).

- (c) In the last case, we compared the M phase against the other three and observed a mixed result: first, the accuracy was comparable to that of S-phase and lower than those for G1 and G2, whereas the precision was comparable to that of G2 and lower than both for G1 and S phases – also, in this case the best recall was achieved (see Table 2).

Comparing the results (see Figure 1), we believe that S-phase, represents the best-case scenario in this study. This can be a result of the distribution of abstracts in Set C (see Table 1). It can also be attributed to the distribution of vectors in each training set (see Table 2; the number of vectors represents the abstracts associated with each set – note that Caipirini does not remove multiple occurrences of abstracts in the training sets). For example, although for M phase there are more training vectors for set A than in the case of S phase, the latter seems to be more robust. Indeed, when comparing with the work from which we got the data set from it becomes clear that for S phase there are many more specific keywords [10]. This indicates that mining the literature for S phase has an advantage in comparison to the other three phases, because this way the SVM can learn better characteristic features and in turn to create a trained model that can separate better the classes.

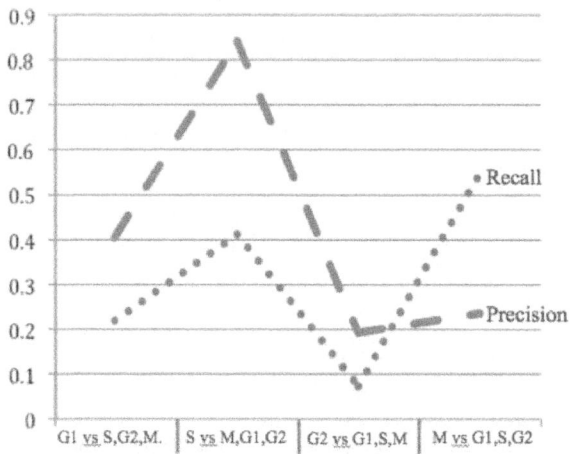

Fig. 1. Precision and Recall for the four experiments. Each case (*x* axis) is named after the phases to which the gene identifiers used in the input sets A and B belonged to.

However, the performance of this categorization can be tested further, along various dimensions: such examples include using different SVM configurations, using different combinations of term types (in the current study all term types were used) and dictionaries, by setting set C otherwise, or by using subsets and/or permutations of each cell cycle phase.

Last, in this work we do not try to interpret further the results since we believe that the comparison of Caipirini with the performance of another somewhat comparable tool [9] already indicated that for this dataset it can be difficult to achieve better results. Nevertheless, we expect that mining literature related to the different phases of the human cell cycle can become a standard case-study used to evaluate and compare new methods and tools, which makes the human cell cycle dataset especially interesting for such tasks. Notably, in order to enable more such scenarios and with many classes of genes, Caipirini's future plans already include the development of an updated version in which multi-class SVM classifiers will also be feasible [9], e.g., in order to distinguish G1, S, G2 and M phases directly 'in one go'.

4   Conclusions

This work does not present novel methods, but rather reports on the performance of Caipirini in mining literature related to different phases of the human cell cycle. First, we verified previous results about S phase and then we expanded further to the remaining three phases. Last, we conclude that this gene set, as proposed in [9] and [10], indeed makes a good benchmark: the findings suggest that the chosen cell cycle data set possesses not only realistic biological scenarios, but also computational characteristics that are challenging for researchers interested in biomedical classification tasks.

Acknowledgements. *Funding:* Georgios A. Pavlopoulos would like to acknowledge support from: Research Council KUL:ProMeta, GOA Ambiorics, GOA MaNet, CoE EF/05/007 SymBioSys en KUL PFV/10/016 SymBioSys , START 1, several PhD/postdoc & fellow grants. Flemish Government: FWO: PhD/postdoc grants, projects   G.0318.05 (subfunctionalization), G.0553.06 (VitamineD), G.0302.07 (SVM/Kernel), research communities (ICCoS, ANMMM, MLDM); G.0733.09 (3UTR); G.082409 (EGFR) IWT: PhD Grants, Silicos; SBO-BioFrame, SBO-MoKa, TBM-IOTA3 FOD:Cancer plans, IBBT. Belgian Federal Science Policy Office: IUAP P6/25 (BioMaGNet, Bioinformatics and Modeling: from Genomes to Networks, 2007- 2011); EU-RTD: ERNSI: European Research Network on System Identification; FP7-HEALTH; CHeartED.

References

1. Krallinger, M., Valencia, A.: Text-mining and information-retrieval services for molecular biology. Genome Biol. 6(7), 224 (2005), doi:10.1186/gb-2005-6-7-224
2. Krallinger, M., Erhardt, R.A., Valencia, A.: Text-mining approaches in molecular biology and biomedicine. Drug Discov. Today 10(6), 439–445 (2005), doi:10.1016/S1359-6446(05)03376-3
3. Lewis, J., Ossowski, S., Hicks, J., Errami, M., Garner, H.R.: Text similarity: an alternative way to search MEDLINE. Bioinformatics 22(18), 2298–2304 (2006), doi:btl388
4. Goetz, T., von der Lieth, C.-W.: PubFinder: a tool for improving retrieval rate of relevant PubMed abstracts. Nucleic Acids Res. 33, W774–W778 (2005)
5. Poulter, G.L., Rubin, D.L., Altman, R.B., Seoighe, C.: MScanner: a classifier for retrieving Medline citations. Bioinformatics 9, 108 (2008), doi:1471-2105-9-108
6. Tuchler, T., Velez, G., Graf, A., Kreil, D.P.: BibGlimpse: the case for a light-weight reprint manager in distributed literature research. BMC Bioinformatics 9, 406 (2008), doi:1471-2105-9-406

7. Nobata, C., Cotter, P., Okazaki, N., Rea, B., Sasak1, Y., Tsuruoka, Y., Tsujii, J.I., Ananiadou, S.: Kleio: A Knowledge-enriched Information Retrieval System for Biology. In: 31st Annual International ACM SIGIR Conference on Research and Development in Information Retrieval, Singapore, pp. 787–788. Association for Computing Machinery (2008)

8. Fontaine, J.F., Barbosa-Silva, A., Schaefer, M., Huska, M.R., Muro, E.M., Andrade-Navarro, M.A.: MedlineRanker: flexible ranking of biomedical literature. Nucleic Acids Res. 37(Web Server issue), W141–W146 (2009), doi:gkp353

9. Soldatos, T.G., O'Donoghue, S.I., Satagopam, V.P., Barbosa-Silva, A., Pavlopoulos, G.A., Wanderley-Nogueira, A.C., Soares-Cavalcanti, N.M., Schneider, R.: Caipirini: using gene sets to rank literature. BioData Mining 5(1), 1 (2012), doi:10.1186/1756-0381-5-1

10. Soldatos, T., O'Donoghue, S.I., Satagopam, V.P., Brown, N.P., Jensen, L.J., Schneider, R.: Martini: using literature keywords to compare gene sets. Nucleic Acid Res. 38(1), 26–38 (2010), doi:10.1093/nar/gkp876

11. Jensen, L.J., Jensen, T.S., de Lichtenberg, U., Brunak, S., Bork, P.: Co-evolution of transcriptional and post-translational cell-cycle regulation. Nature 443(7111), 594–597 (2006), doi:10.1038/nature05186

12. PubMed, http://pubmed.org

13. Entrez gene database, http://www.ncbi.nlm.nih.gov/sites/entrez?db=gene

14. Ensembl, http://ensembl.org

15. Fan, R.-E., Chang, K.W., Hsieh, C.-J., Wang, X.-R., Lin, C.-J.: LIBLINEAR: A library for large linear classification. Journal of Machine Learning Research 9, 1871–1874 (2008)

16. Medical Subject Headings (MeSH) Fact sheet. In: National Library of Medicine (2005)

CW-PRED: A HMM-Based Method for the Classification of Cell Wall-Anchored Proteins of Gram-Positive Bacteria

Danai K. Fimereli[1], Konstantinos D. Tsirigos[1], Zoi I. Litou[1],
Theodore D. Liakopoulos[2], Pantelis G. Bagos[2], and Stavros J. Hamodrakas[1]

[1] Department of Cell Biology and Biophysics, Faculty of Biology,
University of Athens, Athens 157 01, Greece
fdanai@gmail.com, {ktsirig,zlitou,shamodr}@biol.uoa.gr
[2] Department of Computer Science and Biomedical Informatics,
University of Central Greece, Papasiopoulou 2-4 Lamia 35100, Greece
{liakop,pbagos}@ucg.gr

Abstract. Gram-positive bacteria have surface proteins that are often implicated in virulence. A group of extracellular proteins attached to the cell wall contains an LPXTG-like motif that is target for cleavage and covalent coupling to peptidoglycan by sortase enzymes. A Hidden Markov Model (HMM) was developed for predicting the LPXTG and LPXTG-like cell-wall proteins of Gram-positive bacteria. The model is the first capable of predicting alternative (i.e. other than LPXTG-containing) substrates. Our analysis of 177 completely sequenced genomes identified 1456 cell-wall proteins, a number larger compared to the previously available methods. Among these, apart from the previously identified 1283 proteins carrying the LPXTG motif, we identified 39 newly identified proteins carrying NPXTG, 53 carrying LPXTA and 81 carrying the LAXTG motif. The tool is freely available for academic use at http://bioinformatics.biol.uoa.gr/CW-PRED/.

Keywords. Gram-positive bacteria, cell-wall proteins, sortase substrates, LPXTG-like motifs, Hidden Markov Models, proteome analysis.

1   Introduction

Surface proteins of pathogenic bacteria carry out many important functions including invasion of host cells, evasion of the immune response and adhesion to the site of infection and may be used as drugs or vaccine targets [1]. Most of the cell-wall attached proteins have a conserved C-terminal region containing an LPXTG motif, which is required for linking to the cell wall envelope[2, 3]. The C-terminal signal, required for the sorting of the protein to the cell wall, consists of the LPXTG sequence motif (where X denotes any amino acid), followed by a hydrophobic domain and a short positively charged tail[4-6]. Membrane-associated transpeptidases, called sortases, are responsible for the covalent attachment of the LPXTG-like proteins to the Gram-positive bacterial cell wall. Sortases cleave their protein substrate between the threonine (Thr) and glycine (Gly) residues of the LPXTG motif [7] and an amide

I. Maglogiannis, V. Plagianakos, and I. Vlahavas (Eds.): SETN 2012, LNAI 7297, pp. 285–290, 2012.
© Springer-Verlag Berlin Heidelberg 2012

bond is formed between the C-terminal of the threonine and the amino group of the pentaglycine cross-bridge of peptidoglycan. The hydrophobic region of the sorting signal then passes through the plasma membrane and, together with the charged tail, both act as a stop transfer signal [2, 3, 8, 9]. The surface protein linked to peptidoglycan is then displayed on the microbial surface [10].

Apart from SrtA which cleaves LPXTG substrates, it has been shown that other sortases can process proteins that do not fit to the canonical pattern[11-13]. For example, SrtB from *Staphylococcus aureus* recognizes the NPQTN motif [14], whereas SrtC recognizes the LPXTA motif in proteins of *Bacillus anthracis* [10]. Traditionally, LPXTG-like proteins were predicted using regular expression patterns and Hidden Markov Models. Among these methods, CW-PRED has been shown to be the most successful both in terms of sensitivity and specificity [15]. However, the limited number of experimentally verified non-canonical substrates limits also the applicability of such methods in detecting other sortase substrates. This work presents a HMM model, that extends the previous model developed by Litou and coworkers [15] for predicting LPXTG-like cell-wall proteins of Gram-positive bacteria.

2   Materials and Methods

For training the initial version of the model [15], 55 experimentally verified proteins were used, none of which had a sorting signal that differed from the canonical LPXTG motif (SrtA substrates) [16]. In order to extend the model, we performed an extensive literature search in order to find experimentally verified surface proteins. We scrutinized more than 100 published articles published up to October 2010 and we requested experimental evidence for the localization of the protein to the cell-surface. The sequences of these cell-wall anchored proteins were subsequently retrieved from the UNIPROT database, version 14 [17].

We also considered previously described datasets [3] from which we extracted 65 additional experimentally verified cell-wall anchoring proteins of Gram-positive bacteria. After redundancy reduction we finally came up with a total of 132 proteins (the largest set ever compiled), of which 122 had the canonical LPXTG motif, 5 had the NPXTG motif, 3 had the LAXTG motif and 2 had the LPXTA motif. Even though LAXTG-containing proteins are most likely cleaved by SrtA, we considered them as a separate category for computational convenience. In the HMM sub-model that corresponds to the cleavage site pattern, we created four additional branches consisting of states that model the LPXTG, NPXTG, LAXTG and LPXTA variants, while the rest of the states remained the same. The old HMM model was parsimonious in terms of the number of freely estimated parameters, and it has proved to be very sensitive and specific. Thus, we updated only the transition end emission parameters of the HMM that correspond to these states, whereas the other model parameters remained unchanged. The model architecture is shown in Figure 1.

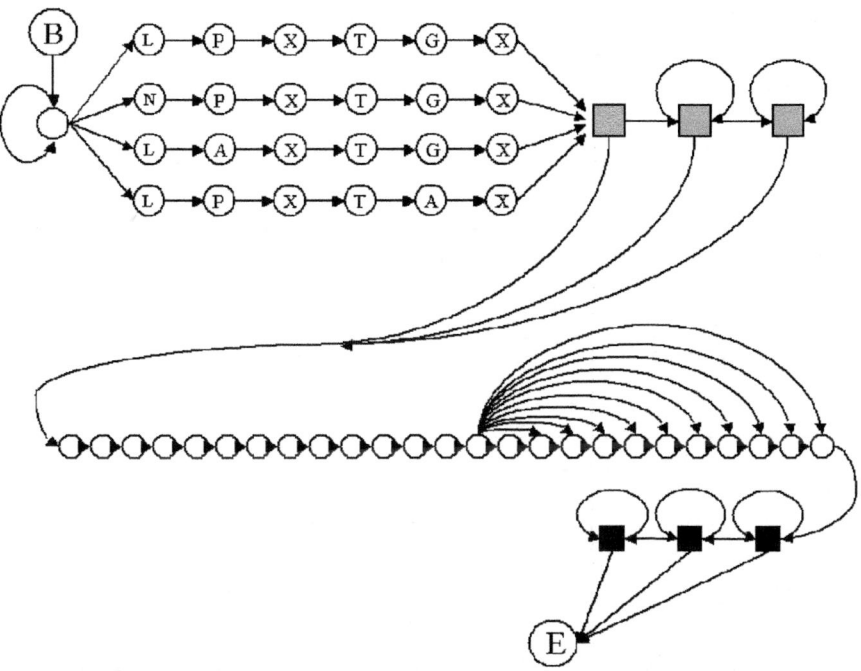

Fig. 1. A graphical representation of the LPXTG anchor submodel of the HMM. Different states are used sequentially to model the LPXTG cleavage site, the variable-length gap region, the hydrophobic helix, and the positively charged tail. Arrows represent allowed transitions among states, and states having the same emission probabilities are depicted using the same shape and color. Regions that are expected to have variable (nonfixed) length are modeled using self-transitioning states. The beginning state is denoted by B, and the end state by E. Different states are used sequentially to model the LPXTG cleavage site (upper left section), the variable-length gap region (upper right section; gray squared states), the hydrophobic helix (middle section; small pointed circle states), and the positively charged tail (bottom dark squared states) [15].

3   Results

The original version of the predictor performs already very well in predicting experimentally verified cell-wall anchored proteins (100% specificity and sensitivity in a 25-fold cross-validation procedure) and this is also the case for the updated version. Due to the lack of an independent test set, we could not measure performance quantitatively. Therefore, as an alternative, we analyzed 177 completely sequenced Gram-positive bacterial genomes retrieved from the NCBI, in order to test the method's prediction accuracy on large, 'unknown' datasets. The detailed results are deposited in a database available as supplementary material in http://bioinformatics.biol.uoa.gr/CW-PRED-results/. The updated HMM predictor identified a total of 1456 proteins, a number larger compared to previously available methods [15]. Apart from the 1283 proteins carrying the LPXTG motif that could be identified by the old model too, by using the new model we identified and classified 39 additional proteins carrying NPXTG, 53 carrying LPXTA and 81 carrying the LAXTG motif.

Table 1. Novel proteins experimentally verified as sortase substrates that are correctly predicted by the CW-PRED algorithm

Protein from Davies, et al. 2009 [18] (Uniprot AC)	Prediction by CW-PRED	Protein from Egan, et al., 2010 [19] (Uniprot AC)	Prediction by CW-PRED
SGO_0854 (A8AWJ3)	Sortase A	sub0135 (B9DT15)	Sortase A
SGO_1148 (A8AXC5)	Sortase A	sub0145 (B9DT25)	Sortase A
SGO_0707 (A8AW49)	Sortase A	sub0207 (B9DT84)	Sortase A
SGO_0210 (A8AUS0)	Sortase A	sub0826 (B9DS05)	Sortase A
SGO_0211 (A8AUS1)	Sortase A	sub0888 (B9DUA9)	Sortase A
SGO_1487 (A8AYA6)	Sortase A	sub1095 (B9DSF3)	Sortase A
SGO_1247 (A8AXM1)	Sortase A	sub1154 (B9DSH4)	Sortase A
SGO_0890 (A8AWM6)	Sortase A	sub1370 (B9DV27)	Sortase A
SGO_2005 (A8AZP4)	Sortase A	sub1730 (B9DW17)	Sortase A
SGO_0966 (A8AWU7)	Sortase A	sub0135 (B9DT15)	Sortase A
SGO_0208 (A8AUR8)	Sortase C	sub0145 (B9DT25)	Sortase A
SGO_0317 (A8AV26)	Sortase A	sub0207 (B9DT84)	Sortase A
SGO_0316 (A8AV25)	Sortase A	sub0826 (B9DS05)	Sortase A
SGO_0388 (A8AV94)	Sortase A	sub0888 (B9DUA9)	Sortase A
SGO_1415 (A8AY35)	Sortase A	sub1095 (B9DSF3)	Sortase A
SGO_0107 (A8AUG9)	Sortase A	sub1154 (B9DSH4)	Sortase A
SGO_0430 (A8AVD6)	Sortase A	AAM99322 (Q8E1E1)	Sortase A
SGO_2004 (A8AZP3)	Sortase A	AAN00204 (Q8DYY9)	Sortase A
SGO_1651 (A8AYR8)	Sortase A	CAW99349 (C0MFU4)	Sortase A
SGO_1650 (A8AYR7)	Sortase A	CAW94597 (C0MAN5)	Sortase A
SGO_1182 (A8AXF9)	Sortase A	CAW92812 (C0M9K8)	Sortase A
		CAW92309 (C0MAH2)	Sortase C
		AAL00574 (Q8DNF3)	Sortase A
		AAT87853 (Q5X9R0)	Sortase A
		AAL97965 (Q8P0G8)	Sortase A

Of the 1456 proteins identified, 778 (53.4%) had an annotation suggesting a definite localization to the bacterial cell wall (cell-wall bound, anchored, LPXTG-bound etc), or belong to families of proteins known to be LPXTG-bound (C5A peptidase, dextranase, sialidase, M protein etc). Furthermore, 171 proteins (11.7%) belong to the same category, having however annotations such as putative, probable or possible. We also identified 40 (mostly extracellular) enzymes (2.8%) without however having any indication as to whether these proteins are cell wall-bound or not, and 30 other proteins (2.1%) of various annotations that may also be LPXTG-bound proteins, but they may also constitute false positive findings. We also identified 419 hypothetical proteins (28.8%), having absolutely no annotation concerning their function or localization. Finally, only 18 proteins (1.2%) possessed an annotation suggesting that they were putative or known transmembrane proteins; this figure should be considered as an estimate for the false positive prediction rate of the method. The majority of proteins with non-canonical motifs are newly identified cell-wall anchored proteins that are presumably cleaved by sortases with different substrate specificities [18]. The annotation was carried out based on the respective Uniprot entries of the proteins.

4   Discussion

We presented a HMM model for predicting the LPXTG-like cell-wall proteins of Gram-positive bacteria. In contrast to the previous HMM model [15], the new model predicts more proteins that contain all possible motifs in their carboxy-terminal, namely the NPXTG, LAXTG and LPXTA motifs, while these proteins are regarded to be cleaved by different sortases. When evaluated at the 94 sequenced genomes previously analyzed [15], the new updated nethod is better at detecting proteins containing non-canonical sortase substrates. Additionally, 83 newly sequenced genomes were also analyzed (a total of 177 sequenced genomes) and proteins having all possible motifs were detected (http://bioinformatics.biol.uoa.gr/CW-PRED-results/). Most importantly, proteins not included in the training set that were identified recently in different organisms using experimental methods [19, 20] were also predicted as sortase substrates by our model (Table 1).

   Taken together, these findings suggest that CW-PRED is a reliable tool for predicting cell-wall proteins of Gram-positive bacteria that contain all possible motifs in their C-terminal. The user may submit either a single sequence and receive detailed results or multiple sequences (up to 1000 per submission) and receive summary prediction in an easily readable format. The prediction method (along with the training set used) and the results from the analysis are freely available for academic users at http://bioinformatics.biol.uoa.gr/CW-PRED/. As far as computational requirements is concerned, a benchmark test on an Intel Xeon CPU server machine with 4GB of RAM memory showed that it takes approximately 15 minutes for a submission of 500 protein sequence entries. This shows that CW-PRED can be used quite efficiently for large genome analysis projects as well.

References

1. Lee, S.G., Pancholi, V., Fischetti, V.A.: Characterization of a unique glycosylated anchor endopeptidase that cleaves the LPXTG sequence motif of cell surface proteins of Gram-positive bacteria. J. Biol. Chem. 277, 46912–46922 (2002)
2. Cabanes, D., Dehoux, P., Dussurget, O., Frangeul, L., Cossart, P.: Surface proteins and the pathogenic potential of Listeria monocytogenes. Trends Microbiol. 10, 238–245 (2002)
3. Navarre, W.W., Schneewind, O.: Surface proteins of gram-positive bacteria and mechanisms of their targeting to the cell wall envelope. Microbiol. Mol. Biol. Rev. 63, 174–229 (1999)

4. Fischetti, V.A., Pancholi, V., Schneewind, O.: Conservation of a hexapeptide sequence in the anchor region of surface proteins from gram-positive cocci. Mol. Microbiol. 4, 1603–1605 (1990)
5. Marraffini, L.A., Dedent, A.C., Schneewind, O.: Sortases and the art of anchoring proteins to the envelopes of gram-positive bacteria. Microbiol. Mol. Biol. Rev. 70, 192–221 (2006)
6. Roche, F.M., Massey, R., Peacock, S.J., Day, N.P., Visai, L., Speziale, P., Lam, A., Pallen, M., Foster, T.J.: Characterization of novel LPXTG-containing proteins of Staphylococcus aureus identified from genome sequences. Microbiology 149, 643–654 (2003)
7. Guttilla, I.K., Gaspar, A.H., Swierczynski, A., Swaminathan, A., Dwivedi, P., Das, A., Ton-That, H.: Acyl enzyme intermediates in sortase-catalyzed pilus morphogenesis in gram-positive bacteria. J. Bacteriol. 191, 5603–5612 (2009)
8. Mazmanian, S.K., Ton-That, H., Su, K., Schneewind, O.: An iron-regulated sortase anchors a class of surface protein during Staphylococcus aureus pathogenesis. Proc. Natl. Acad. Sci. U S A 99, 2293–2298 (2002)
9. Ton-That, H., Mazmanian, S.K., Faull, K.F., Schneewind, O.: Anchoring of surface proteins to the cell wall of Staphylococcus aureus. Sortase catalyzed in vitro transpeptidation reaction using LPXTG peptide and NH(2)-Gly(3) substrates. J. Biol. Chem. 275, 9876–9881 (2000)
10. Marraffini, L.A., Schneewind, O.: Targeting proteins to the cell wall of sporulating Bacillus anthracis. Mol. Microbiol. 62, 1402–1417 (2006)
11. Maresso, A.W., Schneewind, O.: Sortase as a target of anti-infective therapy. Pharmacol. Rev. 60, 128–141 (2008)
12. Ton-That, H., Marraffini, L.A., Schneewind, O.: Protein sorting to the cell wall envelope of Gram-positive bacteria. Biochim. Biophys. Acta 1694, 269–278 (2004)
13. Zhou, M., Boekhorst, J., Francke, C., Siezen, R.J.: LocateP: genome-scale subcellular-location predictor for bacterial proteins. BMC Bioinformatics 9, 173 (2008)
14. Boekhorst, J., de Been, M.W., Kleerebezem, M., Siezen, R.J.: Genome-wide detection and analysis of cell wall-bound proteins with LPxTG-like sorting motifs. J. Bacteriol. 187, 4928–4934 (2005)
15. Litou, Z.I., Bagos, P.G., Tsirigos, K.D., Liakopoulos, T.D., Hamodrakas, S.J.: Prediction of cell wall sorting signals in gram-positive bacteria with a hidden markov model: application to complete genomes. J. Bioinform. Comput. Biol. 6, 387–401 (2008)
16. Hobohm, U., Scharf, M., Schneider, R., Sander, C.: Selection of representative protein data sets. Protein Science: A Publication of the Protein Society 1, 409–417 (1992)
17. Wu, C.H., Apweiler, R., Bairoch, A., Natale, D.A., Barker, W.C., Boeckmann, B., Ferro, S., Gasteiger, E., Huang, H., Lopez, R., Magrane, M., Martin, M.J., Mazumder, R., O'Donovan, C., Redaschi, N., Suzek, B.: The Universal Protein Resource (UniProt): an expanding universe of protein information. Nucleic Acids Res. 34, D187–D191 (2006)
18. Comfort, D., Clubb, R.T.: A comparative genome analysis identifies distinct sorting pathways in gram-positive bacteria. Infect Immun. 72, 2710–2722 (2004)
19. Davies, J.R., Svensater, G., Herzberg, M.C.: Identification of novel LPXTG-linked surface proteins from Streptococcus gordonii. Microbiology 155, 1977–1988 (2009)
20. Egan, S.A., Kurian, D., Ward, P.N., Hunt, L., Leigh, J.A.: Identification of sortase A (SrtA) substrates in Streptococcus uberis: evidence for an additional hexapeptide (LPXXXD) sorting motif. J. Proteome Res. 9, 1088–1095 (2010)

Predicting Human miRNA Target Genes Using a Novel Evolutionary Methodology

Korfiati Aigli[1], Kleftogiannis Dimitris[2], Theofilatos Konstantinos[1],
Likothanassis Spiros[1], Tsakalidis Athanasios[1], and Mavroudi Seferina[1]

[1] Department of Computer Engineering and Informatics, University of Patras, Greece
{korfiati,theofilk,likothan,mavroudi}@ceid.upatras.gr,
tsak@cti.gr
[2] Math. and Computer Sciences and Engineering King Abdullah Univ. of Science and Technology
dimitrios.kleftogiannis@kaust.edu.sa

Abstract. The discovery of miRNAs had great impacts on traditional biology. Typically, miRNAs have the potential to bind to the 3'untraslated region (UTR) of their mRNA target genes for cleavage or translational repression. The experimental identification of their targets has many drawbacks including cost, time and low specificity and these are the reasons why many computational approaches have been developed so far. However, existing computational approaches do not include any advanced feature selection technique and they are facing problems concerning their classification performance and their interpretability. In the present paper, we propose a novel hybrid methodology which combines genetic algorithms and support vector machines in order to locate the optimal feature subset while achieving high classification performance. The proposed methodology was compared with two of the most promising existing methodologies in the problem of predicting human miRNA targets. Our approach outperforms existing methodologies in terms of classification performances while selecting a much smaller feature subset.

Keywords: miRNAs, miRNA targets, genetic algorithms, evolutionary computation, Support Vector Machines, Machine Learning classification, multi-objective optimization.

1 Introduction

In recent years the development of high throughput techniques accelerated the discovery of small non-protein-coding regulatory molecules. One type of these are micro-RNAs (miRNAs). The large family of miRNAs is defined as small (approximately 22 nt) in length, stable molecules which regulate the functions of many other target-genes [1]. Typically, miRNAs have the potential to bind to the 3'untraslated region (UTR) of their mRNA target genes for cleavage or translational repression. The miR-NA class is evolutionary conserved and miRNAs have been discovered in animals, flies, plants and viruses [2]. Their targets range from signaling proteins, metabolic enzymes, transcription factors and so on.

I. Maglogiannis, V. Plagianakos, and I. Vlahavas (Eds.): SETN 2012, LNAI 7297, pp. 291–298, 2012.
© Springer-Verlag Berlin Heidelberg 2012

The very first miRNAs and their targets were discovered experimentally through classical genetic techniques. A description of the experimental techniques and the detailed history of the miRNA genes discovery can be found in [3]. However the experimental identification of miRNA genes and their targets has many drawbacks; cost, time, low specificity are the main technical hurdles.

In order to overcome these limitations and achieve high classification performance many computational approaches have been proposed. The computational methods have proven to be invaluable tools in understanding the biology of miRNAs. Many review papers have already reported the principles of miRNA genes and targets identification and discussed the computational methods that have been applied [4], [5]. Sequence complementarity, thermodynamic stability calculations and evolutionary conservation among species are mainly the most characteristic features which are used to determine the existence of a productive miRNA-mRNA duplex formation [1, 2]. The usage of sequence conservation reduces false positive predictions but some less conserved target sites may be missed leading to low sensitivity. On the other hand, when seed region conservation is not used, the predictors are prone to finding a very large number of predictions and thus to   present a low specificity.

At present, TargetScanS [6], PicTar [7], miRanda [8], DIANA-microT [9], miTarget [10] and NBmiRTar [11] are considered to be the most prevailing algorithmic approaches for the prediction of miRNA targets. Although encouraging results are obtained, still existing computational methodologies for the prediction of miRNA targets mainly fail to handle the trade-offs between sensitivity-specificity and interpretability-prediction performance. Furthermore, they select the features which are going to be used as inputs for the prediction either empirically or using simple filtering methods which are incapable of taking advantage of the mutual information between features and of their rate of ability to link with a specific classifier.

In the present work we present a novel computational machine learning approach for the prediction of miRNA targets, which combines the efficiency of Support Vector Machines with Genetic Algorithms for parameters optimization and feature selection. The proposed methodology presents high classification performance combined with a selection of a much smaller feature subset. Thus, it manages to overcome the main problems of existing computational methodologies for the prediction of miRNA targets.

The rest of the article is organized as follows: section 2 describes the implementation of our method. Section 3 provides the experimental results and section 4 concludes the paper.

2   Methodology

2.1   Dataset

In order to distinguish between real and pseudo targets, our model was trained and tested using a relevant biological data set consisting of both positive and negative examples. To ensure the quality of the training data, experimentally verified microRNAs and their targets were collected from the literature. During the data collection step, sequences which were not verified by wet lab experiments were excluded. Targets whose precise binding sites could not be accurately verified were also excluded. The major criterion for including a target into the dataset was the exact binding site of the miRNA-mRNA duplex to be known.

The human microRNAs were downloaded from miRBase database release 18 [12]. The experimentally verified human microRNA targets were downloaded from TarBase version 5c [13] and miRecords release November 2010 [14] databases. After filtering the target binding sites from these sources, the final dataset consisted of 182 human records of miRNAs and their target mRNA binding sites. From this set, 178 records were positive examples, i.e. true targets and the remaining 4 were negative examples, i.e. pseudo targets. Since the current set of 4 confirmed negative examples was insufficient, additional artificial negative examples were generated following the procedure described in [15].

In specific, 3000 artificial mature miRNAs (30 nt long) were used to produce artificial negative examples. Then, MiRanda [8] is used to generate target predictions for these artificial miRNAs, the target results are assumed to be false positive predictions since the query search did not include true miRNAs. The minimum free energy (MFE) and the miRanda score threshold (SC) (in our case set at 25 kcal/mol and 180, respectively) are two important parameters that should be set to increase the stringency of the predictions and thus decrease the selection of weaker false positive predictions [16]. Since using all 3000 artificial miRNAs yielded a large and unmanageable set of predictions, 100 of them were chosen at random to re-query miRanda and from the whole set of false targets 174 were chosen at random to serve as our negative examples. This method is supposed to be superior to choosing miRNA-mRNA duplexes at random. This is because the artificial negative examples we generated resemble more to true duplexes and will therefore lye, with a good probability, closer to the decision boundary.

Between positive and negative examples a 1:1 proportion was used to guarantee that our classifiers will be trained with equal numbers of positive and negative examples. Finally, in order to create the training and the test sets the whole dataset was divided in half at a random manner.

2.2   Feature Set

In order to train our model, we searched for representative features capable of distinguishing efficiently between real and pseudo microRNA targets. As a result we collected most of the features presented in the literature since our method would extract the optimal subset of them. They can be broadly categorized in structural, thermodynamic, positional and 'motif' [11] based features. Evolutionary conservation was not used in our approach since it would bias the results to evolutionary conserved miRNA and targets. A total number of 124 features were computed and for the computation, RNAfold program from the Vienna RNA package [17] was used as well as scripts written by us.

2.3   Proposed miRNA Target Prediction Method

A hybrid methodology, implemented in Matlab, was designed and developed for the prediction of miRNA target genes, combining Genetic Algorithms (GA) and Support Vector Machine (SVM) classifiers. The SVM algorithm [18] is the most popular kernel based method and it is considered as a state-of-the-art classification technique able to provide accurate classification models with high generalization ability. Genetic Algorithms [19] are search algorithms inspired by the principle of natural selection. They are useful and efficient if the search space is big and complicated or there is not any available mathematical formulation of the problem. It has been shown that GAs can deal with large search spaces and do not get trapped in local optimal solutions like other optimization algorithms [19].

In our hybrid method the genetic algorithm is used to locate the optimal feature subset and on the same time to tune the *parameters* of the Radial Basis Kernel (C and γ) [20] of the SVM classifier. The produced evolutionary hybrid algorithm mainly consists of the iterative application of the evaluation, selection, crossover and mutation steps in a population of candidate solutions (chromosomes) which are initially randomly generated. Each chromosome is consisted of *feature genes* that encode the best feature subset and *parameter genes* that encode the best choice of parameters (binary encoding was used). The proposed method is depicted in detail in Fig.1.

The size of the initial population was set to 20 chromosomes and the termination criterion stops the evolution when the population is deemed as converged. Specifically, the population is deemed as converged when the average fitness across the current population is less than 5% away from its best fitness. Alternatively, the algorithm stops when the maximum number of 100 generations is reached. The proposed fitness function which was used to evaluate each candidate solution is the one described in equation (1):

$$Fitness = 0.5 \cdot Accuracy + 0.5 \cdot GeometricMean - 0.001 \cdot Selected_{Features} - 0.0001 \cdot SupportVectors$$

$$(1)$$

where Accuracy is the SVM's accuracy, GeometricMean is the geometric mean of sensitivity and specificity, Selected_Features is the selected feature subset size and SupportVectors is the number of support vectors included in the trained SVM model. This fitness function is used in order to balance classification performance, sensitivity-specificity tradeoff, the complexity of the feature set (which relates to the interpretability of the model) and the classification model's complexity (and thus its generalization ability). The values for the constant multipliers in our multiobjective fitness function were set as shown in equation (1) to weight our goals in the following order of significance (from the least significant to the most significant):

Simplicity of Classification model< Complexity of feature set <Sensitivity-specificity tradeoff = Classification performance

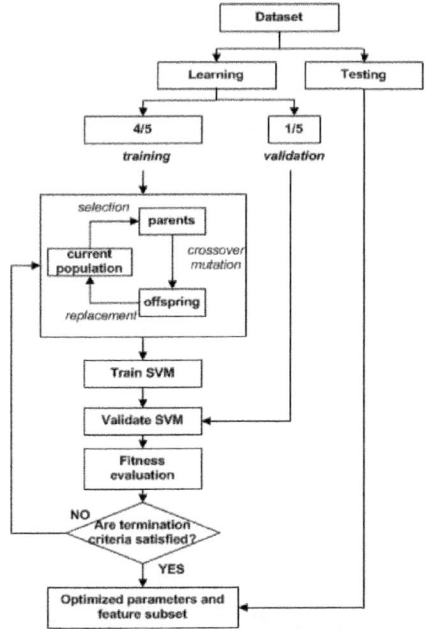

Fig. 1. Flow Chart of the proposed method

The selection scheme which was applied in the proposed hybrid methodology was Rank based roulette wheel selection [21] in order to control the pressure of natural selection. Following, this selection scheme the proposed evolutionary algorithm forces our population to areas of better solutions while minimizing the probability of reducing the population's diversity and thus minimizing the possibility of getting trapped in local optimal.

The two main genetic operators of a Genetic Algorithm are crossover and mutation. For the crossover operator, two-point crossover was used to create two offsprings from every two selected parents. The parents are selected at random, two crossover points are selected at random and two offsprings are made by exchanging genetic material between the two crossover points of the two parents. The crossover probability was set equal to 0.9 to leave some part of the population to survive unchanged to the next generation.

Most studies on the selection of the optimal mutation rate parameter coincide that a time-variable mutation rate scheme is usually preferable than a fixed mutation rate [22]. Accordingly, we propose the dynamic control of the mutation parameter using equation (2):

$$Pm(n) = 0.2 - n \cdot \frac{0.2 - \frac{1}{P_S}}{\mathbf{MAX_G}} \tag{2}$$

where n is the current generation, PS is the size of the population and MAXG is the maximum generation specified by the termination criteria. Using equation (2), we start with a high mutation rate for the first generations and then gradually decrease it over the number of generations. In this way global search characteristics are adopted in the beginning and are gradually switched to local search characteristics for the final iterations. The mutation rate is reduced with a smaller step when a small population size is used in order to avoid stagnation. For bigger population sizes the mutation rate is reduced with a larger step size since a quicker convergence to the global optimum is expected.

3   Results

In order to evaluate the performance of our methodology, we compared its test set performance with the corresponding performance, of the miTarget[10] and NBmiR-Tar[11] classifiers. For the constructed data set, due to the stochastic nature of the proposed methodology and the randomization process for the splitting of training and test sets in every execution, we ran the experiments 20 times and computed the average values. Table 1 summarizes the results achieved.

As we can easily observe in Table 1 our method achieves a significantly better classification performance and at the same time it uses a smaller feature set.

Table 1. Comparative classification performance

Method	Features	Accuracy	Specificity	Sensitivity
miTarget	41	93,93%	89,77%	89,77%
NBmiRTar	67	85,73%	80,13%	91,48%
Proposed Methodology	**38,2**	**99,10%**	**98,24%**	**100,00%**

With a further examination of the frequency of appearance of the extracted features, we observed that the following subset of 5 features had a frequency over 80%:

- number of matches in seed part
- total number of AU matches
- number of bulges of length 5 in out-seed part
- free energy of the out-seed part
- position 3 with a GC match, an AU match, a GU match or a mismatch

These results confirm our hypothesis that the suggested methodology is capable of identifying representative features which optimize the performance. It is also observed that this extracted feature subset contains various types of information, including structural, thermodynamic and positional features. The results also indicate how important for the prediction the out-seed region is, since most of the extracted features concern this region.

4   Conclusion and Future Work

In the present paper we have introduced a novel methodology for the prediction of miRNA targets. This methodology consists of a hybrid combination of a modified genetic algorithm with an SVM classifier using a novel multi-objective fitness function. In contrast to previous approaches where the performance of the classifiers strongly depends on the careful (mostly by hand) pre-selection of the optimal features, our algorithm accepts all available features as input (without any restrictions concerning independency) and automatically generates a small optimal feature subset. At the same time it finds the optimal SVM parameters C and γ for the optimal feature set and produces prediction models of high classification performance.

The proposed methodology was compared with two of the latest existing methodologies and outperformed them in both classification performances and number of the selected features. Using methodologies like the proposed one, that can find a small informative subset of features which does not include features with mutual information or irrelevant features, may help biologists to gain a better understanding of the miRNA targeting procedure.

In order to further enhance the interpretability of our classifier, as future work, we will extract fuzzy rules from the SVM classifier using the methodology described in [23]. Finally, our future plans involve the development of a web-based tool for the online prediction of miRNA targets based on the proposed methodology.

Acknowledgments. (This research has been co-financed by the European Union (European Social Fund - ESF) and Greek national funds through the Operational Program "Education and Lifelong Learning" of the National Strategic Reference Framework (NSRF) - Research Funding Program: Heracleitus II. Investing in knowledge society through the European Social Fund.

References

1. Bartel, D.P.: MicroRNAs: genomics, biogenesis, mechanism, and function. Cell 116(2), 281–297 (2004)
2. Lagos-Quintana, M., Rauhut, R., Meyer, J., Borkhardt, A., Tuschl, T.: New microRNAs from mouse and human. RNA 9(2), 175–179 (2003)
3. Lai, E.C.: microRNAs: runts of the genome assert themselves. Curr. Biol. 13(23), R925–R936 (2003)
4. Mendes, N.D., Freitas, A.T., Sagot, M.-F.: Current tools for the identification of miRNA genes and their targets. Nucleic Acids Res. 37(8), 2419–2433 (2009)
5. Li, L., Xu, J., Yang, D., Tan, X., Wang, H.: Computational approaches for microRNA studies: a review. Mamm. Genome 21(1-2), 1–12 (2010)
6. Lewis, B.P., Burge, C.B.: Conserved seed pairing, often flanked by adenosines, indicates that thousands of human genes are microRNA targets. Cell 120(1), 15–20 (2005)
7. Grun, D., Wang, Y.L., Langenberger, D., Gunsalus, K.C., Rajewsky, N.: MicroRNA target predictions across seven Drosophila species and comparison to mammalian targets. PLoS Comput. Biol. 1(1), 51–66 (2005)
8. Enright, A.J., John, B., Gaul, U., Tuschl, T., Sander, C., Marks, D.S.: MicroRNA targets in Drosophila. Genome Biol. 5(1), R1.1–R1.14 (2005)
9. Kiriakidou, M., Nelson, P.T., Kouranov, A., Fitziev, P., Bouyioukos, C., Mourelatos, Z., Hatzigeorgiou, A.: A combined computational- experimental approach predicts human microRNA targets. Genes Dev. 18, 1165–1178 (2004)

10. Kim, S.K., Nam, J.W., Rhee, J.K., Lee, W.J., Zhang, B.T.: miTarget: microRNA target-gene prediction using a support vector machine. BMC Bioinformatics 7, 411–422 (2006)
11. Malik, Y., Jung, S., Kossenkov, A., Showe, L., Showe, M.: Naïve Bayes for microRNA target predictions—machine learning for microRNA targets. Bioinformatics 23(22), 2987–2992 (2007)
12. Griffiths-Jones, S.: The microRNA Registry. Nucl. Acids Res. 32(suppl. 1), D109–D111 (2004)
13. Papadopoulos, G.L., Reczko, M., Simossis, V.A., Sethupathy, P., Hatzigeorgiou, A.G.: The database of experimentally supported targets: a functional update of TarBase. Nucleic Acids Res. 37, D155–D158 (2009)
14. Xiao, F., Zuo, Z., Cai, G., Kang, S., Gao, X., Li, T.: miRecords: an integrated resource for microRNA-target interactions. Nucleic Acids Res. 37, D105–D110 (2009)
15. Saetrom, O., Snøve, O., Saetrom, P.: Weighted sequence motifs as an improved seeding step in microRNA target prediction algorithms. RNA 11, 995–1003 (2005)
16. Hsu, P.W.: miRNAMAP: genomic maps of microRNA genes and their target genes in mammalian genomes. Nucleic Acids Res. 34, D135–D139 (2006)
17. Hofacker, I.L.: Vienna RNA secondary structure server. Nucleic Acids Res. 31(13), 3429–3431 (2003)
18. Lewis, D.P., Jebara, T., Noble, W.S.: Support vector machine learning from heterogeneous data: an empirical analysis using protein sequence and structure. Bioinformatics 22, 2753–2760 (2006)
19. Holland, J.: Adaptation in natural and artificial systems: an introductory analysis with applications to biology, control, and artificial intelligence. MIT Press, Cambridge (1995)
20. Vapnik, V.N.: The nature of statistical learning theory. Springer (2000)
21. Jadaan, O., Rao, C.R., Rajamani, L.: Parametric Study to Enhance Genetic Algorithm Performance, Using Ranked based Roulette Wheel Selection method. In: InSciT 2006, Merida, Spain, vol. 2, pp. 274–278 (2006)
22. Thierens, D.: Adaptive Mutation Rate Control Schemes in Genetic Algorithms. In: Proceedings of the 2002 IEEE World Congress on Computational Intelligence: Congress on Evolutionary Computation, pp. 980–985 (2002)
23. Mavroudi, S., Katsanos, P., Papadimitriou, S., Likothanassis, S.: Transparent Classification Process of Bioinformatics Data with an Approximated Support Vector Fuzzy Inference System. In: The International Special Topic Conference on Information Technology in Biomedicine (ITAB 2006), Ioannina, Epirus Greece, October 26-28 (2006)

Ontology-Based Automatic Image Annotation Exploiting Generalized Qualitative Spatial Semantics

Christos V. Smailis and Dimitris K. Iakovidis

Dept. of Informatics & Computer Technology, Technol. Educational Institute of Lamia, Greece

Abstract. Ontologies provide a formal approach to knowledge representation suitable for digital content annotation. In the context of image annotation a variety of ontology-based tools has been proposed. Most of them enable manual annotation of the images with higher level concepts whereas many of them are capable of formally representing low-level features as well. However, they either consider specific, usually quantitative, representations of the low-level features, or spatial semantics limited to 2D/3D image spaces. In this paper we propose a novel ontology-based methodology for automatic image annotation that exploits generalized qualitative spatial relations between objects, given an image domain. To represent knowledge for the spatial arrangements, we have implemented an ontology that models spatial relations in multi-dimensional vector spaces. The application of the proposed methodology is demonstrated for automatic annotation of segmented objects in chest radiographs.

1 Introduction

Knowledge authoring in the image domain was traditionally realized by manual segmentation and association of image objects to textual tags, usually arbitrarily selected. Recently, image annotation techniques based on ontologies have been proposed, enabling formal, unambiguous semantic annotation and inference. A problem arises in linking high level semantics such as concepts that are expressed in text form, with low level features of images due to their perceptual nature. This is usually referred to as semantic gap. For this purpose several annotation tools utilize ontologies in order to establish links between MPEG-7 low level feature descriptors and semantics. For example the K-Space Annotation Tool (KAT) [1] implements an ontology-based framework for the semantic annotation of images. KAT's annotation framework is based on the Core Ontology of Multi-Media (COMM) [2]. COMM models the various annotation levels and their linking (e.g. of descriptive and structural annotations), while providing MPEG-7 based structural and media descriptions of formal semantics. Similarly, PhotoStuff [3] is an ontology-based image annotation tool that expresses spatial, temporal or spatioteporal de-composition information, two internal, ontologies are used that model the different multimedia content and segment types in accordance with the MPEG-7 specifications. This provides a simple schema for linking content instances with respective low-level descriptors. A similar annotation scheme is present in M-Ontomat-Annotizer. M-Ontomat-Annotizer enables the ontology-based representation of associations

I. Maglogiannis, V. Plagianakos, and I. Vlahavas (Eds.): SETN 2012, LNAI 7297, pp. 299–306, 2012.
© Springer-Verlag Berlin Heidelberg 2012

between domain specific concepts and their respective low-level visual descriptors. In order to formalize the linking of domain concepts with visual descriptors, M-Ontomat-Annotizer [4] employs the Visual Annotation Ontology (VAO) and the Visual Descriptor Ontology (VDO) [5], both hidden to the user. A survey of the aforementioned tools can be found at [6].

Other studies suggest bridging the semantic gap by describing images through the spatial arrangement of the included objects. Hudelot et al. [7] introduced an ontology of fuzzy 2D/3D directional and topological spatial relations that focuses on the representation of image structural knowledge instead of features such as color and texture. In [8], we presented IROn, an ontology of medical image representations theoretically extending the approach of [7] from image spaces/volumes to multidimensional spaces. However this ontology being rather tied to the medical imaging domain, contains oversimplified concept definitions of spatial relations thus providing limited expressivity.

In this paper we propose a novel methodology for automatic image annotation, based on an ontology we implemented for this purpose that builds on the modeling approach introduced in [8]. This ontology generalizes the ontological representation of spatial relations provided by IROn to any imaging domain. It has enhanced semantic expressivity by being capable of representing qualitative spatial relations not only in 2D/3D spaces, but also in multidimensional vector spaces. Furthermore, the proposed methodology is implemented within our Ratsnake annotation tool [9], enabling it to automatically annotate images. The generalized ontology of spatial relations, the proposed methodology and its application for automatic object annotation are presented in the following paragraphs.

2   Generalized Ontological Representation of Spatial Relations

Our generalized ontological model of spatial relations between objects has been implemented using the web ontology language description logics (OWL DL), which is characterized for its compactness and expressivity of description logics. The modeling approach adopted takes into account the following considerations: a) Spatial relations have their own characteristics, but at the same time act as links between different objects; b) Spatial relations should be independent of vector space dimensionality.

According to this approach, spatial relations are modeled as concepts instead of properties (this reification has been also used in previous studies [7],[8]). To ensure independency from space dimensionality, the spatial relations can only be defined between 1D projections of a reference and a target object, across a certain axis. An axis may participate in the definition of one or more multidimensional spaces. Currently two types of spatial relations have been included in our ontology, namely directional and topological. Each spatial relation can also be linked to its inverse. Directional relations are categorized into positive and negative ones, whereas topological relations are divided into eight main categories that are based on the ones used by region connection calculus 8 (RCC 8). The rest of this section describes the concepts included in our ontology in detail:

• An Object refers to the set of objects that are associated through spatial relations between each other. In description logics syntax [10] this is expressed as:

```
Object ⊑ ⊤
```

• In order to refer to the objects that are used as a reference in the spatial relations, the concept ReferenceObject has been defined:

```
ReferenceObject ≡ Object ⊓
∃ reference.SpatialRelation ⊓ ≥ 1 reference
```

• TargetObject refers to the objects that are used as targets in Spatial Relations:

```
TargetObject ≡ Object ⊓
∃ target.SpatialRelation ⊓ ≥ 1 target
```

The concepts ReferenceObject and TargetObject overlap each other and are subsumed by Object.

• The concept NumericValue, enables the representation of numbers as instances of this concept:

```
NumericValue ⊑ ⊤
```

This is needed in order to represent distinct numeric values regardless of their actual value and to overcome the inability of OWL DL to express numeric datatype properties that can be used for reasoning tasks.

• The concept VectorSpace represents a multi-dimensional vector space. A vector space may be defined by many axes that can also belong to other vector spaces as well:

```
VectorSpace ⊑ (∃ definedBy.Axis) ⊓ (∀ definedBy.Axis)
⊓ (≥ 1 definedBy)
```

• The Axis concept represents an axis that may define one or more vector spaces at the same time:

```
Axis ⊑ (∃ defines.VectorSpace) ⊓ (∀ defines.VectorSpace) ⊓ (≥ 1
defines)
```

• SpatialRelation refers to the set of spatial relations that are defined according to a reference object and a target object across an Axis:

```
SpatialRelation ⊑ (∃ reference.Object) ⊓ (∃ target.Object) ⊓
(∃ hasAxis.Axis) ⊓ (∀ reference.Object) ⊓ (∀ target.Object) ⊓
(∀ hasAxis.Axis) ⊓ (= 1 reference) ⊓ (= 1 target) ⊓ (= 1 hasAx-
is)
```

• The SpatialRelation concept subsumes the concept DirectionalRelation that refers to the set of relations implying direction across an axis. A NumericValue indicating the number of intermediate objects (or their absence if this value represents zero) between the projections of two objects on this axis is required. This way one can uniquely describe the relative position of the target objects in a vector space using a reference object and multiple directional relations.

```
DirectionalRelation ⊑ SpatialRelation ⊓
(∃ numberOfIntermediateObjects.NumericValue) ⊓
(= 1 numberOfIntermediateObjects)
```

DirectionalRelation subsumes the following disjoint concepts: PositiveDirectionalRelation, NegativeDirectionalRelation.

• SpatialRelation also subsumes the concept TopologicalRelation which represents basic relations based on RCC 8. Each topological relation is defined along an axis.

```
TopologicalRelation ⊑ SpatialRelation
```

TopologicalRelation subsumes the following disjoint concepts: Equal, ExternalConnection, Non-TangentialProperPart, Non-TangentialProperPartInverse, PartialOverlap, TangentialProperPart, TangentialProperPartInverse, and Disconnected.

3   Ontology-Based Automatic Image Annotation

Spatial relations are often more reliable descriptors than other object properties in images of static contexts [7]. For example, in chest radiographs the texture of a lung may vary depending on the subject's pathology, whereas its relative position with respect to the spinal cord will remain approximately the same. The methodology presented in this section exploits the semantic description of the spatial arrangement of objects to automatically annotate the objects, within an image or a sequence of images of the same domain, by ontological reasoning. This methodology has been implemented within our Ratsnake annotation tool and enables automatic image annotation within a specified image domain. The whole process is divided in two phases: a training and a labeling phase.

3.1   Training Phase

During the training phase, users must load an image in the annotation tool and annotate objects of interest in the image either manually or by using the semi-automatic image annotation framework proposed in [9]. Each object must be assigned a new textual label or a semantic concept from a domain ontology loaded in the annotation tool. After that, users must specify the image domain, by either submitting a new textual label or by providing a representative concept from one of the loaded ontologies. Then, a new ontology, using the spatial ontology presented in Section 2, is automatically generated to describe the knowledge of the spatial arrangement of objects in the specified domain. This ontology has two parts; a fixed part which holds fundamental concepts regarding the image domain and the segmented image objects, and a dynamically generated part which holds the spatial relations between these objects.

The fixed part of the concept hierarchy in the automatically generated ontology consists of three main classes:

- CoreElements is the superset of all the other classes in the automatically generated ontology.

- Image, in the training phase, represents the training image from which the domain knowledge is extracted.

    `Image ⊑ CoreElements`

- SpatialObject subsumes automatically generated concepts that represent the set of the manually annotated objects on the training image.

    `SpatialObject ⊑ CoreElements`

- ImageDomain represents the image domain specified by the user. Each image domain comprises a set of annotation types that should be contained in images of that domain.

    `ImageDomain ⊑ CoreElements`

In the dynamically generated part user specified image domains are asserted in the ontology as subclasses of the ImageDomain class. The types of annotated image objects are asserted as classes which inherit both the SpatialObject class as well as a subclass of image domain that represents a user specified domain. The instances of the segmented objects in the training image are asserted as individuals of the class that represents the annotation type.

In order to extract the spatial relations between the segmented objects we consider that each object is represented by its center of gravity (CoG). Of course alternative representations of objects could be considered as well. The 1D projection of every segmented image object is spatially related to the 1D projection of a reference object, across each axis of the 2D image plane, using individuals of the subclasses of the SpatialRelation class, defined in the proposed spatial ontology. These include the directional PositiveDirectionalRelation, NegativeDirectionalRelation that can be used to express orientation on an axis and the topological Equal that can be used to assert that the projections of the two objects are located at the same position on an axis. An arbitrarily selected object, that is common for all images of the domain, can be considered as a reference. For images of static context such as the chest radiographs, this reference can be defined as the image center. After this step, the classes that represent annotation types obtain certain restrictions based on the spatial arrangement of the objects. These restrictions define how each instance of a certain annotation type can be related to the reference of that domain thus making the classification of the segmented objects possible.

3.2   Labeling Phase

In the beginning of the labeling phase, images are loaded and segmented in the annotation tool. All segmented ROIs are initially unlabeled. Next, the domain of the images must be specified by the user. Once again spatial relations between the ROIs are extracted with the method used during the training phase. The individuals representing the unlabeled segmented objects are asserted as instances of SpatialObject.

In order to infer the class of the individuals that represent the segmented objects, the restrictions defined in these classes can be exploited by a reasoner, such as FACT++ or Pellet. When instance classification is completed by the reasoner the names of these classes can be assigned as labels to each segmented object. In the following section, both the training and the labeling phases are demonstrated.

4   Automatic Annotation of Objects in Chest Radiographs

We consider the use case of automatic annotation of objects in segmented chest radiographs. For the purposes of our study, we have considered chest radiographs from the publicly available Database of the Japanese Society of Radiological Technology (JSRT) [11]. For each of these images, the ground truth segmented areas from [12] are used. Each image consists of the following objects: heart, left lung, right lung, left clavicle and right clavicle as shown in Fig.2. During the training phase, a random image is selected and its contents are manually annotated by linking them to concepts of the Foundational Model of Anatomy (FMA) [13]. The automatically generated ontology is populated by creating a class for the domain of chest radiographs that subsumes all the classes that represent the types of the segmented objects.

Each class that represents an annotation type obtains restrictions that define how individuals of that class should be related in space to the center of the image across each axis of the 2D plane. For example the left lung is positioned higher in the Y-axis than the center of the image and is on the left of it across the X-axis as shown in Fig.1. Therefore the concept Left_Lung should have the following restrictions which are automatically generated during the training phase:

```
Left_lung ≡ ∃ target ((∃ numberOfIntermediateObjects
{Value-0}) ⊓ (∃ reference ReferenceObject) ⊓ (∃ hasAxis {X-
Axis}) ⊓ NegativeDirectionalRelationship) ⊓ ∃ target ((∃ numbe-
rOfIntermediateObjects {Value-0}) ⊓ (∃ reference ReferenceOb-
ject) ⊓ (∃ hasAxis {Y-Axis}) ⊓ PositiveDirectionalRelationship)
```

The rest of the annotation type classes obtain similar restrictions. Thus, spatial knowledge for the domain is collected. An example of the produced class hierarchy is illustrated in Fig. 2.

During the labeling phase chest radiograph images are segmented while their domain is explicitly defined. Individuals of the type SpatialObject representing the instances of the unclassified segmented objects are then created. Each of them is affiliated to an individual representing the center of the image that belongs to the chest-radiograph domain using instances of the spatial relations defined in our spatial ontology. For example, an individual representing a positive directional relation between the center of an image and a left lung across the axis X is automatically asserted as:

```
NegativeDirectionalRelationX0_ImageCenter-Left_lung:
∃ reference.{ImageCenter-Individual} ⊓  ∃ target.{LeftLung-
Individual} ⊓ ∃ hasAxis.{ X-Axis-Individual} ⊓ ∃ numberOfInter-
mediateObjects.{Value-0}
```

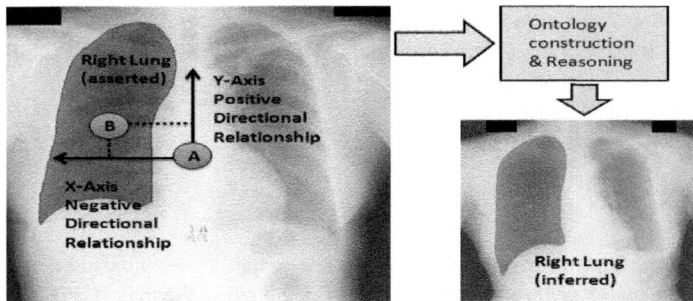

Fig. 1. In the training phase spatial knowledge is extracted from a representative training image. During the labeling phase it is used to infer the annotation types of the segmented objects.

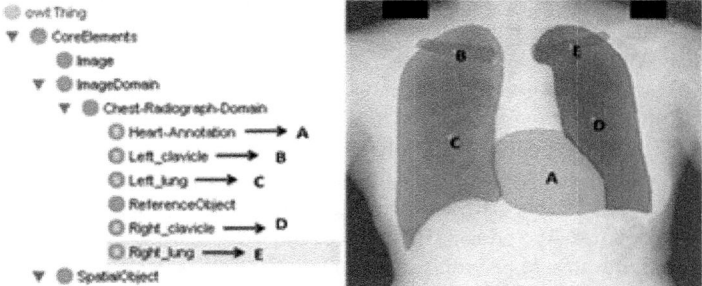

Fig. 2. An example class hierarchy of the automatically generated ontology. Each unlabeled segmented object is assigned to a certain annotation type during the labeling phase.

After this step a reasoner can infer the type of each segmented object thus making possible the labeling of the unclassified objects in each image. In our experiment every segmented object in all of the images of JSRT were successfully labeled.

5   Conclusions

This paper made two contributions. First, it presented a generalized ontology that can describe spatial relations in multidimensional spaces. Then we proposed an automatic annotation methodology that uses the aforementioned ontology to automatically annotate objects that belong to images of the same domain. Advantages of the proposed methodology over conventional approaches include: a) It is non-parametric, b) It does not require any feature normalization since it utilizes relative object descriptions, c) It offers a general framework for bridging the semantic gap, that is particularly suitable for images of static context. Comparative advantages of the proposed approaches over the previous ones, such as M-Ontomat Annotizer [4], include exploitation of the spatial semantics to classify objects and capability to describe spatial relations within feature spaces. Future research directions include the application of the proposed annotation methodology for the automatic annotation of clusters of feature vectors in multidimensional spaces for data mining.

Acknowledgment. This work was realized in the framework of the project DebugIT, co-funded by the EC FP7 grant agreement n° FP7–217139. The EC, DG INFSO, is not liable for any use that may be made of the information in this document. It reflects solely the views of the authors.

References

1. Saathoff, C., Schenk, S., Scherp, A.: Kat: the k-space annotation tool. In: International Conference on Semantic and Digital Media Technologies, Germany (2008)
2. Arndt, R., Troncy, R., Staab, S., Hardman, L., Vacura, M.: COMM: Designing a Well-Founded Multimedia Ontology for the Web. In: Aberer, K., Choi, K.-S., Noy, N., Allemang, D., Lee, K.-I., Nixon, L.J.B., Golbeck, J., Mika, P., Maynard, D., Mizoguchi, R., Schreiber, G., Cudré-Mauroux, P. (eds.) ASWC 2007 and ISWC 2007. LNCS, vol. 4825, pp. 30–43. Springer, Heidelberg (2007)
3. Halaschek-Wiener, C., Golbeck, J., Schain, A., Grove, M., Parsia, B., Hendler, J.A.: PhotoStuff — An Image Annotation Tool for the Semantic Web. In: 4th International Semantic Web Conference Posters, Galway (2005)
4. Petridis, K., Anastasopoulos, D., Saathoff, C., Timmermann, N., Kompatsiaris, Y., Staab, S.: M-OntoMat-Annotizer: Image Annotation Linking Ontologies and Multimedia Low-Level Features. In: Gabrys, B., Howlett, R.J., Jain, L.C. (eds.) KES 2006. LNCS (LNAI), vol. 4253, pp. 633–640. Springer, Heidelberg (2006)
5. Simou, N., Tzouvaras, V., Avrithis, Y., Stamou, G., Kollias, S.: A visual descriptor ontology for multimedia reasoning. In: Workshop on Image Analysis for Multimedia Interactive Services, Montreux (2005)
6. Dasiopoulou, S., Giannakidou, E., Litos, G., Malasioti, P., Kompatsiaris, Y.: A Survey of Semantic Image and Video Annotation Tools. In: Paliouras, G., Spyropoulos, C.D., Tsatsaronis, G. (eds.) Multimedia Information Extraction. LNCS, vol. 6050, pp. 196–239. Springer, Heidelberg (2011)
7. Hudelot, C., Atif, J., Bloch, I.: Fuzzy Spatial Relation Ontology for Image Interpretation. Fuzzy Sets and Systems 159, 1929–1951 (2008)
8. Iakovidis, D.K., Schober, D., Boeker, M., Schulz, S.: An Ontology of Image Representations for Medical Image Mining. In: 9th International Conference on Information Technology and Applications in Biomedicine, Larnaca (2009)
9. Iakovidis, D.K., Smailis, C.V.: Efficient Semantically-Aware Annotation of Images. In: International Conference of Imaging Systems and Tech., Penang, pp. 146–149 (2011)
10. Baader, F., Calvanese, D., McGuinness, D., Nardi, D., Patel-Schneider, P.: The Description Logic Handbook: Theory, Impl. and Appl. Cambridge University Press, Cambridge (2003)
11. Shiraishi, J., et al.: Development of a Digital Image Database for Chest Radiographs with and without a Lung Nodule: Receiver Operating Characteristic Analysis of Radiologists Detection of Pulmonary Nodules. Am. J. Roentgenol. 174, 71–74 (2000)
12. Van Ginneken, B., Stegmann, M.B., Loog, M.: Segmentation of Anatomical Structures in Chest Radiographs using Supervised Methods: a Comparative Study on a Public Database. Medical Image Analysis 10, 19–40 (2006)
13. Golbreich, C., Zhang, S., Bodenreider, O.: The foundational model of anatomy in OWL: Experience and perspectives. Journal of Web Semantics, Web Semantics: Science, Services and Agents on the World Wide Web 4, 181–195 (2006)

Image Interpretation by Combining Ontologies and Bayesian Networks

Spiros Nikolopoulos[1,2], Georgios Th. Papadopoulos[1],
Ioannis Kompatsiaris[1], and Ioannis Patras[2]

[1] CERTH-ITI, Informatics and Telematics Institute, Greece
{nikolopo,papad,ikom}@iti.gr
[2] School of Electronic Engineering and Computer Science, QMUL, UK
i.patras@eecs.qmul.ac.uk

Abstract. A drawback of current computer vision techniques is that, in contrast to human perception that makes use of logic-based rules, they fail to benefit from knowledge that is provided explicitly. In this work we propose a framework that performs knowledge-assisted analysis of visual content using ontologies to model domain knowledge and conditional probabilities to model the application context. A bayesian network (BN) is used for integrating statistical and explicit knowledge and perform hypothesis testing using evidence-driven probabilistic inference. Our results show significant improvements compared to a baseline approach that does not make any use of context or domain knowledge.

1 Introduction

The advances in information technology have reduced the spatial and temporal obstacles in information exchange, allowing users to easily generate and exchange large amounts of digital data. However, the limitations of machine understanding makes it difficult for automated systems to interpret and index all this content in a manner coherent with human cognition. With respect to multimedia, the difficulty of mapping a set of low-level visual features into semantic concepts has motivated the use of domain knowledge.

In our work we introduce a framework for enhancing image analysis using different types of evidence. As evidence we define the information that can be used to support or disproof a hypothesis. In our framework (Fig. 1), we use visual stimulus, application context and domain knowledge to drive a probabilistic inference process that verifies or rejects a hypothesis made about the semantic content of an image. The application context and the domain knowledge are considered to be the a priori/fixed information, while the visual stimulus depends on the examined image and is considered to be the observed/dynamic information. We model the layer of evidence so as to effectively combine both a priori and observed information. More specifically, first we analyze the visual stimulus to obtain conceptual information. Then, we represent domain knowledge and application context in a computationally enabled format. Finally, we combine everything in a bayesian network (BN) that is able to perform inference based

I. Maglogiannis, V. Plagianakos, and I. Vlahavas (Eds.): SETN 2012, LNAI 7297, pp. 307–314, 2012.
© Springer-Verlag Berlin Heidelberg 2012

on soft evidence. In this way, we provide the means to handle aspects like causality (between evidence and hypotheses), uncertainty (of the extracted evidence) and prior knowledge. The main contributions of our work are: a) We combine ontologies and bayesian networks for the purpose of allowing in a probabilistic way the fusion of evidence obtained at different levels of image analysis. b) We show how global and regional evidence can be probabilistically combined within a BN that incorporates domain knowledge and application context.

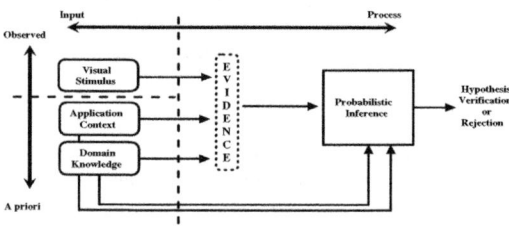

Fig. 1. Functional relations between the different components of our framework

2   Related Work

Semantic image analysis has been addressed by mapping low-level visual features (i.e., color, shape) to high-level descriptions (i.e., concepts), without using domain knowledge or context. Some indicative works include [1] where the authors use the mean of global image features to represent the gist of a scene, and [2] where scene classification is performed using bayesian classifiers. However, the suboptimal performance of these solutions has motivated the exploitation of knowledge and context.

Towards this objective the authors of [3] introduce "Multijects" as a way to map time sequence of multi-modal, low-level features to higher level semantics and "Multinets" for representing higher-level probabilistic dependencies between "Mutlijects". In the same lines, [4] proposes a framework for semantic image understanding that integrates in the same knowledge-based inference framework (based on BNs), both low-level and semantic features. Similarly, [5] uses low-level features and a BN to perform indoor versus outdoor scene categorization. However, the absence of a methodology for integrating domain knowledge into the inference process is what differentiates these works from our approach. Finally there are also works that utilize ontologies as a means to encode domain knowledge. [6] presents a method for combining ontologies and BNs in an effort to introduce uncertainty in ontology reasoning and mapping, while [7] proposes a knowledge assisted image analysis scheme that combines local and global information. However, none of these works attempt to couple ontology-based approaches with probabilistic inference algorithms for combining concept detectors, context and knowledge.

3   Framework Description

Visual Stimulus: For analyzing the visual stimulus we employ supervised learning where a classifier is trained to identify a concept, provided that a sufficiently large number of examples are available. If N_C denotes the set of domain concepts, a concept detector can be implemented using a classifier F_c that is trained to recognize instances of the concept $c \in N_C$. If F_c is a probabilistic classifier, we have $F_c(I_q) = Pr(c|I_q)$. These probabilities $Pr(c|I_q)$ are essentially the soft evidence that are provided to the BN for triggering probabilistic inference.

Domain Knowledge: Let R be the set of binary predicates that are used to denote relations between concepts and O the algebra defining the allowable operators. We use OWL–DL to construct a structure $K_D = S(N_C, R, O)$ that describes how the domain concepts are related to each other. DL stands for "Description Logics" [8] and constitutes a specific set of constructors such as intersection, union, disjoint, complement, etc. Our goal is to use these constructors for explicitly imposing semantic constraints in the process of image interpretation that can not be captured by typical machine learning techniques.

Application Context: Let app denote the application specific information used to guide the analysis mechanism in searching for evidence, and $W = [W_{i,j}]$ the matrix whose elements quantifies the effect of concept c_i on c_j. Then, we consider the application context $X = S(app, W)$ to consists of both app and W. W_{ij} is implicitly extracted from data and encoded into the Conditional Probability Tables (CPTs) of the BN to influence the probabilistic inference process.

Evidence-driven Probabilistic Inference: To perform inference: a) we use K_D to decide which of the concepts should be treated as evidence c^E, b) we use app to decide where to physically search for them, c) we apply F_c on I_q to obtain the degrees of confidence for the concepts in c^E, d) we use app and K_D to decide which of the concepts should constitute the hypotheses set c^H, e) we provide as soft evidence the confidence degrees for the concepts in c^E and trigger probabilistic inference in the BN, f) we propagate evidence beliefs using the network's inference tracks R and the causality quantification functions W_{ij}, and g) we calculate the posterior probabilities for all concepts in c^H. If $\acute{h}(I_q, c_i)$ are the posterior probabilities of the network nodes and $\otimes$ is an operator (e.g., max) that depends on the specifications of the analysis task, semantic image interpretation is achieved based on the formula: $c = \arg \otimes_{c_i \in c^H} (\acute{h}(I_q, c_i))$.

4   Ontology to Bayesian Network Mapping

Our motive for using BNs is to estimate the posterior probabilities of the concepts in the hypothesis set c^H, using the observed confidence degrees of the concepts in the evidence set c^E. The work in [6] describes a probabilistic extension to OWL ontology based on BNs and define a set of structural translation rules to convert this ontology into a directed acyclic graph. Here, we propose an adaptation of this method that learns the network parameters from data.

Network Structure: The transformation of an ontology to a BN takes place in two stages. In the first stage, the BN incorporates the hierarchical information of the ontology by transforming all concepts into nodes (called concept nodes n_{cn}) with two states (i.e., true and false). An arc is drawn between two concept nodes in the network, if and only if they are connected with a superclass-subclass relation in K_D and with the superclass-to-subclass direction. At the second stage, the BN incorporates the semantic constraints of the ontology by creating a control node n_{cl} for each DL constructor (see [6] for details). The constructors that can be handled are owl:intersectionOf, owl:unionOf, owl:complementOf, owl:equivalentClass and owl:disjointWith.

Parameter Learning: Once the structure is fixed, each concept node n_{cn} needs to be assigned a prior probability if it is a root node or a CPT if it is a child node. In [6] these probabilities are set by domain experts. The drawback of this approach is that apart from requiring human intervention when switching to a different domain, it is also likely to introduce bias in the initial conditions of the BN. In our work, we propose a variation of this approach where the necessary probabilities are learned from data (i.e., concept label annotations of the images). The conditional probabilities of all concept nodes are learned by employing the Expectation Maximization (EM) algorithm on sample data. The last step is to manually set the CPTs of all control nodes n_{cl} as shown in [6] and set the belief of the true state equal to 100%. This is done in order to enforce the semantic constraints into the probabilistic inference process.

5   Framework Functional Settings

Our framework implements two different image analysis tasks: (a) **Image categorization** selects the category concept c_i that best describes an image I_q as a whole. In this case, a hypothesis is formulated for each of the category concepts, that is $h(I_q)$. Global classifiers are applied to estimate the initial probability for each hypothesis. For this task, the application context app determines which evidence should be taken from the image local information (e.g., knowing that a region depicts *road* is a piece of contextual information that can help deciding whether the image depicts a *Seaside* or a *Roadside* scene). Local classifiers are applied to the pre-segmented regions $I_q^{s_j}$, in order to generate the pieces of evidence $E(I_q)$ that will be used to trigger probabilistic inference. (b) **Localized region labeling**, assigns labels to pre-segmented image regions with one of the available regional concepts $\acute{c}_i$. In this case, a hypothesis is formulated for each of the available regional concepts and for each of the image segments. Local classifiers are used to estimate the initial probability for each of these hypotheses. Here, the contextual information app is considered to be the image as a whole (e.g., knowing that an image depicts a *Roadside* scene can help in deciding whether a specific region depicts *sea* or *road*). The confidence degrees of the category concepts c_i constitute the pieces of evidence for this task $E(I_q)$, which are used to trigger probabilistic inference. In practice, our framework can be used to improve region labeling when there is a conflict between the decisions suggested by the global and local classifiers by favoring the hypotheses with maximum positive impact on its posterior probability.

The low level processing of visual stimulus consists of visual features extraction, segmentation and learning the concept detection models. Four MPEG-7 visual descriptors [9], namely Scalable Color, Homogeneous Texture, Region Shape, and Edge Histogram, were employed as described in [7]. Segmentation was performed using an extension of the Recursive Shortest Spanning Tree algorithm [10] and Support Vector Machines (SVMs) with a gaussian radial kernel function were employed for learning the concept detection models.

6   Experimental Study

In our study we demonstrate the performance improvements achieved by exploiting context and knowledge compared to baseline detectors that rely solely on visual information. A collection of 648 annotated at global and region detail comprised our dataset[1]. Half of the images were used for training the classifiers F_c and learning the BN parameters and the other half for testing. The resulting BN is depicted in Fig. 2.

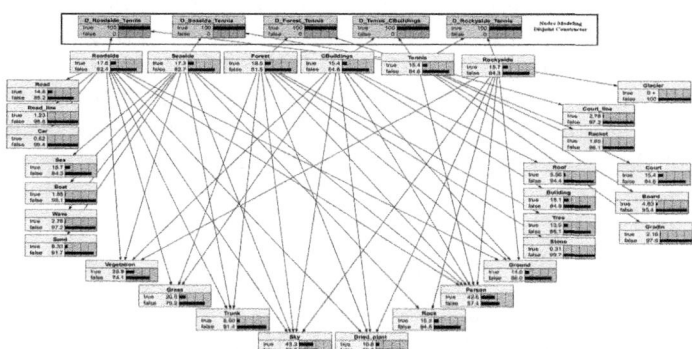

Fig. 2. The nodes in the black frame are used to model the disjointness between the *Tennis* and all other category concepts in the domain

Image categorization is evaluated using three configurations. In the baseline configuration $CON1$ we assess the performance of image categorization based solely on visual stimulus. The second configuration $CON2$ uses context and knowledge in order to extract the existing evidence and facilitate the process of evidence driven probabilistic inference. The BN employed in this configuration is the one depicted in Fig. 2 without the nodes enclosed by the black frame. The third configuration $CON3$ takes into account the semantic constraints of the domain. In this case, the utilized BN is extended with the addition of the

---

[1] http://mklab.iti.gr/project/scef

control nodes (i.e., the nodes enclosed by the black frame of Fig. 2) that are used for modeling the disjointness between *Tennis* and all other category concepts. The reason for treating $CON2$ and $CON3$ as two different configurations was to examine how much of the improvement comes from the use of regional evidence and concept hierarchy information $(CON2)$, and how much comes from the enforcement of the semantic constraints $(CON3)$.

In both $CON2$ and $CON3$ the analysis process unfolds as follows. Initially, we formulate the hypotheses set using all category concepts. Then, we search for all possible regional concepts determined in K_D (i.e., $\forall c_j \in C_L$) before deciding which of them should be used as evidence. This approach requires the application of all available classifiers, global and local, for producing one set of confidence values for the image as a whole, $LK_{global} = \{Pr(c_i|I_q) : \forall c_i \in C_G\}$ and one set per identified image region, $LK_{local} = \{Pr(c_j|I_q^{s_k}) : \forall c_j \in C_L$ & $\forall s_k \in S\}$. All values of LK_{global} and the maximum per column values of LK_{local} are introduced as soft evidence into the BN nodes. Then, the network is updated to propagate evidence impact and the concept corresponding to the node with the highest resulting posterior probability (among the category concepts), is selected to categorize the image (i.e., in this case $\otimes \equiv max$, see Section 3). Fig. 3(a) shows that CON2 outperforms CON1 by $\approx 5\%$ on average. The running example of Fig. 4 demonstrates how evidence collected using regional information $(CON2)$ can correct a decision erroneously taken by a global classifier that relies solely on visual stimulus $(CON1)$. Finally, using CON3 the performance is further increased with an average improvement of $\approx 6.5\%$, compared to the baseline $(CON1)$. Given that the semantic constraint was enforced between the *Tennis* and all other concepts in C_G, the improvement in performance comes from the correction of the test samples that were originally mis-categorized as *Tennis*.

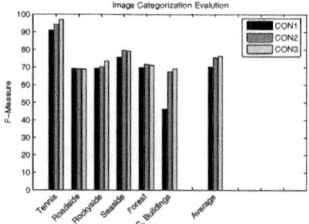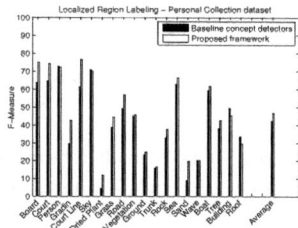

Fig. 3. a) F-Measure scores for image categorization using CON1,CON2 and CON3 configurations, and b) F-Measure scores for localized region labeling

Localized Region Labeling was performed using the BN of Fig. 2 (without the nodes enclosed by the black frame). Our framework is put into force when there is a conflict between the decisions suggested by the global and local classifiers. Let $Child(c_k) = \{c_j : k \rightarrow_{parent} j\}$ be the subset of C_L corresponding to the child nodes of $c_k \in C_G$. Let also $LK_{global} = \{Pr(c_i|I_q) : \forall c_i \in C_G\}$ be the set of global confidence values for image I_q and $LK_{local}^{s_w} = \{Pr(c_j|I_q^{s_w}) : \forall c_j \in C_L\}$ be

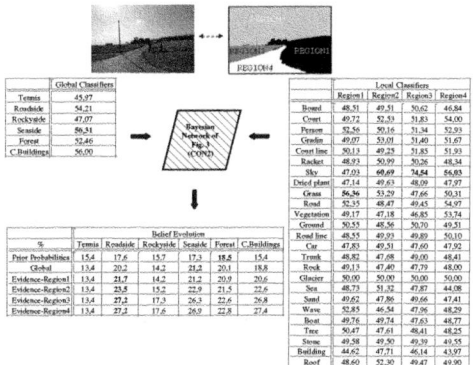

Fig. 4. Running example of image categorization using the framework's $CON2$ configuration. The evidence extracted from image regions help to correct a misclassification error about the image category.

the set of local confidence values for a region $I_q^{s_w}$ of the image. A conflict occurs when $c_l \notin Child(c_g)$ with $g = \arg\max_i(LK_{global})$ and $l = \arg\max_j(LK_{local}^{s_w})$. In the first case we follow the suggestion of the global classifiers and select c_g. Then, the local concept c_l is selected such that $l = \arg\max_j(LK_{local}^{s_w})$ and $c_l \in Child(c_g)$. The confidence values corresponding to c_g and c_l are inserted into the BN as evidence and the overall impact on the posterior probability of the hypothesis that $I_q^{s_w}$ depicts c_l is measured. In the second case, we follow the suggestion of the local classifiers and select $c_{\acute{l}}$, such that $\acute{l} = \arg\max_j(LK_{local}^{s_w})$. The confidence values of the global classifiers are examined and the $c_{\acute{g}}$ with $\acute{g} = \arg\max_i(LK_{global})$ and $c_{\acute{g}} \in F(c_{\acute{l}})$ is selected. The confidence values corresponding to $c_{\acute{l}}$ and $c_{\acute{g}}$ are inserted into the network and the overall impact on the posterior probability of the hypothesis that $I_q^{s_w}$ depicts $c_{\acute{l}}$ is measured. Eventually, the values of the two different cases are compared and depending on the largest, c_l or $c_{\acute{l}}$ is chosen to label the region in question (i.e., this is the functionality of $\otimes$ operator described in Section 3, for this task). If no conflict occurs, the concept corresponding to the local classifier with maximum confidence is selected. Fig. 3(b) shows that when using the proposed framework an

Table 1. Comparison with existing methods in object recognition

	Buildings	Grass	Tree	Cow	Sheep	Sky	Aeroplane	Water	Face	Car	Bicycle	Flower	Sign	Bird	Book	Chair	Road	Cat	Dog	Body	Boat	Average
Textonboost [11]	**62**	**98**	86	58	50	83	60	53	**74**	63	**75**	63	35	**19**	**92**	15	86	**54**	19	**62**	7	58
PLSA-MRF/P [12]	52	87	68	**73**	**84**	94	**88**	**73**	70	68	74	**89**	33	19	78	**34**	**89**	46	**49**	54	**31**	**64**
Prop. Fram.	32	55	**87**	40	73	**96**	57	56	50	**76**	8	64	**38**	12	46	5	51	12	8	29	18	44

average increase of approximately 4.5% is accomplished. Finally, Table 1 shows how our method compares with two state-of-the art methods [11] and [12] on the MSRC dataset[2].

7   Conclusions

Our experiments have shown that the amount and nature of the semantic information that can be used to enhance image interpretation depends on the characteristics of the domain. Although the knowledge structure and the causality relations were useful in all cases, the semantic constraints originating from the domain were only able to help when the imposed rules were sufficiently concrete (e.g., the disjointness between "Tennis" and all other category concepts). On the contrary, attempts to incorporate semantic constraints that were less strict from the visual inference point of view didn't lead to performance improvements.

References

1. Oliva, A., Torralba, A.: Building the gist of a scene: the role of global image features in recognition. Progress in Brain Research (2006)
2. Gokalp, D., Aksoy, S.: Scene classification using bag-of-regions representations. In: CVPR 2007, pp. 1–8 (June 2007)
3. Naphade, M.R., Huang, T.S.: A probabilistic framework for semantic video indexing, filtering, and retrieval. IEEE TMM 3(1), 141–151 (2001)
4. Luo, J., Savakis, A.E., Singhal, A.: A bayesian network-based framework for semantic image understanding. Pattern Recognition 38(6) (2005)
5. Kane, M.J., Savakis, A.E.: Bayesian network structure learning and inference in indoor vs. outdoor image classification. In: ICPR 2004, pp. 479–482 (2004)
6. Ding, Z., Peng, Y., Pan, R.: A bayesian approach to uncertainty modeling in owl ontology. In: Int. Conf. on Adv. in Intel. Sys. - Theory and Applications (2004)
7. Papadopoulos, G.T., Mezaris, V., Kompatsiaris, I., Strintzis, M.G.: Combining global and local information for knowledge-assisted image analysis and classification. EURASIP J. Adv. Sig. Proc. 2007(2), 18 (2007)
8. Horrocks, I.: Description Logics in Ontology Applications. In: Beckert, B. (ed.) TABLEAUX 2005. LNCS (LNAI), vol. 3702, pp. 2–13. Springer, Heidelberg (2005)
9. Manjunath, B.S., Ohm, J.R., Vinod, V.V., Yamada, A.: Colour and texture descriptors. IEEE TCSVT, Special Issue on MPEG-7 11, 703–715 (2001)
10. Adamek, N.M.T., O'Connor, N.: Region-based segmentation of images using syntactic visual features. In: WIAMIS 2005, Montreux, Switzerland (2005)
11. Shotton, J., Winn, J.M., Rother, C., Criminisi, A.: *TextonBoost*: Joint Appearance, Shape and Context Modeling for Multi-class Object Recognition and Segmentation. In: Leonardis, A., Bischof, H., Pinz, A. (eds.) ECCV 2006, Part I. LNCS, vol. 3951, pp. 1–15. Springer, Heidelberg (2006)
12. Verbeek, J., Triggs, B.: Region classification with markov field aspect models. In: CVPR 2007, pp. 1–8 (2007)

---

[2] http://research.microsoft.com/vision/cambridge/recognition

Advanced Cancer Cell Characterization
and Quantification of Microscopy Images

Theodosios Goudas and Ilias Maglogiannis

University of Central Greece
Department of Computer Science and Biomedical Informatics, Lamia, Greece
{goudas,imaglo}@ucg.gr

Abstract. In this paper we present an advanced image analysis tool for the accurate characterization and quantification of cancer and apoptotic cells in microscopy images. Adaptive thresholding and Support Vector Machines classifiers were utilized for this purpose. The segmentation results are improved through the application of morphological operators such as Majority Voting and a Watershed technique. The proposed tool was evaluated on breast cancer images by medical experts and the results were accurate and reproducible.

Keywords: Image Analysis, SVM, Breast Cancer, Cancer cell, Adaptive Thresholding, Watershed, MCF-7.

1 Introduction

The analysis and characterization of biomedical image data is a complex procedure involving several processing phases, like data acquisition, pre-processing, segmentation, feature extraction and classification. The proper combination and parameterization of the above phases enables the development of adjunct tools that can help on the early diagnosis or the monitoring of therapeutic procedures. A specific imaging domain, which image analysis and processing techniques may apply, is that of histological images obtained by optical or electronic microscopy. For instance Loukas et al [6], achieved cell counting in complex large scale histological images by utilizing edge and color information. Saveliev and Pahwa [7] approached the cell counting problem using a topological working algorithm on binary and grayscale images, suitable for different types of cells. Phukpattaranont and Boonyaphiphat [8] presented an algorithm for the segmentation of cancer cells on microscopic images of immunohistologically stained slides from breast cancer. Their method was based on colour contents, neural networks classification and cell size consideration. Maglogiannis et al [9] successfully classified biological microscopic images of lung tissue sections with idiopathic pulmonary fibrosis. Tosun and Gunduz-Demir [10] proposed an effective on histopathological images segmentation algorithm. Especially the evaluation of cancer related pathology images is considered quite important, since it requires years of theoretical and practical training for a pathologist in order to be able to recognize and diagnose fast and accurately the status and the future evolution of a tumor cells.

I. Maglogiannis, V. Plagianakos, and I. Vlahavas (Eds.): SETN 2012, LNAI 7297, pp. 315–322, 2012.

Breast cancer on the other hand is one of the most commonly diagnosed cancer and one of the leading causes of death in United States [1]. Radiotherapy is one of the most common treatments on breast cancer cases [2]. Combined modality treatments are developed through empirical approaches using specific drugs in order to stop the growth of tumors and cause the cancer cell to enter the apoptotic phase with the assistance of the external beam radiation therapy. Researches on Vitamin D [3] proved effectiveness against a broad range of tumor cell types.

The goal of the specific work is the development of an advanced image analysis tool for the accurate quantification of the cancer and the apoptotic cells and the recognition of the corresponding regions in the microscopy image. The tool is used for the evaluation of the influence of the vitamin D3 analogue EB1089 [5] with fractionated radiation on growth and apoptosis human breast cancer tumour MCF-7 [11] cells injected in mice. The rest of the paper is organised as follows; Section II describes the utilized tools and methods for developing the image analysis tool. Section III presents the evaluation, while Section IV concludes the paper.

2   Materials and Methods

Fig. 1 illustrates the block diagram of the proposed tool. Images are first edited by the classification model, which accomplishes the separation of the different type of cells into their respective generated images. The training of the above model is based on the ground truth provided by expert pathologists.

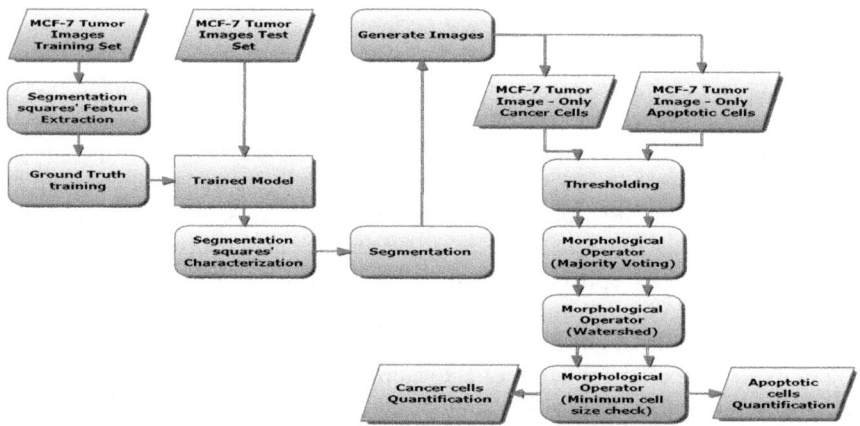

Fig. 1. Data Flow Block Diagram of the Proposed Tool

2.1   Image Dataset Description

The microscopy images dataset was obtained from the National Cancer Institute tumor repository (Frederick, MD) [19]. These images were taken from six week old mices, which were injected the MCF-7 human breast cancer type. Subconfluent cultures, which were grown in RPMI 1640 on 37oC, were fed with fresh medium, washed with PBS, trypsinized, resuspended in medium, and pooled. After centrifugation, cells were resuspended in Matrigel and cold RPMI 1640 for s.c. inoculation in mice.

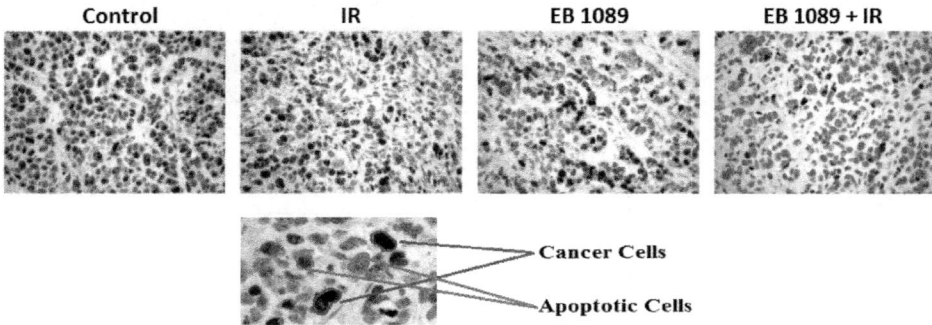

Fig. 2. Four treatment groups of cancer cell images and indication of Cancer and Apoptotic Cells

When the tumor volumes reached 150–200 mm3, tumor-infected mice were randomly selected to receive 3 different treatments. The first group's mice received EB 1089 alone (45 pmol/24 h for 8 days), the second group received radiation alone and the third EB 1089 followed by radiation. So the image dataset provided four groups of datasets, Control, IR (Radiation), EB 1089 (Drug) and EB 1089 + IR combined (see Fig. 2). As also depicted in the second row of Fig. 2, cancer and apoptotic cells have a circular form and sometimes are merged making harder their quantification.

2.2   Feature Extraction and Classification

Customized code was developed, utilizing the ImageJ [12] library, which separates cancer and apoptotic cells from the entire image. While four classifiers were evaluated (Support Vector Machines (SVM), Naïve Bayes, K- Nearest Neighbor and Decision Trees) the SVM classifier was selected since it achieved the higher rates. The mean values of red, green and blue color channels are the features used for the training and testing of the classification model. The ten-fold cross validation has been adopted as a method for testing the accuracy of the classification model. The width of the segmentation square was selected heuristically, from a 2 to 8 pixels range, and set at 2. The case of classifying one by one the pixels was avoided because of the increased processing time during classification and the increased possibility of multiple misclassification issues.

More specifically, the entire image is scanned into segmentation squares classified by the SVM classifier. Each segmentation square belonging to a specific class is assigned with the corresponding color (see Fig. 3). Basically, one class contains everything but apoptotic cells (red segmentation squares in Fig. 3) and the other everything but cancer cells (blue segmentation squares in Fig. 3. The red color segmentation squares generate an image, which discards all the apoptotic class cells (see Fig. 4b). The blue color segmentation squares does the same on the cancer class cells (see Fig. 4c). The result is the generation of two images, each of them containing one kind of cells.

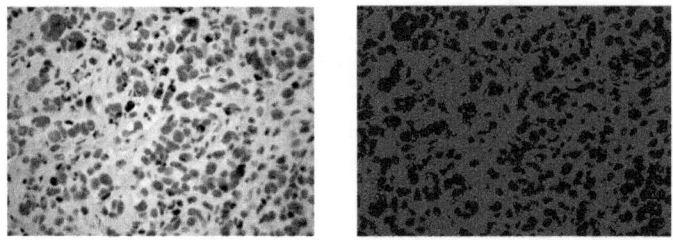

Fig. 3. Original and Segmented Image

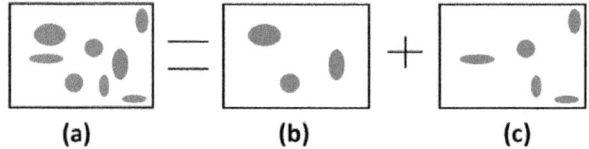

(a)   **(b)**   **(c)**

Fig. 4. a) Original Image b) Red pixels in **Fig. 3** c) Blue pixels in **Fig. 3**

2.3   Thresholding

Adaptive thresholding segmentation is applied on the 8-bit grayscale versions of each of the generated images. Thresholding is one of the most common methods for image segmentation task and it is used in several applications [14]. In order to find the optimal value for thresholding [15] the images, the following procedure is followed: An initial threshold value is set at the minimum possible value (1), which separates the foreground from the background pixels. The average values of the pixels up to the threshold value (the foreground objects) and the pixels above (the background objects) are calculated. Afterwards, threshold value is increased and the process is repeated until the threshold value is greater than the composite average. The optimal threshold for the cancer cells image, utilizing the above technique, is $T1=170$ from the 0-255 scale. Based on the optimal threshold value found a new image is generated by replacing every pixel whose value is lower or equal to $T1=170$ with black, and the pixels over that value with white. The same procedure is applied to the apoptotic image as well. Because the apoptotic cells are lighter than the dark cancer cells require higher values to the threshold in order to distinct them from the background. Therefore, the above procedure ended up with a $T2=196$ threshold value for the apoptotic cells image.

2.4   Noise Removal and Object Quantification

A. Majority Voting Technique
In order to enhance the segmentation results a morphological filtering is required. A simple majority vote technique described in [16] with a dynamic vote limit was utilized in order to accomplish this task. The value of the central segmentation square is set by the majority vote of its eight neighbor segmentation blocks. The limit is set to

five, which means if five or more neighbor segmentation squares have the same value, which differs from the value of the central one; it is automatically set to the same value with its neighbors.

B. Watershed Filtering

The watershed filter is then applied on this image in order to accurately cut the merged particles and provide a clear image for the quantification procedure. Majority vote technique was applied before watershed, since we need first to enhance the foreground objects and then try to separate the merged ones.

C. Size-based Correction and Labeling

Another major factor, except the color, that characterizes a cancer or apoptotic cell is its size. Based on the assistance of our expert pathologists, the size of a valid cancer cell is interpreted as an approximately 100±15 pixels area on the image. For that reason an analyze particle method, similar to a component labeling [18] algorithm was developed. This developed algorithm allows user to set the minimum size of a valid countable cell. More specifically, the developed algorithm scans the image, from right to left beginning from the top and moving to the bottom, until it finds a pixel of a foreground object, in our case a black one since we deal with a binary image. It checks if that pixel belongs to an object that has been already scanned, and if it is it ignores it, otherwise it begins the scanning of a new object by registering it as the first pixel of that object. Afterwards the algorithm will check, based on the previous move of the scanner (in the first step default move is Right), from the westernmost point and moving clockwise to find a pixel of the same color, which has not been visited yet. This loop continues until there is no neighbor point to visit. In the end the entire object will be scanned in a clockwise spiral way. If the size of the object is less than the minimum it turns it to white, and practically it deletes it. This method is as accurate as the Analyze Particles method of imageJ is, plus it requires less memory and it's more simplified than the initial connected component-labeling algorithm. The time required for the proposed tool to complete the above procedures is about 48 seconds on an Intel ® Core™ i7 CPU Q720 at 1.60GHz with 8 GB RAM installed. The whole quantification procedure is depicted in Fig. 5.

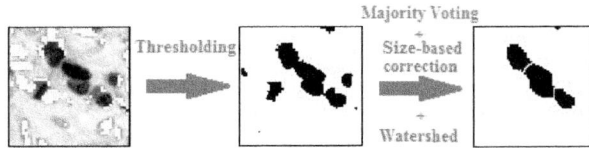

Fig. 5. Example of the proposed Quantification Procedure

3   Experimental Results

The application of the developed tool in 15 images is depicted in Fig. 6. The detection and quantification results are presented in Table 1. As depicted in Table 1, for three images (one of each type), the proposed tool achieved an average of 96.5% accuracy. Likewise, the tool proved sufficient in the testing of all the images of the dataset achieving a 95.37% overall accuracy (see Table 2). Some miscounts may occur due to the existence of extremely merged cells (which look like one round entity), which cannot be separated by the watershed algorithm.

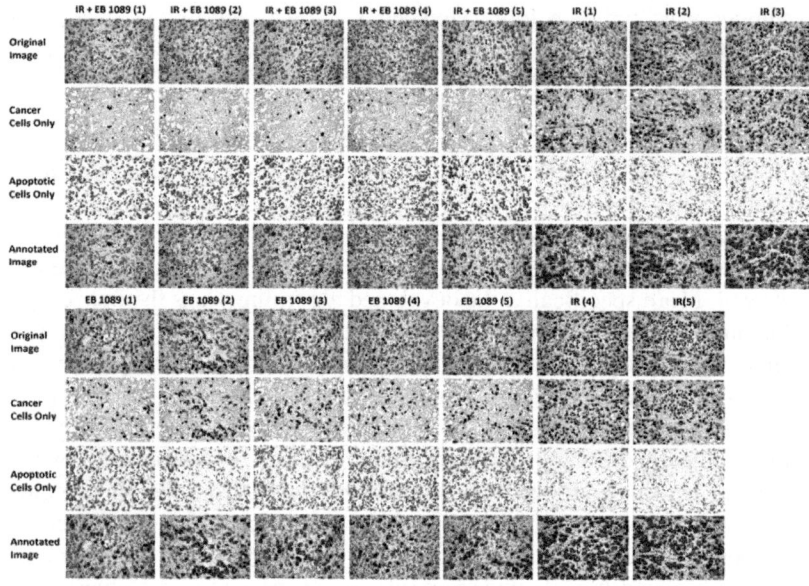

Fig. 6. Visualized Automatic Cell Recognition and Quantification Results

The performed evaluation is in coincidence with the results reported in [15], indicating also the same efficiency of each treatment. In Fig. 6, only the cancer cells are annotated in order to be easier for the physician to obtain an objective perception about the pathogenesis. An option for the annotation of the apoptotic is available as well.

Table 1. Confusion matrices of three random indicative images one of each type (IR+EB 1089(3),IR(1) and EB 1089(2))

IR + EB 1089 (3)	true Cancer cells	true Apoptotic cells	class precision (%)	Total Accuracy (%)	IR (1)	true Cancer cells	true Apoptotic cells	class precision (%)	Total Accuracy (%)	EB 1089 (2)	true Cancer cells	true Apoptotic cells	class precision (%)	Total Accuracy (%)
pred. Cancer cells	13	2	86.67		pred. Cancer cells	147	9	94.23		pred. Cancer cells	109	8	93.16	
pred. Apoptotic cells	1	263	99.62		pred. Apoptotic cells	12	212	94.64		pred. Apoptotic cells	4	203	98.07	
class Recall (%)	92.86	99.25		98.92	class Recall (%)	92.45	95.93		94.47	class Recall (%)	96.46	96.21		96.30

Table 2. Confusion matrix for the whole image dataset (Cell Recognition / Quantification)

ALL images	true Cancer cells	true Apoptotic cells	class precision (%)	Total Accuracy (%)
pred. Cancer cells	1404	132	91.41	
pred. Apoptotic cells	98	3332	97.14	
class Recall (%)	93.48	96.19		95.37

Table 3. Results of the Tool runs in treatment groups

Image	IR + EB 1089 (1)	IR + EB 1089 (2)	IR + EB 1089 (3)	IR + EB 1089 (4)	IR + EB 1089 (5)	IR (1)	IR (2)	IR (3)
Cancer Cells	7	18	13	17	11	147	168	204
Apoptotic Cells	241	265	263	278	229	212	195	165

Image	IR (4)	IR (5)	EB 1089 (1)	EB 1089 (2)	EB 1089 (3)	EB 1089 (4)	EB 1089 (5)
Cancer Cells	228	197	51	109	85	58	91
Apoptotic Cells	119	152	250	203	251	253	256

4   Conclusions

In this paper we proposed a sufficient combination of Support Vector Machines along with Majority Voting and Watershed algorithm, in order to characterize and quantify different types of cells. The simplified connected component-labelling algorithm proved quite fast and sufficient for the quantification of the above cells. The proposed tool was applied on breast cancer biopsy images and provided a ratio of cancer cells over apoptotic cells in order to measure the efficiency of various treatments. The custom code was developed in Java; thus the tool can be easily integrated in an Application Server for web-based execution through Web services.

References

1. German, R.R., Fink, A.K., Heron, M., Johnson, C.J., Finch, J.L., Yin, D.: The Accuracy of Cancer Mortality Group: The accuracy of cancer mortality statistics based on death certificates in the United States. Cancer Epidemiology 35(2), 126–131 (2011)

2. Loncaster, J., Dodwell, D.: Adjuvant radiotherapy in breastcancer. Are there factors that allow selection of patients who do notrequire adjuvant radiotherapy following breast-conserving surgery forbreast cancer? Minerva Med. 93, 101–107 (2002)
3. Chen, A., David, B.H., Bissonnette, M., Scaglione-Sewell, B., Brasitus, T.A.: 1, 25-Dihysdroxyvitamin D3 stimulates activator Protein- 1 dependent Caco-2 cell differentiation. J. Biol. Chem. 274, 35505–35513 (1999)
4. Hansen, C.M., Hamberg, K.J., Binderup, E., Binderup, L.: Seocalcitol (EB 1089): A vitamin D analogue of anticancer potential. Background, design, synthesis, preclinical and clinical evaluation. Curr. Pharm. Design 6, 803–828 (2000)
5. Loukas, C.G., Wilson, G.D., Vojnovic, B., Linney, A.: An image analysis-based approach for automated counting of cancer cell nuclei in tissue sections. Cytometry Part A 55A(1), 30–42 (2003)
6. Saveliev, P., Pahwa, A.: A topological approach to cell counting. In: Proceedings of Workshop on Bio-Image Informatics: Biological Imaging, Computer Vision and Data Mining, Center for Bio-Image Informatics, University of California - Santa Barbara, USA, January 17-18 (2008)
7. Phukpattaranont, P., Boonyaphiphat, P.: Colour based segmentation of nuclear stained breast cancer cell images. ECTI Transactions on Electrical Eng. Electronics and Communications 5(2), 158–164 (2007)
8. Maglogiannis, I., Sarimveis, H., Kiranoudis, C., Chatzioannou, H., Oikonomou, N., Aidinis, V.: Radial Basis Function neural networks classification for the recognition of idiopathic pulmonary fibrosis in microscopic images. IEEE Transactions on Information Technology in Biomedicine 12(1), 42–54 (2008)
9. Tosun, A.B., Gunduz-Demir, C.: Graph Run-Length Matrices for Histopathological Image Segmentation. IEEE Transactions on Medical Imaging 30(3), 721–732 (2011)
10. Soule, H.D., Vazquez, J., Long, A., Albert, S., Brennan, M.: A human cell line from a pleural effusion derived from a breast carcinoma. Journal of the National Cancer Institute 51(5), 1409–1416 (1973)
11. Abramoff, M.D., Magalhaes, P.J., Ram, S.J.: Image Processing with Image. Biophotonics International 11(7), 36–42 (2004)
12. Batenburg, K.J., Sijbers, J.: Adaptive thresholding of tomograms by projection distance minimization. Pattern Recognition 42(10), 2297–2305 (2009)
13. Ridler, T.W., Calvard, S.: Picture thresholding using an iterative selection method. IEEE Trans. System, Man and Cybernetics, SMC 8, 630–632 (1978)
14. Harangi, B., Qureshi, R.J., Csutak, A., Petö, T., Hajdu, A.: Automatic detection of the optic disc using majority voting in a collection of optic disc detectors. In: Proceedings of ISBI 2010, pp. 1329–1332 (2010)
15. Sundaram, S., Sea, A., Feldman, S., Strawbridge, R., Hoopes, P., Demidenko, E., Binderup, L., Gewirtz, A.: The Combination of a Potent Vitamin D3 Analog, EB 1089, with Ionizing Radiation Reduces Tumor Growth and Induces Apoptosis of MCF-7 Breast TumorXenografts in Nude Mice1. Clinical Cancer Research 9, 2350–2356 (2003)
16. Suzuki, K., Horiba, I., Sugie, N.: Linear-time connected-component labeling based on sequential local operations. Computer Vision and Image Understanding 89(1), 1–23 (2003)
17. National Cancer Institute, http://web.ncifcrf.gov/

An Adaptive Dialogue System
with Online Dialogue Policy Learning

Alexandros Papangelis[1,2], Nikolaos Kouroupas[3],
Vangelis Karkaletsis[1], and Fillia Makedon[2]

[1] National Centre for Scientific Research "Demokritos",
Institute of Informatics and Telecommunications
[2] University of Texas at Arlington
Department of Computer Science and Engineering
[3] University of Piraeus, Department of Informatics
alexandros.papangelis@mavs.uta.edu, vangelis@iit.demokritos.gr,
makedon@uta.edu, nick_kouroupas@hotmail.com

Abstract. In this work we present an architecture for Adaptive Dialogue Systems and a novel system that serves as a Museum Guide. It employs several online Reinforcement Learning (RL) techniques to achieve adaptation to the environment as well as to different users. Not many systems have been proposed that apply online RL methods and this is one of the first to fully describe an Adaptive Dialogue System with online dialogue policy learning. We evaluate our system through user simulations and compare the several implemented algorithms on a simple scenario.

Keywords: Adaptive Dialogue Systems, Reinforcement Learning.

1 Introduction

Dialogue Systems (DS) are systems that are able to make human-like conversation with their users and are widely used, mainly as service providers (customer support, flight or hotel booking and others). Such systems, however, are static and inflexible to individual user needs or to changes in their environment, giving rise to a growing need for adaptation in DS. Adaptive Dialogue Systems (ADS) are rapidly becoming smarter and more complex as novel or state of the art Artificial Intelligence (AI) techniques are being applied. AI is a very important part of ADS as it provides methods for learning optimal dialogue policies, Natural Language Understanding (NLU), Natural Language Generation (NLG) strategies and more. In this work we propose an ADS architecture and a system that automatically learns optimal dialogue policies using online RL algorithms.

To the best of our knowledge there is a limited amount of works on dialogue policy learning and due to space constraints we will only mention a few. Cuayáhuitl et al. [2] propose a travel planning DS, that uses hierarchical Reinforcement Learning (RL) to learn dialogue policies for complex actions.

I. Maglogiannis, V. Plagianakos, and I. Vlahavas (Eds.): SETN 2012, LNAI 7297, pp. 323–330, 2012.

Young et al. [14] propose an ADS that provides venue information to tourists in a fictitious city that is able to handle uncertainty and misunderstandings. These systems, however, learn dialogue policies in an offline fashion, meaning that when they interact with real users they actually follow an optimal but static policy. Pietquin et al. [7] propose a system that provides information about restaurants and follow a particle filtering approach to dialogue policy learning. The authors propose the Kalman Temporal Differences algorithm, that is able to learn policies online while also being sample-efficient compared to other methods. Gašić et al. [3] propose a system that provides information about restaurants in Cambridge and applies online RL using Gaussian Processes to learn dialogue policies. These approaches, however, while having many advantages such as handling uncertainty or error recovery, are expensive to run since in [7] many dialogues are required to solve a small problem and in [3] the improvement was not statistically significant over a handcrafted policy.

Our main contribution is that we propose an architecture for ADS that applies several online RL algorithms for dialogue policy learning that are simple to implement and of low cost to run. Such a system is able to learn policies from simulated users for several user categories and these policies are then used as initial policies when the system interacts with a real user. One can also provide handcrafted policies when expert knowledge is available. The system is therefore able to rapidly adapt to a new user since it exploits prior knowledge and continues to learn throughout the interaction.

In the next section we will briefly present some necessary background knowledge, in section 3 we will review the design of our system, in section 4 we will present our evaluation and in section 5 we will discuss the results and conclude.

2   Background

In this section we will briefly provide some details on Markov Decision Processes (MDP), which is the model used by RL, as well as details about RL itself to better understand how it is applied to learn optimal dialogue policies in our system.

A MDP is a tuple $M = \{S, A, P\}$, composed of a non empty set of states S, a non empty set of actions A and a transition probability kernel P that, for each triplet (s_1, a, s_2), models the probability of moving from state s_1 to state s_2 when taking action a. When the system transits from a state to another it receives an immediate feedback value r, called reward. We define a reward function to be the expected value of that reward: $R(s, a) = \mathbb{E}[r(s, a)]$. Here $r(s, a)$ represents the immediate reward the system received after taking action a [11]. A policy π dictates the behaviour of a system and is defined as a mapping from $S \times A$ to a distribution $\pi(s, \alpha)$ that models the probability according to which the system will take action α when it is in state s. A sequence of states and actions until a terminal state is reached defines an episode. For example, a search robot modelled as an MDP may be in a state reflecting its location, and the available actions may be the directions it can go. It will receive positive feedback for finding what it was looking for and negative analogous to the time spent searching. A policy would describe a way of searching the space and RL would try, through the robot's interaction with the environment, to find an optimal way of searching.

More formally, RL tries to find (or learn) an optimal policy π for a system modelled as an MDP. To this aim a function $V(s)$, called *value function*, must be defined that will provide an estimate of how good a policy is $V^{\pi}(s) = \mathbb{E}[\sum_{t=0}^{\infty} \gamma^t r_{t+1} | s_0 = s]$, $s \in S$, i.e. $V^{\pi}(s)$ yields the expected cumulative discounted rewards when the system begins from state s and follows policy π. The discounting factor $\gamma \in [0, 1]$ captures the significance of future rewards. The *return* of a policy π is defined as: $J^{\pi} = \sum_{t=0}^{\infty} \gamma^t r_t(s_t, \pi(s_t))$, where $\pi(s_t) = argmax_{\alpha}\{\pi(s_t, \alpha)\}$. For an optimal policy $\pi^{\star}$ we have that $J^{\pi^{\star}}(s) = V^{\pi^{\star}}(s), \forall s \in S$. The *action-value function* is defined as $Q^{\pi}(s, \alpha) = \mathbb{E}[\sum_{t=0}^{\infty} \gamma^t r_{t+1} | s_0 = s, a_0 = \alpha]$, where $s \in S, \alpha \in A$. Function $Q^{\pi}(s, a)$ provides the expected cumulative discounted rewards when the system begins from state s and takes action α, following policy π. [11]

RL algorithms can be categorised into model-free and model-based algorithms. The first, as the name implies, do not use any model of the environment to aid the learning process, while the latter use interactions with the environment as well as interactions with a model that simulates the world to speed up learning. To implement model-based algorithms we used the Dyna [10] architecture.

3   System Overview

Our system is designed to act as a museum guide and provide descriptions of exhibits in a virtual museum. It is based on the INDIGO [5] system and was implemented using the Olympus [1] platform, which is a platform for developing dialogue systems for research purposes. INDIGO is an affective museum guide dialogue system, able to adapt to different user personalities and user expertise levels. It can assess the user's mood and emotional state and adapt its output accordingly. For dialogue management we used Olympus' RavenClaw Dialogue Manager (DM) and extended it with online RL modules.

Figure 1 depicts the architecture of the proposed Museum Guide dialogue system, where s, a, r are the current state, previous action and reward received respectively and s', a' are the new state and new action. $\tilde{u}_u$ and $\tilde{u}_s$ are the noisy user and system utterances while u_u and u_s are the interpreted user utterance and actual system utterance respectively. The system uses Olympus' NLU and NLG components and also has a learning component, where all learning algorithms are implemented. The DM receives u_u which contains the reward of the last action r. It then sends s, a and r to the learning component and receives back the new system state s' and the new action a' it should take. It then takes action a' and sends a description of the system's utterance u_s to the NLG component. Last, it has an ontology that is based on INDIGO's ontology, which describes museum artefacts, time periods, persons and more and contains information about many exhibits. Museum Guide currently supports one type of query and that is requesting for a description of an exhibit. Search in the ontology is performed by providing values for the exhibit's type, construction time, or time period if it is a person and its physical location.

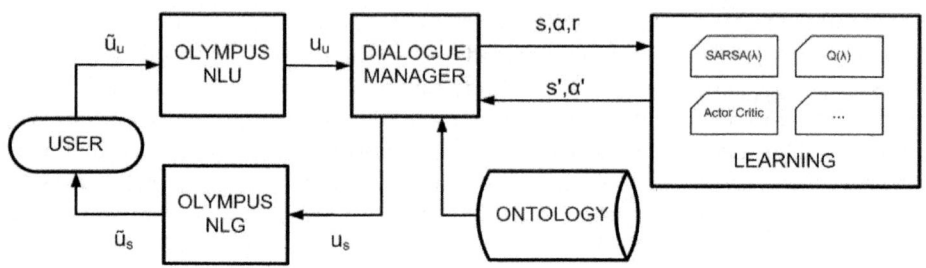

Fig. 1. Architecture of the proposed Museum Guide System

To achieve adaptation in ADS researchers should carefully select methods that are able to tackle the many challenges of this field. RL can successfully handle many of those, such as error recovery and robustness to environmental changes. More specifically, RL can be applied in Dialogue Management (DM) in order to find an optimal dialogue policy that will yield the best action the system should take, depending on the state it is in. Using online RL techniques, the system is able to learn continuously and adapt to changes or different users.

We have implemented a variety of online RL algorithms covering a broad range of the available methods. Our system therefore is able to continue learning as it interacts with real users as well as switch learning methods at will, depending on the problem at hand. Each algorithm's output is in a standardized form and so policies are interchangeable, meaning we can learn a policy using one algorithm and apply it using another. This gives the designer the option of providing a handcrafted policy (modeling prior knowledge) to the system and the system will then optimize that policy according to its current needs. One can also have several user categories and provide handcrafted policies or policies learned through simulations, for each category. The system will be able to use them as initial policies when interacting with appropriate users and refine them to adapt to the specific users' needs. We will now briefly describe the algorithms implemented in our system.

SARSA(λ) (S(λ)) is a very popular RL algorithm, often used in ADS. It applies temporal difference methods for learning and produces an estimate of $Q^\pi(s, a)$, represented as a matrix [10]. λ is a parameter thar controls how much effect will past experience have in future updates. SARSA(λ) is a model-free algorithm, but we also have a model-based version implemented, called DynaSARSA(λ) (DS(λ)).

Q-Learning (Q) was proposed by Watkins [12] and it also learns an estimate of $Q^\pi(s, a)$. The major differences with SARSA(λ) are that it calculates the difference between $Q^\pi(s', a^*)$ and $Q^\pi(s, a)$, where s' is the new state and a^* is the greedily optimal action, that it only updates a single entry of the matrix representing $Q^\pi(s, a)$ at each iteration and does not use eligibility traces, which is a matrix that keeps track of states visited and actions taken. We also have a Dyna version implemented for this algorithm (DQ).

$Q(\lambda)$ is similar to Q-Learning in the sense that it uses the temporal difference between $Q^\pi(s', a^*)$ and $Q^\pi(s, a)$ and similar to SARSA(λ) in the sense that it updates the whole $Q^\pi(s, a)$ matrix at each iteration and uses eligibility traces [12,6]. There is a Dyna version for Q(λ) as well (DQ(λ)).

Actor Critic QV (AC) is an algorithm that uses an actor to follow the policy that is being learned and a critic to evaluate it. This algorithm uses the temporal difference between $Q^\pi(s, a)$ and $V^\pi(s)$ to compute updates for the actor and the critic [13]. We have also implemented a model-based version for this algorithm (DAC).

Our system can operate in two modes. Either in *simulation mode*, where the learning algorithms are trained using simulated users, or in *real user mode* where the system interacts with real users while continuing to learn at a lower pace. A policy learnt using either mode can be saved and loaded for later use again in either mode. During training the system interacts with a real or simulated user and receives a reward after each action (i.e. system utterance). Through this process the system learns which actions bring higher rewards and in what order they should be taken. At the initial stages of training, RL algorithms explore the state-action space and, therefore, make many mistakes. Below we can see example dialogues before training, where actions are taken in a near random way and after training with SARSA(λ):

Dialogue 1: Untrained System
S: Welcome to Museum Guide!
S: What is the location you are looking for?
U: In Athens
S: What is it you'd like to learn about?
U: An altar
S: What is the time period you are looking for?
U: Around 100bc
S: What is the time period you are looking for?
U: Around 100bc
S: What is the location you are looking for?
U: In Athens
S: What is the time period you are looking for?
U: Around 100bc
S: What is the location you are looking for?
U: In Athens
S: Welcome to Museum Guide!

$\vdots$ (omitted)

S: [ITEM DESCRIPTION]
S: You can say, start a new query, or good-bye.
U: bye!
S: Thank you for using Museum Guide, goodbye!

Dialogue 2: Trained System
S: Welcome to Museum Guide!
S: What is it you'd like to learn about?
U: An altar
S: What is the time period you are looking for?
U: Around 100bc
S: What is the location you are looking for?
U: In Athens
S: [ITEM DESCRIPTION]
S: You can say, start a new query, or good-bye.
U: bye!
S: Thank you for using Museum Guide, goodbye!

4   Evaluation

Evaluation of ADS or DS in general is still an open question. Many approaches and methods have been proposed as listed in detail in [8]. When researchers use RL methods the most common approach is to use the reward function $R(s, a)$ as a metric of performance, since it is explicitly defined to minimize or maximize standard metrics such as dialogue length or goal achievement. In our experiments we evaluated each algorithm's speed of convergence, using the reward function $R(d, a)$ as defined later in equation (1). In the rest of this section we will formally model the dialogue problem, describe our experimental setup and present the results of our evaluation, where we focused on the comparison of the different techniques. For simplicity, we opted for a noise free scenario.

The dialogue problem can be formulated as a *slot filling problem*. In such a setting, for example, we have a system that needs to retrieve an exhibit from a database and present it to the user. The user probably has in mind something like: "I want to learn about an *altar*, dating from *500 BC* and located near *Athens*." The information that the system needs (which is item attribute values in its database) are in *italics*, and are called slots. The system must then ask a series of questions in order to retrieve the required information i.e. fill those slots. For different queries the system will require different slots to be filled.

More formally, we can define the problem as: $Z = < z_0, ..., z_N > \in M, M = M_0 \times M_1 \times ... \times M_N, M_i = \{1, ..., |M_i|\}$, where Z are the N slots the user needs to fill and each slot z_i belongs in the set M_i. We can also define the dialogue state as a vector $d \in M$, where the dimensions correspond to slots and their values correspond to the slot values. We also define system actions $A \in \{1, ..., |Z|\}$ to be requests for slots and specifically a_i will request slot z_i. It is possible to define a set of available actions $\tilde{a}_i \subset A$ at each dialogue state d_i but we let $\tilde{a}_i = A$ for simplicity. The user goals are represented by a query vector $q \subset Z$, that represents the slots needed to be filled in order for the system to accurately provide an answer. Please note that we set action a_N to mean *Give Answer*. The reward function in our system is defined as:

$$R(d, a) = \begin{cases} -1, & \text{if} \quad a \neq a_N \\ -100, & \text{if} \quad a = a_N, \exists q_i | q_i = \emptyset \\ 0, & \text{if} \quad a = a_N, \neg\exists q_i | q_i = \emptyset \end{cases} \quad (1)$$

Thus, the optimal reward for each problem is: $-|q|$ since $|q| < |Z|$. Note that this reward function penalises long dialogues and inaccurate responses (i.e. attempts to answer without enough information). It is straightforward to extend this model to account for uncertainty but we will not discuss this in this work.

In our evaluation our problem had 3 slots, *Type, TimePeriod* and *Location*, and typically 6 actions, *Welcome, AskType, AskTimePeriod, AskLocation, Greet-Goodbye* and *GiveAnswer*, out of which we hardcoded the first action to always be *Welcome* and the last to be *GreetGoodbye*. The system then needed to learn how to retrieve the three slots in the most efficient way. We evaluated the system using a simple noise-free user simulator that always responds correctly to any system request. An episode in this problem is over when the system presents the results to the user (which may or may not be the right thing to do). For each algorithm we counted the number of episodes it took to learn the optimal policy and averaged it over 25 runs. Note here that convergence speed is correlated with the average total reward, since the sooner the algorithm converges the higher the reward (it will be performing optimally from the point of convergence and after). The results are shown in Table 1, below.

Table 1. Average learning speed

Alg.	Conv. Ep.
S(λ)	**8.52**
Q	13.8
Q(λ)	12.24
AC	11.6
DS(λ)	31.32
DQ	12.16
DQ(λ)	26.6
DAC	29.04

Table 2. Statistical significance, where $\star$ denotes $p < 0.0001$

Alg.	S(λ)	Q	Q(λ)	AC	DS	DQ	DQ(λ)	DAC
S(λ)	1							
Q	$\star$	1						
Q(λ)	$\star$	**0.0486**	1					
AC	**0.0028**	**0.0352**	0.4961	1				
DS(λ)	$\star$	$\star$	$\star$	$\star$	1			
DQ	**0.0032**	0.1804	0.9443	0.6724	$\star$	1		
DQ(λ)	$\star$	$\star$	$\star$	$\star$	0.1950	$\star$	1	
DAC	$\star$	$\star$	$\star$	$\star$	0.6120	$\star$	0.5355	1

As we can see in Table 1, SARSA(λ) outperforms all algorithms while enjoying statistically significant differences, as shown in Table 2, and DynaQ Learning outperforms the rest model based algorithms. SARSA(λ)'s performance can be in part explained by the eligibility traces that allow past experience to aid the learning process. Model based algorithms evidently do not perform that well, with the statistically insignificant differences (with $p > 0.05$) explained by the fact that these algorithms (including AC) are highly unstable and therefore have very high variance in terms of number of episodes required to converge. We implemented all algorithms in our system to allow the designer freedom of choice (each algorithm is representative of an RL class of methods) and flexibility in unforeseen issues.

5   Concluding Remarks and Future Work

As we can see from Dialogue 1 and 2, there is a clear improvement on the system's behaviour during learning and the optimal dialogue policy resembles one that a human designer would use. While this is a very simple scenario, one can imagine that in a system with many more slots and admissible queries, handcrafted policies are very hard or even impossible to create and inflexible when coming to adapting to users' needs and to abrupt changes in their goals. Online RL can deal with such problems and scale to real world applications thus alleviating the need of huge and complicated handcrafted policies. As mentioned before, our system provides the option of importing a handcrafted policy, that represents prior knowledge that the system may refine to its current needs.

In the future we plan to implement state of the art online RL algorithms, such as Natural Actor Belief Critic [4]. We also plan to apply hierarchical RL to achieve a more natural representation of the system's available actions and the users' goals and also apply techniques such as Complex Action Learning. To this aim we will need to formulate the slot filling problem as a Semi Markov Decision Process (SMDP). SMDPs allow for temporal abstraction in the model, meaning an action can take an arbitrary amount of time to complete and so we can model complex actions. Last we plan to test the Museum Guide system with real users to gain valuable feedback and intuition.

References

1. Bohus, D., Rudnicky, A.I.: The RavenClaw dialog management framework: Architecture and systems. Computer Speech & Language 23(3), 332–361 (2009)
2. Cuayáhuitl, H., Renals, S., Lemon, O., Shimodaira, H.: Evaluation of a hierarchical reinforcement learning spoken dialogue system. Comput. Speech Lang. 24, 395–429 (2010)
3. Gašić, M., Jurčíček, F., Thomson, B., Yu, K., Young, S.: On-line policy optimisation of spoken dialogue systems via live interaction with human subjects. In: Automatic Speech Recognition and Understanding, Hawaii (2011)
4. Jurčíček, F., Thomson, B., Keizer, S., Mairesse, F., Gašić, M., Yu, K., Young, S.: Natural Belief-Critic: A Reinforcement Algorithm for Parameter Estimation in Statistical Spoken Dialogue Systems. International Speech Communication Association 7, 1–26 (2010)
5. Konstantopoulos, S.: An Embodied Dialogue System with Personality and Emotions. In: Proceedings of the 2010 Workshop on Companionable Dialogue Systems, ACL 2010, pp. 31–36 (2010)
6. Peng, J., Williams, R.: Incremental multi-step Q-Learning. Machine Learning, 283–290 (1996)
7. Pietquin, O., Geist, M., Chandramohan, S., Frezza-Buet, H.: Sample-Effcient Batch Reinforcement Learning for Dialogue Management Optimization. ACM Transactions on Speech and Language Processing 7(3), No. 7 (2011)
8. Pietquin, O., Hastie, H.: A survey on metrics for the evaluation of user simulations. The Knowledge Engineering Review (2011) (to appear)
9. Rieser, V., Lemon, O.: Natural Language Generation as Planning Under Uncertainty for Spoken Dialogue Systems. In: EACL 2009, pp. 683–691 (2009)
10. Sutton, R.S., Barto, A.G.: Reinforcement Learning: An Introduction. The MIT Press, Cambridge (1998)
11. Szepesvári, C.: Algorithms for Reinforcement Learning. Synthesis Lectures on Artificial Intelligence and Machine Learning, vol. 4(1), pp. 1–103. Morgan & Claypool Publishers (2010)
12. Watkins, C.J.C.H.: Learning from delayed rewards, PhD Thesis, University of Cambridge, England (1989)
13. Wiering, M.A., Van Hasselt, H.: The QV family compared to other reinforcement learning algorithms. In: IEEE Symposium on Adaptive Dynamic Programming and Reinforcement Learning, pp. 101–108 (2009)
14. Young, S., Gašić, M., Keizer, S., Mairesse, F., Schatzmann, J., Thomson, B., Yu, K.: The Hidden Information State model: A practical framework for POMDP-based spoken dialogue management. Computer Speech & Language 24(2), 150–174 (2010)

Affective, Natural Interaction Using EEG: Sensors, Application and Future Directions

Charline Hondrou and George Caridakis

Image, Video and Multimedia Systems Lab, NTUA
{charline,gcari}@image.ntua.gr

Abstract. ElectroEncephaloGraphy signals have been studied in relation to emotion even prior to the establishment of Affective Computing as a research area. Technological advancements in the sensor and network communication technology allowed EEG collection during interaction with low obtrusiveness levels as opposed to earlier work which classified physiological signals as the most obtrusive modality in affective analysis. The current article provides a critical survey of research work dealing with broadly affective analysis of EEG signals collected during natural or naturalistic interaction. It focuses on sensors that allow such natural interaction (namely NeuroSky and Emotiv), related technological features and affective aspects of applications in several application domains. These aspects include emotion representation approach, induction method and stimuli and annotation chosen for the application. Additionally, machine learning issues related to affective analysis (such as incorporation of multiple modalities and related issues, feature selection for dimensionality reduction and classification architectures) are revised. Finally, future directions of EEG incorporation in affective and natural interaction are discussed.

Keywords: EEG, Affective Computing, Natural Interaction, Affect aware applications.

1 Introduction

The use of ElectroEncephaloGraphy (EEG) to study electrical activity in the human brain was demonstrated for the first time approximately 80 years ago. This development has had far-reaching implications for the study of the human brain's activity changes in response to changes in emotion. Numerous studies have taken place in the last years aiming to understand the correlation between brain signals and emotional states. In EEG, the electrical activity of the brain is observed through scalp electrodes. The 10-20 system [19] is an internationally recognised method to describe and apply the location of the nineteen electrodes used originally. The "10" and "20" refer to the fact that the actual distances between adjacent electrodes are either 10% or 20% respectively of the total front-back or right-left length of the surface of the skull.

I. Maglogiannis, V. Plagianakos, and I. Vlahavas (Eds.): SETN 2012, LNAI 7297, pp. 331–338, 2012.
© Springer-Verlag Berlin Heidelberg 2012

Brain signals are classified in five frequency bands, associated with different mental states. Delta waves (0-3.5 Hz) occur in deep sleep [9]. Theta waves (3.5-7.5 Hz) have been associated with drowsiness, daydreaming, creative inspiration and meditation, arousal [6], sensorimotor processing and mechanisms of learning and memory [10]. Alpha waves (7.5-12 Hz) are present during wakeful relaxation with closed eyes and are reduced with open eyes, drowsiness and sleep. Mu waves (8-13 Hz) are diminished with movement or an intent to move, or when others are observed performing actions. Beta waves (12-30 Hz) are associated with focus, concentration, high alertness, agitation and anxiety. Gamma waves (30-100 Hz) are associated with very high states of consciousness, focus and intellectual acuity, and have a strong presence during meditation.

Finally another important feature measured in EEG studies are Event-Related Potentials (ERP), which are brain responses as a direct result of a thought or perception, and more specifically the P300 signal which is one of the components of an ERP elicited by task-relevant stimuli.

2   Sensors Technology Overview

The first human EEG recording was obtained by Hans Berger in 1924. Since then numerous electroencephalographic studies have taken place using, until a few years ago, caps which were complicated to position on the subject due to their many wires. Recently, the wireless sensors' technology has evolved, making it possible for various systems to be developed. These sensors are inexpensive, easy to set up and are accompanied with out-of-the-box applications or easy to use SDK's, and provide freedom of movement for the user. Industry has shown strong interest in this field. Some examples are Imec, Neurofocus, OCZ, SmartBrain Technologies and QUASAR. Here we will focus on the two most popular, in terms of integration in EEG studies: Emotiv and Neurosky. Depending on the version of these sensors and their SDK there are some variations in the characteristics and properties provided. Here we are presenting the ones that are relative to our theme without separating them according to the edition.

The Neurosky sensor is able to measure frequencies in the range of 0.5-50 Hz and the Emotiv sensor measures frequencies in the range of 0.2-43 Hz. Through both sensors' simple interface the raw EEG, its Fast Fourier Transform and the alpha, beta, gamma, delta and theta waves can be displayed as well as the user's mental state: attention, meditation, anxiety and drowsiness for Neurosky, and long-term excitement, instantanious excitement, engagement, frustration, meditation, boredom for Emotiv. With Emotiv there is also the possibility to monitor the facial expressions (look left/right, blink, left/right wink, raise brow, clench teeth, smile) and the movements of the head calculated from the headset's gyroscope, whereas an animation of "explosions" simulates the action of blinking in Neurosky. The 10-20 system doesn't apply to Neurosky due to the fact that there is only one sensor on the forehead and one "ground" sensor on the earlobe whereas Emotiv is considered partially compliant to the 10-20 system.

3   Affective Aspects of EEG Application

3.1   Emotion Representation

Because of the user-friendly interface these sensors provide, the emotion representation is often quite straightforward. Emotiv provides as direct output frustration and excitement in [11], long-term excitement, instantaneous excitement and engagement in [4, 13] and excitement, engagement, boredom, meditation and frustration in [5] through its simple interface. In some cases information from the Emotiv sensor about the raw EEG and wave variations are combined with the information provided by other biological or non biological sensors, resulting in different types of emotion representation: anger, disgust, fear, happiness, sadness, joy, despisal, stress, concentration and excitement in [8], positive, negative and neutral state of mind in [3, 20]. In cases where the cognitive load of the subject is being studied during a task [7], changes in power of lower frequency (alpha, theta) brain waves detected by Emotiv are analysed in order to determine whether the cognitive load is low, medium or high. Finally, a different approach is adopted when attention or the wink movement is detected. In this case the raw EEG provided by the sensor is processed in order to detect the P300 signal [1, 21] or the signal caused by the winking [1]. The Neurosky sensor outputs, through its intuitive interface as well, attention and meditation in [2], attention level in [22], and relaxation and irritation in [14]. In a fatigue detection system in [12], when three conditions are met simultaneously the user is considered fatigued: a) attention decreases below a certain threshold, b) meditation increases above a threshold and c) either of the delta or theta wave signals maintain the highest value of all frequency bands.

3.2   Annotation

The most common process for annotating experimental corpora is self assessment. This includes questionaires or tasks prior to and/or after the experiment concerning the emotion or the cognitive feature examined [2, 7, 14, 17]. More specifically, certain well-known tasks are given to the subject in order to evaluate the results. As seen in [8, 20], International Affective Picture System (IAPS) is incorporated in order to provide a set of normative emotional stimuli for experimental investigation of emotion and attention. The goal is to develop a large set of standardized, emotionally-evocative, internationally accessible, color images which includes contents across a wide range of semantic categories [15]. In order to measure engagement in [4] the Independent Television Commission-Sense of Presence Inventory (ITC-SOPI) [16] questionnaire was used. This questionnaire offers a valid method of measuring cross-media presence which allows results from different laboratories to be compared. It studies four factors: Sense of Physical Space, Engagement, Ecological Validity, and Negative Effects. In the same study the Self-Assessment Manikin (SAM) is used as well. SAM is a non-verbal pictorial assessment technique that directly measures the pleasure, arousal, and dominance [18] associated with a person's affective reaction to a wide variety of stimuli [15]. Sometimes annotation is provided by the experiment itself. An example of that is [3] where positive, negative and neutral state of mind are measured. During this experiment the participants are asked to control a robot in a maze by thinking about the direction it must take (in reality they can't). The direction in which the robot should move is shown with an arrow. The robot follows a predefined path, sometimes the right one, sometimes the wrong one. When it follows the right path the participant is assumed to be satisfied (positive), when it follows the wrong path the participant is assumed to be unsatisfied (negative) and while the participant is looking at the arrow (before the robot moves) a neutral state is assumed. Another example is [21] where the P300 signal responding to a visual stimulus is measured. In this case the subject is asked to press a button when the stimulus appears. Another article [22] where attention is measured, builds on results from previous studies which suggest that attention is correlated with the errors made and the speed of the activity, as well as whether the participant gave-up or not.

3.3   Stimuli/Induction

The induction of the different mental states detected in EEG studies can be obtained by audio stimuli such as the sounds of a game in a CAVE environment [13] or wind, sea waves and a composition of slow violins, tinkling bells and oboes to induce a positive feeling and musical pop tracks which the subject strongly dislikes to induce a negative feeling like in the case of [14]. Visual stimuli can include displaying pleasant, neutral and unpleasant pictures from the International Affective Picture System [20], visuals in game-playing [13] or a robot's movement [3]. If the P300 signal is to be detected, examples of stimuli can be found in [21] where the subject is looking at a monitor where a ship appears intermittently or in [1] where the photo of each person in a mobile phone's addressbook flashes and when the photo of the person we want to call flashes the signal is detected. Furthermore, examples of interactive Brain Computer Interfaces (BCI) used to induce different emotions are encountered in [4, 8, 11]. Finally, learning activities and tasks such as the Stroop Test, Hanoi Towers, Berg's Card Sorting Task, and seeking information on the web can also be used as stimuli [2, 7, 17, 22].

4   Machine Learning Aspect

4.1   Multimodality

Biomedical studies, in their effort to be more accurate, combine multiple biological signals as well as information coming from the subject's face, voice, body movements and actions on the computer.

EEG information is combined with information taken from the subject's face using visual input or observations in [2, 5, 8, 11, 17]. For the latter, "MindReader" - a system developed at MIT Media Lab - infers emotions from facial expressions and head movements in real-time.

Often EEG is studied in combination with Galvanic Skin Response (GSR), which is a method of measuring the electrical conductance of the skin, which varies with its moisture level. This is of interest because the sweat glands are controlled by the sympathetic nervous system, so skin conductance is used as an indication of psychological or physiological arousal. Examples can be found in [5, 7, 13, 14].

Heart rate measurement is another way to index state of mind and the fusion of it with EEG has been studied in [8, 13, 14].

The eyes' movement is another cue that provides information about the user's attention or focus point. In [5] "Tobii Eye Tracking System" was incorporated in the system, providing data about the user's attention and focus time while performing a task on the computer. This information is combined with the information provided by the EEG sensor. In the case of [7], the eyes' movements and the EEG were used to predict mental states of a person engaged in interactive seeking of information.

Other inputs used to determine mental states can be mouse clicks, keyboard strokes, screen cam recordings [7], body posture, finger pressure (usually on the mouse) [5] and acoustic features [8].

4.2   Feature Processing

Due to the huge variability of features collected in biometric studies, in order to reduce the dimensionality of the problem, eliminate the noise or extract particular characteristics from the signal, the need to preprocess them is common. [20, 21] use Independent Component Analysis (ICA). [14, 20] use Principal Component Analysis (PCA). Noise reduction is also a very important issue in biosignal processing. The use of Notch filters (50 and 60 Hz) and bandpass filters (for example 1-20 Hz in order to isolate the P300) are commonly used.

4.3   Classification

An abundance of classification approaches is being used in EEG research. K-nearest neighbor algorithm and Support Vector Machines (SVM) are incorporated in [11] in order to create predictive models of frustration and excitement, and in [17] to classify numerous features of raw EEG in order to create a model of human academic emotion (boredom, confusion, engagement and frustration). [17] also makes use of a multilayer perceptron (MLP). All of the above classifiers have been used in [14] along with Logistic Regression, Decision Trees, Naïve Bayes and ensemble classifiers.

[11] uses Linear Regression as well and [20] uses the K-means algorithm. [3] makes use of Linear Discriminant Analysis (LDA) to determine the satisfaction level as categorical representation (satisfied, neutral, unsatisfied) and in [21] the Adaptive Neuro Fuzzy Inference System (ANFIS) is used to detect P300-rhythm.

At this point it is worth mentioning that different types of open-source data mining software with embedded algorithms have been a very useful tool for EEG studies. Important examples are "RapidMiner" in [11, 17], and "Weka" in [14].

5   Application Domains

For research purposes various systems have been created in order to study emotion recognition in BCI's [2, 5, 14] as well as attention detection [21]. The main fields in which the wireless EEG sensors find application are games (subsection 5.1), learning (subsection 5.2) and health (subsection 5.3). They are also used in mobile phones [1, 20], Human-Robot Interaction (HRI) [3] and interactive information seeking [7].

5.1   Games

One of the most common fields of use of wireless EEG sensors is game play. The EEG signal is used as feedback to the game so that the game scenario adjusts to the player's needs. For example, detection of boredom will cause changes in the game to make it more challenging whereas detection of anxiety will cause the game to slow down or decrease the levels of difficulty. The portability of these devices is even more useful in cases where they are combined with games played in virtual reality environments. In these cases the player's immersion is augmented further. A good example can be seen in [13] where the environment used is "CAVE" (projectors are directed to three, four, five or six of the walls of a room-sized cube).

5.2   E-Learning

E-Learning is an application domain aiming to create virtual learning environments that will simulate and enhance conventional learning environments [4, 17]. In [11] a tutoring system predicts the student's appraisal of the feedback given and in [22] the system adapts and modifies the learning activity according to the student's level of attention. [8] is proposing a virtual environment for job interview training that senses the applicant's emotions.

5.3   Health and Universal Access

Wireless sensors are now being introduced to the P300 Speller, contributing to its portability. The P300 Speller is a 6x6 matrix of alphanumeric characters where one of its rows or columns flashes randomly. When the character the subject wants flashes, the P300 signal is measured. In this domain we can also find a fatigue detection system proposed by [12].

6   Conclusions and Future Directions

The current article provides a critical survey of research work dealing with broadly affective analysis of EEG signals collected during natural or naturalistic interaction by wireless sensors. EEG analysis in relation to emotion, while having a long history, has always been considered an extremely obtrusive emotional cue capture technique, establishing it as unsuitable for natural interaction. Recent releases of sensors enabling wireless collection of EEG signals enable affect-aware applications using natural interaction. It is expected that application domains such as gaming and e-learning will dominate the field. A related milestone could be the release of a gaming platform with EEG sensors included or at least available as an add-on. As Microsoft's Kinect sensor and OpenNI framework boosted research and applications on Natural Interaction, a similar explosion could follow if a major industry released a gaming platform (similar to the Xbox 360) which would collect EEG data. On the other hand, enabling low-cost and widely available collection of EEG activity during learning activities through e-learning applications would boost research on correlation of brain and cognitive functions as well as adaptive, educational interfaces.

References

[1] Campbell, A., Choudhury, T., Hu, S., Lu, H., Mukerjee, M.K., Rabbi, M., Raizada, R.D.S.: Neurophone: brain-mobile phone interface using a wireless eeg headset. In: Proceedings of the Second ACM SIGCOMM Workshop on Networking, Systems, and Applications on Mobile Handhelds, pp. 3–8. ACM (2010)

[2] Crowley, K., Sliney, A., Pitt, I., Murphy, D.: Evaluating a brain-computer interface to categorise human emotional response. In: 2010 IEEE 10th International Conference on Advanced Learning Technologies (ICALT), pp. 276–278. IEEE (2010)

[3] Esfahani, E.T., Sundararajan, V.: Using brain–computer interfaces to detect human satisfaction in human–robot interaction. Int. J. Human. Robot. 8(01), 87–101 (2011)

[4] Goldberg, B.S., Sottilare, R.A., Brawner, K.W., Holden, H.K.: Predicting Learner Engagement during Well-Defined and Ill-Defined Computer-Based Intercultural Interactions. In: D'Mello, S., Graesser, A., Schuller, B., Martin, J.-C. (eds.) ACII 2011, Part I. LNCS, vol. 6974, pp. 538–547. Springer, Heidelberg (2011)

[5] Gonzalez-Sanchez, J., Chavez-Echeagaray, M.E., Atkinson, R., Burleson, W.: Abe: An agent-based software architecture for a multimodal emotion recognition framework. In: Proc. of 9th Working IEEE/IFIP Conference on Software Architecture, WICSA 2011 (2011)

[6] Green, J.D., Arduini, A.: Hippocampal activity in arousal. Journal of Neurophysiology (1954)

[7] Gwizdka, J., Cole, M.J.: Inferring cognitive states from multimodal measures in information science (2011)

[8] Hamdi, H., Richard, P., Suteau, A., Saleh, M.: Virtual reality and affective computing techniques for face-to-face communication

[9] Hammond, D.C.: What is neurofeedback? Journal of Neurotherapy 10(4), 25 (2006)

[10] Hasselmo, M.E., Eichenbaum, H.: Hippocampal mechanisms for the context-dependent retrieval of episodes. Neural Networks 18(9), 1172–1190 (2005)

[11] Inventado, P.S., Legaspi, R., Bui, T.D., Suarez, M.: Predicting student's appraisal of feedback in an its using previous affective states and continuous affect labels from eeg data. In: Proceedings of the 18th International Conference on Computers in Education, Putrajaya, Malaysia (2010)

[12] Junjian, W., Shujun, X.: Fatigue detecting system. Master's thesis, Linnaeus University (2011)

[13] Koutepova, T., Liu, Y., Lan, X., Jeong, J.: Enhancing video games in real time with biofeedback data. In: ACM SIGGRAPH ASIA 2010 Posters, p. 56. ACM (2010)

[14] Kuncheva, L.I., Christy, T., Pierce, I., Mansoor, S.P.: Multi-modal Biometric Emotion Recognition Using Classifier Ensembles. In: Mehrotra, K.G., Mohan, C.K., Oh, J.C., Varshney, P.K., Ali, M. (eds.) IEA/AIE 2011, Part I. LNCS, vol. 6703, pp. 317–326. Springer, Heidelberg (2011)

[15] Lang, P.J., Bradley, M.M., Cuthbert, B.N.: International affective picture system (iaps): Technical manual and affective ratings (1999)

[16] Lessiter, J., Freeman, J., Keogh, E., Davidoff, J.: A cross-media presence questionnaire: The itc-sense of presence inventory. Presence: Teleoperators & Virtual Environments 10(3), 282–297 (2001)

[17] Mampusti, E.T., Ng, J.S., Quinto, J.J.I., Teng, G.L., Suarez, M.T.C., Trogo, R.S.: Measuring academic affective states of students via brainwave signals. In: 2011 Third International Conference on Knowledge and Systems Engineering (KSE), pp. 226–231. IEEE (2011)

[18] Mehrabian, A.: Pleasure-arousal-dominance: A general framework for describing and measuring individual differences in temperament. Current Psychology 14(4), 261–292 (1996)

[19] Niedermeyer, E., Da Silva, F.H.L.: Electroencephalography: basic principles, clinical applications, and related fields. Lippincott Williams & Wilkins (2005)

[20] Petersen, M.K., Stahlhut, C., Stopczynski, A., Larsen, J.E., Hansen, L.K.: Smartphones Get Emotional: Mind Reading Images and Reconstructing the Neural Sources. In: D'Mello, S., Graesser, A., Schuller, B., Martin, J.-C. (eds.) ACII 2011, Part II. LNCS, vol. 6975, pp. 578–587. Springer, Heidelberg (2011)

[21] Ramirez-Cortes, J.M., Alarcon-Aquino, V., Rosas-Cholula, G., Gomez-Gil, P., Escamilla-Ambrosio, J.: P-300 rhythm detection using anfis algorithm and wavelet feature extraction in eeg signals. In: Proceedings of the World Congress on Engineering and Computer Science, vol. 1 (2010)

[22] Rebolledo-Mendez, G., De Freitas, S.: Attention modeling using inputs from a brain computer interface and user-generated data in second life. In: The Tenth International Conference on Multimodal Interfaces (ICMI 2008), Crete, Greece (2008)

Affective Computing on Elderly Physical and Cognitive Training within Live Social Networks

Evdokimos I. Konstantinidis[*], Antonis Billis, Eirini Grigoriadou,
Stathis Sidiropoulos, Stavroula Fasnaki, and Panagiotis D. Bamidis

Lab of Medical Informatics, Medical School, Aristotle University of Thessaloniki, Greece
{evdokimosk,eirinipsychology,sevifasnaki}@gmail.com,
{ampillis,bamidis}@med.auth.gr, stathsid@auth.gr

Abstract. Emotions play a key role in the user experience, in serious games developed for education, training, assessment, therapy or rehabilitation. Moreover, social network features were recently coined in as key elements for computer based cognitive and physical interventions. In this paper, it is argued that Affective Computing principles may be exploited to increases the motivation of senior users for such computer based interventions. A case study with quantitative results is drawn from the European Commission funded Long Lasting Memories project. Emphasis is placed on how affection, system usability and acceptance might be related to social interaction. Results provide a first evidence that there is indeed a link between how well the intervention and the system is liked when users are placed in groups thereby forming live social networks. It is imperative that such findings could be taken under consideration upon new exergaming designs incorporating social networking capacities over the web.

Keywords: Affective Computing, Social Network, Physical, Cognitive, Intervention.

1 Introduction

Considered as a significant emerging area with enormous research potential and a wide spectrum of prospective applications, Affective Computing (AC) was introduced by Picard in mid-nineties. The term of Affective Computing, i.e., "computing that relates to, arises from, or deliberately influences emotions", was first introduced at Pickard's publication of the Affective Computing book [1]. Acting as the bridge between emotions and computers through the use of theoretical descriptions of human affective states, AC investigates methods in order to establish a complete and reliable layer to support this bridge [2].

One of the fields that AC finds fertile ground is at applications assisting elderly people. Recent literature reveals an increasing number of projects and research targeting to elderly people. This increasing curve stems from the fact that the percentage of elderly living alone also increases gradually. Few of these projects pay attention at the recognition and fewer at influencing elderly people's emotional state. Recent systems

---

[*] Corresponding author.

I. Maglogiannis, V. Plagianakos, and I. Vlahavas (Eds.): SETN 2012, LNAI 7297, pp. 339–344, 2012.

use the technologies of affective computing and fuzzy interpolation to support the judgment of emotion state for elderly living alone [3]. Biosensors, digital cameras, speech treatment (perception/recognition of emotions) and on the other hand robots, avatars, music (expression of emotions) compose the orchestra of affective computing regarding elderly people [4].

On the contrary, the current trends on influencing elderly people's emotional state describe social networks that have been designed especially for elderly people. Such social platforms constituents include communication with relatives and friends and collaboration or competition to achieve goals in form of games. More generally, social networks with these characteristics invest on influencing the seniors' emotional state in order to promote the prosperity on daily life resulting at shielding health and wellness from emotional affection. Additionally, influencing of elderly people's emotional state must be a field of investigation, since there is a direct correlation to elderly health. Comparatively, emotions play a key role in the user experience, for example in serious games developed for education, training, assessment, therapy or rehabilitation [5]. Receiving increasing attention, the importance of emotion in the development of more engaging games [6] has recently been recognized by the gaming community. Nowadays, several games targeting at adopting the gameplay to the user's state (adjust difficulty level etc.) [6].

As it can be argued, in case of serious games targeting to therapy and training, AC increases the motivation to conform to therapy schedule and as a consequence better health results with successful training. On the other hand, findings in the literature denote the lack of motivation, stemming from affective computing, at physical and cognitive training. Nevertheless, collaborative serious games and or games promoting the competition may enrich the level of motivation.

Therefore, the main objective of the current piece of work is to highlight the importance of affective components' integration into a human-computer interaction system with the aim to enhance the usability perception of end-users, such as seniors [7]. In the context of the Long Lasting Memories (LLM) project funded by the European Commission, the approach of combining physical and cognitive training within an independent living platform was adopted [8]. The focus of this paper is to demonstrate how attention is paid to the relationship between affection produced by the game play and intervention groups (during trials) forming social networks.

2   Materials and Methods

2.1   Long Lasting Memories Trials

The Long Lasting Memories evaluates and validates the intervention by trials that take place during the project duration. The sample is consisted of elderly individuals, either healthy or Alzheimer's patients [9], and, alongside the literature, on Mild Cognitive Impairment (MCI) and dementia patients [10] with a Mini Mental State Examination score (MMSE) ≥ 25 and a Montreal Cognitive Assessment (MoCA) score ≥ 23; an Instrumental Activities of Daily Living (IADL) score ≤ 16, and aged 60 or older [7] (inclusion criteria). Consent from a cardiologist confirming the physical ability of the participant to exercise was also required. The trials were executed at 5 iterations each of them having duration 8 weeks. The seniors were presented at the trial site five days per week and the threshold for a successful intervention was 24 intervention days. The trials sites were different from iteration to iteration according to seniors needs during recruitment. The group of seniors performing the intervention at the same geo-location at the same time was variable from 1 to 12 users per group.

2.2   Physical Training

FitForAll (FFA) is an exergaming platform, for supporting seniors' physical training [10]. Seniors' interaction with the platform is realized through innovative low-cost game peripherals, such as Nintendo Wii™ Remote and Balance Board. Following user-centered game design principles, FFA aims at the alleviation of existing deficits of the Third Age. Moreover, taking into account the significant role affection (stress, disappointment) plays for seniors, when they come across new technology and computers, FFA is strongly built upon accessibility and user acceptance guidelines, by emphasizing on the users' impairments and limitations. Passive AC components of the platform, along with active AC components [7] allow users to maintain their self-esteem communicating with the system and its dynamic content respectively.

3   Results

3.1   Physical Training

FFA has been validated regarding its usability and mainly for its affective impact on seniors, in terms of a questionnaire, including items from: the Exercise Induced Feeling Inventory [11-12], the Physical Activity Enjoyment Scale [13], all validated and reliable measures of emotional states produced by exercise [14]. Ten items declaring 5 positive and 5 negative affective states were included and a Likert scale (from 1=not at all to 7=very much) was used to reply [7].

Table 1. Summary of results of 14 participants in the usability survey. A p value < 0.05 indicates significant difference between the mean and the neutral mean for each section (aRange = the possible minimum and maximum score for each section, [b]SD= standard deviation, [c]Neutral Mean= the value that would be anticipated if all the answers indicated a rating that was equally positive or negative. [d,e,f] significant at the 0.05 level)

Section	Range[a] (min-max score)	Mean (SD)[b]	Neutral Mean[c]	p value
Affective	10 – 70	57.43 (5.64)	30.00	$p < .00001^d$
Usability	5 – 34	28.21 (3.29)	17.00	$p < .00001^e$
Satisfaction	7 – 35	28.43 (3.72)	14.00	$p < .00001^f$

As it is evident, the difference between participants' ratings in each section and the Neutral Mean for that section were highly significant [10].

3.2   Live Social Network

During the Long Lasting Memories (LLM) trials the intervention was organized in groups of elderly. The capacity of the groups was not constant and was depending to the time of the day, the geographical location, capacity of LLM systems (PC) and the senior likes. Thus, the trials results in small social groups from 1 to 12 users. During the LLM trials all subjects were conformed into 46 groups at 5 iterations (phased pilots).

Table 2. The number of groups according to group attendance

Seniors per Group	1	2	3	4	5	6	7	8	9	10	11	12
Number of Groups	2	8	5	5	2	5	6	6	3	-	2	2

In line with Table 2, Fig 1 shows drop out percentages during the Long Lasting memories trials. A drop out is considered when a subject was not able to fulfill the threshold in terms intervention days. There was no group with ten (10) seniors and therefore, the value for it is considered as 0%.

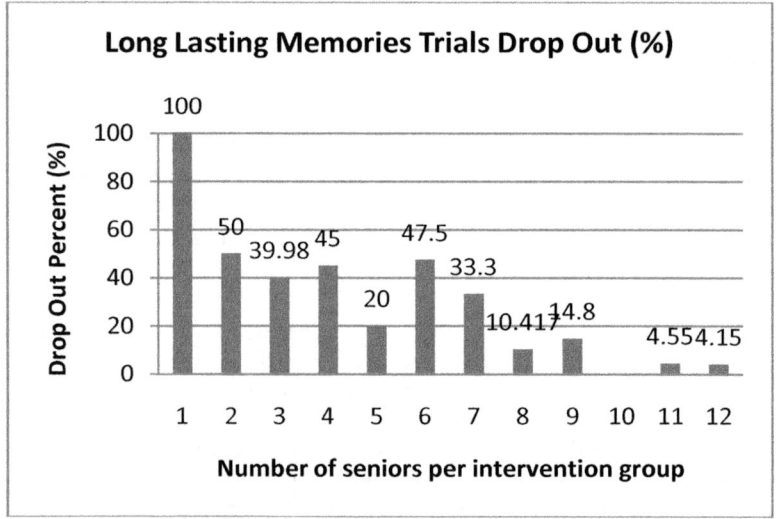

Fig. 1. Drop out during the LLM compared to the number of participants per group

4   Discussion

Many of the AC notions applied in the various elderly applications so far have been on what is called passive AC. Results obtained so far, indicate that there is strong evidence that the entertainment/joy received through the interaction within a social group affects the affective state of the user; these in turn play a crucial role in the acceptability of a human-computer interactive system like that used in FFA. Extensive analysis of the statistical interaction between the affective survey results (snapshot presented in Table 1) and the dropout curves (snapshot in Figure 1) are under way. Such results will definitely confirm the exact relationship between affect perceived through system interaction, joy received from social interaction, and system acceptance (defined as non-drop-out system usage).

Therefore, future research on the physical training platform shall focus on enriching current passive AC elements with more active AC. In addition, FFA affective concept motivates elderly people to continue an intensive (5 days a week) cognitive and physical therapy in form of training. Furthermore, the AC aspects of the physical training system are enriched by the "social network" aspect of the intervention groups (e.g. competition-like goals and rewards (virtual daily tasks, e.g. collection of apples of a tree), social context during training (e.g. seniors providing advice to an another on how to win the game). Designed to promote the collaboration and/or competition, FitForAll finds fertile ground in case of "large" social network (more than 7 seniors per group).

On the other hand, it is revealed that the emotional state of the seniors play vital role in motivating and encouraging them to continue and intensive intervention based on serious games. Considering that more seniors per group means more competition and thus more positive emotional state, Fig. 1 depicts that an active emotional state motivates and encourages elderly people to continue with their intervention.

Consequently, the preliminary findings, regarding the correlation between real social networks and affective computing in case of serious games, must be analyzed so as to produce guidelines for incorporating virtual social networks capabilities and features in the training and therapy computing systems. Consequently, elderly people that perform a serious game intervention at home residential setting will take advantage of this as if they were performing in day care centers intervention programs. Finally, a continuously research on the discussed field will introduce a preliminary work of affective social computing systems.

Further future work will mainly cover the development of a social cloud platform which will provide a virtual environment for supporting physical training and enhancing social relations among seniors. A client of this platform will provide access in already existing social networking cloud services/applications. The data will be refreshed in real time so as a Senior could play his serious game in FFA and simultaneously communicate or be aware about his/her friends – users via social network services without geographical limits.

References

1. Picard, R.W.: Affective Computing, 1st edn. The MIT Press (1997)
2. Luneski, A., Konstantinidis, E.I., Bamidis, P.D.: Affective Medicine: a review of Affective Computing efforts in Medical Informatics. Methods of Information in Medicine 49(3), 207–218

3. Chang Hsu, C., Chien, Y.Y.: An Intelligent Fuzzy Affective Computing System for Elderly Living Alone. In: Ninth International Conference on Hybrid Intelligent Systems, HIS 2009, Shenyang, August 12-14, pp. 293–297 (2009)
4. Camarinha-Matos, L., Afsarmanesh, H.: The Need for a Strategic R&D Roadmap for Active Ageing. In: Camarinha-Matos, L.M., Paraskakis, I., Afsarmanesh, H. (eds.) PRO-VE 2009. IFIP AICT, vol. 307, pp. 669–681. Springer, Heidelberg (2009), doi:10.1007/978-3-642-04568-4_69
5. Hudlicka, E.: Affective game engines: motivation and requirements. In: Proceedings of the 4th International Conference on Foundations of Digital Games (FDG 2009), pp. 299–306. ACM, New York (2009), doi:10.1145/1536513.1536565
6. Gilleade, K., Dix, A., Allanson, J.: Affective Videogames and Modes of Affective Gaming: Assist Me, Challenge Me, Emote Me. In: DIGRA, Vancouver, BC, Canada (2005)
7. Billis, A.S., Konstantinidis, E.I., Ladas, A.I., Tsolaki, M.N., Pappas, C., Bamidis, P.D.: Evaluating affective usability experiences of an exergaming platform for seniors. In: 10th International Workshop on Biomedical Engineering, Kos Island, Greece, October 5-7 (2011)
8. The Long Lasting Memories Project, http://www.longlastingmemories.eu (last visit April 14, 2011)
9. Folstein, M.F., Folstein, S.E., McHugh, P.R.: Mini-mental state A practical method for grading the cognitive state of patients for the clinician. Psychiatr Res., 189–198 (1975)
10. Nasreddine, M.D., Ziad, S., Natalie, A., Bédirian, V., Charbonneau, S., Whitehead, V., Collin, I., Jeffrey, L., Chertkow, H.: The Montreal Cognitive Assessment, MoCA: A Brief Screening Tool For Mild Cognitive Impairment. Journal of the American Geriatrics Society 53(4), 695–699(5) (2005)
11. Billis, A.S., Konstantinidis, E.I., Mouzakidis, C., Tsolaki, M.N., Pappas, C., Bamidis, P.D.: A game-like interface for training seniors' dynamic balance and coordination. In: XII Mediterranean Conference on Medical and Biological Engineering and Computing, MEDICON 2010. IFMBE Proceedings, vol. 29, pp. 691–694 (2010)
12. Gauvin, L., Rejeski, W.J.: The Exercise-Induced Feeling Inventory: Development and initial validation. Journal of Sport and Exercise Psychology 15, 403–423 (1993)
13. Kendzierski, D., DeCarlo, K.J.: Physical Activity Enjoyment Scale: Two Validation Studies. Journal of Sport and Exercise Phychology
14. Paxton, R.J., Nigg, C., Motl, R.W., Yamashita, M., Chung, R., Battista, J., et al.: Physical activity enjoyment scale short form–does it fit for children? Research Quarterly for Exercise and Sport (2008)

Semantic Video Abstracting: Automatic Generation of Movie Trailers Based on Video Patterns

Till von Wenzlawowicz and Otthein Herzog

Technologie-Zentrum Informatik und Informationstechnik,
Universität Bremen, Am Fallturm 1, 28359 Bremen, Germany
{tillvw,herzog}@tzi.de

Abstract. Summarizing and abstracting of multimedia data is a field of great research interest, especially for multiple video platforms. In this paper we describe a system capable of generating Hollywood movie trailers automatically by using audio and video processing algorithms, combined with ontology-based knowledge and CLIPS, a rule based system. We show that the system is capable of generating convincing movie trailers for the action genre. Further work has been done to extend the results to other movie genres.

Keywords: video analysis, semantic representation of video, video abstracting, video synthesis, movie trailer generation.

1 Introduction

The recent progress in automatic video and audio processing enables multiple application fields. A classical case of video abstracting are movie trailers, used to attract people to watch a movie by summarizing the content to some extent and to create excitement and expectations. The rather artistical task of creating a trailer, nowadays perfected by the movie industry, is challenged by the automatic approach outlined in this paper. By using video and audio analysis techniques various low-level features of video files can be extracted and combined to higher level semantic features. Our approach deals with the combination and processing of these features and semantic knowledge about trailer structures to automatically generate trailers.

The paper is structured as follows: First related techniques and systems are described. Then the structure of a typical Hollywood trailer is described. The subsequent section discusses the approach and the software system used to generate trailers. The paper concludes with an evaluation of the generated trailers and the conclusion.

2 Related Work

The general problem of creating a video abstract, the summarization of the content of the video, is an emerging research field. Different ways of video abstracting are described by Truong and Venkatesh[8]. Two main approaches are

I. Maglogiannis, V. Plagianakos, and I. Vlahavas (Eds.): SETN 2012, LNAI 7297, pp. 345–352, 2012.

named, keyframing and video-skimming. Keyframing summarizes the content of a video in one or more still images while video skimming provides a shorter version of the video. A summarization of multi-view videos is described and applied to surveillance camera footage by Fu et al. in [3]. The task of finding specific actions in movies is described in [4] where the action *drinking* can be recognized. The term *trailer generation* is explicitly mentioned by Lienhart et al. in [6] and Chen et al. [2], both using film theory in order to select footage without focusing on the generation of trailers.

3   Trailer Structure

In modern cinema the trailer is one of the most important ways to advertise an upcoming film. It therefore has the task to attract a broad audience and convince people to watch the movie. A common trailer introduces the setting, location and characters of the story to be told, and presents elements of the basic plot of the movie.

These characteristics can be found in the selection of scenes and their arrangement. In a typical Hollywood trailer for an action movie five different phases can be identified:

1. Intro: The people, setting and location are introduced.
2. Story: The problem or task to be solved or challenged is portrayed and the relationships between the characters are shown.
3. Break: A dramatic moment, often combined with a dramatic comment by a main character.
4. Action: Fast and loud, spectacular scenes to draw attention.
5. Outro: Mostly calm and slow footage, often showing a main character in a closeup shot and making a tough or comic comment, followed by the title, credits and a release date.

In order to be able to describe the structure in a computable way a corresponding representation was developed, the *trailer grammar*. This grammar consists of syntactic elements and semantic rules.

The basic elements of a video are usually *shots* and *transitions*, thus they can be defined also as the syntactic elements of a trailer. In order to distinguish between shots in the movie and shots used in the trailer grammar the latter ones are called *clips*.

The semantic rules for the composition of the trailer are defined in a generic hierarchical structure displayed in Figure 1. The structure consists of *patterns* and *pattern lists*. The first level is the *trailer pattern*, which consists of five *phases patterns*, corresponding to the phases described above. Each phase contains *sequence patterns* which are constructed of *clip/transition pairs*, the syntactic elements described before. This generic structure allows the modeling of a specific trailer model incorporating semantic knowledge.

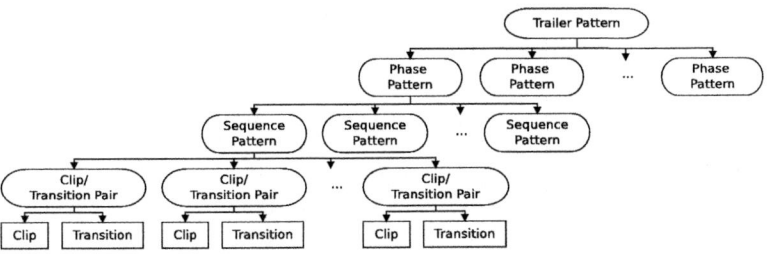

Fig. 1. The hierarchical trailer structure, shown is a branch of the generic model (taken from [1], page 149)

3.1 Action Trailers

The first kind of trailers chosen to be analyzed and generated are the trailers of a typical Hollywood action movie. A trailer of this genre usually focuses on spectacular shots and scenes like explosions, gunshots, fights and less on a story-based narrative structure. These spectacular scenes are defined by features which can be automatically detected and used as elemental parts for the decomposition of a video.

3.2 Other Genres

Trailers for other genres than action movies mostly tell more about the characters of the movie. This is very challenging for automatic detection and generation as it requires a system to research the narrative units used to tell the story of the movie. An interesting question is how a trailer for a non-action genre can be generated using an adapted model for action trailers.

4 Automatic Trailer Generation System

In order to automatically generate trailers, a movie needs to be segmented into shots, which can then be categorized into a list of pre-defined shottypes. Using the semantic rules defined in the trailer grammar these shots can then be arranged and composed to generate a new video, the trailer.

4.1 Approach

For the automatic generation the syntactic elements and the semantic rules for action trailers must be defined to build a specific trailer model. This was done in a first step by a manual shot-by-shot analysis of 11 action trailer movies and resulted in a system of 19 clip categories (see Table 1) and a set of semantic rules, describing from which category clips should be arranged. Additional seven categories for non-movie footage were defined, containing textual animations for the title of the movie, the main actors, the credits and a few others.

Table 1. Clip Categories

Footage Clip			Animation Clip
Character1CUSilent	PersonSpeaking	SlowAction	ActorName
Character1CUSpeaking	Quote	Spectacular	CompanyName
Characer1Silent	QuoteLong	Shout	Credits
Character1Speaking	Explosion	Scream	DirectorProducer
PersonCUSilent	Fire	Setting	Greenscreen
PersonCUSpeaking	Gunshot		Tagline
PersonSilent	FastAction		Title

In order to automatically classify the shots of a movie into semantic categories a two step method is used. First various audio and video processing algorithms analyze the movie for low-level features, such as the motion in a certain frame range or the loudness of the audio track. The results are then combined to improve the classification and find higher-level features. A shot classified in the category *PersonSpeaking* for example needs to show a face in small size, has speech present in the audio track and should not exceed a certain length.

Once the shots of the movie are categorized, a *trailer template*, derived from the specific trailer structure and described by the trailer grammar, can be filled with corresponding clips. The animations can be generated and and the trailer video file, together with trailer music and sound effects, can be composed.

4.2   Architecture

The software system can be split into two parts: The first part is a set of video and audio processing tools, which analyze a movie. The second part consists of the generator module. The main parts of the generator are an ontology, where the knowledge about the categories and about the semantic trailer structure are stored using the trailer grammar, and a CLIPS[1] component which performs the actual generation. Additionally the generator controls the rendering module and the final composition of a trailer.

The analyzer modules are mostly based on open-source software and described briefly below. A detailed description of the system is available in [1].

Shot detection. The shot detection is using a tool developed in[7]. It performs the basic segmentation of the movie into shots based on gray-level histogram changes.

Motion-based segmentation. Using the Lucas Kanade feature tracker provided in the OpenCV library[2] this module calculates the motion in the movie and segments it into frame ranges with similar optical flow characteristics.

---

[1] http://clipsrules.sourceforge.net/
[2] http://opencv.willowgarage.com/wiki/

Face detection. This module performs a face detection in the movie using the Haarcascade classifier[5] from OpenCV.

Face recognition. The results of the face detection are clustered by using PCA and k-means clustering. The output is the frame range where a certain character is detected.

Text detection. The text detection is based on a tool described in[9]. It filters frames containing text to avoid them during the generation of the trailer.

Sound volume-based segmentation. This module assists the visual detection of loud events like explosions and action sequences, and indicates dialogues and calm clips with a lower volume.

Sudden volume change detection. A sudden change in volume indicates surprising and spectacular clips.

Speech detection. It is important to know whether a character is speaking or not, because seeing a person speaking while not hearing it is irritating. The speech detection uses the CMU Sphinx speech recognition system[3] together with the included HUB4 acoustic model and AN4 3gram language model. The module determines the frame ranges with speech, while content of the speech is not important.

Speech recognition. The speech recognition module finds famous quotes by a character in the movie. It takes a set of quotes, taken from the Internet Movie Database[4] and converts them into a word-phoneme dictionary by using addttp4[5]. This allows the module to search the audio track of the movie for the quote and enables the system to include the corresponding clip into the trailer later on.

Shout detection. This module looks for loud passages in the results of the speech detection, which are categorized as shouts.

Music detection. Using stable power spectrum peaks as an indication for music this module looks for parts of the movie where music is present to avoid mixing movie music and trailer music.

Sound event detection. The sound event detection module is used to find pre-trained sound-samples for gunshots, explosions, crashes and screams. This is done by using a Support Vector Machine[6] approach on feature vectors extracted from the soundtrack.

---

[3] http://cmusphinx.sourceforge.net/

[4] http://www.imdb.com

[5] http://www.nist.gov/speech/tools/addttp4-11tarZ.html

[6] http://www.csie.ntu.edu.tw/~cjlin/libsvm/

The output of the detection modules is merged into one xml file per movie. The file contains the results from all detectors and additional metadata such as resolution and length of the video file. It also contains data about the movie which is obtained from the Internet Movie Database like the director, year of production and the most important actors.

The generator part of the movie takes the movie file and the corresponding analyzer data as input and assigns the movie shots to their clip categories (see Table 1). In the ontology the categories are defined via *category parameters*. These parameters determine the properties the footage needs to have in order to be classified into the category, for example a maximum length or volume.

After the categorization process is finished the CLIPS-based system determines a suited trailer template from the hierarchical trailer model in the ontology by selecting a valid instance using the predefined rules. Then the system fills the leafs of the hierarchy with categorized clips. In the case of a requested category without clips left alternatives are searched in a similar category.

Requested animation clips are generated using information from the metadata and the open source 3D-modeling software Blender[7].

Music and sound effects are selected from a pool of audio files containing typical trailer music and sound effects. The music is arranged according to the phases described above and selected randomly while following certain rules in the ontology to guarantee a harmonic soundtrack.

The movie and the additional media files are then merged into the final trailer video file using avisynth[8] and virtualdub[9]. Figure 4.2 shows an excerpt of a automatically generated trailer for the movie *Terminator 2*.

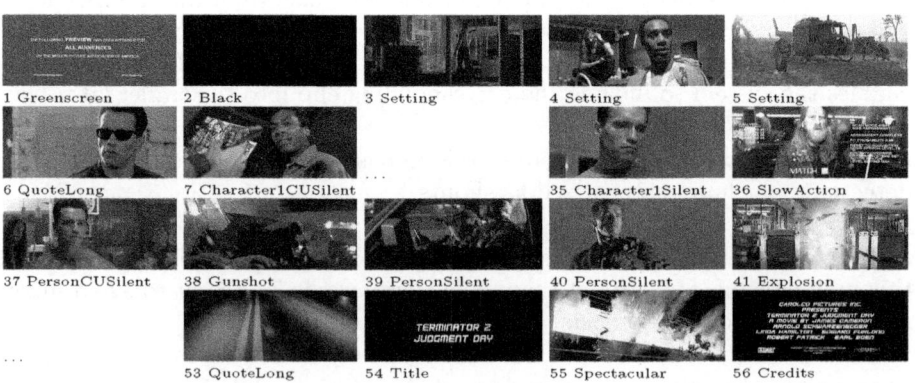

Fig. 2. 18 of 56 clips showing parts of our automatically generated *Terminator 2* trailer (complete Intro Phase: 1-6, middle part of the Action Phase: 35-41, and complete Outro Phase: 53-56). The corresponding type of category is given below each clip.

---

[7] http://www.blender.org

[8] http://avisynth.org/

[9] http://www.virtualdub.org/

4.3   Applying to Different Genres

We applied the automatic trailer generation to movies of genres other than action as well. The nature documentary *Earth* was chosen to look how our action trailer model would apply on such a movie. First we started generating trailers using the action trailer template together with the action music pool. In a second step we chose a different set of music files containing classical music which would be a better fit to the genre. Finally we developed a new trailer model by only using the categories *slow action, fast action* and *setting* and omitting categories which focus on human characters and action specific features like explosions and gunshots.

5   Evaluation

The automatically generated action trailers were evaluated by showing a test set of seven different trailers to a user group of 59 people. The participants of the study should then give a rating for the quality of the trailer. The test set consisted of two professional trailers, *War Of The Worlds* and *Miami Vice*, a trailer for *The Transporter* generated by the video generation software *movee*, two trailers generated by our system, *Bad Boys* and *Blade*, with a random selection of shots and finally two trailers, *Transporter 2* and *Terminator 2* based on the trailer patterns defined in the system.

The results are shown in Figure 3. The automatically generated trailers with a given score of 7.29 and 7.26 compete well in comparison to the professional Hollywood trailers (scored 7.86 and 4,92 by the participants). The evaluation shows that our trailer model is well superior to a random selection of shots.

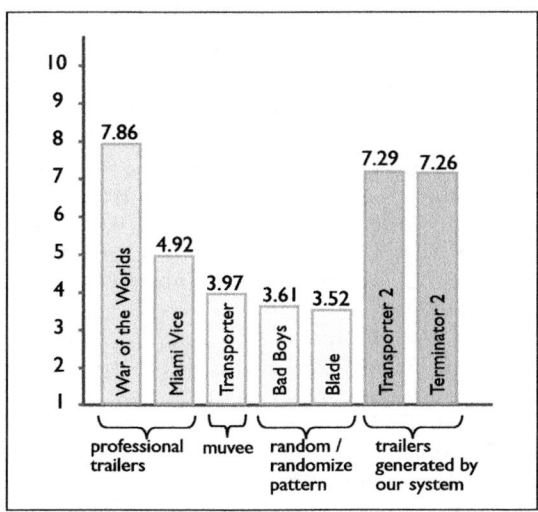

Fig. 3. Mean score of the evaluated trailers

Preliminary results for the application of our action model the genre of nature documentary appear promising. A spontaneous evaluation in our group rated the trailer with classical music convincing and pointed out that the choice of music is important for the impression of the trailer.

6   Conclusion

In this paper we presented a fully automatic system capable of generating Hollywood like trailers for action movies. We described the basic structure of such a trailer and our implementation of the knowledge using an ontology-based trailer model. The evaluation shows that the quality of the automatically generated trailers can compete with professional composed ones.

Acknowledgements. We would like to thank the Graduate School*Advances in Digital Media*, funded by the *Klaus Tschira Foundation*, and the participants of the master project *Semantic Video Patterns* on which results this paper is based:

Christoph Brachmann, Hashim Iqbal Chunpir, Silke Gennies, Benjamin Haller, Philipp Kehl, Astrid Paramita Mochtarram, Daniel Möhlmann, Christian Schrumpf, Christopher Schultz, Björn Stolper, Benjamin Walther-Franks, Arne Jacobs, and Thorsten Hermes.

References

1. Brachmann, C., Chunpir, H.I., Gennies, S., Haller, B., Kehl, P., Mochtarram, A.P., Möhlmann, D., Schrumpf, C., Schultz, C., Stolper, B., Walther-Franks, B., Jacobs, A., Hermes, T., Herzog, O.: Automatic Movie Trailer Generation Based on Semantic Video Patterns, Media Upheavals, vol. 27, pp. 145–158. Transcript Verlag (2009)
2. Chen, H.W., Kuo, J.H., Chu, W.T., Wu, J.L.: Action movies segmentation and summarization based on tempo analysis. In: MIR 2004: Proceedings of the 6th ACM SIGMM International Workshop on Multimedia Information Retrieval, pp. 251–258. ACM Press, New York (2004)
3. Fu, Y., Guo, Y., Zhu, Y., Liu, F., Song, C., Zhou, Z.H.: Multi-view video summarization. IEEE Transactions on Multimedia 12(7), 717–729 (2010)
4. Laptev, I., Perez, P.: Retrieving actions in movies. In: IEEE 11th International Conference on Computer Vision, ICCV 2007, pp. 1–8 (October 2007)
5. Lienhart, R., Maydt, J.: An extended set of haar-like features for rapid object detection. In: IEEE ICIP, vol. 1, pp. 900–903 (September 2002)
6. Lienhart, R., Pfeiffer, S., Effelsberg, W.: Video abstracting. Communications of the ACM 40(12), 54–62 (1997)
7. Miene, A., Dammeyer, A., Hermes, T., Herzog, O.: Advanced and adapted shot boundary detection. In: Fellner, D.W., Fuhr, N., Witten, I. (eds.) Proc. of ECDL WS Generalized Documents, pp. 39–43 (2001)
8. Truong, B.T., Venkatesh, S.: Video abstraction: A systematic review and classification. ACM Trans. Multimedia Comput. Commun. Appl. 3 (February 2007), http://doi.acm.org/10.1145/1198302.1198305
9. Wilkens, N.: Detektion von Videoframes mit Texteinblendungen in Echtzeit. Master's thesis, Universität Bremen (2003)

Learning to Case-Tag Modern Greek Text

Antonis Koursoumis, Evangelia Gkatzou, Antigoni M. Founta, Vassiliki I. Mavriki,
Karolos Talvis, Spyros Mprilis, Ahmad A. Aliwat, and Katia Lida Kermanidis

Ionian University, Department of Informatics
7 Tsirigoti Square, 49100, Corfu, Greece
kerman@ionio.gr

Abstract. Morphological case tagging is essential for the identification of the
syntactic and semantic roles of sentence constituents in most inflectional
languages. Although it is usually viewed as a side-task of general tagging
applications, it is addressed in the present work as an individual, stand-alone
application. Supervised learning is applied to Modern Greek textual data in order
to case-tag declinable words using merely elementary lexical information and
local context. Several experiments with various context window sizes, as well as
base- and meta-learning schemata, were run with promising results.

Keywords: tagging, morphological case, supervised learning, ensemble learning,
Modern Greek.

1   Introduction

Tagging is the process of assigning morphological attributes to words in natural
language text. Tagged text can then be utilized for further analysis, i.e. parsing,
information extraction etc. A significant part of previous approaches to automatic
tagging have focused on the identification of the part-of-speech (pos) tag of a word
using rule-based systems, statistical models, supervised and unsupervised learning
algorithms, and combinations of the above. Another set of approaches addresses
broader morphological information, where the tag set includes gender, number, case,
person, voice, word type and other elements of grammatical information.

Only very limited approaches have given special attention to or, much less, have
focused solely on case tagging. These approaches addressed morphologically rich,
inflectional languages, where words in certain pos categories (usually nominals) may
appear in several cases. The most usual grammatical cases, that are present in the vast
majority of inflectional languages, are the nominative, the genitive and the accusative.
However, certain languages, contemporary or ancient, have special cases, like the
dative, the vocative, the ablative, the instrumental, the locative.

The grammatical case of a nominal element is quite significant as it determines the
relationship between the nominal and its head (e.g. a noun with the main verb, a
modifier with the noun it modifies etc.), and it is therefore essential for identifying the
syntactic and semantic roles of the elements in a sentence.

Unlike previous approaches, the present work focuses solely on case tagging for
the first time in Modern Greek (MG). The methodology makes use of low-level

I. Maglogiannis, V. Plagianakos, and I. Vlahavas (Eds.): SETN 2012, LNAI 7297, pp. 353–360, 2012.
© Springer-Verlag Berlin Heidelberg 2012

information, i.e. elementary morphological information. No lexica, lemmatizers, stemmers, or stress identification tools are made use of. The context is taken into account, without exploiting any kind of information regarding its syntactic structure. Thereby, the methodology is not resource-demanding and may easily be adapted to other languages that have a case-based morphology. Supervised learning has been employed for the prediction of the correct grammatical case value. A novel feature-vector structure has been proposed for the learning instances and a set of state-of-the-art learning algorithms, stand-alone- as well as meta-classifiers, have been experimented with, and their performance is compared.

The rest of this paper is organized as follows. Section 2 describes previous approaches related to case tagging. Section 3 introduces some important MG properties that affect the task. The dataset, the experimental setup and the results are presented and discussed in section 4. The paper concludes in the last section.

2   Related Work

As mentioned before, there are significant ambiguity problems during the process of tagging because of the idiosyncrasies of some languages. This kind of problem does not seem to appear only in MG, but in many morphologically rich languages like Arabic, Turkish, Dutch and Icelandic. Several efforts have been made in the last decade to address this problem.

In Icelandic, a case tagging approach has been proposed [2], who developed a case tagger for non-local case and gender decisions, using 639 tags and approximately a corpus of 590.000 tokens. The approach achieved an accuracy of 97.48%.

In the case of Arabic, a memory-based learning for morphological analysis and pos tagging has been proposed, using as input unvoweled words [8]. The tagger reaches an accuracy rate of 93.3% for known and 66.4% for unknown words.

A similar approach has been proposed for a morphosyntactic tagger and dependency parser for Dutch called TADPOLE [16]. TADPOLE is 96.5% correct on known and 79.0% on unseen words.

When it comes to the Greek language, many difficulties are yet to be surpassed, although certain important approaches have already been published [9][10][11][12], focusing almost exclusively on pos tagging.

Finally, for the Turkish language some approaches have been proposed in the past years. The most important attempt implemented a system that extracts a corpus from the Web, annotates its sentences with case information and uses the Naïve Bayes classifier to convey subcategorization frames (SFs) on Turkish verbs [15] with promising results, taking into account the properties of the language.

3   Morphological Case in Modern Greek

MG has a complex inflectional system. The morphological richness allows for a relatively free-word-order syntax, where the role of each constituent is determined by its morphological features rather than by its position in the sentence.

There are eleven different pos categories in MG, six declinable (articles, nouns, adjectives, pronouns, verbs and numerals), and five indeclinable (adverbs, prepositions, conjunctions, interjections and particles). All indeclinable words plus articles and pronouns form closed sets of words, while nouns, adjectives, and verbs form open sets. Nouns, adjectives, pronouns, numerals and participles are characterized by the case attribute. Its possible values are: nominative, genitive, accusative and vocative. The dative case was extensively used in Ancient Greek, but its function has been taken over either by other cases or by other syntactic structures (e.g. certain prepositional phrases) in MG ("Syncretism").

Morphological cases indicate types of syntactic relations. A nominal element in the nominative case denotes a subject, or the copula of a linking verb, the accusative case denotes a direct object or a temporal expression, while the genitive case denotes possession or an indirect object. In prepositional phrases, the case of the nominal element (genitive or accusative) depends on the preposition introducing the phrase.

The morphological richness renders pos ambiguity a less significant research challenge than case ambiguity in MG. The same word form may often be found in text associated with different sets of morphological features. In other words, the same word form can appear in texts having three different case values. Very often declinable words have the same orthographic form in the nominative and in the accusative case. This holds for almost all nouns, adjectives, articles, pronouns and ordinal numerals, feminine and neutral, singular and plural. For example, the phrase

```
         Ακούει        το      παιδί
(S(he))  listens       the     child
```

has two different meanings: "The child is listening" and "Someone is listening to the child". The first meaning sets the noun phrase "το παιδί" (the child) in the nominative case (the child as a subject), while, the second, in the accusative (the child as the object). Another common ambiguity is the genitive and the accusative case. This holds for most singular masculine and neutral nouns and adjectives. Also, the vocative case shares the same orthographic form with the genitive and the accusative and the genitive case in several masculine nouns and adjectives, and with the nominative and accusative case in several feminine and neutral nouns and adjectives.

4   Morphological Case Learning

The MG corpus used for the experiments comes from the Greek daily newspaper "Eleftherotypia" [3]. The subset of the corpus (250K words) used for the experiments described herein is manually annotated with morphological information.

The dataset we use for our calculations and experiments consists of 65535 instances. Each instance corresponds to a specific word in the corpus that has a case; it holds info referring to the two words following and the two words preceding the focus word. The dataset uses thirty four different attributes, one of which is the class of the focus word. The attributes are listed in Table 1. The class of the focus word takes three different values: "n", "g", "a", "v" and "d", corresponding to the nominative, genitive, accusative, vocative and dative case respectively. The analysis of the dataset shows that 30,7% of the words are in the nominative, 26,2% in the genitive and 42,9% in the accusative case. The vocative and dative instances are extremely rare, i.e. 0,04% and 0,06% respectively.

Table 1. The features of the learning vector

	Feature Description		Feature Description
1	last three letters of the focus word	18	last three letters of word+1
2	last two letters of the focus word	19	last two letters of word+1
3	focus word pos	20	word+1 pos
4	focus word gender	21	word+1gender
5	focus word number	22	word+1 number
6	last three letters of word-1	23	last three letters of word+2
7	last two letters word-1	24	last two letters of word+2
8	word-1pos	25	word+2 pos
9	word-1 gender	26	word+2 gender
10	word-1 number	27	word+2 number
11	word-1 case (manual)	28	position of the closest previous verb
12	last three letters of word-2	29	number of the closest previous verb
13	last two letters of word-2	30	voice of the closest previous verb
14	word-2 pos	31	position of the closest next verb
15	word-2 gender	32	number of the closest next verb
16	word-2 number	33	voice of the closest next verb
17	word-2 case (manual)	34	focus word case (class)

State-of-the-art learning algorithms have been experimented with. The Weka workbench (http://www.cs.waikato.ac.nz/ml/weka) was used for the experiments presented herein. Tests were run with instance-based learning (k-NN) in order to determine the best value for k. Decision trees (C4.5 for unpruned trees as well as with reduced error pruning) were created; the Naive Bayes classifier was also tested. Apart from these stand-alone classifiers, ensemble learning schemata have also been experimented with. Stacking, boosting and bagging were run on the data with promising results. For stacking, the prediction results of three stand-alone classifiers (Naïve Bayes, 7-NN and C4.5) are taken as input to the meta-learner (C4.5). For bagging, C4.5 was applied iteratively ten times, each time to a randomly chosen portion (60%) of the data. For boosting, AdaBoost was run with C4.5 and reduced-error pruning. The context window size has been experimented with as well: four different datasets were created, i.e. (-2,+2), (-1,+1), (-2,0), (-1,0). Validation was performed using 10-fold cross validation. Classification results (precision and recall for all class values, classifiers and context window sizes) are shown in Figure 1.

As is to be expected, results for the vocative and dative cases are poor due to their sparse occurrence in the data. The dative case scores somewhat better and in some cases (e.g. with C4.5) quite well, because of the characteristic orthographic endings of the words in this case (usually archaic expressions from Ancient Greek or other earlier versions of the Greek language, that are still used). The advanced meta-learning schemata are also able to capture these orthographic idiosyncrasies quite well despite its sparseness. The majority of vocative examples are classified as nominative, due to the large ambiguity problem, as described in section 3, on top of the sparseness. Regarding the remaining cases, the genitive achieves the highest results, i.e. 98% with boosting. The genitive is rarely mistaken as one of the other cases; the ambiguity is slightly higher between the nominative and the accusative.

Regarding the context window, preceding words are more important than the ones following the focus word, probably due to the preceding articles, modifiers and determiners that often share their case with the following headword. The following words, and especially word+2, seem to be more misleading than helpful. According to the information gain ratio, the most important features for learning are the ending letters and pos of the focus word as well as the morphological features of the previous words (especially the word-1 case), the ending letters of word-1 and the voice of the closest verb.

Concerning the algorithms, the larger the learning vector, the more neighbors are required for accurate instance-based learning. Using the two preceding words, and a large number of neighbors, k-NN is able to learn the sparse cases with flawless precision. Pruned C4.5 performs significantly better than without pruning, especially for the sparse cases. Naïve Bayes leads to the poorest overall results, while the metalearners (especially boosting) lead to the best results regarding the vocative case.

Placing the current approach on the map of related MG text tagging approaches [9][10][11][12], the results reported herein are comparable to the ones reported in the

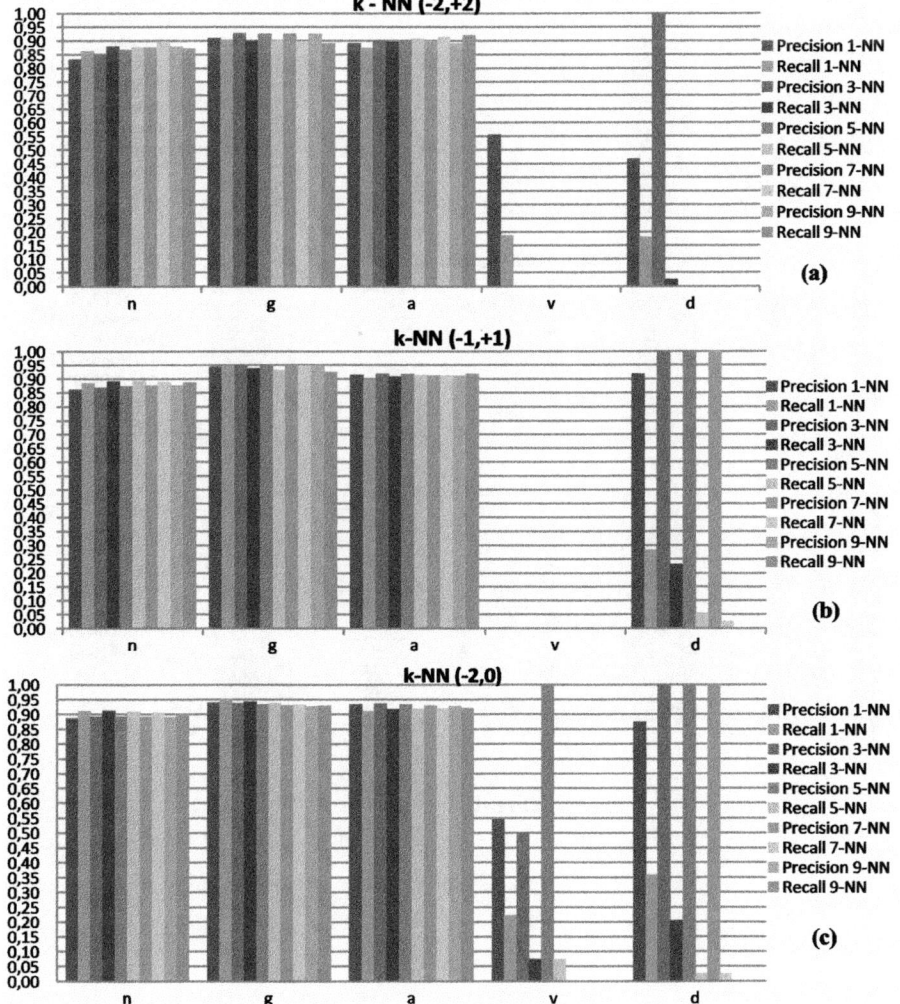

Fig. 1. (a)-(j). Experimental results

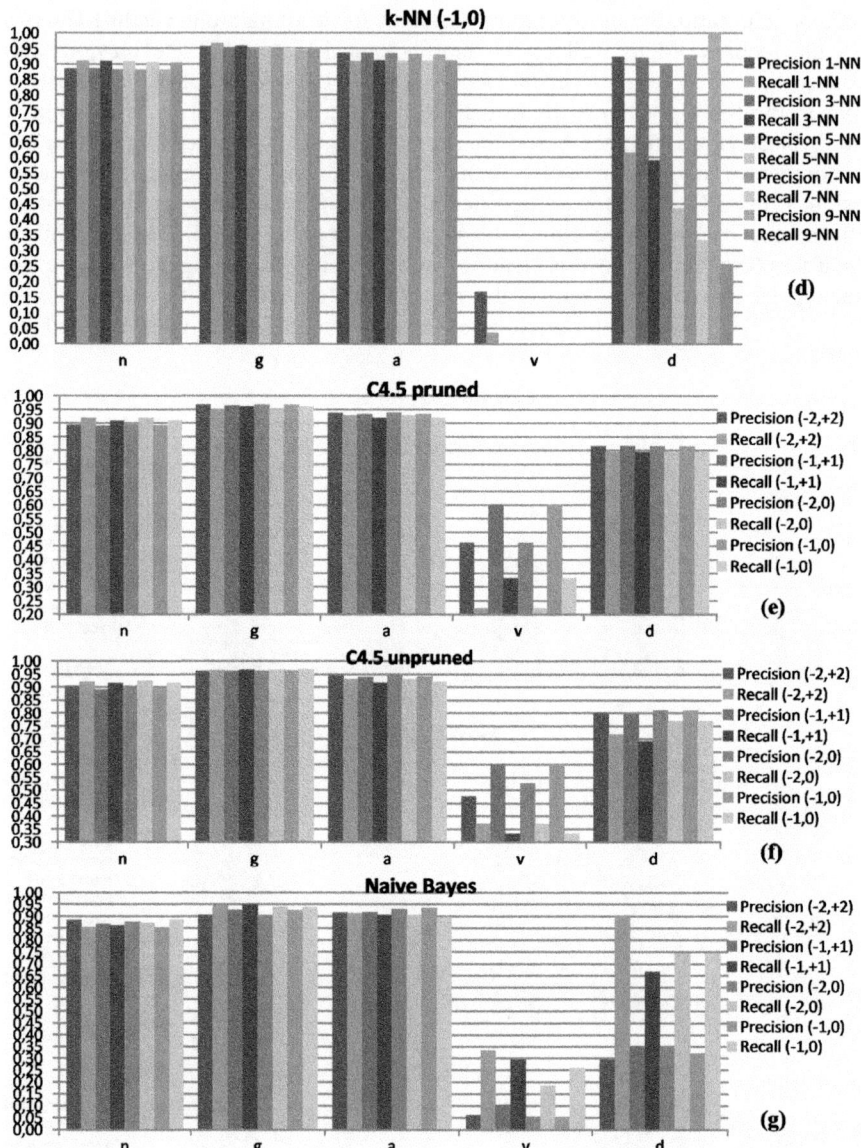

Fig. 1. (*continued*)

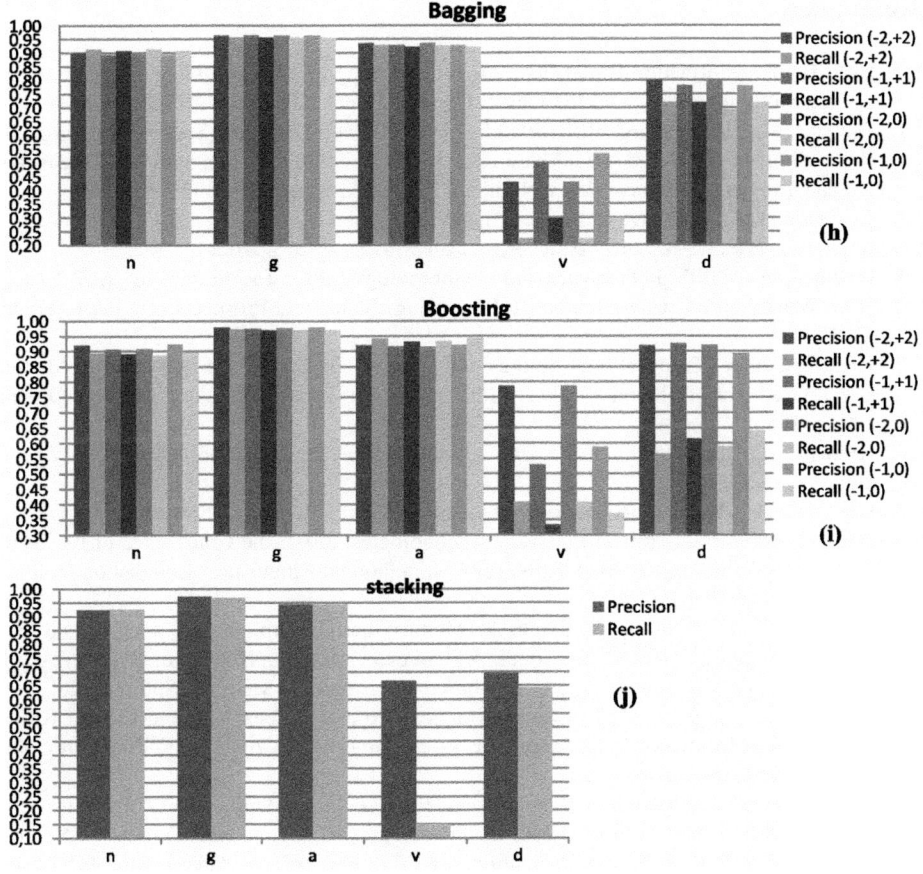

Fig. 1. (*continued*)

literature, even though no direct comparison is feasible, as most previous work is on pos tagging. Their reported accuracy varies from 85% to 98.2%, the corpus sizes vary from 140K to 1.9M words (much larger than ours), and employed resources include stemming (prefix and suffix identification), stress information, and/or morphological lexica, none of which is available in the present approach.

5   Conclusion

A methodology exclusively for morphological case tagging of MG has been presented. It relies on minimal resources, i.e. morphological and context information, and addresses satisfactorily the free word order of MG, as well as its rich inflectional system. Several learning algorithms and the context window surrounding the focus word have been experimented with, and the features that are significant for case learning have been investigated. Special morphosyntactic features that might help learning the sparse cases, feature selection pre-processing, higher-level resources (e.g. lemmatization, syntactic structures) would be interesting future research aspects to explore.

References

1. Brill, E.: Transformation-Based Error-Driven Learning and Natural Language Processing: A Case Study in Part of Speech Tagging. Computational Linguistics 21(24) (1995)
2. Dredze, M., Wallenberg, J.: Icelandic Data Driven Part of Speech Tagging. In: Proceedings of the 46th Annual Meeting of the Association for Computational Linguistics: Human Language Technologies, Columbus, OH, USA, Short Papers 33–36 (2008)
3. Evaluations and Language Resources Distribution Agency, http://www.elda.fr/catalogue/en/text/W0022.html
4. Freeman, A.: Brill's POS tagger and a morphology parser for Arabic. In: ACL/EACL-2001 Workshop on Arabic Language Processing: Status and Prospects, Toulouse, France (2001)
5. KEME (Center of Educational Studies and Training in Education): Revision of Modern Greek Grammar of Manolis Triantafillidis (in Greek). Didactic Books Publishing Organization (1983)
6. Kramarczyk, I.: Improving the tagging accuracy of Icelandic text. MSc Thesis, Reykjavík University (2009)
7. Loftsson, H.: Tagging Icelandic Text using a Linguistic and a Statistical Tagger. In: NAACL-Short 2007 Human Language Technologies 2007: The Conference of the North American Chapter of the Association for Computational Linguistics, Companion Volume, Short Papers 105–108 (2007)
8. Marsi, E., Van den Bosch, A., Soudi, A.: Memory-based morphological analysis and part-of-speech tagging of Arabic. In: Soudi, A., van den Bosch, A., Neumann, G. (eds.) Arabic Computational Morphology Knowledge-based and Empirical Methods. Springer (2007)
9. Orphanos, G., Tsalidis, C.: Combining Handcrafted and Corpus-Acquired Lexical Knowledge into a Morphosyntactic Tagger. In: Proceedings of the 2nd CLUK Research Colloquium, Essex, UK (1999)
10. Papageorgiou, H., Prokopidis, P., Giouli, V., Piperidis, S.: A Unified POS Tagging Architecture and its Application to Greek. In: Proceedings of Second International Conference on Language Resources and Evaluation, LREC 2000, Athens, Greece, pp. 1455–1462 (2000)
11. Papakitsos, E., Grigoriadou, M., Ralli, A.: Lazy Tagging with Functional Decomposition And Matrix Lexica: An Implementation in Modern Greek. Literary and Linguistic Computing 13(4), 187–194 (1998)
12. Petasis, G., Paliouras, G., Karkaletsis, V., Spyropoulos, C., Androutsopoulos, I.: Resolving Part-of-Speech Ambiguity in the Greek Language Using Learning Techniques. In: Proc. of the ECCAI Advanced Course on Artificial Intelligence, Chania, Greece (1999)
13. Shen, L., Satta, G., Joshi, A.K.: Guided learning for bidirectional sequence classification. In: ACL (2007)
14. Triantafillidis, M.: Modern Greek Grammar (Dimotiki) (in Greek). Reprint with corrections 1978. Institute of Modern Greek Studies, Thessaloniki (1941)
15. Usun, E., et al.: Web-based Acquisition of Subcategorization Frames for Turkish. In: 9th International Conference on Artificial Intelligence and Soft Computing. IEEE Computational Intelligence Society, Los Alamitos (2008)
16. Van den Bosch, A., Busser, G.J., Daelemans, W., Canisius, S.: An efficient memory-based morphosyntactic tagger and parser for Dutch. Selected Papers of the 17th Computational Linguistics in the Netherlands Meeting, Leuven, Belgium, pp. 99–114 (2007)

Understanding How Visual Context Influences Multimedia Content Analysis Problems

Phivos Mylonas

Image, Video and Multimedia Laboratory,
Department of Computer Science
School of Electrical and Computer Engineering
National Technical University of Athens
P.C. 15773, Athens, Greece
fmylonas@image.ntua.gr

Abstract. The importance of context in modern multimedia computing applications is widely acknowledged and has become a major topic of interest in multimedia content analysis systems. In this paper we focus on visual context, tackling it from the scope of its utilization within the above framework. We present a brief review of visual context modeling methods and identify and discriminate its useful types within multimedia applications, envisioning possible usage scenarios for contextual information. Finally, a representation of visual context modeling is reviewed, being suitable for aiding in the case of common multimedia analysis problems, such as object detection and scene classification.

Keywords: visual context, multimedia analysis, knowledge representation, context representation and analysis, context-driven multimedia analysis.

1   Introduction

The polysemy of the term *context* is widely acknowledged and currently there is no solid definition that covers its usage within most multimedia analysis efforts. In the field of computer science, the interest in contextual information is of great importance in fields like artificial intelligence, information search and retrieval, as well as image and video analysis [2]. Still, effective use of available contextual information within multimedia structures remains an open and challenging problem, although a categorization of context-aware applications according to subjective criteria has been tried out [10].

A fundamental problem tackled via access to and processing of contextual information is the bridging of two fundamental gaps in the literature; the *semantic* and *sensory gap* [4]. The *semantic gap*, an issue inherent in most multimedia applications, is described as the gap between high-level semantic descriptions humans ascribe to images and low-level features machines can automatically parse. The *sensory gap* is described as the gap between an object and the computer's ability to sense and describe this object. It is contextual knowledge that may enable computational systems to bridge both gaps. With the advent of all kind of new multimedia-enabled devices

I. Maglogiannis, V. Plagianakos, and I. Vlahavas (Eds.): SETN 2012, LNAI 7297, pp. 361–368, 2012.

and multimedia-based systems, new opportunities arise to infer media semantics and contextual metadata are capable of playing the important role of a "semantic mediator".

It is common knowledge, though, that context itself appears in various forms and modifications and researchers commonly emphasize distinctions between different types of context. This paper provides an overview on the definition of one basic aspect of context exploited within multimedia systems and applications, namely the aspect of context summarized in the term: *visual context*. It's efforts are directed towards the fields of scene classification and object detection in multimedia analysis, introducing envisioned usage scenarios in the area.

The rest of this paper is organized as follows: in Section 2, after underlining the importance of context identification, two useful types of context utilized within the scope of multimedia content-based systems are identified, namely *context of content analysis* and *context of use*. Section 3 deals with visual context in typical image analysis problems, such as scene classification and object detection/recognition. Section 4 addresses the problem of visual context modeling, whereas final comments on the topic and conclusions are drawn in Section 5.

2   Visual Context Identification

The task of suitable visual context definition and identification is very important, because all knowledge required for multimedia content analysis is thought to be context-sensitive, thus resulting in a specific need for formal definitions of context structures prior to any static or dynamic context analysis. The first objective formed within this task is the definition of the suitable aspect of context at hand, providing conceptual and audiovisual information. We may introduce two types of context: the *context of content analysis* and the *context of use*. *Context of content analysis* refers to the context during the initial content analysis phase. It is intended to be used to aid the extraction of semantic metadata both at the level of simple concepts and at the level of composite events and higher level concepts. For instance, during scene classification it is used to detect whether a picture or video clip represents *city* or *landscape* content, essentially aiding the analysis process. On the other hand, *context of use* is related to the use of content by search/retrieval and personalization applications. In this case, given the multimedia content and metadata, contextual information from external sources are utilized, consisting mainly of information about the particular user, network and client device.

In multimedia computing applications the aspects of context, which are thought to be the most suitable and appropriate for research and progress, are the ones described above. Therefore, from now on we shall present them under a common approach, summarized in the notion of *visual context*. *Visual context* forms a rather classical approach to context, tackling it from the scope of environmental or physical parameters in multimedia applications. Different architectures, conceptual approaches and models support dynamic and adaptive modeling of visual context. One of the main objectives in the field is the combination of context parameters extracted from low level visual features with higher level concepts and interpretation (e.g. fuzzy set theory) to support additional knowledge processing tasks like reasoning. Specifically, it is wise for a context description to support fuzziness, in order for it to face the uncertainty introduced by content analysis or the lack of knowledge. Such a context representation also supports audiovisual information (e.g. lighting conditions, information about the environment, e.t.c.) and is separately handled by visual context models. The second objective is visual context analysis, i.e. to take into account the extracted/recognized concepts during content analysis in order to find the specific context, express it in a structural description form, and use it for improving or continuing the content analysis, indexing and searching procedures, as well as for personalization purposes.

In terms of knowledge-assisted content analysis and processing, a set of core visual context functionalities of the multimedia application requires to be defined, regarding the way such a system is expected to execute knowledge-assisted image analysis functions automatically or in a supervised mode, so as to either detect or to recognize parts of content. Additionally, context is thought to generate or assist end-users classify their contents and metadata, through suggestions or sorting being performed in a sophisticated way, making quite naturally implicit use of its analysis functionalities. For example, in a face recognition scenario, visual clues may help the system detect the right person. Issues relating more to the automatic creation of metadata even after analysis, e.g. through inference, make use of context, as different sources of information (different analysis modules, textual inputs) may also be integrated.

As far as retrieval is concerned, a set of core visual context functionalities of a multimedia search and retrieval system need to be also defined; there are many distinct aspects suggested and commented by users, regarding the way of performing searches, the type of searches they expect to have and the constraints they imagine. Organizing multimedia data into meaningful categories marked by end-users as being important, could exploit contextual information. Retrieval is especially related to context, when tackling textual query analysis, search by semantic, visual or metadata similarity, semantic grouping, browsing and rendering of retrieved content, personalization and relevance feedback. However, user browsing capabilities, together with retrieval capabilities, suppose detection of common metadata, which is not considered to be related to the notion of visual context discussed herein. Another form of context, dealing mostly with the semantic part of the analysis would be more useful in this case [14]. In any case, research efforts focusing on search by visual similarity [3] may definitely benefit from the use of visual context information, as in the case of scene classification and object detection discussed in the following.

3 Visual Context in Image Analysis

By visual context in the sequel we will refer to all information related to the visual scene content of a still image or video sequence that may be useful for its analysis. Although image analysis deals with several well-known research problems, visual context is mostly related to *scene classification* and *object detection*. *Scene classification* forms a top-down approach where low-level visual features are employed to globally analyse the scene content and classify it in one of a number of pre-defined categories, e.g. indoor/outdoor, city/landscape, and so on. On the other hand, *object detection/recognition* is a bottom-up approach that focuses on local analysis to detect and recognise specific objects in limited regions of an image, without explicit knowledge of the surrounding context, e.g. recognise a building or a tree. These two major fields of image analysis actually comprise a chicken-and-egg problem, as, for instance, detection of a building in the middle of an image might imply a picture of a city with a high probability, whereas pre-classification of the picture as "city" would favor the recognition of a building vs. a tree. Solution to the above problem can be dealt through modeling of visual concept descriptors in one or more context domain ontologies and ontology learning/visual concept detection techniques that would utilize visual context information.

Attempts worth mentioning in the area include the one proposed in [7], where a list of semantic objects is used in a framework for semantic indexing and retrieval of video. As expected, colour has also been one of the central features of existing work on natural object detection. For example, in [9] *colour classification* is utilized in order to detect sky. In the context of content-based image retrieval, Smith and Li [12] assumed that a blue extended patch at the top of an image is likely to represent clear sky. An exemplar-based approach is presented more recently that uses a combination of colour and texture features to classify sub-blocks in an outdoor scene as sky or vegetation, assuming correct image orientation [13]. The latter brings up the issue of utilizing context orientation information in object class detection algorithms, a task that is generally avoided due to the fact that such contextual information is not always available and the performance of the algorithms is more than adequate despite this shortcoming.

However, none of the above methods and techniques utilizes visual context in the form we defined it herein. This tends to be the main drawback of these individual object detectors, since they only examine isolated strips of pure object materials, without taking into consideration the context of the scene or individual objects themselves. This is very important and also extremely challenging even for human observers. The notion of visual context is able to aid in the direction of natural object detection methodologies, simulating the human approach to similar problems. Many object materials can have the same appearance in terms of colour and texture, while the same object may have different appearances under different imaging conditions (e.g. lighting, magnification). However, one important trait of humans is that they examine all the objects in the scene before making a final decision on the identity of individual objects. The use of visual context forms the key for this unambiguous recognition process, as it refers to the relationships among the location of different objects in the scene. In this manner, it is useful in many cases to reduce the ambiguity among conflicting detectors and eliminate improbable spatial configurations in object detection.

3.1   The Role of Spatial Context

An important variation of visual context is *spatial context*; *spatial context* is associated to spatial relationships between objects or regions in a still image or video sequence. One may identify two types of spatial contextual relationships:

- Relationships that exist between co-occurrence of objects in natural images.
- Relationships that exist between spatial locations of certain objects in an image.

The definition of spatial context is an important issue for the notion of visual context in general. In order to be able to use context in applications, a mechanism to sense the current context - when thought as location, identities of nearby people or objects and changes to those objects - and deliver it to the application is crucial and must be present. A significant distinction exists between methods trying to determine location in computing applications and research fields. On the one hand, most of the existing approaches tend to restrict themselves, trying to infer the location where the image was taken (i.e., camera location); inferring the location of what the image was taken of (i.e., image content location) is a rather difficult and more complex task tackled by much less approaches. In [2], this challenge is addressed by leveraging regularities in a given user's and in a community of users' photo taking behaviors. Suitable weights, based on past experience and intuition, are chosen in order to assist in the process of location-determining features and then adjusted through a process of trial and error. An example describing the notion behind the method considers the following: it seems rather intuitive that if two pictures are being taken in the same location within a certain time frame (e.g., a few minutes for pedestrian users), they are probably in or around the same location.

Another factor to be considered is the intersection of spatial metadata in determining the location of image content. For example, patterns of being in certain locations at certain times with certain people will help determine the probability of which building in an area a user might be in. Information on whether this particular building is the place he/she works in can also be derived in such a case. Rule-based constraint and inference engines can also be used to aid reasoning, as well as machine learning algorithms to learn from past performance to optimize and adjust the relative importance of the various location-determining features. Taking the process a step further into the field of context modeling, transforms the problem into how to represent the contextual information in a way that can help bridging the gap between applications using contextual information and the deployment of context-aware services. The development of such applications requires tools that are based on clearly defined models of context. A simple approach is to use a plain model with context being maintained by a set of environment variables.

3.2   The Role of Scene Context

Visual context information may also be derived from the overall description of the entire scene; the so-called *scene context*. In a number of studies the context provided by a real-world scene has been claimed to have a mandatory, perceptual effect on the identification of individual objects in such a scene. This claim has provided a basis for challenging widely accepted data-driven models of visual perception. The so far discussed visual context, defined by normal relationships among the locations of different materials in the scene without knowing exactly what the scene type is, is referred to as spatial context, and it the one that is going to be used mostly in a multimedia system application. In the sequel, visual context analysis is discussed in relation to the problems of scene classification and object detection.

Given the increase in the number and size of digital archives and libraries, there is a clear need for automated, flexible, and reliable image search and retrieval algorithms, as well as for image and video database indexing. Scene classification provides solutions in the means of suitable applications for all of these problems. The ultimate goal is to classify scenes based on their content. However, scene classification remains a major open challenge. Most solutions proposed so far, such as those based on colour histograms and local texture statistics [1][11], lack the ability to capture a scene's global configuration, which is critical in perceptual judgments of scene similarity. On the other hand, common standard approaches to object detection usually look at local pieces of an image in isolation when deciding if the object is present or not at a particular location. Of course, this is suboptimal and can be easily illustrated in the following example: consider the problem of finding a table in an office. A table is typically covered with other objects; indeed almost none of the table itself may be visible, and the parts that may be visible, such as its edge, are fairly generic features that may occur in many images. However, the table can be identified using contextual cues of various kinds. Of course, this problem is not restricted to tables, or occluded objects: almost any object, when seen at a large enough distance, becomes impossible to recognize without using visual context.

However, most techniques utilized in the field have usually positive results only in case of objects which have well-defined boundaries. Consequently, such strategies are not well suited for complex scenes, especially those which consist mostly of natural objects. The main difference between scene classification and object recognition techniques relies in the latter statement. Given these difficulties inherent in individual object recognition, scene classification approaches usually classify scenes without first attempting to recognize their components. Also, efforts have been made in using scene classification to facilitate object detection, and vice versa [5].

As already discussed in this section, several approaches of analyzing the content of images exist in the literature and many aspects of context are identified aiding in the process of image analysis. One of the main goals in the field is the effective combination of local and global information, towards implementing robust methods to use in typical image analysis problems. It should be clear by now, that visual context can play a key role in the procedure of combining this information; context should actually stand in the middle, being able to handle both types of information and providing the means to achieve better coherence and reliable research results. In order to achieve the latter, appropriate visual context models should be selected and designed in a straightforward and productive manner, utilizing the variations of the particular aspects of visual context.

4   Visual Context Modeling

Focusing our efforts in providing a robust context model capable of handling both local and global information in image analysis, resulted in the ascertainment that the only way to achieve this is to actually model the relationships between the information and not the information themselves, with respect to the level of details present in each relationship. In this manner, at least two types of meaningful visual (spatial) contextual relationships are identified in digital images: a) relationships exist between co-occurrence of certain objects in the image; e.g. detection of *snow* with high probability would imply low *grass* probability, b) relationships exist between spatial locations of certain objects within an image; e.g. *grass* tends to occur below *sky*, *sky* above *snow*. The goal is, of course, to develop a non-scene specific method for generating spatial context models useful for general scene understanding problems.

In general, spatial context modeling refers to the process of building relationship models that define the spatial arrangement and distribution of objects of interest in a scene. There has been prior work on using high-level scene models for spatial context-based material detection [8]. However, the main limitation of such techniques is the need for constructing a different model for each scene type, thus restricting its applicability to a general scene understanding application. Other researchers propose different approaches for spatial context modeling, e.g. configuration-based scene modeling, targeted towards content-based indexing and retrieval applications [4]. In this work, the qualitative and photometric relationships between various objects in a scene are modeled in a spatial sense, and these relationships are used to retrieve other scenes with semantically similar content.

Extending this technique in the case of scene classification, the approach is different in the concept that a top-down technique is necessary, since information is not available in the form of objects, but in the form of regions. Towards fulfilling the ultimate goal of this task, i.e. , classification of images or video sequences based on their content, most of the strategies implemented use aggregate measures of an image's colour and texture as a signature for the image and compare these signatures afterwards in order to achieve levels of similarity between the images. However, this is not adequate in the case images' components vary significantly in colour distribution, texture, illumination or even spatial layout. In such cases the aid of visual context is more than evident as depicted in [6].

5   Conclusions and Future Work

Structures and techniques for representing and exploiting visual contextual information are necessary preconditions for the smooth operability of multimedia analysis. In this work we attempted to introduce suitable types of visual context and context models; we identified two types of context, namely context of content analysis and context of use. We observed why visual context information may be extremely helpful in knowledge extraction, especially when handling typical multimedia analysis problems like scene classification and object detection.

As part of a future avocation scene classification and/or object detection techniques may benefit from available visual contextual information, in order to provide information about indoor/outdoor scenery at the metadata level. Also information about the mood of depicted persons or of the depicted scene as a whole may be tackled by means of analyzing visual context. The latter can also aid towards satisfying simple user requests such as the orientation of a multimedia item. As far as retrieval is concerned, closest match search capabilities together with image search by visual similarity depict clearly possible future benefits from exploiting visual context information parameters. In the field of a multimedia system's content adaptation, the task of correction of image orientation or even general enhancements is tackled by methods dealing to a great degree with visual context.

References

1. Ashley, J., Flickner, M., Lee, D., Niblack, W., Petkovic, D.: Query by image content and its applications. IBM Research Report, RJ 9947 (87906) Computer Science/Mathematics (March 1995)
2. Davis, M., Good, N., Sarvas, R.: From Context to Content: Leveraging Context for Mobile Media Metadata (2004)
3. Kalantidis, Y., Tolias, G., Avrithis, Y., Phinikettos, M., Spyrou, E., Mylonas, P., Kollias, S.: VIRaL: Visual Image Retrieval and Localization. Multimedia Tools and Applications 51(2), 555–592 (2011)
4. Lipson, P., Grimson, E., Sinha, P.: Configuration based scene classification and image indexing. In: IEEE International Conference on Computer Vision & Pattern Recognition (1997)
5. Murphy, K., Torralba, A., Freeman, B.: Using the Forest to See the Trees: A Graphical Model Relating Features, Objects, and Scenes. In: NIPS 2003 (2003)
6. Mylonas, P., Spyrou, E., Avrithis, Y., Kollias, S.: Using Visual Context and Region Semantics for High-Level Concept Detection. IEEE Transactions on Multimedia 11(11), 229–243 (2009)
7. Naphade, M., Huang, T.S.: A factor graph framework for semantic indexing and retrieval in video. In: CVPR Workshop on Content-based Image and Video Retrieval (2000)
8. Ohta, Y.: Knowledge-based interpretation of outdoor natural color scenes. Pitman Advanced Publishing Program, Boston (1983)
9. Saber, E., Tekalp, A.M., Eschbach, R., Knox, K.: Automatic image annotation using adaptive colour classification. CVGIP: Graphical Models and Image Processing 58, 115–126 (1996)
10. Schilit, B., Adams, N., Want, R.: Context-Aware Computing Applications. In: IEEE Workshop on Mobile Computing Systems and Applications, Santa Cruz, CA (1994)
11. Smith, J.R., Chang, S.: Local color and texture extraction and spatial query. In: IEEE International Conference on Image Processing (1996)
12. Smith, J.R., Li, C.-S.: Decoding image semantics using composite region templates. In: IEEE Int. Workshop on Content-based Access of Image & Video Database (1998)
13. Vailaya, A., Jain, A.: Detecting sky and vegetation in outdoor images. In: SPIE, vol. 3972 (January 2000)
14. Wallace, M., Akrivas, G., Mylonas, P., Avrithis, Y., Kollias, S.: Using context and fuzzy relations to interpret multimedia content. In: 3rd International Workshop on Content-Based Multimedia Indexing (CBMI), IRISA, Rennes, France (September 2003)

Block Operator Context Scanning for Commercial Tracking

Ioannis Giannoukos[1], Vassilis Vrachnakis[1], Christos-Nikolaos Anagnostopoulos[2], Ioannis Anagnostopoulos[3], and Vassili Loumos[1]

[1] Electrical & Computer Engineering School, National Technical University of Athens
[2] Cultural Technology and Communication Dpt., University of the Aegean
[3] Computer Science and Biomedical Informatics Dpt., University of Central Greece
igiann@medialab.ntua.gr, canag@ct.aegean.gr, janag@ucg.gr,
loumos@cs.ntua.gr

Abstract. The industry that designs and promotes advertising products in television channels is constantly growing. For effective market analysis and contract validation, various commercial tracker systems are employed. However, these systems mostly rely on heuristics and, since commercial broadcasting varies significantly, are often inaccurate. This paper proposes a commercial tracker system based on the Block Operator Context Scanning (Block - OCS) algorithm, which is both accurate and fast. The proposed method, similar to coarse-to-fine strategies, skips a large portion of the image sequences by focusing only on Regions of Interest. In this paper, a video matching algorithm is also proposed, which compares image sequences using time sliding windows of frames. Experimental results showed 100% accuracy and 50% speed increase compared to traditional block-based processing methods.

Keywords: Block-Operator Context Scanning, Commercial Tracking, Sliding Windows, Video Matching.

1 Introduction

The advertising industry functions as an intermediate between the manufacturers and the customers, creating products of substantial cost. In this industry, broadcast monitoring for commercial detection and tracking are crucial tools for contract validation and market analysis. These applications monitor TV channels to detect how many times a commercial clip is broadcasted and in which time zone. This information is extremely useful for copyright owners to collect royalties and for advertisers to efficiently manage the commercial broadcasting for the validation of their contracts with the television networks. This process, however, introduces a high computational cost, making it inappropriate for real-world applications.

This paper presents an accurate and fast commercial tracking system which implements a modified version of the Operator Context Scanning (OCS) algorithm, proposed in our previous works [1-3]. This algorithm acts as an alternative to the traditional exhaustive block-based processing. It uses operators in the form of sliding windows and skips a large portion of the input image pixel space, focusing only on

I. Maglogiannis, V. Plagianakos, and I. Vlahavas (Eds.): SETN 2012, LNAI 7297, pp. 369–374, 2012.

Regions of Interest. The Regions of Interest in an image are defined by the sliding window operator and present the features that the operator is searching for. To further improve the speed and accuracy of the system, a novel video matching method is proposed that uses temporally sliding windows, which group consecutive adjacent frames of the stored video clips.

2   Block Operator Context Scanning

The OCS algorithm uses pixel operators in the form of sliding windows, which associate a pixel neighborhood to the possibility of belonging to a Region of Interest (RoI). It focuses the processing of an image on the regions that have a large density of the desired features and uses a low sampling rate for the rest of the image regions.

Specifically, the Block-OCS algorithm can be formulated as follows. Let I be an image, which can be divided into K sub-regions, arranged in M columns and N rows. Therefore, each image sub-region size is $\frac{W}{M} \times \frac{H}{N}$, where W and H is the width and the height of image I respectively. Additionally, let $V=[v_1, v_2,..., v_n]$ be a feature vector that a Sliding Windows OPerator (SWOP) of size $\frac{W}{M} \times \frac{H}{N}$ is extracting. The SWOP operator evaluates a fitness function f in the region, based on the feature vector V, and when f exceeds a predefined threshold, R is marked as that of a Region of Interest (SWOP=1); otherwise the SWOP output is '0'. Therefore, the Block-OCS algorithm produces a binary mask, the positive pixels of which indicate the Regions of Interest.

The main advantage of the algorithm is the introduction of the factor of velocity during image scanning. The algorithm velocity is manipulated using an Additive Increase Multiplicative Decrease (AIMD) window-based control scheme, which is commonly used to prevent data traffic congestion on computer networks [4]. Specifically, if the currently processed region centroid is (x, y), the next region centroid to be scanned in the horizontal direction will be (x,y'), assuming for simplicity that y'<H. The new vertical coordinate y' is calculated as follows (equation 1):

$$y'= y + v_H(p) \tag{1}$$

where v_H is, the "velocity" parameter of the Block-OCS algorithm defined in the horizontal axis, $v_{H,max} \geq v_H \geq W/M$, $v_H \in N$, and $v_{H,max}$ the maximum value of the velocity parameter in the horizontal axis. The parameter p in the aforementioned equation refers to the pth region that the Block-OCS examines in the image I and $1 \leq p \leq K$, $p \in N$. Compared to the original OCS, the velocity in the Block-OCS cannot be assigned values in the range [0, W/M), since the factor of the minimum vertical velocity $v_{min,H}=W/M$ prevents the re-calculation of feature vector V multiple times in the same region. The values of parameter v_H follow the pattern of equation 2.

$$v_H(p+1) = \begin{cases} v_{min,H} + a + v_H(p), \text{ if } SWOP(x,y) = 0, \\ (additive\ increase),\ a > 0 \\ \\ v_{min,H} + d \cdot v_H(p), \text{ if } SWOP(x,y) = 1, \\ (multiplicative\ decrease),\ 1 > d > 0 \end{cases} \tag{2}$$

where α is the "acceleration" parameter and d refers to the "deceleration". In accordance with the AIMD scheme [4], the Block-OCS algorithm considers the high density SWOP zero outputs as "data" to be "transmitted" as fast as possible. Thus, it searches for "traffic congestion", since this would indicate a Region of Interest. Similar to the AIMD scheme, the Block-OCS velocity parameter value is directly correlated to the appropriate window size that is required to achieve the optimal transmission rate. Consequently, a large portion of the image is skipped, reducing in this way the computational cost of the image segmentation method.

The aforementioned process, described for the horizontal axis, is also applicable to the vertical axis of the image. If the SWOP operator detects a small number of candidate pixels after scanning an image row, then a number of image rows are skipped according to the vertical velocity parameter. Additionally, a minimum vertical velocity factor $v_{min,V}=H/N$ is also considered in the vertical axis of the image.

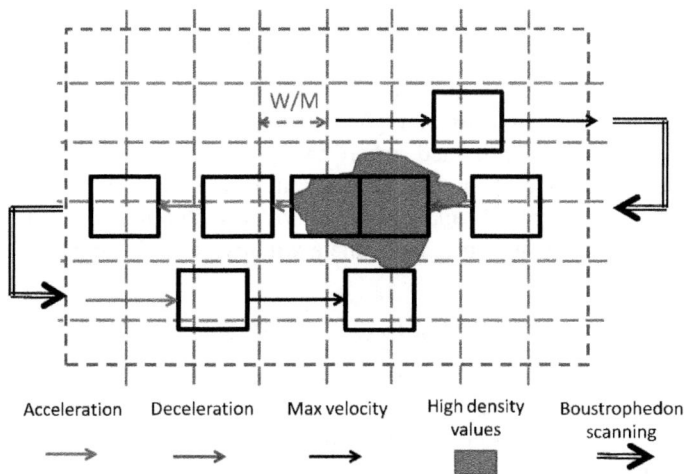

Fig. 1. Block Operator Context Scanning algorithm

The Block-OCS algorithm scans the image following a "boustrophedon" scheme, which was introduced in the original OCS (as seen in Figure 1). In this scheme, the scanning window slides in alternating opposite directions in a descending series of horizontal lines, like the course of plough in successive furrows. This way, the velocity does not reset after scanning an image row, since the next region to be processed is always near the previous pixel neighborhood.

3   Video Matching Algorithm

The video matching algorithm compares a video stream to a database of stored image sequences. The algorithm reduces search space using the temporal information of the stored image sequences. In the following, the proposed algorithm is described in detail.

Let H_{Block} be the block histogram of image I that contains K bins, corresponding to K sub-images of the image, arranged in M columns and N rows. A block in coordinates (i,j) corresponds to the [(i-1) * M +j] bin of the histogram. Each bin contains an activation value, which describes the area coverage of the feature that is searched. This value is derived from the Block-OCS algorithm, that is, the number of pixels that present the desired features in the region defined by the operator. When the operator finds a Region of Interest, it distributes the number of candidate pixels found to the respective histogram bins, according to the percentage coverage of the operator region surface to the MxN sub-images of image I.

To compare two frames, the Mean Square Error (MSE) of the respective histograms is used. Specifically, let H_{in} be the histogram of an input frame of the TV program and H_c (where $0 \leq c \leq C$) the histogram of the cth stored commercial in the database. Each histogram contains K bins. Then, a frame in the database is compared to the current frame of the input sequence as follows:

$$MSE\left(H_{in}, H_c\right) = \frac{1}{K}\sum_{j=1}^{K}(H_{in}^j - H_c^j)^2 \tag{3}$$

However, the frame that presents the minimum MSE does not always correspond to the correct commercial. So, instead of finding the frame with the minimum MSE value, a threshold MSE_{thres} is defined, where every commercial with frames below this threshold is considered a candidate. In addition, time sliding windows are applied in order to exploit temporal information during video matching. More specifically, this technique groups adjacent frames to define a window with the length of 2m+1 frames ($m \in \mathbb{N}$), as follows:

$$W_t = [H_{t-m}, H_{t-m-1},\dots H_t, H_{t+1}, \dots, H_{t+m}] \tag{4}$$

This time sliding window is applied to both input stream (TV broadcast) and the stored image sequences. The proposed algorithm compares the frames of the input stream only to the stored frames defined by the time sliding windows. A number of candidate commercials may be indicated by this process. Then, the windows of both the input stream and the stored commercials slide, by t_{step} seconds, to include the next group of frames (Fig. 2).

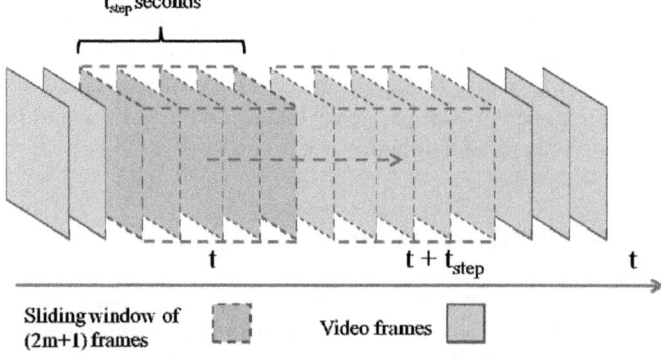

Fig. 2. Time sliding window technique

To match an entire commercial to the input stream, a novel algorithm is used, which utilizes the temporal information of the stored image sequences. This algorithm categorizes the stored commercials into three sets, namely, true candidates (corresponding to set T), false candidates (set F) and rejected (set R). The goal of the algorithm is to filter the stored sequences and find the candidate which best matches the input stream.

Initially, all stored image sequences are included in set F and the time sliding windows contain their first $2m+1$ frames. The filtering process initiates when, compared to the input stream, a number of commercials present a MSE below the threshold and are transferred to set T. In the next steps, the following actions may be taken: a commercial in set T which exceeds the threshold MSE_{thres} is moved to set F, a commercial in set F that presents a MSE below the threshold is transferred to set T and a commercial that remains in set F for a time period $t > t_{thres}$ is rejected (sent to set R). All the commercial clips in set R are not processed further. As far as the time sliding windows are concerned, they slide for $2m+1$ frames, corresponding to t_{step} seconds, at each step of the algorithm until they reach the end of the respective image sequences. The procedure ends when no commercials remain in sets T and F, or when the time sliding windows reach the end of the image sequences in the database. Then, the image sequence that has appeared the most in set T is matched to the input stream. When this procedure finishes, the algorithm resets and restarts.

In parallel, the timestamps that correspond to the beginning and to the end of the input stream and the found commercials are compared. If the identified commercial has the same duration in both the input stream and the database, then it is considered a positive match. On the contrary, if the duration is not the same, a warning is issued. This warning could mean that either a shortened or a longer version of the stored commercial was aired.

4   Experimental Results

One hundred forty seven (147) commercial clips were collected from the video sample, including clips that were aired on different channels. Approximately 80% of those (116 commercial clips) were stored in a database. To evaluate the proposed method, two test cases were designed. The first included non-commercial program (a talk show), commercial clips previously stored in the database and other commercials (unknown to the system). Therefore, the first test case is considered to be a typical example of normal TV broadcast. The second test case contained commercials that were deliberately shortened; commercial shortening may occur in TV channel broadcast, in order to save broadcast time. This test case was designed to evaluate the proposed system in terms of estimating the duration of the commercials aired.

In both test cases, all the commercials stored in the database were accurately identified in the input stream, including those that were aired by a different TV channel. Additionally, the non-commercial program and the unknown commercials were correctly classified as unknown video streams. As far as shortened commercials are concerned, the method correctly identified 14 as the shortened versions of known commercials and 10 were classified as unknown. The values of the method parameters were as follows. The Block-OCS max velocity parameter was assigned the value 20, to produce an image histogram of K=99 blocks. The time sliding window had a length of 5 frames (m=2) corresponding to 0.5 seconds. The threshold t_{thres} over which a commercial is rejected was 3, corresponding to 1.5 seconds of broadcast time.

5   Discussion

This paper presents a commercial tracker system that measures how many times a commercial clip stored in a database has been aired and calculates its broadcast duration. The system is based on the Block Operator Context Scanning algorithm which uses pixel operators to process the image sequences in a coarse-to-fine manner. The algorithm uses the popular Canny edge detector to find Regions of Interest that include edges in high density. The main advantage of Block-OCS is that it focuses only on Regions of Interest, by applying a low sampling rate to the rest. Compared to typical block based processing, the method was found to be 50% faster (9 frames per second instead of 6 which is found in the literature). The personal computer used in the experiments has a Core 2 Duo processor at 2GHz and 4GB RAM. The system was developed using the Open Computer Vision [5] library and the MySQL database management system [6].

References

1. Giannoukos, I., Anagnostopoulos, C.-N., Loumos, V., Kayafas, E.: Operator context scanning to support high segmentation rates for real time license plate recognition. Pattern Recognition 43, 3866–3878 (2010)
2. Anagnostopoulos, C.N., Anagnostopoulos, I., Kayafas, E., Loumos, V.: A license plate recognition algorithm for Intelligent Transportation System applications. IEEE Transactions on Intelligent Transportation Systems 7(3), 377–392 (2006)
3. Anagnostopoulos, C., Anagnostopoulos, I., Vergados, D., Kayafas, E., Loumos, V.: Sliding Windows: A software method for real-time inspection in textile surface. Textile Research Journal 74(7), 646–651 (2004)
4. Chiu, D.M., Jain, R.: Analysis of the increase and decrease algorithms for congestion avoidance in computer networks. Computer Networks and ISDN Systems 17, 1–14 (1989)
5. OpenCV. Open Computer Vision Library (February 1, 2012)
   http://sourceforge.net/projects/opencv/
6. MySQL. MySQL relational database management system (February 1, 2012),
   http://www.mysql.com/

Identifying Conceptual Layers in the Ontology Development Process

Manolis Wallace[1], Panos Alexopoulos[2],
and Phivos Mylonas[3]

[1] Department of Computer Science and Technology,
University of Peloponnese, End of Karaiskaki st., 22100, Tripolis, Greece
wallace@uop.gr
[2] iSOCO, Av. del Partenn, 16-18, 1° 7ª Campo de las Naciones 28042 Madrid, Spain
p.alexopoulos@gmail.com
[3] Department of Informatics, Ionian University, 7 Tsirigoti Square, 49100,
Corfu, Greece
fmylonas@ionio.gr

Abstract. Whilst a variety of ontological engineering methodologies exist, their actual application is far from trivial, mainly due to the widely diverse nature of the steps involved, that require different forms of expertise, typically possessed by different individuals. In order to address this, in this work we propose the separation between the conceptualization and formalization parts of the process. As proof of concept we apply the proposed approach to the IKARUS methodology, develop a graphical tool to support the resulting methodology and present results from its experimental application. Early results show that the separation of the conceptualization and formalization parts of the ontological engineering methodologies can greatly facilitate the efficiency and effectiveness of the resulting methodologies.

1 Introduction

The field of ontological engineering has played a revitalizing role in various aspects of computer science, by providing a paradigm shift in the way problems are approached and tackled. Such applications range from semantic annotation [16], and document clustering [7] to decision support [5] and knowledge management [11] to list just a few. A more recent and certainly far more challenging field of application for ontologies is that of multimedia processing, where consideration of the semantic layer has provided for the generation of a promising new field, that of semantic multimedia [12]. In this context the complexity and sensitivity of the intended application domain augments demands on the quality of considered ontologies, making development of such ontologies, as for example [3], an even more strenuous task.

On the technical side significant results have been presented with regards to design of ontology representation languages capable of describing the semantics of common, and not so common, human knowledge [15][8], as well as on

I. Maglogiannis, V. Plagianakos, and I. Vlahavas (Eds.): SETN 2012, LNAI 7297, pp. 375–382, 2012.

theoretical aspects such as consistency of representations [4] and computability regarding its implicitly contained knowledge [2] .

But as more progress was made with respect to the technical side of ontological computing, the more evident it became that we were lacking on the methodological side. Although we had the languages to represent human knowledge and algorithms and tools to exploit it, we were still missing the ability to develop extensive, detailed, complete, consistent and correct ontologies. As a response to this gap, we have seen the development of a sequence of methodologies that formalize the ontology development, extension and adaptation processes by organizing them in specific steps and tasks, such as METHONTOLOGY [6], DILIGENT [17], DOGMA[10] and HCOME [13].

Still, even with these methodologies in hand, the actual development of a truly efficient ontology remains a challenging task, not only because tasks comprising these methodologies are quite abstract in their nature, but also because they are quite diverse. Whilst it may be easy to identify experts who can specify fine differences between different types of red wines or others who can select the ideal ontological description structures for every situation, it is quite difficult to find people who combine such skills.

With this in mind, in this paper we shift our focus to characteristics of the ontology development process and to human skills that are associated with them. What we propose is the separation between conceptualization and formalization layers of the process. Based on the characteristics of these layers, any ontology development methodology can be properly adjusted, so that different layers may be implemented by different individuals, who hold different types of expertise needed to be involved for a successful process completion. As proof of concept, we examine a specific ontology engineering methodology, IKARUS-Onto [1], and provide required adaptations. In addition, we develop a simple yet characteristic user interface in order to support users in the cooperative application of the developed methodology.

The remainder of this paper is organized as follows: Section 2 presents the core proposal of this work, i.e. the distinction between conceptualization and formalization layers of ontological engineering. Building on this, in section 3 we review the methodology that will be used in the application example and associate the tasks it comprises to the aforementioned layers. Section 4 presents a graphical tool developed in order to support users in this cooperative ontology engineering task, whilst section 5 lists our concluding remarks.

2   Conceptualization and Formalization Layers

An ontology engineering methodology may be viewed as an abstract description of a process that transfers knowledge from humans to a machine readable formalized structure. Intuitively, we may conclude that for such a process to be successful, we need at least one person that holds the knowledge ontology, a way to extract this knowledge from humans and a way to structure it within an ontology.

Whilst the first component is an individual, commonly referred to as "domain expert", the other two are actions that have to be applied: extraction of knowledge and modeling of the extracted knowledge as a formal ontology. And while identifying a domain expert for a given field is typically a straightforward task, it is these two additional aforementioned components that determine the actual success of the ontology development process. The role of ontology engineering methodologies is to structure the way these actions are implemented, aiming into assisting implementers in achieving better results with less effort.

One problem with existing ontology engineering methodologies is that both actions are treated in a homogeneous approach and the same person is expected to be in a position to implement both efficiently. This is even the case with collaborative approaches (e.g. see [14] and [9]) where multiple users are considered in order to either divide the volume of work or to verify results, but still all users are expected to work on all parts of the ontology engineering process. Unfortunately, as we explain below, this is inherently problematic in any ontology engineering effort that is referred to any domain other than ontology engineering itself.

The choice of the ontology representation language itself is an important task that has a major influence on the applicability and effectiveness of the resulting ontology driven application. What is needed is an expert that will be able to select from the variety of available representation options (i.e. OWL, RDF, f-SHIN, Fuzzy OWL, etc.) the one that best fits the application requirements to be developed, as well as the nature of the available knowledge. This person is commonly referred to as "knowledge engineer". In addition to this rather simplistic example of language selection, a knowledge engineer makes a series of other critical decisions in the ontology engineering process (e.g. which type of structure to use in each case, what to model as a number and what not, when to consider probabilities, when to consider uncertainty and so on). Consequently, for the ontology engineering process to be successful, the person implementing it needs to combine properties of domain expert and ontology engineer.

Although "intermediate experts" have been considered (i.e. people who to some degree understand both the domain at hand and the ontology engineering procedure and may be able to facilitate the overall exchange of information), this has not been proven efficient in practice, since: i) inclusion of an additional person adds to process overhead and ii) specific person abilities limit the work of both the domain expert and the ontology engineer. An ideal answer would be a methodological tool, i.e. a formal ontology development methodology, that is well defined and designed in a way that is understandable and applicable for both types of experts. This tool would need to provide maximum independence between the work of the two different experts and assist them in understanding each other's role and needs in the process, so that their cooperation may be facilitated.

Our proposal is that the conceptualization part of the process, i.e. the part that involves a knowledge elicitation task, should be disconnected from the formalization part, i.e. the part that involves a representation of this knowledge using a formal ontology representation language. This would allow for development of ontological engineering methodologies that can be implemented cooperatively by individuals with different backgrounds and types of expertise; both of them required for the overall process to be completed successfully. In such an approach, a domain expert would be allowed to express his knowledge in some generic form, unconstrained from specific formalization limitations. Then, an ontology engineer would examine this knowledge against the intended application and would select a proper formalization. To further elaborate on this statement, in the following section we focus on IKARUS-Onto, a detailed methodology for development of fuzzy ontologies.

3   IKARUS-Onto and Expert Roles

IKARUS-Onto assumes that a conventional ontology is available and describes the actions needed in order to generate its extended fuzzy version. Whilst at first this may strike one as a limited example of the aforementioned approach, it is worth noting that IKARUS-Onto is quite similar to conventional ontology engineering methodologies. In fact, it inherits the structure of METHONTOLOGY, which is one of the most acknowledged and applied ontology engineering methodologies [6]. In order to incorporate in IKARUS-Onto the theory discussed within the previous section, we examine each step in order to identify whether it is a conceptualization or a formalization step. Contrary to what one might expect, it is not possible to simply split the overall process in two distinct phases, one for each layer. Still, it is possible to identify the layers involved and thus the associated roles (domain expert or ontology engineer) that need to implement them. Even if the steps are interleaved, having a clear view of "who should do what" greatly facilitates the effective cooperation of both of them.

In Fig. 1 we summarize the steps comprising IKARUS-Onto. Step 0 corresponds to the development of the original conventional ontology and therefore falls outside the core of the proposed methodology. It is worth noting though, that it is a step that, as has already been mentioned earlier, cannot be perfectly executed by either an ontology engineer or a domain expert alone; their combined expertise is absolutely required. Step 1 refers to establishing the need for fuzziness, and therefore the need to actually apply the rest of the methodology and develop a fuzzy version of the ontology. Broken into distinct actions, this step includes a check that the intended application of the ontology is one where vagueness would play a role, i.e. a task for the ontology engineer, and a check that the specific domain is characterized by vagueness, i.e. a task for the domain expert.

Step 2 is concerned with the actual specification of domain vagueness in fuzzy terms. This forms the core of the work to be performed. When analyzed into distinct tasks, this step may be broken down into:

- Identification of areas of the original ontology where vagueness actually exists, which is a task ideally performed by the domain expert.

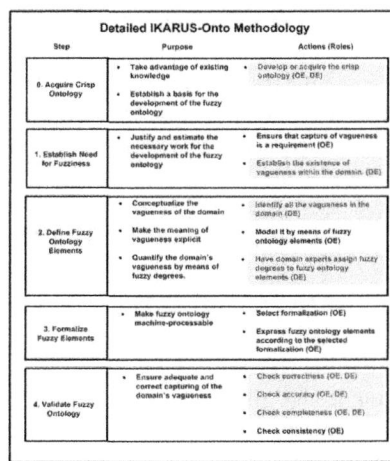

IKARUS-Onto Methodology

Step	Purpose
0. Acquire Crisp Ontology	• Take advantage of existing knowledge • Establish a basis for the development of the fuzzy ontology
1. Establish Need for Fuzziness	• Justify and estimate the necessary work for the development of the fuzzy ontology
2. Define Fuzzy Ontology Elements	• Conceptualize the vagueness of the domain • Make the meaning of vagueness explicit • Quantify the domain's vagueness by means of fuzzy degrees
3. Formalize Fuzzy Elements	• Make fuzzy ontology machine-processable
4. Validate Fuzzy Ontology	• Ensure adequate and correct capturing of the domain's vagueness

Fig. 1. Outline of the IKARUS-Onto methodology

Detailed IKARUS-Onto Methodology

Step	Purpose	Actions (Roles)
0. Acquire Crisp Ontology	• Take advantage of existing knowledge • Establish a basis for the development of the fuzzy ontology	• Develop or acquire the crisp ontology (OE, DE)
1. Establish Need for Fuzziness	• Justify and estimate the necessary work for the development of the fuzzy ontology	• Ensure that capture of vagueness is a requirement (OE) • Establish the existence of vagueness within the domain. (DE)
2. Define Fuzzy Ontology Elements	• Conceptualize the vagueness of the domain • Make the meaning of vagueness explicit • Quantify the domain's vagueness by means of fuzzy degrees.	• Identify all the vagueness in the domain (DE) • Model it by means of fuzzy ontology elements (OE) • Have domain experts assign fuzzy degrees to fuzzy ontology elements (DE)
3. Formalize Fuzzy Elements	• Make fuzzy ontology machine-processable	• Select formalization (OE) • Express fuzzy ontology elements according to the selected formalization (OE)
4. Validate Fuzzy Ontology	• Ensure adequate and correct capturing of the domain's vagueness	• Check correctness (OE, DE) • Check accuracy (OE, DE) • Check completeness (OE, DE) • Check consistency (OE)

Fig. 2. Detailed IKARUS-Onto methodology with reference to user roles

– Selection of the mathematical model and ontological structure that best match each case of vagueness, when considering both the semantics of the vagueness and the actual limitations or requirements of the intended application; a task that may only be performed by the ontology engineer.
– Specification of the exact fuzzy degree(s) that should be associated with each case of vagueness (a task to be performed by a domain expert), assuming of course that the domain expert is aware of the meaning that these degrees are expected to carry and the way in which these degrees will be interpreted when the ontology is put into practical application.

Clearly, step 2 cannot be performed by an ontology engineer or a domain expert alone. Step 3 refers to the selection of the most suitable ontology representation language for the generated ontology. This selection is determined by the nature of ontological structures that have been used in the previous steps, as well as by technical specification of the application in which the fuzzy ontology will be used. This is a clearly technical step that can be performed by an ontology engineer alone. Finally, step 4, often omitted as optional, is the validation step, in which the output of the aforementioned tasks is checked for correctness, consistency, etc.. These checks range from purely technical ones, such as the consistency check, to heavily semantic ones, such as the accuracy check, and as a result are again performed by a collaboration between domain experts and ontology engineers.

In Fig. 2 we present a graphical representation of the IKARUS-Onto methodology, on which tasks to be implemented by domain experts are highlighted. One may easily observer that the role of the domain expert is not limited to a single continuous segment of the process, but is instead closely intertwined with the work of the ontology engineer. Hence, the need for organization of the cooperation between users performing the two roles is evident. Further to the abstract description of the methodology including the consideration of the conceptualization and formalization layers, a graphical tool that would organize the work would further facilitate the cooperation. We present a first development attempt of such a tool in the following section 4.

4   Ontology Fuzzification Tool

In order to apply the theory proposed herein in an experimental framework we developed a graphical tool that implements the IKARUS-Onto methodology, while also taking into consideration and supporting distinct user roles that implement the different layers of the process. Specifically, the tool aims to organize the ontology fuzzification work around the IKARUS-Onto methodology, while at the same time support domain experts in their role. Emphasis is put on the conceptualization layer, since, on one hand, there is already an abundance of tools to support the ontology engineer in his task and on the other hand, an ontology engineer needs far less support due to the nature of his work.

The ontology fuzzification tool is set up as a standalone web interface in which a crisp ontology may be loaded. This ontology is visualized, so that users may graphically review it and specify any required updates and/or extensions. The visual approach to ontological editing makes it possible for domain experts, who are laymen when it comes to computing, to participate in the process. Additionally, it is also worth mentioning that the visual portion of the ontological editing process is not bound to a specific notation or ontology description language. Therefore the domain expert does not need to comprehend or even worry about specific language characteristics or limitations.

As already discussed, step 0 of the methodology presented in section 3, forms a preparatory step that lies outside the core scope of IKARUS-Onto. Tasks included in steps 1 and 2 of the methodology are supported in greater detail, since they are the main tasks of the ontology fuzzification process. As can be seen in Fig. 2, work in steps 1 and 2 of the methodology can be organized as four intermittent phases of ontology engineer and domain expert work. This exact structure is followed by the developed tool. Specifically, the visualized ontology is first presented to the ontology engineer, so that he may assess the need to capture the related vagueness. Assuming the decision is to go ahead with the fuzzification process, the visualized ontology is presented to the domain expert in the User Interface (UI) shown in Fig. 3. In this UI the domain expert can visually specify elements of the ontology for which some type of vagueness will need to be captured and modeled in the ontology.

Following the structure of the IKARUS-Onto methodology, the work is then transfered to the UI presented in Fig. 4. Here the ontology engineer is presented with elements that have been "highlighted" by the domain expert. For each one of them, the ontology engineer may select the most suitable structure to model its vagueness. Additionally, the ontology engineer "annotates" his work by explaining the meaning of the specified degrees and the way they will be

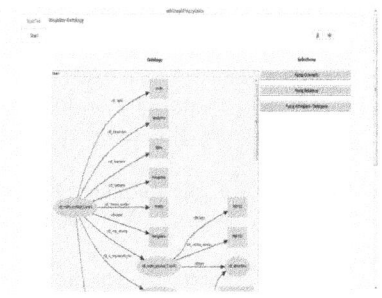
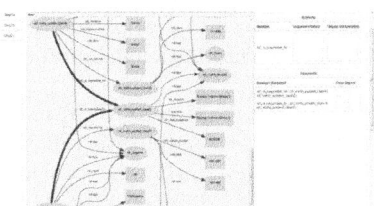

Fig. 3. The domain expert is assisted in identifying the elements to fuzzify

Fig. 4. The ontology engineer specifies the type of fuzziness for each element and its meaning

interpreted, when the ontology is put to actual use. It is exactly this information that will assist the domain expert during the next step to specify the fuzzy degrees in a meaningful, consistent and efficient manner.

5   Discussion and Conclusions

In this paper we discussed fundamentally different types of tasks that are involved in the ontology development process and may be identified into two distinct layers, namely conceptualization and formalization. As we explained, by separating tasks associated with each layer, any conventional ontology engineering methodology may be modified to facilitate efficient collaboration between a domain expert and an ontology engineer, thus optimizing the overall process with respect to both effort and quality of results.

Continuing, we applied our proposal specifically within the IKARUS-Onto methodology framework. The result of this analysis has been an updated version of the methodology that is designed specifically for cooperative and interdisciplinary ontological engineering, as well as a first version of the graphical tool that supports it. It is worth noting that, although much of the analysis has been focused specifically on IKARUS-Onto, the core of our proposal is directly applicable in any ontological engineering methodology. In fact, as part of our immediate future work we plan to apply our cooperative and interdisciplinary modifications to other methodologies, such as METHONTOLOGY, whereas corresponding versions of our tool will also be developed.

References

1. Alexopoulos, P., Wallace, M., Kafentzis, K., Askounis, D.: IKARUS-Onto: a methodology to develop fuzzy ontologies from crisp ones. Knowledge and Information Systems, doi:10.1007/s10115-011-0457-6

2. Analyti A., Antoniou G., Damsio C.V., Wagner G., Computability and Complexity Issues of Extended RDF. In: Proceedings of the 18th European Conference on Artificial Intelligence (2008)
3. Arndt, R., Troncy, R., Staab, S., Hardman, L.: COMM: A Core Ontology for Multimedia Annotation. In: Staab, S., Studer, R. (eds.) Handbook on Ontologies, 2nd edn. International Handbooks on Information Systems, pp. 403–421. Springer (2009)
4. Baclawski, K., Kokar, M.M., Waldinger, R., Kogut, P.A.: Consistency checking of semantic web ontologies. In: Horrocks, I., Hendler, J. (eds.) ISWC 2002. LNCS, vol. 2342, pp. 454–459. Springer, Heidelberg (2002)
5. Bouamrane, M.-M., Rector, A., Hurrell, M.: Using OWL ontologies for adaptive patient information modelling and preoperative clinical decision support. Knowledge and Information Systems, 1–14 (2010)
6. Fernandez Lopez, M., Gomez Perez, A., Juristo, N.: Methontology: From ontological art towards ontological engineering. In: Proceedings of the Spring Symposium on Ontological Engineering of AAAI (1997)
7. Fodeh, S., Punch, B., Tan, P.-N.: On ontology-driven document clustering using core semantic features. Knowledge and Information Systems, 1–27 (2011)
8. Horrocks, I., Patel-Schneider, P.F., van Harmelen, F.: From SHIQ and RDF to OWL: the making of a Web Ontology Language. Web Semantics: Science, Services and Agents on the World Wide Web 1(1), 7–26 (2003)
9. Hu, H., Zhao, Y., Wang, Y., Li, M., Wang, D., Wu, W., He, J., Du, X., Wang, S.: Cooperative Ontology Development Environment CODE and a Demo Semantic Web on Economics. In: Zhang, Y., Tanaka, K., Yu, J.X., Wang, S., Li, M. (eds.) APWeb 2005. LNCS, vol. 3399, pp. 1049–1052. Springer, Heidelberg (2005)
10. Jarrar, M., Meersman, R.: Ontology Engineering -The DOGMA Approach. In: Dillon, T.S., Chang, E., Meersman, R., Sycara, K. (eds.) Advances in Web Semantics I. LNCS, vol. 4891, pp. 7–34. Springer, Heidelberg (2008)
11. Jurisica, I., Mylopoulos, J., Yu, E.: Ontologies for Knowledge Management: An Information Systems Perspective. Knowledge and Information Systems 6(4), 380–401 (2004)
12. Kompatsiaris, Y., Hobson, P. (eds.): Semantic Multimedia and Ontologies: Theory and Applications. Springer (March 2008)
13. Kotis, K., Vouros, G.: Human-Centered Ontology Engineering: the HCOME Methodology. International Journal of Knowledge and Information Systems (KAIS) 10, 109–131 (2006)
14. Maedche, A., Staab, S.: Ontology Learning for the Semantic Web. IEEE Intelligent Systems 16(2), 72–79 (2001)
15. McGuinness, D.L., Fikes, R., Hendler, J., Stein, L.A.: DAML+OIL: An Ontology Language for the Semantic Web. IEEE Intelligent Systems 17(5), 72–80 (2002)
16. Sanchez, D., Isern, D., Millan, M.: Content annotation for the semantic web: an automatic web-based approach. Knowledge and Information Systems, 1–26 (2010)
17. Vrandecic, D., Pinto, H.S., Sure, Y., Tempich, C.: The DILIGENT knowledge processes. Journal of Knowledge Management 9(5) (2005)

Author Index